EIGHTY YEARS' PROGRESS

OF

THE UNITED STATES:

A FAMILY RECORD

OF AMERICAN INDUSTRY, ENERGY AND ENTERPRISE:

SHOWING

THE VARIOUS CHANNELS OF INDUSTRY AND EDUCATION THROUGH WHICH THE PEOPLE OF THE UNITED STATES HAVE ARISEN FROM A BRITISH COLONY TO THEIR PRESENT NATIONAL IMPORTANCE;

GIVING, IN AN HISTORICAL FORM,

THE VAST IMPROVEMENTS IN MINING INDUSTRY, SETTLEMENT OF NEW LANDS, INTERNAL TRADE, BANKING, INSURANCE, EMIGRATION, SOCIAL AND DOMESTIC LIFE, LITERATURE, TELEGRAPHING, FINE ARTS, EDUCATION, EDUCATIONAL AND HUMANE INSTITUTIONS, ETC., ETC.

WITH A LARGE AMOUNT OF STATISTICAL INFORMATION,

SHOWING THE COMPARATIVE PROGRESS OF THE DIFFERENT STATES WITH EACH OTHER, AND, TO SOME EXTENT, THIS COUNTRY WITH OTHER NATIONS.

BY EMINENT LITERARY MEN,

WHO HAVE MADE THE SUBJECTS OF WHICH THEY HAVE WRITTEN THEIR SPECIAL STUDY.

EXTENSIVELY EMBELLISHED WITH STEEL AND ELECTROTYPE PLATE ENGRAVINGS,

EXECUTED BY THE FIRST ARTISTS IN THE COUNTRY, ILLUSTRATING THE PROGRESS OF THE VARIOUS INTERESTS TREATED OF.

FURNISHED BY AGE[illegible]

VOL. II.

HARTFORD, CO[illegible]
PUBLISHED BY L. STEBBINS.
1867.

SUBJECTS AND AUTHORS.

MINING INDUSTRY OF THE UNITED STATES,

Including Gold, Silver, Copper, Lead, Zinc, Iron, Coal, Petroleum, &c., showing the Localities, Richness of Ores, Methods of Mining, Smelting, and applying the different Minerals to practical uses, with their values, &c., &c.

FUR TRADE, various kinds and values of Furs.

HAT MANUFACTURE.

By JAMES T. HODGE, Geologist,

Of the late Pennsylvania, and other Geological Surveys; Contributor to Appleton's "New American Cyclopædia" on the same Subjects.

LAND, SETTLEMENT, INTERNAL TRADE.

Western Settlement, Population, and Land Sales, Canals and Railroads, Expenditures, Lake Cities, Reciprocity, Annual Sales of Land by the Government, River Cities, Atlantic Cities, Date of Settlement, Population, Valuation, Manufactures, Exports, Imports, Growth of New York, Express Business.

BANKS, UNITED STATES MINT, AND INSURANCE.

Bills of Credit, Government Issues, United States Bank, State Banks, Suffolk System, Safety Fund, Banks, Free Banks, Number of Banks in each State, Aggregate Capital, Clearing Houses, Private Banking, New National System, &c., Establishment of Mint, Standard of Coins, Laws Regulating Coinage, Precious Metals in the Country, Insurance,—Fire, Marine, Life, Accident, &c.

EMIGRATION.

General Migrations, Colonies and United States, Number of Aliens arrived in the United States from 1820 to 1856, and their Nationalities, Landing in New York, Future Homes.

AUTHORS, BOOKS, NEWSPAPERS, BOOK-BINDING, PRINTING PRESSES, TELEGRAPH.

Writers,—including Theologians, Statesmen, Novelists, Historians,—Short Sketches of their Lives, their Literary Productions; Newspapers,—Dailies, Weeklies, Periodicals, Book Trade, Publishing, Jobbing, Retailing, Selling by Subscription, Book-Binding, Printing Presses, Telegraph.

By THOMAS P. KETTELL

SOCIAL AND DOMESTIC LIFE.

Domestic Architecture, Furniture, Food, Dress, Social Culture, &c.

By FREDERICK B. PERKINS.

ARTS OF DESIGN.

Painters, Sculptors, Engravers, &c.

By T. ADDISON RICHARDS, Artist,

Editor of Appleton's "Railway Guide," Correspondent of "Harper's Magazine."

EDUCATION,

Including the History and Statistics of Free Schools, Common Schools, Grammar Schools, Academies, Colleges, Professional Schools of Theology, Law, Medicine, War, Teaching, Engineering, Agriculture, Mechanics and Fine Arts; with Special Schools for Deaf Mutes, Blind, Idiots, Juvenile Criminals and Orphans, and Supplementary Educational Agencies and Libraries, Lyceums, Lectures, &c.

By HENRY BARNARD, LL. D.,

Superintendent of Common Schools in Connecticut and Rhode Island; Chancellor of the State University of Wisconsin; and Editor of the "American Journal of Education."

CONTENTS OF VOLUME II.

MINING INDUSTRY.

	PAGE
Introductory Remarks	17
Iron Works in Virginia previous to 1622	17
First Blast Furnace in 1702	17
IRON	18
First Trial of Anthracite Coal for manufac-facturing	18
Great Britian produces more than half of the whole product of the world	19
Iron produced from 1828 to 1840	20
MATERIALS EMPLOYED IN THE MANUFACTURE	20
Ore in Pennsylvania, Maryland, Tennessee, New York, Canada, and Wisconsin	21
Consumption of Charcoal per Ton of Iron	22
Quantities of Air used in Blast Furnaces	23
Furnaces in the Lehigh Valley	23
DISTRIBUTION OF ORES	24
Ores in New Jersey	25
Ores in Pennsylvania	26
Great Chestnut Hill Ore-bed	27
Ores in Maryland	28
Ores in Southern States	28
Ores in Western States	29
IRON MANUFACTURE	32
Description of Blast Furnaces	32
WROUGHT IRON	36
PUDDLING	37
List of Rolling Mills in 1856	40
Mills making Railroad Iron in 1856	40
Boiler Plate and Sheet Iron Manufactories in 1856	41
IRON WIRE	41
NAILS	41
List of Nail Manufactories in 1856	42
STEEL	43
Cast Steel	44
Table of Iron Works in operation and abandoned in 1856	45
Production of Pig Iron	46
Distribution of Furnaces by States	46
Product of Wrought Iron	46
Value of the Iron product in 1856	47
COPPER	48
New Jersey Mines	49
Tennessee Mines	50
Lake Superior Mines	51
Product of the Pittsburgh and Boston Company Mines from 1852 to 1860	53
Minesota Company	55
Product of do from 1848 to 1860	56
Statistics of Lake Superior Mines	57
COPPER SMELTING	58
USEFUL APPLICATIONS OF COPPER	60
Cost of Smelting Copper	60
Manufacture of Brass	62
GOLD	63
Vermont Mines	64
Virginia do	64
North Carolina Mines	69
Georgia do	69
Pike's Peak do	70
California do	71
Australia do	71
Annual production of Gold in the World at the time of its discovery in California	71
Length and Cost of Artificial Water-courses in California	72
Quartz Mining	73
Table of annual productions of the Mines of California from 1848 to 1857	73

PAGE
Various Machines for Mining purposes ... 74
Tables showing the amount of Gold coined by the U.S. Government, and where produced 78-9
The uses of Gold ... 80
LEAD ... 81
Localities of Mines ... 82
Iowa Mines ... 84
Table showing the shipments of Lead from the Upper Mississippi from 1821 to 1841. 85
Table showing the production and importation of Lead from 1832 to 1858 ... 87
LEAD SMELTING ... 87
USEFUL APPLICATIONS OF LEAD ... 91
Lead Pipe ... 91
Shot and Bullets ... 92
American process of making Shot, ... 93
WHITE LEAD ... 94
List of American White Lead Works ... 96
ZINC ... 96
New Jersey Mines ... 96
Pennsylvania do. ... 97
METALLURGIC TREATMENT AND USES ... 98
EUROPEAN MANUFACTURE ... 100
List of the Silesian Company Works ... 102
Schedule of the cost of Zinc Ore on shipboard at Antwerp ... 103
ZINC PAINT ... 103
Description of Manufacture ... 104
PLATINUM ... 107
IRIDIUM AND OSMIUM ... 110
MERCURY ... 110
California Mines ... 111
Almaden Mine in Spain ... 111
Total annual production of various Mines .. 111
METALLURGIC TREATMENT ... 114
USEFUL APPLICATIONS OF MERCURY ... 114
SILVER ... 115
COBALT ... 116
NICKEL ... 117
CHROME OR CHROMIUM ... 118
MANGANESE ... 119
TIN ... 119
COAL ... 120
VARIETIES OF COAL ... 121
Relative value of different kinds of Coal ... 124
GEOLOGICAL AND GEOGRAPHICAL DISTRIBUTION OF COAL ... 124
AMOUNT OF AVAILABLE COAL ... 133
Extent of Coal Fields in different States ... 133
Relative amount of Coal Fields of Europe and America ... 134
Table showing annual amount of Lead produced in Pennsylvania and Maryland from 1820 to 1860 ... 134

PAGE
TRANSPORTATION OF COAL TO MARKET ... 135
Table of Railroads and Canals constructed for transporting Coal ... 142
USEFUL APPLICATIONS OF COAL ... 146
ILLUMINATING GAS ... 147
List of Gas Co.'s, with amount of Capital, &c. 148
Process of making Gas ... 152
GAS FOR STEAMBOATS AND RAILROAD CARS ... 156
HYDROCARBON OR COAL OILS ... 156
Table of Coal Oil Works in the United States 157
History and method of manufacture ... 158
PETROLEUM OR ROCK OIL ... 163
Petroleum in the United States ... 164
Daily yield of seventy-four Oil Wells ... 165
List of Petroleum Refining works ... 170
LAND SETTLEMENT, INTERNAL TRADE ... 169
Land Sales in Ohio ... 170
Canals in the West ... 172
First Locomotive built in this Country ... 174
Population of Land States in 1830 and in 1860 175
Detroit and Chicago ... 177
RIVER CITIES, ATLANTIC CITIES ... 180
Statistics of New Orleans ... 182
NEW YORK, TELEGRAPH, GOLD ... 185
Comparative Exports of the Atlantic Cities 187
Harnden Express ... 188
Growth of New York ... 190
Bulls and Bears ... 195
Hotels in New York ... 197

BANKS IN THE UNITED STATES.

BILLS OF CREDIT ... 198
Congress Issues, $358,465,000 ... 199
Ten Thousand Dollars for a Cocked Hat ... 199
First Bank of the United States ... 201
One Hundred and Twenty Banks go into operation in four years ... 201
Table of relative growth of Banks ... 203
Table of Number of Banks, and Capital ... 204
Banks Located in New York ... 204
Alabama with Carolina, do ... 208
Clearing House System ... 209
Table of Capital of all Banks ... 209

UNITED STATES MINT.

ESTABLISHMENT OF THE MINT, STANDARD OF COIN, &c ... 212
Value of the Dollar and the Pound Sterling in Colonial Paper Money ... 213
Alloy of Gold Coin ... 214
United States Coinage ... 214
California Gold ... 215
Weight of Silver Coin ... 216

PAGE
Amount of New Silver Coin.............. 216
Deposit of Domestic Gold at United States Mint and Branches.................... 216
Amount of Specie in 1821................ 217

INSURANCE.

Fire, Marine, and Life................... 219
Number and Capital of New York Companies 222
Capital, Premiums, and Risks of the Fire Companies of the United States............. 223
Marine Insurance....................... 224
Life Insurance........................... 225
Comparative Rates of Domestic Life Insurance 226

IMMIGRATION.

General Migration...................... 228
Colonies of the United States............. 228
Early Immigration....................... 229
Naturalization Laws..................... 230
Number of Immigrants for the last forty years, with their Birth-places............ 231
European Migration—French and German. 232
Decrease in Population of Ireland.......... 235
Allowance on Passage................... 236
Saving part of the Passage Money......... 239
Landing in New York—Future Homes..... 240
Table of Immigration.................... 240
Location of Immigrants in the United States 242
Amount of Money received in the United States by Immigrants.................. 243
Amount of Money remitted by Friends in aid of Immigration..................... 243
Number of Natives arriving from abroad... 244

SOCIAL AND DOMESTIC LIFE.

Introduction............................ 245
Domestic Architecture................... 245
Description of Buildings.................. 246
Houses South........................... 247
Introduction of Anthracite Coal............ 248
Nott's Stoves........................... 248
Furniture, Furnishing Goods, &c.......... 249
China, Glass, Silver Forks, &c............. 251
Food, Cooking, &c....................... 252
Cooking Stoves.......................... 253
Dress................................... 253
Social and Mental Culture............... 259

BOOKS.

Book Trade, Publishing, &c............... 262
First Booksellers in America.............. 263
American Bible Society.................. 264
Harper and Brothers, Appletons.......... 264
Number of Book Publishers in the United States.................................. 265
Gift-Book Sales.......................... 265
Sale of Old Books....................... 266
Subscription Sales....................... 267
Circulation of Popular Works............. 267
School Book Trade....................... 268
Reprints and American Books............. 269
Book Binding............................ 269
Books of Wood and Metal................ 272
Description of Binding................... 273
Writers of America...................... 274
Theologians, Statesmen, Novelists, Historians.................................. 274
Early Founders of the Colony Good Writers................................... 274
Works of James Madison................. 275
Judge Marshall, Story, Wheaton, John Quincy Adams, and others..................... 276
Cooper, Hawthorne, Willis........... 279–280
Prescott and Bancroft.................... 284
Lady Authors............................ 285
Printing Press.......................... 286
Franklin's Press......................... 286
Hoe and Adams Presses.................. 297
Types.................................. 298
Machines for Casting Types.............. 298
Stereotype, Electrotype.................. 300
Newspapers............................. 301
City Papers............................. 303
Number of Papers in the United States.... 307
Telegraph—Origin....................... 308
Morse, House, and Hughes Machines...... 311
First Lines.............................. 313
Various Lines and Companies............. 313
Penalty for refusing to transmit Messages.. 314
Comparison between Telegraphs and Couriers 315

THE ARTS OF DESIGN IN AMERICA.

Horace Walpole......................... 316
American Art begins with Benjamin West.. 317
Stuart, Robert Fulton.................... 318
Sketches of the Lives of Prominent Painters 318 to 325
Sculptors....................... 326 to 328
Engraving.............................. 332
Dr. Anderson........................... 332
Copper-Plate Engraving.................. 333
American Bank Note Company............ 333
Descriptions of Engraving................ 334
Lithography, Daguerreotype, Academies of Art, &c............................... 335

PAGE

EDUCATION AND EDUCATIONAL INSTITUTIONS.

DEVELOPMENT IN THE COLONIAL PERIOD 337
Early Efforts in Virginia.................. 337
do do in New York............... 338
Early Efforts in Colonies of Massachusetts and Connecticut....................... 338
Town Action in behalf of Schools.......... 339
COLONIAL LEGISLATION AND ACTION IN THE ORDER OF THEIR SETTLEMENT............ 341
Virginia................................ 341
Massachusetts........................... 342
Rhode Island, Connecticut................ 344
New Hampshire........................... 345
New York................................ 346
Maryland................................ 347
New Jersey, Pennsylvania................ 348
Delaware, North Carolina................. 349
South Carolina, Georgia.................. 350
RESULTS AT THE CLOSE OF OUR COLONIAL HISTORY................................ 350
REVOLUTIONARY AND TRANSITION PERIOD..... 351
Opinions and Efforts of Noah Webster, George Washington, John Adams, Thomas Jefferson................................ 352
Opinions and Efforts of James Madison, John Quincy Adams, Benjamin Rush, John Jay, De Witt Clinton, Chancellor Kent, Daniel Webster............................ 353
PROGRESS OF COMMON OR ELEMENTARY SCHOOLS 355
Letter from Noah Webster................ 355
do do Heman Humphrey........... 356
do do Joseph T. Buckingham........ 359
do do Dr. Nott..................... 362
Recollections of Peter Parley............. 363
The Homespun Era of Common Schools, by Horace Bushnell, D.D.................... 369
Letter from William Darlington, M.D., LL.D. 370
Schools in Philadelphia.................... 371
School Holiday in Georgia................ 373
Old Field School or Academy in Virginia... 377
Remarks................................. 380
What is Education?..................... 383
Remarks on the Common School System in the United States....................... 384
ACADEMIES, HIGH SCHOOLS, &C.............. 388
Letter of Josiah Quincy.................. 389
Address of Hon. Edward Everett........... 391
COLLEGES................................ 392
PROFESSIONAL, SCIENTIFIC AND SPECIAL SCHOOLS 393
THEOLOGICAL SCHOOLS..................... 393
LAW SCHOOLS............................. 394
MEDICAL SCHOOLS......................... 394
MILITARY AND NAVAL SCHOOLS.............. 395
NORMAL SCHOOLS, &C...................... 397
SCHOOLS OF SCIENCE FOR ENGINEERS, &C...... 400
The Lawrence School..................... 401
SCHOOLS OF AGRICULTURE.................. 402
COMMERCIAL SCHOOLS...................... 403
SCHOOLS FOR MECHANICS................... 403
FINE ARTS—FEMALE EDUCATION............. 404
SCHOOL-HOUSES, APPARATUS, AND TEXT-BOOKS 406
The Horn-Book........................... 413
New England Primer...................... 414
Webster's Spelling Book.................. 416
School Apparatus........................ 422
LIBRARIES............................... 423
Astor Library, Boston City Library........ 424
New York Mercantile Library............ 425
Table of Libraries in the United States...... 429
LYCEUMS, &C............................. 432
INSTITUTIONS FOR THE INSTRUCTION OF DEAF AND DUMB............................. 434
Rev. Thomas H. Gallaudet................ 435
INSTITUTIONS FOR THE BLIND............... 439
INSTITUTIONS FOR IDIOTS.................. 440
INSTITUTIONS FOR EDUCATION OF ORPHANS.... 445
REFORMATORY INSTITUTIONS................ 446
Educational Statistics of the United States.. 451
Table of American Colleges............... 452
do Theological Schools............... 454
do Law Schools, Medical Schools..... 455
do Deaf and Dumb Institutions...... 456
do Blind Institutions............... 457

LIST OF ILLUSTRATIONS.

PAGE.

1, Fancy Title,. . . . . . (*Steel Plate.*)
2, Chestnut Hill Mine, ... 27
3, Blast Furnace, ... (*Fig. A,*) 35
4, " " . . . .(*Fig. B,*) 35
5, Hydraulic Mining, ... 65
6, Tunneling at Table Mountain, Cal. 66
7, Large Rocker, ... 67
8, Stamps for Crushing Gold Ores, . 68
9, Burke Rocker, ... 74
10, Crushing Mill, or Arrastre, ... 75
11, Scotch Hearth Furnace, ... 88
12, Apparatus for working Platinum, . 108
13, View of New Almaden Quick Silver Mine, ... 113
Map of the Anthracite region, Pa., Mines, ... 126
14, Map showing Different Strata, in Coal Regions, Pa., ... 130
15, Map showing Different Strata in Coal Regions, Pa., ... 132
16, Mt. Pisgah Plane, Mauch Chunk, Pa. 137
17, Great Open Quarry of the Lehigh, 138
18, Baltimore Company's Mine, Pa., . 139
19, Colliery Slope,. 140
20, View at Mauch Chunk, ... 141
21, View on the Upper Mississippi, (*Steel Plate,*) 182
22, View, United States Bank, Pa., (*Steel Plate,*) 206
23, Buildings on Fire, ... 219
24, Fashion, 1776, ... 255
25, Evening Dress, 1780, ... 255
26, Fashion, 1780, ... 255
27, " 1785, ... 255

PAGE.

28, Evening Dress, 1795, ... 255
29, " " 1797, ... 255
30, Fashion, 1800, ... 255
31, " 1805, ... 255
32, Children, 1805, ... 255
33, Fashions, 1812, ... 255
34, Boys, 1812, ... 255
35, Men, 1812, ... 255
36, Women, 1815, ... 256
37, Men, 1818, ... 256
38, Women, 1820, ... 256
39, Men, 1825, ... 256
40, " 1828, ... 256
41, Winter Dress, 1833, ... 256
42, Boys and Girls, 1833, ... 256
43, Men, 1833, ... 256
44, Women, 1833, ... 256
45, " 1840, ... 256
46, Men, 1844, ... 256
47, Women, 1850, ... 256
48, Franklin Press, ... 289
49, Washington Press, ... 289
50, Hand Press, Steam Inking machine, 290
51, Improved Inking Apparatus, ... 290
52, Patent Single Cylinder Machine, . 291
53, Eight Cylinder Machine, ... 292
54, Ten Cylinder Machine, ... 293
55, Four Color Machine, ... 294
56, Bed and Platen Power Machine, . 295
57, Railroad Ticket Machine, ... 296
58, Morse' Telegraph Apparatus, ... 309
59, Fishing at Newport, ... 330
60, Country View, ... 330
61, Spring, ... 331

PAGE.
62, Summer, ... 331
63, Fall, ... 331
64, School Houses as they were, ... 406
65, " " " 406
66, " " as they are, ... 407
67, Village School House, ... 407
68, View of Girard College, ... 408
69, Packer Collegiate Institute, ... 409
70, " " Garden Front, . 410
71, " " Interior, ... 410
72, Norwich Free Academy, ... 411
73, Chicago City University, ... 412
74, Horn Book of 18th Century, ... 413
75, John Hancock, ... 414
76, Burning of John Rogers at the Stake, ... 414
77, In Adam's Fall we sinned all, ... 415
78, Heaven to Find, the Bible mind, . 415
79, Christ Crucified, for Sinners died, 415
80, The Deluge Drowned, the Earth around, ... 415
81, Elijah hid, by Ravens fed, ... 415
82, The Judgment made Felix afraid, 415
83, As Runs the Glass, ... 415
84, My Book and Heart must never part, ... 415
85. Job feels the Rod, ... 415
86, Proud Korah's troop was swallowed up, ... 415
87, Lot fled to Zoar, ... 415
88, Moses was he who Israel's host led through the Sea, ... 415
89, Noah did view the Old World and New, ... 415
90, Young Obadias, David, Josias, ... 415
91, Peter denied his Lord and cried, . 415
92, Queen Esther sues, ... 415
PAGE.
93, Young pious Ruth left all for Truth, 415
94, Young Samuel dear, the Lord did fear, ... 415
95, Young Timothy learnt Sin to fly, . 415
96, Vasthi for Pride was set aside, ... 415
97, Whales in the Sea, ... 415
98, Xerxes did die, ... 415
99, While Youth doth cheer Death may be near, ... 415
100, Zaccheus he did climb the Tree, . 415
101, The Boy that Stole Apples, ... 416
102, Country Maid, ... 417
103, Cat and Rat, ... 417
104, Fox and Swallow, ... 418
105, Fox and Bramble, ... 418
106, The Partial Judge, ... 418
107, Bear and Two Friends, ... 419
108, Two Dogs, ... 419
109, Eye, Nose, &c., ... 420
110, Arm, Hand, &c., ... 420
111, Eagle's Nest, ... 420
112, Vertebrates, ... 420
113, Articulates, ... 420
114, Mollusks, ... 420
115, Radiates, ... 420
116, Animals of the Seal Kind, ... 420
117, Birds, ... 421
118, Flowers, ... 421
119, Geological Chart, ... 421
120, School Apparatus as it was, ... 422
121, School Apparatus as it is, ... 422
122, Boston City Library. Exterior, . 425
123, Boston City Library. Interior, . 426
124, American Asylum for Deaf and Dumb, ... 437
125, Pennsylvania Asylum for Blind, . 440
126, Asylum for Idiots, Syracuse, N. Y. 444

MINING INDUSTRY OF THE UNITED STATES.

INTRODUCTORY REMARKS.

The mineral wealth of the American colonies does not appear to have been an object of much interest to the early settlers. Congregated near the coast, they were little likely to become acquainted with many of the mineral localities, most of which are in the interior, in regions long occupied by the Indian tribes. The settlers, moreover, probably possessed little knowledge of mining, and certainly lacked capital which they could appropriate in this direction. Some discoveries, however, were made by them very soon after their settlement, the earliest of which were on the James river, in Virginia. Beverly, in his "History of the Present State of Virginia," published in London in 1705, makes mention of iron works which were commenced on Falling Creek, and of glass-houses which were about to be constructed at Jamestown just previous to the great massacre by the Indians, in 1622. This undertaking at Falling Creek is referred to by other historians, as by Stith, in his "History of Virginia" (1753), p. 279. A Captain Nathaniel Butler, it appears, presented to the king, in 1623, a very disparaging account of the condition of the colony, mentioning, among other matters, that "the Iron Works were utterly wasted, and the People dead; the Glass Furnaces at a stand, and in small Hopes of proceeding." The committee of the company, in their reply to this, affirm that "great Sums had been expended, and infinite Care and Diligence bestowed by the Officers and Company for setting forward various Commodities and Manufactures; as Iron Works," etc., etc. Salmon, in his "Modern History" (1746), vol. iii, pp. 439 and 468, refers to the statement of Beverly, mentioning that "an iron work was set up on Falling Creek, in James River, where they found the iron ore good, and had near brought that work to perfection. The iron proved reasonably good; but before they got into the body of the mine, the people were cut off in that fatal massacre (of March, 1622), and the project has never been set on foot since, until of late; but it has not had its full trial." This author also refers to the representations of the Board of Trade to the House of Commons, in 1732, as containing notices of the iron works in operation in New England. From various reports of the governor of Massachusetts Bay and other officials of this colony, there appear to have been, in 1731, as many as six furnaces and nineteen forges for making iron in New England, as also a slitting mill and nail factory connected with it.

The first blast furnace in the colonies appears to have been built in 1702, by Lambert Despard, at the outlet of Mattakeeset pond, in Plymouth County, Massachusetts, and a number more were afterward set in operation to work the bog ores of that district. Their operations are described in the "Collections of the Massachusetts Historical Society" for 1804, by James Thacher, M. D., who was himself engaged in the manufacture. In Rhode Island and Providence Plantations, the same kinds of ore were found and worked at about the same period. Alexander gives the year 1715 as the epoch of blast furnaces in Maryland, Virginia, and Pennsylvania. These enterprises were regarded with great disfavor in the mother country. In 1719 an act was brought forward in the House of Lords, forbidding the erection of rolling or slitting mills in the American colonies, and in 1750 this was made a law.

In Connecticut, Governor Winthrop was much interested in investigating the character of the minerals about Haddam and Middletown. In 1651 he obtained a license giving him almost unlimited privileges for working any mines of "lead, copper, or tin, or any minerals; as antimony, vitriol, black lead, alum, salt, salt springs, or any other the like, * * * to enjoy forever said mines, with the lands, woods, timber, and water within two or three miles of said mines." And in 1661, another special grant was made to him of any mines he might discover in the neighborhood of Middletown. It does not appear, however, that he derived any special advantage from these privileges, although he used to make frequent excursions to the different localities of minerals, especially to the Governor's Ring, a mountain in the north-west corner of East Haddam, and spend three weeks at a time there with his servant, engaged, as told by Governor Trumbull to President Styles, and recorded in his diary, in "roasting ores, assaying metals, and casting gold rings." John Winthrop, F.R.S., grandson of Governor Winthrop, was evidently well acquainted with many localities of different ores in Connecticut, and sent to the Royal Society a considerable collection of specimens he had made. It is supposed that among them Hatchett found the mineral columbite, and detected the new metal which he named columbium. At Middletown, an argentiferous lead mine was worked, it is supposed, at this period, by the Winthrops, and the men employed were evidently skilful miners. When the mine was reopened in 1852, shafts were found well timbered and in good preservation, that had been sunk to the depth of 120 feet, and, with the other workings, amounted in all to 1,500 feet of excavation. The oldest American charter for a mining company was granted in 1709, for working the copper ores at Simsbury, Connecticut. Operations were carried on here for a number of years, the ore raised being shipped to England, and a similar mining enterprise was undertaken in 1719, at Belleville, in New Jersey, about six miles from Jersey City. The products of the so-called Schuyler mine at this place amounted, before the year 1731, to 1,386 tons of ore, all of which were shipped to England. At this period (1732) the Gap mine, in Lancaster county, Pennsylvania, was first opened and worked for copper, and about the middle of the century various other copper mines were opened in New Jersey; also, the lead mine at Southampton, Mass., and the cobalt mine at Chatham, Conn. In 1754 a lead mine was successfully worked in Wythe county, in south-western Virginia, and this is still productive. It is probable that, by reason of the higher value of copper at that period, and the lower price paid for labor than at present, some of the copper mines may have proved profitable to work, though it is certain this has not been the case with them of late years. The existence of copper in the region about Lake Superior was known, from the reports of the Jesuit missionaries, in 1660, and one or two unsuccessful attempts were made to work it during the last century by parties of Englishmen. The lead mines of the upper Mississippi, discovered by Le Sueur in his exploring voyage up the river in 1700 and 1701, were first worked by Dubuque, a French miner, in 1788, upon the tract of land now occupied by the city in Iowa bearing his name.

Such, in general, was the extent to which this branch of industry had been carried up to the close of the last century. The only coal mines worked were some on the James river, twelve miles above Richmond, and the capacity of these for adding to the wealth of the country was not by any means appreciated. The gold mines were entirely unknown, and the dependence of the country upon Great Britain for the supply of iron had so checked the development of this branch of manufacture, that comparatively nothing was known of our own resources in the mines of this metal. The most important establishments for its manufacture were small blast furnaces, working bog ores, and the bloomaries of New York and New Jersey, making bar iron direct from the rich magnetic ores.

The progress of the United States in these branches will be traced in the succeeding chapters, one of which will be devoted to each of the principal metals.

CHAPTER I.

IRON.

The early history of the iron manufacture in the American colonies has been noticed in the introductory remarks which precede this chapter. Since the year 1750 the restrictions imposed upon the business by the mother country had limited the operations to the production of pig iron and castings, and a few blast furnaces were employed in New England and the middle Atlantic states. A considerable portion of the pig iron was exported to Great Britain, where it was admitted free of duty, and articles of wrought iron and steel were returned from that country. In 1771 the shipment of pig iron from the colonies amounted to 7,525 tons. By the sudden cessation of commercial relations on the breaking out of the war, the country was thrown upon its own resources, but was illy prepared to meet the new and extraordinary demands for iron. The skill, experience, and capital for this business were all alike wanting, and even the casting of cannon was an undertaking that few of the furnace masters were prepared to venture upon. The bog ores found in Plymouth county, Mass., together with supplies from New Jersey, sustained ten furnaces; and in Bridgewater, cannon were successfully cast and bored by Hon. Hugh Orr, for the supply of the army. They were also made at Westville, Conn., by Mr. Elijah Bachus, who welded together bars of iron for the purpose. The Continental Congress, also, was forced to establish and carry on works for furnishing iron and steel, and in the northern part of New Jersey, the highlands of New York, and the valley of the Housatonic in Connecticut, they found abundance of rich ores, and forests of the best wood for the charcoal required in the manufacture. At their armory at Carlisle, Pa., the first trials of anthracite for manufacturing purposes were made in 1775. But the condition of the country was little favorable for the development of this branch of industry, and after the war, without capital, a currency, or facilities of transportation, the iron business long continued of little more than local importance. The chief supplies were again furnished from the iron works of Great Britain, the establishment of which had in great part been owing to the restrictions placed upon the development of our own resources; and while that country continued to protect their own interest by prohibitory duties that for a long period excluded all foreign competition, the iron interest of the United States languished under a policy that fostered rather the carrying trade between the two countries than the building up of highly important manufactories, and the establishment around them of permanent agricultural settlements through the home market they should secure. Hence it was that the manufacture in Great Britain was rapidly accelerated, improved by new inventions, strengthened by accumulated capital, and sustained by the use of mineral coal for fuel, almost a century before we had learned in the discouraging condition of the art, that this cheap fuel, mines of which were worked near Richmond in Virginia, before 1790, could be advantageously employed in the manufacture. The natural advantages possessed by Great Britain powerfully co-operated with her wise legislation; and as her rich deposits of iron ore and coal were developed in close juxtaposition, and in localities not far removed from the coast, the iron interest became so firmly established that no nation accessible to her ships could successfully engage in the same pursuit, until, by following the example set by Great Britain, its own mines and resources might be in like manner developed. Thus encouraged and supported, the iron interest of Great Britain has prospered at the expense of that of all other nations, till her annual production amounts to more than one-half of the seven millions or eight millions of tons produced throughout the world; and the products of her mines and furnaces have, until quite recently, been better known, even in the extreme western states, where the cost of "Scotch pig iron" has been more than doubled by the transportation, than has that of the rich ores of these very states. And thus it is the annual production of the United States scarcely yet amounts to 1,000,000 tons, notwithstanding the abundance and richness of her mines, both of iron ores and of coal, and the immense demands of iron for her own consumption. So great are the advantages she possesses in the quality of these essential materials in the production of iron, that according to the statement of an able writer upon this subject, who is himself largely engaged in the manufacture, less than half the quantity of raw materials is required in this country to the ton of iron, that is required in Great Britain, "thus economizing labor to an enormous extent. In point of fact, the materials for making a ton of iron can be laid down in the United States at the furnace with less expenditure of human labor than in any part of the known world, with the possible exception of Scotland." ("On the Statistics and Geography of the Production of Iron," by Abram S. Hewitt, N. Y., 1856, p. 20). The tables presented by this writer, of the annual production, show striking vicissitudes in the trade, which is to be accounted for chiefly by the fluctuations in prices in the English market depressing or encouraging our own manufacture, and by the frequent changes in our tariff.

"In 1810 the production of iron, entirely charcoal, was 54,000 tons. In 1820, in consequence of the commercial ruin which swept over the country just before, the business was in a state of comparative ruin, and not over 20,000 tons were produced.

In 1828	the product	was	130,000	tons.
" 1829	"	"	"	142,000	"
" 1830	"	"	"	165,000	"
" 1831	"	"	"	191,000	"
" 1832	"	"	"	200,000	"
" 1840	"	"	"	315,000	"

In 1842 it fell to less than 230,000 tons, the result of the remission of duties under the compromise tariff. In 1846 Secretary Walker estimated it to be 765,000 tons, the result of the combined action of the high tariff of 1842 and the high prices in England, caused by the new demand for railways. In 1847 and 1848 it reached 800,000 tons. In 1849 it fell to 650,000 tons. In 1850, by the census returns it was reduced to 564,755 tons; and it continued to fall off until the first of January, 1853, when the whole product did not exceed 500,000 tons; still leaving it, even at the lowest point, second only to Great Britain. The make then began to increase, so that in 1855 it had reached at least 1,000,000 of tons. This estimate is not confirmed in the tables prepared by the committee of the Association of Iron Manufacturers for 1856, which will be presented in more detail in the course of this chapter. Not reckoning the bar and blooms made direct from the ore, which in 1856 is given as 28,633 tons, the production of pig metal in 1854 was 724,833 tons; in 1855, 728,973 tons; and in 1856, 812,917 tons. The annual production at the present time probably falls short of this amount.

Until the year 1840, charcoal had been the only fuel used in the manufacture of iron; and while it produced a metal far superior in quality to that made with coke, the great demands of the trade were for cheap irons, and the market was chiefly supplied with these from Great Britain. The introduction of anthracite for smelting iron ores in 1840 marked a new era in the manufacture, though its influence was not decidedly felt for several years afterward.

MATERIALS EMPLOYED IN THE MANUFACTURE.

Before attempting to exhibit the resources of the United States for making iron, and the methods of conducting the manufacture, it is well to give some account of the materials employed, and explain the conditions upon which this manufacture depends. Three elements are essential in the great branch of the business—that of producing pig iron, viz: ores, fuel to reduce them, and a suitable flux to aid the process by melting with and removing the earthy impurities of the ore in a freely flowing, glassy cinder. The flux is usually limestone, and by a wise provision, evidently in view of the uses to which this would be applied, limestone is almost universally found conveniently near to iron ores; so also are stores of fuel commensurate with the abundance of the ores.

The principal ores are hematites, magnetic and specular ores, the red oxides of the secondary rocks, and the carbonates. Probably more than three-quarters of the iron made in the United States is from the first three varieties named, and a much larger proportion of the English iron is from the last—from the magnetic and specular ores none. Hematites, wherever known, are favorite ores. They are met with in great irregular-shaped deposits (apparently derived from other forms in which the iron was distributed), intermixed with ochres, clays, and sands, sometimes in scattered lumps and blocks, and sometimes in massive ledges; they also occur in beds interstratified among the mica slates. Although the deposits are regarded as of limited capacity, they are often worked to the depth of more than 100 feet; in one instance in Berks county, Penn., to 165 feet; and when abandoned, as they sometimes are, it is questionable whether this is not rather owing to the increased expenses incurred in continuing the enormous excavations at such depths, than from failure of the ore. Mines of hematite have proved the most valuable mines in the United States. At Salisbury, in Connecticut, they have been worked almost uninterruptedly for more than 100 years, supplying the means for supporting an active industry in the country around, and enriching generation after generation of proprietors. The great group of mines at Chestnut Hill, in Columbia county, Penn., and others in Berks and Lehigh counties in the same state, are of similar character.

The ore is a hydrated peroxide of iron, consisting of from 72 to 85 per cent. of peroxide of iron (which corresponds to about 50 to 60 per cent. of iron), and from 10 to 14 per cent. of water. Silica and alumina, phosphoric acid, and peroxide of manganese are one or more present in very small quantities; but the impurities are rarely such as to interfere with the production of very excellent iron, either for foundry or forge purposes—that is, for castings or bar iron. It is easily and cheaply mined, and works easily in the blast furnace. On account of its deficiency in silica it is necessary to use a limestone containing this ingredient, that the elements of a glassy cinder may be provided, which is the first requisite in smelting iron; or the same end may be more advantageously attained by adding a portion of magnetic ore, which is almost always mixed with silica in the form of quartz; and these two ores are consequently very generally worked together—the hematites making two-thirds or three-quarters of the charge, and the magnetic ores the remainder.

Magnetic ore is the richest possible combination of iron, the proportion of which cannot exceed 72.4 per cent., combined with 27.6 per cent of oxygen. It is a heavy, black ore, compact or in coarse crystalline grains, and commonly mixed with quartz and other minerals. It affects the magnetic needle, and pieces of it often support small bits of iron, as nails. Such ore is the loadstone. It is obtained of various qualities; some sorts work with great difficulty in the blast furnace, and others are more easily managed and make excellent iron for any use; but all do better mixed with hematite. The magnetic ores have been largely employed in the ancient processes of making malleable iron direct from the ore in the open forge, the Catalan forge, etc., and at the present time they are so used in the bloomary fires. They are found in inexhaustible beds of all dimensions lying among the micaceous slates and gneiss rocks. These beds are sometimes so extensive that they appear to make up the greater part of the mountains in which they lie, and in common language the mountains are said to be all ore.

Specular ore, or specular iron, is so named from the shining, mirror-like plates in which it is often found. The common ore is sometimes red, steel gray, or iron black, and all these varieties are distinguished by the bright red color of the powder of the ore, which is that of peroxide of iron. Magnetic ore gives a black powder, which is that of a less oxidized combination. The specular ore thus contains less iron and more oxygen than the magnetic; the proportions of its ingredients are 70 parts in 100 of iron, and 30 of oxygen. Though the difference seems slight, the qualities of the two ores are quite distinct. The peroxide makes iron fast, but some sorts of it produce an inferior quality of iron to that from the hematite and magnetic ores, and better adapted for castings than for converting into malleable iron. The pure, rich ores, however, are many of them unsurpassed. It is found in beds of all dimensions, and though in the eastern part of the United States they prove of limited extent, those of Missouri and Lake Superior are inexhaustible. Magnetic and specular ores are associated together in the same district, and sometimes are accompanied by hematite beds; and it is also the case, that iron districts are characterized by the prevalence of one kind only of these ores, to the exclusion of the others.

The red oxides of the secondary rocks consist, for the most part, of the red fossiliferous and oolitic ores that accompany the so-called Clinton group of calcareous shales, sandstones, and argillaceous limestones of the upper silurian along their lines of outcrop in Pennsylvania, Maryland, and eastern Tennessee, and from Oneida county, N. Y., westward past Niagara Falls, and through Canada even to Wisconsin. The ore is found in one or two bands, rarely more than one or two feet thick, and the sandstone strata with which they are associated are sometimes so ferruginous as to be themselves workable ores. The true ores are sometimes entirely made up of the forms of fossil marine shells, the original material of which has been gradually replaced by peroxide of iron. The oolitic variety is composed of fine globular particles, united together like the roe of a fish. The ore is also found in compact forms, and in Wisconsin it is in the condition of fine sand or seed. Its composition is very variable, and its per-centage of iron ranges from 40 to 60. By reason of the carbonate of lime diffused through some of the varieties, these work in the blast furnace very freely, and serve extremely well to mix with the silicious ores.

Of the varieties of carbonate of iron, the only ones of practical importance in the United States are the silicious and argillaceous carbonates of the coal formation, and the similar ores of purer character found among the tertiary clays on the western shores of Chesapeake Bay. The former varieties are the chief dependence of the iron furnaces of Great Britain, where they abundantly occur in layers among the shales of the coal formation, interstratified with the beds of coal—the shafts that are sunk for the exploration of one also penetrating beds of the other. The layers of ore are in flattened blocks, balls, and kidney-shaped lumps, which are picked out from the shales as the beds of these are excavated. The ore is lean, affording from 30 to 40 per cent. of iron; but it is of easy reduction, and makes, when properly treated, iron of fair quality. In Pennsylvania, Ohio, western Virginia, Kentucky, and Tennessee, the ores occur with the same associations as in England; but the supply is, for the most part, very precarious, and many furnaces that have depended upon them are now kept in operation only by drawing a considerable portion of their supplies from the mines of Lake Superior, more than one thousand miles off. Among the horizontally stratified rocks west of the Alleghanies, the same bands of ore are traced over extensive districts, and are even recognized in several of the different states named. One of the most important of these bands is the buhrstone ore, so called from a cellular, flinty accompaniment which usually underlies it, the whole contained in a bed of peculiar fossiliferous limestone. So much carbonate of lime is sometimes present in the ore, that it requires no other flux in the blast furnace. Its per-centage of iron is from 25 to 35. Along the line of outcrop of some of the carbonates are found deposits of hematite ores, the result of superficial changes in the former, due to atmospheric agencies long continued. In southern Ohio, at Hanging Rock particularly, numerous furnaces have been supported by these ores, and have furnished much of the best iron produced at the west.

The carbonates of the tertiary are found in blocks and lumps among the clays along the shores of the Chesapeake at Baltimore, and its vicinity. The ores are of excellent character, work easily in the furnace, make a kind of iron highly esteemed—particularly for the manufacture of nails—and are so abundant that they have long sustained a considerable number of furnaces. They lie near the surface, and are collected by excavating the clay beds and sorting out the balls of ore. The excavations have been carried out in some places on the shore below the level of tide, the water being kept back by coffer dams and steam pumps.

Bog ores, with which the earliest furnaces in the country were supplied, are now little used. They are rarely found in quantities sufficient for running the large furnaces of the present day, and, moreover, make but an inferior, brittle quality of cast iron. They are chiefly found near the coast, and being easily dug, and also reduced to metal with great facility, they proved very convenient for temporary use before the great bodies of ore in the interior were reached. Some furnaces are still running on these ores in the south-west part of New Jersey, and at Snowhill, on the eastern shore of Maryland, and the iron they make is used to advantage in mixing at the great stove foundries in Albany and Troy with other varieties of cast iron. It increases the fluidity of these, and produces with them a mixture that will flow into and take the forms of the minutest markings of the mould.

Charcoal has been the only fuel employed in the manufacture of iron until anthracite was applied to this purpose, about the year 1840, and still later—in the United States—coke and bituminous coal. So long as wood continued abundant in the iron districts, it was preferred to the mineral fuel, as in the early experience of the use of the latter the quality of the iron it produced was inferior to that made from the same ores with charcoal, and even at the present time, most of the highest-priced irons are made with charcoal. The hard woods make the best coal, and after these, the yellow pine. Hemlock and chestnut are largely used, because of their abundance and cheapness. The charcoal furnaces are of small size compared with those using the denser mineral coal, and their capacity rarely exceeds a production of ten or twelve tons of pig iron in twenty-four hours. In 1840 they seldom made more than four tons a day; the difference is owing to larger furnaces, the use of hot blast, and much more efficient blowing machinery. The consumption of charcoal to the ton of iron is one hundred bushels of hard-wood coal at a minimum, and from this running up to one hundred and fifty bushels or more, according to the quality of the coal and the skill of the manager. The economy of the business depends, in great part, upon the convenience of the supplies of fuel and of ores, of each of which rather more than two tons weight are consumed to every ton of pig iron. As the woods are cut off in the vicinity of the furnaces, the supplies are gradually drawn from greater distances, till at last they are sometimes hauled from ten to fourteen miles. The furnaces near Baltimore have been supplied with pine wood discharged from vessels at the coaling kilns close by the furnaces. Transportation of the fuel in such cases is a matter of secondary importance.

The mineral coals are a more certain dependence in this manufacture, and are cheaply conveyed from the mines on the great lines of transportation, so that furnaces may be placed anywhere upon these lines, with reference more especially to proximity of ores. Thus they can be grouped together in greater numbers than is practicable with charcoal furnaces. Their establishment, however, involves the outlay of much capital, for the anthracite furnaces are all built upon a large scale, with a capacity of producing from twenty to thirty tons of pig iron a day. This requires machinery of great power to furnish the immense quantities of air, amounting in the large stacks to fifteen tons or more every hour, and propel it through the dense column, of fifty to sixty feet in height, of heavy materials that fill the furnace. The air actually exceeds in weight all the other materials introduced into the furnace, and its efficiency in promoting combustion and generating intensity of heat is greatly increased by the concentration to which it is subjected when blown in under a pressure of six or eight pounds to the square inch. It is rendered still more efficient by being heated to temperature sufficient to melt lead before it is introduced into the furnace; and this demands the construction of heating ovens, through which the blast is forced from the blowing cylinders in a series of iron pipes, arranged so as to absorb as much as possible of the waste heat from the combustible gases that issue from the top of the stack, and are led through these ovens before they are finally allowed to escape. The weight of anthracite consumed is not far from double that of the iron made, and the ores usually exceed in weight the fuel. The flux is a small and cheap item, its weight ranging from one-eighth to one-third that of the ores.

The location of furnaces with reference to the market for the iron is a consideration of no small importance, for the advantages of cheap material may be overbalanced by the difference of a few dollars in the cost of placing in market a product of so little value to the ton weight as pig iron.

The following statement presents the cost of the materials and of other items which go to make up the total expense of the production at different localities near the sea-board. The general expenses at the localities named are reduced to a low amount by the large scale upon which the business is conducted.

At different points on the Hudson river, anthracite furnaces are in operation, which are supplied with hematites from Columbia and Dutchess counties, N. Y., and from the neighboring counties in Massachusetts, at prices varying from $2.25 to $3.00 per ton; averaging about $2.50. They also use magnetic ores from Lake Champlain, and some from the Highlands below West Point, the latter costing $2.50, and the former $3.50 to $4.50 per ton; the average being about $3.50. The quantities of these ores purchased for the ton of iron produced are about two tons of hematite and one of magnetic ore, making the cost for the ores $6.75. Two tons of anthracite cost usually $9, and the flux for fuel about 35 cents. Actual contract prices for labor and superintendence have been $4 per ton. Thus the total expense for the ton of pig iron is about $20.10; or, allowing for repairs and interest on capital, full $21.

In the Lehigh valley, in Pennsylvania, are numerous furnaces, which are supplied with anthracite at the low rate of $3 per ton, or $6 to the ton of iron. The ores are mixed magnetic and hematites, averaging in the proportions used about $3 per ton, or, at the rate consumed of 2½ tons, $7.50 to the ton of iron. Allowing the same amount—$4.35—for other items, as at the Hudson river furnaces, the total cost is $17.85; or, with interest and repairs, nearly $19 per ton. The difference is in great part made up to the furnaces on the Hudson by their convenience to the great markets of New York, Troy, and Albany.

The charcoal iron made near Baltimore shows a higher cost of production than either of the above, and it is also subject to greater expenses of transportation to market, which is chiefly at the rolling mills and nail factories of Massachusetts. Its superior quality causes a demand for the product and sustains the business. For this iron per ton 2½ tons of ore are consumed, costing $3.62½ per ton, or $9.06; fuel, 3½ cords at $2.50, $8.75; flux, oyster shells, 30 cts.; labor (including $1.50 for charring) $2.75; other expenses, $2; total, $22.86.

At many localities in the interior of Pennsylvania and Ohio, iron is made at less cost, but their advantages are often counterbalanced by additional expenses incurred in delivering the metal, and obtaining the proceeds of its sale. Increased facilities of transportation, however, are rapidly removing these distinctions. At Danville, on the Susquehanna river, Columbia county, Pennsylvania, the cost of production has been reduced to an unusually low amount, by reason of large supplies of ore close at hand, the cheapness of anthracite, and the very large scale of the operations. Pig iron, as shown by the books of the company, has been made for $11 per ton. Its quality, however, was inferior, so that, with the expenses of transportation added, it could not be placed in the eastern markets to compete with other irons. The rolling mills connected with the furnaces afforded the means of converting it into railroad bars, with which, from the increased value of the iron, the cost of transportation was of less moment.

DISTRIBUTION OF THE ORES.

The magnetic and specular ores of the United States are found in the belt of metamorphic rocks—the gneiss, quartz rock, mica and talcose slates, and limestones—which ranges along to the east of the Alleghanies, and spreads over the principal part of the New England states. It is only, however, in certain districts, that this belt is productive in iron ores. The hematites belong to the same group, and the important districts of the three ores may be noticed in the order in which they are met from Canada to Alabama. Similar ores are also abundant in Missouri, and to the south of Lake Superior.

New England States.—In New Hampshire magnetic and specular ores are found in large quantities in a high granitic hill called the Baldface Mountain, in the town of Bartlett. The locality is not conveniently accessible, and its remoteness from coal mines will probably long keep the ore, rich and abundant as it is, of no practical value. At Piermont, on the western border of the state, specular ore, very rich and pure, is also abundant, but not worked. At Franconia a small furnace, erected in 1811, was run many years upon magnetic ores, obtained from a bed of moderate size, and which in 1824 had been worked to the depth of 200 feet. In 1830 the iron establishments of this place were still objects of considerable interest, though from the accounts of them published in the *American Journal of Science* of that year, it appears that the annual production of the blast furnace for the preceding nine years had averaged only about "216 tons of cast iron in hollow ware, stoves, machinery, and pig iron"—a less quantity than is now produced in a week by some of the anthracite furnaces. One forge making bar iron direct from the ore produced forty tons annually, and another 100 tons, consuming 550 bushels of charcoal to the ton. The cost of this, fortunately, was only from $3.75 to $4.00 per hundred bushels. A portion of the product was transported to Boston, the freight alone costing $25 per ton.

In Vermont these ores are found in the metamorphic slates of the Green Mountains, and are worked to some extent for mixing with the hematite ores, which are more abundant, being found in many of the towns through the central portion of the state, from Canada to Massachusetts. In 1850 the number of blast furnaces was ten, but their production probably did not reach 4,000 tons per annum, and has since dwindled away to a much less amount. At the same time there were seven furnaces in Berkshire, Mass., near the hematite beds that are found in the towns along the western line of the state. These had a working capacity of about 12,000 tons of pig iron annually, and this being made from excellent ores, with charcoal for fuel, its reputation was high and the prices remunerative; but as charcoal increased in price, and the cheaper anthracite-made iron improved in quality, the business became unprofitable; so that the extensive hematite beds are now chiefly valuable for furnishing ores to the furnaces upon the Hudson river, where anthracite is delivered from the boats that have come through the Delaware and Hudson canal, and magnetic ores are brought by similar cheap conveyance from the mines on the west side of Lake Champlain. Through Connecticut, down the Housatonic valley, very extensive beds of hematite have supplied the sixteen furnaces which were in operation ten years ago. The great Salisbury bed has already been named. In the first half of the present century it produced from 250,000 to 300,000 tons of the very best ore; the iron from which, when made with cold blast, readily brought from $6 to $10 per ton more than the ordinary kinds of pig iron. The Kent ore bed was of similar character, though not so extensive.

New York.—Across the New York state line, a number of other very extensive deposits of hematite supported seven blast furnaces in Columbia and Dutchess counties, and now furnish supplies to those along the Hudson river. In Putnam county, magnetic ores succeed the hematites, and are developed in considerable beds in Putnam Valley, east from Cold Spring, where they were worked for the supply of forges during the last century. These beds can again furnish large quantities of rich ore. On the other side of the river, very productive mines of magnetic ore have been worked near Fort Montgomery, six miles west from the river. At the Greenwood furnace, back from West Point, was produced the strongest cast iron ever tested, which, according to the report of the officers of the ordnance department, made to Congress in 1856, after being remelted several times to increase its density, exhibited a tenacity of 45,970 lbs. to the square inch. The beds at Monroe, near the New Jersey line, are of vast extent; but a small portion of the enormous quantities of ore in sight, however, makes the best iron. Mining was commenced here in 1750, and a furnace was built in 1751, but operations have never been carried on upon a scale commensurate with the abundance of the ores. In the northern counties of New York, near Lake Champlain, are numerous mines of rich magnetic ores. Some of the most extensive bloomary establishments in the United States are supported by them in Clinton county, and many smaller forges are scattered along the course of the Ausable river, where water power near some of the ore beds presents a favorable site. Bar iron is made at these establishments direct from the ores; and at Keeseville nail factories are in operation, converting a portion of the iron into nails. In Essex county there are also many very productive mines of the same kind of ore, and Port Henry and its vicinity has furnished large quantities, not only to the blast furnaces that were formerly in operation here, but to those on the Hudson, and to puddling furnaces in different parts of the country, particularly about Boston. In the interior of Essex county, forty miles back from the lake, are the extensive mines of the Adirondac. The ores are rich as well as inexhaustible, but the remoteness of the locality, and the difficulty attending the working of them, owing to their contamination with titanium, detract greatly from their importance. On the other side of the Adirondac mountains, in St. Lawrence county, near Lake Ontario, are found large beds of specular ores, which have been worked to some extent in several blast furnaces. They occur along the line of junction of the granite and the Potsdam sandstone. The iron they make is inferior—suitable only for castings. The only other ores of any importance in the state are the fossiliferous ores of the Clinton group, which are worked near Oneida Lake, and at several points along a narrow belt of country near the south shore of Lake Ontario. They have sustained five blast furnaces in this region, and are transported in large quantities by canal to the anthracite furnaces at Scranton, in Pennsylvania, the boats returning with mineral coal for the furnaces near Oneida Lake.

New Jersey.—From Orange county, in New York, the range of gneiss and hornblende rocks, which contain the magnetic and specular ores, passes into New Jersey, and spreads over a large part of Passaic and Morris, and the eastern parts of Sussex and Warren counties. The beds of magnetic ore are very large and numerous, and have been worked to great extent, especially about Ringwood, Dover, Rockaway, Boonton, and other towns, both in blast furnaces and in bloomaries. At Andover, in Sussex county, a great body of specular ores furnished for a number of years the chief supplies for the furnaces of the Trenton Iron Company, situated at Philipsburg, opposite the mouth of the Lehigh. On the range of this ore, a few miles to the north-east, are extensive deposits of Franklinite iron ore accompanying the zinc ore of this region. This unusual variety of ore consists of peroxide of iron about 66 per cent., oxide of zinc 17, and oxide of manganese 16. It is smelted at the works of the New Jersey Zinc Company at Newark, producing annually about 2,000 tons of pig iron. The metal is remarkable for its large crystalline faces and hardness, and is particularly adapted for the manufacture of steel, as well as for producing bar iron of great strength.

As the forests, which formerly supplied abundant fuel for the iron works of this region, disappeared before the increasing demands, attention was directed to the inexhaustible sources of anthracite up the Lehigh valley in Pennsylvania, with which this iron region was connected by the Morris canal and the Lehigh canal; and almost the first successful application of this fuel to the smelting of iron ores upon a large scale was made at Stanhope, by Mr. Edwin Post. A new era in the iron manufacture was thus introduced, and an immense increase in the production soon followed, as the charcoal furnaces gave place to larger ones constructed for anthracite. The Lehigh valley, lying on the range of the iron ores toward the southwest, also produced large quantities of ore, which, however, was almost exclusively hematite. Hence, an interchange of ores has been largely carried on for furnishing the best mixtures to the furnaces of the two portions of this iron district; and the operations of the two must necessarily be considered together. The annual production, including that of the bloomaries of New Jersey, has reached, within a few years, about 140,000 tons of iron. But in a prosperous condition of the iron business this can be largely increased without greatly adding to the works already established, while the capacity of the iron mines and supplies of fuel are unlimited. The proximity of this district to the great cities, New York and Philadelphia, adds greatly to its importance.

Pennsylvania.—Although about one-third of all the iron manufactured in the United States is the product of the mines of Pennsylvania, and of the ores carried into the state, the comparative importance of her mines has been greatly overrated, and their large development is rather owing to the abundant supplies of mineral coal conveniently at hand for working the ores, and, as remarked by Mr. Lesley ("Iron Manufacturer's Guide," p. 433), "to the energetic, persevering German use for a century of years of what ores do exist, than to any extraordinary wealth of iron of which she can boast. Her reputation for iron is certainly not derived from any actual pre-eminence of mineral over her sister states. New York, New Jersey, Virginia, and North Carolina, are far more liberally endowed by nature in this respect than she. The immense magnetic deposits of New York and New Jersey almost disappear just after entering her limits. The brown hematite beds of her great valley will not seem extraordinary to one who has become familiar with those of New York, Massachusetts, Vermont, Virginia, and Tennessee. Her fossil ores are lean and uncertain compared with those of the south; and the carbonate and hematized carbonate outcrops in and under her coal measures will hardly bear comparison with those of the grander outspread of the same formations in Ohio, Kentucky, and western Virginia." The principal sources of iron in the state are, first, the hematites of Lehigh and Berks counties—the range continuing productive through Lancaster, also on the other side of the intervening district of the new red sandstone formation. The ores are found in large beds in the limestone valley, between the South and the Kittatinny mountains; those nearest the Lehigh supply the furnaces on that river, already amounting to twenty-three in operation and four more in course of construction, and those nearer the Schuylkill supply the furnaces along this river. The largest bed is the Moselem, in Berks county, six miles west-south-west from Kutztown. It has been very extensively worked, partly in open excavation and partly by underground mining, the workings reaching to the depth of 165 feet. Over 20,000 tons a year of ore have been produced, at a cost of from $1.30 to $1.50 per ton.

Magnetic ores are found upon the Lehigh, or South mountain, the margin on the south of the fertile limestone valley which contains the hematite beds. These, however, are quite unimportant, the dependence of the great iron furnaces of the Lehigh for these ores being on the more extensive mines of New Jersey; while the only supplies of magnetic ores to the furnaces of the Schuylkill and the Susquehanna are from the great Cornwall mines, four miles south of Lebanon. An immense body of magnetic iron ore, associated with copper ores, has been worked for a long time at this place, at the junction of the lower silurian limestones and the red sandstone formation. The bed lies between dikes of trap, and exhibits peculiarities that distinguish it from the other bodies of iron ore on this range. The Warwick, or Jones' mine, in the south corner of Berks county, resembles it in some particulars. Its geological position is in the upper slaty layers of the Potsdam sandstone, near the meeting of this formation with the new red sandstone. Trap dikes penetrate the ore and the slates, and the best ore is found at both mines near the trap. Copper ores are also found in connection with the iron ores, but not in workable quantities. The Warwick mine has been worked more than seventy-five years, and has yielded for twenty years together an average of 7,000 tons of ore. Other magnetic ores are found in Lancaster and Chester counties, but are quite unimportant as sources of iron. Along the Maryland line, on both sides of the Susquehanna, chrome iron has been found in considerable abundance in the serpentine rocks, and has been largely and very profitably mined for home consumption and for exportation. It furnishes the different chrome pigments, and their preparation has been carried on chiefly at Baltimore.

A portion of the hematites which supply the furnaces on the Schuylkill, occur along a narrow limestone belt of about a mile in width, that crosses the Schuylkill at Spring Mill, and extends north-east into Montgomery county, and south-west into Chester county. Their production has been very large, and that of the furnaces of the Schuylkill valley dependent upon these and the other mines of this region has been rated at 100,000 tons of iron annually.

The great Chestnut hill hematite ore bed, three and a half miles north-east of Columbia, Lancaster county, covers about twelve acres of surface, and has been worked in numerous great open excavations to about 100 feet in depth, the ore prevailing throughout among the clays and sands from top to bottom. "The floor of the mine is hard, white Potsdam sandstone, or the gray slaty layers over it. The walls show horizontal wavy layers of blue, yellow, and white laminated, unctuous clays, from forty to sixty feet deep, containing ore, and under these an irregular layer of hard concretionary, cellular, fibrous, brown hematite from ten to thirty feet thick down to the sandstone." ("Iron Manufacturer's Guide, p. 562.") In the accompanying wood-cut, the darkly shaded portions represent the hematites, while the lighter portions above are chiefly clays. Professor Rogers supposes that the ore has leached down from the upper slaty beds through which it was originally diffused, and has collected upon the impervious sandstone, which in this vicinity is the first water bearing stratum for the wells.

CHESTNUT HILL MINE.

The repeated occurrence of the lower silurian limestones and sandstones along the valleys of central Pennsylvania, from the Susquehanna to the base of the Alleghany mountain, is accompanied through these valleys with numerous beds of hematite; and to the supplies of ore they have furnished for great numbers of furnaces, is added the fossiliferous ore of the Clinton group, the outcrop of which is along the slopes of the ridges and around their ends. Many furnaces have depended upon this source of supply alone. As stated by Lesley, there were, in 1857, 14 anthracite furnaces that used no other, and 11 anthracite furnaces which mixed it either with magnetic ore or hematite, or with both. Montour's ridge, at Danville, Columbia county, referred to on page 24, is one of the most remarkable localities of this ore. Professor Rogers estimated, in 1847, that there were 20 furnaces then dependent upon the mines of this place, and producing annually an average of 3,000 tons of iron each, with a consumption of 9,000 tons of ore, or a total annual consumption of 180,000 tons. At this rate, he calculated that the available ore would be exhausted in 20 years.

Between the Clinton group and the coal measures are successive formations of limestones, sandstones, shales, etc., which form a portion of the geological column of many thousand feet in thickness; and among these strata, ores like the carbonates of the coal measures are occasionally developed, and these are recognized and worked at many localities along the outcrop of the formations to which they belong. Though of some local importance, they do not add very largely to the iron production of the state. Along the summit of the Alleghany mountain the base of the coal measures is reached, which thence spread over the western portion of the state, nearly to its northern line. The ores which belong to this formation are chiefly contained among its lower members, and found in the outcrop of these around the margin of the basin. At some localities they have been obtained in considerable abundance, and many furnaces have run upon them alone; but for large establishments of several furnaces together, they prove a very uncertain dependence.

MARYLAND.—The metamorphic belt crosses this state back of Baltimore, and is productive in chromic iron and copper ores, rather than in magnetic and specular ores. Some of the former, highly titaniferous, have been worked near the northern line of the state, on the west side of the Susquehanna; and at Sykesville, on the Potomac, a furnace has been supplied with specular ores from its vicinity. Several hematite beds within twenty miles of Baltimore have supplied considerable quantities of ore for mixture with the tertiary carbonates, upon which the iron production of the state chiefly depends. Beds of these occur near the bay from Havre de Grace to the District of Columbia. In the western part of the state large furnaces were built at Mount Savage and Lonaconing to work the ores of the coal formation; but the supply has proved insufficient to sustain them. In 1853 the capacity of the blast furnaces of the state was equal to a production of over 70,000 tons of iron. This, however, has never been realized.

SOUTHERN STATES.—South of Maryland the same iron belt continues through Virginia, the Carolinas, and Georgia; and although it is often as productive in immense beds of the three varieties of ore—the magnetic, specular, and hematite—as in the other states along its range, these resources add comparatively little to the material wealth of the states to which they belong. Through Virginia, east and west of the Blue Ridge, hematite ores abound in the limestone valleys, and magnetic ores are often in convenient proximity to them. Many small furnaces have worked them at different times, but their product was always small. Three belts of magnetic ore, associated with specular iron and hematites, are traced across the midland counties of North Carolina, and have furnished supplies for furnaces and forges in a number of counties—as Lincoln, Cleveland, Rutherford, Stokes, Surry, Yadkin, Catawba; and Chatham, Wake, and Orange counties upon the eastern belt. The belt of ore from Lincoln county passes into South Carolina, and through York, Union, and Spartanburg districts. It crosses the Broad River at the Cherokee ford, and though the whole belt is only half a mile wide, it presents numerous localities of the three kinds of ore, and of limestone also in close proximity, and finely situated for working. Several other localities are noticed in the "State Geological Report," by M. Tuomey, who remarks, on page 278, that "if iron is not manfactured in the state as successfully as elsewhere, it is certainly not due to any deficiency in natural advantages." In northern Georgia the ferruginous belt is productive in immense bodies of hematite, associated with magnetic and specular ores, in the Allatoona hills, near the Etowah river, in Cherokee and Cass counties. This, which appears to be one of the great iron districts of the United States, though bountifully provided with all the materials required in the manufacture, and traversed by a railroad which connects it with the bituminous coal mines of eastern Tennessee, supports only six small charcoal furnaces of average capacity, not exceeding 600 or 700 tons per annum each. In Alabama, hematites and specular ores accompany the belt of silurian rocks to its southern termination, and are worked in a few bloomary fires and two or three blast furnaces. The fossiliferous ore of the Clinton group is also worked in this state.

TENNESSEE in 1840 ranked as the third iron-producing state in the Union. The counties ranging along her eastern border produced hematite ores, continuing the range of the silurian belt of the great valley of Virginia; those bordering the Clinch river produced the fossil ore of the Clinton group, there known as the dyestone ore; and western Tennessee presented a very interesting and important district of hematites belonging to the subcarboniferous limestone in the region lying east of the Tennessee and south of the Cumberland river.* The

* "It is remarkable that most of these deposits

furnaces of this district, which have numbered 42 in all, were the greater part of them in Dickson, Montgomery, and Stewart counties. They were all supplied with charcoal for fuel, at a cost of $4 per hundred bushels. In 1854 the product of pig iron was 37,918 tons; but it gradually declined to 27,050 tons in 1857; and in August, 1858, only 15 furnaces were in operation. The secretary of the American Iron Association, in his report of 1858, remarks that in spite of the old establishments of the manufacture, and wealth of ore deposits south of the Kentucky-Tennessee line, the capital and energy of the trade is moving northward down the two great rivers of that region toward the Ohio and its rolling mills.

Kentucky.—The western part of this state contains, in the counties of Calloway, Trigg, Lyon, Caldwell, Livingston, and Crittenden, an important district of hematite ores—the continuation northward of that of Tennessee. In 1857 10 charcoal furnaces produced 15,600 tons of iron. Eastern Kentucky, however, has a much more productive district in the counties of Carter and Greenup, which is an extension south of the Ohio of the Hanging Rock iron district of Ohio. The ores are carbonates and hematite outcrops of carbonates, belonging to the coal measures and the subcarboniferous limestone. They are in great abundance; a section of 740 feet of strata terminating below with the limestone named, presenting no less than 14 distinct beds of ore, from three inches to four feet each, and yielding from 25 to 60 per cent. of iron. One bed of 32 per cent. iron contains also 11 per cent. bitumen—a composition like that of the Scotch "black band" ore. Others contain so much lime, that the ores are valuable for fluxing as well as for producing iron. The furnaces use charcoal and coke. Their production, taken with that of the same district in Ohio, places this region, as will be seen in the tables to follow, among the first in importance in the United States.

Ohio.—The ores of this state, like those of Kentucky, belong almost exclusively to the coal measures and the limestone formations beneath. In both states some of the fossiliferous ore also is found, but it is comparatively unimportant. The productive beds are near the base of the coal formation, ranging from the Hanging Rock district of Scioto and Lawrence counties north-east through Jackson, Hocking, Athens, Perry, Muskingum, Tuscarawas, Mahoning, and Trumbull counties, to the line of Mercer county in Pennsylvania. The uncertain character of the ores, both as to supply and quality, is strikingly shown by the fact that many of the furnaces of the more northern counties depend for a considerable portion —one-fourth or more—of the ores they use upon the rich varieties from Lake Superior and Lake Champlain. Although the long transportation makes these ores cost nearly three times as much per ton as those of the coal formation, some furnaces find it more profitable to use the former, even in the proportion of three-fourths, on account of the much better iron produced, the greater number of tons per day, and the less consumption of fuel to the ton. The fuel employed is charcoal in many of the furnaces; some have introduced raw bituminous coal to good advantage.

Indiana, Illinois, and Iowa contain no important bodies of iron ore. The coal measures, which cover large portions of these states, are productive in some small quantities of the carbonates, in the two former, which give support to a very few furnaces; but in Iowa they contain no workable beds at all.

Michigan.—The iron region of this state is in the upper peninsula, between Green Bay and Lake Superior. Magnetic and specular ores are found throughout a large portion of this wild territory, in beds more extensive than are seen in any other part of the United States—perhaps than are anywhere known. The district approaches within twelve miles of the coast of Lake Superior, from which it is more conveniently reached than from the south side of the peninsula. The ores are found in a belt of crystalline slates, of six to ten miles in

are of what is called pot ore, that is, hollow balls of ore, which, when broken open, look like broken caldrons. One of them, preserved by Mr. Lewis, is 8 feet across the rim! Another is six feet across. The majority are crossed within by purple diaphragms or partitions of ore, and the interstitial spaces are filled with yellow ochre. Some, like the great eight-foot pot, are found to be full of water. The inside surface is mammillary, irregular, sometimes botryoidal or knobby, but the outside is pretty smooth and regular. All these pots were undoubtedly once balls of carbonates of lime and iron segregated in the original deposit. . . . Gypsum and pyrites are both often found in these Tennessee pots."—*Iron Manufacturer's Guide*, p. 603.

width, that extends west from the lake shore, and is bounded north and south by a granitic district. They are developed in connection with great dikes and ridges of trap, which range east and west, and dip with the slates at a high angle toward the north. The ores also have the same direction and dip. Localities of them are of frequent occurrence for eighteen miles in a westerly direction from the point of their nearest approach to Lake Superior. A second range of the beds is found along the southern margin of the slate district; and about thirty miles back from the lake, where the slates extend south into Wisconsin, similar developments of ore accompany them to the Menomonee river and toward Green Bay. The quality of the ore found at different places varies according to the amount of quartz, jasper, hornblende, or feldspar that may be mixed with it; but enormous bodies are nearly pure ore, yielding from 68 to 70 per cent. of iron, and free from a trace even of manganese, sulphur, phosphorus, or titanium. A single ridge, traced for about six miles, rising to a maximum height ot fifty feet above its base, and spreading out to a width of one thousand feet, has been found to consist of great longitudinal bands of ore, much of which is of this perfectly pure character. Another ridge presents precipitous walls fifty feet high, composed in part of pure specular ore, fine grained, of imperfect slaty structure, and interspersed with minute crystals of magnetic oxide; and in part of these minute crystals alone. Another body of one thousand feet in width, and more than a mile long, forms a hill one hundred and eighty feet high, which is made up of alternate bands of pure, fine grained, steel-gray peroxide of iron, and deep red jaspery ore—the layers generally less than a fourth of an inch in thickness, and curiously contorted. Their appearance is very beautiful in the almost vertical walls. On one of the head branches of the Esconaba is a cascade of thirty-seven feet in height, the ledge over which the water falls being a bed of peroxide of iron, intermixed with silicious matter.

For the supply of the few furnaces and bloomary establishments already in operation in this district, and for the larger demands of distant localities, the ores are collected from open quarries, and from the loose masses lying around. A railroad affords the means of transporting them to Marquette, on the lake shore, whence they are shipped by vessels down the lake. The business already amounts to more than 100,000 tons per annum, and is increasing very rapidly. The name Bay de Noquet and Marquette railroad suggests a southern terminus of this road on Green Bay, and when an outlet is opened in this direction, the production of iron ores will no doubt exceed that of any other region upon the globe. Large quantities will be reduced with charcoal in blast furnaces and bloomaries in the region itself; and when the forests in the vicinity of the works are cut off, the extensive timbered lands around Lake Michigan and Lake Huron will furnish inexhaustible supplies of fuel, which may be brought in vessels to the furnaces, as the pine wood from the forests around Chesapeake Bay has long been delivered to the furnaces on its western shore. Anthracite and bituminous coal will also be brought back as return cargoes by the vessels that carry the ores to the coal fields of Ohio and Pennsylvania. With its vast inland navigation and wonderful resources of iron and of copper also, the north-western portion of our country promises to be the scene of a more extended and active industry than has ever grown out of the mines of any part of the world.

Wisconsin.—Magnetic and specular ores in bodies, somewhat resembling those of the region just described, are found in the extreme northern part of Wisconsin, upon what is known as the Penokie range, distant about 25 miles from Chegwomigon Bay, Lake Superior. Bad River and Montreal River drain this district. The ores, from their remoteness, are not soon likely to be of practical importance. Other immense bodies of these ores, estimated to contain many millions of tons, are found on Black River, which empties into the Mississippi below St. Croix river, on the line of the Land Grant Branch railroad. A furnace has been built by a German company to work these mines. In the eastern part of Wisconsin the oolitic ore of the Clinton group is met with in Dodge and Washington counties, and again at Depere, seven miles south-east of Green Bay. In the town of Hubbard, Dodge county, forty miles west from Lake Michigan, is the largest deposit of this ore ever discovered. It spreads in a layer ten feet thick over 500 acres, and is estimated to contain 27,000,000 tons. It is in grains, like sand, of glistening red color, staining the hands. Each grain has a minute nucleus of silex, around which the oxide of iron collected. The per-centage of metal is about fifty. This ore will probably be worked near Milwaukee with Lake Superior ores, the La Crosse railroad, which passes by the locality, already affording the means of cheap transportation.

Missouri.—This state must be classed among the first in the abundance of its iron ores, though up to this time comparatively little has been done in the development of its mines. The ores are exclusively hematites, and the magnetic and specular, and all occur in the isolated district of silurian rocks—formations which almost everywhere else in the western middle states are concealed beneath the more recent formations. In the counties along the line of the Pacific railroad south-west branch, Prof. Swallow, the state geologist, reports no less than ninety localities of hematite. These are in Jefferson, Franklin, Crawford, Phelps, Pulaski, Marion, Green, and other counties. The first attempts to melt iron in Missouri, and probably in any state west of Ohio, were made in Washington county, in 1823 or 1824, and with the hematites of the locality were mixed magnetic ores from the Iron mountain. In Franklin county there is but one furnace, though on both sides of the Maramec are beds of hematite pipe ore, which cover hundreds of acres. The Iron mountain district is about sixty miles back from the Mississippi river (the nearest point on which is St. Genevieve), and extends from the Iron mountain in the south-east part of Washington county into Madison county. It includes three important localities of specular ore: the Iron Mountain, Pilot Knob, and Shepherd mountain. The first is a hill of gentle slopes, 228 feet high above its base, and covering about 500 acres—a spur of the porphyritic and syenitic range on the east side of Bellevue valley. In its original state, as seen by the writer in 1841, it presented no appearance of rock in place, its surface was covered with a forest of oak, the trees thriving in a soil wholly composed of fragments of peroxide of iron, comminuted and coarse mixed together. Loose lumps of the ore were scattered around on every side but the north, and upon the top were loose blocks of many tons weight each. Mining operations, commenced in 1845, developed only loose ore closely packed with a little red clay. An Artesian well was afterward sunk to the depth of 152 feet. It passed through the following strata in succession: iron ore and clay, 16 feet; sandstone, 34 feet; magnesian limestone, 7½ inches; gray sandstone, 7½ inches; "hard blue rock," 37 feet; "pure iron ore," 5 feet; porphyritic rock, 7 feet; iron ore 50 feet to the bottom. The ore appears to be interstratified with the silicious rocks with which it is associated in a similar manner to its occurrence at the other localities, and data are yet wanting to determine how much may exist in the hill itself, as well as below it. Enough is seen to justify any operations, however extensive, that depend merely upon continued supplies of ore. In quality the ore is a very pure peroxide; it melts easily in the furnace, making a strong forge pig, well adapted for bar iron and steel. Two charcoal furnaces have been in operation for a number of years, and up to the close of 1854 had produced 24,600 tons of iron. The flux is obtained from the magnesian limestone, which spreads over the adjoining valley in horizontal strata.

Pilot Knob is a conical hill of 580 feet height above its base, situated six miles south of the Iron mountain. Its sides are steep, and present bold ledges of hard, slaty, silicious rock, which lie inclined at an angle of 25° to 30° toward the south-west. Near the top the strata are more or less charged with the red peroxide of iron, and loose blocks of great size are seen scattered around, some of them pure ore, and some ore and rock mixed. At the height of 440 feet above the base, where the horizontal section of the mountain is equal to an area of fifty-three acres, a bed of ore is exposed to view on the north side, which extends 273 feet along its line of outcrop, and is from nineteen to twenty-four feet in thickness. It is included in the slaty rocks, and dips with them. Other similar beds are said to occur lower down the hill; and higher up others are met with to the very summit. The peak of the mountain is a craggy knob of gray rocks of ore, rising sixty feet in height, and forming so conspicuous an object as to have suggested the name by which the hill is called. The ore is generally of more slaty structure than that of the Iron mountain, and some of it has a micaceous appearance. The quantity of very pure ore conveniently at hand is inexhaustible. The production of iron will be limited more for want of abundance of fuel than of ore. Charcoal, however, may be obtained in abundance for many years to come, and bituminous coal may also be brought from the coal mines of Missouri and Illinois, as the ores also can be carried to the river to meet there the fuel. The locality is already connected with St. Louis by a railroad. A blast furnace was built here in 1846, and another in 1855. A bloomary with six fires was started in 1850, and has produced blooms at an estimated cost of $30 per ton.

Shepherd mountain, about a mile distant from the Pilot Knob toward the south-west, is composed of porphyritic rocks, which are penetrated with veins or dikes of both magnetic and specular ores. These run in various directions, and the ores they afford are of great purity. They are mined to work together with those of the Pilot Knob. The mountain covers about 800 acres, and rises to the height of 660 feet above its base. Other localities of these ores are also known, and the occurrence of specular ore is reported by the state geologists in several other counties, as Phelps, Crawford, Pulaski, La Clede, etc.

In other parts of the United States and its territories great bodies of iron ore are known to exist, which will probably become valuable at some future time. In Arkansas are found very pure magnetic ores, remarkable for their high magnetic property. Near Santa Fé, in New Mexico, specular ores abound, which must before long be used to furnish the iron required for that region, instead of transporting it, as at present, at heavy cost from the iron districts near the Mississippi river. In California reports are made of the existence of masses of rich ores, comparable in extent even with those of Lake Superior.

IRON MANUFACTURE.

Iron is known in the arts chiefly in three forms—cast iron, steel, and wrought iron. The first is a combination of metallic iron, with from 1½ to 5 or 5½ per cent. of carbon; the second is metallic iron combined with ½ to 1½ per cent. of carbon; and the third is metallic iron, free as may be from foreign substances. These differences of composition are accompanied with remarkable differences in the qualities of the metal, by which its usefulness is greatly multiplied. The three sorts are producible as desired directly from the ores, and they are also convertible one into the other; so that the methods of manufacture are numerous, and new processes are continually introduced. The production of wrought iron direct from the rich natural oxides, was until modern times the only method of obtaining the metal. Cast iron was unknown until the 15th century. Rude nations early learned the simple method of separating the oxygen from the ores by heating them in the midst of burning charcoal; the effect of which is to cause the oxygen to unite with the carbon in the form of carbonic acid or carbonic oxide gas, and escape, leaving the iron free, and in a condition to be hammered at once into bars. The heat they could command in their small fires was insufficient to effect the combination of the iron, too, with the carbon, and produce the fusible compound known as cast iron. In modern times the great branch of the business is the production of pig metal or cast iron in blast furnaces; and this is afterward remelted and cast in moulds into the forms required, or it is converted into wrought iron to serve some of the innumerable uses of this kind of iron, or to be changed again into steel. In this order the principal branches of the manufacture will be noticed.

The production of pig metal in blast furnaces is the most economical mode of separating iron from its ores, especially if these are not extremely rich. The process requiring little labor, except in charging the furnaces, and this being done in great part by labor-saving machines, it can be carried on upon an immense scale with the employment of few persons, and most of those ordinary laborers. The business, moreover, has been greatly simplified and its scale enlarged by the substitution of mineral coal for charcoal—the latter fuel, indeed, could never have been supplied to meet the modern demands of the manufacture.

Blast furnaces are heavy structures of stone work, usually in pyramidal form, built upon a base of 30 to 45 feet square, and from 30 to 60 feet in height. The outer walls, constructed with immense solidity and firmly bound together, inclose a central cavity, which extends from top to bottom and is lined with large fire brick of the most refractory character, and specially adapted in their shapes to the required contour of the interior. The form of this cavity is circular in its horizontal section, and from the top goes on enlarging to the lower portion, where it begins to draw in by the walls changing their slope toward the centre. This forms what are called the boshes of the furnace—the part which supports the great weight of the ores and fuel that fill the interior. For ores that melt easily and fast they are made steeper than for those which are slowly reduced. The boshes open below into the hearth—the central contracted space which the French name the crucible of the furnace. The walls of this are constructed of the most refractory stones of large size, carefully selected for their power to resist the action of fire, and seasoned by exposure for a year or more after being taken from the quarry. Being the first portion to give out, the stack is built so that they can be replaced when necessary. The hearth is reached on each side of the stack by an arch, extending in from the outside. On three sides the blast is introduced by iron pipes that pass through the hearthstones, and terminate in a hollow tuyere, which is kept from melting by a current of water brought by a lead pipe, and made to flow continually through and around its hollow shell. (See fig. *d.*) The fourth side is the front or working-arch of the furnace, at the bottom of which access is had to the melted materials as they collect in the receptacle provided for them at the base of the hearth or crucible. This arch opens out into the casting-house, upon the floor of which are the beds in the sand for moulding the pigs into which the iron is to be cast. Upon the top of the stack around the central cavity are constructed, in first-class furnaces, large flues, which open into this cavity for the purpose of taking off a portion of the heated gaseous mixtures, that they may be conveyed under the boilers, to be there more effectually consumed, and furnish the heat for raising steam for the engines. A portion of the gases is also led into a large heating-oven, usually built on the top of the stack, in which the blast (distributed through a series of cast iron pipes) is heated by the combustion. These pipes are then concentrated into one main, which passes down the stack and delivers the heated air to the tuyeres, thus returning to the furnace a large portion of the heat which would otherwise escape at the top, and adding powerfully to the efficiency of the blast by its high temperature. The boilers, also conveniently arranged on the top of the furnace, especially when two furnaces are constructed near together, are heated by the escape gases without extra expense of fuel, and they furnish steam to the engines, which are usually placed below them. On account of the enormous volume of air, and the great pressure at which it is blown into the furnace, the engines are of the most powerful kind, and the blowing cylinders are of great dimensions and strength. Some of the large anthracite furnaces employ cylinders 7½ feet diameter, and 9 feet stroke. One of these running at the rate of 9 revolutions per minute, and its piston acting in both directions, should propel every minute 7,128 cubic feet of air (less the loss by leakage) into the furnace—a much greater weight than that of all the other materials introduced. It is, moreover, driven in at a pressure (produced by the contracted aperture of the nozzle of the tuyeres in relation to the great volume of air) of 7 or 8 lbs. upon the square inch. Two such cylinders answer for a pair of the largest furnaces, and should be driven by separate engines, so that in case of accident the available power may be extended to either or both furnaces. It is apparent that the engines, too, should be of the largest class and most perfect construction; for the blast is designed to be continued with only temporary interruptions that rarely exceed an hour at a time, so long as the hearth may remain in running order—a period, it may be, of 18 months, or even 4 or 5 years. Furnaces were formerly built against a high bank, upon the top of which the stock of ore and coal was accumulated, and thence carried across a bridge, to be delivered into the tunnel-head or mouth of the furnace. The more common arrangement at present is to construct, a little to one side, an elevator, provided with two platforms of sufficient size to receive several barrows. The moving power is the weight of a body of water let into a reservoir under the platform when it is at the top. This being allowed to descend with the empty barrows, draws up the other platform with its load, and the water is discharged by a self-regulating valve at the bottom. The supply of water is furnished to a tank in the top either by pumps connected with the steam engine or by the head of its source.

The furnaces of the United States, though not congregated together in such large numbers as at some of the great establishments in England and Scotland, are unsurpassed in the perfection of their construction, apparatus, and capacity; and none of large size are probably worked in any part of Europe with such economy of materials. The accompanying wood-cut (fig. *a*) will give an idea of the form and dimensions of one of first class, and may be taken to represent one of the pair of furnaces belonging to the Thomas Iron Company, in the Lehigh valley, Pennsylvania, though the plan is so far modified in the cut as to place the working-arch and casting-house upon a different side. The boiler-stack, which extends 80 feet in length along the level of the oven, O, for heating the blast, is not represented. A duplicate boiler-stack and heating-oven, connected with the other furnace, also stand upon the high platform, which extends from the top of one furnace-stack to that of the other—a distance of about 110 feet, and at an elevation above the bottom of the hearth of 45 feet. The furnace is carried 15 feet higher than this by a low, dome-like structure, in fire brick, which contains an annular flue, EE, 6 feet high and 4 feet wide, into which the gaseous products of combustion are drawn through the horizontal flues, FF, 8 in all. From the annular ring one-fourth of the gases pass into the heating-oven, O, and are burned around the pipes, sufficient atmospheric air being admitted for their combustion; and the other three-fourths flow under the five boilers, and are consumed in the great chamber, 80 feet long, 6 feet high, and about 16 feet wide, beneath them. This is seen in fig. *b*, which is a horizontal section on the top of the stacks.

In fig. *a*, A is the central cavity of the furnace, 60 feet in height, 18 feet in diameter at the top of the boshes, BB (14 feet above the bottom), and 8 feet in diameter at the tunnel-head, on the level of the charging platform, P. The boshes form a cone like a funnel, and the hearth, H, then represents the neck of the funnel. This is 5 feet high, and 7 feet across. The blast is admitted on three sides, by four tuyeres, side by side, in each arch. It is brought down from the heating-oven by the main pipe, *y*, which is 18 inches in diameter. On the fourth side of the furnace is the working-arch, W, by which access is had to the hearth for letting out the cinder and metal. The former flows from time to time over the dam-stone, *d*, and down the cinder-slope, *m*, and the latter is let out through an opening under the dam-stone as often as it rises so as to threaten running over. The block, T, in front of the hearth, is supported by the side stones, and stretches across from one to the other. Under this the workmen thrust long iron bars, and pry up and loosen the cinder whenever it gets thick and endangers obstruction of the blast. The lining of furnaces is made of the best of fire brick, a foot or more deep, moulded in shapes for the circle. Behind this lining is a narrow space filled with sand, and back of this is another fire-brick lining. The heating-oven, as designed in the cut, is 25 feet high, and about the same length, by 10 feet wide. This gives abundant space for the gases to circulate freely and be thoroughly consumed before escaping through the chimneys on the top. In this oven are 5 rows of arched oval pipes, 12 in each row. They stand 10 feet high, arranged on 6 bed-pipes, and their size is 8 by 4 inches. The blast set in operation in the space below the platform, is conducted into the receiver, R, which is a cylinder of boiler-plate iron, 108 feet long and 6½ feet diameter, designed to give uniformity of pressure to the current of air which passes from it to the heating-oven, and thence into the furnace. These receivers are of various forms, and are necessarily of great strength, to resist the pressure of the blast over their expanded surface. The chimney, S, in the cut, is connected with one of the boiler-stacks. This is more clearly seen in fig. *b*. The half omitted is a duplicate of that drawn, and would, if completed, show the other furnace to which the boilers and the chimney, S, belong. The other boilers, *b b*, are connected with the furnace, A. The manner of introducing the blast through the sides of the hearth is shown in fig. *c*, which is a horizontal section through the tuyeres, *t*.

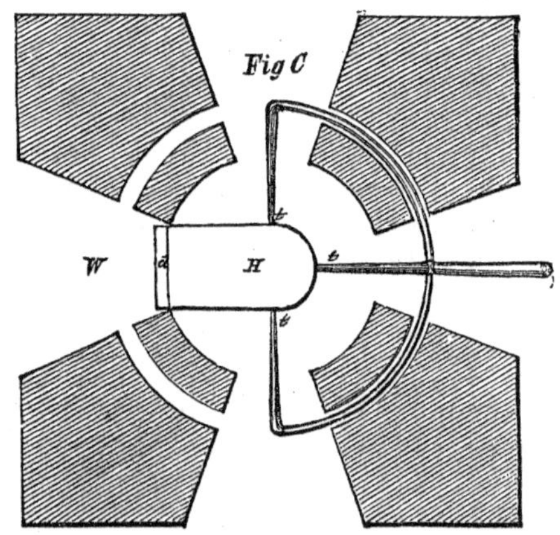

Fig. a.

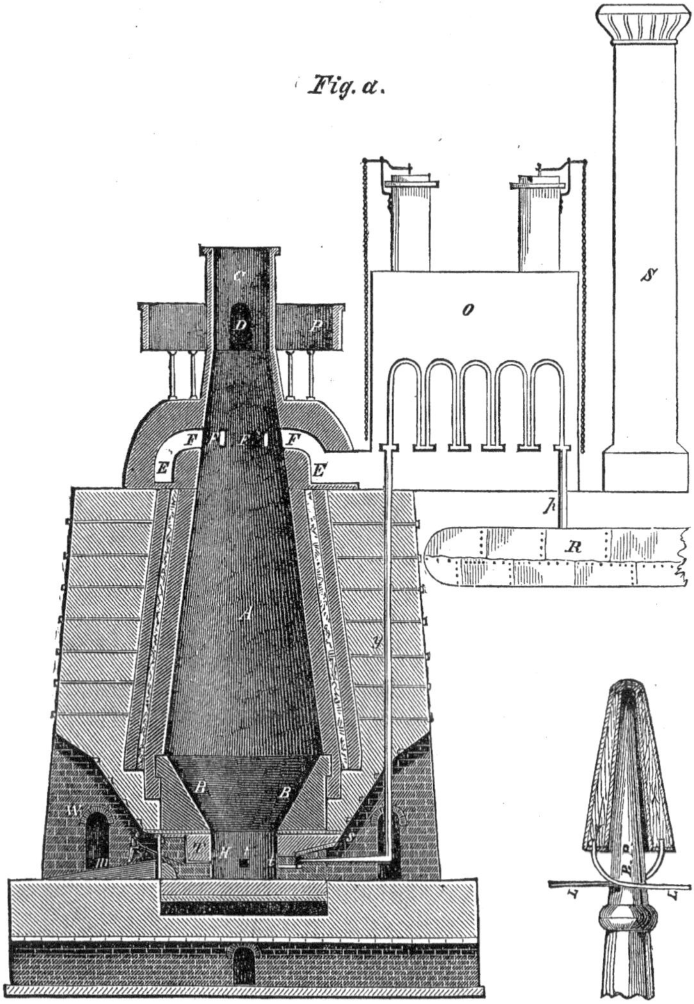

Fig. b.

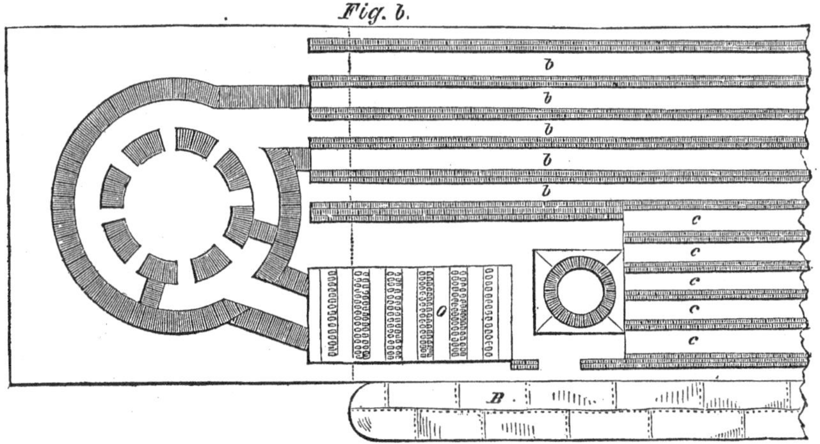

Pig iron, as obtained from the blast furnaces, is classed as forge pig and foundry iron. The one kind is especially fitted for puddling, and not for recasting; while the other is suited for the latter purpose, and is kept for the use of the foundry. This is an establishment for remelting iron and casting it into moulded forms, as pipes, cannon, stoves, machinery, and the innumerable other articles which are made of cast iron. It is often connected with blast furnaces, but is also to be found in almost every large town, and in some the business is carried on upon a very extensive scale, the supplies of both crude iron and fuel being conveyed from a distance. The most extensive foundries in the United States are those of Albany and Troy, the great business of which is the manufacture of stoves. In the former city it has been stated that about 200,000 stoves are made every year. Cannon are cast at the foundries in Boston and Pittsburg, and other places in the United States. The property of cast iron to melt readily and take the form of the mould into which it is poured renders this of great value, especially for multiplying in great numbers the same object. But this kind of iron being brittle, it is not suited to a great variety of articles which require some strength, and which, on account of their complicated forms and great numbers, it would be very desirable to make by some cheaper method than by hammering them out of wrought iron. To meet this want a method was invented of removing from small articles in cast iron the carbon, which makes the distinction between this and malleable iron, and of doing this without affecting the shape of the article. As hitherto practised, the articles to be decarbonized, as the crooked mountings of harness, the elbows of pipes, and numerous other things, are placed upon shelves in an oven, and covered with some pulverized oxide of iron, as common iron rust. Here they are kept hot for ten days to two weeks, when it is found the oxygen of the iron rust and the carbon of the cast iron have disappeared—united together and gone off in the state of a gaseous mixture of the two elements—leaving the castings in a malleable state, and the rust in the form of a metallic incrustation adhering to them. Although the process is slow and imperfect, the metallic crust as it forms interposing itself between the carbon and oxygen remaining, and the results of a heat are often unsatisfactory, the business has been prosecuted with great success in many towns in New England and the middle states. But by the inventions of Prof. A. K. Eaton, of New York, its character now promises to be essentially modified. The first object was to find some oxide, the base of which was also volatile, so that when decomposed all of it would escape, leaving room for fresh oxide to reach the cast iron. The oxide of zinc was found to answer this purpose, especially when used in the form of the native carbonate of the oxide. This being substituted for the oxide of iron, the decarbonization was rapidly effected, from 18 to 24 hours being sufficient to accomplish what required by the other method 10 days to two weeks. The process, moreover, effected another result. The vapors of zinc were collected and condensed in water, and thus this metal was obtained from its ore. By another very recent discovery of the same chemist, it appears that carbonate of soda, or crude soda ash, has a property, scarcely ever before recognized, of removing carbon from cast iron which is immersed in the fused alkali; and as the sodium generated in the process tends to combine with and remove from the iron the phosphorus, sulphur, and silicon, which in very small quantity materially injure its quality, this method is likely to prove still more important than the other. It is applicable also to the production of steel from cast iron, as will be noticed in treating of this article.

WROUGHT IRON.

Of the various methods of producing wrought iron direct from the ore, the most simple and the one in most extensive use is that of the bloomary fire. It consists of a receptacle, open in front, of about three feet from front to back, two feet in width, and depth below the opening one and a half feet. A tuyere for the blast enters on one side at this height above the bottom, and is connected with the pipes for heating the blast, which are arranged in the wide chimney that completes the top of the structure. The receptacle is filled with rich ores, freed as much as possible from all foreign mixtures, and mixed with sufficient charcoal to effect their reduction. This being fired, the blast is let on, and as the mass becomes softened by the heat, it is stirred up by heavy ringers or iron pokers, and the particles of iron are brought together and made to cohere in one lump or loup. This is then taken out and immediately placed under the forge hammer, or passed through the squeezer, by either of which processes it is freed from the cinder and oxide of iron, and converted into a bloom, an oblong block of wrought iron of convenient size for handling or for transportation. The process is not adapted for ores of less than sixty-five per cent. of iron, and even with these the waste is very great, two tons and a half being required to make one ton of blooms. The consumption of charcoal is about 250 bushels. Each fire can produce about one ton in twenty-four hours; or with rich magnetic ores in coarse particles, one hundred pounds per hour may be obtained. Two men are required to each fire, and their wages by contract are eleven dollars per ton of blooms. With ores costing nine dollars, and charcoal from fifteen to seventeen dollars for 250 bushels—rates which are common in northern New York—the cost of a ton of blooms is from thirty-five to thirty-seven dollars. The quality of the iron is better than the ores can be made to produce by other processes; for at the moderate heat employed, some of the foreign metallic bases present escape reduction, and do not combine with the iron, as they are likely to do in the high heat of the blast furnace. But on the other hand the quantity of iron lost in the cinder is large, and so is the consumption of fuel. The process is particularly adapted to thinly inhabited districts, where magnetic ores abound, water power can be had upon almost every stream, and charcoal is worth little more than the labor of preparing and hauling it to the works. A bloomary fire requires little capital to start it, and new ones can be added as fast as the business warrants the increase. As this declines, the fires may be stopped for a longer or shorter time without involving the serious losses occasioned by the interruption of the blast of the smelting furnace. The extent to which the business can be increased in any locality is limited by the necessary dependence of each fire upon two experienced workmen (in case it is run night and day), which is equivalent to the employment of two skilful men for every ton of iron made per day. Where such labor is not abundant, great difficulty may be experienced in keeping the works in operation. The great districts for bloomaries are the counties of Clinton and Essex, New York, northern New Jersey, and recently the iron district of Lake Superior. In 1850 there were no less than two hundred fires in the two counties named above, of which number twenty-one were in one establishment.

In order to reheat the blooms for hammering them into bars, a separate fire was formerly employed; but by a recent improvement the gaseous products of combustion that escape from the bloomary fire are conveyed into a reheating furnace, in which the blooms are placed, and into which the hot-air blast is blown through a large number of tuyeres, so as to introduce its oxygen throughout the partially consumed gaseous mixture. By this means an intense heat is generated, without extra expense of fuel, and two bloomary fires supply sufficient gases for one reheating furnace.

A great number of processes have been patented for making wrought iron direct from the ore, most of which are based on the general plan introduced by Mr. Clay, of Great Britain. The ore, pulverized and screened, is mixed with two-fifths of its weight of bituminous coal, and the whole is introduced into a side chamber connected with a puddling furnace. There being heated, and partially deoxidized by the reaction of the carbon of the coal, it is brought into a condition ready for being balled up into a loup in the puddling furnace, into which the charge is transferred. Renton's plan, which has been in use in New Jersey, is to introduce the finely pulverized ore, mixed with twenty per cent. of charcoal, into vertical fire-brick tubes, arranged over a puddling furnace and heated by its escape heat. These tubes are twelve feet long, and five by eighteen inches in section; open at top, and so contrived at bottom that the charge can be let out as desired into the puddling furnace. In Harvey's or Salter's process the ore, pulverized and mixed with charcoal, was spread upon an inclined shelf in the upper part of the chimney of the puddling furnace; and after being partially heated, it was pushed off on to a lower and hotter shelf; and so it was kept gradually moving down till it was at last delivered into the puddling furnace, new charges being introduced at the top to keep the charges full.

Puddling.—The great supplies of wrought iron are obtained from pig metal by the process called puddling. The principle of this operation is the removal of the carbon from the pig iron by exposing the melted metal to the action of the oxygen of the air, and causing it to escape in combination with this in the form of carbonic acid gas. The furnaces employed are reverberatory; the fire, of bituminous coal, wood, peat, or anthracite,being at one end, and the flame from it playing over a bridge from which it impinges upon the roof of a long, low oven, and is reflected down upon the floor of this, where the metal to be melted is placed. By thus separating the fuel from the metal, this is kept free from any injurious mixtures which might be introduced with the former. The best fuels are those which give the most flame, and when anthracite is used it is necessary to increase the draught by means of a fan blower; and in the United States this is commonly employed with bituminous coals also. The puddling furnaces are either single or double. The former are only worked on one side, and have a hearth area of sixteen to twenty-four square feet; while the double furnaces have a hearth area of about forty feet, and are worked from two opposite sides. Fire brick is used in their construction, and the whole is incased in cast iron plates, which are securely bound together with bars of iron. The floor of the hearth is formed of cast iron plates, covered with pulverized cinder in sufficient quantity to make, when it is melted, a complete layer of two or three inches in thickness. Around the hearth are hollow boshes of cast iron, left open at the ends for the free circulation of air to prevent their being overheated. Sometimes the blast is passed through them, thus taking away a portion of the heat to be returned to the fire. The hearth occupies a depression of about six inches in depth below the sill of the working-door. When the bed of cinder has become hard by cooling, some iron scales or forge cinder are added to it, and usually some pulverized magnetic iron ore also. It is then ready for the cast iron, which may be either in pieces of the original pigs, or in plate metal, which is pig iron partially refined by melting it in a refinery fire, in which it is exposed for a time to a current of air, and then running it out into flat cakes, and chilling these with cold water. The metal is improved in quality by this preliminary operation, and where fuel is cheap it is advantageously practised. In Pennsylvania it is done in small furnaces, called run-out fires. The charge of a single puddling furnace is from 350 to 500 pounds; the double furnace is charged with twice as much. The pieces are all less than twenty-eight pounds each. Before being introduced they are economically heated in an oven in the chimney. After being placed on the hearth, the doors are tightly closed, and a brisk fire is kept up for about a quarter of an hour, until the pieces are at a bright red heat. Through the hole in the side-door the workman then places them by means of an iron bar in the best position for being uniformly heated to the temperature required. In less than half an hour the pieces are so softened, that they can be broken into fragments by the bar working through the same hole in the door. When they are just ready to melt, the fire is checked by closing the damper on the top of the chimney, and water is thrown in, a little at a time, to cool the charge; or pulverized iron ore, or iron scales, or cinder are used instead of water. The workman then begins to stir the pieces about, beating the fragments with his hook or bar, until they are all reduced to powder. The fire is then gradually increased by raising the damper and adding fuel, while the stirring of the metal is continued. In less than an hour from the beginning the iron commences to form soft, spongy lumps, which, if well worked at sufficiently high heat, adhere to each other, so that they may be collected into balls of any size. This is what is called "coming to nature." The making up of the iron into balls requires active work, which must be continued without cessation till the whole is converted into these globular masses of seventy to one hundred pounds weight each. The balls as they are made are laid up against the fire bridge to protect them from the oxidizing action of the flame, as well as to get them out of the way; and when all are ready the furnace is closed for a few minutes to give them a thorough heat. They are then taken out one by one, and dragged in tongs or upon a car to the hammer or squeezer, to be forged into blooms. The time consumed in the puddling for each heat is usually an hour and a half, but sometimes much longer. As soon as one charge is out another is introduced, and the furnace is kept in constant operation, thus avoiding the loss of fuel that would attend its cooling.

A method of puddling is much practised, which is called boiling. The furnace used for this purpose is like the puddling furnace, except that the hearth is deeper, in order to give capacity for a greater quantity of forge cinder, upon a large supply of which the operation depends. This is spread over the bottom in sufficient quantity to form a layer 4 inches deep, and as it begins to cool, it is drawn up around the sides, so as to leave a depression in the centre. In this the iron is placed, and as soon as may be is melted down. The damper is then closed to keep the temperature uniform, and the iron and cinder are busily stirred; at the same time more cinder is thrown in—a handful at a time—till the contents begin to swell up and boil. This is owing to the formation of carbonic oxide from the carbon of the pig iron and the oxygen of the iron scales of the cinder, and as this gas rises it burns with a blue flame. Gradually the boiling subsides, by reason of the removal of the carbon, and the cinder settles down, leaving the iron in spongy masses, which would unite into one body if not worked over and broken up as in ordinary puddling. This being thoroughly done, it is then well heated and made up into balls for the hammer. The process requires more time, labor, and fuel than the other; but it produces better iron, and more of it from the same quantity of crude metal. Thus 95 per cent. is sometimes obtained from metal which, when treated by the other method, may yield only 80 per cent. The extent, however, to which the operation may be carried on is limited by the amount of cinder available, which is supplied wholly from the puddling furnaces.

The consumption of fuel in puddling is from 1,700 to 2,240 lbs. of anthracite or of bituminous coal to the ton of rough bars obtained. The waste of the metal is in great part made up, and sometimes wholly so, by the addition of rich ores to the charge. This plan was first adopted in the United States, and is now generally practised wherever such ores can be obtained. The cost of the labor employed in puddling is from $3.50 to $4 per ton. The forging of puddlers' balls into blooms is called shingling, and was formerly performed altogether under the forge hammer. This, however, is now very generally supplanted by the squeezer, of which there are two sorts—one a ponderous lever, the short arm of which, shaped like the upper jaw of a crocodile, opens and closes over a fixed lower jaw. The ball being placed between these is powerfully compressed, and being properly handled at the same time is made to receive the desired shape. A more perfect machine is the rotary squeezer invented by Mr. Henry Burden, of Troy. It consists of an upright cylinder of cast iron about 4 feet in diameter, the same height as the length of a bloom, and its face

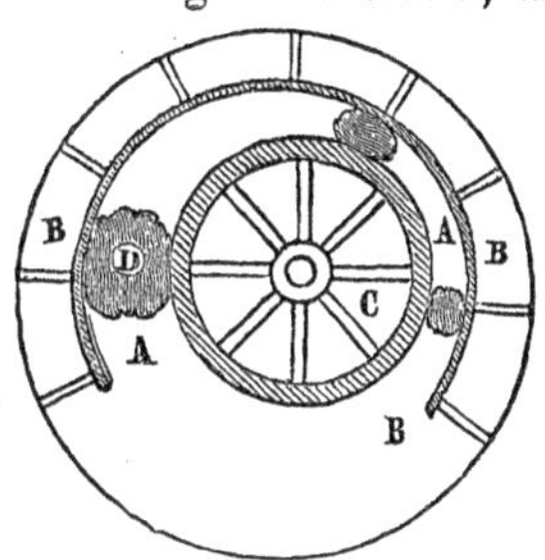

serrated with vertical grooves. It is made to revolve within an elliptical shell, which is open on one side to receive the ball. As this is presented at the larger aperture on one side of the opening, it is drawn in by the revolution of the cylinder, and thoroughly squeezed, as it is rolled around between the two serrated faces. The space between these grows narrower by the slight eccentricity of the shell, and when the ball is brought round to the other side of the revolution of the cylinder and is there discharged, it is greatly reduced in diameter, and enlongated in the form of a cylindrical block.

The next process is to reduce this into rough bars. The bloom, without reheating, is taken directly to the roughing rolls, and passed between these; first through the largest space, and then successively through smaller and smaller grooves, until it is drawn out in the shape required. The iron is still very imperfect, being hard and brittle, with many flaws and imperfections. To convert it into merchantable iron, it is cut into short lengths by shears worked by machinery; and the pieces are made up into piles or faggots, which are placed upon the hearth of a "reheating furnace." This is made like a puddling furnace, with a very low roof, so designed that the space may be entirely occupied by the gaseous products of combustion to the exclusion of atmospheric air, the effect of which would be to oxidize and waste the metal, besides injuring its quality by introducing scales of the oxide. The hearth is made to slope toward the base of the chimney-flue at the back end, and being covered with pure silicious sand, the oxide of iron which forms combines with this, and flows down as a silicate of the protoxide of iron in a liquid cinder. When at a good welding heat the piles or faggots are taken out, and passed through the finishing rolls, which are of much superior construction to the roughing rolls, their faces being smooth and polished, and the shape of the grooves made as perfect as possible, to give all the forms of iron required in merchant bars. From faggots thus made the iron is prepared for railroad bars, the peculiar forms of which require rolls of complicated designs.

The rolling mills of the United States, in operation in 1856, were as follows:—

No. of Mills.	States.	Product. Tons.
1	Maine	4,500
19	Massachusetts	55,292
2	Rhode Island	4,475
5	Connecticut	5,759
1	Vermont	500
13	New York	55,172
10	New Jersey	28,403
91	Pennsylvania	241,484
4	Delaware	2,211
13	Maryland	14,812
12	Virginia	26,355
1	North Carolina	215
3	South Carolina	1,210
1	Georgia	900
3	Tennessee	2,680
15	Ohio	30,980
7	Kentucky	16,865
1	Indiana	Unfinished.
1	Illinois	"
4	Missouri	4,420
2	Michigan	1,848

The mills making railroad iron at the same time were the following, producing the quantities given:—

	Tons of Rails.
The Bay State, South Boston	17,871
" Rensselaer, Troy, N. Y.	13,512
" Trenton, N. J., about	13,000
" Phœnixville, Pennsylvania	18,592
" Pottsville, Schuylkill Co., Penn	3,021
" Lackawanna, Luzerne Co., Penn	11,338
" Rough and Ready, Danville, Penn	5,259
" Montour, Danville, Penn	17,538
" Safe Harbor, Lancaster Co., Penn	7,347
" Mount Savage, Cumberland, Maryland	7,159
" Cambria, Cambria Co., Penn	13,206
" Brady's Bend, Armstrong Co., Penn	7,533
" Cosalo, Lawrence Co., Penn	0
" Washington, Wheeling, Va	2,355
" McNickle, Covington, Ky	1,976
" Newbury, near Cleveland, Ohio	0
" Railroad Mill, Cleveland, Ohio	0
" Wyandotte, near Detroit, Mich	1,848
" Chicago, Ill	0
" Indianapolis, Indiana	0
	141,555

About 1,000 tons in addition to the above were rolled at Pottsville, in the Palo Alto mill; making a total production of 142,555 tons of railroad iron, two-thirds of which were made in Pennsylvania.

Sheet Iron.—For making sheet iron the bars are gradually spread out between smooth rolls, which are brought nearer together as the metal grows thinner. The Russians have a method of giving to sheet iron a beautifully polished surface, and a pliability and durability which no other people have been able to imitate. All attempts that have been made to learn the secret of this process have entirely failed, and the business remains a monopoly with the Russians. The nearest imitation of this iron is produced at Pittsburg, Pennsylvania, and several eastern establishments, by what is called Wood's process. This consists in rolling the common sheet at a certain temperature while it is covered with linseed oil. A very fine surface is thus produced, but the pliability and toughness of the Russian iron are wanting, even though the sheets are often annealed in close vessels, and the glaze and color are also inferior. Sheet iron is now extensively prepared for roofing, and other uses requiring exposure to the weather, by protecting its surface with a coating of zinc. This application is an American invention, having been discovered in 1827, by the late Prof. John W. Revere, of New York. In March, 1859, he exhibited, at a meeting of the Lyceum of Natural History, specimens of iron thus protected, which had been exposed for two years to the action of salt water without rusting. He recommended it as a means of protecting the iron fastenings of ships, and introduced the process into Great Britain. Sheets thus coated are known as galvanized iron, though the iron is now coated with zinc by other means as well as by the galvanic current. One method, that of Mallet, is to place the sheets, after they are well cleaned by acid and scrubbed with emery and sand, in a saturated solution of hydrochlorate of zinc and sulphate of ammonia; and after this in a bath composed of 202 parts of mercury and 1,292 of zinc, to every ton weight of which a pound of potassium or sodium is added. The compound fuses at 680° Fahrenheit, and the zinc is immediately deposited upon the iron surface. Another method is to stir the sheets in a bath of melted zinc, the surface of which is covered with sal ammoniac.

The use of heavy sheets or plates for building purposes is also a recent application of iron, that adds considerably to the demand for the metal. The plates are stiffened by the fluting, or corrugating, which they receive in a powerful machine, and may be protected by a coating of zinc. Their preparation is largely carried on in Philadelphia; and in the same works a great variety of other articles of malleable iron, for domestic and other uses, are similarly protected with zinc, as window shutters, water and gas pipes, coal scuttles, chains for pumps, bolts for ships' use, hoop iron, and telegraph and other wire.

The production of the principal boiler-plate and sheet iron establishments of the United States is thus given for the year 1856:—

	Tons.
East of the Delaware there are but two mills, both of which are in Jersey City. Product in 1856	550
In E. Pennsylvania, on the Schuylkill and lower Susquehanna, 25 mills	21,218
Near Wilmington, Delaware, 3 mills	1,374
Between Wilmington and Baltimore, 7 mills.	2,998
Pittsburg, Penn., 14 mills. Sheet iron, 6,437; boiler iron, 3,212; besides bars, rods, hoops, and nails	9,649
Sheet iron at the Sharon mill, Mercer Co. Penn.	500
Bloom mill, Portsmouth, S. Ohio, and Globe mill, Cincinnati, about	2,000
	38,289

A mill for boiler plate has been erected at St. Louis.

Iron Wire.—The uses of iron wire have greatly increased within a few years past. The telegraph has created a large demand for it; and with the demand the manufacture has been so much improved, especially in this country, that the wire has been found applicable to many purposes for which brass or copper wire was before required. It is prepared from small rods, which are passed through a succession of holes, of decreasing sizes, made in steel plates, the wire being annealed as often as may be necessary to prevent its becoming brittle. In this branch the American manufacturers have attained the highest perfection. The iron prepared from our magnetic and specular ore is unequalled in the combined qualities of strength and flexibility, and is used almost exclusively for purposes in which these qualities are essential. But where stiffness combined with strength is more important, Swedish and Norwegian iron also are used. Much of the iron wire now made is almost as pliable as copper wire, while its strength is about 50 per cent. greater. In Worcester, Mass., a large contract has been satisfactorily filled for No. 10 wire, one of the conditions of which was that the wire, when cold, might be tightly wound around another wire of the same size without cracking or becoming rough on the surface. Such wire is an excellent material for ropes, and considerable American iron is already required for this use, especially for suspension bridges. Wires are also used for fences, and are ingeniously woven into ornamental patterns. The so-called "netting fence," thus made, can be rolled up like a carpet. For heavier railing and fences, as for the front yards of houses, for balconies, window guards, etc., iron bars and rods are now worked into ornamental open designs, by powerfully crimping them and weaving them together like wires.

Nails.—Among the multitude of other important applications of malleable iron, that of nail making is particularly worthy of notice, as being in the machine branch of it—the preparation of cut nails—entirely an American process. Our advance in this department is ascribed to the great demand for nails among us in the construction of wooden houses. In England, even into the present century, nails were wrought only by hand, employing a large population. In the vicinity of Birmingham it was estimated that 60,000 persons were occupied wholly in nail making. Females and children, as well as men, worked in the shop, forging the nails upon anvils, from the "split iron rods" furnished for the purpose from the neighboring iron works. The contrast is very striking between their operations and those of the great establishments in Pennsylvania, consisting of the blast furnaces, in which the ores are converted into pig; of the puddling furnaces, in which this is made into wrought iron; of the rolling and slitting mills, by which the malleable iron is made into nail-plates; and of the nail machines, which cut up the plates and turn them into nails—all going on consecutively under the same roof, and not allowing time for the iron to cool until it is in the finished state, and single establishments producing more nails than the greater part of the workshops of Birmingham fifty years ago. Public attention was directed to machine-made nails as long ago as 1810, by a report of the secretary of the treasury, in which he referred to the success already attained in their manufacture in Massachusetts. "Twenty years ago," he states, "some men, now unknown, then in obscurity, began by cutting slices out of old hoops, and, by a common vice gripping these pieces, headed them with several strokes of the hammer. By progressive improvements, slitting mills were built, and the shears and the heading tools were perfected, yet much labor and expense were requisite to make nails. In a little time, Jacob Perkins, Jonathan Ellis, and a few others, put into execution the thought of cutting and of heading nails by water; but being more intent upon their machinery than upon their pecuniary affairs, they were unable to prosecute the business. At different times other men have spent fortunes in improvements, and it may be said with truth that more than a million of dollars have been expended; but at length these joint efforts are crowned with complete success, and we are now able to manufacture, at about one-third of the expense that wrought nails can be manufactured for, nails which are superior to them for at least three-fourths of the purposes to which nails are applied, and for most of those purposes they are full as good. The machines made use of by Odiorne, those invented by Jonathan Ellis, and a few others, present very fine specimens of American genius." The report then describes the peculiar character of the cut nail—that it was used by northern carpenters without their having to bore a hole to prevent its splitting the wood; that it would penetrate harder wood than the wrought nail, etc. At that time, it states, there were twelve rolling and slitting mills in Massachusetts, chiefly employed in rolling nail plates, making nail rods, hoops, tires, sheet iron, and copper, and turning out about 3,500 tons, of which about 2,400 tons were cut up into nails and brads. From that time to the present the manufacture of nails by machinery has been a profitable branch of industry in the south-eastern part of Massachusetts, the iron and the coal being furnished from the middle Atlantic states, and the nails, in great part, finding a market at the south. The following table presents the number of nail mills in operation in 1856. The smaller establishments are gradually going out of the business, and this is becoming more concentrated in the coal and iron regions, thus saving the cost of transportation in these heavy articles. The manufacturers of New England, however, ingeniously divert a part of their operations to the production of smaller articles, with which the cost of transportation is a less item in proportion to their value, such as tacks, rivets, screws, butts, wire, and numerous finished articles, the value of which consists more in the labor performed upon them and in the use of ingenious machinery than in the cost of the crude materials employed.

NAIL FACTORIES IN THE UNITED STATES, AND THEIR PRODUCTION IN 1856.

	Tons.
In south New England, 12 mills, nails principally	25,000
Troy, New York	4,000
Rockaway, Boonton, New Jersey, nails and spikes	8,250
Southern New Jersey	4,167
On the Schuylkill, 5 mills, about	9,000
On the lower Susquehanna, 2 mills, about	2,600
Middle Pennsylvania, 2 mills, about	2,000
Maryland, 2 mills	2,155
Richmond, 1 mill	1,075
Pittsburg, 14 mills, nails, spikes, rivets, tacks	14,195
Wheeling, 2 mills	6,465
Ironton, southern Ohio, 1 mill	775
Mahoning Co., N. E. Ohio, 1 mill	380
Buffalo	1,400
Total	81,462

The number of nail machines employed in these mills was 2,645.

A great variety of machines have been devised for nail making, very ingenious in their designs, and all too complicated for description. The iron is rolled out into bars for this manufacture, of 10 or 12 feet in length, and wide enough to make three or more strips, each one of which is as wide as the length of the nail it is to make. The cutting of these strips from the wider bars is the special work of the slitting mill, which is, in fact, but a branch of the rolling operation, and carried on in conjunction with it. The slitting machine consists of a pair of rolls, one above the other, each having 5 or 6 steel disks upon its axis, set as far apart as the width required for the nail-rod. Those upon one roll interlock with those upon the other, so that when the wide bar is introduced it is pressed into the grooves above and below, and cut into as many strips as there are spaces between the disks. This work is done with wonderful rapidity, several bars being passed through at once. In the nail factory each nail-making machine works upon one of these strips, or nail-rods, at a time, first clipping off a piece from the end presented to it, and immediately another, as the flat rod is turned over and the end is again presented to the cutter. The reason of turning it over for each successive cut is because the piece cut off for the nail is tapering, in order to make it a little wider at the end intended for the head than at the other, and thus, making the wider cut on alternate sides of the rod, this is regularly worked up into pieces of the proper shape. In the older operations a workman always sat in front of each machine, holding the rod and turning it over with every clip; but by a modern improvement this work is also done by mechanical contrivance. Each piece, as fast as it is clipped off, disappears in the machine. There it is seized between powerful jaws, and the head is pressed up from the large end by the short, powerful motion imparted to the piece of apparatus called the header. As it is released, it slides down and drops upon the floor, or in a vessel placed to receive the nails.

Machinery has been applied in the United States to the manufacture of horse-shoe nails, according to a number of patented plans. Of these, the most successful is probably that invented about the year 1848, by Mr. L. G. Reynolds, of Providence; also the inventor of the solid-headed pin. The form of this nail could not be given as in ordinary cut nails by the cutter, but the sides required to be pressed as well as the head. This involved the use of movable plates of suitable figure; and as it was found that the nails could not be shaped except when the metal was softened by heat, the plates must necessarily be of the hardest steel, and protected as effectually as possible from the effects of constant working of heated iron. These difficulties were fully overcome, and the nails, after being turned out, were toughened by annealing, giving them all the excellent qualities of hand-made nails, with the advantage of perfect uniformity of size, so that one nail answers as well as another for the holes in the horse-shoes. They are, moreover, made with great rapidity, each machine producing half a ton of nails in 12 hours. The process has been taken to Europe, and is there in successful operation. Spikes, also, have been made and headed in similar machines; and among all small articles in iron, none, perhaps, has proved so profitable to the inventor as the hook-headed spike, used for holding down, by its projecting head, the edge of the iron rails to the sill. This was the invention of Mr. Henry Burden, of Troy, whose machines for wrought-iron spikes and for horse-shoes have also proved very successful. By the latter, perfect shoes are turned out at the rate of 60 in a minute. This process has been introduced in most of the European countries.

STEEL.

As already remarked, steel differs in composition from metallic iron only by containing from ½ to 1½ per cent. of carbon, and from cast-iron by the latter containing a larger proportion of carbon, which may amount to 5.5 per cent. To readily convert these varieties into each other is an object of no small importance, for their properties are so entirely distinct, that they really serve the purposes of three different metals. Steel is particularly valuable for its extreme hardness, fine grain, and compact texture, which admits of its receiving a high polish. It is the most elastic of metals, and much less liable to rust than iron. It has the peculiar property of assuming different degrees of hardness, according to the rapidity with which it is chilled when heated; and it may be melted and run into moulds like cast iron, and the ingots thus prepared may be hammered, rolled, and forged into shapes like wrought iron; and these may finally be tempered to any degree of hardness desired. Differing so little in composition from metallic iron and from cast iron, and being so universally in demand for a multitude of uses, it would seem that it ought to be produced as cheaply as one or the other of the varieties, between which its composition places it. But this is far from being the case. While pig iron is worth only $20 to $30 per ton, and bar iron $60 to $90, cast steel in bars is worth from $250 to $300 per ton. This is chiefly owing to the difficulty of procuring in large quantities steel of uniform character, which the consumers of the article can purchase with perfect confidence that it is what they require and have been accustomed to use. The English boast, with good reason, of the position they occupy in this manufacture, which is almost a monopoly of the steel trade of the whole world. Though producing themselves little or no iron fit for making alone the best steel, they have imported enough of the Swedish and Norwegian bar iron to insure a good quality, and have been especially cautious to render this as uniform as possible. Their method of manufacture is to introduce carbon into the wrought iron by what is called the cementing process. On the continent of Europe steel is made to some extent, in Silesia and Styria, by removing from cast iron enough of its carbon to leave the proper proportion for steel, and then melting the product and casting it into ingot moulds. But this cheaper method does not appear to have been taken up in Great Britain. In the United States several processes are in operation, two of which are peculiarly American. The cementing method, as conducted in England, has been longest known, and will be first described. The cementing furnace is a sort of oven, furnished with troughs or shelves, upon which charcoal dust is laid for receiving the bars. These are placed edgewise in the charcoal, half an inch apart, and the spaces are filled in with more sifted coal. Enough is added to cover the bars, and upon this a second tier is laid in the same way, and so on till the trough is filled with several tons of iron, all of which is perfectly excluded from the air. The trough being secured with others in the oven, a fire is started under them. In about six days the bars have absorbed enough carbon to acquire the properties of the softer kinds of steel, such as are used for saws and springs. In a day or two longer it answers for cutting instruments, and some time after this it gains in hardness, so as to be fitted for cold chisels, for drills such as miners use, etc. Its character is ascertained at any time by drawing out one of the bars. After the change is effected the fire is extinguished, and about a week is allowed for the furnace and its contents to cool. When at last the bars are obtained, their surface is found to be covered with blisters, whence the steel is called blistered steel. The fibrous texture of the iron has given place to a granular structure, but is so irregular and uneven that the metal requires further treatment to perfect it. To make the English shear-steel, so called from its being originally employed for shears used in sheep-shearing, the bars are cut into lengths of a foot and a half, and a number of these are bound together to make a faggot. This is brought to a welding heat, and drawn down first under a forge-hammer, and then under the tilt-hammer. This weighs from 150 to 200 pounds, and strikes from 150 to 360 strokes a minute. The rapidity of the work keeps the steel at a glowing heat, and it is soon fashioned into a dense bar of smooth surface, susceptible of a polish, and suited for the manufacture of cutting instruments. Sometimes it is cut into pieces to be refaggoted, and drawn down again into bars, which are then called double-shear.

Cast steel is a still more dense and perfect variety. It is prepared by melting, in large crucibles, blistered steel broken into small pieces, and pouring the metal into moulds. These are then worked into shapes by the forge hammer and the rolls.

The American methods of making steel were discovered by Prof. A. K. Eaton, of New York, and the one now employed by the Damascus Steel Company was practically demonstrated by him in Rochester and its vicinity in 1851 and 1852. This consists in carbonizing and melting malleable iron in crucibles at one operation, by introducing into the pot with the pieces of iron a carbonaceous salt, such as the ferro-cyanide of potassium, either alone or in combination with charcoal powder. At an intense heat this salt rapidly carbonizes the iron, which thus first becomes steel, then fuses, and is poured into moulds. The quantity of the salt employed is proportional to the quantity of the iron and the quality of the steel required. The operation is successfully carried on in different establishments in New Jersey, New York, and Pennsylvania, and cast steel of the very best quality is produced at less expense than the article has ever before cost in this country. For bar steel, according to the prospectus of the company, the best charcoal-made iron is employed, costing $85 per ton, and this, together with the coal used for fuel, the chemical materials, the melting, crucibles, and hammering, make the whole cost about $142 per ton, while that of the imported article is $300 or more. The great difficulty in the process is to obtain suitable crucibles for withstanding the intense heat required to melt the charge of 60 lbs. of malleable iron. Those in use are blue-pots, costing $1.60 each. Though made of the best of plumbago, they stand only two or three meltings.

The other process, which is just now introduced into practice, is based upon the property of carbonate of soda to remove from cast iron the carbon it contains, when the metal is kept for a few hours in a bath of the melted alkali. The decarbonizing effect is in part due to the action of the oxygen of the alkaline base, which is given up to the carbon of highly heated cast iron, but principally to the decomposition of the combined carbonic acid, which gives to the carbon one of its atoms of oxygen, and is resolved into carbonic oxide. This property of soda was discovered by Prof. Eaton in 1856, but the fact that the carbonated or bicarbonated alkalies act principally by virtue of their carbonic acid, was only recently recognized and made practically available by him. The action of soda or its carbonates is not limited to the removal of the excess of carbon in cast iron. It combines with and removes those impurities which would prove fatal to the quality of the steel if remaining in it, as sulphur, phosphorus, and silicon; and the method thus admits of the use of crude irons, such as could never be applied to this manufacture by any other mode. The cast iron, in the form of thin plates, having been kept at a bright red heat in the bath of melted carbonate for a sufficient time, which is determined by occasionally taking out and testing some of the pieces, is transferred to the crucible, and is then melted and poured into moulds, as in the ordinary method of making cast steel. The crucibles, not being subjected to greater heat than is required for melting cast steel, endure much longer than when employed for melting wrought iron in the carbonizing process; thus a great saving is effected in the expense of the conversion; and this economy is still further increased by the use of a crude material, costing only from $20 to $30 per ton, in place of the superior qualities of wrought iron, worth $85 per ton. So great, indeed, is the saving, that the cost of the cast steel, when obtained in ingots, is found not to exceed the cost of the malleable iron employed in the other process.

Statistics.—The records of the production of iron of the United States are very incomplete up to the year 1854. Even the census returns are highly defective, as they often make no distinction between iron made from the ore and the products of the secondary operations of remelting and puddling. The first systematic attempts to obtain complete accounts of the business, as conducted in Pennsylvania, were made in 1850 by the Association of Iron Manufacturers, organized in Philadelphia. Mr. Charles E. Smith collected the returns, and published them in a small volume, together with other papers relating to the manufacture. In 1856 the association, through their secretary, Mr. J. P. Lesley, and their treasurer, Mr. C. E. Smith, obtained full returns from 832 blast furnaces, 488 forges, and 225 rolling mills in the United States, besides others in Canada, exhibiting their operations for the preceding three years. Some of these results are presented in the following tables:—

NO 1.—TABLE OF IRON WORKS IN OPERATION AND ABANDONED IN 1858.

	Anthracite Furnaces.	Charcoal and Coke Furnaces.	Abandoned Furnaces.	Bloomary Forges.	Abandoned Bloomaries.	Refinery Forges.	Abandoned Refineries.	Rolling Mills.	Abandoned.
Maine	..	1	..	..	..	..	..	1	..
New Hampshire	..	1	..	..	..	1	..	..	..
Vermont	..	5	..	5	..	..	..	1	..
Massachusetts	3	7	..	..	..	5	1	19	..
Rhode Island	..	..	..	..	..	..	..	2	..
Connecticut	1	14	..	..	..	6	..	5	..
New York	14	29	6	42	1	3	2	11	5
New Jersey	4	6	12	48	29	2	..	10	1
Pennsylvania	93	150	102	1	3	110	44	91	5
Delaware	..	..	1	..	..	..	..	4	..
Maryland	6	24	7	..	..	..	..	13	..
Virginia	..	39	56	..	..	43	..	12	..
North Carolina	..	3	3	36	..	..	..	1	1
South Carolina	..	4	4	2	..	..	..	3	..
Georgia	..	7	1	4	..	..	..	2	..
Alabama	..	3	1	14	..	..	..	..	..
Tennessee	..	41	33	50	2	9	3	3	2
Kentucky	..	30	17	..	..	4	9	8	..
Ohio	..	54	26	..	..	..	5	15	..
Indiana	..	2	3	..	..	..	..	1	..
Illinois	..	2	..	..	..	..	..	1	..
Michigan	..	7	..	3	..	..	..	2	..
Wisconsin	..	3	..	..	..	..	..	..	..
Missouri	..	7	..	..	..	3	..	5	1
Arkansas	..	..	..	1	..	..	..	..	..
Total	121	439	272	206	35	186	64	210	15

	Furnaces		Forges		Rolling Mills.		Total
In working order,	560	Furnaces,	389	Forges,	210	Rolling Mills.	Total, 1,159
Abandoned,	272	"	99	"	15	"	" 386
In all,	832	"	488	"	225	"	" 1,545

The production of the blast furnaces in the different iron districts for the years 1854, 1855, and 1856, is exhibited in Table No. 2; their arrangement being according to the fuel employed and the quantities of iron produced in each district in 1856:—

TABLE NO. 2.—PRODUCTION OF PIG IRON.

Fuel.	District.	1854.		1855.		1856.	
Anthracite	Pennsylvania	....	208,603	....	255,326	....	306,972
"	Out of Pennsylvania	....	99,007	...	87,779	....	87,537
Charcoal and Coke	S. Ohio	56,081	79,010	47,982	64,162	70.455	92,116
" " "	E. Kentucky	22,929		16,180		21,661	
" " "	W. Pennsylvania	78.927	90,216	59,388	69,314	59,597	76,653
" " "	N. Ohio	11,289		9,926		17,056	
" " "	E. Pennsylvania	....	62,724	....	60,596	....	52,775
Charcoal	W. Tennessee	37,918	53,054	33,683	50,347	32,162	50,664
"	W. Kentucky	12,236		13,664		14,902	
"	S. Indiana	1,400		1,500		1,800	
"	S. Illinois	1,500		1,500		1,800	
Charcoal and Coke	S. W. Pennsylvania	11,052	12,982	18,217	20,559	29,400	30,867
" " "	N. W. Virginia	1,930		2,342		1,467	
" " "	Maryland	....	36,658	....	36,309	....	30,998
Charcoal	E. of the Hudson	....	30,420	....	32,826	..	29,937
"	N. and W. New York	....	19,197	....	19,736	....	18,847
"	Missouri	....	7,591	....	10,181	....	10,138
"	S. New York and N. New Jersey	....	13,435	....	7,901	....	5,683
"	E. and Middle Virginia	....	5,880	....	6,926	....	5,730
"	North and South Carolina	1,820	6,056	1,830	6,061	1,956	7,694
"	Georgia	2,391		2,715		2,807	
"	E. Tennessee and Alabama.	1,845		1,516		2,931	
"	Michigan	....	990	....	9[illegible]0	3,678	6,178
"	Wisconsin	....	....	....	....	2,500	
Total production of pig iron in the United States	Tons .		725,823		728,973		812,789

TABLE NO. 3.—DISTRIBUTION OF THE FURNACES BY STATES.

I. ANTHRACITE FURNACES.

No.	States.	Product. Tons.
3	Massachusetts	4,443
1	Connecticut	0
14	New York	47,257
4	New Jersey	26,117
93	Pennsylvania	306,972
6	Maryland	10,720
121		394,509

II. COKE FURNACES.

No.	States.	Product. Tons.
21	Pennsylvania	39,953
3	Maryland	4,528
24		44,481

III. RAW BITUMINOUS COAL FURNACES.

No.	States.	Product. Tons.
6	Pennsylvania	8,417
13	Ohio	16,656
19		25,073

IV. CHARCOAL FURNACES.

No.	States.	Product. Tons.
1	Maine	2,100
1	New Hampshire	0
5	Vermont	2,420
7	Massachusetts	8,564
14	Connecticut	12,876
29	New York	21,774
6	New Jersey	2,100
143	Pennsylvania	96,154
21	Maryland	26,470
39	Virginia	14,828
3	North Carolina	450
4	South Carolina	1,506
7	Georgia	2,807
3	Alabama	1,495
41	Tennessee	28,476
30	Kentucky	36,563
41	Ohio	70,355
2	Indiana	1,800
2	Illinois	1,900
7	Missouri	10,138
3	Wisconsin	2,500
7	Michigan	3,678
416		348,954

	No. of Furnaces.	Tons.
Anthracite, as above	121	394,509
Coke, "	24	44,481
Raw Coal, "	19	25,073
Charcoal, "	416	348,954
Total pig	580	813,017

TABLE NO. 4.—PRODUCT OF WROUGHT IRON DIRECT FROM THE ORE, 1856.

Bloomaries.	States.	Product. Tons.
5	Vermont	1,650
42	New York	18,710
48	New Jersey	4,487
36	North Carolina	1,182
2	South Carolina	640
4	Georgia	40
14	Alabama	252
50	Tennessee	1,222
3	Michigan	450
204		28,633
Pig iron as above		812,917
Grand total production of iron from the ore in 1856		841,550

In addition to this amount, the importations for the year 1856 of iron designed for manufacture are estimated at 363,998 tons, consisting of Scotch pig, 55,403 tons; rolled and hammered iron, 298,275 tons; and scraps, 10,320 tons; and if to this be added for old rails reworked, 100,000 tons, and for scrap, 25,000 tons, the total amount of iron entering into domestic consumption was 1,330,548 tons. The importation of railroad iron not included in the above was 167,400 tons. The proportion of foreign iron introduced into the general consumption, not including rails, was about 30 per cent.

The value of the immediate products of the manufacture of domestic iron is thus given at the prices current in 1856:—

Foundry pig	302,154 tons	a $27,	$8,158,158
Foundry cold-blast charcoal iron for car wheels, &c.	35,000 "	a 35,	1,225,000
Rails	142,555 "	a 63,	8,980,965
Boiler and sheet	38,639 "	a 120,	4,636,680
Nails	81,462 "	a 84,	6,842,808
Bar, rod, hoop, and band	235,425 "	a 65,	15,302,625
Hammered iron	21,000 "	a 125,	2,625,000
Total			$47,771,236

Mr. Smith presents the following conclusion to the "Statistical Report of the Iron Manufacture:" "The great facts demonstrated are, that we have nearly 1,200 efficient works in the Union; that these produce annually about 850,000 tons of iron, the value of which in an ordinary year is $50,000,000; of this amount the portion expended for labor alone is about $35,000,000."

Since 1856 no attempts have been made to collect the statistics of the iron business of the United States, and consequently but a very general statement can be given of the changes which have taken place. The total annual production has probably not varied much from 800,000 tons—exceeding rather than falling short of this amount. In the Lehigh valley the business is rapidly increasing, while the charcoal iron manufacture in different parts of the country is steadily diminishing. In the vicinity of Baltimore only one furnace was in operation in November, 1860; and besides another at Texas, in Baltimore county, and one of the bog ore furnaces on the eastern shore, it is believed all the rest, including those in the bituminous coal region, were out of blast. The business, however, in general is in a sound condition, and great improvements have been made in diminishing the cost of the manufacture, by means of more care in the superintendence and by reducing the general expenses and the number of hands employed to the ton of iron produced.

The census of 1860 gives the following statistics of the iron production and manufacture of that year. There had been very little progress in the production of iron in the country for several years previous, in consequence of the very low rate of duty at which foreign railroad and other iron was admitted.

Iron blooms, valued at	$2,623,178
Pig iron	20,870,120
Bar, sheet and railroad iron	31,888,705
Iron wire	1,643,857
Iron forgings	1,907,460
Car wheels	2,083,350
Iron castings of all kinds	36,132,033
	$97,148,705

The opening of the war, in 1861, gave an extraordinary impetus to iron production and manufacture. The tariff and other causes reduced the importation to a minimum, while the demand for iron for the fabrication of small arms and cannon; for the construction of the large fleet of iron-clads, and for the other war vessels; for the building of locomotives, the casting of car wheels and furnishing the vast quantity of railroad iron needed to repair the old tracks destroyed by the contending armies, and to lay the tracks of new roads, extended the business vastly beyond all former precedent; and the requirement that the Pacific railroad and its branches shall be constructed solely of American iron, as well as the increase in its use for buildings, and for shipping, have maintained it in a prosperous condition.

The manufacture of steel and the other manufactures of iron, aside from those already enumerated, brought the aggregate production and manufacture of iron and steel, in 1860, up to $285,879,510. The revenue tax paid on iron and steel manufactures in 1864 indicates that the product of the branches taxed amounted to about $123,000,000. This estimate was far below the production, as many branches were not taxed, and the returns of that year were imperfect. The production and manufacture of 1865 were not less than 400 millions of dollars. There is every reason to expect that the development of the iron mines will be pushed forward with constantly increasing energy, and that the time is not far distant when many of the great repositories of ores we have described—now almost untouched—will be the seats of an active industry and centres of a thriving population, supported by the home markets they will create. The great valley of the west, when filled with the population it is capable of supporting, and intersected in every direction with the vast system of railroads, of which the present lines form but the mere outlines, will itself require more iron than the world now produces, and the transportation of large portions of this from the great iron regions of northern Michigan and Wisconsin, and of coal back to the mines, will sustain larger lines of transportation than have ever yet been employed in conveying to their markets the most important products of the country. The importation of foreign iron—already falling off in proportion to the increased consumption—must, before many years, cease, and be succeeded by exports for the supplies of other nations less bountifully provided for in this respect than the United States and Great Britain.

CHAPTER II.

COPPER.

The early attempts to work copper mines in the United States have already been alluded to in the introductory remarks to the department of this work relating to mining industry. The ores of this metal are widely distributed throughout the country, and in almost every one of the states have been found in quantities that encouraged their exploration—in the great majority of cases to the loss of those interested. The metal is met with in all the New England states, but only those localities need be named which have at times been looked upon as important.

Copper occurs in a native or metallic state, and also in a variety of ores, or combinations of the metal with other substances. In these forms the metallic appearance is lost, and the metal is obtained by different metallurgical operations, an account of some of which will be presented in the course of this chapter. Until the discovery of the Lake Superior mines, native copper, from its scarcity, was regarded rather as a curiosity than as an important source of supply. The workable ores were chiefly pyritous copper, vitreous copper, variegated copper, the red oxide, the green carbonate or malachite, and chrysocolla. The first named, though containing the least proportion of copper, has furnished more of the metal than all the other ores together, and is the chief dependence of most of the mines. It is a double sulphuret of copper and iron, of bright yellow color, and consists, when pure, of about 34 per cent. of copper, 35 of sulphur, and 30 of iron. But the ore is always intermixed with quartz or other earthy minerals, by which its richness is greatly reduced. As brought out from the mine it may not contain more than 1 per cent. of copper, and when freed as far as practicable from foreign substances by the mechanical processes of assorting, crushing, washing, jigging, etc., and brought up to a percentage of 6 or 7 of copper, it is in Cornwall a merchantable ore, and the mine producing in large quantity the poor material from which it is obtained may be a profitable one. Vitreous copper, known also as copper glance, and sulphuret of copper, is a lead gray ore, very soft, and contains 79.8 per cent. of copper, united with 20.2 per cent. of sulphur. It is not often found in large quantity. Variegated or purple copper is distinguished by its various shades of color and brittle texture. It yields, when pure, from 56 to 63 per cent. of copper, 21 to 28 of sulphur, and 7 to 14 of iron. The red oxide is a beautiful ore of ruby red color, and consists of 88.8 per cent. of copper and 11.2 per cent. of oxygen. It is rarely found in sufficient quantity to add much to the products of the mines. Green malachite is a highly ornamental stone, of richly variegated shades of green, famous as the material of costly vases, tables, etc., manufactured in Siberia for the Russian government. It is always met with in copper mines, especially near the surface, but rarely in large or handsome masses. It consists of copper 57.5, oxygen 14.4, carbonic acid 19.9, and water 8.2 per cent. Chrysocolla is a combination of oxide of copper and silica, of greenish shades, and is met with as an incrustation upon other copper ores. It often closely resembles the malachite in appearance. It contains about 36 per cent. of copper.

The first mines worked in the United States were peculiar for the rich character of their ores. These were, in great part, vitreous and variegated copper, with some malachite, and were found in beds, strings, and bunches in the red sandstone formation, especially along its line of contact with the gneiss and granitic rocks in Connecticut, and with the trap rocks in New Jersey. The mine at Simsbury, in Connecticut, furnished a considerable amount of such ores from the year 1709 till it was purchased, about the middle of the last century, by the state, from which time it was occupied for sixty years as a prison, and worked by the convicts; not, however, to much profit. In 1830 it came into possession of a company, but was only worked for a short time afterward. On the same geological range, but lying chiefly in the gneiss rocks, the most productive of these mines was opened in

1836, in Bristol, Conn. It was vigorously worked from 1847 to 1857, and produced larger amounts of rich vitreous and pyritous ores than have been obtained from any other mine in the United States. No expense was spared in prosecuting the mining, and in furnishing the most efficient machinery for dressing the ores. It is stated that full 1,800 tons of ore were sent to market, which produced over $200,000, the yield ranging from 18 to 50 per cent. of copper. The mine was finally abandoned in 1857.

The New Jersey mines have all failed, from insufficient supply of the ores. The Schuyler mine, at Belleville, produced rich vitreous copper and chrysocolla, disseminated through a stratum of light brown sandstone, of 20 to 30 feet in thickness, and dipping at an angle of 12°. During the periods of its being worked in the last century, the excavations reached the depth of 200 feet, and were carried to great distances on the course of the metalliferous stratum. The mine was then so highly valued that an offer of £500,000, made for it by an English company, was refused by the proprietor, Mr. Schuyler. In 1857–58 attempts were made by a New York company to work the mine again, but the enterprise soon failed. Among the other mines which have been worked to considerable extent in New Jersey are the Flemington mine, which resembled in the character of its ore the Schuyler mine, and the Bridgewater mine, near Somerville, at which native copper in some quantity was found in the last century; two pieces met with in 1754 weighing together, it was reported, 1,900 lbs. A mine near New Brunswick also furnished many lumps of native copper, and thin sheets of the metal were found included in the sandstone. At different times this mine has been thoroughly explored, to the loss of those engaged in the enterprise. In Somerset county, the Franklin mine, near Griggstown, has been worked to the depth of 100 feet. Carbonate and red oxide of copper were found in the shales near the trap, but not in quantity sufficient to pay expenses. In Pennsylvania, near the Schuylkill river, in Montgomery and Chester counties, many mines have been worked for copper and lead at the junction of the red sandstone and gneiss. Those veins included wholly in the shales of the red sandstone group were found to produce copper chiefly, while those in the gneiss were productive in lead ores. At the Perkiomen and Ecton mines—both upon the same lode —extensive mining operations have been carried on; a shaft upon the latter having reached in 1853 the depth of 396 feet. The sales of copper ores during the three years the mines were actively worked amounted to over $40,500; but the product was not sufficient to meet the expenditures.

The mines in Frederick county, Maryland, in the neighborhood of Liberty, were near the red sandstone formation, though included in argillaceous and talcose slates. A number of them have been worked at different times up to the year 1853, when they were finally given up as unprofitable.

A more newly discovered and richer copper district in Maryland is near Sykesville, on the Baltimore and Ohio railroad, 32 miles from Baltimore, in a region of micaceous, talcose, and chloritic slates. A large bed of specular iron ore lying between the slates was found to contain, at some depth below the surface, carbonates and silicates of copper, and still further down copper pyrites. In the twelve months preceding April 1, 1857, 300 tons had been mined and sent to market, the value of which was $17,896.92, and the mine was reported as improving. The ore sent to the smelting works at Baltimore, in December of that year, yielded 16.03 per cent. of copper. Within seven miles of Baltimore the Bare Hill mine has produced considerable copper, associated with the chromic iron of that region.

Like the last two named, all the other localities of copper ores of any importance along the Appalachian chain and east of it are remote from the range of the red sandstone, and belong to older rock formations. In the granites of New Hampshire, pyritous copper has been found in many places, but has nowhere been mined to any extent. In Vermont, mining operations have been carried on to some extent upon a large and very promising lode of pyritous copper, which is traced several miles through Vershire and Corinth. At Strafford, pyritous ores were worked in 1829 and afterward, both for copperas and copper. In New York, excellent pyritous ores were produced at the Ulster lead mine in 1853. Among other sales of similar qualities of ore, one lot of 50 tons produced 24.3 per cent. of copper.

In Virginia, rich ores of red oxide of copper, associated with native copper and pyritous copper, are found in the metamorphic slates at Manasses Gap, and also in many other places further south along the Blue

Ridge. The very promising appearance of the ores, and their numerous localities, would encourage one to believe that this will prove to be a copper region, were it not that, when explored, the ores do not seem to lie in any regular form of vein. In the southern part of the state, in Carroll, Floyd, and Grayson counties, copper was discovered in 1852, and mines were soon after opened in a district of metamorphic slates, near their junction with the lower silurian limestones. The copper was met with in the form of pyritous ore, red oxide, and black copper, beneath large outcropping masses of hematite iron ore, or gossan. Some of the shipments are said to have yielded over 20 per cent. of copper. The amount of ores sent east, over the Virginia and Tennessee railroad, in 1855, was 1,931,403 lbs.; in 1856, 1,972,834 lbs.; and in the nine months ending June 30, 1857, 1,085,997 lbs.; 1858, 688,418 lbs.; 1859, 1,151,132 lbs.; and 1860, 2,679,673 lbs. Copper ores are very generally met with in the gold mines of this state, and further south, but the only one of them that has been worked expressly for copper is that of the North Carolina Copper Company, in Guilford county. From this a considerable amount of pyritous copper ores were sent to the north in 1852 and 1853.

In Tennessee, an important copper region lies along the southern line of Polk county, and extends into Gilmer county, Georgia. The ore was first found in 1847, associated with masses of hematite iron ores, which formed great outcropping ledges, traceable for miles from south-west to north-east along the range of the micaceous and talcose slates. An examination of the ores, made to ascertain the cause of their working badly in the furnace, was the means of corroborating or giving importance to the discovery of the copper. In 1851 copper mining was commenced, and afterward prosecuted with great activity by a number of companies. The ore was found in seven or eight parallel lodes of the ferruginous matters, all within a belt of a mile in width. At the surface there was no appearance of it, but as the explorations reached the depth of seventy-five or one hundred feet below the surface of the hills, it was met with in various forms, resulting from the decomposition of pyritous copper, and much mixed with the ochreous matters derived from a similar source. In a soft black mass, easily worked by the pick, and of extraordinary dimensions, were found intermixed different oxides and other ores of copper, yielding various proportions of metal, and much of it producing 20 per cent. and more, fit to be barrelled up at once for transportation. This ore spread out in a sheet, varying in width at the different mines; at the Eureka mine it was 50 feet wide, and at the Hiwassee 45 feet, while at the Isabella mine the excavations have been extended between two walls 250 feet apart. In depth this ore is limited to a few feet only, except as it forms bunches running up into the gossan or ochreous ores. Below the black ore is the undecomposed lode, consisting of quartz, more or less charged with pyritous copper, red oxide, green carbonate, and gray sulphuret of copper; and it is upon these the permanent success of the mines must depend. About 14 mining companies have been engaged in this district, and the production of the most successful of them was as follows, up to the year 1858: Isabella, 2,500 tons; Calloway, 200; Mary's, 1,500; Polk county, 2,100; Tennessee, 2,200; Hiwassee, 2,500; Hancock, 2,000—making a total of 13,000 tons, yielding from 15 to 40 per cent. of copper, and worth $100 per ton, or $1,300,000. In addition to this, the products of the London mine, yielding an average of 45 per cent. of copper, amounted to over $200,000 in value; and the products of the Eureka mine were rated for 1855 at $86,000; for 1856 at $123,000; and for 1857 at $136,000. The value of the ores remaining at the mines too poor to transport, but valuable to smelt in furnaces on the spot, was estimated at $200,000 more. Furnaces for smelting, on the German plan, were in operation in 1857, and produced the next year 850 tons of matt, or regulus. At the Eureka mine, in 1858, there were 4 reverberatory furnaces, 2 blast, and 2 calcining furnaces. The fuel employed is wood and charcoal. By the introduction of smelting operations, ores of 5 to 6 per cent. are now advantageously reduced.

In 1857 the mines of a large portion of this district were incorporated into the so-called Union Consolidated Mining Company, and most of the other mines were taken up by the Burra Burra Company and the Polk County Company. The principal interests in the last two are held in New Orleans. The first named own 11 mines, of which they are working three only, with a monthly production of 750 to 800 tons of 12 per cent. copper, besides 5 or 6 tons of precipitate copper. This is metallic copper, precipitated from the waters of the mine by means of scrap iron thrown into the vats in which these waters are collected. The iron being taken up by the acids which hold the copper in solution, the latter is set free, and deposited in fine metallic powder. The ore is smelted in furnaces constructed on the German plan, and being put through twice, produce a regulus of 55 per cent. As soon as the proper furnaces and refineries can be constructed, it is intended to make ingot copper, and by working more of the mines belonging to the company it is expected the monthly production will soon be raised to 2,000 tons of 10 to 12 per cent. ore.

The two other companies have erected extensive smelting works; and the mines of the Burra Burra are producing 450 to 500 tons per month of 14 per cent. ore, and those of the Polk County Company about 300 tons of 15 per cent. ore. Both companies will soon be able to make ingot copper. The report of the Union Consolidated Company for the first year of their operations presents, against expenditures amounting to $307,182.77, receipts of $457,803.73, leaving a profit of $150,620.96. A large portion of the regulus is shipped to England for sale.

The profits of these mines were greatly reduced the first few years of their operation by the necessity of transporting the ores 40 miles to a railroad, and thence more than 1,000 miles by land and water to the northern smelting works. The establishment of furnaces at the mines not only reduces this source of loss, but renders the great body of poorer ores available, which they were not before. A railroad is now in process of construction to connect the mines with the Georgia railroads.

West of the Alleghanies, the only copper mines, besides those of Lake Superior, are in the lead region of Wisconsin, Iowa, and Missouri. A considerable number of them have been worked to limited extent, and small blast furnaces have been in operation smelting the ores. These were found only near the surface, in the crevices that contained the lead ores; and in Missouri, in horizontal beds in the limestone, along the line of contact of the granite. The ores were mixed pyritous copper and carbonate, always in very limited quantity. The amount of copper produced has been unimportant, and it is not likely that any considerable increase in the supply of the metal will be derived from this source.

The existence of native copper on the shores of Lake Superior, is noticed in the reports of the Jesuit missionaries of 1659 and 1666. Pieces of the metal 10 to 20 lbs. in weight were seen, which it is said the Indians reverenced as sacred; similar reports were brought by Father Dablou in 1670, and by Charlevoix in 1744. An attempt was made in 1771 by an Englishman, named Alexander Henry, to open a mine near the forks of the Ontonagon, on the bank of the river, where a large mass of the metal lay exposed. He had visited the region in 1763, and returned with a party prepared for more thoroughly exploring its resources. They, however, found no more copper besides the loose mass, which they were unable to remove. They then went over to the north shore of the lake, but met with no better success there. General Cass and Mr. H. R. Schoolcraft visited the region in 1819, and reported on the great mass upon the Ontonagon. Major Long, also, in 1823, bore witness to the occurrence of the metal along the shores of the lake. The country, till the ratification of the treaty with the Chippewa Indians in 1842, was scarcely ever visited except by hunters and fur-traders, and was only accessible by a tedious voyage in canoes from Mackinaw. The fur companies discouraged, and could exclude from the territory, all explorers not going there under their auspices. Dr. Douglass Houghton, the state geologist of Michigan, in the territory of which these Indian lands were included, made the first scientific examination of the country in 1841, and his reports first drew public attention to its great resources in copper. His explorations were continued both under the state and general government until they were suddenly terminated with his life by the unfortunate swamping of his boat in the lake, near Eagle river, October 13, 1845.

In 1844 adventurers from the eastern states began to pour into the country, and mining operations were commenced at various places near the shore, on Keweenaw Point. The companies took possession under permits from the general land office, in anticipation of the regular surveys, when the tracts could be properly designated for sale. Nearly one thousand tracts, of one mile square each, were selected—the greater part of them at random, and afterward explored and abandoned. In 1846 a geological survey of the region was authorized by Congress, which was commenced under Dr. C. T. Jackson, and completed by Messrs. Foster and Whitney in 1850. At this time many mines were in full operation, and titles to them had been acquired at the government sales.

The copper region, as indicated by Dr. Houghton, was found to be nearly limited to the range of trap hills, which are traced from the termination of Keweenaw Point toward the south-west in a belt of not more than two miles in width, gradually receding from the lake shore. The upper portion of the hills is of trap rock, lying in beds which dip toward the lake, and pass in this direction under others of sandstone, the outcrop of which is along the northern flanks of the hills. Isle Royale, near the north shore of the lake, is made up of similar formations, which dip toward the south. These rocks thus appear to form the basin in which the portion of Lake Superior lying between is held. The trap hills are traced from Keweenaw Point in two or three parallel ridges of 500 to 1,000 feet elevation, crossing Portage lake not far from the shore of Lake Superior, and the Ontonagon river about 13 miles from its mouth. They thence reach further back into the country beyond Agogebic lake, full 120 miles from the north-eastern termination. Another group of trap hills, known as the Porcupine mountains, comes out to the lake shore some 20 miles above the mouth of the Ontonagon, and this also contains veins of copper, which have been little developed until the explorations commenced near Carp lake in these mountains in 1859. These have resulted in a shipment of over 20 tons of rough copper in 1860, and give encouragement to this proving a copper-producing district. The formations upon Isle Royale, which is within the boundary of the United States, although they are similar to those of the south shore, and contain copper veins upon which explorations were vigorously prosecuted, have not proved of importance, and no mines are now worked there. The productive mines are comprised in three districts along the main range of the trap hills. The first is on Keweenaw Point, the second about Portage lake, and the third near the Ontonagon river. All the veins are remarkable for producing native copper alone, the only ores of the metal being chiefly of vitreous copper found in a range of hills on the south side of Keweenaw Point, and nowhere in quantities to justify the continuation of mining operations that were commenced upon them. The veins on Keweenaw Point cross the ridges nearly at right angles, penetrating almost vertically through the trap and the sandstones. Their productiveness is, for the most part, limited to certain amygdaloidal belts of the trap, which alternate with other unproductive beds of gray compact trap, and the mining explorations follow the former down their slope of 40°, more or less, toward the north. The thickness of the veins is very variable, and also their richness, even in the amygdaloid. The copper is found interspersed in pieces of all sizes through the quartz vein stones and among the calcareous spar, laumonite, prehnite, and other minerals associated with the quartz. These being extracted, piles are made of the poorer sorts, in which the metal is not sufficiently clear of stone for shipment, and these are roasted by firing the wood intermixed through the heaps. By this process the stone entangled among the copper is more readily broken and removed. The lumps that will go into barrels are called "barrel work," and are packed in this way for shipment. Larger ones, called "masses," some of which are huge, irregular-shaped blocks of clean copper, are cut into pieces that can be conveniently transported, as of one to three tons weight each. This is done by means of a long chisel with a bit three-fourths of an inch wide, which is held by one man and struck in turns by two others with a hammer weighing 7 or 8 lbs. A groove is thus cut across the narrowest part of the mass, turning out long chips of copper one-fourth of an inch thick, and with each succeeding cut the groove is deepened to the same extent until it reaches through the mass. The process is slow and tedious, a single cut sometimes occupying the continual labor of three men for as many weeks, or even longer. This work is done in great part before the masses can be got out of the mine. The masses are found in working the vein, often occupying the whole space between the walls of trap rock, standing upon their edges, and shut in as solidly as if all were one material. To remove one of the very large masses is a work of many months. It is first laid bare along one side by extending the level or drift of the mine through the trap rock. The excavation is carried high enough to expose its upper edge and down to its lower line; but on account of irregular shape and projecting arms of copper, which often stretch forward, and up and down, connecting with other masses, it requires long and tedious mining operations to determine its dimensions. When it is supposed to be nearly freed along one side, very heavy charges of powder are introduced in the rock behind the mass, with the view of starting it from its bed. When cracks are produced by these, heavier charges are introduced in the form of sand-blasts, and these are repeated until the mass is thrown partly over on its side as well as the space excavated will admit. In speaking further of the Minesota mine, the enormous sizes of some of the masses, and the amount of powder consumed in loosening them, will be more particularly noticed.

To separate the finer particles of copper from the stones in which they are contained, these, after being roasted, are crushed under heavy stamps to the condition of fine sand, and this is then washed after the usual method of washing fine ores, until the earthy matters are removed and the metallic particles are left behind. This is shovelled into small casks for shipment, and is known as stamp copper. The stamping and crushing machinery, such as have long been used at the mining establishments of other countries, were found to be entirely too slow for the requirements of these mines, and they have been replaced by new apparatus of American contrivance, which is far more efficient than any thing of the kind ever before applied to such operations. The stamps heretofore in use have been of 100 lbs. to 300 lbs. weight, and at the California mines were first introduced of 800 lbs. to 1,000 lbs. weight. At Lake Superior they are in use on the plan of the steam hammer, weighing, with the rod or stamp-leg, 2,500 lbs. and making 90 to 100 strokes in a minute. The capacity of each stamp is to crush over one ton of hard trap rock every hour. It falls upon a large mortar that rests upon springs of vulcanized rubber, and the force of its fall is increased by the pressure of steam applied above the piston to throw it more suddenly down. The stamp-head covers about one-fourth of the face of the mortar, and with every succeeding stroke it moves to the adjoining quarter, covering the whole face in four strokes.

The only other metal found with the copper is silver, and this does not occur as an alloy, but the two are as if welded together, and neither, when assayed, gives more than a trace of the other. It is evident from this that they cannot have been in a fused state in contact. The quantity of silver is small; the largest piece ever found weighing a little more than 8 lbs. troy. This was met with at the mines near the mouth of Eagle river, where a considerable number of loose pieces, together with loose masses of copper, were obtained in exploring deep under the bed of the stream an ancient deposit of rounded boulders of sandstone and trap. The veins of even the trap rocks themselves of this locality exhibited so much silver that in the early operations of the mines a very high value was set upon them on this account. But at none of the Lake Superior mines has the silver collected paid the proprietors for the loss it has occasioned by distracting the attention of the miners, and leading them to seek for it with the purpose of appropriating it to their own use. Probably they have carried away much the greater part of this metal; at least until the stamp mills were in operation.

The principal mine of this district is the Cliff mine of the Pittsburg and Boston Company, opened in 1845, and steadily worked ever since. In 1858 the extent of the horizontal workings on the vein had amounted to 12,368 feet, besides 831 feet in cross-cuts. Five shafts had been sunk, one of which was 817 feet deep, 587 feet being below the adit level, and 230 feet being from this level to the summit of the ridge. The shaft of least depth was sunk 422 feet.

The production of the mine from the year 1853 is exhibited in the following table:—

Year.	Mineral produced. lbs.	Refined copper. lbs.	Yield per cent.	Price per lb. deducting cost of smelting.	Value realized.
1853,	2,268,182	1,071,288	47.83	cts. 27.32	$292,647 05
1854,	2,332,614	1,315,808	56.35	24.38	320,783 01
1855,	2,995,837	1,874,197	62.56	25 33	475,911 26
1856,	3,291,239	2,220,934	67.48	24.12	535,848 67
1857,	8,363,557	2,863,850	70.28	20.44	497,870 47
1858,	8,183,085	2,331.964	71.00	21.03	475,321 89
1859,	2,189,632	1,415,007	64.35	20.50	290,097 97
1860	2,805,442	..	..	..	..
	22,374,588	..	..	..	..
Product from accumulated slags....		71,530, exclusive of slags.			

The quantities of the different sorts for the year 1857 are as follows:—

941 masses	1,958,181 lbs.
869 bbls. of barrel work	613,731 "
1,020 " of stampings	791,645 "
Total	3,363,557 "

The Portage lake mining district is from twenty to twenty-five miles west from the

Cliff mine on the same range of hills. This region is of more recent development, the explorations having been attended with little success previous to 1854. The veins are here found productive in a gray variety of trap as well as the amygdaloidal, and instead of lying across the ridges, follow the same course with them, and dip in general with the slope of the strata. Some of the larger veins consist in great part of epidote, and the copper in these is much less dense than in the quartz veins, forming tangled masses which are rarely of any considerable size. On the eastern side of this lake are worked, among other mines, the Quincy, Pewabic, and Franklin, and on the opposite side the Isle Royale, Portage, and Columbian mines. The most successful of these has been the Pewabic. Operations were commenced here in 1855 upon an unimproved tract, requiring the construction of roads and buildings, clearing of land, etc. etc., all involving for several years a continued heavy outlay. The immediate and rapid production of the mine required the construction of costly mills, without which a large proportion of the copper would be unavailable for the market. The first three years the assessments were $50,000, and the shipments of barrel and mass copper were in 1856 $97\frac{856}{2000}$ tons; in 1857, $209\frac{329}{2000}$ tons; in 1858, 402 tons; in 1859, $813\frac{778}{2000}$ tons. The proceeds from the sales up to this time paid off all the expenditures, and left besides a considerable surplus. The Franklin Company, working the same lode upon the adjoining location, commenced operations in July, 1857, and that year shipped 20 tons of copper, the next year 110 tons, and in 1859, 218 tons; the total amount in capital furnished by assessments was $10,000. These two mines have been the most rapidly developed of any of the Lake Superior mines.

The Ontonagon river crosses the trap hills about forty miles south-west from Portage lake, and the mines worked in the Ontonagon district are scattered along the hills north-east from the river for a distance of nearly twenty miles. The outlet for the greater number of them is by a road through the woods to the village at the mouth of the river. The veins of this district also lie along the course of the ridges, and dip with the trap rocks toward the lake. As they are worked, however, they are found occasionally to cut across the strata, and neighboring veins to run into each other. In some places copper occurs in masses scattered through the trap rock with no sign of a vein, not even a seam or crevice connecting one mass with another. They appear, however, to be ranged on the general course of the strata. At the Adventure mine they were so abundant, that it has been found profitable to collect them, and the cliffs of the trap rock present a curious appearance, studded over with numerous dark cavities in apparently inaccessible places leading into the solid face of the mountain.

The great mine of this district is the Minesota, two miles east from the Ontonagon river. The attention of the explorers in this region in the winter of 1847–48 was attracted by parallel lines of trenches, extending for miles along the trap hills, evidently made by man at some distant period. They were so well marked, as to be noticed even under a cover of three feet depth of snow. On examination they proved to be on the course of veins of copper, and the excavations were found to extend down into the solid rock, portions of which were sometimes left standing over the workings. When these pits were afterward explored, there were found in them large quantities of rude hammers, made of the hardest kind of greenstone, from the trap rocks of the neighborhood. These were of all sizes, ranging from four to forty pounds weight, and of the same general shape—one end being rounded off for the end of the hammer, and the other shaped like a wedge. Around the middle was a groove—the large hammers had two—evidently intended for securing the handle by

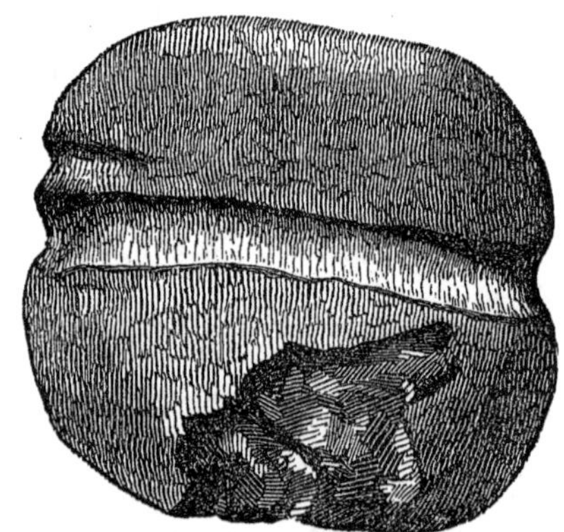

STONE HAMMER.

which they were wielded. In every instance the hammers were more or less broken, evidently in service. One of them brought from the mine by the writer, and now in the collection of the Cooper Union of New York, is represented in the accompanying sketch. It measures 6½ inches in length, the same in breadth, and 2½ inches in thickness.

The quantity of hammers found in these old workings was so great that they were collected by cart-loads. How they could have been made with such tools as the ancient miners had, is unaccountable, for the stone itself is the hardest material they could find. And it is not any more clear, how they applied such clumsy tools to excavating solid rock nearly as hard as the hammers themselves. Every hammer is broken on the edge, as if worn out in service. The only tools found besides these were a copper gad or wedge, a copper chisel with a socket head, and a wooden bowl. The great extent of the ancient mining operations indicates that the country must have been long occupied by an industrious people, possessed of more mechanical skill than the present race of Indians. They must also have spread over the whole of the copper region, for similar evidences of their occupancy are found about all the copper mines, and even upon Isle Royale. It is not improbable that they belonged to the race of the mound builders of the western states, among the vestiges of whom, found in the mounds, various utensils of copper have been met with. But of the period when they lived, the copper mines afford no more evidence than the mounds. Some of the trenches at the Minesota mine, originally excavated to the depth of more than twenty-five feet, have since filled up with gravel and rubbish to within a few feet of the surface, a work which in this region would seem to require centuries; and upon the surface of this material large trees are now standing, and stumps of much older ones are seen, that have long been rotting. In clearing out the pits a mass of copper was discovered, buried in the gravel nearly twenty feet below the surface, which the ancients had entirely separated from the vein. They had supported it upon blocks of wood, and, probably by means of fire and their hammers, had removed from it all the adhering stone and projecting points of copper. Under it were quantities of ashes and charred wood. The weight of the mass, after all their attempts to reduce it, appears to have been too great for them to raise; and when it was finally taken out in 1848, it was found to weigh over six tons. It was about ten feet long, three feet wide, and nearly two feet thick. Beneath this spot the vein afterward proved extremely rich, affording many masses of great size.

The veins worked by the Minesota Company all lie along the southern slope of the northern trap ridge, not far below the summit. Three veins have been discovered which lie nearly parallel to each other. The lowest one is along the contact of the gray trap of the upper part of the hill and a stratum of conglomerate which underlies this. It dips with the slope of this rock toward the north-north-west at an angle of about 46° with the horizon. The next upper vein outcropping, 80 or 90 feet further up the hill, dips about 61°, and falls into the lower vein along a very irregular line. Both veins are worked, and the greatest yield of the mine has been near their line of meeting.

The position of the veins along the range of the rocks, instead of across them, gives to the mines of this character a great advantage, as their productiveness is not limited to the thickness of any one belt which proves favorable for the occurrence of the metal; and the outcrop of the vein can be traced a great distance along the surface, affording convenient opportunities for sinking directly upon it at any point.

The Minesota Company, having abundant room, have been able to sink a large number of shafts along a line of outcrop of 1,800 feet, and several of the levels below extend considerably further than this entire length. In 1858 nine shafts were in operation, and ten levels were driven on the vein, the deepest at 535 feet down the slope. The ten fathom level at that time was 1,960 feet in length. This mine is remarkable for the enormous size and great number of its masses. The largest one of these, taken out during the year 1857, after being uncovered along its side, refused to give way, though 1,450 pounds of powder had been exploded behind it in five successive sand-blasts. A charge of 625 pounds being then fired beneath it, the mass was so much loosened that by a succeeding blast of 750 pounds it was torn off from the masses with which it connected, and thrown over in one immense piece. It measured forty-five feet in length, and its greatest thickness was over eight feet. Its weight was estimated at about 500 tons. What it proved to be is not certain, as no account was preserved of the pieces into which it was cut, but it is known to have exceeded 400 tons. Other masses have been taken out which presented a thickness of over five feet solid copper. The value of the silver picked out from among the copper has amounted in one year to about $1,000.

The reports of the company present the following statistics of the mine from its earliest operations:—

Years.	No. of men employed.	Expenditure.	Mineral product. Tons.	Per-centage	Value of Copper.	Assessments paid.	Dividends.
1848,	20	$14,000	6½	..	$1,700	$10,500	..
1849,	60	28,000	52	..	14,000	16,500	..
1850,	90	58,000	103	..	29,000	36,000	..
1851,	175	88,000	307½	..	90,000	3,000	..
1852,	212	108,000	520	..	196,000	..	$30,000
1853,	280	168,000	523	..	210,000	..	60,000
1854,	392	218,000	763	..	290,000	..	90,000
1855,	471	280,933	1,434	71	549,876	..	200,000
1856,	537	356,541	1,859	72.5	701,906	..	300,000
1857,	615	402,538	2,058	74	736,000	..	300,000
1858,	713	384,827	1,833	70.1	595,000	..	180,000
1859,	718	384,394	1,626	71	515,786	..	120,000
1860,	8 months to Sept. 1......		1,431				
	Estimate, for the year....		2,250				

In consequence of recent discoveries of masses of copper running into the sandstone off from the vein itself, the product of the year 1860 will considerably exceed that of any other year; the profits, however, are not proportionally large, owing to the low price of copper. To this the diminished profits of 1858 and 1859 are partly to be attributed. The product for 1857, 1858, and 1859 was divided as follows:—

Years.	Masses. lbs.	Barrel work. lbs.	Stamp work. lbs.
1857,	3,015,581	819,900	280,512
1858,	2,429,989	903,871	333,352
1859,	2,040,454	929,571	282,092

Besides the dividends named, the original stockholders have derived large profits from the sale of portions of the extensive territory, three miles square, which belonged to the company, and the organization upon these tracts of new companies.

Before the completion of the St. Mary's Canal, no exact records were preserved of the amount of copper sent from Lake Superior. But up to the close of navigation in 1854 it is supposed the total shipments from the commencement of mining in 1845 had been about 7642 tons of pure copper.

Since that time, the annual product of rough copper has been as follows:—

Districts.	1855.	1856.	1857.	1858.	1859.	1860.
Keweenaw....................	2,245	2,128	2,200	2,125	1,910.3	1,910.8
Portage......................	315	462	704	1,116	1,533.1	3,064.8
Ontonagon....................	1,984	2,767	3,190	2,655	2,597.6	3,588.7
Porcupine, Mo., etc..........	..	..	..	..	..	28.1
Total................	4,544	5,357	6,094	5,896	6,041.0	8,543.4

The condition of the Lake Superior mines at the close of the year 1860 is well presented in the business circular of Messrs. Dupee, Beck, & Sayles, of Boston, received since the preceding pages passed through the hands of the printer and stereotyper. From this we introduce the following additional matter. The depreciation in the price of copper from a maximum of 29½ cents a pound of the few preceding years to a maximum of 24½ cents and a minimum of 19 cents, had induced increased economy and care in the administration of the mines, the good effects of which were already beginning to be experienced:—

"Freights to and from the mines from May to September were 25 per cent. less than in 1859. The transportation of a ton of copper from the lake shore to Boston, cost, after the opening of St. Mary's Canal, 1855, $20; in 1860, to Boston, $11, and to New York, $9. The substitution of bituminous coal for wood, which has been delivered during the past summer at the wharves of Portage Lake for $3.25 per ton, will save much money and leave the forests of the country for building materials and for timbering of the mines. With the wants of a rapidly increasing population, new and cheaper sources of supply are constantly opening in the region itself. Many agricultural products, hitherto sent up at great cost from Lower Michigan, are now raised in the neighborhood of the mines, and at the new settlements on the south-western shores of the lake, cheaply and abundantly. At Portage Lake, a machine shop, an iron foundry, and a manufactory of doors, sashes, blinds, etc., have been put in operation during 1860. The smelting works of the Portage Lake Company are now successfully refining the products of that district. These works consist of four reverberatory and two cupola furnaces, capable of refining 6000 tons per annum. The buildings are of the most thorough and substantial character, and the location of the works accessible, at a very small cost of transportation, to all the mines now wrought, or likely to be wrought for many years hence, in that neighborhood. Hitherto, to save cost of transportation to the smelting companies in other states, it has been necessary to dress the rough copper to an average probably of 70 per cent. Now, by the proximity of the furnaces to the mines, a dressing of 50 per cent. will answer the same purpose, while the refined copper, hitherto rarely ready for the market before the 1st to 15th July, will be sent directly from the lake to New York or Boston, arriving there in ordinary seasons by the 1st of June. Further, there will be added the new facility of obtaining cash advances through the winter on the warehouse receipts of the smelting company.

"The opening of the entry into Portage Lake during the past season has been one of the greatest improvements in the navigation of the Lake Superior region since the completion of the ship canal around the falls of St. Mary's river. At the comparatively small cost of $50,000, steamers of the largest class able to pass through the St. Mary's Canal may now enter Portage Lake, and discharge their cargoes at the docks of the several companies located on its shores. Besides avoiding the loss of time and expense of transhipment hitherto necessary, the opening of Portage Lake has provided one of the most capacious and safest harbors in the world.

"In the Ontonagon district, a plank road has been completed recently, facilitating to a very great extent the transportation to and from the Minesota, National, Rockland, and Superior mines.

"The iron interests of Lake Superior are rapidly attaining great importance. The amount brought down to Marquette, the port of shipment, in 1860, was: of iron ore from the Jackson Company, 62,980 tons; Cleveland Company, 47,889; Lake Superior Company, 39,394; total, 150,263. Of pig iron, Pioneer Company, 3050 tons; S. R. Gay, 1800; Northern Company, 650; total, 6500. Ore valued at $3; pig at $25; aggregate value, $588,289."

The following statistics are presented of the principal mines:—

COMPARATIVE TABLE OF SHIPMENTS OF ROUGH COPPER FROM LAKE SUPERIOR DURING THE SEASONS OF 1859 AND 1860.

The weights of the barrels have been deducted, and the results are given in tons (2000 lbs.) and tenths.

	1859.	1860.
KEWEENAW DISTRICT.		
Central	172.3	78.6
Clark	5.6	7.2
Connecticut	24.	5.3
Copper Falls	329.4	328.
Eagle River	6.	..
North American	8.7	..
Northwest	73.8	103.5
Phœnix	32.	31.2
Pittsburg and Boston	1,254.5	1,357.
Summit	4.	..
	1,910.3	1,910.8
PORTAGE DISTRICT.		
C. C. Douglass	..	24.
Isle Royale	241.3	458.6
Franklin	204.7	267.
Hancock	..	7.2
Huron	7.4	78.
Mesnard	.6	..
Pewabic	734.4	1,363.8
Portage	8.7	..
Quincy	336.	866.2
	1,533.1	3,064.8
ONTONAGON DISTRICT.		
Adventure	139,4	29.7
Aztec	15.3	4.9
Bohemian	3.	..
Evergreen Bluff	27.	41.9
Hamilton	.7	7.9
Mass	12.3	..
Minesota	1,623.6	2,183.4
National	323.2	727.8
Nebraska	9.8	26.4
Norwich	22.	..
Ogima	35.4	..
Ridge	27.8	..
Rockland	347.	552.7
Superior	1.7	14.
Toltec	9.4	..
	2,597.6	3,588.7
Keweenaw District	1,910.3	1,910.8
Portage	1,533.1	3,050.8
Ontonagon	2,597.6	3,553.7
Porcupine Mountain	..	20.5
Sundry mines	..	7.6
	6,041.0	8,543.4

Franklin: the product for the year ending November 30 has been 112 masses, weighing 72,166 lbs.; 721 barrels of barrel work, 469,116 lbs.; and 67 barrels stamp work, 63,816 lbs. Total, 605,098 lbs., equal to $180\frac{7}{10}$ tons refined copper. The actual shipments were about 267 tons rough, or 158 tons ingot copper. The stamps are Ball's, consisting of two pairs of two heads each. They did not commence work till November 19.

Huron: total shipments this year, $65\frac{4}{10}$ tons of $64\frac{1}{2}$ per cent. barrel work, and 12,311 lbs. of refined copper, smelted at the Portage Lake works. There is ready for the stamps an amount equivalent, at a fair estimate, to the quantity shipped this season.

Isle Royale: total shipments this season $458\frac{6}{10}$ tons, averaging over 70 per cent. Preparations have been made for opening a large amount of ground during the winter, with a view to large shipments at the opening of navigation.

Minesota: November returns, 150 tons. The total shipments in 1860 were 1992 masses, and 2127 barrels of barrel and stamp work. Net weight, 4,366,718 lbs. This is the largest shipment made in one year by any mine at the lake. The promise for future production is as great, at least, as the result for this year.

Pewabic: November product, $304\frac{8}{10}$ tons. The actual shipments for the season have been 2,727,632 lbs. The product for one year to November 30 was as follows: 467 masses, weighing 348,658 lbs.; 2294 barrels kiln or barrel work, weighing net, 1,450,778 lbs.; 342 barrels No. 1, stamp, 379,718 lbs.; 399 barrels No. 2, stamp, 389,973 lbs.; 401 barrels No. 3, stamp, 346,912 lbs.; add on tributers' account, 27,428. Total, 2,943,467 lbs.

The smelting returns are not yet all made, but on an estimate based on past experience, the result will not vary much from 2,030,992 lbs., or about 1000 tons of ingot copper.

During the year there have been shipped 1533 ounces of silver.

Pittsburg and Boston: November product, 114 tons. Total shipments, 1357 tons. Total product for the year, 1402 tons. The annual report recently published gives the result of the year ending December 1, 1859. The product for that year was $1,099\frac{8}{10}$ tons, yielding $64\frac{35}{100}$ per cent., or $707\frac{5}{10}$ tons ingot copper. The receipts, including $2,405 17 from sales of silver, were $292,503 14. The expenditures were $272,175 75, leaving net profit, $20,327 39.

COPPER SMELTING

The ores of copper, unlike those of most of the other metals, are not in general reduced at the mines; but after being concentrated by mechanical processes called dressing—which consist in assorting the piles according to their qualities, and crushing, jigging, and otherwise washing the poorer sorts—they are sold to the smelters, whose establishments may be at great distances off, even on the other side of the globe. The richer ores, worth per ton three or four times as many dollars as the figures that represent their percentage of metal, well repay the cost of transportation, and are conveniently reduced at smelting works situated on the coast near the markets for copper, and where the fuel required for their reduction is cheap. At Swansea, in South Wales, there are eight great smelting establishments, to which all the ores from Cornwall and Devon are carried, and which receive other ores from almost all parts of the world. It is stated that in this district there are nearly 600 furnaces employed, which consume about 500,000 tons of coal per annum, and give employment to about 4,000 persons besides colliers. The amount of copper they supply is more than half of that consumed by all nations. The total product of fine copper produced by all the smelting establishments of Great Britain for 1857 is stated to be 18,238 tons, worth £2,079,323.

The copper smelting works of the United States are those upon the coast, depending chiefly upon foreign supplies of ores, and those of the interior for melting and refining the Lake Superior copper. There are also the furnaces at the Tennessee mines, which have been already noticed. The former are situated at the following localities: At Point Shirley, in Boston harbor, are the furnaces of the Revere Copper Company, which also has rolling mills and other works connected with the manufacture of copper at Canton, on the Boston and Providence railroad. At Taunton, Mass., a similar establishment to that at Canton is owned by the Messrs. Crocker, of that town. There are smelting furnaces at New Haven, Conn.; at Bergen Point, in New York harbor; and at Baltimore, on a point in the outer harbor.

The furnaces established for working the Lake Superior copper are at Detroit, Cleveland, and Pittsburg. At the last named are two separate establishments, with each of which is connected a rolling mill, at which the ingot copper is converted into sheets for home consumption and the eastern market. A furnace was also built at Portage lake, Lake Superior, in 1860, of capacity equal to melting 6000 tons of copper annually. The details and extent of the operations carried on by the smelting works appear to have been carefully kept from publication. In a work on "Copper and Copper Smelting," by A. Snowdon Piggott, M. D., who had charge of the chemical assays, etc., for the Baltimore Company, published in 1858, while the English processes are fully described, no information is given as to the methods adopted at the American works; and of their production all the information is contained in the two closing sentences of the appendix, as follows: "Of the copper-smelting establishments of the United States I have no statistics. Baltimore turns out about 8,000,000 pounds of refined copper annually." Applications which have been made by the writer to the proprietors of several of the establishments for information as to the business, have been entirely unsuccessful. The total production of copper in 1858 was supposed to be about 13,000 tons per annum; and of this about 7000 tons were required by the rolling mills for making sheet copper, sheet brass, and yellow metal.

The French treatise on Metallurgy by Professor Rivot contains the only published description of the American method of smelting copper. By the English process, the separation of the metal from its ores is a long and tedious series of alternate roastings or calcinations, and fusions in reverberatory furnaces. The system is particularly applicable to the treatment of poor, sulphurous ores contaminated with other metals, as iron, arsenic, etc., and can only be conducted to advantage where fuel is very cheap, the consumption of this being at the rate of about 20 tons to the ton of copper obtained. The process employed in Germany is much more simple, and the methods in use at the American smelting works are more upon the plan of these. Blast or cupola furnaces supply at some of them the place of reverberatories, and the separation of the metal is completed in great part by one or two smeltings. The treatment of the Lake Superior copper is comparatively an easy operation. For this large reverberatory furnaces are employed, through the roof of which is an opening large enough to admit masses of 3 to 3½ tons weight, which are raised by cranes and lowered into the furnace. The barrels of barrel work are introduced in the same way, and left in the furnace without unpacking. When the furnace is charged, the opening in the top is securely closed by fire-proof masonry, and the fire of bituminous coal is started, the flame from which plays over the bridge, and, reflected from the roof, strikes upon the copper, causing it gradually to sink down and at last flow in a liquid mass. A small portion of the copper by the oxidizing action of the heated gases is converted into a suboxide, which is partially reduced again, and in part goes into the slags in the condition of a silicate of copper, the metal of which is not entirely recovered. The mixture of quartz, calcareous spar, and epidote accompanying the copper, is sometimes such as to melt and form a good cinder without addition of any other substance, but usually some limestone or other suitable material is added as a flux. Complete fusion is effected in 12 to 15 hours according to the size of the masses, and this is kept up for about an hour in order that the fine particles of copper may find their way through the fluid slag, which floats upon the metal. Working tools called rabbles are then introduced through the side-doors of the furnace, and the charge is stirred up and the slag is drawn out through the door. It falls upon the ground, and is taken when sufficiently cool to the cupola or slag furnaces where it is chilled with water to render it easy to break up. Those portions which contain as much as one fourth per cent. of copper are reserved to be passed through the slag furnace. The total amount of slag is usually less than 20 per cent. of the whole charge. In the melting the copper absorbs carbon, which if allowed to remain would render it brittle and unfit for use. To remove it the fire is so arranged that the gases pass through with much unconsumed air; this playing on the surface of the copper produces a suboxide of the metal, which in the course of half an hour is quite taken up by the copper, and coming in contact with the particles of carbon the oxygen combines with this, and removes it in the form of carbonic acid gas.

It now remains to remove the excess of oxygen introduced, which is effected by the ordinary method of refining. A large proportion of fuel is employed on the grate for the amount of air admitted through it, so that the flames as they pass over the bridge convey little free oxygen, and the surface of the metal is covered with fine charcoal. After a little time a pole of green wood is thrust into the melted copper and stirred about so long as gases escape from the surface. It is then taken out, and if on testing the copper some suboxide still remains, the refining is cautiously continued with charcoal, and just when, as appears by the tests, all the oxide is reduced, the work of dipping out the metal is commenced. This is done by large iron ladles, the whole set of men employed at two furnaces, to the number of about 12, coming to this work and taking turns in the severe task. They protect themselves from the intense heat by wet cloths about their arms, and as quickly as possible bale out a ladle full of copper and empty it into one or more of the ingot moulds, of which 36 are arranged in front of the furnace-door upon three parallel bars over a trough of water. As the metal becomes solid in each mould, this is upset, letting the ingot fall into the water. The weight of the ingot being 20 pounds, the filling of them all removes 720 pounds of copper from the furnace. The metal that remains is then tested, and according to its condition the discharging may be continued or it may be necessary to oxidize the copper again and repeat the refining, or merely to throw more charcoal upon the surface and increase the heat. The time required to ladle out the whole charge is from four to six hours. When this is completed the sole of the furnace is repaired, by stopping the cracks with sand and smoothing the surface to get all ready for the next charge; and at the same time the second furnace has reached the refining stage of the process. One charge to a furnace is made every evening, and as in the night it is necessary only to keep up the fires, the great labor of the process comes wholly in the day time.

The following is the estimated cost at Detroit of the smelting, on a basis of two furnaces, each of which is charged with four and a half to five tons of mass copper, consuming two and a half tons of coal, and producing from three to three and a half tons of ingots:—

Labor, 15 hands, at $1.50	$22.50
Bituminous coal, 5 tons, at $5	25.00
Wood and charcoal	1.25
Repairs to furnace, average for the season	2.00
	$50.75

To this should be added, for superintendence, office, and general expenses, perhaps ten dollars more, which would make the cost for six or seven tons of ingot copper, $60.75, or $9 to $10 per ton. At Pittsburg the rate charged has been $11 per ton; and fuel is there afforded at about one third the amount allowed in the above estimate.

The cupola furnaces for treating the slags are of very simple plan and construction. They are of cylindrical form, about ten feet high, and three feet diameter inside. Their walls, the thickness of a single length of fire brick, are incased in boiler-plate iron, and stand upon a cast-iron ring, which is itself supported upon four cast-iron columns about three feet above the ground. Transverse iron bars support a circular plate, and upon this the refractory sand for the sole of the furnace is placed, and well beaten down to the thickness of a foot, with a sharp slope toward the tapping hole. A low chimney conveys away the gaseous products of combustion, and through the base of it the workmen introduce the charges. The blast is introduced by three tuyeres a foot above the sole; but before it enters the furnace it is heated by passing through a channel around the furnace. A steady current is obtained by the use of three double acting blowing cylinders, which give a pressure equal to about three and a half inches of mercury.

The hands employed at the Detroit establishment, besides the superintendent and head smelter, are eighteen furnace men and from five to ten workmen, according to the arrivals of copper during the season of navigation. After the stock thus received is worked up, the furnaces remain idle during the remainder of the winter.

USEFUL APPLICATIONS OF COPPER.

The uses of copper are so numerous and important that the metal must rank next in value to iron. In ancient times, indeed, it was the more useful metal of the two, being abundant among many nations to whom iron was not known. In the ancient Scandinavian tumuli recently opened in Denmark, among the various implements of stone were found swords, daggers, and knives, the blades of which were, in some instances, of copper, and in some of gold, while the cutting edges were formed of iron, showing that this was more rare and valuable than either copper or gold. It has been supposed that several of the ancient nations, as the Egyptians, Greeks, etc., possessed the art of hardening copper, so as to make it serve the purposes of steel. That they employed it for such uses as those to which we now apply tools of steel is certain, and also that the specimens of some of their copper tools are considerably harder than any we make of the same metal. These are found, on analysis, to contain about one part in ten of tin, which, it is known, increases, when added in small proportions, the hardness of copper, and this was probably still further added to by hammering.

Among the most important uses of the metal at present is that of sheathing the bottoms of ships in order to protect the timbers from the ravages of marine animals, and present a smooth surface for the easy passage of the vessel through the water. The metal is well adapted, from its softness and tenacity, for rolling into sheets, and these were first prepared for this use for the Alarm frigate of the royal navy, in 1761. Sheet lead had been in use before this time, but was soon after given up for copper. On account of the rapid deterioration of the copper by the action of the sea-water, the naval department of the British government applied, in 1823, to the Royal Society for some method of preserving the metal. This was furnished by Sir Humphry Davy, who recommended applying strips of cast iron under the copper sheets, which, by the galvanic current excited, would be corroded instead of the copper. The application answered the purpose intended, but soon had to be given up, for the copper, protected from chemical action, it was found, became covered with barnacles and other shell-fish, so as seriously to impair the sailing qualities of the vessels, and for this reason it has been found necessary to submit to the natural wasting of the metal, and replace the sheets as fast as they become corroded.

Various alloys have been proposed as substitutes for copper. That known as yellow metal, or Muntz's, has been the most successful and has been very generally introduced. It consists of copper alloyed with about 40 per cent. of zinc, and is prepared by plunging cakes of zinc into a bath of melted copper contained in a reverberatory furnace. The volatilization of the zinc and oxidation of the metals is guarded against by a covering of fine charcoal kept upon the melted surface. The bolts, nails, and other fastenings for the sheathing, and for various other parts of the ship, are made also of copper and of yellow metal; and to secure the greatest strength, they should be cast at once in the forms in which they are to be used. The manufacture of all these articles is extensively carried on at the different copper establishments in Massachusetts, Connecticut, and Baltimore.

Sheet copper is also applied to many other very important uses, as for copper boilers and pipes, for large stills and condensers, the vacuum pans of sugar refineries, and a multitude of utensils for domestic purposes, and for employment in the different arts. For engraving upon it is prepared of the purest quality and of different thicknesses, according to the kind of engraving for which it is to be used. The engraver cuts it to the size he requires, planishes it, and gives to it the dead smooth surface peculiar to engraving plates. The smaller utensils of sheet copper, as urns, vases, etc., are very ingeniously hammered out from a flat circular sheet. As the hammering is first applied to the central portion, this spreads and takes the form of a bowl. As the metal becomes harder and brittle by the operation, its softness and ductility are restored by annealing, a process that must often be repeated as the hammering is continued, and toward the last, when the metal has become more susceptible to the change induced by the application of the hammer, the annealing must be very carefully attended to, and the whole process be conducted with much skill and judgment acquired by long experience.

For larger and more common hollow articles, the sheet copper is folded around, and lapped by various sorts of joints, some of which are secured by rivets, and some by a double lap, the two edges locking into each other, and made close by hammering. The edges are also soldered either with soft or hard solder. For the latter an alloy is made for the purpose, by melting in a crucible a quantity of brass, and then stirring in one-half or one-third as much zinc, until the blue flame disappears. The mixture is then turned out into a shallow pan, and when cold the plate is heated nearly red hot, and beaten on an anvil or in a mortar. This is the hard solder of the braziers.

A still more important application of the

copper is in the manufacture of the alloy known as brass; and that called bronze also serves many useful purposes. The former is composed of copper and zinc, the latter of copper and tin. It is a curious fact in metallurgy that brass was extensively manufactured, and used more commonly than any single metal or other alloy, many centuries before the existence of such a metal as zinc was known. It was prepared by melting copper and introducing fragments of the *lapis calaminaris*, an ore of zinc, in which the oxide of the metal is combined with carbonic acid. Charcoal was also added to the mixture, and by the reaction with this the zinc ore was reduced to the metallic state, and at once united with the copper, without appearing as a distinct metal. This process is still in use for making brass, but the more common method is to introduce slips of copper into melted zinc, or to plunge beneath melted copper lumps of zinc held in iron tongs. The proportion of the two metals is always uncertain, owing to the unknown quantity of zinc that is consumed and escapes in fumes This is prevented as much as possible by covering the melted metal with fine charcoal, and by throwing in pieces of glass, which melt and cover the mixture with a thin protecting layer. Old brass is much used in making new, and the addition of quantities of this to the pot containing the other ingredients, adds to the uncertainty of the composition. The best proportion of the two metals is believed to be two parts of copper to one of zinc, which is expressed by the term " eight-ounce brass," meaning eight ounces of zinc to sixteen of copper. Sixteen-ounce brass—the two metals being equal—is a beautiful golden yellow alloy, called prince's metal. But all brass of more than ten ounces of zinc to the pound of copper is whitish, crystalline, hard, and brittle; of less than ten ounces it is malleable, soft, and ductile. The alloys known as pinchbeck, Manheim gold, bath metal, etc., formerly much in use as imitations of gold, are about three to four ounce brass.

Brass combines a great number of excellent qualities, which render it adapted for a multitude of uses. Its compactness, durability, strength, and softness, render it an excellent material for fine work, and nothing, except tin, perhaps, is a more agreeable substance for shaping in the lathe. In use it is not liable to rust by exposure, is easily kept clean, and takes a polish almost as beautiful as that of gold. It is hence a favorite material for the works of watches and clocks, almost all sorts of instruments in which great hardness is not essential, and for various household utensils, and ornaments upon furniture. In thin plates it is stamped and embossed in figures, and is thus cheaply applied to many useful and ornamental purposes. Its ductility is such, that those sorts containing little zinc can be beaten out, as will be described in the account of gold-beating, almost like gold-leaf itself, so as to be used as a cheap substitute for this in gilding in some cases. It is also drawn out into wire, often of great fineness; and of the suitable sizes of this there is a very large consumption in the manufacture of pins, and hooks and eyes. The consumption of copper alone for these articles at the factories at Waterbury, Connecticut, has amounted for some years past to more than a ton a day. By ingenious machinery the brass wires are clipped to their proper length for pins, pointed, headed, and after being tinned, are stuck in paper, with very little attention from the workmen. This manufacture used often to be cited as an example of the economical division of labor, showing the great number of workmen through whose hands a single pin passed before it was completed. It serves better now to exemplify the perfection of machinery, and some of the most admirable of this, particularly that by which the finished pins are stuck in their papers, is a peculiarly American invention, and worth, to the manufacturers at Waterbury alone, many thousand dollars annually. The solid-headed pin, made somewhat after the manner in which cut nails are headed, was invented by two citizens of Rhode Island, Mr. Slocum and Mr. S. G. Reynolds. This was before the year 1840. The covering of the brass pins and hooks and eyes with the slight coating of tin is effected by placing a quantity of them in a scouring barrel, together with about twice their weight of tin in grains, several ounces of cream of tartar, and several gallons of warm water. The barrel is then made to revolve upon its axis, until the pins or other articles are perfectly clean. After this they are boiled in a similar mixture.

Much of the brass of the ancients was properly bronze—that is, a compound of copper and tin. This alloy, in different proportions of its ingredients, is still of very great service. Gun metal—the material of the so-called brass cannon—is composed of copper

96 to 108 parts, and tin 11 parts. The compound resists wear extremely well, but its strength is only about one-half that of wrought iron. Statues, and hard castings for machinery, are formed of this alloy, and the former have very commonly been cast from cannon captured in the victories of the commander in whose honor the statues were made. One of the most noted foundries for the casting of cannon, statues, and bronze ornaments in the United States is that of the Messrs. Ames, at Chicopee, Mass. The equestrian statue of Washington, in Union square, New York, is one of their most successful productions. The French bronze contains 2 parts of tin, 1 of lead, 6 of zinc, and 91 of copper. Bell-metal is a bronze usually consisting of 7 parts of copper and 22 of tin. Their manufacture has been carried on at different copper foundries in the United States for many years. The largest bell in the country, that upon the City Hall, in New York, weighs 23,000 pounds, and was cast in Boston. The largest number of bells is probably produced at the foundry of the Messrs. Meneely, at Troy, N. Y. The Chinese gong is now an American manufacture, composed of bell-metal, which, after being cast, is forged under the hammer, between two disks of iron. The casting is made malleable by plunging, while hot, into cold water.

As with zinc copper forms an alloy made to imitate gold, so with tin and nickel it is made to form a combination resembling silver, and known as German silver. The proportions of the metals are 8 parts of copper to either 3 or 4 each of the two other metals. This is a very useful alloy, answering as a cheap substitute for silver in spoons, forks, and other utensils, and for brass in various instruments. It takes the place of the old-fashioned pewter, and, being cheaply electro-plated with silver, is made as beautiful as the genuine articles of the richer metal.

Another alloy of the copper and tin is the telescope or speculum metal, which consists of about one-third tin and two-thirds copper. It is of a steel-white color, very hard and brittle, and susceptible of a high polish, which is not soon tarnished, qualities that cause it to be used for the mirrors of telescopes.

In coinage copper is largely employed —in the old cent unalloyed, and in the new combined with 12 parts in 100 of nickel.

CHAPTER III.

GOLD.

Although the discovery of gold mines was the chief motive that led to the settlement of the American continent, those of the United States appear to have escaped notice until the present century. The only exception to this may be in the discovery made by some Europeans of the gold region of northern Georgia at a period long antecedent to the occupation of this district by the whites. Of this fact no written record is preserved; but in working the deposit mines of the Nacoochee valley, in Habersham county, there were discovered, about the year 1842, various utensils and vestiges of huts, which evidently had been constructed by civilized men, and had been buried there several centuries. It is supposed they belonged to De Soto's party, which passed through this region in the sixteenth century on their exploring expedition from Florida to the Mississippi river. The earlier historians hardly mention gold as even being supposed to exist in the colonies. Salmon, in the third volume of his "Modern History," 1746, merely alludes to a gold mine in Virginia, which of late "had made much noise," but does not even name the locality, and evidently attaches no importance to it. In Jefferson's "Notes on Virginia" mention is made of the discovery of a piece of gold of 17 dwts. near the Rappahannock. In 1799, as mentioned by Wheeler in his "History of North Carolina," a son of Conrad Reed picked up a piece of gold as large as a small smoothing iron from the bed of a brook on his father's farm, in Cabarrus county, and its value not being known it was kept for several years in the house to hold the door open, and was then sold to a silversmith for $3.50. In Drayton's "View of South Carolina," 1802, the metal is stated to have been found on Paris Mountain, in Greenville district. About this time it began to be met with in considerable lumps in Cabarrus county, N. C., and not long afterward in Montgomery and Anson counties. At Reed's mine, in Cabarrus, the discovery by a negro of a lump weighing 28 lbs. avoirdupois, near the same stream already referred to, led to increased activity in exploring the gravelly deposits along the courses of the brooks and rivers of this region, and numerous new localities of the metal were rapidly discovered. A much larger proportion of gold was collected, during these earlier workings, in coarse lumps than in the operations of later times—pieces of metal of one to several pounds weight being often found. Before the year 1820, as stated in *Bruce's Mineralogical Journal* (vol. i., p. 125), the quantity of American gold received at the mint at Philadelphia amounted to $43,689. All of this was from North Carolina. In 1827 there had been received from the same source $110,000. But besides this amount, a considerable proportion of the gold product was consumed by jewellers, who paid a better price than was received from the mint, and was retained by the banks, in which it was deposited. It also circulated to some extent as a medium of exchange in the mining region, being carried about in quills, and received by the merchants usually at the rate of ninety cents a dwt. The total product of the mines must, therefore, have been much larger than appears from the mint returns. In 1829, Virginia and South Carolina began to appear as gold-producing states—there being deposited in the mint from the former gold to the value of $2,500, and from the latter of $3,500. The same year the rich gold deposits of northern Georgia were discovered, and suddenly became very productive, so that the receipts at the mint from this state for the year 1830 amounted to $212,000. Gold mining had now become an established branch of the productive industry of the states, and as its importance increased, the necessity was felt of the establishment of branch mints in the mining region. One was constructed by act of Congress at Dahlonega, Lumpkin county, Georgia, and another at Charlotte, Mecklenburg county, N. C.; and both commenced coining gold in 1838. From the irregular manner in which the gold deposits were worked, and their uncertain yield, the annual production of the mines was very variable. In a single year the mint at Dahlonega received and coined gold to the value of $600,000; and until the discovery of the California gold mines, the American production was estimated to average annually about $100,000. It was, however, gradually declining in importance from the year 1845; and of late years has dwindled away, so as not to amount to enough for the support of the branch mints, the abolition of which by act of Congress was generally looked for in 1857 and 1858. The late introduction at the mines of North Carolina and Georgia of the hydraulic and sluice washing, which has proved highly successful in California, gives encouragement that these mines may again soon became as productive as before.

The rock formations of the United States, in which gold mines are worked, follow the range of the Appalachians, and are productive chiefly along their eastern side in a belt of country sometimes attaining a width of 75 miles, as along the southern part of North Carolina, and in Georgia in two distinct belts which are separated by a district of formations unproductive in gold. The extreme northern gold mines on this range are in Canada East, upon the Chaudiere river and its tributaries, the Du Loup and the Touffe des Pins. In 1851 and 1852, deposits were worked upon these streams, and about 1,900 dwts. were collected — found among the gravel which lay in the crevices formed by the ragged edges of the upturned argillaceous and talcose slates. The pieces were all small, only one weighing as much as 4 ounces. The returns were not sufficient to cover the outlays, and the working was consequently abandoned.

The next localities on the range toward the south which have furnished gold are in Vermont, on the western border of Windsor county, in the towns of Bridgewater and Plymouth. At Newfane, in Windham county, a piece of gold was found in 1826, which weighed 8½ oz.; but the only successful attempts to work the deposits were commenced in 1859, in Windsor county, and have since been prosecuted to limited extent. At Bridgewater, the gold has been found in place, in a quartz vein, associated with galena, and pyritous copper, and iron. It has not proved sufficiently rich to work. Through western Massachusetts and Connecticut, and the south-east part of New York, and through New Jersey and Pennsylvania, the talcose and argillaceous slates, and the other rocks of the gold belt, appear to be unproductive in this metal, a little gold only having been met with in some of the ores worked for lead and copper in Lancaster county, near the borders of Maryland. Specimens of quartz rich in gold have been found in Montgomery county, in the last-named state; but no mine has been worked there.

In Virginia the deposit mines of Louisa county especially were very productive even in 1833, and they had not been worked long before rich veins were found, and operations

HYDRAULIC MINING.

By this operation, as described in the text, hills of loose materials or of decomposed slates and other rocks containing gold, are washed down, and the earthy matters are swept away through the sluices made either of wooden troughs or by excavating channels in the bed-rock. In these the coarse gold is caught against the bars placed at intervals across the sluices. This is a purely Californian method, and has proved so effectual in collecting the little gold buried in large bodies of earth, that it is now generally adopted in other gold regions in which the conditions are favorable for its practice.

TUNNELLING AT TABLE MOUNTAIN, CALIFORNIA.

This represents a common method of reaching beds of rich ores that lie at considerable depths below the surface, by which the labor of removing the superficial deposits is avoided. Veins of ores, whether lying at a steep or gentle inclination, are often explored by such tunnels driven in upon their course. The sides and roof may be protected or not, as the ground is soft or solid, by timbering.

At the outside of the tunnel below the railroad track is the machine called the "long tom," a shallow trough, ten to twenty feet long, and about sixteen inches wide. The lower end, which turns up gently from the plane of the bottom, is shod with iron and perforated with holes. The water from the mine is turned on the upper end, and flows up this slope and through the holes, carrying with it the finer mud and sand which are continually thrown into the tom. One man at the lower end keeps the mud in motion and removes the coarse lumps. Under the lower end of the tom is placed a "riffle box," in which mercury may be used to advantage if the gold is in fine particles.

LARGE ROCKER USED IN CALIFORNIA WITH QUICKSILVER.

The above cut represents a rocker of unusual dimensions, which has been introduced in some places in California, and is employed particularly for auriferous deposits in which the gold is in too fine particles to be caught in the long tom. It is slightly inclined, and is rocked by one man while the others collect the gravel and throw it upon the perforated iron plate. Across the bottom of the trough are placed "riffle bars," and behind each one of these some mercury. The fine particles of gold coming in contact with this are caught and retained in the form of amalgam. The coarse gravel falls off the lower end of the plate, while the fine mud and sand are washed by the water through the holes in the plate.

STAMPS FOR CRUSHING GOLD ORES.

This cut represents a common form of stamps, such as are used for pulverizing auriferous quartz or other ores. They are variously arranged at different mills; sometimes four or five running in one set, and several sets being placed on the same line, but separate from each other. This arrangement is more convenient for stopping a portion at a time as may be required for repairs or for collecting the very coarse gold under the stamps which cannot pass through the grating or the plates, perforated with many holes, that are usually employed in front of the stamps.

upon these had been carried on to considerable extent previous to 1836, principally in the counties of Spottsylvania, Orange, Louisa, Fluvanna, and Buckingham. Some of the mines produced at times very rich returns, but their yield was, for the most part, exceedingly irregular, the gold occurring in rich pockets or nests, very unequally scattered in the vein. The occasional richness of the veins caused the attention of wealthy capitalists in this country and in England to be directed to this region, and large outlays were made, in providing powerful engines and other suitable machinery for working the ores, and in opening the mines. But, although the operations have been directed by the best mining skill, supported by abundant capital, the enterprise, on the whole, has not proved successful, and since 1853 the business has greatly declined in importance.

In North Carolina numerous quartz veins have been worked during the last 30 years, and operations are still carried on with moderate success at several mines in Guilford, Davidson, Montgomery, Cabarrus, Rowan, and Mecklenburg counties. Deposit mines have been worked with great success, also, in Burke, Rutherford, and McDowell counties. At a single time, it is stated, there might have been seen, from one point of view in McDowell county, no less than 3,000 persons engaged in washing the deposits. In this district sluice-washing has recently been successfully introduced by Dr. Van Dyke, who is also engaged in the same process in Georgia. The most important group of mines is at Gold Hill, on the southern line of Rowan and Cabarrus counties. Mining operations were begun here in 1843, and for 10 years the annual product averaged about $100,000; the last four years of this period more than one-third of all the gold coined at the Charlotte mint was from Gold Hill. In 1853 the property was purchased by a New York company, by which it has since been worked, but with greatly reduced profits, although the mines have been furnished with the most efficient machinery. These are the deepest gold mines in the Atlantic states, one of the shafts having now reached the depth of 680 feet. The ore is pyritous iron, containing gold in particles rarely visible, and probably chemically combined with the iron and sulphur in the form of a double sulphuret. It is separated with difficulty, and very imperfectly, by the processes of crushing and amalgamating; and the immense heaps of tailings collected below the mines, amounting probably to over two million bushels, still retain quantities of gold worth from fifty cents to two dollars the bushel. In Davidson county a mine was opened in 1839, which produced in the three succeeding years about $7,000 worth of gold, when the ore was proved to be more valuable for silver than for gold. These metals were associated with a variety of metallic ores, among which the sulphuret, carbonate, and phosphate of lead were especially abundant. Furnaces were constructed for reducing these, and separating the silver obtained with the lead. This is the only mine east of the Rocky Mountains which has furnished any considerable amount of silver to the mint. It is now known as the Washington mine.

Although many gold mines have been worked in South Carolina, the only one of much note is the Dorn mine, in Abbeville district. In 1850 this mine, then quite new, produced gold to the value of $19,000, and in 1852 the production rose to $202,216, although the mine was provided with very imperfect machinery and worked in a very rude manner. This large yield was, however, of short duration, the gold occurring in great quantity only in streaks or pockets upon a short portion of the vein.

The Georgia gold mines, first worked in the north-east part of the state in 1829, were soon found to extend south-west into the country beyond the Chestatee river, which was then possessed by the Cherokee Indians. In 1830 the borders of this territory were overrun by a reckless set of adventurers, notwithstanding the attempts made, first by a force of United States troops stationed for the protection of the Indians, and afterward by Georgia troops, when the state extended her laws in 1830 over the Cherokee country. On the removal of the Indians, their lands were distributed in 40 acre lots, by lottery, among the inhabitants of the state, and thus titles were obtained to the gold mines. The deposit mines yielded richly for a few years, and the whole product of gold for the first ten years of their working is supposed to have amounted to $16,000,000, a large portion of which never reached the United States mints, but was distributed in barter throughout the neighboring states and worked up in jewelry. From 1839 to 1849 the production did not probably exceed $4,000,000. A number of quartz veins were opened in Habersham, Lumpkin, Cherokee, Carroll, Columbia, and other counties, and considerable amounts of gold were obtained from these. They were, however, generally abandoned when the workings reached a depth at which machinery would be required for draining the mines. In Columbia county, about 20 miles from Augusta, the McCormack mine has been worked without interruption for about 20 years steadily, producing very fair profits. The gold is found in small particles in a honey-combed quartz, which contains but little pyrites and some galena. Nearly all the gold was obtained within 70 feet of the surface.

In Lumpkin county the gold is found in immense beds of decomposed micaceous and talcose slates, which, too poor to be worked by the slow process of crushing the whole material in mills and then washing away the earthy matter, will probably well repay the more thorough system of operations according to the California hydraulic process. After these beds had remained neglected for many years, Dr. H. M. Van Dyke, who had gained experience in California, and already applied it in introducing the system into North California, found in Boston, Mass., capitalists who agreed to furnish the money required for securing the richest tracts in the vicinity of Dahlonega, and conveying to them the water for washing down the hills on the plan, which will be more particularly noticed in speaking of the California mines. In 1858 he commenced operations, which have since been actively conducted; taking the water of the Yahoola river at a point about 13 miles above the spot where it will be first used, and conveying it by a canal or ditch over the more elevated portion of the country, crossing the valleys by means of sluices supported upon trestle-work, the height of which gradually increases with the descent of the streams, until at the crossing of the Yahoola near Dahlonega the high trestle now in construction is at the level of 240 feet above the bed of the river, with a span between the hills of 1,400 feet. Beyond this crossing the canal is to be extended two miles further, to reach the rich deposits upon which the hose washing will be first applied. It is expected that the arrangements will be completed early in 1861, and that from the numerous localities controlled by the company, at which the water can be used to advantage, the proceeds will revive the reputation of the Georgia gold mines.

Another association was formed in Boston in 1857, called the Nacoochee Hydraulic Mining Company, for the purpose of applying the same system to the high grounds in White county, recently a part of Habersham, in which are the mines of the Nacoochee valley and its vicinity, at one period highly productive, and where many deposits exist at so great an elevation, that no water has heretofore been brought to bear upon them. By damming the Nacoochee river, this company can carry water to these points; and their arrangements are already nearly completed. In some experimental trials they have, by the use of a current of water that would flow through a six-inch pipe, obtained several hundred dollars per week with the labor of two miners. From one spot more than 1,500 dwts. were washed out in small nuggets, several of about 100 dwts. each, and one of 387 dwts. The value of these is $1 the dwt., and of the gold dust 97 cents. The auriferous belt of rocks consists of alternating beds of micaceous, hornblende, and talcose slates and gneiss, which stand nearly vertically, and contain between their layers bands of quartz. The gold is found in the quartz and in the auriferous pyrites accompanying it, and to some extent in the slates also. Detached or "free" gold is also met with, derived, no doubt, from pyrites which has decomposed and disappeared. From the general disintegration of the edges of these strata, gold has been distributed in the deposits around.

From Georgia, the gold-bearing rocks are traced into eastern Tennessee, where they have been worked along the range of the Coweta and Smoky Mountains; and from the south side of the Blue Ridge, in Georgia, they have proved productive in a south-west direction, through Carroll county, into Alabama; but the formation is soon lost in the last-named state.

The gold regions along both slopes of the Rocky Mountains are, however, the most remarkable yet discovered on this continent. In COLORADO, "the whole range of mountains seems crowded with veins of rich mineral ore. They run into and through the hill sides like the bars of a gridiron—every hundred feet, every fifty feet, every twenty feet." The first and largest development of these mines lies along and up the Clear Creek and centres around its sources. The principal mining villages of this section are Central City, Black Hawk and Nevada. Another centre of productive mining interests is in the South Park. The gold in Colorado is combined with sulphur and forms a sort of pyrites. This renders its extraction more difficult; but processes have lately been devised which, without increasing materially the expense, will raise the production of gold per cord of ore to three or five-fold what it has hitherto been. There are also large deposits of gold in New Mexico and Utah, which are not yet developed to any considerable extent.

IDAHO and MONTANA are also immensely rich in gold mines and placers. The Boise Basin, in Idaho, has yielded, and still yields to the placer miner in many parts a fair return for his labor, and possesses, beside, many valuable gold-bearing quartz leads. The South Boise has also many valuable leads. The Owyhee mines, sixty miles south of Boise City. They are almost entirely silver-producing, though some gold is extracted from the silver. In Montana, the placer diggings are yet paying largely, and the quartz leads are richer in gold than in any section yet discovered; and the two localities which have been thus far principally worked, Alder Gulch, and the vicinity of Helena, about one hundred and fifty miles apart, are yielding both gold and silver in great profusion.

Still another region rich in gold, richer perhaps than either of the others, though as yet developed with difficulty, on account of the hostile and treacherous Indians who roam over it, is the Territory of Arizona. Its gulches and cañons abound in the precious metal, and it cannot be long before they yield in profusion their long hidden wealth. The completion of the Pacific railroad will soon make this wealth available.

The most important gold region of the United States and of the world is that of California. Its development has not only largely multiplied the previous gold production of the globe, but it has been the means of rapidly bringing into the use of civilized nations large territories of productive lands, which before were an unprofitable wilderness, founding new states, enlarging the commerce of the world, and bringing into closer intercourse nations which before were the most widely separated. At the period when the wealth of the gold mines of California began to be realized, the annual production of gold throughout the world had gradually fallen to about $20,000,000, and more than half of this was furnished by Russia alone. In 1853, only five years later, California produced an amount estimated at $70,000,000, and the total production, through the supplies, nearly as large, furnished at the same time by Australia, had increased to almost double this amount. Little was known of California previous to the discovery of gold at Sutter's mill, on the American fork of the Sacramento, in February, 1848; yet its being a country containing gold was made known by Hakluyt in his account of Drake's expedition of 1577–9, and by Cavello, a Jesuit priest of San José, Bay of Francisco, who published a work on the country in Spain in 1690. Reports from later travellers confirmed these statements at various times, and in *Hunt's Merchants' Magazine* for April, 1847, a report is presented by Mr. Sloat, which speaks in very decided terms of the richness of the gold placers of the country, as noticed by him during his observations of the two preceding years. The Rev. C. S. Lyman, in a letter written to the editor of the *American Journal of Science* from San José, in March 1848, notices the discovery of the preceding month as very promising. In August of that year it was reported that four thousand men were engaged in working the deposits on the American fork, and were taking out from $30,000 to $40,000 a day. This comprised a large portion of the population of California. San Francisco was almost deserted, and people were pouring in from distant regions. The next year the emigration commenced in the United States, both by sea around Cape Horn, and across the plains and Rocky Mountains in large parties. By the close of the year 1849 the number of persons engaged in mining was estimated at from 40,000 to 50,000 Americans, and about 5,000 foreigners: the total product of gold at about $40,000,000. The mining district was traced up the valley of the Sacramento toward the north, and the continuation of the same formations up that of the San Joaquin in the opposite direction was also beginning to be understood. Along the valleys of the streams, which flowed into these rivers from the Sierra Nevada range to the east, gold was almost everywhere found, and upon the hills and elevated plains it was met with beneath the sands and clays which covered the surface to the depth of fifteen to thirty feet or more; all the materials, earthy and metallic, appearing either to have been derived from the superficial disintegration of the slaty formations, or to have been deposited by ancient rivers, which have since been diverted in other directions. Deposits of this character were called dry diggings, and, except in the wet season, were worked to great disadvantage for the want of water to separate the earthy matters from the gold. In the bottoms of the streams the deposits contained much coarse gold, derived from the wearing down of the slate formations through which they had made their way in their rapid descent from the Sierra Nevada mountains. By the excavation of the vast gulches or ravines of these streams, some of which presented precipitous walls of about 3,000 feet in height, an immense amount of gold must have been removed from its original beds, which, as the lighter earthy matters were swept down the rivers, remained behind, forming the riches of the auriferous deposits. The country of this peculiar character was found to extend along the western slopes of the Sierra Nevada for 400 or 500 miles, and the gold-bearing slates to spread over a width of from forty to sixty miles.

Whether or no the natural processes by which the gold had been collected from its original beds suggested to the California miner an improved method of washing the auriferous formations upon a gigantic scale, it was soon found that the richness of the deposits would justify, especially in the dry diggings, large outlays in conveying water from great distances by canals or ditches, and applying this, either under the pressure of a great head, to tear up the material from its bed and wash away the earthy portions, or to wash the auriferous gravels as these were carried to the water sluices and thrown into them for this purpose. On this plan hydraulic operations were soon laid out of extraordinary extent. Currents were diverted well up the slope of the Sierra Nevada mountains, and conveyed in canals along the sides of the hills, and in sluices, supported upon trestle-work, from one hill to another, sometimes at a height of more than 200 feet above the bottoms. On the hills where the water was required for "hose washing," it was taken from the canal or sluice in a large and strong canvas hose, to the lower end of which a nozzle, like that of a fire engine, was attached. The least head for efficient service was about 60 feet, and a head of 100 feet was used where it could be had and the hose would bear it. Large hose and nozzles proved much more efficient than several smaller ones of equal or even greater capacity. As estimated by Mr. Wm. P. Blake, with a pipe of an inch and a half or two inches aperture, and a pressure of 90 feet head, a boy can excavate and wash as much auriferous earth as 10 or 15 men by the ordinary methods. In suitable places, where the waste water can flow rapidly away though the sluices made for its channel and for catching the gold, the jet of water is directed against the side of a hill, which it rapidly excavates, sweeping off the earthy portions, undermining the trees, and rolling down the loose stones, and, where the ground is favorable for the operation, cutting every thing away, it may be to a depth of 100 feet from the top to the bottom of the excavation, leaving behind barren acres of loose stone in unsightly piles—a perfect picture of desolation. At the close of the year 1858 it was estimated that the artificial water-courses already constructed for mining purposes in California amounted to 5,726 miles in length, and their cost to $13,575,400; and besides these there were branches not enumerated, and others in construction, to the extent of about 1,000 miles more. Among the principal of these canals are the Columbia and Stanislaus, in Tuolumne county, which is 80 miles long, and cost $600,000; the Butte, in Amador county, 50 miles long, cost $400,000; that of the Union Water Company, in Calaveras county, 78 miles long, cost $320,000; and that of the Tuolumne Hydraulic Company, 60 miles long, cost $300,000. Notwithstanding the cost of these enterprises, they have proved in general highly profitable, paying, after deducting the expenses of keeping them up, from one to more than five per cent. a month. The water is sold to the miners by the canal companies at so much per inch of the discharge—this being from a horizontal aperture, one inch high, at the bottom of a box in which the water is kept six inches deep. The length of the aperture is regulated by a slide. The price has fallen from $3.00 an inch per day in 1851, to 50 cents in 1854, and is now still less.

Sluice-washing, which is a necessary part of the hydraulic or hose process, is also carried on independently of it, and by a method which was first adopted in California. Channels are made sometimes upon the surface of the slaty beds in place, the ragged edges of which are very favorable for catching the gold, or sometimes of boards, in the form of an open trough, a foot or 15 inches in width, and 8 or ten inches deep, which are extended to several hundred feet in length. These are set at a suitable slope, usually about one in twelve, and "riffle" bars are laid across to obstruct the flow of the heavy metallic particles which sweep along the bottom, while the muddy portions and stones are carried over with the flow of the water, and discharged at the lower end. Fresh gravel is continually shovelled into the sluices, and once a day, or oftener, these are cleaned up to collect the gold from the riffles and pools, which are sometimes used at the head of one joint of the sluice to receive the discharge from the next one above. Where the descent is rapid enough to keep the pool "in a boil," a considerable portion of the gold may be caught in it, especially if mercury be introduced.

In 1851 attention began to be turned to the quartz veins, or "ledges," as they were called, and numerous companies were soon established in the United States and in England for carrying on regular mining operations upon these. Within five years after, many deep shafts had been sunk upon veins in different parts of the country, and mills were in operation, furnished with the most efficient machinery for crushing and washing the ore. The uncertain supply of water, and the great expense attending the procuring it by canals from a distance, have operated strongly against the success of these works. They have, however, added considerably to the production of gold, and are still vigorously prosecuted. Upon the estate of Col. Fremont, in Mariposa county, several veins are worked to considerable extent on the northern ridge of Mount Bullion, and the quartz is transported to the Benton Mills, on Bear River, and to the steam mills at Bear Valley, Ophir, Guadaloupe, and Agua Fria. The principal vein, called the Pine Tree, has been traced about 20 miles from Mount Ophir, through Bear Valley, and along Mount Bullion to Merced River, with an average thickness of 30 feet. Among its contents are found oxides and carbonates of copper, and its ores are often exceedingly rich in gold. Those of the neighboring vein, called the Josephine, are variously valued at from $50 to $2,000 per ton. On account of the precipitous character of the hills, the transportation of the ore was almost impracticable until Col. Fremont had constructed a railroad, 3¾ miles long, down the steep slopes, in zigzag lines, upon grades varying from 2 to 7½ feet in 100, and with 17 curves of radii, varying from 53 to 84 feet. The width of the track is 36 inches, and the rails are of iron bars set on edge. The cars carry each 2½ tons of rock, and are run down in 45 minutes, their movement being regulated by a brake. By the construction of this road and the completion of new mills, furnished with powerful stamping machinery, and with inexhaustible supplies of ore at command, Col. Fremont is now in a position to thoroughly test the question as to the dependence that may be placed upon quartz mining in California as a permanent business.

The total production of the mines of California, as nearly as can be made up from the official returns, has been presented in the following values, in pounds sterling, for the years named:—

1848......	£11,700	1853......	£12,500,000
1849......	1,612,000	1854......	14,100,000
1850......	5,000,000	1855......	13,400,000
1851......	8,250,000	1856......	14,000,000
1852......	11,700,000	1857......	13,110,000

The quantities deposited in the mints of the United States will be given, together with those from other states, in the course of this article.

Gold is almost universally found native, or uncombined with other substances, and the processes for separating it from the stony matters with which it is associated may be, and commonly are, wholly mechanical. It occurs in the alluvial deposits, mixed with their lowest beds of sand and gravel; also in veins, usually of quartz, which often contain various metallic ores besides the gold; and it is disseminated through the mass of great beds of slate, which are frequently in a more or less decomposed condition. From such beds it is often distributed in fine particles through the soil in their vicinity. Not subject to be chemically affected by any of the ordinary agents of change, the particles of gold, large or small, remain unaltered in the soil, always seeking by their great weight the lowest level; and they may at any time be collected by washing away the earthy matters. New localities are tested by trying the earth in different places, by washing it in an iron pan or upon the blade of a shovel, an experienced hand readily throwing the heavy particles by themselves, while the lighter are allowed to flow away. This method is one of the means in use for collecting gold upon a small scale, and the Mexicans of the gold regions, by long practice, are particularly expert in it. If a vein is to be tested, the quartz is finely crushed, and the powder is then washed in the same manner. Gold may be thus brought to view when none was visible in the stones, however closely examined. By placing a little mercury or quicksilver in the pan, the gold will be more perfectly secured, as, by coming in contact with each other, these metals instantly unite to form a heavy amalgam, and the mercury thus holds the finest particles of gold so that they cannot escape. The mixture, separated from the sand, is squeezed in a piece of thick linen or deerskin, through which the excess of mercury escapes, leaving the amalgam. This may then be heated on a shovel, when the mercury goes off in vapor, and the gold is left in its original-shaped particles, cohering together in a cake. If the quantity of amalgam is considerable, it is distilled in a retort, and the mercury is condensed to be used again. This amalgamation fails entirely if the slightest quantity of any greasy substance is present, as a film of the grease coats every portion of the mercury, and effectually prevents its contact with the gold. These processes contain the principles of nearly all the methods in use for separating gold. A great variety of machines have been based upon them, the simplest of which have proved the most valuable. The Burke rocker has always been a favorite machine in the southern states, and has been largely used in California by small companies of miners, and in localities where operations were not carried on upon a very extensive scale. It is a cradle-shaped trough, about six feet long, set on two rockers, the upper end a few inches higher than the lower, and placed so as to receive at its head a current of water from the end of a leading trough above. This falls upon a perforated iron plate, set as a shelf in the machine, and upon this the auriferous gravel is thrown. The finer particles fall through as the rocker is kept in motion by hand, and the coarse gravel rolls down to the lower end, and falls off upon the ground. Across the bottom of the rocker are placed, at intervals of 6 or 8 inches, low bars or partitions which catch the heavy sands, and prevent their being washed out of the lower end with the water and mud. This lower portion is sometimes arranged as a drawer, which can be secured by a lock, so that the gold which falls into it is safe against robbery. The drawer is called the "riffle box." Some rockers are mere open troughs without a shelf. The "tom" is often preferred to the rocker, which it resembles, except in its being a trough without rockers, on the plan of the sluices already described. Both it and the rocker are of convenient size for moving about from one place to another, as the working of the deposit advances.

BURKE ROCKER.

Vein mining requires more efficient machinery, and stamping mills are constructed as near as may be to the mines, for reducing the stony materials to powder, and the sands from the stamps are passed through a variety of machines designed to catch the gold. Stamps are solid blocks of the heaviest cast iron attached to the end of a wooden or iron rod called the leg, to which the lifting cam is applied for raising them. They commonly weigh about 300 lbs. each, though in California they are made of twice and even three times this weight. Several of them are set together in a frame side by side, and are lifted in succession by the cams upon a horizontal shaft, which revolves in front of them. The bed in which they stand, and into which the ore to be crushed is thrown, is sometimes a massive anvil, hollow in the top, firmly imbedded in a heavy stick of timber, or is formed of stones, beaten by the stamps themselves into a solid bed. Water is usually supplied in small currents to the stamps, and sometimes mercury also is poured into the bed. The only exit for the crushed materials is through small holes punched in a sheet of copper, of which the side of the boxing around the stamps is formed, opposite to that at which the ore is fed. Through these holes the mud and water are projected with every blow into a capacious box, the floor of which inclines gently back toward the stamp, and contains along this edge a quantity of mercury, in which a considerable portion of the gold is caught. From the box a spout leads the current into the other machines, often through an inclined trough, in the bottom of which baize or blanket stuff is laid for the purpose of entangling in its fibres the particles of gold that are swept along. These are frequently taken up and cleaned. Much of the gold, however, always escapes them, and the current is variously treated before it is finally allowed to flow away. The sands require to be more finely pulverized, and the current first flows into mills of some sort, as the Chilian mill, arrastre, etc. The former consists of a pair of heavy wheels of granite, from four to six feet in diameter when new, set in a horizontal frame, one on each side of an upright shaft, and carried around with the shaft as it revolves upon its axis. The stones They revolve in a water-tight box or tub upon a granite floor. Sometimes they are used in the place of stamps for breaking up the coarse ore; and worked at the rate of eight to twelve revolutions a minute, they should crush to fine sand from one to two tons of quartz in twelve hours. The water, which flows in one side the tub, passes out over the opposite edge with the light slime and fine mud, while much of the gold remains in the bottom, caught by the mercury placed there to secure it. The arrastre is something like the Chilian mill, only instead of revolving stones, heavy flat ones are dragged round with the shaft by chains, secured to the horizontal arms. These machines in Mexico are worked by horses or mules, but in this country by water or steam power. The slowness of their operation is not regarded as an objectionable feature, but on the contrary is favorable for effectually securing the gold. Among the simplest and best contrivances employed below the Chilian mill are the "shaking tables." These are platforms seven or eight feet long, of plank in a single piece, as wide as can be procured.

CRUSHING MILL, OR ARRASTRE.

being as close as possible to the shaft, have a twisting motion which acts powerfully to grind the particles crushed by their weight. The planks, of two inches thickness, are worked down from a line across the middle to a thin edge at one end, and from the other end they are made to diminish to half an inch thickness at the line across the middle. Each one is furnished with sides, and a strip across the thin end of six inches in height, the joining made perfectly tight, and is then swung between four posts in a horizontal position by four rods or chains, which should be at least eight feet long. Mercury is poured into the two divisions, until they are more than half filled. The sands are made to flow in upon the thin end, and are received upon the face of the mercury; and the table is made to swing forward and back by the revolution of a crank. By the motion the sands are mixed in with the mercury, and swept along in successive waves, and falling over the middle ridge are treated in the same manner in the succeeding division. The mercury is retained by its weight in the depressed portions of the table, and the water and sands are discharged over the open end. Many machines designed for effecting the amalgamation of the gold in the most thorough manner have been patented within the last few years, and have been introduced at the mines under various names; few of them, however, involve any new principles, but are merely modified forms of the old contrivances. The use of hot water was found several years ago to hasten the amalgamation, and the employment of steam engines provided a cheap way of obtaining it in the large quantities required. Prof. A. K. Eaton, of New York, found that amalgamated metallic surfaces could be made to collect most completely the very fine particles of gold, which by all other processes it has been found impossible to secure. The use of copper, brass, or zinc proved troublesome and impracticable from the rapidity with which they were dissolved in the mercury, adulterating the amalgam. An amalgamated iron surface proved to be free from this objection, and the following description of apparatus was finally decided on as the most efficient: A circular plate of wrought iron is amalgamated over what is intended to be its inferior surface, and an open tube is fixed in its centre, rising three or four feet high, and furnished at the top with a bowl or funnel. This tube and disk are supported upon a surface of mercury contained in a shallow tub of larger diameter than the disk, a frame-work being attached to the tub for this purpose. A pulley is fixed upon the hollow shaft, so that a belt may be attached for causing the disk to rotate upon the mercury. The sands are fed with water into the funnel at the top of the tube, and the pressure caused by the height of the column carries them down upon the mercurial surface, and, by reason of this pressure and the centrifugal action of the revolving disk, they gradually work outward between this surface and the amalgamated surface above, being pressed and rubbed between them till they escape round the circumference of the disk, and flow over the edge of the tub. Hot water, as in all other modes of amalgamating, is preferable to cold. By this process all free gold, however fine the particles, must come in contact with the amalgamated surface, and be taken up by the mercury. It perfectly separates the gold that in other machines floats off in the fine slime, for the reason that simply pressed into the mercury and left to themselves, the impalpable particles immediately rise upon its surface, without coming into actual contact with the fluid metal. In gold ores, especially those of sulphurous character, much of the gold is so fine that it remains suspended a long time in water, and is entirely lost. The important feature of this invention is the use of an inferior amalgamated surface, against which these floating particles are pressed. The pressure is secured by any desired depth of the mercury, but in practice less than an inch above the lower edge of the plate is found to be sufficient. The efficiency of the machine was fully tested in November, 1860, at the Gold Hill mine, in North Carolina, where better results were obtained with it than by any other machine ever before applied to the separation of the gold from its pyritous sands. In the same month it was tried at the United States assay office, in New York city, upon the tailings of the sweeps from which all the gold had been extracted that could be removed by the amalgamating machines in use, and from these it readily separated the remaining portion.

As remarked in the mention made of the Gold Hill mines, when gold is associated with iron and copper pyrites it is held very tenaciously, as if combined itself with the sulphur, like the other metals. However finely such ores are pulverized, every microscopic particle of pyrites appears to retain a portion of gold, and prevent its uniting with the mercury. This portion of the gold, consequently, escapes in the tailings; and if these are kept in refuse heaps, exposed to the weather, the pyrites slowly decompose, and more gold is continually set free. Thus it is the heaps may be washed over with profit for many successive years. Artificial roasting of the ores is recommended by high authorities as a sure method of freeing the gold at once, the effect of it being to break up the sulphurets, causing the sulphur to escape in vapor, and the iron to crumble down in the state of an oxide, or an ochreous powder, from which the gold is readily separated by the ordinary methods. This is objected to by others, who assert that it involves a great loss of gold, which is volatilized or carried off mechanically in the sulphur fumes. In California complete separation is sought to be attained by long-continued and most thorough pulverization of the ores, the heavy sands of the first concentration being received into Chilian or other mills, and repeatedly ground to the extreme of fineness, and always in the presence of mercury. Various chemical processes have been devised for the treatment of these ores, and in Russia it has been proposed to smelt the sands after they had been concentrated, and cause the gold to be taken up by iron reduced by the same smelting operation from its ores. The mechanical and amalgamating treatment, however, appears to be the only one in successful use.

The great value of gold renders it profitable to work deposits and ores which contain an exceedingly small per-centage of metal. In the "branch mining" of the southern states, deposits worked by the rocker are regarded as profitable which pay a pennyweight or nearly one dollar per day to the hand employed. The yield is always uncertain, and sometimes runs up, for a short time, to very large amounts; but it has, for the most part, ceased to be followed as a regular pursuit. The production of the ores is quite as uncertain as that of the deposits, and their value depends upon a variety of circumstances: as the hardness of the material, the tenacity with which it holds the fine gold when crushed, the convenience of the locality to mills, and the expenses attending the working of the mines. The great beds of decomposed slates of Georgia can be worked to profit when they yield from four to five cents worth of gold to the bushel of stuff, or about 100 lbs. weight; but the mill for crushing and washing it must then be close at hand. The proportion of the gold, in this case, is less than 2 parts in 1,000,000. The hard quartz ores must contain nearly or quite 20 cents worth of gold in the bushel, especially if they are pyritiferous.

Although the gold is obtained in a metallic state, it differs very much in value in different localities. That of the deposits is the proper representative of the character of the gold of any district, and always brings a higher price at the mint than the imperfectly cleaned gold derived from the veins of the same locality. It has peculiarities in its appearance by which its source may often be recognized. This is commonly owing to the different proportions of silver with which it is alloyed. Deposit gold from the vicinity of Dahlonega, in Georgia, is worth 93 cents the pennyweight; that of Hart county, in the same state, 98 cents; of Carroll county, Georgia, and Chesterfield district, South Carolina, $1.02; of Union county, Georgia, or the Tennessee line, 72 cents; Charlotte, North Carolina, $1.00; and that of Burke county, North Carolina, only 50 cents. The value appears to decrease toward the western margin of the gold region. The average fineness of California gold is found to be from 875 to 885 parts in 1,000, which is very near that of our gold coin, viz., 900 in 1,000. The native gold from Australia has from 960 to 966 parts in 1,000 pure gold, and some from the Chaudiere, in Canada, 877.3 pure gold, and 122.3 silver; another specimen 892.4, silver 107.6. The specific gravity of the metal has been increased by casting from 14.6 in the native state to 17.48.

At the mint and branch mints of the United States, records are preserved of the source whence the gold offered for coinage is obtained, and tables are thus prepared, copies of which are given on the succeeding pages. These are interesting for reference, although they can hardly be regarded as presenting even an approximate estimate of the amount of gold derived from the mines of the United States. As already stated, considerable portions of this never reach the mints; and from California particularly large quantities have been carried to Europe in the form of gold dust. The product of its mines is more nearly presented in the tables accompanying the description of the gold-mining operations of that region. Gold has been coined at private mints in California and at Pike's Peak; but this coinage, not recognized by the government, after circulating for a time, finds its way to the government mint, and the gold is credited in the accounts as the production of the region where it was converted into coin.

1.—MINT OF THE UNITED STATES, PHILADELPHIA.

Period.	Virginia.	North Carolina.	South Carolina.	Georgia.	Tennessee.	Alabama.	New Mexico.	California.	Oregon.	Kansas.	Other sources.	Total.
1804 to 1827	..	$110,000 00	..	..	..	..	..	..	..	..	..	$110,000 00
1828 to 1837	$427,000 00	2,519,500 00	$327 500	$1,763,900 00	$12,400	..	..	..	..	..	$13,200	5,063,500 00
1838 to 1847	518,294 00	1,303,636 00	152,366	566,316 00	16,499	$45,493	..	..	..	..	21,037	2,623,641 00
1848	57,886 00	109,034 00	19,228	3,370 00	3,497	3,670	$682	$44,177 00	..	..	..	241,544 00
1849	129,382 00	102,688 00	4,309	10,525 00	2,739	2,977	32,889	5,481,439 00	..	..	144	5,767,092 00
1850	65,991 00	43,734 00	759	5,114 00	307	1,178	5,392	31,667,505 00	..	..	326	31,790,306 00
1851	69,052 00	49,440 00	12,338	2,490 00	126	817	890	46,939,367 00	..	..	..	47,074,520 00
1852	83,626 00	65,248 00	4,505	3,420 00	..	254	814	49,663,623 00	..	..	..	49,821,490 00
1853	52,200 00	45,690 00	3,522	1,912 00	..	..	3,632	52,732,227 00	13,535	..	5,213	52,857,931 00
1854	23,347 00	9,062 00	1,220	7,561 00	..	245	738	35,671,185 00	..	..	..	35,713,358 00
1855	28,895 50	22,626 00	1,200	1,733 50	..	310	900	2,634,297 63	..	..	1,535	2,691,497 63
1856	21,607 00	12,910 00	5,980	4,910 00	..	..	2,460	1,440,134 58	40,750	..	..	1,528,751 58
1857	2,505 00	6,805 00	2,565	3,542 00	..	..	..	565,566 41	..	..	..	580,983 41
1858	18,377 00	15,175 00	300	18,365 00	..	..	..	1,372,506 07	3,600	..	..	1,428,323 07
1859	15,720 00	9,305 00	4,675	20,190 00	240	..	275	959,191 79	2,960	$145	..	1,012,701 79
Total	$1,513,882 50	4,424,853 00	540,467	2,413,348 50	35,808	54,944	48,672	229,171,219 48	60,845	145	41,455	238,305,639 48

2.—BRANCH MINT, SAN FRANCISCO.

Period.	California.	Period.	California.	Period.	California.
1854	$10,842,281 23	1856	29,209,218 24	1858	19,104,369 99
1855	20,860,437 20	1857	12,526,826 93	1859	14,098,564 14
		Total			$106,641,697 73

3.—BRANCH MINT, NEW ORLEANS.

Period.	North Carolina.	South Carolina.	Georgia.	Tennessee.	Alabama.	California.	Other sources.	Total.
1838 to 1847	$741	$14,306	$37,364	$1,772 00	$61,903	..	$3,613	$119,699 00
1848	..	1,488	2,317	947 00	6,717	$1,124 00	..	12,593 00
1849	..	423	..	..	4,062	669,921 00	2,733	677,189 00
1850	..	..	..	..	3,560	4,575,576 00	894	4,580,030 00
1851	..	..	..	..	1,040	8,764,682 00	..	8,770,772 00
1852	..	..	..	..	..	3,777,784 00	..	3,777,784 00
1853	..	..	..	..	..	2,006,673 00	..	2,006,673 00
1854	..	..	..	..	..	981,511 00	..	981,511 00
1855	..	..	..	..	..	411,517 24	..	411,517 24
1856	..	..	..	..	..	283,344 91	..	283,344 91
1857	..	..	..	..	..	129,328 39	..	129,328 39
1858	..	..	1,560	164 12	..	448,439 84	..	450,163 96
1859	..	..	..	..	..	93,272 41	..	93,272 41
Total	$741	16,217	41,241	2,883 12	77,282	22,148,173 79	7,290	22,293,827 91

4. BRANCH MINT, CHARLOTTE, NORTH CAROLINA.

Period.	N. Carolina.	S. Carolina.	California.	Total.
1838 to 1847	$1,529,777 00	$143,941 00	..	$1,673,718 00
1848	359,075 00	11,710 00	..	370,785 00
1849	378,223 00	12,509 00	..	390,732 00
1850	307,289 00	13,000 00	..	320,289 00
1851	275,742 00	25,478 00	$15,111 00	316,061 00
1852	337,604 00	64,934 00	28,362 00	430,900 00
1853	227,847 00	61,845 00	15,465 00	305,157 00
1854	$188,277 00	$19,006 00	$6,328 00	$213,606 00
1855	196,894 03	14,277 17	5,817 66	216,988 86
1856	157,355 18	..	16,237 35	173,592 53
1857	170,560 33	5,807 16	..	176,067 49
1858	75,376 47	..	..	75,376 47
1859	182,489 61	22,762 71	..	205,252 32
Total	$4,386,239 62	$394,965 04	$87,321 01	$4,868,525 67

5. BRANCH MINT, DAHLONEGA, GEORGIA.

Period.	N. Carolina.	S. Carolina.	Georgia.	Tennessee.	Alabama.	California.	Kansas.	Other sources.	Total.
1838 to 1847	$64,351 00	$95,427 00	$2,978,353 00	$32,175 00	$47,711 00	..	..	..	$3,218,017 00
1848	5,434 00	8,151 00	251,376 00	2,717 00	4,075 00	..	..	..	271,753 00
1849	4,882 00	7,323 00	225,824 00	2,441 00	3,661 00	..	..	..	244,131 00
1850	4,500 00	5,700 00	204,473 00	1,200 00	1,800 00	$30,025 00	..	..	247,698 00
1851	1,971 00	3,236 00	154,723 00	2,251 00	2,105 00	214,072 00	..	$951 00	379,309 00
1852	443 00	57,543 00	93,122 00	750 00	..	324,931 00	..	..	476,789 00
1853	2,085 00	33,950 00	56,984 00	149 00	..	359,122 00	..	..	452,290 00
1854	5,818 00	15,988 00	47,027 00	223 00	..	211,169 00	..	..	280,225 00
1855	3,145 82	9,113 27	56,686 36	..	277 92	47,428 70	..	..	116,652 07
1856	..	25,723 75	44,107 99	106 42	..	81,467 10	..	..	101,405 26
1857	..	8,083 89	25,097 63	..	..	6,498 42	..	..	39,679 54
1858	..	32,322 28	57,891 45	107 33	..	5,293 52	..	..	95,614 58
1859	2,656 88	4,310 35	57,023 12	..	..	699 19	$82 70	..	65,072 24
Total	$95,286 70	$307,171 54	$4,252,688 55	$42,119 75	$59,629 92	$1,230,705 53	$82 70	$951 00	$5,988,635 69

6. ASSAY OFFICE, NEW YORK.

Period.	Virginia.	N. Carolina.	S. Carolina.	Georgia.	Alabama.	California.	Kansas.	Oregon.	Other sources.	Total.
1854	$167 00	$3,916 00	$395 00	$1,242 00	..	$9,221,457 00	..	..	..	$9,227,177 00
1855	2,370 00	3,750 00	7,620 00	13,100 00	$350 00	25,025,896 11	..	..	$1,600 00	25,054,686 11
1856	6,928 00	805 07	4,052 29	41,101 28	233 62	16,259,008 90	..	..	..	16,582,129 16
1857	1,531 00	1,689 00	2,663 00	10,451 00	1,545 00	9,899,957 00	..	..	..	9,917,836 00
1858	501 00	7,007 00	6,354 00	12,951 00	2,181 00	19,660,551 46	..	$5,581 00	27,523 00	19,722,629 46
1859	436 00	20,122 00	700 00	14,756 00	593 00	11,694,872 25	$3,944 00	2,866 00	405 00	11,738,694 25
Total	$11,933 00	$37,289 07	$21,784 29	$93,601 28	$4,902 62	$92,031,722 72	$3,944 00	$8,447 00	$29,528 00	$92,243,151 98

7. SUMMARY EXHIBIT OF THE ENTIRE DEPOSITS OF DOMESTIC GOLD AT THE UNITED STATES MINT AND BRANCTES, TO JUNE 30, 1859.

Mints.	Virginia.	N. Carolina.	S. Carolina.	Georgia.	Tennessee.	Alabama.	New Mexico.	California.	Kansas.	Oregon.	Other sources.	Total.
Philadelphia	$1,513,582 50	$4,424,853 00	$540,467 00	$2,413,348 50	$35,808 00	$54,944 00	$48,672 00	$229,171,219 48	$145 00	$60,845 00	$41,455 00	$238,305,639 48
San Francisco	..	..	..	..	..	..	..	106,641,697 73	..	..	..	106,640,697 73
New Orleans	..	741 00	16,217 00	41,241 00	2,883 12	77,282 00	..	22,148,173 79	..	..	7,290 00	22,293,827 91
Charlotte	..	4,386,239 62	394,965 04	..	..	..	..	87,321 01	..	..	..	4,868,525 67
Dahlonega	..	95,286 70	307,171 54	4,252,688 55	42,119 75	59,629 92	..	1,230,705 53	82 70	..	951 00	5,988,635 69
Assay Office	11,933 00	37,289 07	21,784 29	93,601 28	..	4,902 62	..	92,031,722 72	3,944 00	8,447 00	29,528 00	92,243,151 98
Total	$1,525,515 50	$8,944,409 39	$1,280,604 87	$6,800,879 83	$80,810 87	$196,758 54	$48,672 00	$451,310,840 26	$4,171 70	$69,292 00	$79,224 00	$470,340,478 46

The most important use of gold is as a medium of exchange. For this purpose it is converted into coin at the mints, and into bars or bullion at the government assay office. In this form a large portion of the receipts from California is immediately exported from New York to make up the balance of foreign trade. Each bar is stamped with marks, representing its fineness and weight, and may continue to be thus used, or when received at foreign mints, is converted into coin. A large amount of gold is consumed in jewelry, trinkets, watches, and plate, and still more in the form of gold-leaf. This last being worn out in the using, or being distributed in too small quantities together to pay for recovering it, is altogether lost to the community, after the articles have served the purpose intended. This loss in the time of James I. was considered so serious, that a special act was passed, restricting the use of gold and silver-leaf, except for specified objects, which, singularly enough, were chiefly for military accoutrements. Gold employed in the recently invented process of electrotyping, in which large quantities are consumed, is similarly lost in the using.

Besides the use of gold-leaf in gilding, it is employed quite largely by dentists as the best material for filling teeth. They also use much gold plate and wire for securing the artificial sets in the mouth. In book-binding, gold is consumed to considerable extent for lettering and ornamenting the backs of the books. The manufacture of gold-leaf is carried on in various places, both in the cities and country. It is a simple process, known in ancient times, but only of late years carried to a high degree of perfection. The ingots, moulded for the purpose, and annealed in hot ashes, are rolled between rollers of polished steel, until the sheet is reduced from its original thickness of half an inch to a little more than $\frac{1}{800}$ of an inch, an ounce weight making a strip ten feet long and $1\frac{1}{2}$ inches wide. This is annealed and cut into pieces an inch square, each weighing about six grains. A pile is then made of 150 of these pieces, alternating with leaves of fine calf-skin vellum, each one of which is four inches square, and a number of extra leaves of the vellum are added at the top and bottom of the pile. The heap, called a tool or kutch, is slipped into a parchment case open at the two ends, and this into a similar one, so that each side of the pack is protected by one of the case. It is placed upon a block of marble, and then beaten with a hammer weighing sixteen pounds, and furnished with a convex face, the effect of which is to cause the gold to spread more rapidly. The workman wields this with great dexterity, shifting it from one hand to the other, without interfering with the regularity of the blow. The pack is occasionally turned over, and is bent and rolled in the hands to cause the gold to extend freely between the leaves, as it is expanded. The gold-leaves are also interchanged to expose them all equally to the beating. When they have attained the full size of the vellum, which is done in about twenty minutes, they are taken apart, and cut each one into four pieces, making 600 of the original 150. These are packed in gold-beater's skin, and the pack is beaten as before, but with a lighter hammer, until they are extended again to sixteen square inches. This occupies about two hours. The gold-leaves are then taken out, and spread singly upon a leather cushion, where they are cut into four squares by two sharp edges of cane, arranged in the form of a cross. To any other kind of a knife the gold would adhere. These leaves are again packed, 800 together, in the finest kind of gold-beater's skin, and expanded till each leaf is from 3 to $3\frac{1}{2}$ inches square. The aggregate surface is about 192 times larger than that of the original sheet, and the thickness is reduced to about the $\frac{1}{150000}$ of an inch. The beating is sometimes carried further than this, especially by the French, so that an ounce of gold is extended over 160 square feet, and its thickness is reduced to $\frac{1}{234000}$ of an inch, or even to $\frac{1}{2500000}$. When the pack is opened, the leaves are carefully lifted by a pair of wooden pliers, spread upon a leather cushion by the aid of the breath, and cut into four squares of about $3\frac{1}{4}$ inches each, which are immediately transferred one by one between the leaves of a little book of smooth paper, which are prevented from adhering to the gold-leaves by an application of red ochre or red chalk. Twenty-five leaves are put into each book, and when filled, it is pressed hard, and all projecting edges of the gold are wiped away with a bit of linen. The books are then put up in packages of a dozen together for sale.

An imitation gold-leaf, called Dutch gold-leaf, is used to some extent. It is prepared from sheets of brass, which are gilded, and beaten down in the manner already described. When new it appears like genuine gold-leaf, but soon becomes tarnished in use. Party gold-leaf is formed of leaves of gold and of silver, laid together and made to unite by beating and hammering. It is then beaten down like gold-leaf.

The gold-beater's skin used in this manufacture is a peculiar preparation made from the cæcum of the ox. The membrane is doubled together, the two mucous surfaces face to face, in which state they unite firmly. It is then treated with preparations of alum, isinglass, whites of eggs, etc., sometimes with creosote, and after being beaten between folds of paper to expel the grease, is pressed and dried. In this way leaves are obtained $5\frac{1}{8}$ inches square, of which moulds are made up, containing each 850 leaves. After being used for a considerable time, the leaves become dry and stiff, so that the gold cannot spread freely between them. To remedy this, they are moistened with wine or with vinegar and water, laid between parchment, and thoroughly beaten. They are then dusted over with calcined selenite or gypsum, reduced to a fine powder. The vellum, which is used before the gold-beater's skin, is selected from the finest varieties, and this, too, after being well washed and dried under a press, is brushed over with pulverized gypsum.

In the great exhibition at London in 1851, machines were exhibited from the United States, and also from Paris, which were designed for gold-beating, and it was supposed they would take the place of the hand process. They have been put into operation at Hartford, in Connecticut, but after being tried, they have been laid aside for the old method.

CHAPTER IV.

LEAD.

Lead is met with in a great number of combinations, and has also been found in small quantity, at a few localities in Europe, in a native state. The common ore, from which nearly all the lead of commerce is obtained, is the sulphuret, called galena, a combination of 86.55 per cent. of lead and 13.45 of sulphur. It is a steel gray mineral of brilliant metallic lustre when freshly broken, and is often obtained in large cubical crystals: the fragments of these are all in cubical forms. The ore is also sometimes in masses of granular structure. Very frequently galena contains silver in the form of sulphuret of that metal, and gold, too, has often been detected in it. The quantity of silver is estimated by the number of ounces to the ton, and this may amount to 100 or 200, or even more; but when lead contains three ounces of silver to the ton this may be profitably separated. Ores of this character are known as argentiferous galena; if the silver is more valuable than the lead they are more properly called silver ores. In Mexico and Germany such are worked, but not in the United States. Galena is easily melted, and in contact with charcoal the sulphur is expelled and the lead obtained. The ore is found in veins in rocks of different geological formations, as in the metamorphic rocks of New England, the lower silurian rocks of Iowa, Wisconsin, and Missouri, in limestones and sandstones of later age in New York and the middle states, belonging to higher groups of the Appalachian system of rocks, and in the new red sandstone of Pennsylvania at its contact with the gneiss.

Carbonate of lead is another ore often associated with galena, though usually in small quantity. It is of light color, whitish or grayish, commonly crystallized, and in an impure form is sometimes obtained in an earthy powder. At St. Lawrence county, New York, large quantities of it have been collected for smelting, and were called lead ashes. The ore may escape notice from its unmetallic appearance, and at the Missouri mines large quantities were formerly thrown aside as worthless. It contains 77.5 per cent. of lead combined with 6 per cent. of oxygen, and this compound with 16.5 per cent. of carbonic acid. Beautiful crystals of the ore, some transparent, have been obtained at the mines on the Schuylkill, near Phœnixville, Pennsylvania; the Washington mine, Davidson county, North Carolina; and Mine La Motte, Missouri.

Another ore, the phosphate or pyromorphite, has been known only as a rare mineral until it was produced at the Phœnixville mines so abundantly as to constitute much the larger portion of the ores smelted. It is obtained in masses of small crystals of a green color, and sometimes of other shades, as yellow, orange, brown, etc., derived from the minute portions of chrome in combination. With these a variety of other compounds of lead are mixed, together with phosphate of lime and fluoride of calcium, so that the percentage of the metal is variable. The compounds of lead met with at these mines are the sulphuret, sulphate, carbonate, phosphate, arseniate, molybdate, chromate, chromo-molybdate, arsenio-phosphate, and antimonial argentiferous. Besides all these, a single vein contained native silver, native copper, and native sulphur, three compounds of zinc, four of copper, four of iron, black oxide of manganese, sulphate of barytes, and quartz.

The eastern portion of the United States is supplied with lead almost exclusively from Spain and Great Britain, but the western states are furnished with this metal from mines in Iowa, Wisconsin, and Missouri. The lead veins of the eastern and southern states are of little importance. In Maine the ores are found in Cobscook Bay, near Lubec and Eastport, in limestone rocks near dikes of trap. A mine was opened in 1832, and a drift was carried in about 155 feet at the base of a rocky cliff on the course of the vein; it was then abandoned, but operations have recently been recommenced. In New Hampshire argentiferous galena is found in numerous places, but always in too small quantity to pay the expenses of extraction. At Shelburne a large quartz vein was worked from 1846 to 1849, and three shafts were sunk, one of them 275 feet in depth. The ore was found in bunches and narrow streaks, but in small quantity. Some of it was smelted on the spot, and five tons were shipped to England, which sold for £16 per ton. The richest yielded 84 ounces of silver to the ton. Another vein of argentiferous galena has been partially explored at Eaton, and this is most likely of any to prove valuable.

Massachusetts, also, contains a number of lead veins, none of which have proved profitable, though some of them have been worked to considerable extent. The most noted are those of Southampton and Easthampton. Operations were commenced at the former place in 1765 upon a great lode of quartz containing galena, blende, copper pyrites, and sulphate of barytes. It is in a coarse granitic rock near its contact with the red sandstone of the Connecticut valley. About the year 1810 an adit level was boldly laid out to be driven in from 1,100 to 1,200 feet, to intersect the vein at 140 feet below the surface. A single miner is said to have worked at it till his death, in 1828, when it had reached the length of 900 feet. At different times this adit has been pushed on, and when last abandoned, in 1854, it was supposed to be within a few feet of the vein. The rock was so excessively hard that the cost of driving the adit was about $25 per foot. Lead veins are found in Whately, Hatfield, and other towns in Hampshire county.

In Connecticut, also, several veins have been worked to some extent. That at Middletown, referred to in the introductory remarks as one of the earliest opened mines in the United States, is the most noticeable. It is unknown when this mine was first worked. In 1852 operations were renewed upon it, and a shaft sunk 120 feet below the old workings. The vein is among strata of a silicious slate, in some places quite rich, but on the whole it has proved too poor to work. The ore contained silver to the value of from $25 to $75 to the ton of lead.

Lead mines have been opened in New York, in Dutchess, Columbia, Washington, Rensselaer, Ulster, and St. Lawrence counties. In the first four of these the ore is found in veins near the junction of the metamorphic slates and limestones. The Ancram or Livingston mine, in Columbia county, has been worked at different times at considerable expense, but with no returns. A mine in Northeast, Dutchess county, was first opened by some German miners in 1740, and ore from it was exported. The Committee of Public Safety, during the revolutionary war, sought to obtain supplies of lead from it. The lead veins of this part of New York have attracted more interest, on account of their highly argentiferous character, than the quantity of ore they promise would justify; but it seems to be almost universally the case throughout the United States that the galena yielding much silver fails in quantity. The Ulster county mines are found on the west side of the Shawangunk mountain in the strata of hard grit rock which cover its western slope. At different places along this ridge veins have been found cutting across the strata in nearly vertical lines, and have produced some lead, zinc, and copper. The Montgomery mine, near Wurtsboro, in Sullivan county, was chiefly productive in zinc. Near Ellenville, Ulster county, several veins have been followed into the mountain, and one of these, which was worked in 1853, afforded for a short time considerable quantities of rich lead and copper ores. From the former there were smelted about 459,000 pounds of lead, and the sales of the latter amounted to from 60 to 70 tons, of which 50 tons yielded 24.3 per cent. of copper. Where the vein was productive it contained the rich ores unmixed with stony gangues, and sometimes presenting a thickness of five feet of pure ore; where it became poor it closed in sometimes to a mere crack in the grit rock, and then the expense of extending the workings became very great from the extreme hardness of this rock. Open fissures were met with, one of which was more than 100 feet long and deep, and in places 12 feet or more wide. It was partially filled with tough yellow clay, through which were dispersed fragments of sandstone, magnificent bunches of quartz crystals, and lumps of lead and copper ores. The walls on the sides also presented a lining in places of the same ores. A drift was run into the base of the mountain about 200 feet, and a shaft was sunk at the foot of the slope about 100 feet. The expense of working in the hard rock proved to be too great for the amount of ore obtained, and the mine was abandoned in 1854, although its production, for the extent of ground opened, has been exceeded by but few other mines in the eastern states. The most promising veins in the state are those of St. Lawrence county in the vicinity of Rossie. They occur in gneiss rock, which they cut in nearly vertical lines. One of these was opened along the summit of Coal Hill, and was worked in 1837 and 1838 by an open cut of 440 feet in length, to the depth, in some places, of 180 feet. In 1839 the mine was abandoned, after the company had realized about $241,000 by the sale of some 1,800 tons of lead they had extracted. The galena was remarkably free from blende, and from pyritous iron and copper, which (especially the first-named) are so often associated with the ore, rendering it difficult to smelt. Calcareous spar, often finely crystallized, formed the gangue of the vein. A nearly transparent crystal, weighing 165 lbs., is preserved in the cabinet of Yale College. Other attempts have been made to work the mine; and the cause of its being allowed to lie idle appears to be the difficulty of negotiating a mining right with the proprietors.

In Pennsylvania the most productive lead mines are those of Montgomery and Chester counties, found in a small district of 5 or 6 miles in length by 2 or 3 in width, at the line of contact of the gneiss, and red shale and sandstone. About 12 parallel veins have been discovered, extending north 32° to 35° east, and dipping steeply south-east. In the gneiss they are productive in lead ores, and in the red shale in copper. The gneiss is decomposed, and the vein itself is in considerable part ochreous and earthy, owing to decomposition of pyritous ores. In this material, called by the miners gossan, silver has been discovered amounting to 10 ounces to the ton. The two principal mines of this group are the Wheatley and the Chester County. The former was opened in 1851, and up to September, 1854, had produced 1,800 tons of ore, principally phosphate, estimated to yield 60 per cent. of metal. In this vein the great number of varieties of lead and other ores enumerated above were met with. The Chester County Mining Company commenced operations in 1850, and up to November, 1851, had raised and smelted 190,400 lbs. of ore, almost exclusively phosphate, which produced about 47 per cent. of lead. The silver in this ore amounted to about 1.6 ounce in 2,000 lbs.; in the galena associated with it the silver was found in quantities varying from 11.9 to 16.2 ounces; the coarser grained galena giving the most, and the fine grained the least. In connection with the furnaces for smelting the ores, was one for separating the silver by cupellation, and a considerable amount of silver was obtained before the mining operations were abandoned, in 1854.

Lead ores are found along the Blue Ridge, in Virginia, and at one point, near the central portion of its range across the state, a mine has been worked for a number of years. They are also met with in several of the gold mines, but not in workable quantities. In south-west Virginia and east Tennessee the ores are found in the silurian limestones, and a considerable number of mines have been worked to moderate extent in both states. The most important one is the Wythe lead mine, 16 miles from Wytheville, which was worked in 1754. It is in a steep hill on the border of New River, a fall upon which, near the mine, affords power for raising the water required in dressing the ores, and also for producing the blast for the furnace. Several shafts have been sunk, one of which extending down to the adit—a depth of 225 feet—is used as a shot tower. The ores are galena, with more or less carbonates intermixed. The product for 1855 is stated to have been 500 tons of lead. The transportation of lead, in pigs, bars, and shot, from the south-west part of Virginia toward the east, by the

Virginia and Tennessee railroad, for the years named, has been as follows:—

	1856. lbs.	1857. lbs.	1858. lbs.	1859. lbs.
Pig Lead	409,649	514,878	163,405	854,695
Bar Lead	..	234,087	52,230	22,580
Shot	364,660	120,142	104,623	254,970
Total	774,309	869,057	320,258	1,132,245

In the other direction the transportation of the same articles was comparatively unimportant.

South of Virginia the only lead mine of importance is the Washington mine, Davidson county, N. C. This was opened in 1836, in the silicious and talcose slates of the gold region, and was worked for the carbonate of lead, which was found in a dull, heavy ore of earthy appearance, with which were intermixed glassy crystals of the same mineral. Some galena and phosphate of lead were also met with. After a time native silver was detected, and the lead that had been obtained was found to be rich in silver. Till 1844 the mine continued to produce ores containing much silver, and afforded the first deposits of this metal in the mint from domestic mines. The character of the ores changed, however, below the depth of 125 feet, the silver almost disappearing. The actual product of the mine is not known. That of 1844 is said to have been $24,209 in value of silver, and $7,253 of gold, obtained from 160,000 lbs. of lead—an average of 240 oz. of auriferous silver to 2,000 lbs. of metal. In 1851 the production was 56,896 lbs. of lead and 7,942.16 oz. of auriferous silver—equal to 279 oz. to the ton of metal. Zinc blende and galena became at last the prevailing ores, the silver varying from 2.5 to 195 oz. to the ton; and the workings were extended upon two parallel veins which lay near each other in the slates. In 1852 mining operations were abandoned as unprofitable, but were soon after renewed, and are still continued.

The great lead mines of the United States are the upper mines, in a district near the Mississippi, in Iowa, the south-west part of Wisconsin, and the north-west part of Illinois; and the lower mines, in Missouri. The existence of lead ores in the upper district was made known by Le Sueur, who discovered them in his voyage up the Mississippi in 1700 and 1701. They attracted no further attention, however, till a French miner, Julien Dubuque, commenced to work them in 1788; and in this employment he continued, on the spot where now stands the city in Iowa bearing his name, until his death in 1809. When the United States acquired possession of the country in 1807, the mineral lands were reserved from the sales, and leases of mining rights were authorized. These were not, however, issued until 1822, and little mining was done before 1826. From that time the production of lead rapidly increased; and the government for a time received the regular rates for the leases. But after 1834 the miners and smelters refused to pay them any longer, on account of so many sales having been made and patents granted of mineral lands in Wisconsin. In 1839 the United States government authorized a geological survey of the lead region, in order to designate precisely the mineral tracts, and this was accomplished the same year by Dr. D. D. Owen, with the aid of 139 assistants. In 1844 it was decided to abandon the leasing system, and throw all the lands into the market. The lead region, according to the report of Dr. Owen, extends over about 62 townships in Wisconsin, 10 in the north-west corner of Illinois, and 8 in Iowa—a territory altogether of about 2,880 square miles. Its western limit is about 12 miles from the Mississippi river; to the north it extends nearly to Wisconsin river; south to Apple river, in Illinois; and east to the east branch of the Pekatonica. From east to west it is 87 miles across, and from north to south 54 miles. Much of the region is a rolling prairie, with a few isolated hills, called mounds, scattered upon its surface, the highest of them rising scarcely more than 200 feet above the general level. The prevailing limestone formations give fertility to the soil, and the country is well watered by numerous small streams, which flow in valleys excavated from 100 to 150 feet below the higher levels. The limestone, of gray and yellowish gray colors, lies in nearly horizontal strata, and the portion which contains the lead veins hardly exceeds 50 feet in thickness. Beneath it is a sandstone of the age of the Potsdam sandstone, and above it are strata of limestone recognized as belonging to the Trenton limestone, so that it proves to be a formation interposed between these, quite western in character, as it is not met with east of Wisconsin. The veins occupy straight vertical fissures, and several near together sometimes extend nearly a mile in an east and west direction. They never reach downward into the sandstone, but are lost in the lower strata of the limestone, and where the upper strata of the formation appear, these cover over the veins, and are consequently known as the cap-rock. In the fissures or crevices the galena is found, sometimes in loose sheets and lumps embedded in clay and earthy oxide of iron, and sometimes attached to one or both walls. It is rarely so much as a foot thick. No other ores are found with it, except some zinc blende and calamine, and occasionally pyritous iron and copper. The lead contains but a trace of silver. The fissures, as they are followed beneath the surface, sometimes expand in width till they form what is called an "opening;" and the hollow space may go on enlarging till it becomes a cave of several hundred feet in length and 30 or 40 in width. Their dimensions are, however, usually within 40 or 50 feet in length, 4 to 8 in width, and as many in height. The walls of the openings often afford a thick incrustation of galena, besides more or less loose mineral in the clay, among the fragments of rock, with all of which the caves are partially filled. Flat sheets of ore often extend from the vertical fissures between the horizontal limestone strata; these are more apt to contain blende, and pyrites, and calcareous spar than the ore of the vertical crevices. Besides these modes of occurrence, galena is found in loose lumps in the clayey loam of the prairies. This is called float mineral, and is regarded as an evidence of productive fissures in the vicinity.

The galena occurs under a variety of singular forms in the crevices. It lines curious cavities which extend up in the cap-rock, terminating above in a point, and which are known as chimneys. Upon the roofs of the openings it is found in large bunches of cubical crystals, and the same are obtained lying in the clays of the same openings. A flat sheet of the ore was worked in Iowa that was more than 20 feet across and from 2 to 3 feet thick, each side of which turned down in a vertical sheet, gradually diminishing in thickness. It yielded 1,200,000 lbs. of rich galena, and more still remained behind in sight. The crevices near Dubuque are the most regular and productive of any in the district. One called the Langworthy, on a length of about three-fourths of a mile, has produced 10,000,000 lbs. of ore. On the main fissure there were usually three ranges of crevices one above another, widening out to 15 or 20 feet.

The smelters of this region form a distinct class from the miners, of whom the former buy the ores as these are raised, and convert them into metal in the little smelting establishments scattered through the country. The lead has been principally sent down the Mississippi river to Saint Louis and New Orleans; but a portion has always been consumed in the country, and some has been wagoned across to Milwaukee before the construction of railroads, which since 1853 have afforded increased facilities for distributing in different directions the product of the mines. The only records of the amount of lead obtained are those of the shipments down the river. The following table presents the number of pigs shipped from the earlier workings to 1857; the figures for 1841 to 1850, inclusive, being furnished to Dr. Owen's Report of 1852 by Mr. James Carter, of Galena. The pigs weigh about 70 lbs. each.

SHIPMENTS OF LEAD FROM THE UPPER MISSISSIPPI.

Years.	Pigs.	Years.	Pigs.
1821 to 1823	4,790	1842	447,859
1824	2,503	1843	561,321
1825	9,490	1844	624,601
1826	13,700	1845	778,460
1827	74,130	1846	730,714
1828	158,655	1847	771,679
1829	190,620	1848	680,245
1830	119,060	1849	628,934
1831	91,170	1850	569,521
1832	61,164	1851	474,115
1833	113,440	1852	408,628
1834	113,648	1853	425,814
1835	158,330	1854	423,617
1836	191,750	1855	430,365
1837	219,360	1856	435,654
1838	200,465	1857	485,475
1839	357,785	1858	
1840	317,845	1859	
1841	452,814		

The lead region of Missouri was first brought into public notice by the explorations of the French adventurer, Renault, who was sent out from Paris in 1720, with a party of miners, to search for precious metals in the territory of Louisiana, under a patent granted by the French government to the famous company of John Law. Their investigations were carried on in the region lying near the Mississippi and south of the Missouri river; and here, though they failed to find the precious metals they were in search of, they discovered and opened many mines of lead ore. A large mining tract in the northern part of Madison county is still called by the name of their mineralogist, La Motte. Their operations, however, were altogether superficial, and the lead they obtained was wholly by the rude and wasteful process of smelting the ores upon open log-heaps—a practice which even of late years is followed to some extent. Up to Renault's return to France, in 1742, little progress had been made in the development of this mining district. The next step was made by one Moses Austin, of Virginia, who obtained from the Spanish government a grant of land near Potosi, and commenced in 1798 regular mining operations by sinking a shaft. He also started a reverberatory furnace and built a shot tower. Schoolcraft states in his "View of the Lead Mines of Missouri," that there were in 1819 forty-five mines in operation, giving employment to 1,100 persons. Mine á Burton and the Potosi diggings had produced from 1798 to 1816 an annual average amount exceeding 500,000 pounds; and in 1811 the production of Mine Shibboleth was 3,125,000 pounds of lead from 5,000,000 pounds of ore. At a later period, from 1834 to 1837, the several mines of the La Motte tract produced, it is estimated, 1,035,820 pounds of lead per annum. From 1840 to 1854 the total yield of all the mines is stated by Dr. Litton in the state geological report to amount to over 3,833,121 pounds annually. At the close of this period it had, however, greatly fallen off, there being at that time scarcely 200 persons engaged in mining, besides those employed at the three mines known as Perry's, Vallé's, and Skewers'. The principal mines have been in Washington, St. Francis, and other neighboring counties. The ores are found in strata of magnesian limestone of an older date than the galena limestone of Wisconsin, and supposed to lie, with the sandstones with which they alternate, on the same geological horizon as the calciferous sand rock, which is found in the eastern states overlying the Potsdam sandstone. Some of the mines are at the contact of the horizontal limestone with granite rocks, but the ores in this position are only in superficial deposits or in layers included in the limestone. In their general features the veins do not differ greatly from those of the northern mines. Some of them, however, contain a larger proportion of other ores besides galena, as well as a greater variety of them. Carbonate of lead, called by the Miners dry bone and white mineral, is more abundant, and also blende, called by them black jack, and the silicate of zinc. Iron and copper pyrites are often seen, and at Mine la Motte are found the black oxides of cobalt and manganese associated with the carbonates of lead and copper. Nearly all the mining operations have been mere superficial excavations in the clay, which were soon exhausted of the loose ore and abandoned. But to this there are some remarkable exceptions of deeper and more permanent mines than are known in the northern lead regions. Such are Vallé's and Perry's mines, both situated on the same group of veins, which form a network of fissures and openings running in every direction and spreading over an area of about 1,500 feet in length by 500 in breadth, the extension of which is from north-west to south-east. These mines have been steadily worked since 1824, and 22 shafts have been sunk upon the fissures, six of which are over 110 feet deep, one is 170 feet deep, and only two are less than 50 feet. For the first 10 to 30 feet they pass through gravel and clay, below this through a silicious magnesian limestone of light color, and then enter a very close-grained variety of the same, called by the miners the cast steel rock. A succession of openings are encountered, which are distributed with considerable regularity upon three different levels. Those of the middle series have been the most productive. Sometimes chimneys connect them with the caves of the tier above or below. The portion of these mines on the Vallé tract produced, according to the state report, from 1824 to 1834 about 10,000,000 pounds of lead, and in the succeeding 20 years about as much more; and Perry's mine from 1839 to 1854 has produced about 18,000,000 pounds.

No accurate estimates have been preserved of the total production of the Missouri mines. This has always fallen far short of the yield of the northern mines. From 1832 to 1843 it is reported as running from 2,500 to 3,700 tons per annum, while that of the northern mines in the same time was from 5,500 to 14,000 tons, and in 1845 it even exceeded 24,000 tons. In 1852 Mr. J. D. Whitney estimated that the production in Missouri had fallen to 1,500 tons, or less; and from that period it has probably not advanced. As this decrease in the supply has been going on while the price of lead has risen to nearly three times what it was in 1842, the cause is probably owing to the mines themselves being in great part exhausted. The only sufficient sources known from which the increasing supplies required from year to year can be furnished, are the mines of Great Britain and Spain, though should the argentiferous lead mines of Mexico ever be worked for the lead as well as the silver they contain, they might furnish large quantities of the former metal. As the production of the United States has fallen off, that of Great Britain has increased from 64,000 tons in 1850 to 73,129 tons in 1856, and 96,266 tons in 1857, thus considerably exceeding one-half of the whole production of the globe in this metal, which in 1854 was rated at about 133,000 tons. At that time the production of Spain was rated at 30,000 tons, and of the United States at 15,000 tons. The following table, from *Hunt's Merchants' Magazine*, of July, 1859, presents several features of interest in the history of this business. The amount of domestic lead received at St. Louis and New Orleans is not, however, a true index of the production of the American mines, and the falling off of the figures in the second column for several years past, is properly accounted for to some extent by the new outlets opened from the northern mines eastward, and also by the largely increased consumption of the metal in the western states.

Years.	Pig lead from American mines received at St. Louis and New Orleans. lbs.	Pig, bar, and sheet lead imported. lbs.	Invoice value of yearly importations.	Average rate of duty per 100 lbs.	White and red lead imported lbs.	Invoice value of yearly importations.
1832......	8,540,000	5,333,588	$124,311	$3.00	557,781	$30,791
1833......	12,600,000	2,282,068	60,660	3.00	625,069	36,049
1834......	14,140,000	4,997,293	168,811	2.77	1,024,663	57,572
1835......	16,000,000	1,006,472	35,663	2.77	832,215	50,225
1836......	18,000,000	919,087	35,283	2.55	908,105	62,237
1837......	20,000,000	335,772	13,871	2.57	599,980	47,316
1838......	20,860,000	165,844	6,573	2.34	522,681	38,683
1839......	24.000,000	528,922	18,631	2.31	720,408	50,905
1840......	27,000,000	519,343	18,111	2.08	643,418	41,043
1841......	30,000,000	62,246	2,605	2.07	532,122	31,617
1842......	33,110,000	4,689	155	3.00	479,738	28,747
1843......	39,970,000	290	3	3.00	93,166	5,600
1844......	44,730,000	..	..	3.00	..	..
1845......	51,240,000	19,609	458	3.00	231,171	14,744
1846......	54,950,000	214	6	3.00	215,434	15,685
1847......	46,130,000	224,905	6,288	0.56	298,387	15,228
1848......	42,420,000	2,684,700	85,387	0.64	318,781	19,703
1849......	35,560,000	..	..	..	..	..
1850......	40,313,910	36,997,751	1,182,597	0.64	853,463	43,756
1851......	34,934,480	43,470,210	1,517,603	0.70	1,105,852	52,631
1852......	28,593,180	37,544,588	1,283,331	0.70	842,521	43,365
1853......	31,497,950	43,174,447	1,618,058	0.70	1,224,068	69,058
1854......	21,472,990	47,714,140	2,095,039	0.90	1,865,893	102,812
1855......	21,441,140	56,745,247	2,556,523	0.90	2,319,099	134,855
1856......	15,347,880	55,294,256	2,528,014	0.91	3,548,409	174,125
1857......	14,028,140	47,947.698	2,305,768	0.72	1,793,377	113,075
1858......	21,210,420	41,230,019	1,972,243	0.72	1,785,851	109,426

For the year ending June 30, 1859, the imports of lead are given at 64,000,000 pounds, worth nearly $2,700,000. Of this about $57,000 worth were re-exported to foreign countries, besides American lead to the value of $30,000, and a small amount of manufactured lead.

Lead Smelting. The lead mines of the United States being scattered over wide territories, and their products being nowhere brought together in large quantities, the process of reducing the ores has been conducted in small establishments and by the most simple methods. The earlier operations were limited to smelting the ores in log furnaces. Upon a layer of logs placed in an inclosure of logs or stones piled up, split wood was set on end and covered with the ore, and over this small wood again. The pile was fired through an opening in front. The combustion of the small wood removed from the ore a portion of the sulphur, and the reduction was completed by the greater heat arising from the burning of the logs. The lead run down to the bottom and out in front into a basin, whence it was ladled into the moulds. The loss of metal was of course very large; but a portion was recovered by treating the residue in what was called an ash furnace. The process is still resorted to in places where no furnaces are within reach. But wherever mines are opened that promise sufficient supplies of ore, furnaces are soon constructed in their vicinity. Those in use are of two sorts: the Scotch hearth and the reverberatory. Besides these, another small furnace is often built for melting over the slags. This is little else than a crucible built in brick-work, and arranged for the blast to enter by an aperture in the back, and for the metal to flow out by another opening in front.

The Scotch hearth is a small blast furnace, but resembles the open forge or bloomary fire for iron ores. It has long been in use in Europe, and is the most common furnace at our own mines. In this country it has been greatly improved by the introduction of hot blast; and in its most perfect form is represented in the accompanying figures; figure *a* being a vertical section from front to back, and figure *b* a horizontal section.

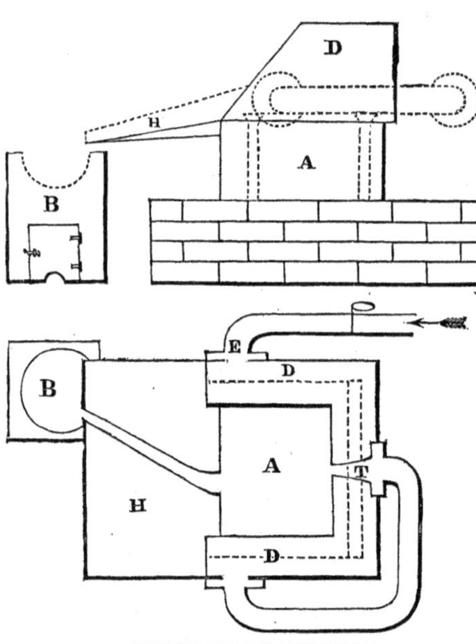

SCOTCH HEARTH FURNACE.

A is the reservoir of lead of the furnace, consisting of a box, open at top, about two feet square and one foot deep, formed of cast iron 2 inches thick. From its upper front edge a sloping hearth, H, is fixed so as to receive the melted lead that overflows, and conduct it by the groove into the basin, B. In this it is kept in a melted state by a little fire beneath, and, as convenient, the lead is ladled out and poured into moulds. D is a hollow shell of cast iron $\frac{3}{4}$ of an inch thick, its inner and outer sides inclosing a space of 4 inches width. Into this space the blast is introduced at E, and becoming heated, passes out at F, and thence through the curved pipe into a tuyere, T, cast in the air-chest 2 inches above the level of the lead reservoir. Before commencing operations this reservoir is to be filled with lead, and is thus kept so long as the furnace is in use; the process being conducted upon the surface of the melted metal. The furnace may be kept in continual operation by adding new charges of galena every ten or fifteen minutes, and working them down after they have become roasted at the surface. The fuel employed is dry pine wood split into small pieces, and billets of these are thrown in against the tuyere just before each new charge of ore, that already in the furnace being raked forward upon the hearth to make room for the fuel, and the blast being temporarily turned off. The old charge is then thrown, together with fresh ore, upon the wood, and the blast is let on, when the heat and flame immediately spread through the materials. The sulphur in the ore serves itself as fuel, accelerating the process by its combustion, and in a few minutes the whole charge is stirred up, spread out on the hearth, and the hard, unreduced fragments are broken in pieces by blows of the shovel. Slaked lime is sometimes added in small quantity when the partially reduced ore becomes too soft and pasty by excess of heat. Its effect is to lessen this tendency rather by mechanical than chemical action. If any flux is used, it is fluor spar, blacksmith's cinders, or bits of iron. The latter hasten the reduction by the affinity of the iron for the sulphur of the ore. The cast iron of the air-chest is protected from the action of the sulphur by the cooling influence of the air blown in; and this is also advantageous by its keeping the furnace from becoming so hot, that the galena would melt before losing its sulphur, and thus form combinations of exceedingly difficult reduction. A fan, run by steam or water power, is commonly employed for raising the blast; but as this gives little pressure, it is replaced to great advantage by blowing cylinders, with an air-receiver for giving regularity to the current of air. With such an apparatus, the smelter can apply the blast with great advantage at times to help loosen up the charge and throw the flame through every part of it. The ores are prepared for smelting by separating from them all the stony and clayey particles, and as much as possible of the blende and other impurities that may accompany them. This may require a succession of mechanical processes, in which the ores are crushed to fine fragments and dressed by jigging and screening under water. Not only is the labor and cost of smelting reduced by the purity of the ore, and especially its freedom from blende and pyrites, but the quality also of the metal is thereby improved. Lead that contains iron is not adapted for the manufacture of white-lead. The American metal being generally free from this brings a higher price than Spanish or English lead. With pure ore a cord of wood may be made to produce four tons of lead; and each furnace 7,500 lbs. every 24 hours; a smelter and his assistant managing the operation for 12 hours. At Rossie large quantities of lead have thus been smelted at a daily cost for labor of $5, and for fuel of $1.50, making $1.75 per ton. In Wisconsin, before the use of the hot blast, each furnace-shift was continued from 8 to 10 hours, until 30 pigs of lead were produced of 2,100 lbs. weight, at an expense of about $4 for labor, and $1.50 for fuel.

The other form of furnace—the reverberatory—resembles others of this class employed in smelting copper ores. The sole, or hearth, upon which the ores are spread, is about 8 feet in length by 6 in breadth, and is made to incline rapidly toward an aperture on one side, or at the end under the chimney, and out of which the lead is allowed at the end of each smelting to flow into a receiver outside. The charge is supplied either through a hopper in the arched roof, or through the holes in the sides, which also serve for admitting the pokers used by the workmen to stir up the charge. Unless the galena has been previously calcined or roasted—a process necessary for poor ores only—this is the first thing to be attended to in all the smelting operations. In the large charge of 30 cwt. of ore this usually takes the first two hours of the process, and is effected in great part by the heat remaining in the furnace from the preceding operation, the doors at the sides being kept open at the same time to allow free access of air. The oxidation of the sulphur is expedited by almost constant stirring of the charge, which brings fresh portions to the surface, causing an evolution of white fumes. As these begin to diminish, the fire is started on the grate, and the heat is raised till the charge softens and the pieces of ore adhere to the rake. The doors are then closed, and the fire is urged for a quarter of an hour, when the smelter opens the door to see if the metal separates and flows down the inclined hearth. If the separation does not go on well, it is hastened by opening one of the doors, partially cooling the furnace, and stirring the charge. The fire is then again urged. If the slags which form seem to require it, he treats them with a few shovelfuls of lime and fine coal; and when, after having flowed down into the lower portion of the hearth, they are brought into a doughy consistency, the smelter pushes the slag to the opposite upper edge of the hearth, from which it is taken out through a door on that side by his assistant, while he lets off the lead into the receiver.

The separation by this method is not so perfect as by the Scotch hearth, and the expense of fuel is greater; but the reverberatory is worked without the necessity of steam or water power, which is required to raise the blast for the other process. The slags of the reverberatory contain so much lead that they are always remelted in the slag furnace. Those of the Scotch hearth, when pure ores are employed, are sufficiently clear of metal without further reduction. In Europe other sorts of furnaces are in use, which are adapted particularly for ores of poorer quality than are ever smelted in the United States.

In the Hartz mountains, at Clausthal, argentiferous silver ores containing much silica are worked in close cupola furnaces, into which only enough air is admitted to consume the fuel. The object is not to roast out the sulphur, but to cause this to combine with the granulated cast iron or with the quick-lime, either of which is mixed with the ores to flux them and form a fusible compound with the sulphur, through which the metallic lead can easily find its way to the bottom. The production of a silicate of lead is thus avoided, which is a difficult compound to reduce, and is always formed when much silica is present. This process will probably be applied to some of the silicious ores of the United States, and may be particularly suited to the Washoe ores of California.

By all the methods of reducing lead a great loss is incurred by the volatilization of a portion of the lead in white fumes, called lead ashes. These are carried up through the chimney of the furnace and fall upon the ground in the neighborhood, poisoning the vegetation and the water by the carbonate of lead, which results from the fumes. Trees even are killed, and the dogs die off, and also the cattle. In Scotland the lead has been detected in chemical examinations of the bodies of animals thus killed, and it was particularly noticeable in the spleen. For the injury thus occasioned at the furnaces of the United States no remedy has been applied, but at many of the great establishments in Europe, where the loss of lead and the damage to the neighborhood is much more serious, attempts have been made to arrest the fumes, by causing them to pass through long flues in the chimney stacks, in which the particles on cooling would settle down; and their cooling has been hastened by showers of water falling among the vapors. Flues have been extended great distances beyond the works, and have been found much more efficient than any form of condensation by sudden cooling. Some of the works constructed for this purpose are very remarkable for their great extent and the saving they have effected, and similar ones may perhaps be found well worthy of construction at some of the smelting establishments in the United States. At the works of Mr. Beaumont, in Northumberland, England, horizontal or slightly inclined galleries have been completed in stonework, 8 feet high and 6 feet wide, for an extent of 8,789 yards (nearly five miles). This is from one mill alone. The same proprietor has connected with other mills in the same district and in Durham four miles of galleries for the same purpose. The writer who gives the account of these in the recent edition of Ure's Dictionary, by Robert Hunt, remarks: "The value of the lead thus saved from being totally dissipated and dispersed, and obtained from what in common parlance might be called chimney sweepings, considerably exceeds £10,000 sterling annually, and forms a striking illustration of the importance of economizing our waste products." Not only is lead lost in the fumes, but in the working of argentiferous lead ores, a portion of the silver too is carried off and deposited with them. The fumes collected at the works of the Duke of Buccleuch yield one-third their weight of lead, and five ounces of silver to the ton. The loss of silver is of little importance in this country, where this metal is not obtained at the present time, unless it be at the Washington mine, in North Carolina, and at the Washoe mines, in California; and consequently methods of separating it from the lead possess little more than scientific interest. In the smelting of argentiferous lead ores, the silver goes with the lead, being completely dissolved and diffused throughout its substance. The usual way of separating it is founded on the principle of the lead being a metal easily oxidized and converted into the substance called litharge, in which condition it lets go the silver, which has no affinity either for the new compound of oxygen and lead, or for the oxygen alone. The change is effected by melting the lead in the shallow basins called cupels, formed of a porous earthy material, as the pulverized ashes of burned bones, kneaded with water, and mixed in a framework of iron. When dried, these are set in a reverberatory furnace, and the pigs of lead are melted upon their surface. After being thoroughly heated, a current of air is made to draw through an opening in the side of the furnace directly upon the face of the melted metal. This oxidizes the lead, and the yellow litharge with more or less red oxide, called minium, collects in a thin film upon its surface, and floats off to the edge, sinking into and incrusting the cupel and falling over its side into a receptacle placed to receive it. This process goes on, the lead gradually disappearing as the oxygen combines with it, till with the removal of the last films of oxide the melted silver suddenly presents its brilliant, perfectly unsullied face. The oxide of lead may be collected and sold for the purposes of litharge, as for a pigment, for use in the manufacture of glass, etc.; or it may be mixed with fine coal and converted back into lead, the carbon of the coal effecting this change by the greater affinity it has at a high heat for the oxygen, than the lead has to retain it. By this process, known as cupellation, lead is hardly worth treating for silver, unless it contain about 10 ounces to the ton of the precious metal; and it was therefore an important object to devise a method of saving with economy the silver lost in the large quantities of the poorer argentiferous leads. Such a method was accidentally discovered in 1829 by Mr. Pattinson, of Newcastle, and is now extensively in use in Europe for the poorer silver-leads, cupellation being preferred for the richer. He observed that when the lead containing silver forms crystals, as it is stirred while in a melted state, the crystals contain little or none of the silver, and may be removed, thus concentrating the silver in the portions left behind. This crystallizing process is applied in the large way as follows: Cast iron pots are set in brickwork side by side, capable of holding each one 4 or 5 tons of lead. The middle one is first charged, and when the lead is melted and stirred, the fire is removed under the next pot to the right; and into this crystals of lead as they form are ladled by means of a sort of cullender, which lets the fluid lead fall back. This instrument is kept hotter than the lead by frequently dipping it in a pot of lead over a separate fire. When four-fifths of the lead have been transferred to the pot to the right, the remainder, which contains all the silver, is removed to the next pot to the left, and the middle pot is then charged with fresh lead, which is treated in the same manner. The process is repeated with each pot, as it becomes full, four-fifths of its contents going to the next pot to the right, and one-fifth to the next to the left, and thus the lead is finally discharged into moulds at one end, and the argentiferous alloy, concentrated to the richness of 300 ounces of silver to the ton, is run into bars about 2 inches square. From these the silver is obtained by cupellation. At one establishment in England, that of Messrs. Walker, Parker & Co., the weekly product of silver is from 8,000 to 10,000 ounces. Whenever the lead mines of the eastern states are made to yield regular returns of lead, the separation of its silver is likely to be carried on in independent establishments, supplied like the copper-smelting works with material from various sources. Works having these objects in view were established in the fall of 1860, at Brooklyn, New York, by Messrs. Bloodgood & Ambler, and will commence operations with the smelting of the Washoe silver-lead ores from California, of which over sixty tons have been delivered at the works for reduction. Their successful treatment will no doubt be followed by the shipment of other ores of the different metals from various sources; and it is to be hoped that it will hereafter be found more advantageous to send ores to New York to be reduced, than to the smelting establishments on the other side of the Atlantic.

Useful Applications of Lead.—A considerable part of the lead product of the world is converted into the carbonate, known as white lead, and used as a paint. The principal articles of metallic lead are sheet lead, lead pipe, and shot. Sheet lead is manufactured in two ways. The melted lead is upset from a trough suspended over a perfectly level table, covered with fine sand, and furnished with a raised margin; and when the metal has spread over this, a couple of workmen, one on each side, carry along a bar supported upon the margin, pushing forward the excess of lead above that necessary for the required thickness, till it falls over the end of the table. By the other method, called milling, the lead is cast in a plate, 6 or 7 feet square, and 6 inches thick, and this being taken up by a crane, is placed upon a line of wooden rollers, which form a flooring for the length it may be of 70 or 80 feet and a width of 8 feet. Across the middle of this line are set the two heavy iron rolls by which the lead plate is compressed, as it is passed between them. The top of the lower roll is on a level with the top of the wooden rollers, and the upper roll is so arranged that it can be set nearer to or further from the lower one, as the thickness of the plate requires.

Lead pipe was formerly made by turning up sheet lead and soldering the edges; and is still prepared in this way for the large sizes, as those over six inches diameter. After this a method was contrived of casting the lead in a hollow cylindrical plug, its inner diameter of the bore required, and then drawing this down through slightly conical dies of decreasing diameter, a mandril or steel rod being inserted to retain the uniform diameter of the bore. Pipes made in this way were limited to 15 to 18 feet in length, and the metal was full of flaws. Many attempts have been made to cast long lengths of lead pipe, all of which have proved unsuccessful. In 1820 Thomas Burr, of England, first applied the hydraulic press to forcing lead, when beginning to solidify in cooling, through an annular space between a hollow ring and a solid core secured in its centre. He thus produced pipes of considerable length. The method of forcing the liquid metal through dies to form pipes was, however, first patented in 1797 by Bramah, who used a pump for this purpose. The process was introduced into this country in 1840–41 by Messrs. Tatham & Brothers, now of New York, who invented and patented an important improvement in the method of securing the die and core. In this operation the melted lead is made to flow from the furnace into a cylindrical cavity in a block of cast iron, which may be of 1800 lbs. weight, and from this, when cooled to the proper temperature, it is forced out through the die by a closely-fitting piston. By one process the piston, starting from the bottom of the cylindrical cavity, moves upward, carrying with it the slender core or rod which determines the diameter of the bore of the pipe, and pushes the melted lead before it through the die fixed in the top of the cast iron block. The pipe as it is formed passes out from the top of the machine, and is coiled around a receiving drum. By the machine contrived by Mr. Cornell of New York, the great iron block containing the lead rises by the pressure of the hydraulic machine, and the piston which is fixed above it enters the cavity. The piston in this case is hollow and the die is set in its lower end. The core is secured in the bottom of the block, and is carried upward as this rises. The pressure applied in this operation amounts to 200 to 300 tons. Dies are used of a great variety of sizes, according to the kind of pipe required. Lead wire is made in this way with a die of very small size without a core. It is used for securing vines and attaching tags to fruit trees and shrubs. The principal works in the United States engaged in the manufacture of sheet lead and lead pipe are in New York, Boston, Philadelphia, Chicago, Cincinnati, and Saint Louis.

Lead pipe is in general use as the most convenient conduit for water for domestic purposes. It is readily bent to any angle, and is made to adapt itself to any position. When water freezes within and bursts it, the damage is easily repaired; joints are also made with little trouble. The lead is not liable to become rusty like iron, and is cheaper than tin or copper. These qualities give to it a preference over other kinds of pipe, notwithstanding the very serious objection that the lead is often acted upon by the water, and produces poisonous salts of a very dangerous character. Some waters more than others have a tendency to promote the oxidation of the lead. This is particularly likely to occur with nearly all waters in pipes which are alternately exposed to the action of air and water, as when the water being drawn out, the air enters and takes its place. The oxide of lead is converted by carbonic acid gas, which is present in almost all water, into a carbonate of lead which is soluble to some extent in an excess of the gas, and is carried along, bearing no indication of its presence, while the lead pipe continues to be corroded until it may be in places eaten nearly through. The water used for drinking and for culinary purposes is thus continually introducing an insidious poison into the system, the effect of which is at last experienced in the disease known as the painters' colic, often followed by paralysis. As this occurs without a suspicion being awakened of the real source of the disease, and is produced by quantities so small as from $\frac{1}{10}$ to $\frac{1}{20}$ of a grain in the gallon, the use of lead pipe is properly regarded by scientific men as always unsafe; and some substitute for this metal in pipes and in sheets used for lining water cisterns, is highly desirable. It has been proposed to coat the pipe with some insoluble lining; but such an application necessarily increases its cost, it may perhaps be removed by hot water flowing through the pipe, and the purchaser may have no confidence in the coating being faithfully applied, or as certain to be efficient during long-continued use. Block tin is perfectly safe, but it is expensive, and is moreover likely to be alloyed with the cheaper metal lead, which in this condition is thought to be equally dangerous as when used alone. As no popular substitute for lead is provided, it is a reasonable precaution for those employing it to be always watchful and on their guard against its evil effects—using as little of it as necessary, causing the water to be occasionally tested, and, whenever opportunity offers, cutting open and examining pieces of the pipe to see whether its internal surface is corroded, and every morning before using the water that has stood in the pipes, to cause this to flow away together with enough more to thoroughly wash out the pipes and remove any salts of lead that may have formed in them during the night.

Large quantities of lead are consumed in the United States in the manufacture of shot and bullets; and one ingenious method of producing shot is an American invention.

The quality of the lead employed for this purpose is of little importance. The harder and inferior sorts, which would not answer for the white lead manufacture, are economically diverted to this object. If too brittle, from the iron and antimony combined with the lead, the metal is made to assume the right quality by mixing with it a small proportion of arsenic, which, for most kinds of lead, may amount to one per cent. To introduce this into the lead a large pot of the metal is melted, and powdered charcoal or ashes is laid around its edge. The arsenical compound, either of white arsenic or of orpiment (the sulphuret of arsenic), is then stirred into the centre of the mass, and a cover is tightly luted over the pot. In the course of a few hours, the mixture being kept hot, the combination of the lead with the arsenic is completed, and a portion of litharge floats upon the surface. This is formed from the oxygen of the white arsenic uniting with some of the lead, and it retains a portion of the arsenic. The alloy is now tried by letting a small quantity of it fall from a moderate height through a strainer into water. From the appearance of the globules the quality of the mixture is judged of. If they are lens-shaped, too much arsenic has been used; but if they are flattened on the side, or hollowed in the middle, or drag with a tail behind them, the proportion of arsenic is too small. When a proper mixture is obtained it is run into bars, and these are taken to the top of a tower, from 100 to 200 feet high, where the lead is melted and poured through cullenders, which are kept hot by being placed in a sort of chafing-dish containing burning charcoal. The lead is thus divided into drops that fall to the bottom, and are received in a vessel of water. Each cullender has holes all of the same size, which is considerably less than that of the shot produced by them. This is owing to the drop of melted lead first assuming an elongated form, which is concentrated into the globular by the air impinging equally upon all sides in the course of its descent. When it reaches the water, it is important that it should have cooled throughout, so that no solid crust be suddenly formed over a fluid interior; and hence, for large shot it is evident the height of the fall must be greater than is required for small shot. The temperature of the lead also, when it is dropped, must vary according to the size of the shot; for the largest size being so low that a straw is hardly browned when thrust into it. A portion of the lead becomes oxidized and is caught in the cullender, the bottom of which it coats, and serves a useful purpose by checking the too rapid flow of the melted lead through the holes. The holes vary in size, from $\frac{1}{50}$ of an inch for shot larger than No. 1, to $\frac{1}{360}$ of an inch for No. 9. The shot being taken out of the water and dried upon the surface of a long steam chest, are transferred to an iron cask suspended upon an axis passing through its ends, and a little plumbago being introduced with them, the cask is made to revolve until the shot are thoroughly cleaned and polished. The next operation is to separate the imperfect ones from the good. This is done by rolling them all together down a succession of inclined platforms, separated by a narrow space between each. The good shot clear these spaces and are caught below, while the bad ones fall through upon the floor. The good are then introduced into the sifters for assorting them according to their sizes. Several sieves are arranged like drawers in a case; the coarsest above, and finer ones succeeding below. The upper tier of sieves being charged, the case is set rocking, and the shot are soon assorted, and are then ready for packing in bags. Bullets and buck-shot are moulded by hand from a large pot of the metal into moulds with many receptacles.

The American process of shot-making was invented in 1848 by David Smith, of the firm of T. O. Leroy & Co., of New York, by whom it is exclusively used. Its object is to dispense with the use of the costly high towers, by substituting for them a lower fall against an ascending current of air. This current is produced by a fan-blower operating at the base of an upright hollow shaft into which the shot are dropped from a moderate height. The power required to run the fan is not much more than that ordinarily expended in raising the lead to the top of the high towers; and it is found that the lead, in consequence of its being more rapidly and equally cooled in the short descent against the current of air, may be used at a higher temperature than is practicable with that dropped from high towers; and thus it may not only be poured more rapidly, but it has not the tendency to burst in falling and form imperfect shot, as is the case with that dropped from high towers, to guard against which the lead is kept at a low temperature.

There are in New York city, besides this operation, which is carried on by Messrs. Leroy, in Water street, three shot towers, and a fourth is nearly completed on Staten Island. The ordinary capacity of these is from 3000 to 4000 tons of shot per annum. The annual shot production of St. Louis is about the same as that of New York, though there is now only one shot tower in use. There were formerly seven more on the river bluffs below the city, but these have hardly been used since 1847. In Baltimore is a tower the height of which, including ten feet constructed below the surface of the ground, is 256 feet, which exceeds by one foot the height of the famous tower in Vienna, described by Dr. Ure as the highest structure of the kind in the world, being 249 feet above the surface of the ground. Its production is stated to be about 400 tons per annum. In Philadelphia there is one tower which makes about 300 tons annually; in Wythe county, Virginia, is one formed in one of the shafts of the mine, making about 200 tons; and on the Wisconsin river, at Helena, is a small tower probably making about as much more. The actual production of the country in shot and bullets is supposed to be about 7000 tons, and to have made but little advance for many years past.

White Lead.—Before the introduction of the oxide of zinc as a paint, one of the most important uses of lead was its conversion into the carbonate or white lead. The manufacture was originally carried on almost exclusively in Holland; and it was not until near the close of the last century that it was introduced into England. In the United States it was unknown until after the late war, and being first undertaken in Philadelphia, it was afterward extended to New York and Brooklyn, and in the latter city has prospered more than in any other part of the country. Various attempts have been made to introduce new methods of manufacture, but the old Dutch process has continued in general use; the modifications of it which have raised the manufacture in this country to a higher state of perfection than in any other part of the world being merely improvements in the details, by which ingenious machinery has been made to diminish the labor expended in the process.

White lead is a combination of oxide of lead with carbonic acid, and is obtained in the form of a soft, very white, and heavy powder. It mixes readily with oil, giving to it a drying property, spreads well under the brush, and perfectly covers the surfaces to which it is applied. It is not only employed alone as the best sort of white paint, but is the general material or body of a great number of paints, the colors of which are produced by mixing suitable coloring matters with the white lead. Besides its use as a paint it is also in demand to a considerable extent as an ingredient in the so-called vulcanized india-rubber. To prepare it, the purest pig lead, such as the refined foreign lead and the metal from the upper mines of the Mississippi, is almost exclusively used. This was by the old methods made in thin sheets, and these into small rolls, to be subjected to the chemical treatment. But according to the American method devised by Mr. Augustus Graham of Brooklyn, and now generally adopted, the lead is cast into circular gratings or "buckles," which closely resemble in form the large old-fashioned shoe-buckles, from which they receive their name. They are six or eight inches in diameter, and the lead hardly exceeds one sixth of an inch in thickness. Ingenious methods of casting them are in use in the American factories, by which the lead is run upon moulds directly from the furnace, and the buckles are separated from each other and delivered without handling into the vessels for receiving them. They are then packed in earthen pots shaped like flower-pots, each of which is provided with a ledge or three projecting points in the inside, intended to keep the pieces above the bottom, in which is placed some strong vinegar or acetic acid. It is recommended that on one side the pot should be partially open above the ledge, and if made full all round, it is well to knock out a piece in order to admit a freer circulation of vapors through the lead. In large establishments an immense supply of these pots is kept on hand, the number at one of the Brooklyn works being reckoned at not less than 150,000. They continue constantly in use till accidentally broken below the ledge. Being packed with the buckles and the acid, they are set close together in rows upon a bed of spent tan, a foot to two feet thick, and thin sheets of lead are laid among and over the pots in several thicknesses, but always so as to leave open spaces among them. An area is thus covered, it may be twenty feet square or of less dimensions, and is enclosed by board partitions, which, upon suitable framework, can be carried up twenty-five feet high if required. When the pots and the interstices among them are well packed with lead, a flooring of boards is laid over them, and upon this is spread another layer of tan; and in the same manner eight or ten courses are built up, containing in all, it may be, 12,000 pots and 50 or 60 tons of lead, all of which are buried beneath an upper layer of tan. As the process of conversion requires from eight to twelve weeks, the large factories have a succession of these stacks which are charged one after another, so that when the process is completed in one, and the pots and lead have been removed and the chamber is recharged, another is ready for the same operation.

The conversion of metallic lead into carbonate is induced by the fermenting action, which commences in the tan soon after the pile is completed. The heat thus generated evaporates the vinegar, and the vapors of water and acetic acid rising among the lead oxidize its surface and convert it externally into a subacetate of lead; at the same time carbonic acid evolved from the tan circulates among the lead and transforms the acetate into carbonate of the oxide, setting the acetic acid free to renew its office upon fresh surfaces of lead. When the tan ceases to ferment the process is at an end, and the stack may then be taken to pieces. The lead is found in its original forms, but of increased bulk and weight, and more or less completely converted into the white carbonate. The thoroughness of the operation depends upon a variety of circumstances; even the weather and season of the year having an influence upon it. The pieces not entirely converted have a core of metallic or "blue" lead beneath the white carbonate crust. The separation is made by beating off the white portion, and this being done upon perforated copper shelves set in large wooden tanks and covered with water, the escape of the fine metallic dust is entirely prevented and its noxious effect upon the health of the workmen is avoided. In Europe, rolling machines closely covered are applied to the same purpose, but less effectually. The white lead thus collected is next ground with water between millstones to a thin paste, and by repeated grindings and washings this is reduced to an impalpable consistency. The water is next to be removed, and, according to the European plan, the creamy mixture is next turned into earthen pots, and these are exposed upon shelves to a temperature not exceeding 300° until perfectly dry. Instead of this laborious method, the plan is adopted in the American works of employing shallow pans of sheet copper, provided with a false bottom, beneath which steam from the exhaust-pipe of the engine is admitted to promote evaporation. These pans or "drying kilns" are sometimes 100 feet long and 6 feet broad, and several are set in the building one above another. The liquid lead paste is pumped up into large tanks, and the heavier portion settling down, is drawn off into the pans, while the thinner liquid from the surface is returned to be mixed with fresh portions of white lead. Beside pans, tile tables heated by flues in the masonry of which they are built, are also employed. From four to six days are required for thoroughly drying the white lead. This is the finishing process, after which the lead is ready for packing in small casks for the market.

The manufacture of white lead, which was formerly an unhealthy and even dangerous occupation, has been so much improved by the expedients for keeping the material wet and thus preventing the rising of the fine dust, that the peculiar lead disease now rarely attacks the workmen. The business is conducted altogether upon a large scale, and though diminishing in importance, still supports a number of extensive factories in different parts of the country. Some of these have arrangements for converting-stacks that extend under cover 200 feet in length, and their facilities for grinding and drying are proportionally extensive. These and the time required for fully completing the process and getting the white lead ready for market—which is from three to four months—involve the use of large capital and tend to keep the business in few hands.

There is still a considerable demand for pure white lead, and the competition and watchfulness of the trade insure the genuineness of the article thus warranted by the manufacturers. The large class of customers, the grinders, who form a distinct trade, can use and mix the pure article with other substances and with coloring matters to suit their purposes. The mineral, sulphate of barytes or heavy spar, is the chief article used to adulterate white lead, and for this purpose it is obtained from mines in

Connecticut and other places, and is extensively ground in mills for this use alone. When perfectly pure, the powder is absolutely white; it has about the same weight as white lead, and is quite as indestructible; it is, indeed, less acted upon or discolored by noxious vapors. It lacks, however, the body of white lead, and is not so brilliant: hence it may be used in such proportion as to materially injure the paint in those good qualities. Oxide of zinc is also largely mixed with white lead, as will be noticed more particularly in the succeeding chapter.

The principal white lead works, together with the probable amount of their annual production, in the United States are as follows:—

	No. of Works.	Tons.
Brooklyn, N. Y.	3	6000
Staten Island, N. Y.	1	1000
Hudson River (Saugerties), N. Y.	2	1000
Buffalo, N. Y.	1	1000
Philadelphia, Pa.	2	3000
Pittsburg, "	1	
Baltimore, Md.	1	600
Boston, Mass.	1	1500
Salem, "	1	
Cincinnati, O.	2	
Louisville, Ky.	1	
Chicago, Ill.	1	
St. Louis, Mo.	1	

CHAPTER V.

ZINC.

WHILE the production of the lead mines has been falling off in the United States, that of the zinc mines has been steadily increasing since they were first worked about ten years since; and the metal is applied to many purposes for which lead has heretofore been almost exclusively used. The growing importance of this product in the United States will justify a reference to the zinc manufacture of Europe.

The metal, as mentioned in the chapter on COPPER, very curiously escaped the notice of the ancients, though they obtained it from its ores in preparing brass, an alloy of copper and zinc. In the metallurgical processes it is readily sublimed by heat, and when its fumes come in contact with the air they are immediately oxidized, burning with a greenish white flame, and are then converted into the white oxide of zinc—a compound of one equivalent of the metal = 34, and one of oxygen = 8; which correspond respectively to 81 and 9 per cent. These fumes when collected are found to be a white flocculent powder, now known as the white oxide of zinc, or zinc paint. If the vapor of zinc be protected from contact of air and passed through pipes into water, it is condensed into metallic drops, and these may be melted in close vessels and poured into moulds. Cast zinc is a brittle metal of bluish white color and greater lustre than that of lead. By heating it to the temperature of 212° to 300° F. it entirely loses its brittleness, and is made malleable and ductile, so that it can be rolled out into sheets. Its melting point is 680°, while that of lead is 608°.

A variety of ores are worked for this metal; as the sulphuret, called blende; the carbonate, called smithsonite; and the silicate of zinc, or calamine. The last two usually occur associated together. The red oxide is an important ore, but found only in New Jersey. Blende almost universally accompanies galena, and in some lead mines is the prevailing ore. The miners call it black jack. When pure, it consists of zinc 67, sulphur 33. Being more difficult to reduce than the other ores, it has been comparatively little used, though the Chinese are known to have been successful in their management of it. In the United States it lies valueless in immense quantities about many of the lead mines; but it is not improbable the old refuse heaps will yet be turned to profit. At the zinc works near Swansea, in Wales, it has been worked for many years; and in England it has for a few years past come into use. In 1855, it is reported that 9620 tons of this ore from various mines were sold; while of the calamine ores, the produce of the Alston Moor mines, sales of only 182 tons were reported. More ores of each sort were no doubt smelted, but the proportion of each was probably not very different from that stated. Dr. Ure, in his Dictionary, speaks of this ore selling at Holywell for £3 per ton. In France there are now five establishments working blende; while in 1840 all the zinc consumed in the country was imported. Smithsonite resembles some yellowish or whitish limestones, and usually accompanies these rocks, being irregularly bedded among their strata. In its best condition it is obtained in large blocks of botryoidal and reniform shapes, sometimes crystallized. But usually it is in porous crumbly masses, much mixed and stained with reddish oxide of iron. The pure ore contains 65 per cent. of oxide of zinc (which is equivalent to 52 of the metal) and 35 of carbonic acid. The silicate of zinc is found intermixed with the carbonate, which it resembles in appearance. It contains, when pure, silica 25.1, water 7.5, and oxide of zinc 67.4, corresponding to 54 per cent. of the metal. The red oxide is found only at Mine Hill and Stirling Hill, near Franklin, in the extreme northern county of New Jersey. The pure oxide, of which it is almost exclusively composed, contains 80.26 per cent. of zinc and 19.74 of oxygen. The bright red color is probably derived from the small quantity of oxide of manganese present. The ore is mixed with franklinite iron ore, each being in distinct grains, one red and the other black; and with these is associated a white crystalline limestone, either in disseminated grains with the ores, or forming the ground through which they are dispersed. Two beds, consisting of the zinc and iron ores, lie in contact with each other along the south-eastern slope of the Stirling Hill, between the limestone of the valley and the gneiss of the ridge, dipping with the slope of these rocks about 40° toward the valley, and ranging north-east and south-west. The upper bed, varying from 3 to 8 feet in thickness, consists of more than 50 per cent. red oxide of zinc; and the lower bed, which is 12 feet thick and in some places more than this, is chiefly franklinite, changing to limestone below, interspersed with imperfect crystals of franklinite. At Mine Hill, 1½ miles north-east from Stirling Hill, two distinct beds are again found together, that containing the most zinc in this case being the under one of the two, lying next the gneiss. These localities have been well explored; the beds have been traced considerable distances along their line of outcrop; and at Stirling Hill the red oxide of zinc has been mined for more than ten years by the New Jersey Zinc Company. Their workings have reached to a depth of about 250 feet, and have afforded the finest specimens of zinc ore ever seen. A single mass of the red oxide was sent in 1851 to the Great Exhibition in London, which weighed 16,400 lbs., and attracted no little attention, from the purity, rarity, and extraordinary size of the specimen. The Passaic Mining and Manufacturing Company also have opened two beds of the same ore on their property at Stirling Hill, adjoining that of the New Jersey Zinc Company, and since June, 1854, have taken out about 30,000 tons of rich and lean ores. At the depth of 178 feet, the principal bed is 21 feet wide, of which about 2½ feet is rich ore, and the rest limestone sufficiently interspersed with oxide of zinc to render it worth dressing. This company have recently completed at the mines very extensive works for dressing the lean ores before they are shipped to their furnaces at Jersey City. The principal supplies of their ores for the last year have been of the smithsonite and calamine from the mines in the Saucon valley, Lehigh county, Pennsylvania, of which they have mined about 5000 tons during the year 1860. These ores are extensively worked to the north of Friedensville, both by this company and the Pennsylvania and Lehigh Zinc Company, whose furnaces are at Bethlehem, in Lehigh county. The mines of the two companies, which are near together, are known as the Saucon mine and the Lehigh Zinc Company's mine. They were first opened in 1853. The two kinds of ore are found together, as is common in the European mines, and more or less blende is interspersed among them. They form very large irregular beds in limestone of the lower Silurian period, and are penetrated by veins of quartz, which traverse both the ore and limestone. Huge masses of limestone lie interspersed among the ores. The deepest workings at the Saucon mine are about 100 feet below the surface; and from this depth galleries have been run in every direction, exposing to view more than 50,000 tons of ore. The ores of best quality are found in the lower workings.

About the same time that these mines were opened in Lehigh county, another, producing similar kinds of zinc ore, was discovered near Lancaster, in Pennsylvania; but after being explored it was found to contain so much blende and galena, that it was abandoned as worthless. Large deposits of the same varieties of zinc ore are known to exist in Tennessee; one locality at Mossy Creek, a few miles north-east of Knoxville, and another at Powell's river, a branch of the Clinch river, in Campbell county, about 40 miles north of Knoxville. These beds, examined by the writer in 1858, unquestionably contain very large quantities of excellent ore. The former, being close to the East Tennessee and Virginia railroad, is very conveniently situated; and the other is within half a mile of a river navigable at certain seasons by flat-boats. Below its junction with the Clinch river are beds of bituminous coal, and the river is thence navigable by steamboats. At Kingston it is crossed by a railroad.

Very pure ores of similar character have been found in Arkansas. The localities are in a lead mining region in Lawrence, Marion, and Independence counties; but chiefly in the first named. The ores occur in a formation of magnesian limestone, imbedded in red ferruginous clay. They are almost exclusively smithsonite, containing very small proportions of silicate of zinc. Crystals of smithsonite and of blende are found upon the lumps of pure, flesh-colored ore. The district promises to become an important one for the supply of zinc to the western states.

The following are analyses of ores from the Saucon valley mines; the first three by Prof. John Torrey, of the New York Assay Office, being of specimens, and the last two of samples of large shipments. No. 4 was made at the Assay Office, Hatton Gardens, London; and No. 5 in Paris.

No. 1.

Oxide of zinc	48.90
Carbonic acid	26 40
Peroxide of iron	3.15
Carbonate of magnesia	.62
Silica	18.50
Water	.30
Loss	2.13
	100.00
Metallic zinc	39.30

No. 2.—*Granular Sulphuret of Zinc.*

Sulphuret of zinc	73.27
Sulphuret of iron	1.49
Silica	25.50
	100.26
Metallic zinc	49.09

No. 3.—*Waxy Sulphuret of Zinc.*

Sulphuret of zinc	97.63
Sulphuret of iron	1.54
Silica	1.40
	100.57
Metallic zinc	65.41

No. 4.—*Mixture of Blende and Carbonate of Zinc.*

Zinc	61.70
Sulphur	19.82
Iron	4.76
Silica	1.00
Carbonic acid	9.90
Phosphate of lime	.88
Oxygen, water, and loss	1.94
	100.00

Contains of silver 4.15 ozs. to the ton of 20 cwt.

No. 5.

Zinc	Carbonate of zinc, 75.1	42.0
Oxygen		10.5
Carbonic acid		22.6
Protoxide of iron	Carb. of iron, 10.2	7.3
Carbonic acid		2.9
Silica		11.8
Moisture		2.9
		100.0

METALLURGIC TREATMENT AND USES.

Zinc ores are applied to practical purposes, not only to produce the metal, but also the white oxide of zinc, which is largely employed as a paint. The ancients used an ore they called *lapis calaminaris*, to make brass, by melting it with copper in crucibles, not knowing that another metal was thus formed which produced an alloy with the copper. Although the metal was discovered in the 16th century, the nature of its ores was little known before the middle of the last century. It is now prepared upon a large scale in Belgium and Silesia, and small quantities are produced in England, France, and different parts of Germany. The simple method of obtaining zinc from its ores, called distillation *per descensum*, was introduced into England about the year 1740, and was derived from the Chinese, who appear to have been acquainted with the metal long before it was known to the Europeans. As now practised in Great Britain, the ores are first calcined, the effect of which is to expel a portion of the water, carbonic acid, and sulphur they contain. They are then ground to powder, and mixed with fine charcoal, or mineral coal, and introduced into stationary earthen pots, or crucibles. When set in the furnace, an iron pipe, passing up through the bottom of the hearth, enters the crucible, and connects with an open vessel directly beneath. About six pots are set together under a low dome of brick-work, through which apertures are left for filling them. Each one has a cover, which is luted down with fire clay; and the iron tube in each is stopped with a wooden plug, which, as the operation goes on, becomes charred and porous, so as to admit through it the passage of the zinc vapors. The tubes are prevented from being clogged with depositions of the condensed zinc, by occasionally running a rod through them from the lower end. The zinc collects in the dishes under the tubes, in the form of drops and powder, a portion of which is oxidized. The whole is transferred to melting-pots, and the oxide which swims upon the surface of the melted metal is skimmed off and returned to the reducing crucibles, while the metal is run into moulds. The ingots are known in commerce as spelter.

In the United States zinc was first made by Mr. John Hitz, under the direction of Mr. Hassler, who, by order of Congress, was engaged about the year 1838 to manufacture standard weights and measures for the custom-houses. The work was done at the U. S. arsenal at Washington, the ores used being the red oxide of New Jersey. The expense exceeded the value of the metal obtained, and it has generally been supposed that we could not produce spelter so cheaply as it can be imported from Europe. The next experiments were made at the works of the New Jersey Zinc Company, 1850, on the Belgian plan. In these great difficulties were experienced for want of retorts of sufficiently refractory character to withstand the high temperature and the chemical action of the constituents of the ore. The franklinite, which always accompanies the red oxide ores, was particularly injurious by reason of the oxide of iron forming a fusible silicate with the substance of the retorts These trials consequently failed after the expenditure of large sums of money. The next important trial was made in 1856, by a Mr. Hoofstetter, who built a Silesian furnace of 20 muffles for the Pennsylvania and Lehigh Zinc Company at their mine near Friedensville. This proved a total failure, and seemed almost to establish the impracticability of producing spelter with the American ores, clays, and anthracite. About this time Mr. Joseph Wharton, the general manager of the Pennsylvania and Lehigh Zinc Company, and Mr. Samuel Wetherill, of Bethlehem, both hit upon the same plan of treating zinc ores in an open furnace, and leading the volatile products through incandescent coal, in order to reduce the zinc oxide so formed, and draw only metallic and carbonaceous vapors into the condensing apparatus. Mr. Wharton constructed his furnace in Philadelphia, and Mr. Wetherill his in Bethlehem. The former having completed his trials, filed a caveat for the process, but soon after abandoned it as economically impracticable. The latter continued his operations, patented the method, and produced some zinc, eight or ten tons of which were sold to the U. S. Assay Office in New York. The manufacture was not, however, long continued. In 1858, Mr. Wetherill recommenced the production of zinc, adopting a plan of upright retorts, somewhat like that in use in Carinthia, in Austria, and that of the English patent of James Graham. Mr. Wetherill had succeeded in procuring good mixtures of fire clays, and his retorts made of these and holding each a charge of 400 lbs. of ore, proved sufficiently refractory for the operation. The works now under his charge at Bethlehem, erected in 1858–9, and belonging to the owners of the Saucon mine, have a capacity of about two tons of metal daily.

Mr. Wharton, after abandoning the method of reduction by incandescent coals, continued his experiments on different plans, and finally decided on the Belgian furnace as the best, after having actually made spelter from silicate of zinc, with anthracite, in muffles of American clays, at a cost below its market value. These trials were made in the zinc oxide works of the Pennsylvania and Lehigh Zinc Company. Their success encouraged the company to construct a factory at Bethlehem for reducing zinc ores, and this was done under the direction of Mr. Wharton in 1860. The capacity of the works is about 2000 tons per annum, and their actual daily product in the winter of 1860–1, is over three tons. Four stacks or blocks are constructed, each containing four furnaces. To each furnace there are 56 retorts, making in all 896, working two charges in twenty-four hours. Their total capacity is about five tons of metal. Besides the ordinary spelter of this manufacture, which, as will be seen by the remarks that follow, is remarkable for its freedom from injurious mixtures, and is the best commercial zinc in the world, Mr. Wharton also prepares from selected ores a pure zinc for the use of chemists, and for purposes in which a high degree of purity is essential. This is cast in ingots of about nine pounds each, and is sold at the price of ten cents per pound. For the supply of chemists, and for the batteries employed by the telegraph companies, the American zinc of this manufacture is preferred to all others. The total annual consumption of crude spelter in the United States amounts to the value of about $600,000; and the value of sheet zinc, nails, etc., is about as much more.

The commercial zincs, it has long been known, are contaminated by various foreign substances, the existence of some of which is indicated in the finely divided black substance which remains floating or sinking in the liquid, when the metal is dissolved in dilute acids. The impurities have been stated by different chemists to consist of a great variety of substances, such as lead, cadmium, arsenic, tin, iron, manganese, carbon, etc. They injuriously affect the quality of the metal for many of its uses; and the presence of one of them, arsenic, is fatal to the highly important use of zinc by chemists, as a reagent in the detection of arsenic in other substances. Arsenic in the form of a sulphuret often accompanies the native sulphurets of zinc, and its oxide, being volatile, is readily carried over with the zinc fumes in the metallurgic treatment of blende, and may thus be introduced into the spelter. It is evidently, therefore, a matter of consequence to know the qualities of the different zincs of commerce, and the exact nature of the impurities they contain. Very thorough investigations having these objects in view have recently been made in Cambridge, Massachusetts, by Messrs. Charles W. Eliot and Frank H. Storer of Boston, and the results of these, with a full description of their methods of examination, were communicated, May 29, 1860, to the American Academy of Arts and Sciences, and published in the eighth volume of the new series of their Memoirs. Eleven varieties of zinc from different parts of Europe, and made from the ores of New Jersey, and of the Saucon valley, Pennsylvania, were experimented upon, of all of which large samples were at hand. These varieties were the following: 1, Silesian zinc; 2, Vieille Montagne zinc; 3, New Jersey zinc; 4, Pennsylvanian zinc, Bethlehem, Pennsylvania; 5, Vieille Montagne zinc, employed at the United States mint, Philadelphia; 6, zinc of MM. Rousseau, Frères, Paris, labelled and sold as *zinc pur;* 7, sheet zinc obtained in Berlin, Prussia; 8, zinc made near Wrexham, North Wales; 9, zinc from the Mines Royal, Neath, South Wales; 10, zinc from the works of Dillwyn & Co., Swansea, South Wales; 11, zinc from the works of Messrs. Vivian, Swansea. All of these, except the Pennsylvania zinc, furnished an insoluble residue, which was found to consist chiefly of metallic lead, and this proved to be the principal impurity of all the samples examined; "the carbon, tin, copper, iron, arsenic, and other impurities found in the metal by previous observers, occur either in very minute quantities, or rarely, and doubtless accidentally." The proportions of lead present in 100 parts of each of the varieties examined were respectively as follows: in No. 1, 1.46; 2, 0.292; 3, 0.079; 4, 0.000; 5, 0.494; 6, 0.106; 7, 1.297; 8, 1.192; 9, 0.823; 10, 1.661; 11, 1.516. The New Jersey zinc was found to contain a sensible quantity of tin, copper amounting to 0.1298 per cent., iron 0.2088 per cent., and an unusually large amount of arsenic. Traces of this were also detected in the white oxide prepared from the ores of the New Jersey mines, and in the red oxide ore itself; but the same ore afforded no clue as to the source whence the copper was derived, a metal of which not the slightest traces were discoverable in the other zincs. None of the samples contained sufficient arsenic to admit of its proportion being determined, and some were entirely free from it, as some of the Belgian and Pennsylvania spelter, but traces of it were met with in other samples from the same regions, indicating that the occasional use of inferior ores, such as blende, intermixed with the carbonates and silicates, might introduce this substance, or possibly it might come over only in the first part of the distillation, and the zinc collected in the latter part might be quite free from it. The Silesian zinc contained minute quantities of sulphur and arsenic; and the English zinc more arsenic than any other, except perhaps the New Jersey. The purest of all the samples was that from Bethlehem, Pennsylvania, some of it yielding no impurity, except a trace of cadmium. The source of a trace of arsenic in another sample is supposed to be in the use of the crust of oxide of zinc from the operations connected with the manufacture of white oxide of zinc, no particular care being taken in that process to reject inferior ores, and this crust being taken to the other works where the metal is prepared and mixed with the selected ores employed for this use, it has thus introduced the arsenic. As the authors of the paper remark, there seems to be no reason why zinc of uniform purity should not be obtained from the excellent ores of the Saucon valley mines.

EUROPEAN MANUFACTURE.

A large portion of the zinc of commerce is furnished by the works of the Vieille Montagne Company, established near the frontier of Belgium and Prussia, chiefly in the province of Liege of the former country. A large number of mines are worked in this region, the most important of which is that of the Vieille Montagne or Altenberg, situated in the village of Moresnet, between Aix-la-Chapelle and the town of Liege. It is said that the great body of carbonate of zinc found here was worked as long ago as the year 1435, and that for four centuries it was not known that the ore was of metallic character, but it was used as a peculiar earth adapted for converting copper into brass. The ore lies in a basin-like depression in strata of magnesian limestone, and is much mixed with beds of clay intercalated among its layers. The ore is chiefly carbonate mixed with the silicate and oxide of zinc. Some of it is red, from the oxide of iron intermixed, and this produces only about 33 per cent. of metal. The purer white ore yields about 46 per cent., and is moreover much preferred on account of its working better in the retorts. The furnaces employed in the distillation of these ores are constructed upon a very large scale, and on a different plan from those in use in Great Britain. The general character of the operations, however, is the same. The ores are first calcined, losing about one fifth of their weight. They are then ground in mills, and charges are made up of 1100 lbs. of the powdered ore mixed with 550 lbs. of fine coal. The mixture being well moistened with water, is introduced into cylindrical retorts, which are three feet 8 inches long and 6 inches diameter inside, set inclining outward, to the number of 42 in a single furnace, and 4 such furnaces are constructed in one stack. The open end of each retort connects, by means of an iron adapter 16 inches long, with a wrought-iron cone, the little end of which, projecting out from the furnace, is only an inch in diameter. After the charges have been sufficiently heated, the sublimed zinc condenses in the neck of the retort and in the adapter and cone. The last two are then removed, and the zinc and oxide are collected from them, and the liquid metal in the neck of the retorts is drawn out and caught in a large ladle, from which it is poured into moulds. The zinc thus obtained is remelted before it is rolled. Two charges are run through in twenty-four hours, each furnace producing from 2200 lbs. of ore about 620 lbs. of metal, which is about 30 per cent. From a late report of these operations it appears that there are seven large smelting establishments belonging to the Vieille Montagne Zinc Mining Company, on the borders of Belgium and Prussia, comprising 230 furnaces. The annual product of these is 29,000 tons of spelter, of which 23,000 tons are converted into sheet zinc, and about 7000 tons are rolled at mills not the property of the company. They also manufacture oxide of zinc in three establishments devoted to this operation, to the amount of about 6000 tons annually. The company also purchases spelter very largely.

The metallurgy of zinc has, within a few years past, become an important branch of industry in Upper Silesia on the borders of Poland, and not far from Cracow. In 1857 there were no less than 47 zinc works in this part of Prussia, one of which, named Lydogniahütte, at Königshütte, belonged to the government, and the remainder were owned by private companies and individuals. In that year their total production was 31,480 tons of spelter, valued at about 17,660,000 francs. Many of the establishments belong to the Silesian Company, which also owns several coal mines near their works, and a number of zinc mines. The government works are supplied with ores from their own mines, and also from all the others, being entitled to one twentieth of their product. From a description of the operations published in the sixteenth volume of the *Annales des Mines*, fifth series, 1859, it appears that the processes are the same which had been employed for full twenty years previously, and each establishment presents little else than a repetition of the works of the others. The furnace in use is a double stack, furnished along each side with horizontal ovens, into each of which three muffles or retorts are introduced. These are constructed of refractory fire clays, and are charged, like the retorts of gas furnaces, by conveying the material upon a long charger or spoon into the interior. Their dimensions are about 4 feet long, 22 inches high, and 8½ inches wide, and the weight of the charge introduced is only about 55 pounds. The ovens on each side of the stacks contain as many as 20 and sometimes 30 retorts. The same stack contains besides, 1st, an oven in which the ores belonging to it are roasted for expelling the water and a portion of the carbonic acid they contain (a process in which they lose about ⅓ their weight); 2d, an oven for baking the retorts, each establishment making its own; and 3d, a furnace for remelting and purifying the zinc obtained from the retorts. Several stacks are arranged in a large building with close walls and open along the top of the roof to allow the smoke to escape. On one side, connected with it, are the workshops in which the muffles are made and various other operations are carried on.

The principal zinc mines are in the vicinity of Beuthen, and are found in the magnesian limestones of the new red sandstone formation. They are connected with the zinc works, which are principally near Königshütte, by branch railroads connecting with the principal line of road between Tarnowitz and Kattowitz. The ores are chiefly carbonates, always mixed with much oxide of iron, which is sometimes present to the extent of 20 per cent., and with them is also associated more or less silicate of zinc, blende, galena, and cadmium. Their percentage of zinc is very variable, rarely reaching 35, and probably averaging 21 or 22 per cent. Much that is worked does not exceed 12 per cent. They lie in irregular deposits, and it is found that their yield of zinc has been gradually falling off, so that it is now only about two fifths of what it was formerly. This low yield involves a large consumption of fuel, which is 20 tons for one of zinc obtained; and if this deterioration continues, the mines must some time hence be abandoned. The coal employed in working the ores is of poor quality, burning without flame; but it leaves no cinder, and is procured from mines very near the works, and at the extraordinary low price of 6 to 7 francs the 1000 kilogrammes (about one ton). The retorts are charged every 24 hours with roasted ore reduced to the size of nuts, and mixed with oxide of zinc from previous operations, with the dross from the crucible employed in remelting, with the incrustations from the muffles and their connections outside the furnaces, and in fine with cinders that have fallen through the grates, these last making about ⅓ the bulk of the charge. The workmen having discharged a muffle of the liquid zinc and oxide remaining from the previous operation by drawing them forward, so that they fall upon an iron shelf placed below to catch them, and having repaired any cracks and holes in the muffle, they introduce the new charge in small portions at a time, and immediately adjust the outer connection, which is also of earthenware bent down at a right angle, and close up the openings in front. The zinc soon begins to distil over, and drops down upon the iron shelf, forming pieces of all shapes; and it is more or less mixed with oxide colored yellow by the oxide of cadmium. When remelted and run into moulds, the spelter is stated to have about the following composition: zinc, 97.50, cadmium, 1.00, lead, 0.20, arsenic, 0.84, sulphur, 0.05, together with traces of tin, iron, and carbon; but the character and proportion of the impurities are probably very variable. The expenses of the manufacture at the royal works amounted for the year 1856 to 48.60 francs the metrical quintal (220.47 lbs.), and in 1858 to 54.84 francs; consisting in the latter year of the following items: ore, 26.84; fuel, 14.30; labor, 7.00; materials employed, 3.70; general expenses, 3.00. The operations of the Silesian Company at their several works for the first half of the year 1858 are thus presented:—

COST OF THE SEVERAL ITEMS PER METRICAL QUINTAL OF PRODUCT.

Name of Works.	Ores treated. Met. quint.	Zinc obtained. Met. quint.	Cost of labor. Francs.	Fuel. Francs.	Ores. Francs.	Sundry expenses. Francs.	Total cost. Francs.
Gabor Silesia	112,399	19,703	4.98	10.35	11.40	4.27	31.00
Paulshütte	40,784	4,928	7.10	14.69	14.24	4.77	40.80
Thurzohütte	37,458	4,495	7.57	12.08	12.92	4.90	37.47
Friedenshütte	15,345	2,346	5.96	10.66	13.98	4.62	35.22
Stanislashütte	40,534	3,978	8.83	16.18	15.66	6.23	46.90
Carlshütte	45,918	5,723	6.06	14.80	13.23	6.91	41.00
	292,438	41,173					

The general consumption of spelter throughout the world is estimated in the report to which we have already referred, relating to the Vieille Montagne Company, to be about 67,000 tons, of which about 44,000 tons are sheet zinc applied as follows:—

	Tons.
For roofing and architectural purposes	23,000
" sheathing of ships	3,500
" lining packing cases	2,500
" domestic utensils	12,000
" stamped ornaments	1,500
" miscellaneous uses	1,500
	44,000

The estimate of 67,000 tons as the total annual production of zinc is probably too small for Europe alone. Taking the product above given of the works of the Vieille Montagne Company, viz., 29,000 tons, and that of the Silesian furnaces, 31,480 tons, there remain only 6,520 tons to be divided among the other zinc-producing countries. These are Poland, on the borders of Silesia, the annual production of which is usually given as 4000 tons; England, which has rapidly advanced from 1000 tons of spelter per annum to 6900 tons in 1858; Austria, which produces 1500 tons; Sweden, 40 tons; and the Hartz 10 tons. Zinc, it is believed, is also manufactured to some extent in Spain. The European production would, therefore, seem to exceed 73,000 tons, and for the total production of the world, that of the United States and of China should be added. Of the extent of the manufacture of the latter country we know nothing. The United States produces of oxide of zinc and spelter over 7000 tons annually.

The value of the ores at different costs of the metal is given in the following recently prepared table from one of the European houses:—

SCHEDULE OF THE COST OF ZINC ORE ON SHIPBOARD AT ANTWERP.

CARBONATE OF ZINC.

	Metal worth 50 francs the 100 kilogrammes.	Metal worth 55 f. the 100 kilogrammes.	Metal worth 60 f. the 100 kilogrammes.
Percentage of zinc by analysis.	Value of 100 kilogrammes. Francs.	Value of 100 kilogrammes. Francs.	Value of 100 kilogrammes. Francs.
40	80.00	94.50	109.00
45	102.50	119.50	136.50
50	125.00	144.50	164.00
55	147.50	169.50	191.50
60	170.00	194.50	219.00
65	192.50	219.50	246.50
70	215.00	244.50	274.00
SILICATE OF ZINC.			
40	45.00	57.00	69.00
45	67.50	82.00	96.50
50	90.00	107.00	124.00
55	112.50	132.00	151.50
60	135.00	157.00	179.00
65	157.50	182.00	206.50
70	180.00	207.00	234.00

A kilogramme is equivalent to 2205 lbs. avoirdupois.

Fifteen years ago the quantity of zinc used for roofing did not exceed 5000 tons per annum, and no zinc was employed for sheathing ships, or lining packing cases. The stamped ornaments in this metal only came into use in 1852. In Germany zinc is now very generally used for roofing; and in Paris it has been employed for nearly every roof constructed during the last fifteen years. In laying the sheets great care is taken that the metal has sufficient room to expand and contract by change of temperature; and especially that it is fastened with zinc nails, and is allowed to come nowhere in contact with iron—even with nail heads. The purer the metal the longer it lasts. It is supposed the English do not apply it much to roofing on account of the poor success attending the use of bad metal, such as they manufacture from inferior ores.

Besides the uses named for this metal, it is employed for coating sheet iron, making what is called galvanized iron, though the use of the galvanic current is now dispensed with in its preparation; for pipes for conveying liquids; for baths, water-tanks, milk pans and pails, plates for engraving upon; for galvanic batteries; for nails, spikes, and wire, which is made of great flexibility and of all sizes. It has also been cast into statues, and made to imitate bronze. The Vieille Montagne Company sent to the Great Exhibition in London a statue of Queen Victoria, which with its pedestal of zinc was twenty-one feet high. Zinc is also an important reagent in chemical operations, and is especially employed with sulphuric acid to decompose water for obtaining hydrogen gas.

ZINC PAINT.

White oxide of zinc was first recommended as a substitute for white lead by the celebrated Guyton de Morveau about the close of the last century, during his investigations on the subject of lead poisoning; and to him it was suggested by Courtois, a manufacturer at Dijon. The high price of zinc at that time, and ignorance respecting the proper manner of using the oxide of zinc, prevented its introduction. It was many years after this that methods of producing it as cheaply as white lead were devised by M. Leclaire, a house-painter of Paris; and he also first prepared to use with it a series of yellow and green unchangeable colors, to replace those before in use having noxious bases of lead, copper, or arsenic; and also a drying oil, prepared by boiling linseed oil with about five per cent. of oxide of manganese. His process, which is still the one in general use in Europe, is based on the treatment of the metal instead of the ore, as practised in this country, and scarcely any white oxide of zinc is there made by any other method. The furnaces employed are similar to those for producing the metal, or like those of the gas works. When the retorts set in these furnaces have become very hot, they are charged with the ingots of zinc. The metal soon melts, and its vapor passes off through the outlets of the retorts, where it meets a current of air, and both together are drawn on through the condensing apparatus either by the draught of a chimney, or by an exhausting fan at the further extremity of the apparatus. The metallic vapors become oxidized by mixing with the air, and are converted into a light, flaky, white powder, which is the oxide of zinc. The arrangements for condensing and collecting this are similar in principle to those employed for the same purposes in the American process. By making use of the metal in retorts, instead of subliming it from ores contaminated with their own impurities, and mixed with the coal required for conducting the process, a much purer oxide of zinc is obtained; and by selecting the purest sorts of spelter, the beautiful article, called by the French *blanc de neige*, or "snow-white," is produced, which is employed by painters in the place of the "silver-white." With the use of other zinc, the product is fit to be substituted for the best white lead. But if the metal has been made from ores containing cadmium or iron, or if old zinc has been introduced to which any solder adheres, according to the French chemists oxides of other metals are produced, and are taken up in small quantities with the zinc vapors, imparting to the oxide a slightly yellow or greenish tint, which if not very decided may however disappear when the paint is mixed; but the experience of American manufacturers does not accord with this explanation.

The manufacture of white oxide of zinc direct from the ore is a purely American process, established by the experiments of Mr. Richard Jones of Philadelphia in the year 1850. The great bodies of the rich ores of northern New Jersey had at various times, for the past two centuries, attracted the attention of many persons interested in metallurgical operations; and of late years numerous attempts had been made to devise some method of converting them to useful purposes. Zinc, however, was a metal not much in demand, and nothing was known of the useful qualities of the white oxide. When the value of this had been demonstrated in Europe, and the practicability of producing it economically from the red oxide was shown, a company was organized in New York under the name of the New Jersey Zinc Company, for the purpose of carrying on this manufacture upon a large scale. This association was incorporated by the Legislature of New Jersey, February 15, 1849, and the report of their operations, made December 31, 1853, by their president, C. E. Detmold, Esq., showed a production, for 1852, of 2,425,506 lbs. of oxide; and for 1853, of 4,043,415 lbs.; and the total production for 10 years, ending with 1860, has amounted to above 19,500 tons. Their works were established at Newark, N. J., to which place the ores are brought by the Morris and Essex canal; and the anthracite consumed in the manufacture is also delivered by water transportation. The company has forty furnaces, that may be kept in constant operation. The character of the process is like that which will be given below, as conducted by the Passaic Mining and Manufacturing Company.

The success of the enterprise of the New Jersey Zinc Company, and the discovery in 1853 of the great beds of silicate and carbonate of zinc in the Saucon valley, Pennsylvania, led to the organization in that year of the Pennsylvania and Lehigh Zinc Company, and the erection of furnaces for making the oxide at Bethlehem, on the Lehigh river. The operations were conducted by Samuel Wetherill, Esq., by a patented process of his own invention, and at a contract price of $50 per ton; the ore being delivered by the company at the works for $1.50 per ton. About four tons are consumed to the ton of oxide. The company have mined up to the present time about 60,000 tons of ore, and are manufacturing about 320,000 lbs. of oxide of zinc per month.

A third company was established in 1855, called the Passaic Mining and Manufacturing Company, and their works, constructed at Communipaw, on the Morris canal near Jersey City, went into operation in June of that year. They obtain their ores both from the mines of red oxide in Sussex county, and from the Saucon valley mines in Pennsylvania. They employ 24 furnaces, built in 3 stacks, of 8 each, in which they are arranged like ovens, half of them opening on one side and half on the opposite side. Each one is about 6 feet in depth (from front to back), 4 feet in width, and about $3\frac{1}{2}$ feet in height. The roof is arched, with an opening through it for the pipe which conveys away the vapor and products of combustion. The sole is formed of cast-iron plates, which are perforated full of small holes for admitting the blast to penetrate every portion of the charge, as the wind is driven by two large fan-blowers into the receptacle under the furnace corresponding to the ash pit. The ores are prepared by first crushing them to powder, which is done by passing them through two pairs of Cornish rolls, and then mixing them thoroughly with about half their weight of the dust of anthracite. A fire is kindled upon the grate-bars of 250 lbs. of pea coal, and when ignited to full whiteness the charge of 600 lbs. of ore, mixed with 300 of coal dust, is added, and when exhausted the charge is withdrawn, leaving only sufficient coal to ignite the next charge, thus working off 4 charges in every 24 hours. The proportion of oxide obtained from the ore is variable, as the charge is not of uniform quality; but it is usually between 30 and 40 per cent. As the coal rapidly consumes from the effect of the blast, the ores are decomposed, and metallic zinc sublimes. The vapor rises with the gaseous products of combustion, and all are carried up the pipe, which just above the roof of the stack terminates under an inverted funnel, the base of which covers the lower pipe like a hood, and the upper portion is a pipe like that below. A strong current of air is created by two exhausting fan-blowers at the other extremity of the apparatus, and the vapors are drawn up together with much air which flows in around the open base of the funnel, and causes at this point a vivid combustion of the zinc vapors, which burn with a pale blue flame, and are thus converted into oxide. The appearance presented by this combustion actively going on in full view under each hood is very striking, and is far from suggesting to an observer unacquainted with the process, the possibility that from the pale flames rushing up the pipes any valuable product can be recovered. The pipes connect above with a cylindrical sheet-iron receiver that extends over the three stacks, so as to secure the products of all the furnaces. It is a huge pipe, $6\frac{1}{2}$ feet in diameter, and 130 feet long, and passes along under the roof, against a line of windows on each side, through which air is admitted for hastening the cooling of the products. The pipe discharges into a square tower in masonry, and in this the particles are washed and cooled by a continual falling sheet of water. The light flocculent oxide of zinc is not carried down by this to any great extent, but is drawn on by the exhaust through 3 large pipes to a second tower with three divisions, in which the fans are placed that create the draught. From this the current, still propelled by the fans, moves on through other pipes that connect with the system of flannel bags, which in great numbers, and of extraordinary sizes, are suspended throughout the portion of the building devoted to the final cooling of the oxide, and filtering it from the gaseous matters intermixed. Some of the bags extend the whole length of the rooms, which are 120 feet long by 64 wide, and the diameter of the largest of them is over 4 feet. They are arranged near together, and some are carried vertically from the horizontal ones up to the roof. Through the pores of the flannel the gases escape, and the oxide of zinc remains thoroughly purified. Nearly 200,000 square feet of flannel are worked into these bags; and one person is almost constantly employed with a sewing machine, and two others working by hand, in making and repairing them. Along the under side of the horizontal bags pipes of cotton cloth, ten or twelve inches in diameter, reach down nearly to the floor, and are kept tied around their lower ends. These are called the teats; and the oxide of zinc is collected by lifting up the portions of the bags where it has settled, and shaking these so as to make it fall into the teats. The ends of these are then opened, and the white zinc is received in strong bags, which being tied up are laid upon a truck, and this is run by steam power back and forth under a compressing roller. The air dispersed through it, rendering it so light and bulky, is thus expelled, and the oxide is converted into a dense, heavy powder. The last process is to grind this with bleached linseed oil, which is done in the ordinary paint mills. The paint is then transferred into small kegs for the market.

The residuum of the furnace charge, when of red oxide, consists of some unsublimed zinc ore mixed with franklinite and more or less unconsumed coal. It is raked out in the form of slags, and is accumulated in immense piles about the works. In 1853, Mr. Detmold succeeded in using this as an iron ore, and produced excellent iron which proved to be also well adapted for the manufacture of steel. The iron manufacture has been continued, and has become a profitable branch of the operations of the United States Zinc Company, producing about 2000 tons of zinc per annum. The franklinite itself had been used a year earlier for the same purposes by Mr. Edwin Post, at Stanhope, and from this he obtained both iron and steel; but when the manufacture was undertaken upon a large scale by the New Jersey Franklinite Company, at Franklin, New Jersey, it proved unsuccessful in practice.

The product of the zinc works of the Passaic Company for the year 1856, was 2,327,920 lbs. of oxide of zinc; and the monthly production for the year 1860 has been about 400,000 lbs. from 16 furnaces. With the 24 in blast their monthly capacity is from 280 to 300 tons of 2000 lbs. to the ton. The total annual product of the three establishments is from 6000 to 7000 tons of oxide; and the consumption of this large quantity in the United States is good evidence of the importance of this paint, and of the great extent to which it must have superseded the use of white lead.

The items which make up its cost are of such nature that no exact estimate can be given of this. The ores are of no definite composition, and according to their percentage, as obtained from the mine or afterward dressed, the quantity required to produce a ton of oxide must vary, while with poor ores a proportionably larger amount of fuel is consumed than that required for rich ores. These items consequently vary between considerable extremes; and then the cost of the bags, barrels for packing, and the numerous incidentals, including repairs and general expenses, can only be arrived at by a careful computation of the operations of each establishment. The market price of the oxide is from 4½ to 5½ cents per lb.

The importance of the application of white zinc to painting in the place of white lead appears to have been much more fully appreciated in France and the United States than in Great Britain. Soon after the discoveries of Leclaire that white oxide of zinc could be thus used, and produce, with the colored bases he prepared of this and other innocuous oxides, all the tints required, the French government, recognizing the importance of his inventions, conferred upon him the cross of the Legion of Honor, and adopted the paints for the public buildings. By the year 1849, over 6000 public and private buildings had been painted with his preparations, and the testimony was very strong in their favor. Not one of his workmen had been attacked by the painter's colic, though previously a dozen or more suffered every year from it. The colors were pronounced more solid and durable than the old, were made brighter by washing, and were not tarnished by sulphuretted hydrogen, as occurs to white lead. The best white paint was moreover so pure and brilliant a white, that it made the best white lead paint by its side look disagreeably yellow and gray. No difficulty was experienced in making the new colors, mixed with the prepared oil, dry rapidly without the use of the ordinary dryers of lead compound; and used in equal weight with lead, the zinc was found to cover better, and was, consequently, more economical at equal prices per lb. The English, however, found many objectionable qualities in the new paint. Its transparency, which is the cause of its brilliancy, by reflecting instead of absorbing the light, was regarded as a defect, and the painters complained that it had not the body or covering properties of the carbonate of lead. It would not dry rapidly for the second coat without the use of the patent dryers, which contain lead, and therefore it was no better than the lead. Messrs. Coates & Co., who now import into Great Britain about 1000 tons of oxide of zinc per annum, wrote to the editor of the *Lancet* in March, 1860, that the consumption of white lead is still nearly 100 to 1 of white zinc, and that in 1856 the importation of the latter amounted to only 235 tons. They ascribe the real cause of the larger consumption of white lead, to the almost entire exclusion of zinc, to the fact, that white lead can be adulterated with barytes and other cheap ingredients without the adulteration being detected by the eye, thus securing large profits to the manufacturer and contractor, which cannot be realized in the use of zinc paint, for the reason that it has little affinity for foreign substances. The experience of the manufacturers of the United States does not substantiate this statement as to the difficulty of using the oxide of zinc in mixture with other substances. It is employed not only alone, but mixed with either barytes or white lead, or with both of them; and large quantities are thus sold and give satisfaction to consumers, who would reject the paint, if they supposed it to be any thing else than white lead. As to its covering quality, it is found that the oxide of zinc varies according to the manner in which it has been prepared. The light flocculent oxide mixes readily with oil without grinding; but though pressed, it covers much less surface than the same oxide moulded when moistened with water, and dried by artificial heat. This preparation also causes any yellowish or greenish tints to disappear, and the article may be supplied to the consumer in cakes, which when ground with oil will cover more surface than the same weight of white lead. The body of the white zinc may be still further improved by calcination before grinding.

The inferior colored sorts of oxide of zinc, such as are collected in the iron receivers near the furnaces, and that made from the pulverized ores of zinc, have been largely employed for painting iron surfaces, especially on board of ships, the paint being found to possess a peculiar quality of protecting the iron it covers from rusting.

Besides its use as a paint, oxide of zinc is applied to the preparation of the mastic for rendering metallic joints tight; and to that of glazed papers and cards, for which white lead and carbonate of barytes have heretofore been used. The French use it in preparing the paste for artificial crystals instead of oxide of lead or other metallic oxides; and they have also made with it some of the finest sorts of cut glass and especially lenses. In the Great Exhibition of 1851, an award was made to specimens of zinc glass which presented a very pleasing and white appearance, and were regarded as especially suited to achromatic purposes. It was remarkable for its being purer and more pellucid than lead glass, and also of greater specific gravity.

A patent has been granted in the United States for the manufacture of flint glass with oxide of zinc, and specimens of glass were produced with it in 1860, which were remarkable for their brilliancy and beautiful surface, or "skin," as it is called. The glass is more infusible than that made with oxide of lead, and there seems to be no good reason to prevent it coming rapidly into use.

CHAPTER VI.

PLATINUM.

Although this metal is not obtained in large quantity in the United States, it is found associated with the gold in many localities in California and Oregon, and has been detected in Rutherford county, North Carolina, and in traces in the lead and copper ores of Lancaster county, Pennsylvania. From the states on the Pacific it has been supposed that it would yet be afforded as a commercial article. It is a metal of considerable interest from the extent to which it is used in the United States, and the success that has attended the attempts to work it in Philadelphia and New York. The metal is supplied to commerce from no certain source, and finds its way into the United States in a great variety of forms, as in native grains found in washing the gold deposits of Cauca on the western coast of South America, of Brazil, and Oregon, and in manufactured articles imported from Europe and chiefly from France. Russia produced between the years 1824 and 1845 many times as much platinum as all the rest of the world, and introduced the metal into her coinage; but after 1845 it was no longer coined, and the yield of the deposits in the Ural has dwindled away to almost nothing. The supply from Borneo has been very large for some years, the whole product of the island sometimes amounting to 600 lbs. a year. It is found in small grains and lumps in the sands that are washed for gold; and pieces of several pounds have been met with in Siberia, the largest weighing over 22 lbs. troy. The properties which give to the metal its great value, as its power of resisting the effects of heat and many of the most powerful chemical agents, also render it exceedingly difficult to work and to convert into useful shapes. The crude grains are generally alloyed to the amount of about 20 per cent. of their weight with the very refractory metal iridium, with osmium, rhodium, iron, and sometimes other metals also. It is separated from the chief part of these and purified by dissolving the grains in *aqua regia*, a mixture of nitric and hydrochloric acid, and causing the metal to be precipitated by sal-ammoniac. It falls in a yellowish powder, which is a compound of platinum, ammonia, and chlorine. To decompose this the compound is separated from the liquid, and being well washed and dried, is heated red hot in a cast-iron crucible. This drives off the ammonia and chlorine, and the platinum remains in the crucible in a spongy condition. This is condensed into solid metal by repeated heatings and hammerings. It has always been a matter of great difficulty to raise

OXI GEN
HYDRO GEN
E.A.L. ROBERTS.
N.Y.
3
4
5
6
7
8
10
10

sufficient heat to soften the platinum, even in quantities less than an ounce, so that it could be worked under the hammer. It used formerly to be brought into a metallic cake by making a fusible alloy of it with arsenic, and then burning out the latter as much as possible, and hammering or rolling the cake into sheets, but the arsenic remaining in the platinum always injures its quality. Dr. Robert Hare, of Philadelphia, was the first to fuse the metal for any practical purpose, and in May, 1838, he exhibited a cake of about 23 ounces, which was run together from grains and scraps by means of the intense heat produced by his oxy-hydrogen blowpipe. From a reservoir of oxygen, and from another of hydrogen, a gas-pipe conveyed the gases into one tube, in which they were mixed just back of the igniting jets; and in this the explosive mixture was kept cool by ice around the tube. Explosion was moreover guarded against by the extreme fineness of the apertures through which the gases were made to pass.

This means of working platinum has been applied very successfully by Dr. E. A. L. Roberts, of Bond street, New York, in the preparation of platinum plate and various articles in this metal employed by dentists, such as the plates and fastenings for sets of artificial teeth, and the little pins which secure each tooth in its setting. The annual consumption of these last, it is estimated, amounts throughout the United States to about $60,000 in value, which is nearly ⅛ of the annual supply of the metal. The apparatus consists of two cylindrical copper gas-holders, one for hydrogen, holding 220 gallons, and one for oxygen, holding 80 gallons. The Croton water, with a pressure of about 60 lbs. upon the square inch, is admitted into the bottom of these gas-receivers, for propelling the gases as they are required. The discharge pipes have each at their extremity a short brass tube, which is full of pieces of wire of nearly the same length as the tube, jammed in very tightly. These unite in another brass tube which is packed in a similar way, and connects by a metallic pipe of only ¼ inch bore, with the burner. This is a little platinum box, one end of which terminates in a disk of platinum or copper ½ by ¼ inch in size, perforated with 21 very minute holes in 3 rows. This box is buried in plaster of Paris mixed up with fibres of asbestus, forming a lump sufficiently large to contain around the box a receptacle into which, by means of flexible pipes, a current of water is admitted and discharged on the same principle that the water-tuyeres of iron forges and furnaces are constructed and kept cool while in use. The burner points downward, so that the jet is directed immediately upon the face of the metal held up beneath it. The method of using the apparatus is as follows: the platinum scraps being first consolidated by pressure in moulds into compact cakes of 10 to 20 ounces each, these are placed upon a plate of fire-brick, and brought to a full white heat in a powerful wind furnace. The plate with the platinum is then removed from the furnace and set in a large tin pan thickly lined with asbestus and plaster of Paris, and is brought directly under the jet, which at the same time is ignited. The platinum immediately begins to melt upon the surface, and the pieces gradually run together into one mass as the different parts of the cakes are brought successively under the jet. Though the metal melts and flows upon itself, it cools too rapidly to be cast in a mould; nor is this necessary or desirable for the uses to which it is applied. These require a soft and tough material, while the fused metal is hard and sonorous, and of crystalline texture, breaking like spelter. It is made malleable and tough by repeated heatings and hammerings. It is introduced into the muffle of the assay furnace constructed by Dr. Roberts especially for producing the high heat required in these and similar operations, and is heated so intensely that when the door of the furnace is opened the cake of metal is too dazzlingly hot to be visible. It is then taken out with tongs plated with platinum, and hammered with a perfectly clean hammer upon a clean anvil, both of which should be as hot as possible without drawing the temper of the steel. If the process is one of welding, when the platinum has cooled so as to be distinctly visible, it should be heated again, for in this condition every blow tends to shatter and shake it to pieces. The lump is forged by hammering it to a thickness of about ¼ of an inch, and then being again heated very hot, is passed instantly through the rolls. It is thus obtained in sheets, which are easily converted into the various uses to which the metal is applied.

Upon the opposite page, the apparatus employed and manner of conducting the operations are exhibited in the wood-cut;

and the articles designated by the figures are thus explained:—

1. Reservoir for oxygen.
2. " " hydrogen.
3. Hydrogen generator.
4. Oxygen "
5. Blowpipe.
6. Tuyere.
7. Rolls for converting the metal into sheets.
8. Gasometer.
9. Water pipes.
10. Pan.
11. Moulds in which the loose pieces of metal are compressed.

Crucibles for chemical use are prepared by the ingenious method called spinning. A disk of the metal is securely fixed against the end of the mandrel of a lathe, and, as it revolves rapidly, a blunt point is pressed upon its surface, causing the plate to gradually bend over and assume the desired form. The large platinum retorts used in the manufacture of sulphuric acid are imported from Paris. The whole amount of platinum brought to the United States for the year 1850 was 34,000 oz. troy, which, at the custom-house valuation of $6.10 per oz., amounts to $200,000. Probably the whole amount of native metal worked over does not exceed 1500 oz. The amount of scraps remelted by Dr. Roberts is about 1000 oz. a year.

IRIDIUM AND OSMIUM.

An alloy of these metals in fine grains of excessive hardness is found very frequently with platinum and with the gold which is refined at the mints. It is of interest from the use to which it is applied in forming the nibs of gold pens; and for this purpose the small grains are purchased by the pen-makers sometimes at the rate of $250 an ounce. From this quantity they may select from 8000 to 12,000 points of suitable size and shape for use. The alloy is known as iridosmium, and is also very generally called iridium. At some seasons it has been quite abundant in the gold presented at the New York assay office; but recently it is more rare. As it does not fuse and alloy with the gold, it appears in specks upon the bars of this metal. The method of separating it is to melt the gold with a certain portion of silver, as in the usual refining process. The alloy thus obtained being less dense than the melted gold, the particles of iridium settle in the lower portions; the upper is then ladled off, and the metals are parted. More of the impure gold is added, and the process thus goes on till a considerable amount of iridium is concentrated into the alloy of gold and silver, from which it is at last obtained by dissolving these metals. According to the statement of Dr. Thèvenet published in the *Annales des Mines* (vol. xvi., 1859), iridium is collected at the gold-washings along the sea-coast of Oregon, and is sometimes quite equal in quantity to the gold. He describes it as white, glistening, very heavy, its specific gravity being 20 to 21, very hard, and resembling sand, its angles slightly flattened and rounded by friction. It is accompanied by platinum and rhodium. After one of the storms that prevail along this coast, the miners at low tide collect the black sand and carry it to the washing and amalgamating apparatus, in which it is stirred with mercury and then treated upon the shaking tables. Though by their rude processes they probably lose ⅓ of the precious metals, they sometimes collect several ounces a day of gold to the man. Near Fort Orford, to the north of Rogue River, about 15 per cent. of iridium is found with the gold. Still further north, between Cape Blanco and Coquille, the metals collected consist of about 45 per cent. iridium and 5 per cent. platinum. Between Randolph and Cape Arago the metallic grains are very light and in extremely thin scales; they consist of 70 per cent. iridium and 6 per cent. platinum. Further north, the iridium continues almost as abundantly, but mostly in very fine particles. One piece was shown to Dr. Thèvenet as a great curiosity which was as large as a grain of rice. In sifting more than 50 lbs. of iridium, he states that he had not seen a single specimen of one quarter this size.

CHAPTER VII.

MERCURY.

THIS metal, which is extensively employed in the arts, especially in the treatment of gold and silver ores by amalgamation, in the combination of amalgams for coating mirrors, etc., in the construction of barometers and thermometers, and other philosophical instruments, in the manufacture of the paint called vermilion, for several medicinal preparations, and for a variety of other purposes, was not classed among the productions of the United States until after the acquisition of California, when mines of its principal ore were opened, which have been extensively worked, as will be described below. Mercury, which is the only fluid metal, is found both in a native state, dispersed in drops among the slates that contain the veins of its ores, and also occurs in combination with sulphur in the ore called cinnabar, a compound of one atom of mercury and one of sulphur, or of 86.2 per cent. of the former, and 13.8 per cent. of the latter. Some other natural compounds are known, which are not, however, of much importance. Cinnabar is almost the exclusive source of the metal. This is a very heavy, brilliant ore of different shades of red; s readily volatilized at a red heat, giving off umes, when exposed to the air, both mercurial and sulphurous; but in tight vessels it ublimes without decomposition, and if lime or iron be introduced with the ore into reorts, the sulphur is retained in combination vith the new element, and the mercury escapes in vapor, which may be condensed and recovered in the metallic state. On his principle the process for collecting merury is based. The ores of mercury are ound in almost all the geological formations, ut the productive mines are only in the netamorphic or lowest stratified rocks, and in he bituminous slates of the coal measures.

In order to appreciate the importance of he mines of California, it is necessary to unlerstand the extent of the demand for this netal, and the sources which have supplied it. From the time of the ancient Greeks and Ronans, mercury has been held in high estimaion, and has been furnished from the same nines, which have ever since produced the hief part of the product of the world. Pliny tates that the Greeks imported red cinnabar rom Almaden in Spain, 700 years before he Christian era, and in his own time it was rought to Rome from the same mines to he amount of 700,000 lbs. annually. In nodern times the production amounts to ,700,000 to 3,456,000 lbs. per annum, and s chiefly obtained from two veins, one bout 2 feet, and the other 14 feet thick, which, meeting in a hill about 125 feet high, pread out to a thickness of nearly 100 feet. The ores are of small percentage, yielding bout $\frac{1}{10}$ only of mercury. The greatest lepth of the workings was only about 330 ards several years ago. After the metal has een extracted from the ores, it is packed in ron bottles or flasks holding 76½ lbs. each, nd is taken to Cadiz for shipment. For many years past, the lessees from the Spanish government, in whom the title is vested, have been the Rothschilds and other bankers of Europe; but their contracts with the government have varied from time to time, thus affecting the price at which the product was held.*

The mines next in importance have been those of Idria in Carniola, belonging to the Austrian government. These, for some years previous to 1847, had produced an annual average of 358,281 lbs. of mercury, and since that time, the production has varied, sometimes reaching 600,000, and even over 1,000,000 lbs. per annum. The other mines of Europe do not probably produce 200,000 lbs. On the American continent many localities of the ores have been worked to some extent; but although the consumption is very great at the silver mines of Mexico, amounting, as estimated by Humboldt, to 16,000 quintals of 200 lbs. each, three fourths of the supply was then derived from the European mines. In 1782, mercury was even brought to South America from China, where it was formerly largely extracted in the province of Yunnan. Yet in the early years of the Spanish conquest Peru was a large producer of the metal, its most important mines being in the province of Huancavelica, where no less than 41 different localities of the ore have been known; but at present the whole product of the country is supposed not to exceed 200,000 lbs. A large portion of this product is from the Santa Barbara, or the "Great Mine," which has been worked since 1566. The mines of Chili and the numerous localities at which the ores have been found in Mexico supply no metal of consequence. Dumas estimated, not long since, the total annual production as follows:—

	lbs. avoirdupois.	
Almaden, Spain	2,700,000	to 3,456,000
Idria	648,000	" 1,080,000
Hungary and Transylvania	75,600	" 97,200
Deux Ponts	42,200	" 54,000
Palatinate	19,400	" 21,600
Huancavelica	..	324,000
California	..	2,000,000
Total		7,032,800

* In 1839 the royalty demanded by the government was $59 per quintal of 106 lbs., to which it had reached by successive advances from $51.25; and in 1843 it had advanced to $82.50 per quintal. The opening of the California mines soon caused this to be considerably reduced.

In California the existence of large quantities of cinnabar was known long before the real character of the ore was understood. It was found along a range of hills on the southern side of the valley of San José, about 60 miles south-east from San Francisco. For an unknown period the Indians had frequented the locality, coming to it from distant places, even from the Columbia river, to obtain the bright vermilion paint with which to ornament their persons. With rude implements, such as the stones they picked from the streams, they extracted the ore from the flinty slates and shales in which it was found, and in their search for it they excavated a passage into the mountain of about sixty feet in length. In 1824 the attention of the whites began to be directed to this curious ore, and some of the Mexicans sought to extract from it gold or silver. Other trials made of it in 1845 resulted in the discovery of its true character, and operations were thereupon commenced to work it by one Andres Castillero. Owing, however, to the disturbed state of the country, little was done until 1850, when a company of Mexicans and English engaged vigorously in the extraction and metallurgical treatment of the ore, and established the mine which they called the New Almaden. In 1858 a stop was put upon their further proceedings by an injunction issued by the United States court on the question of defective title. From the testimony presented in the trial, it appeared that the company in the course of eight years had produced full 20,000,000 lbs. of metal, and realized a profit of more than $1,000,000 annually. The Americans who claimed the mine directed their attention to the discovery of new localities of the ore, and succeeded in finding it upon the same range of hills within less than a mile of the old workings. Here they opened a new mine in December, 1858, which they named the Enrequita, and in June, 1860, a company was formed in New York for working it under the name of the "California Quicksilver Mining Association." The following are the returns of their operations to the latest dates: in September, 1859, the product of mercury was 14,400 lbs.; October, 28,650; November, 27,525; December, 28,425; January, 1860, 27,000; February, 16,950; March, 25,500; April, 33,700; May, 46,275; June, 48,750; July, 50,000; August, 79,866; September, 66,096. The increase of production, hereafter, will be limited rather by the capacity of the reducing apparatus than by that of the mine. Twenty-four retorts for distilling the mercury are now in operation, 6 of which have been started since August, 1860. From the report of October 11, 1860, it appears that a new vein has also been opened, in which 20 men are employed, working in solid cinnabar without having encountered the boundary walls of the lode. The total expenditure for mining, for machinery, etc., up to October 15, 1860, had amounted to $275,000, all of which has been paid out of the proceeds of the mine, leaving a considerable balance on hand. The company owns another mine also, called the Providencia, which has produced some cinnabar.

The operations at the Enrequita mine are carried on from the face of the hill, some 5 or 6 levels one above another being carried into the mountain up and down its slope. The most extensive of these is the adit level at the base, which is about 600 feet long. Shafts are sunk from this to the depth of about 50 feet; but the principal workings are in the upper levels for 300 feet over the adit. These are exceedingly irregular, owing to the unequal distribution of the ore through the argillaceous slates. It lies in beds included between the strata of these lower silurian rocks, dipping with them at a very steep angle, and winding with the contortions of the strata. The workings follow the bunches of ore as they lead up or down, and to the right or left. Shafts occasionally penetrate from one level to another, but no regular system of working appears to have been adopted. With the cinnabar is intermixed some arsenical iron and copper pyrites, and the ore and slates are both traversed by veins of carbonate of lime, some of which are retained in hand specimens of the cinnabar.

On the same range of hills, at its western extremity, the Santa Clara Mining Company, of Baltimore, has opened a mine called the Guadalupe, the product of which for the year 1860 was about 200,000 lbs.

The total production of the quicksilver mines, derived from the custom-house returns and the supposed consumption of 35,576 flasks in California, has been estimated to amount, from the commencement of 1853 to near the close of 1858, to about 177,578 flasks, or 13,318,350 lbs.

NEW ALMADEN QUICKSILVER MINE.

METALLURGIC TREATMENT.

From cinnabar not contaminated with strange metals, the method of obtaining the fluid mercury is very simple. In the early workings of the New Almaden mine, the clean ores were placed in the common "try pots," such as are used by the whalers, and a cover being tightly luted on, a fire was started under them, and the mercurial vapors escaped through a tube inserted in the lid and were condensed in cold vessels. Afterward furnaces were constructed in brick-work upon a large scale, each one provided with a chamber or oven 7 feet long, 4 feet wide, and 5 feet high, corresponding to the chamber of the reverberatory furnaces; and into this was introduced a charge of 10,000 lbs. of clean ore separated from the poorer portions after the whole had been broken up. With the ore was mixed a portion of lime to combine with and retain the sulphur. A partition of brick-work separated the oven from the fire-room, and the bricks in this partition were so laid as to leave open spaces for the flame from the burning wood to pass through. On the opposite side of the oven another partition separated this from a chamber of its own size, the only communication between them being by a square hole in one of the corners close to the roof. This chamber connected with another by an opening in the opposite corner near the floor, and this arrangement was extended through eight chambers. Between the last one and the tall wooden flues through which the smoke and vapors finally passed out into the open air was placed a long wooden box provided with a showering apparatus. As the cinnabar was volatilized by the flame playing over the charge, the vapors were carried through the condensing chambers, depositing in each a portion of mercury, and in the showering box they underwent their final condensation. From the bottom of each chamber the metal flowed in gutters to the main conduit which led to the great iron reservoir sunk in the ground. From this it was poured into flasks through brushes which intercepted the scum of oxide of mercury. The method proved very wasteful, from the leakage of the vapors through the brick-work; and it has been abandoned for an improved process, in which the pulverized ores mixed with quicklime are charged into large cast-iron retorts very similar in their form and setting to those employed at the gas-works. Three are set together in a bench of brick-work, and each one is furnished with an eduction pipe inserted in the end and leading down into water contained in a large cylindrical condenser of iron. This is placed along the front line of the furnace, so as to receive the vapors from all the retorts. The mercury, as it is condensed, falls down to the bottom, and is let out through a pipe by a contrivance that prevents the water flowing with it from the condenser. At the Enrequita mine each bench of three retorts requires a little over a cord of oak wood a day for heating. Four benches, in operation from September, 1859, employed 6 men in charging and discharging, working in 2 shifts of 3 men, besides 3 firemen, each working 8 hours. Two men besides these were employed in mixing the ores for the retorts. In June, 1860, the production of these furnaces, from 1000 cargas of ore of 300 lbs. each, was about 50,000 lbs., or about 17 per cent.

In conducting the furnaces, the workmen are seriously affected by inhaling the mercurial vapors. They are sometimes even salivated, and are often obliged to abandon the business for a time. The horses and mules also suffer from the noxious fumes, and many are lost in consequence. But no injurious effects are experienced among those employed in the mines, the cinnabar being always handled with impunity.

The view of the works presents their appearance in 1852, as sketched by J. R. Bartlett, Esq. It was first published in his "Personal Narrative" (New York, 1854).

USEFUL APPLICATIONS OF MERCURY.

The principal uses to which mercury is applied have already been named. The largest quantities are consumed in working gold and silver ores. The principle of the amalgamating process is explained in the account of the treatment of gold ores. In the arts amalgams are applied to many useful purposes, of which the most important is coating the backs of looking-glass plates with tin amalgam. Silver was originally employed instead of tin, and the process is still called "silvering." It is conducted at several establishments in the United States on the old Venetian plan, which has been in use for 300 years. The largest mirrors are prepared by Messrs. Roosevelt & Sons, in New York, from the French plates which they import. The process is a simple one, but is attended with some difficulties arising from the imperfections which will sometimes appear upon the coating, notwithstanding the particular care taken to avoid them. The health of the workmen also suffers, so that they cannot pursue the business more than a few years. The only precaution taken to protect them from the effects of the mercury is thorough ventilation. Frequent use of sulphur baths also is very beneficial. The method of silvering is as follows: tables are prepared of stone made perfectly smooth, with grooves sunk around the edges. These are set horizontally, but can be raised a little at one end by a screw. Each table is covered with tinfoil carefully spread out over a larger surface than the plate will cover, and slips of glass being laid around three of the sides, the mercury is poured on till it covers the foil to the depth of about ¼ of an inch. Its affinity for the tin, and the slips of glass, prevent its flowing off. The glass plate rendered perfectly clean is then slidden along the open side, the advancing edge being kept in the mercury, so that no air nor oxide of the metal can get between the plate and the amalgam. The plate, when in place, is secured and pressed down by weights laid upon it, and the table is raised a little to allow the excess of mercury to trickle off by the grooves and collect in a vessel placed on the floor to receive it. After remaining thus for several hours, the plate is taken off and turned over upon a frame. After several weeks the amalgam becomes hard, and the glass may then be set on edge.

Amalgams of the precious metals are used for what are called the water-gilding and water-silvering methods of gilding and silvering applied to buttons and various other metallic articles. These, being made chemically clean, are washed over with the amalgam contained in a large excess of mercury, and are then placed in a furnace and heated till the mercury is driven off by the heat, leaving a thin film of the precious metal, which may then be burnished.

Mercurial medicines, as calomel, (the chloride,) and blue mass, which is the metal reduced to fine particles by long-continued trituration, and incorporated with twice its weight of confection of roses and liquorice root, are very largely prepared, especially for the southern and western states and the West India islands. The labor of triturating the mercury for blue mass has led to the introduction of ingenious machinery for the purpose, invented by Mr. J. W. W. Gordon of Baltimore, and by Dr. E. R. Squibb of Brooklyn, and worked by the latter at his pharmaceutical laboratory by steam power.

CHAPTER VIII.

SILVER—COBALT—NICKEL—CHROME—MANGANESE—TIN.

But few other ores of much importance are found in the United States, besides those of which accounts have been given; and it remains to describe the occurrence and applications of the ores of those metals only which are comprised in the heading of this chapter.

SILVER.

The occurrence of this metal in the United States is chiefly limited to some of the lead ores; and in very few of these, as noted in the chapter upon lead, has it been found in sufficient quantity to justify the working of the mines and separation of the silver. The Washington mine in Davidson co., N. C., is still worked with moderate success for both metals; but the only promising silver mines are those of Arizona, near the Gila river in New Mexico, and the Washoe mines on the extreme western verge of the Utah territory.

In the territory of Arizona, especially in that portion of it ceded to the United States under the Gadsden treaty, are numerous mines productive in silver, some of which were worked when the territory belonged to old Spain. These are now attracting the attention of Americans, and in 1859 and 1860, companies were organized in Cincinnati, New York, and St. Louis, for exploring and working them. The principal mine is that of the Sonora Company, of Cincinnati. The locality is about 75 miles south of Tucson, and about 270 miles north of Guaymas, which is the chief port of the Gulf of California. Several mines in the vicinity were formerly worked by the Mexicans for silver, and abandoned in consequence of Indian depredations and political troubles. The Sonora Company commenced operations in 1858 upon a new discovery, and have produced a considerable amount of silver, reduced from the ores at their works, at Arivaca, 7 miles from the mines. Seventy miles north of Tucson, operations were commenced in 1860, in another locality, on the same mining range, by a company organized in New York, called the Maricopa Mining Company. Their mine affords rich argentiferous copper ores, samples of which have been brought to New York, and assayed by Prof. John Torrey, and other chemists. They proved to be vitreous copper, associated with carbonates, and yielded an average of over 50 per cent. of copper. The metal contained variable amounts of silver, worth from $40 to $80 per ton. Gold was also detected in it. The outlet for this is also by Guaymas, 420 miles distant, through a region easily traversed by wagons, and upon long-established routes. The cost of transportation, by contracts of Mexicans, is at the rate of 5¼ cents per lb., for the whole distance. In the vicinity of the mines, on the Gila river, it is proposed to reduce the ores. The region is on the Pacific slope of the range of the silver mining districts of Sonora and Durango, and its rock formations are granitic and metamorphic, traversed by dikes of trap, and containing beds of quartz.

On the Rio Mimbres, 240 miles east of Tucson, are the Santa Rita del Cobre and Mimbres mines, from which 333,000 lbs. of copper are reported as having been delivered in New York in 1860. The metal was smelted at the mines, transported through Texas to Port Lavacca, and thence to New York. Whether the ores contain silver or not, is not known. Besides the operations above named, others are in progress in Arizona, of which we have no details. The region is described in the "Personal Narrative" of J. R. Bartlett, Esq., and in the Congressional Pacific Railroad reports.

The Washoe ores are argentiferous galenas of richness varying between great extremes, some of the best sorts which have been shipped to New York, and thence to England, containing enough silver to give them a value of $2000 per ton. The mines are in the inferior range of hills along the eastern base of the Sierra Nevada, and are met with over an extensive territory in the valley of the upper portion of Carson's River and many miles beyond this to the north. Those of most importance are in the vicinity of several new towns, called Virginia City, Silver City, Carson City, etc., about 160 miles north-east from Sacramento. From that point the crest of the Sierra Nevada is reached in 100 miles, nearly due east, and the remaining 60 miles is down the valley of Carson's River. The discoveries of the silver ores were made the latter part of the year 1859, but it was known before this that gold existed in the valley, and that the value of this metal was deteriorated by the silver with which it was usually alloyed. The opening of permanent veins of silver ores produced a great excitement throughout California, and led to an extraordinary emigration to the new mining district, and rapid development during the year 1860 of its resources. The considerable number of mines already in operation, upon veins of unquestionable permanency, and the great richness of some of the ores, together with the variety of those already found, leave no room for doubting that this is a mining region of great importance, and must largely add to the metallic productions of the extreme western states.

The ores, on account of their complex character, are difficult to reduce with economy, and the ordinary methods of obtaining the lead fail, when applied to compounds like these, which contain a large proportion of silica, from which the galena cannot be mechanically separated. The German method of treating such ores, employed at Clausthal, is to reduce them in small blast furnaces, with a flux of granulated cast iron, or of iron turnings, admitting only air enough to keep up the combustion of the fuel. The lead and silver are set free by the sulphur of the ore combining with the iron, and the formation of infusible silicates of oxide of lead is prevented by guarding against the oxidation of lead, through too great access of air. The separation is, however, very imperfect in a single operation, and the rich slags obtained are roasted in order to convert the sulphuret of iron into oxide of iron, which, combining with the silicates of the scoriæ, forms very fusible compounds, which are then returned to the furnace mixed with fresh charges of ore. The silver goes with the lead, and is separated by cupellation.

COBALT.

The ores of this metal are of rather rare occurrence, and are applied to practical purposes not to furnish the metal but its oxide, which is of value for its property of giving a beautiful blue color to glass with which it is melted, and of producing other fine colors when mixed with some other substances. The ores are sought for all over the world for the supply of the British manufactories of porcelain, stained glass, etc. They are chiefly combinations of cobalt with arsenic, sulphur, and sometimes with nickel and iron. The compound known as smaltine, or arsenical cobalt, was obtained at Chatham, Conn., as far back as 1787, and the mine has been worked for cobalt at different times in the present century. The cobalt in the ore is associated with about an equal amount of nickel, and its proportion is said to have been less than two per cent. Cobaltine, which is a compound of sulphur 19.3 per cent., arsenic 45.2, and cobalt 35.5, is the most productive ore of this metal, but is not met with in this country. Varieties of pyritous cobalt have been found in Maryland in quantities too small for working; and also at Mine la Motte in Missouri, associated with a black earthy oxide of cobalt and black oxide of manganese. In other places, also, oxide of cobalt, in small quantity, is a frequent accompaniment of manganese ores. Mine la Motte has furnished a considerable amount of the cobalt oxide, but the beds in which it is found are not of permanent character, and are so far exhausted as to be no longer worked with profit. A similar ore, accompanied with nickel, appears to be very abundantly distributed among the talcose and quartzose slates in Gaston and Lincoln counties, North Carolina. It is thrown out with a variety of other ores, as galena, blende, titaniferous iron, etc.. in working the gold mines of this region; and it is mixed among the great beds of hematite, found in the same district, which are the product of the decomposition of beds of pyritous iron. In some places it is so abundant that the strata containing it are conspicuous where the roads pass over them, by the blackness of the gossan (decomposed ore) or wad. Prof. H. Wurtz, who describes these localities (see "American Journal of Science," 2d series, vol. xxvii., p. 24), is of opinion that the earthy oxide of cobalt is the gossan of the sulphuret of this metal, existing unaltered in the rocks below.

Oxide of cobalt, obtained in a crude state from the washed arsenical ores, is known as zaffre or saflor, and in this condition it is a commercial article. It is refined by separating the arsenic, iron, and other foreign substances, by precipitating them from the solution in hydrochloric acid; and the oxide is finally obtained by precipitating with chloride of lime, and heating the product to redness. Smalt is a preparation of cobalt largely used in the arts as a coloring material, and consists of silicate of potash and cobalt. It is in fact a potash glass colored by silicate of cobalt, and is prepared as follows: Zaffre is melted in pots, with suitable proportions of pure sand and potash and a little saltpetre. The other metals combine together and sink in a metallic mass, which is called speiss. The glass containing the oxide of cobalt is ladled out and poured into water to granulate it, and is then ground to powder. This being introduced into vats of water, the colored glass subsides in deposits, which gradually diminish in their proportions of oxide of cobalt. The first are of the deepest blue, and are called azure; but of this, and of the succeeding fainter shades, there are many varieties, distinguished by peculiar names. When finely powdered, smalt is applied to coloring wall papers, and blueing linen, besides being incorporated with porcelain to impart to it permanent blue shades. The great value of oxide of cobalt, amounting to several dollars per lb., renders it an important object to fully develop the resources of the country in its ores, as well for export as for domestic use. In 1856 there were imported into Great Britain 428 tons of cobalt ore, and 34 tons of oxide of cobalt.

NICKEL.

Nickel is a metal of some commercial importance, and is employed chiefly for producing, with copper and zinc, the alloy known as German silver. The proportions of these metals are not constant, but the most common in use are eight parts of copper to three each of nickel and zinc. The larger the proportion of copper, the more easily the plates are rolled; but if more is used than the relative amounts named, the copper soon becomes apparent in use. The new cent contains 12 parts of nickel to 88 of copper, and the manufacture of this adds somewhat to the demand. The metal has been mined at Chatham, Conn., and is met with at Mine la Motte and other localities where cobalt is found. It occurs in greatest abundance at an old mine in Lancaster county, Penn., where it is associated with copper ores. The mine was originally worked for copper, it is said, more than one hundred and thirty years ago, and was reopened for supplying nickel for the U. S. Mint, on the introduction of the new cent in 1857. The sulphuret of nickel, containing, when pure, 64.9 per cent. of nickel, and 35.1 per cent. of sulphur, is in very large quantity, in two veins of great size, one of which has been traced over 600 feet, and the other over 900 feet in length. In 1859 it was producing at the rate of 200 tons of nickel ore and ten tons of copper ore per month. A pyritous variety of nickel ore, called siegenite, is found at Mine la Motte, Missouri, and in Carroll county, Maryland. In Gaston and Lincoln counties, North Carolina, similar ore was found by Prof. Wurtz, as noticed in the remarks on cobalt, above.

CHROME OR CHROMIUM.

The ore of this metal, known as chromic iron or chromate of iron, has been mined for many years in the United States, both for exportation and domestic use. It is the source whence the chrome colors are obtained that are largely used in the arts, especially in dyeing and calico printing. The name of the metal, from a Greek word meaning color, was given in consequence of the fine colors of its compounds. It usually consists of the sesquioxide of chromium in proportion varying from 36 to 60 per cent., protoxide of iron from 20 to 37 per cent., alumina sometimes exceeding 20 per cent., and more or less silica, and sometimes magnesia. Its value consists only in the first-named ingredient. The localities of the ore are in the serpentine rocks of different parts of the United States, as in the Bare Hills, near Baltimore, and near the Maryland state line on the southern edge of Chester and Lancaster counties, Pennsylvania. In small quantities the ore is met with at Hoboken, Staten Island, and other places near New York city. It is found in several towns in Vermont, but the largest veins of it are in Jay, in the northern part of the state. The composition of this ore was found by Mr. T. S. Hunt to be 49.9 of green oxide or sesquioxide of chromium, 48.96 of protoxide of iron, and 4.14 per cent. of alumina, silica, and magnesia. Though the quantity of the ore in this region is reported to be large, the principal supplies of the country have been obtained in Maryland, and from the mines just over the state line in Pennsylvania. The ore, as recently as 1854, was found in loose fragments among the disintegrated materials of the serpentine upon the tracts called the barrens, and was gathered up from the valleys and ravines, and dug out in sinking shallow pits and trenches over the surface. The ore thus obtained was called "sand chrome," and for a time it had been worth $45 per ton, and thousands of tons had been collected and shipped, principally to Baltimore. At the period named these superficial deposits were mostly exhausted, and the value of the ore was only about $25 per ton. This, however, was sufficient to sustain regular mining operations, which were then carried on upon the veins found in the serpentine, a little west of the east branch of the Octorara Creek. Wood's chrome mine, near the Horse-shoe Ford, was at that time about 150 feet deep, and the workings had been extended north-east and south-west about 300 feet, upon an irregular vein of chrome ore, which lay at an inclination of about 45° with the horizon toward the north-west. The ore, in places, formed bunches, which attained a width of 20 feet, and then thinned away to nothing. Four men obtained from the mine 7 or 8 tons of excellent ore a day, the best of which was directly placed in barrels for the foreign market, and the poorer was dressed and washed for the Baltimore, and other home markets. The state line mine, in the same vicinity, worked to about the same depth, had produced several thousand tons. The supplies of this ore are always of uncertain continuance.

Useful Applications. — Chromate of iron is used chiefly in the production of chromate of potash, and from this the other useful chromatic salts are obtained. The object in view in the chemical treatment of the ore is to convert the sesquioxide of chromium into the peroxide or chromic acid, and cause this to combine with potash. This may be effected by various methods, as by exposing a mixture of the pulverized ore and of saltpetre (nitrate of potash) to a strong heat for some hours. The chrome is peroxidized at the expense of the oxygen of the nitric acid of the saltpetre, and the chromic acid combines with the potash; or if the ore is mixed with carbonate of potash and calcined, the peroxidation of the chrome is effected by admission of air into the furnace, and the same product is obtained as in the employment of saltpetre. The introduction of lime hastens the operation. Other mixtures also are used for the same purpose. When the calcined matter, having been drawn out from the furnace, is lixiviated with water, the chromate of potash is dissolved and washed out, and is afterward recovered in the form of yellow crystals on evaporating the water. From chromate of potash the other salts are readily produced. Chrome yellow, used as a paint, is prepared by mixing chromate of potash with a soluble salt of lead, and collecting the yellow precipitate of chromate of lead which falls. A bright red precipitate is obtained by thus employing a salt of mercury, and a deep red with salts of silver. Chrome green is produced by mixing Prussian blue with chrome yellow. Some new and very interesting compounds of the sesquioxide of chromium with different bases have been recently obtained by Prof. A. K. Eaton of New York, and in consequence of their decided colors and the extraordinary permanency of these against powerful reagents applied to remove them, the salts were employed for printing bank-notes. Though they proved to be all that was required as to the colors themselves, the steel plates were so rapidly cut by the excessively sharp and hard powders, however finely they were ground, that it was found necessary to abandon their use. The new salts were chromites—that of iron having a dark purple color; of manganese, a lighter shade of the same; of copper, a rich blueish black; of zinc, a golden brown; of alumina, a green, somewhat paler than that of the sesquioxide.

MANGANESE.

Though this is a metal of no value of itself, one of its ores, called pyrolusite, is a mineral of some commercial importance, chiefly on account of the large proportion of oxygen it contains, part of which it can be easily made to give up when simply heated in an iron retort. The composition of pyrolusite, or black oxide of manganese, is 63.4 per cent. of manganese, and 36.6 per cent. of oxygen. It is a hard, steel-gray ore, resembling some of the magnetic iron ores, and is often found accompanying iron ores, especially the hematites. In the United States it is met with in various localities along the range of the hematites, from Canada to Alabama, and has been mined to considerable extent at Chittenden and Bennington, Vermont; West Stockbridge and Sheffield, Mass.; on the Delaware river, and near Kutztown, Berks co., Penn.; and abounds in different parts of the gold region, as on Hard-labor Creek, Edgefield District, S. C. Usually the ore is found in loose pieces among the clays which fill the irregular cavities between the limestone strata; its quantity is of course very uncertain, and its mines are far from being of a permanent character. Oxide of iron is commonly mixed with the manganese ore, reducing its richness, and at the same time seriously injuring it for some of the purposes to which it is applied. As obtained from the mines, the assorted ore is packed in barrels and sent to the chemical establishments, where it is employed principally in the manufacture of chloride of lime or bleaching powder. For this purpose the pulverized black oxide of manganese is introduced into hydrochloric acid, and this being heated a double decomposition takes place, a portion of its chlorine is expelled, and the hydrogen that was combined with it unites with a part of the oxygen of the pyrolusite. The chlorine, which it was the object of the process to obtain, is then brought in contact with hydrate of lime, and uniting with the calcium base, forms the bleaching powder. A similar result is obtained by mixing the oxide of manganese with chloride of sodium (common salt), and adding sulphuric acid. By these operations a weight of oxygen equal to about one third that of the pure ore may be obtained, and this may be applied to any of the purposes for which oxygen not absolutely pure is required. Black oxide of manganese is also used to decolorize glass stained green by the presence of the protoxide of iron. Its own amethystine tint is supposed to neutralize the optical effect of the greenish hue of the iron. The market for manganese ore is as uncertain as the supply, and the price varies greatly with the quality of the ore. Pure pyrolusite, free from iron, might be shipped to profit to Liverpool, where it is worth $35 to $40 per ton, but inferior ore would involve bills of cost.

TIN.

The very useful metal, tin, is not one of the products of this country, and there is no encouragement for hoping that its ores will ever be found in workable quantity. Its presence has been recognized in a few small crystals of oxide of tin, found in Chesterfield and Goshen, Mass., and it has been detected as a mere trace in the iron ores of the Hudson, and iron and zinc ores of New Jersey; it is also associated with some of the gold ores of Virginia. In the town of Jackson, N. H., is a vein of arsenical iron, containing thin streaks of oxide of tin; and this is the only place that has afforded enough of the ore for crucible experiments. The commercial supplies are furnished chiefly from the mines of Cornwall, England, and from Banca, and other islands of the Malay archipelago. The United States is one of the largest consumers of tin of any nation, sheet tin having been applied, through the industry and ingenuity of the workers of this article in Connecticut, to the manufacture of a great variety of useful utensils, which have been widely distributed throughout the states. What is called sheet tin is really sheet iron coated with a very thin layer of tin. The sheets are prepared in England by dipping the brightened iron sheets into a bath of melted tin. The process has been applied to coating various articles made of iron, which are thus protected from rusting; and zinc is also used for similar purposes. Such are stirrups, bridle-bits, etc. Cast-iron pots and saucepans are tinned on the inside by melted tin being poured in and made to flow over the surface, which has been made chemically clean to receive the metal. The surface is then rubbed with cloth or tow. Tin is imported in blocks or ingots, and the metal is applied to the preparation of various alloys, as bronze or bell-metal, composed of copper and tin in variable proportions, commonly of 78 parts of copper, and 22 of tin; gun-metal, copper 90, and tin 10; pewter, of various proportions of tin and lead, or when designed for pewter plates, of tin 100, antimony 8, bismuth 2, and copper 2; and soft solder, consisting of tin and lead, usually of two parts of the former to one of the latter. Bismuth is sometimes added to increase the fusibility of the alloy.

CHAPTER IX.

COAL.

To the early settlers of the American colonies the beds of mineral coal they met with were of no interest. In the abundance of the forests around them, and with no manufacturing operations that involved large consumption of fuel, they attached no value to the black stony coal, the real importance of which was not in fact appreciated even in Europe until after the invention of the steam engine. The earliest use of mineral coal was probably of the anthracite of the Lehigh region, though it may be that the James River bituminous coal mines, 12 miles above Richmond, were worked at an earlier period than the Pennsylvania anthracites. The region containing the latter belonged to the tribes of the Six Nations, until their title was extinguished and the proprietary government obtained possession, in 1749, of a territory of 3750 square miles, including the southern and middle of the three anthracite coal-fields. In 1768 possession was acquired of the northern coal-field, and at the same time of the great bituminous region west of the Alleghany mountains. The existence of coal in the anthracite region could not have escaped the notice of the whites who had explored the country, for its great beds were exposed in many of the natural sections of the river banks and precipitous hills, and down the mountain streams pieces of coal, washed out from the beds, were abundantly scattered. The oldest maps now known, dating as far back as 1770, and compiled from still older ones, designate in this region localities of "coal;" but these were probably not regarded as giving any additional value to the territory. The first recorded notice of its use was in the northern basin by some blacksmiths in 1770, only two years after the whites came in possession; and in 1775 a boat load of it was sent down from Wilkesbarre to the Continental armory at Carlisle. This was two years after the laying out of the borough of Wilkesbarre by the Susquehanna Land Company of Connecticut. From this time the coal continued to be used for mechanical operations by smiths, distillers, etc.; and according to numerous certificates from these, published in 1815, in a pamphlet by Mr. Zachariah Cist of Wilkesbarre, they had found it very much better for their purposes, and more economical to use than Virginia bituminous coal, though at the enormous price of 90 cents a bushel. Gunsmiths found it very convenient for their small fires, and one of them, dating his certificate December 9, 1814, stated that he had used it for 20 years, consuming about a peck a day to a fire, which was sufficient for manufacturing 8 musket-barrels, each barrel thus requiring a quart of coal. Oliver Evans, the inventor of the steam engine, certifies in the same pamphlet to his having used it for raising steam, for which it possessed properties superior to those of any other fuel. Judge Fell of Wilkesbarre applied it to warming houses in 1808, and contrived suitable grates for this use of it; but the cheapness of wood and the greater convenience of a fuel which every one understood how to use, long prevented its general adoption. In the first volume of the "Memoirs of the Historical Society of Pennsylvania," T. C. James, M.D., gives "a brief account of the discovery of anthracite coal on the Lehigh," in which he describes a visit he made to the Mauch Chunk mountain in 1804, where he saw the immense body of anthracite, into which several small pits had then been sunk, and which was afterward worked, as it is still, as an open quarry. He states that he commenced to burn the coal that year, and had continued to use it to the time of making this communication in 1826. The discovery of this famous mass of coal was made in 1791, and in 1793 the "Lehigh Coal Mine Company" was formed to work it. But as there were no facilities for transporting the coal down the valley of the Lehigh, nothing was done until 1814, when, at great labor and expense, 20 tons were got down the river and were delivered in Philadelphia. Two years before this a few wagon loads had been received there from the Schuylkill mines; but the regular trade can hardly be said to have commenced until 1820, when the receipts in Philadelphia amounted to 365 tons. Such was the commencement of the great anthracite trade of Pennsylvania, which in the course of 40 years has been steadily increasing, till it now reaches the enormous amount of 8,450,053 tons for the year 1860, and sustains numerous branches of metallurgical and mechanical industry, the possible dependence of which upon this fuel and source of power was hardly dreamed of when its mines were first opened.

The existence of bituminous coal west of the Alleghanies was probably known as early as was that of anthracite in the eastern part of Pennsylvania; and on the western rivers it could not fail to have been noticed by the early missionaries, voyageurs, and hunters. In the old maps of 1770 and 1777 the occurrence of coal is noted at several points on the Ohio. A tract of coal land was taken up in 1785 near the present town of Clearfield, on the head-waters of the west branch of the Susquehanna, by Mr. S. Boyd, and in 1804 he sent an ark load of the coal down the Susquehanna to Columbia, Lancaster county, which, he states, caused much surprise to the inhabitants, that "an article with which they were wholly unacquainted should be thus brought to their own doors." This was the commencement of a trade which has since been prosecuted to some extent by running rafts of timber loaded with coal, and sometimes with pig iron also, from the head-waters to the lower portion of the Susquehanna. The bituminous coal mines on the James River, 12 miles above Richmond, in Virginia, were also worked during the last century, but at how early a period we are ignorant. In an account of them in the first volume of the "American Journal of Science," published in 1818, they are spoken of as already having been worked 30 years.

VARIETIES OF COAL.

The mineral coals are found of various sorts, which are distinguished by peculiarities of appearance, composition, and properties. Derived from vegetable matters, they exhibit in their varieties the successive changes which these have undergone from the condition of peaty beds or deposits of ligneous materials—first into the variety known as brown coal or lignite, in which the bituminous property appears, while the fibre and structure of the original woody masses is fully retained; next in beds of bituminous coal comprised between strata of shales, fire-clay, and sandstones; and thence through several gradations of diminishing proportions of bitumen to the hard stony anthracite, the composition of which is nearly pure carbon; and last of all in this series of steps attending the conversion of wood into rock, the vegetable carbon is locked up in the mineral graphite or plumbago. These steps are clearly traceable in nature, and in all of them the strata which include the carbonaceous beds have undergone corresponding changes. The clayey substratum that supports the peat appears under the beds of mineral coal in the stony material called fire-clay (used when ground to make fire-brick); the muddy sediments such as are found over some of the great modern peat deposits, appear in the form of black shales or slates, which when pulverized return to their muddy consistency; the beds of sand, such as are met with in some of the peat districts of Europe interstratified with different peat beds, are seen in the coal-measures in beds of sandstones; and the limestones which also occur in the same group of strata, represent ancient beds of calcareous marls. The slow progression of these changes is indicated by the different ages of the geological formations in which the several varieties occur. Beds of peat are of recent formation, though some of them are still so old, that they are found at different depths, one below another, separated by intervening layers of sand, clay, and earth. Brown coal, or lignite, is commonly included among the strata of the tertiary period; the bituminous coals are in the secondary formations; and the anthracites, though contained in the same geological group with the great bituminous coal formation, are in localities where the strata have all been subjected to the action of powerful agents which have more or less metamorphosed them and expelled the volatile bitumen from the coal. The graphite or plumbago is in still older groups, or in those which have been still more metamorphosed by heat.

All these varieties of fossil fuel are found in the United States. Peat beds of small extent are common in the northern portion of the country, and in some parts of New England are much used for fuel, and the muck, or decomposed peat, as a fertilizer to the soil. In the great swamps of southern Virginia, the Carolinas, and Georgia, vegetable deposits of similar nature are found upon a scale more commensurate with the extent of the ancient coal-beds. Lignite is not found in workable beds, as in some parts of Germany and England, but in scattered deposits of small extent among the tertiary clays, chiefly near the coast of New Jersey, Delaware, and Maryland, and in the western territories. The distribution of the true coal formations will be pointed out after designating more particularly the characters of the different coals. All of these consist of the elements carbon, hydrogen, oxygen, and nitrogen; the carbon being in part free, and in part combined with the other elements to form the volatile compounds that exist to some extent in all coals. Earthy matters which form the ash of coals are always intermixed in some proportion with the combustible ingredients, and water, also, is present. When coals are analyzed for the purpose of indicating their heating quality by their composition, it is enough to determine the proportions of fixed carbon, of volatile matter, and of ash which they contain. How the combined carbon, hydrogen, oxygen, and the little nitrogen in their composition, may be distributed in the forms of carburetted hydrogen, ammonia, the bituminous oils, etc., cannot be ascertained by analysis, as the means employed to separate most of these compounds cause their elements to form other combinations among themselves: the determination of the ultimate proportions of all the elements would serve no practical purpose. So, if it be required to prove the fitness of any coal for affording illuminating gas, or the coal oils, it must be submitted to experiments having such objects only in view; and even their capacity for generating heat is better determined by comparative experiments in evaporating water, than by any other mode. The bituminous coals are characterized by their large proportion of volatile matter, which, when they are heated, is expelled in various inflammable compounds, that take fire and burn, accompanied by a dense, black smoke and a peculiar odor known as bituminous. If the operation is conducted without access of air, as in a closed platinum crucible, the fixed carbon remains behind in the form of coke; and by removing the cover to admit air, this may next be consumed, and the residuum of ash be obtained. By several weighings the proportions are indicated. Coals containing 18 per cent. or more of volatile matter are classed among the bituminous varieties; but as the proportion of this may amount to 70 per cent. or more, there is necessarily a considerable difference in the characters of these coals, though their most marked peculiarities are not always owing to the different amounts of volatile matter they contain. Thus, some sorts, called the "fat bituminous," and "caking coals," that melt and run together in burning, and are especially suitable for making coke, contain about the same proportion of volatile matter with the "dry coals," as some of the cannel and other varieties, which burn without melting, and do not make good coke. Other varieties are especially distinguished for their large proportion of volatile ingredients; such are the best cannels, and those light coals which have sometimes been mistaken for asphaltum, as the Albert coal of the province of New Brunswick. These varieties are eminently qualified for producing gas or the coal oils; but have little fixed carbon, and consequently can produce little coke. Coals that contain from 11 to 18 per cent. volatile matter, are known as semi-bituminous, and partake both of the qualities of the true bituminous coals, in igniting and burning freely, and of the anthracite in the condensed and long-continued heat they produce. The Maryland coals, and the Lykens valley coal of Pennsylvania, are of this character. The true anthracites contain from 2 to 6 per cent. of gaseous matters, which by heat are evolved in carburetted hydrogen and water, even when the coal has been first freed from the water mechanically held. Their greatest proportion of solid carbon is about 95 per cent. There remains a class which has been designated as semi-anthracite, containing from 6 to 11 per cent. of combustible volatile matter. These coals burn with a yellowish flame, until the gas derived from the combination of its elements is consumed.

The earthy ingredients in coals, forming their ash, are derived from the original wood and from foreign substances introduced among the collections of ligneous matters that make up the coal-beds. The ash is unimportant, excepting as the material which produces it takes the place of so much combustible matter. In some coals, especially those of the Schuylkill region, it is red, from the presence of oxide of iron, and in others it is gray, as in the Lehigh coals. This distinction is used to designate some of the varieties of anthracite; but the quality of these coals is more dependent on the quantity of the ash, than on its color. From numerous analyses of the Schuylkill red ash coals an average of 7.29 per cent. of ash was obtained, and of the white ash anthracite, 4.62 per cent. Coals producing red ash are more likely to clinker in burning than those containing an equal amount of white ash. In some varieties of coal the proportion of earthy matter is so great that the substance approaches the character of the bituminous shales, and may be called indifferently either shale or coal. Though such materials make but poor fuel, some of them have proved very valuable from the large amount of gas and of oily matters they afford. The most remarkable of this class is that known as the Boghead cannel. This is largely mined near Glasgow, in Scotland, and is imported into New York to be used in the manufacture of coal oil. It is a dull black, stony-looking substance, having little resemblance to the ordinary kinds of coal. Its composition is given for comparison with that of other coals, in the following table:—

		Localities.	Authority.	Specific Gravity.	Carbon.	Water and other Vol. Mat.	Ashes.
ANTHRACITE.	RED ASH.	Shenowith Vein, Penn	H. D. Rogers	1.50	94.10	1.40	4.50
		Peach Mountain, Penn.; mean of 40 analyses	W. R. Johnson	1.46	86.09	6.96	6.95
	WHITE ASH.	Lackawanna	W. R. Johnson	1.42	88.98	6.36	4.66
		Beaver Meadow	"	1.56	91.64	6.89	1.47
		Price's Mountain, Montgomery Co., Virginia	A. H. Everett	1.37	89.25	2.44	8.30
		Portsmouth, Rhode Island	Dr. C. T. Jackson	1.85	85.84	10.50	3.66
		Mansfield, Mass	"	1.69	87.40	6.20	6.40
SEMI-BITUMINOUS.		Atkinson's and Templeman's, Maryland; average of 2 specimens	W. R. Johnson	1.313	76.69	15.53	7.83
		George's Creek, Maryland	"	1.35	70.75	16.03	13.22
BITUMINOUS.		Pittsburg, Pennsylvania	B. Silliman, jr.	..	64.72	32.95	2.31
		Cannelton, Indiana	W. R. Johnson	1.272	59.47	36.59	3.94
		Black Heath, James River, Virginia	"	..	58.79	32.57	8.64
		Monroe Co., S. Illinois	J. G. Norwood	1.246	58.70	36.20	4.50
		La Salle Co., N. Illinois	"	1.287	55.10	39.90	3.00
		Albert Coal, New Brunswick	B. Silliman, jr.	1.129	36.04	61.74	2.22
		Grayson (Ky.) cannel	"	1.371	14.36	62.03	23.62
		Breckenridge (Ky.) cannel	"	1.150	27.16	64.30	8.48
		Boghead, black cannel	Dr. Penny	1.218	9.25	62.70	26.50
		Boghead, brown	"	1.160	7.10	71.06	26.20

A complete description of the coals, such as may be found in the Report of Prof. Walter R. Johnson (Senate Document, 28th Congress, No. 386), and presented, in a condensed form, in Johnson's Edition of "Knapp's Chemical Technology," presents many other features affecting the qualities of the coals, and their adaptation to special uses. Such are—1, their capacity for raising steam quickly; 2, for raising it abundantly for the quantity used; 3, freedom from dense smoke in their combustion; 4, freedom from tendency to crumble in handling; 5, capacity, by reason of their density, and the shapes assumed by their fragments, of close stowage; and 6, freedom from sulphur. The last is an important consideration, affecting the value of coals proposed for use in the iron manufacture, sulphur, which is often present in coal in the form of sulphuret of iron, having a very injurious effect upon the iron with which it is brought in contact when heated. It is again to be cautiously guarded against in selecting bituminous coals to be employed in steam navigation; for by the heat generated by spontaneous decomposition of the iron pyrites, the easily ignited bituminous coals may be readily set on fire. This phenomenon is of frequent occurrence in the waste heaps about coal mines, and large bodies of coal stored in yards and on board ships have been thus inflamed, involving the most disastrous consequences. In stowage capacity coals differ greatly, and this should be attended to in selecting them for use in long voyages. Tendency to crumble involves waste. Dense smoke in consuming is objectionable in coals required for vessels-of-war in actual service, as it must expose their position when it may be important to conceal it. The following table was prepared by Prof. Johnson to present some of the general results in these particulars of his experiments:—

GENERAL SCALE OF RELATIVE VALUES FORMED FROM THE AVERAGES OF EACH CLASS OF COAL SUBJECTED TO TRIAL.

	1.	2.	3.	4.	5.
Maryland free-burning coals	1000	1000	395	880	682
Pennsylvania anthracite	977	986	1000	893	319
Pennsylvania bituminous	951	938	390	1000	914
Virginia (James River) bituminous	850	757	242	948	730
Foreign bituminous	801	741	331	948	1000

Column 1 gives the relative evaporative powers of equal weights of the coals; 2, the same of equal bulks; 3, their relative freedom from tendency to clinker; 4, rapidity of action in evaporating water; 5, facility of ignition, or readiness with which steam is gotten up. The general results of experience in use, as well as of special trials systematically conducted upon a large scale, agree in these particulars—that while the bituminous coals are valuable for the greater variety of uses to which they are applicable, and especially for all purposes requiring flame and a diffusive heat, as under large boilers; and while they are quickly brought into a state of combustion, rendering the heat they produce more readily available; the anthracites afford a more condensed and lasting heat, and are to be preferred in many metallurgical operations, especially where great intensity of temperature is required. And for many purposes, the free-burning, semi-bituminous coals, which combine the useful properties of both varieties, are found most economical in use.

GEOLOGICAL AND GEOGRAPHICAL DISTRIBUTION.

The United States is supplied with coal from a number of coal-fields belonging to what are called the true coal-measures, or the carboniferous group, a series of strata sometimes amounting, in aggregate thickness, to 2000 and even 3000 feet, and whether found in this country or in Europe, readily recognized by the resemblance in the various members of its formation, its fossil organic remains, its mineral accompaniments, and by its position relative to the other groups of rock which overlie and underlie it. The principal one of these fields or basins is that known as the Appalachian, which, commencing in the north-eastern part of Pennsylvania, stretches over nearly all the state west of the main Alleghany ridge, and takes in the eastern portion of Ohio, parts of Maryland, Virginia, Kentucky, Tennessee, the north-west corner of Georgia, and extends into Alabama as far as Tuscaloosa. Its total area, including a number of neighboring basins, as those of the anthracite region to the east of the Alleghany ridge, which were originally a part of the same great field, is estimated at about 70,000 square miles. A second great basin is that which includes the larger part of Illinois, and the western portion of Indiana and of Kentucky. Its area is estimated at about 50,000 square miles; but its coal-beds are few and thin compared with those of the great Appalachian coal-field. The same may be said of the third coal-field, on the other side of the Mississippi. This extends over a large part of Iowa and of Missouri, and to the Red River in the western part of Arkansas. The Kansas coal-beds are contained in this field, which along its western borders is more or less broken up at the surface by patches of rock of later formation, as the cretaceous and middle secondary. Beneath these groups, the coal-bearing strata disappear toward the great plains. The

Copied by permission

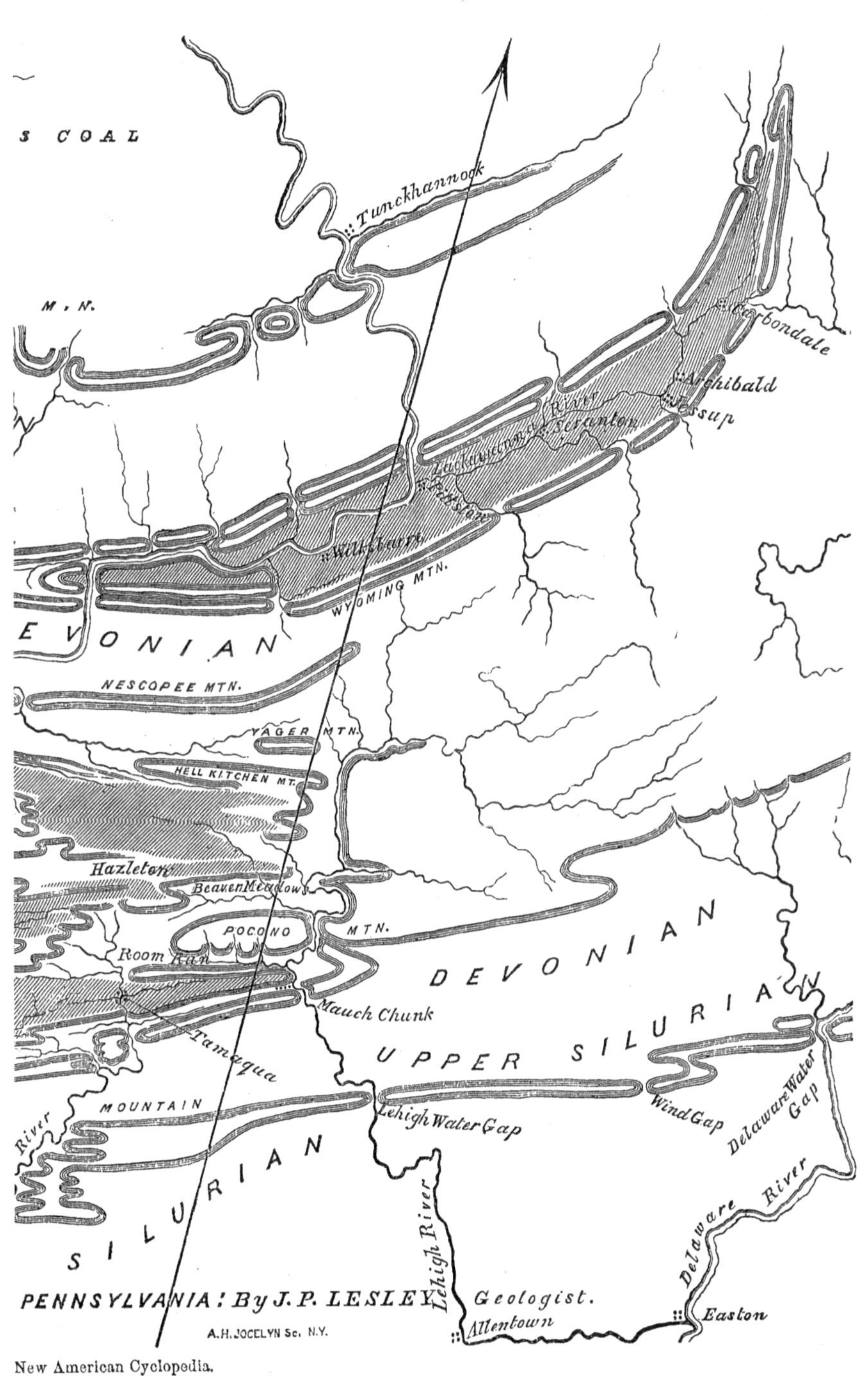

New American Cyclopedia.

whole area of this field has been computed at 57,000 square miles; but its limits have never been accurately defined. A fourth coal-field occupies the central portion of the southern peninsula of Michigan, its area being about 13,350 square miles. Several small beds of bituminous coal are worked in this district, but they have only local importance. A fifth coal-field is that of Rhode Island and south-eastern Massachusetts. The strata of this district are considered as belonging to the true coal-measures, although, from the metamorphic action to which they have been subjected, their true character is very obscure. They contain a few beds of anthracite, very irregular in their dimensions, and much crushed. A number of mines have been opened, but the only one now worked is at Portsmouth, 8 miles north of Newport. In south-eastern Virginia is a bituminous coal-field, lying on both sides of the James River, a few miles above Richmond. The strata which contain the coal-beds of this district are recognized as members of later formation than those of the true coal-measures, being classed with the geological group known as the oolite, or lias; and the coal-beds of central North Carolina, on Deep River, probably belong to the same position in the geological column. Notwithstanding the limited area of this coal-field in Virginia, which is only about 25 miles long and 8 to 10 miles wide, it has produced for more than sixty years past large quantities of coal chiefly for the supply of iron manufacturing establishments, and the gas-works along the seaboard to the north. The strata of these coal-measures occupy a deep depression in the granitic rocks of this region, attaining in the centre of the basin a thickness of nearly 2000 feet. They consist in great part of a micaceous sandstone, and the two or three coal-beds are contained in the lower 150 feet. A great bed at the bottom, which in some places exceeds 40 feet in thickness, and in others dwindles away to 4 or 5 feet only, appears to have been deposited upon the uneven granitic floor, from which it is separated by only a few inches of slate. Shafts have been sunk near the east border of the coal-field to the depth of nearly 900 feet. The amount of coal obtained of late years does not probably exceed 130,000 tons per annum. A singular phenomenon is observed at one point in this district, where a coal-bed is penetrated and overlaid by a body of trap-rock. The coal near this rock is converted into a mass of coke, resembling that artificially produced, except that it is more compact and of a duller lustre.

A large amount of bituminous coal has been brought to Boston and New York, for many years past, from a coal-field belonging to the true coal-measures, in Nova Scotia and Cape Breton. The same formation extends into New Brunswick, and ranges along the western part of Newfoundland, and has been estimated as comprising in all an area of 9000 square miles. The productive portions, however, are limited to a few localities upon the coast of Nova Scotia and Cape Breton, and at these, beds of great thickness have been opened, and worked to the depth of from 200 to 450 feet. At the Pictou mines, opposite the southern point of Prince Edward's Island, one bed is 29 feet thick. Another bed, at the Albion mines, 8½ miles from Pictou, affords 24 feet of good coal, and 12 more of inferior quality; and in Sydney, Cape Breton, are beds of 11 feet, 9 feet, and 6 feet, besides at least 11 others of less thickness. At the South Joggins cliffs, in Nova Scotia, the total thickness of all the strata of the coal-measures was found by Mr. Logan to amount to 14,571 feet, very much exceeding the thickness of the formation as observed in other places on the American continent.

The strata which make up the coal formation, the principal varieties of which have already been named, are regularly laid one upon another in no particular order, and amount in aggregate thickness to several thousand feet, rarely exceeding in the United States 3000 feet. Their thickness is ascertained by sections measured at different localities, some giving one part of the column, and others other portions. In western Pennsylvania the nearly horizontal beds of rock are often exposed in the sides of the precipitous hills, so that sections of several hundred feet may be fully made up. Any peculiar member of the pile, as a bed of limestone, occurring near the top of the section, may be recognized in other localities, where by the dip of the strata it is brought to the lower levels, and the hills above it then present the succession of the higher members of the column; or if the layer taken as the starting point be in the one case at the base, it will be found in the direction of the rising of the strata, at higher and higher elevations, and the lower mem-

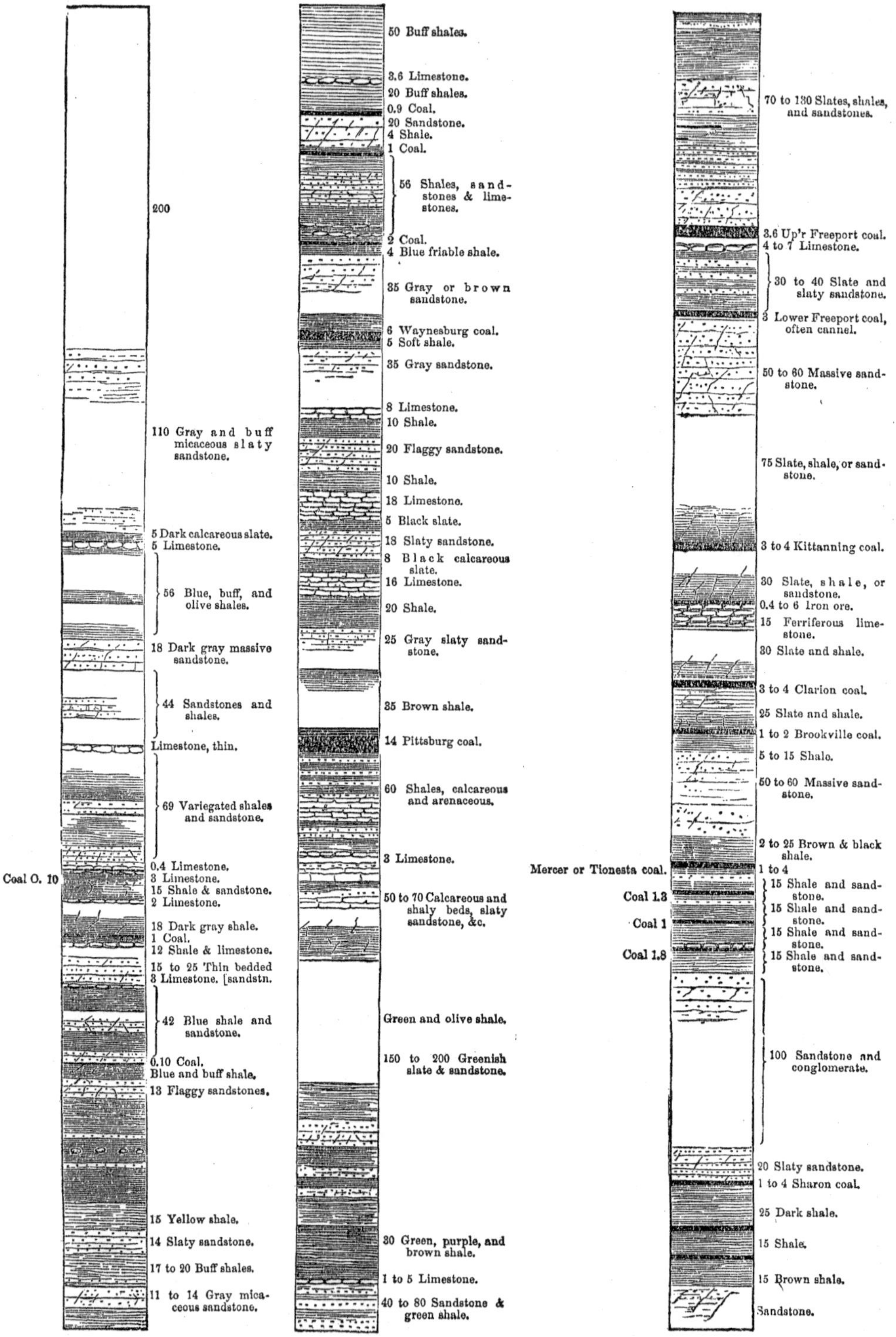

200

110 Gray and buff micaceous slaty sandstone.

5 Dark calcareous slate.
5 Limestone.

56 Blue, buff, and olive shales.

18 Dark gray massive sandstone.

44 Sandstones and shales.

Limestone, thin.

69 Variegated shales and sandstone.

0.4 Limestone.
Coal O. 10 3 Limestone.
15 Shale & sandstone.
2 Limestone.
18 Dark gray shale.
1 Coal.
12 Shale & limestone.
15 to 25 Thin bedded sandstn.
3 Limestone.

42 Blue shale and sandstone.

0.10 Coal.
Blue and buff shale.
13 Flaggy sandstones.

15 Yellow shale.
14 Slaty sandstone.
17 to 20 Buff shales.
11 to 14 Gray micaceous sandstone.

50 Buff shales.

3.6 Limestone.
20 Buff shales.
0.9 Coal.
20 Sandstone.
4 Shale.
1 Coal.

56 Shales, sandstones & limestones.

2 Coal.
4 Blue friable shale.

35 Gray or brown sandstone.

6 Waynesburg coal.
5 Soft shale.
35 Gray sandstone.

8 Limestone.
10 Shale.
20 Flaggy sandstone.
10 Shale.
18 Limestone.
5 Black slate.
18 Slaty sandstone.
8 Black calcareous slate.
16 Limestone.
20 Shale.
25 Gray slaty sandstone.

35 Brown shale.

14 Pittsburg coal.

60 Shales, calcareous and arenaceous.

3 Limestone.

50 to 70 Calcareous and shaly beds, slaty sandstone, &c.

Green and olive shale.

150 to 200 Greenish slate & sandstone.

30 Green, purple, and brown shale.
1 to 5 Limestone.
40 to 80 Sandstone & green shale.

70 to 130 Slates, shales, and sandstones.

3.6 Up'r Freeport coal.
4 to 7 Limestone.

30 to 40 Slate and slaty sandstone.

3 Lower Freeport coal, often cannel.

50 to 60 Massive sandstone.

75 Slate, shale, or sandstone.

3 to 4 Kittanning coal.

30 Slate, shale, or sandstone.
0.4 to 6 Iron ore.
15 Ferriferous limestone.
30 Slate and shale.

3 to 4 Clarion coal.
25 Slate and shale.
1 to 2 Brookville coal.
5 to 15 Shale.
50 to 60 Massive sandstone.

2 to 25 Brown & black shale.
Mercer or Tionesta coal. 1 to 4
15 Shale and sandstone.
Coal 1.3
15 Shale and sandstone.
Coal 1
15 Shale and sandstone.
Coal 1.8
15 Shale and sandstone.

100 Sandstone and conglomerate.

20 Slaty sandstone.
1 to 4 Sharon coal.
25 Dark shale.
15 Shale.
15 Brown shale.
Sandstone.

ərs of the column will then be brought ıto view at the base of the hills. Thus, at ittsburg, the hills opposite the city afford section of 300 or 400 feet, and the marked ;ratum is here the great coal-bed, which up ıe Alleghany river toward the north rises) higher and higher levels in the hills, and ɔward the south, up the Monongahela, sinks ɔ lower levels, till it passes beneath the bed f the stream. By extending these obser-ations over the coal-field, it is found that ıe whole series of strata maintain their eneral arrangement, and the principal mem-ers of the group, such as an important coal-ed, a peculiar bed of limestone, etc., may be lentified over areas of thousands of square ıiles. It is thus the sections have been pre-ared at many localities to complete the eries, as presented on the opposite page, f the bituminous coal-measures of the ex-reme western part of Pennsylvania. The oal-beds introduced are those which are ersistent over the greatest areas. Others ccasionally appear in different parts of the olumn, and various other local differences ıay be detected, owing to the irregularities n the stratification; thus sandstones and lates often thin out, and even gradually ass from one into the other. By their hinning out beds of coal separated by them n one locality may come together in another, ,nd form one large bed; and again, large coal-eds may be split by hardly perceptible di-isional seams of slate or shale, which may ;radually increase, till they become thick trata, separating what was one coal-bed nto two or more. The limestones, though ;enerally thin, maintain their peculiar char-cters much better than the great beds of andstone or shale, and are consequently he best guides for designating in the col-ımns the position of the strata which ac-ompany them, above and below. The fire lay is almost universally the underlying stratum of the coal-beds. In the sections t is not distinguished from the shale-beds. Γhe total thickness of all the measures, is rom 2000 to 2500 feet.

Such is the general system of the coal-bearing formation west of the Alleghan-ies. Every farm and every hill in the coal-field is likely to contain one or more beds of coal, of limestone, of good sandstone for building purposes, of fire clay, and some iron ore; and below the surface, the series is continued down to the group of conglom-erates and sandstones, which come up around the margins of the coal-fields and define their limits. At Pittsburg this group, it is found by boring, as well as by the measurements of the strata in the hills toward the north, is about 600 feet below the level of the river. The coal-measures in this portion of the country are the high-est rock formation; but in the western terri-tories beyond the Mississippi they pass under later geological groups, as the creta-ceous and the tertiary. All the coals are bituminous, and the strata in which they are found are little moved from the horizontal position in which they were originally de-posited. They have been uplifted with the continent itself, and have not been subjected to any local disturbences, such as in other regions have disarranged and metamorphosed the strata.

East of the Alleghanies, in the narrow, elongated coal-fields of the anthracite re-gion, a marked difference is perceived in the position assumed by the strata, and also in the character of the individual beds. They evidently belong to the same geological se-ries as the bituminous coal-measures, and the same succession of conglomerates, sand-stones, and red shales, is recognized below them; but the strata have been tilted at va-rious angles from their original horizontal position, and the formation is broken up and distributed in a number of basins, or canal-shaped troughs, separated from each other by the lower rocks, which, rising to the surface, form long narrow ridges outside of and around each coal-field. Those on each side being composed of the same rocks, sim-ilarly arranged, and all having been sub-jected to similar denuding action, a striking resemblance is observed, even on the map, in their outlines; and in the ridges them-selves this is so remarkable that their shapes alone correctly suggest at once to those fa miliar with the geology of the country, the rocks of which they are composed. Upon the accompanying map, from the first vol. of the "New American Cyclopædia," these ba-sins are represented by the shaded portions, and the long, narrow ridges which surround the basins, and meet in a sharp curve at their ends, are indicated by the groups of four parallel lines. Within the marginal hills the strata of the coal-measures, and of the underlying formations, while retaining their arrangement in parallel sheets, are raised upon their edges and thrown into undulat-ing lines and sharp flexures; and the extrac-

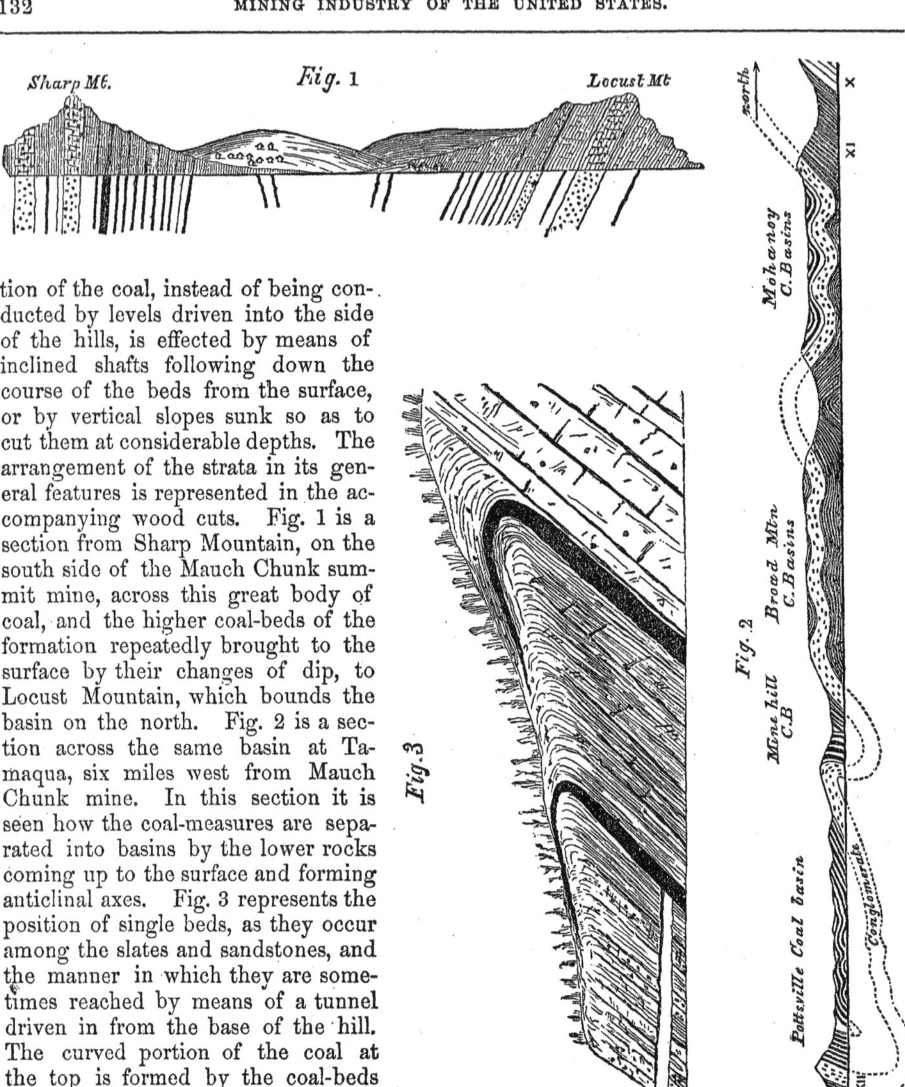

tion of the coal, instead of being conducted by levels driven into the side of the hills, is effected by means of inclined shafts following down the course of the beds from the surface, or by vertical slopes sunk so as to cut them at considerable depths. The arrangement of the strata in its general features is represented in the accompanying wood cuts. Fig. 1 is a section from Sharp Mountain, on the south side of the Mauch Chunk summit mine, across this great body of coal, and the higher coal-beds of the formation repeatedly brought to the surface by their changes of dip, to Locust Mountain, which bounds the basin on the north. Fig. 2 is a section across the same basin at Tamaqua, six miles west from Mauch Chunk mine. In this section it is seen how the coal-measures are separated into basins by the lower rocks coming up to the surface and forming anticlinal axes. Fig. 3 represents the position of single beds, as they occur among the slates and sandstones, and the manner in which they are sometimes reached by means of a tunnel driven in from the base of the hill. The curved portion of the coal at the top is formed by the coal-beds at their outcrop becoming disintegrated, and their fragments and decomposed smut being spread down the slope of the hill. The Roman numerals, "IX," "X," "XI," "XII," in fig. 2, designate the lower formations of rock, known respectively as the red sandstones (corresponding to the "Old Red Sandstone"); a series of gray sandstones; one of red shales; and lastly, the conglomerate. The dotted lines above and below the section mark the continuity of the conglomerate beneath the base of the section and its original course above the present surface before this portion had been removed by diluvial action. The other formations obviously accompany the conglomerate with similar flexures.

The same cause, that threw the strata into their inclined and contorted positions, no doubt changed the character of the coal by dispelling its volatile portions, converting it in fact into coke, while the pressure of the superincumbent beds of rock prevented the swelling up of the material, as occurs in the ordinary process of producing coke from bituminous coal, and caused it to assume the dense and compact structure of anthracite. As the anthracite basins are traced westward, it is observed that the coals in those districts which have been less disturbed, retain somewhat of the bituminous character; and if the continuity were uninterrupted between the anthracite and the bituminous coal-fields, there is no doubt that a gradual passage would be observed from the one kind of coal to the other, and that this would be accompanied by an amount of disturbance in the strata corresponding to the degree in which the coal is deficient in bitumen.

AMOUNT OF AVAILABLE COAL.

In estimating the quantities of workable coal in any district, several points are to be taken into consideration besides the amount of surface covered by the coal-measures and the aggregate thickness of all the beds they contain. Where the strata spread out horizontally, as in the western coal-fields, extensive regions may be covered with a very thin portion of the coal-bearing strata, especially near the margins of the coal-fields; while in the deep basins, like those of the anthracite region, a number of large beds may be accumulated together in very limited districts. Then again, out of the total number of coal-beds, there are more or less of them that must be excluded from the estimate, on account of their being too thin to work; and as the thickness of all of them varies in different localities, a fair average thickness of workable beds is as difficult to arrive at as a fair average area into which this thickness is to be multiplied. The problem is rendered still more complex by the slopes and flexures of the strata in the districts east of the Alleghanies, and by the gaps between the hills which cut off the beds whose plane is above the lowest levels. The great depth at which lie the lower beds in the central parts of the Appalachian coal-field must probably prevent their ever being worked; but for this no allowance is ever made in the estimates of quantities of coal.

The most careful and complete computations of this nature which have been made are those of Professor H. D. Rogers, in vol. ii. of the Geology of Pennsylvania, page 1015. From this source we obtain the following estimates:—

EXTENT OF COAL-FIELD IN THE SEVERAL STATES POSSESSING THE COAL FORMATION.

	Sq. miles.
Massachusetts and Rhode Island	100
Pennsylvania	12,656
Ohio	7,100
Maryland	550
Virginia	15,900
Kentucky	13,700
Tennessee	3,700
Alabama	6,130
Georgia	170
Indiana	6,700
Illinois	40,000
Michigan	13,350
Iowa	24,000
Missouri	21,329
Nebraska	3,712
Kansas	11,880
Arkansas	12,597
Indian Territory	10,395
Texas	2,970
Total	196,939

In the anthracite basins of Pennsylvania the number of workable beds varies from 2 or 3 to 25, according to the depth of the basin; the average number is supposed to be 10 or 12. The maximum thickness of coal is in the Pottsville basin, and amounts to 207 feet. Rejecting the thin seams, the average thickness in the south anthracite field is reckoned at 100 feet; in the middle or north field at about 60 feet; and the general average of the whole, 70 feet.

The maximum thickness of the 15 or 16 coal-beds of the central part of the Appalachian coal-field is about 40 feet, but the average of the whole basin is considered to be 25 feet.

The basin extending over Illinois and into Indiana and Kentucky, contains in the last-named state 16 or 17 workable beds, with a maximum thickness of about 50 feet. The average over the whole area is supposed to be 20 or 25 feet.

The basin of Iowa, Missouri, and Arkansas contains only 2 or 3 workable beds, of total thickness not exceeding 10 feet; while the average for the whole area must be considerably less.

The following estimates of the number and thickness of the beds in some of the British coal-fields are introduced for comparison. The great coal-field of South Wales contains 23 workable beds of 92 feet thickness, averaging over the whole area probably 60 feet. The coal-beds in the South Staffordshire basin amount to 57 feet in thickness, and in one quarter to 70 feet. The average for the whole area is assumed to be 40 feet. The Derbyshire coal-field has about 20 workable beds; aggregate thickness 66 feet, average 40 feet. The Lancashire and Cheshire coal-field in one district has 150 feet of coal in 75 beds, and in another 93 feet in 36 beds, some of which are too thin to be worked. Average thickness of workable coal over the whole field is supposed to be 50 or 60 feet. The Durham and Newcastle coal-field has total thickness of coal 60 feet, of workable coal 30 feet, and average about 20 feet. Over a total area of coal-fields in Great Britain, amounting to 5400 square miles, the average thickness of workable coal is supposed to be 35 feet. Extending these computations to Belgium and France also, Prof. Rogers presented the results of his calculations in tons as follows:—

RELATIVE AMOUNT OF COAL IN THE SEVERAL GREAT COAL-FIELDS OF EUROPE AND AMERICA.

	Tons.	Ratio.
Belgium (assuming an average thickness of about 60 feet of coal) contains about	36,000,000,000	1
France (with same thickness) contains about	59,000,000,000	1.64
The British Islands (averaging 35 feet thickness) contain nearly	190,000,000,000	5.28
Pennsylvania (averaging 25 feet thickness) contains	316,400,000,000	8.8
The great Appalachian coal-field (including Pennsylvania, averaging 25 feet)	1,387,500,000,000	38.5
Coal-field of Indiana, Illinois, and western Kentucky (average thickness 25 feet)	1,277,500,000,000	35.5
The Missouri and Arkansas basin (averaging 10 feet)	739,000,000,000	20.5
All the productive coal-fields of North America (with an assumed thickness of 20 feet of coal, and a productive area of 200,000 square miles)	4,000,000,000,000	111.
All the coal-fields of Europe	..	8.75

The following table contains the yearly returns of the coal product of eastern Pennsylvania and Maryland, from the commencement of the trade in 1820:—

STATISTICS OF PRODUCTION.

Year.	SCHUYLKILL.			WYOMING REGION.				
	Canal.	Railroad.	Total.	Del. & Hud. Coal Co.	Penn. Coal Co.	By canal.	D. L. & W. railroad.	Total tons.
1820	..	..	..	..	..	..	..	..
1821	..	..	..	..	..	..	..	..
1822	1,480	..	1,480	..	..	..	..	..
1823	1,128	..	1,128	..	..	..	..	..
1824	1,587	..	1,587	..	..	..	..	..
1825	6,500	..	6,500	..	..	..	..	..
1826	16,763	..	16,763	..	..	..	..	..
1827	31,360	..	31,360	..	..	..	..	..
1828	47,284	..	47,284	..	..	..	..	..
1829	79,973	..	79,973	7,000	..	..	..	7,000
1830	89,984	..	89,984	43,000	..	..	..	43,000
1831	81,854	..	81,854	54,000	..	..	..	54,000
1832	209,271	..	209,271	84,600	..	..	..	84,600
1833	252,971	..	252,971	111,777	..	..	..	111,777
1834	226,692	..	226,692	43,700	..	..	..	43,700
1835	339,508	..	339,508	90,000	..	..	..	90,000
1836	432,045	..	432,054	103,851	..	..	..	103,861
1837	523,152	..	523,152	115,387	..	..	..	115,387
1838	433,875	..	433,875	78,207	..	..	..	78,207
1839	442,608	..	442,608	122,300	..	..	..	122,300
1840	452,291	..	452,291	148,470	..	..	..	148,470
1841	514,692	850	515,542	192,270	..	..	..	192,270
1842	461,602	49,902	502,504	205,253	..	47,346	..	252,599
1843	447,058	230,254	677,312	227,605	..	58,000	..	285,605
1844	393,887	441,491	835,288	251,005	..	114,906	..	365,911
1845	263,587	820,237	1,083,824	273,435	..	178,401	..	451,836
1846	3,440	1,263,144	1,266,584	320,000	..	192,503	..	512,503
1847	222,693	1,360,361	1,583,054	388,203	..	284,398	..	672,601
1848	436,602	1,216,233	1,652,835	437,500	..	237,271	..	674,771
1849	489,208	1,115,918	1,605,126	454,240	..	259,080	..	713,320
1850	288,080	1,423,977	1,712,057	441,403	111,014	243,250	..	795,667
1851	579,156	1,602,727	2,181,883	479,078	316,017	336,000	6,000	1,131,095
1852	800,932	1,663,117	2,464,049	497,105	426,164	319,341	67,487	1,310,097
1853	888,869	1,587,211	2,476,080	494,327	512,659	442,511	97,358	1,546,855
1854	907,854	1,983,478	2,890,832	440,944	496,648	492,689	133,964	1,564,245
1855	1,105,263	2,213,292	3,319,555	565,460	504,803	464,039	188,865	1,723,167
1856	1,169,286	2,148,903	3,318,189	499,650	612,500	510,631	296,232	1,919,013
1857	1,275,989	1,672,544	2,948,533	480,677	543,873	405,822	490,023	1,920,395
1858	1,323,804	1,542,592	2,866,396	348,789	630,056	350,000	680,500	2,009,345
1859	1,371,753	1,633,150	3,004,903	590,839	688,855	433,548	830,000	2,543,242
1860	1,356,688	1,878,867	3,235,555	499,568	691,465	430,242	1,077,500	2,698,775
Total,	17,970,239	25,848,158	43,818,382	9,089,643	5,534,054	5,799,978	3,867,929	24,291,6[illegible]4

STATISTICS OF PRODUCTION.—Continued.

Year.	LEHIGH.			SEMI-ANTHRACITE.					BITUMINOUS.		Aggregate.
	Canal.	Railroad.	Total.	Shamokin.	Lykens Valley.	Dauphin & S. R.	Trevorton.	Broad-top.	Blossburg.	Barclay.	
1820	365	..	365	..	..	..	..	..	..	..	365
1821	1,073	..	1,073	..	.	..	..	..	..	..	1,073
1822	2,240	..	2,240	..	..	..	..	..	..	..	3,720
1823	5,823	..	5,823	..	..	..	..	..	..	..	6,951
1824	9,541	..	9,541	..	..	..	..	..	..	..	11,108
1825	28,393	..	28,393	..	..	..	..	..	..	..	34,893
1826	31,280	..	31,280	..	..	..	..	..	..	..	48,043
1827	32,074	..	32,074	..	..	..	..	..	..	..	63 430
1828	30,232	..	30,232	..	..	..	..	..	..	..	84.613
1829	25,110	..	25,110	..	..	..	..	..	..	..	148.083
1830	41,750	..	41,750	..	..	..	..	..	..	..	185.734
1831	40,966	..	40,966	..	..	..	..	..	..	..	207,420
1832	70,000	..	70,000	..	..	..	..	..	..	..	363,871
1833	123,000	..	123,000	..	..	..	..	..	..	..	487,748
1834	106,244	..	106,244	..	..	..	..	..	..	..	376,636
1835	131,250	..	131,250	..	..	..	..	..	..	..	560,758
1836	148,211	..	148,211	..	..	..	..	..	..	..	684,126
1837	223,902	..	223,902	..	..	..	..	..	..	..	862,441
1838	213,615	..	213,615	..	..	..	..	..	..	..	725,697
1839	221,025	..	221,025	11,930	..	..	..	..	..	..	797,863
1840	225.318	.	225,318	15,505	..	..	..	..	4,235	..	845,819
1841	143,037	..	143,037	21,463	..	..	..	..	25,966	..	898,278
1842	272,546	..	272,546	10,000	..	..	..	..	13,164	..	1,050,813
1843	267,793	..	267,793	10,000	..	..	..	..	6,268	..	1,246,978
1844	377,002	..	377,002	18,087	..	..	..	..	14,234	..	1,605,522
1845	429,453	..	429,453	10,000	..	..	..	..	29.836	..	2,004,949
1846	517,116	..	517,116	12,572	..	..	..	..	16,509	..	2,325,284
1847	633,507	..	633,507	14,904	..	..	..	..	29,087	..	2.923,153
1848	670,321	..	670,321	19,356	..	..	..	..	33,762	..	3,042,045
1849	781,656	..	781,656	19,650	25,325	..	..	..	32,095	..	3,177,172
1850	690,456	..	690,456	19,921	37,763	..	..	..	23,161	..	3,279,025
1851	964.224	..	964,224	24,899	52,060	20,000	..	..	25,000	..	4,400,161
1852	1,072,136	..	1,072,136	25,846	55,000	33,639	..	..	20,000	..	4,980,767
1853	1,054,309	..	1,054,309	15,500	60,000	29,000	..	..	45,571	..	5,227,315
1854	1,207,186	..	1,207,186	63,500	53,000	63,000	..	..	70.554	..	5,912,317
1855	1,275,050	9,063	1,284,113	116,117	112.000	52,494	..	..	73,201	..	6,680,647
1856	1,186,230	165,740	1,354,970	117,406	100,000	77,307	73,142	42,000	70,670	4,115	7,106,782
1857	900,314	418,236	1,318,550	153,525	121.550	82,285	110,711	78,812	94,314	6,239	6,834,914
1858	908,800	471,029	1,379,829	137,000	127,750	..	106,686	105,478	40,001	18,000	6,790,485
1859	1,050,592	577,651	1,628,243	180,000	139,200	..	124,250	130,387	..	30,143	7,780,368
1860	1,091,032	730,642	1,821,674	211,100	176,290	..	89,515	188,250	..	30,000	8,451,159
Total,	17,204,172	2,372,361	19,576,533	1,253,281	1,059,938	357,725	504,274	544,927	667,626	88,597	92,222,526

In presenting the statistics of the product of the principal coal districts of the United States, it will be observed that these are limited to the eastern portion of Pennsylvania and the Cumberland district of Maryland. It is from these sources almost exclusively that the great markets of the New England states, of the states of New York and New Jersey, and of the eastern portion of Pennsylvania and Maryland have been supplied; and it is from the records preserved by the lines of transportation from the mines that any statistics of the coal products are now available. In the Western states, where the bituminous coal-beds are very generally distributed over large territories, there exists no concentration of the business, as at the East, and no means are afforded of obtaining even an approximate estimate of the amount of coal annually mined.

TRANSPORTATION OF COAL TO MARKET.

The first anthracite from the Schuylkill mines was brought to Philadelphia in wagons. The navigation of the river and canal was hardly practicable for boats previous to the year 1822; and though from that year anthracite was conveyed to Philadelphia and the trade continued to increase, it was not until after the improvements were completed in 1825, that a large amount of coal could be transported by this route. The effect of these improvements was experienced in the transportation of 6500 tons in 1825, which was more than four times the business of 1824; and in 1826 it increased to 16,763, and this nearly doubled in the succeeding year. As for successive years the trade steadily and rapidly increased in importance, the capacity of the canal proved at last insufficient for it, and the Reading railroad was laid out especially for its accommodation, and constructed with a uniform descending grade from the mining region at Pottsville to the Delaware river. This went into operation in 1841, and proved a formidable competitor to the Schuylkill canal, but the still increasing trade has well nigh reached the capacity of both these routes. The greatest amount of coal transported in one year by any one line was in 1855 over the Reading road, being 2,213,392 tons. The number of tons carried by canal the same year was 1,105,263 tons. Since that time the business has been more equally divided between them, the railroad still doing the larger portion of it.

As seen by the table, the first shipments of anthracite were from the Lehigh region, two years before any were sent from the Schuylkill. The transportation was effected by arks or large boxes built of plank, and run down the rapid and shoal river with no little risk. To return with them was impracticable, nor was this desired, for the arks themselves were constructed of the product of the forests, which in this form was most conveniently got to market. They had before been the chief means of conveyance down into the Delaware of the products of the country, which indeed were little else than lumber. As the coal trade increased in importance, the improvement of the river was undertaken by the Lehigh Coal and Navigation Company to insure greater facility in running the arks. They constructed dams across the shoaler places in the river, by which the water was held back, thus increasing the depth above. As the arks coming down the river reached one of these dams, the sluice gates were opened and the boats descended into the next division in which the water was kept up by the next dam below. At first two arks were used together, being connected by hinges at the ends; and as the facilities for running them were improved, more of them were thus joined together, till they reached nearly 200 feet in length. In 1831 the slack-water navigation of the Lehigh was so far perfected, that it was used by canal boats ascending and descending through regular locks.

Up to the year 1827 the transportation of anthracite to Mauch Chunk from the mines, nine miles distant, had been by a wagon road. In January of that year the construction of a railroad was commenced, and in May the road was completed. This was the second railroad built in the United States, the first one being a short road from the granite quarries in Quincy, Massachusetts. The Mauch Chunk road was made with a descending grade all the way, averaging about 100 feet to the mile, so that the loaded cars ran down by gravity. Each train carried down with it in cars appropriated to this use the mules for drawing the empty cars back; and it is stated that after the animals once became accustomed to the routine of their duties they could never be made to travel down the road if accidentally left behind. The trade before many years outgrew these increased facilities of transporting the coal, and it was found essential to provide a new track, upon which the empty cars could be returned by some more economical method. On account of the heavy up-grade, locomotives, it was concluded, could not be advantageously employed, and hence a system of inclined planes and gravity roads was devised, by which the cars hoisted by stationary power to the summit of the planes and thence descending the gravity roads might be returned to the mines, and the use of mules and horses be entirely dispensed with. In the accompanying sketches a part of this arrangement of roads is exhibited.

The high hill called Mount Pisgah, above the village of Mauch Chunk, is the terminating point at the Lehigh river of the long ridge called Sharp Mountain. The great mines of the Lehigh are on its summit about nine miles west of the village. The lower road seen in the sketch is called the loaded track. The cars come by this from the mines, and being let down the inclined plane at its terminus, their loads are discharged into the great bins over the edge of the river. They are then hauled a short distance to the foot of the long plane that reaches to the summit of Mount Pisgah, and by the stationary steam engine are drawn up in about six minutes to an elevation 850 feet above that at the foot. The length of this plane is 2250 feet. From its summit the empty cars run down the inclined road constructed along the south side of the ridge, and at the distance of six miles, having descended about 300 feet, they reach the foot of another inclined plane at Mount Jefferson. This plane is 2070 feet long, rising 462 feet. The ascent is accomplished in three minutes, and from the top another gravity road extends about a mile, descending 44 feet to the Summit Hill village. From this point branch roads lead to the different mines in Panther Creek valley; and all meet again in the loaded track road by which the cars return to Mauch Chunk.

The transportation of coal from Mauch Chunk was conducted by the river and canal

MOUNT PISGAH PLANE, MAUCH CHUNK, PA.

THE GREAT OPEN QUARRY OF THE LEHIGH.

In working this great quarry of anthracite at the Summit mine, above Mauch Chunk, blocks of coal were occasionally left standing for a time, one of which, surmounted by the soil of the original surface and the relics of the vegetation, is represented in the above cut. In this block are discerned the lines of stratification of the coal; and an idea of its extraordinary thickness and extent is conveyed by the appearance of the cliffs upon the further side of the excavated area. Upon the floor of the quarry are seen the mining wagons used for conveying away upon temporary tracks the coal and rubbish of the excavations.

BALTIMORE COMPANY'S MINE, WILKESBARRE, PA.

COLLIERY SLOPE AND BREAKER AT TUSCARORA, PA.

MOUNT PISGAH PLANES AND THE GRAVITY RAILROAD, MAUCH CHUNK.

exclusively until the partial construction of the Lehigh railroad in 1846. But it was not until its completion in 1855, that this began to be an important outlet of the coal region and a powerful competitor for the trade with the canal.

A considerable amount of anthracite finds a market on the borders of Chesapeake Bay, being transported from the mines near the Susquehanna river by the Susquehanna tide-water canal, and by the Baltimore and Susquehanna railroad. Its consumption is extending in this region by its use in the blast furnaces in the place of charcoal, for smelting iron ores, and the receipts of this fuel in the city of Baltimore are steadily gaining upon those of the semi-bituminous coals of the Cumberland region, which are brought to the city by the Baltimore and Ohio railroad. For four years past these receipts have been as follows:—

	1857. Tons.	1858. Tons.	1859. Tons.	1860. Tons.
Bituminous..	443,782	331,865	344,223	397,684
Anthracite.........	257,334	277,967	258,189	325,129
	701,116	609,832	602,412	722,813

The principal outlet of the Northern coal-field had been from 1829 to 1850 by the Delaware and Hudson canal. Since 1847 there have been taken every year to the Hudson river by this route from about 440,000 to 499,650 tons, except in 1855, when the quantity was 565,460 tons. A number of railroads now connect this basin with the central railroad across northern New Jersey, and in other directions it is connected both by railroad and canals with the Erie railroad to the North and the Susquehanna river to the South-west. As large an amount of coal is now transported over each one of three of these lines as by the Delaware and Hudson canal.

The various railroads and canals which have been constructed with especial reference to the transportation of anthracite, are more than 40 in number, and have cost about $93,000,000. Most of them are presented in the following table; of some of them only those portions which may fairly be counted as constructed for coal purposes:—

Names of railroads and canals.	Canals. No. miles.	Railroads. No. miles.	Total cost.
Lehigh Navigation	87	..	$4,455,000
Lehigh and Susquehanna railroad	..	20	1,350,000
Mauch Chunk and Summit railroads	..	36	831,684
Delaware division of the Pennsylvania canal	43	..	1,734,958
Beaver Meadow railroad and branch	..	38	360,000
Hazleton railroad	..	10	120,000
Buck Mountain railroad	..	4	40,000
Summit railroad	..	2	20,000
Lehigh Valley railroad	..	45	3,500,000
Delaware and Hudson canal	108	..	3,250,000
Morris canal	102	..	4,000,000
The Schuylkill Navigation	108	..	5,785,000
Reading and Pottsville railroad	..	98	19,004,000
Shamokin and Pottsville Valley railroad	..	30	900,000
Little Schuylkill railroad	..	28	1,416,187
Danville and Pottsville railroad (44½ miles unfinished)	..	29	680,000
Mine Hill and Schuylkill Haven railroad and branches	..	100	2,800,000
Mount Carbon railroad	..	7	155,000
Port Carbon railroad	..	2	120,000
Schuylkill Valley railroad and branches	..	25	300,000
Mill Creek railroad	..	6	120,000
Lykens Valley railroad	..	16	200,000
Wiconisco canal	12	..	370,000
Swatara railroad	..	4	20,000
North Branch canal	163	..	3,790,310
Union canal and Pine Grove branch	90	..	1,000,000
Schuylkill and Susquehanna railroad	..	52	1,500,000
Northern Central railroad	..	60	1,000,000
Pennsylvania canal (from Wilkesbarre to Columbia)	100	..	3,000,000
Susquehanna tidewater canal	45	..	1,000,000
York and Cumberland railroad	..	26	600,000
Cumberland Valley railroad	..	56	1,192,111
Franklin railroad	..	22	450,000
Nesquehoning railroad	..	5	50,000
Room Run railway	..	6	40,000
Delaware, Lackawanna, and Western railroad	..	170	9,995,000
Lackawanna and Bloomsburg railroad	..	68	1,600,000
Quakake railroad	..	14	280,000
Catawissa, Williamsport, and Erie railroad	..	65	4,145,096
Elmira and Williamsport	..	78	2,000,000
Pennsylvania Coal Company's railroad	..	52	3,745,500
New Jersey Central railroad	..	63	5,746,366
Railroads by individuals	..	120	180,000
Underground railroads	..	200	75,000
Total	858	1,557	$92,921,212

COAL MINING.

Coal-beds are discovered and worked by different methods, varying according to the circumstances under which they occur. In regions where they lie among the piles of strata horizontally arranged, and passing with the other members of the group upon a level or nearly so through the hills, their exact position is often detected by their exposure in the precipitous walls of rock along the rivers; or it is indicated by peculiar indentations, known as "benches," around their line of outcrop, caused by their crumbling and wearing away more rapidly than the harder strata above and below them; and again by the recurrence of springs of water and wet places at the foot of the benches, which point to an impervious stratum within the hill that prevents the water percolating any further down; and lastly, in the little gorges worn by the "runs," the beds are often uncovered, and loose pieces of coal washed down lead to their original source above. However discovered, the method of working them is simple. A convenient place is selected upon the side of a hill, and an excavation called a drift, usually about four feet wide, is made into the coal-bed. The height of the drift is governed by the thickness of the coal-bed and the nature of the overlying slate. Miners sometimes work in drifts only 2½ feet high. Coal-beds three or four feet thick are very common, and are worked without the necessity of removing the overhanging slate, unless it is too unsound to serve as a roof. Beds of ten feet thickness or more require much additional care over those of smaller size, both in removing the coal and supporting the roof; and in many cases it is found expedient to leave a portion of the bed, either at the top or bottom, untouched, especially if the upper layers contain, as they often do, sound sheets of slate. At the entrance of the mines, and in general in all places where the cover is not sound, the materials overhead are prevented from falling by timbers across the top of the drifts, rudely framed into posts set up against the walls on each side; and where the strata are very loose, slabs are driven in over the cross timbers and behind the posts. In such ground the coal cannot be excavated over large areas without leaving frequent pillars of coal and introducing great numbers of posts or props. But previous to abandoning the mine the pillars may be removed, commencing with those furthest in, and all the strata above are thus allowed to settle gradually down. When drifts or gangways have been extended into the coal-beds far enough to be under good cover, branches are commenced at right angles, and a system of chambers is laid out for excavation, leaving sufficient blocks or pillars of coal to provide for the support of the overlying strata. Thus the work is carried on, ventilation being secured by connections made within the hill with gangways passing out in different directions, and sometimes also by shafts sunk from the surface above, or, when these means are not practicable, by ventilating fans worked by hand, and thus forcing air through long wooden boxes which lead into the interior of the mine. Drainage is often a serious trouble, and unless the strata slope toward the outlet of the mine, it can be effected only by a channel cut to the required depth for the water to flow out, or else by the use of pumping machinery. When the strata lie nearly upon a horizontal plane, it is very common for a slight descent to be found from the exterior of a hill toward its centre, as if the beds of rock had been compressed and settled by their greater weight in the middle of the hill. In such positions the coal is extracted with much expense for drainage, and it is therefore an important consideration in judging of the value of coal-beds to ascertain whether or no the water will flow freely out from the excavations. In the bituminous coal-fields west of the Alleghanies, owing to the general distribution of the coal-beds above the level of the water-courses, it has not yet been found worth while to work any of the beds that are known to lie below this level. Coal must reach a much higher value before beds of the moderate size of those in that region can be profitably explored below water level.

It is rare that bituminous coal is obtained by open quarrying. Where the beds lie near the surface, so that they might be uncovered, the coal is almost invariably in a rotten condition and worthless. Consequently one of the first points to be assured of in judging of the value of a coal-bed is that it has sufficient rock cover. After this may be considered the quality of the coal, its freedom from sulphur, etc., the soundness of its roof, and the facilities offered for drainage and ventilation. The quality of a coal-bed undergoes little or no change after it is once reached under good cover beyond atmospheric influences; and hence no encouragement can be given to continue to work a poor bed in hopes of its improving.

Coal is excavated chiefly by light, slender picks. With one of these a miner makes a shallow, horizontal cut as far as he can reach under the wall of coal before him, stretching himself out upon the floor to do this work, and then he proceeds to make a vertical cut extending from each end of that along the floor up to the roof. By another horizontal cut along the roof, a cubical block of coal is thus entirely separated from the bed, except on the back side which cannot be reached. The separation is completed by wedges driven into the upper crevice, or sometimes by small charges of powder. By this means blocks of coal are thrown down amounting to 70 or 80 tons in weight, and with the least possible loss by the reduction of portions of it to dust and fine coal.

The cost of mining and delivering coal at the mouth of the mines, varies with the size and character of the beds. Under the most favorable conditions the horizontal beds of bituminous coal, as those in the hills opposite Pittsburg, have been worked and the coal delivered outside for $1\frac{1}{2}$ cents a bushel, or 45 cents a ton; but in general the total expenses are nearly double this rate. In estimating the capacity of production of coal-beds it is usual to allow a ton of coal to every cubic yard, and a bed of coal a yard thick should consequently contain a ton to every square yard, or 4840 tons to the acre: but the actual product that can be depended on, after the loss by fine coal, by pillars left standing, etc., may not safely be reckoned at more than 3000 tons, or for every foot thickness of the bed 1000 tons.

In the anthracite region, and in other coal districts where the beds are of large size and lie at various degrees of inclination with the horizon, the methods of mining differ more or less from those described. The anthracite beds frequently extend in parallel layers longitudinally through the long ridges, dipping, it may be, nearly with the outer slope, and descending to great depths below the surface. In such positions they are conveniently reached at the ends of the ridges and in the gaps across these, by a level driven on the course of the bed, and rising just enough for the water to drain freely. A level or gangway of this sort is the great road of the mine, by which all the coal is to be brought out in case other similar gangways are not driven into the same bed at points further up or down its slope. Unless the dip is very gentle, one at the lowest point should be sufficient. At different points along its extension passageways are cut in the coal, directed at right angles up the slope of the bed, and as soon as one of them can be brought through to the surface, a ventilating current of air is established, which may afterward be diverted through all the workings. The passageways together with other levels above divide the coal-bed into great blocks, and also serve as shutes by which the coal excavated above is sent down to the main gangway. At the bottom of each shute a bin is constructed for arresting the coal and discharging it, as required, into the wagons which are run in beneath on the tracks laid for this purpose. Coal-beds in this position are also worked from the gangway by broad excavations carried up the "breast" or face of the bed, sufficient pillars of coal from 12 to 25 feet long being left in either case to support the roof. These pillars usually occupy the most room just above the gangways, and on passing up between them, the chambers are made to widen out till they attain a breadth of about 40 feet, and thus the breast is extended up to the next level. Props are introduced wherever required to support the roof, and the rubbish, slates, etc., are stacked up for the same purpose, as well as to get them out of the way.

It often occurs that coal-beds within the ridges can be reached only by a tunnel driven in from the side of the mountain across their line of bearing. Tunnels of this kind are sometimes extended till they cut two or more parallel coal-beds. Each one may then be worked by gangways leaving the tunnel at right angles and following the coal-beds, and the tunnel continues to be the main outlet of them all.

When it is desirable to obtain the coal from the portion of the bed below the level of the gangway, preparations must first be made for raising the water, which may be done for a time by bucket and windlass, and as the slope is carried down and the flow of water increases, then by mining pumps worked by horse or steam power. The slope may commence from the exterior surface or from the lower gangway of a mine already in operation, and is made large enough to admit wagons, which ascend and descend upon two tracks extending down its floor. At the depth of 200 or 300 feet a gangway is driven at right angles with the slope in each direction on the course of the bed, and from this the workings are carried up the breast as already described. Other gangways are started at lower levels of 100 feet or more each, dividing the mine into so many stories or floors. The coal above each gangway is sent down to its level and is received into wagons. By these it is conveyed to the slope, and here running upon a turn-table, each wagon is set upon the track in the slope and is immediately taken by the steam engine to the surface, another car at the same time coming down on the other track. Reservoirs are constructed upon the different levels to arrest the water, that it may not all have to be raised up from the bottom, and the pumps are constructed so as to lift the water from the lower into the higher reservoirs and thence to the surface. Many mines of this character are opened from the surface, one of which is represented in the cut of the "Colliery Slope and Breaker, at Tuscarora, Pennsylvania." An empty wagon is seen in this cut descending the track from the engine house down into the mouth of the pit, and through the end of the building passes the pump rod which by means of a vibrating "bob" is turned down the pit and works by the side of the track. The men pass down into the mines of this character, sometimes by the wagons, and sometimes by ladders or steps arranged for the purpose between the two tracks. Though the opening, as represented, appears insignificant for an important mine, such a slope may extend several hundred feet in depth, and many gangways may branch off from it to the right and left, extending several miles under ground in nearly straight lines along the course of the bed. These, however, to secure ventilation, must have other slopes coming out to the surface, and at these may be other arrangements for discharging the coal and water. In extensive mines the gangways are made wide and capacious for the continual passing back and forth of the wagons drawn by mules. These animals once lowered into the mine are kept constantly under ground, where they are provided with convenient stables excavated from the coal and rock. The men continue at work from eight to ten hours, and in well-ventilated mines the employment is neither very laborious, hazardous, nor disagreeable. The pursuit has, however, little attraction for Americans, and is mostly monopolized by Welsh, English, Irish, and German miners.

In the anthracite region there have been some remarkable instances of open quarries of coal. That of the Summit mine of the Lehigh is unsurpassed in the history of coal mining, for the enormous body of coal exposed to view. The great coal-bed, which appears to have been formed by a number of beds coming together through the thinning out of the slates that separated them, arches over the ridge, forming the uppermost layers of rock, and dipping down the sides at a steeper angle than their inclination. It thus passes beneath the higher strata. On the summit a thin soil, formed chiefly of the decomposed coal itself, covered the beds and supported a growth of forest trees. For several feet down the coal was loose and broken before the solid anthracite was reached. As the excavations were commenced and carried on from this point, it appeared as if the whole mountain was coal. Shafts were sunk into it and penetrated repeated layers of anthracite, separated by thin seams of slate, to the depth, in some places, of more than 55 feet. The work of stripping off and removing the covering of yellow and greenish sandstones and refuse coal was carried on, till the quarry had extended over about 50 acres, and on the north side the overlying sandstone, which had been steadily increasing in thickness, presented a wall of 30 to 40 feet in height. Over this area rail tracks were laid for removing the waste northward to the slope of the hill toward the Panther Creek valley; and when the piles thus formed had grown into large hills, the rubbish was deposited in the spaces left after the coal had been removed. During the progress of this work the scenes presented were of the most picturesque and novel character. The area laid bare was irregularly excavated into steps, upon which temporary rail tracks were laid in every direction. Upon these the wagons were kept busily running, some carrying off the coal, some loaded with slates and waste, and others returning empty for their loads. Here and there stood huge isolated masses of anthracite, with their covering of sandstone, soil, and the relics of the original forest growth, reaching to the height of 50 or 60 feet, monuments of the vast amount of excavation that had been carried on, and presenting in their naked, vertical walls, fine representations of the extraordinary thickness of the bed and of the alternating layers of slate and coal of which it was composed. In the accompanying cut of the great open quarry of the Lehigh is represented one of these blocks. Gradually these masses disappeared as the miners continued their operations; but in the boundary walls of the quarry there are still to be seen black cliffs of solid coal more than 50 feet high, and overtopped by a wall of yellow sandstone of nearly equal additional height. Under these walls operations have been carried on by the regular system of underground mining. From ten acres of the quarry it has been estimated that 850,000 tons of coal have been sent away, the value of which in the ground at the usual rate of 30 cents per ton, would be $255,000, or $25,500 per acre. Estimating the average working thickness of the coal in this part of the coal-field, from the Little Schuylkill to Nesquehoning, at 40 feet, which according to the report of the state geologist is not exaggerated, every available acre contains not less than 65,000 tons. The expense of extracting and preparing the coal from the great bed for market, is stated by the same authority to be 37½ cents per ton for mining and delivering ready for breaking and cleaning. For this operation 12½ cents; and for raising it to the summit and running it to Mauch Chunk 25 cents.

Another locality where coal has been

worked by open quarrying is at the mines of the Baltimore Company, near Wilkesbarre. Here, too, an immense bed of coal was found so close to the surface that it was easily uncovered over a considerable area. As the overlying slates and sandstone increased in thickness, it was found at last more economical to follow the coal under cover; and it was then worked after the manner of mining the bituminous coal-beds west of the Alleghany Mountains. Horizontal drifts 25 feet high, which was the thickness of the bed, were carried in from the abrupt wall, several of them near together and separated by great pillars of coal left to support the roof. The gangways were so broad and spacious that a locomotive and train of cars might have been run into the mine. Within they were crossed by a succession of other levels, and through the wide spaces thus left open, the light of day penetrated far into the interior of the hill, gradually disappearing among the forest of black pillars by which it was obstructed and absorbed.

In the anthracite region, several coal-beds of workable dimensions are often found in close proximity, so that when dipping at a high angle they are penetrated in succession by a tunnel driven across their line of bearing. Larger quantities of coal are thus concentrated in the same area than are ever met with in the bituminous coal-field. In the northern coal-fields, between Scranton and Carbondale, tracts have brought $800 or more per acre, and single tracts of 650 to 700 acres are reported upon by competent mining engineers as containing five workable beds, estimated to yield as follows—each one over nearly the whole area: one bed working 7 feet, 11,200 tons per acre; a second, working 8 feet, 12,800 tons per acre; a third, 6 feet, 9600 tons per acre; a fourth, the same; and a fifth, 3 feet, 4800 tons—altogether equalling a production of 48,000 tons per acre, from which 20 per cent. should be deducted for mine waste, pillars, etc.

The anthracite as usually brought out from the mines is mostly in large lumps of inconvenient size to handle. In this shape it was originally sent to market, and when sold to consumers a man was sent with the coal to break it up in small pieces with a hammer. At present every mine is supplied with an apparatus called a coal-breaker, which is run by steam power, and which crushes the large pieces of coal in fragments. It consists of two rollers of cast iron, one solid, with its surface armed with powerful teeth, and the other of open basket-work structure. These revolve near together, and the coal, fed from a hopper above, is broken between them, and the pieces discharged below into another hopper are delivered into the upper end of a revolving cylindrical screen, made of stout iron wire, and set on a gentle incline. The meshes of this screen are of four or more degrees of coarseness. At the upper end the finer particles only drop through; passing this portion of the screen, the coarser meshes which succeed let through the stove coal sizes, next the "egg coal," and next the "broken coal," while the coarsest pieces of all, called "lump coal," are discharged through the lower end of the screen. Under the screen are bins or shutes, separated by partitions, so as to keep each size by itself. Their floor slopes down to the railway track, and each bin at its lower end is provided with a trap-door, through which the coal is delivered as required into the wagons. The general plan of this arrangement is seen in the preceding wood-cut of the Colliery Slope and Breaker at Tuscarora. The coal wagons are here run from the mine up into the top of the engine house, and thence through the building to the breaker at the upper end of the slope over the shutes. As the coal falls from the screen into these, boys are employed, one in each bin, to pick out and throw away the pieces of slate and stone that may be mixed with the coal. This they soon learn to do very thoroughly and with great activity; and upon the faithfulness with which their work is done depends in no small measure the reputation of the coal.

USEFUL APPLICATIONS.

While anthracite, by reason of its simple composition, is fitted only for those uses in which the combustion or oxidation of its carbon is required to generate heat, or else to extract oxygen from other substances, the bituminous coals, containing a greater variety of ingredients, serve to produce from their volatile ingredients illuminating gas and coal oils. These two subjects will be treated in distinct chapters, and that upon the oils may properly include an account of the wells of natural oil recently developed in the north-west part of Pennsylvania, and in neighboring districts in New York and Ohio, as also in Virginia and Kentucky.

CHAPTER X.

ILLUMINATING GAS.

THE supply of artificial light in abundance and at little cost is one of the most important benefits which science and mechanics can confer. It contributes not merely to physical comfort and luxurious living, but supplies the means to multitudes of obtaining instruction during those hours after the cessation of their daily labors, which are not required for sleep, and which among the poor have in great measure been spent in darkness, on account of the expense of artificial light. At the present day it is not unusual, in the less cultivated portions of the country, to see a farmer's family at night gathered around a blazing fire, and some among them seeking by its fitful light to extract the news from a public journal, or perhaps conning their school tasks, and making some attempts at writing or ciphering; and when the hour to retire has come, the younger members disappear in the dark, and the more honored are favored with a home-made tallow candle, just sufficient for this use, and endurable only to those who are unaccustomed to a more cleanly and efficient method of illumination. With the advance of cultivation and learning, the demand for better light has increased the more rapidly it has been met. The sea has been almost exhausted of whales for furnishing supplies of oil. The pork of the West has been largely converted by new chemical processes into lard oil and the hard stearine for candles; and numerous preparations of spirits of turpentine, under the name of camphene and burning fluid, have been devised and largely introduced with ingenious lamps contrived to secure the excellent light they furnish, with the least possible risk of the awful explosions to which these fluids are liable when their vapor comes in contact with fire. The bituminous coals have been made to give up their volatile portions—by one process to afford an illuminating gas, and by another to produce burning oils; and the earth itself is bored by deep wells to exhaust the newly-found supplies of oil gathered beneath the surface at unknown periods by natural processes of distillation. The resinous products of the pine tree are applied to the production of oil and gas for the same purposes; and peat, wood, and other combustible bodies—even water itself—are all resorted to as sources from which the cry for "more light" shall be satisfied.

The distillation of carbonaceous and bituminous substances to obtain an illuminating gas is a process, the practical application of which hardly dates back of the present century. The escape of inflammable gases from the earth, in different parts of the world, had been observed, and the phenomenon had been applied to superstitious ceremonials, especially at Bakoo on the shores of the Caspian. The Chinese are said to have applied such natural jets of gas to purposes of both illumination and heating; but the first attempts to light buildings by gas distilled from bituminous coal were made about the year 1798 by Mr. Murdock in the manufactory of Messrs. Boulton and Watt, at Soho, England, and about the same time in France by a Frenchman named Le Bow. The London and Westminster Chartered Gas Light and Coke Company was incorporated in 1810, and Westminster bridge was lighted with gas, Dec. 31, 1813. The process was introduced into this country about the year 1821. Some attempts had been made at an earlier date, as in Baltimore according to some statements in 1816, and in New York four years before this. In the New York *News* of August 15, 1859, is an account of the efforts made by Mr. David Melville of that city to establish the use of coal gas in 1812. He lighted his own house with it, and then a factory at Pawtucket. He also succeeded in having it applied to one of the lighthouses on the coast of Rhode Island, and for one year its use was continued with success. But on account of the disturbed state of the times and the prejudices against the use of a new material, the enterprise fell through. In 1822 the manufacture of gas was undertaken in Boston; and the next year the New York Gas Light Company was incorporated with a capital of $1,000,000. The works, however, were not completed and in operation until 1827. Another company, called the Manhattan Gas Light Company, was incorporated in 1830 with a capital of $500,000, which has since been increased to $4,000,000. Such were the beginnings of this branch of manufacture, which has of late rapidly extended itself throughout all the cities and many of the towns of the United States, having works in operation representing a capital of more than $35,000,000, which in 1859 were owned by 237 companies. Some of these works are among the largest and most expensive manufacturing establishments of any kind in the country, including besides the apparatus employed for generating and holding the gas, the pipes extending throughout the cities for the supply of consumers. In New York city the pipes belonging to the Manhattan Gas Light Company, of diameters varying from 3 to 20 inches, amounted in 1858 to 207 miles in length; and those of the New York Gas Light Company, of diameters from 4 to 18 inches, amounted to 138 miles. The former company supplies that portion of the city which lies above Grand street as far as Seventy-ninth street, and the latter that portion below Grand street.

Within the last few years the use of gas has increased with great rapidity throughout the cities and towns of the United States, till the number of companies in operation in the year 1860 amounted to 381, according to the statistics published in July of that year, in the *American Gas Light Journal.* These companies represented a capital of $47,911,215; and it is since ascertained that this sum must be considerably increased by adding to the list over 50 other companies from which no returns had then been received. The interest it appears must already rank among the important branches of industry of the country. For much of the statistical information on this subject we are chiefly indebted to the records collected for the journal above named. The first table below will serve to present some idea of the extent of the larger establishments, and the range in the cost of gas, which varies according to the cost of the coal employed, the scale of the operations, etc. The lowest price paid for gas is at Pittsburg, Pennsylvania, $1.50 per 1000 cubic feet, the bituminous coal employed costing only $1.25 per ton. In many of the smaller towns $7 is the price, which is the maximum on the Atlantic side of the continent.

The second table gives the aggregate number of gas works in the several states, amount of capital invested, etc.

SOME OF THE PRINCIPAL GAS LIGHT COMPANIES IN THE UNITED STATES.

Chartered.	Localities.	Chartered capital.	Approximate annual production. Cubic feet.	Prices to private consumers per 1000 cubic feet.	Average cost of coal used per ton.
1830,	Manhattan, N. Y.	$4,000,000	725,321,000	$2 50	$6 50 to $11 00
1823,	New York, N. Y.	1,000,000	430,000,000	2 50	.. ..
1825,	Brooklyn, N. Y.	2,000,000	163,000,000	2 00	7 28 to 8 15
1859,	Citizens' Co., Brooklyn.	1,000,000	..	2 00	.. ..
1841,	Philadelphia	3,000,000	432,000,000	2 25	6 50 ..
	Northern Liberties	400,000	70,000,000	2 50	6 29 ..
1822,	Boston, Mass.	1,000,000	200,000,000	2 50	5 00 to 12 00
1851,	Cincinnati, Ohio	1,600,000	96,708,900	2 50	3 40 ..
1849,	Chicago, Ill.	1,300,000	86,250,810	3 50	5 78 ..
1846,	Charleston, S. C.	723,800	..	4 00	.. ..
1839,	St. Louis, Mo.	600,000	74,500,000	3 50	7 50 ..
1835,	Pittsburg, Penn.	300,000	54,720,000	1 50	1 25 ..
1848,	Providence, R. I.	1,000,000	41,437,883	3 00	7 20 ..
1845,	Albany, N. Y.	250,000	40,250,000	3 00	6 75 to 8 00
1838,	Louisville, Ky.	600,000	33,750,000	2 70	.. ..
1850,	Williamsburg, N. Y.	500,000	33,493,082	3 50	6 25 to 9 50
1848,	Troy, N. Y.	200,000	28,000,000	3 60	7 20 ..
1851,	Richmond, Va.	341,975	27,000,000	3 00	4 15 ..
1852,	Rochester, N. Y.	200,000	25,000,000	2 50	5 38 ..
1849,	Lowell, Mass.	200,000	21,000,000	3 25	6 50 ..
1848,	Cleveland, Ohio	200,000	20,000,000	3 00	4 25 ..
1849,	Detroit, Mich.	500,000	20,000,000	3 50	5 00 ..
1853,	Jersey City, N. J.	300,000	19,234,000	3 00	7 89 ..
	Milwaukee, Wis.	400,009	19,049,560	3 50	6 00 ..
1849,	Hartford, Conn.	200,000	15,000,000	3 00	8 68 ..
1849,	Portland, Maine	250,000	..	3 50	.. ..
1857,	Columbia, California	50,000	..	10 00	.. ..
1852,	San Francisco, "	1,000,000	..	8 00	.. ..
1858,	Marysville, "	50,000	..	12 50	.. ..
	Stockton, "	50,000	..	10 00	.. ..
1857,	Sacramento, "	500,000	..	10 00	.. ..

TOTAL OF GAS COMPANIES IN THE UNITED STATES FROM RETURNS OF JULY, 1860.

State.	Companies.	Capital.	Coal gas.	Average price.	Rosin gas.	Average price.
Alabama	3	$320,000	3	$5 16	..	..
Arkansas	None.	..	..	..	..	..
California	9	1,790,000	9	10 05	..	..
Connecticut	14	953,000	14	3 83	..	..
Delaware	3	244,300	3	3 50	..	..
District of Columbia	1	500,000	1	3 25	..	..
Florida	1	30,000	1	7 00	..	..
Georgia	6	559,160	4	4 68	2	$6 50
Illinois	13	2,595,000	13	3 91	..	..
Indiana	7	605,000	7	3 97	..	..
Iowa	5	355,000	5	4 40	..	..
Kansas	1	200,000	1	5 00	..	..
Kentucky	5	905,000	5	4 04	..	..
Louisiana	2	1,540,000	2	4 50	..	..
Maine	10	905,300	9	3 90	1	7 00
Maryland	6	780,000	3	3 49	3	6 60
Massachusetts	49	4,759,000	45	3 43	4	6 37
Michigan	8	745,000	8	3 78	..	..
Minnesota	1	200,000	1	6 00	..	..
Mississippi	4	212,000	4	4 75	..	..
Missouri	4	775,000	4	4 50	..	..
New Hampshire	9	425,000	9	3 98	..	..
New Jersey	19	1,849,610	17	3 72	2	6 50
New York	71	12,780,250	61	3 70	10	6 70
North Carolina	8	187,000	..	..	8	5 93
Ohio	30	3,338,600	29	3 85	1	7 00
Oregon	1	50,000	1	8 00	..	..
Pennsylvania	48	5,657,700	48	3 55	..	..
Rhode Island	7	1,344,000	6	3 58	1	7 00
South Carolina	2	767,800	2	5 00	..	..
Tennessee	4	663,000	4	4 00	..	..
Texas	3	225,000	3	6 33	..	..
Vermont	8	216,000	6	4 25	2	6 50
Virginia	11	1,030,000	10	3 68	1	7 00
Wisconsin	8	778,500	8	4 44	..	..
Grand total	381	$47,911,215	346	..	35	..

The preparation of illuminating gas from bituminous coal, wood, rosin, and other bodies of organic nature, is a chemical process, too complicated to be very fully treated in this place. When such bodies are introduced into a retort and subjected to strong heat, the elements of which they consist, as carbon, hydrogen, oxygen, and nitrogen, resolve themselves into a great variety of compounds, and escape (with the exception of a fixed carbonaceous residue of charcoal or of coke) through the neck of the retort in the form of gas or vapors, some of the latter of which condense on cooling into liquids and solids. These compounds are rendered more complicated by appropriating the elements of air and moisture that may be present in the retort or in the crude material, and also of the foreign substances or impurities contained in the latter. In processes of this kind, the products vary greatly in their character and relative proportions according to the degree of heat employed, and the rapidity with which the operation is conducted. The object in this special distillation is to obtain the largest proportion of the gases richest in carbon, particularly that known as olefiant gas, which consists of 86 parts by weight of carbon and 14 of hydrogen, represented by the formula $C_4 H_4$. This and some other gaseous hydrocarbons of similar composition, or even containing a much larger amount of carbon in the same volume, and hence having a correspondingly greater illuminating capacity, it is found, are produced most freely from carbonaceous substances which contain a large proportion of hydrogen compared with that of oxygen. Many of the common bituminous coals contain about 5·5 per cent. each of hydrogen and oxygen, the rest being carbon. Boghead cannel of Scotland contains 11 per cent. of hydrogen and 6·7 of oxygen; rosin 10 per cent. hydrogen and 10·6 oxygen; wood 5·5 hydrogen and 44·5 oxygen. Of such compounds the cannel yields the richest gas and in largest quantity. Still, as will be more fully explained hereafter, the process may be so conducted as to obtain chiefly liquid instead of gaseous products. With the olefiant gas and the others of similar composition, a number of other gases also appear, some of which seem to be essential for producing the effect required in illuminating gas, though they do not themselves afford light by their combustion. Their part is rather like that of nitrogen in the atmosphere, to moderate the intensity of the more active agent of the mixture. Such are the light carburetted hydrogen, carbonic oxide, and hydrogen, all of which are inflammable, but possess little or no illuminating power. The first named contains in an equal volume only half as much carbon as olefiant gas, its composition being represented by the formula C_2 H_4, and if its proportion is too great for the purpose it serves as a diluent, the quality of the gas is impaired, and must be corrected by the use of richer material or increased care in the process.

The light produced by the combustion of gas is variable, not only according to the quality of the gas, but also according to the manner in which it is burned. If its elements undergo the chemical changes which constitute combustion simultaneously, the hydrogen combining with the oxygen of the air to form aqueous vapor, and the carbon with oxygen to produce carbonic acid, no yellow flame appears, but instead of this, a pale blue flame like that of hydrogen alone. Such an effect is produced when air is thoroughly intermixed with the gas as it passes through a tube to the jet where it is ignited. But if the conditions of the combustion are such that the hydrogen burns first and appropriates the oxygen in contact with the gas, the particles of carbon are brought to an incandescent state and produce the yellow light before they reach the oxygen with which they combine. The particles may even be arrested while *in transitu* and be deposited upon a cold surface in the form of soot. The greatest heat is produced with the most thorough mode of combustion and the appearance of the pale blue flame; and lamps designed to give great heat are now in general use among chemists, in which gas is burned in this manner. When the air is impelled by a bellows they even produce an intensity of heat sufficient for many crucible operations.

If too much carbon be present a part of it escapes unconsumed and produces a smoky flame, hence the necessity of the diluents or gases deficient in carbon for neutralizing the too large proportion of those gases richest in carbon. The noxious compounds in illuminating gas, and which should be as far as possible extracted from it before it is delivered for consumption, are the sulphurous ingredients formed by the combination of the sulphur of the iron pyrites commonly present in bituminous coals with the carbon, and with the hydrogen and the ammoniacal products. They are the highly offensive sulphurets of carbon, the sulphuretted hydrogen, etc. Carbonic acid, nitrogen, oxygen, carbonate of ammonia and aqueous vapors are to be regarded as foreign substances, though always present to some extent in the gas.

The liquids generated by the distillation mostly condense in two layers on cooling, the upper an aqueous fluid, rendered strongly alkaline by the ammoniacal compounds in solution; and the lower a black tarry mixture commonly known as coal tar, which is composed of more than a dozen different oily hydrocarbons, as benzole, tuluole, etc., and contain in solution the solid oily compounds of carbon and hydrogen, as naphthaline, para-naphthaline, and several others. Many of these are likely to prove of considerable practical importance. Benzole is a highly volatile fluid, a powerful solvent of the resins, india-rubber, gutta percha, greasy matters, etc. A most beautiful light is produced by the flame of benzole mixed with due proportions of common air, and the mixture is effected by passing a current of air through the fluid, the vapor of which it takes up and carries along with it. The difficulty attending this application is the condensation of the benzole and its separation from the air at temperatures below 50°. Above 70° too much vapor is taken up, and the effect is a smoky flame. In Europe much attention has been directed to the separation of the more hidden products of coal tar; and among these the following are enumerated in a statement exemplifying the rapid increase in the value of these products as they are obtained by more extended researches. Benzole worth about 25 cents a pound; nitro-benzole, a substance having the odor and taste of bitter almonds and used as a flavoring, worth, crude, 70 cents, or refined, $1.50 per pound. The ordinary aniline dye for producing the mauve color, $4.50 to $8 per pound, and the pure aniline violet in powder $240 to $325 per pound, or about its weight in gold.

Gas works established in cities and towns are commonly built in places where the property and buildings around are least likely to be injured by the escape of the products, and rather upon a low than a high level, for the reason that the gas on account of its lightness compared with the atmospheric air ascends more freely than it descends to its points of communication with the external air. The works consist of the apparatus for distilling the coal and receiving the products of the distillation, that for purifying the gas, and that for conveying it to the places where it is consumed, and there measuring the quantities supplied to each customer. The retorts in general use are either of cast iron or of fire clay. The latter are a late improvement highly recommended, and introduced at the present time into a few of the gas works. Various forms have been tried; the most approved are of ⌂ shape, 7 to 9 feet long, 1 or 2 feet wide, and 12 or 15 inches high. They are set in the furnace stacks, commonly two on the same horizontal plane, two more over these, and a fifth at the top. A single furnace fire below is sufficient for heating them, and the capacity of the works is increased by multiplying these fires along the length of the stacks. Sometimes the stacks are made double, so as to take two retorts set end to end, each opening on opposite sides of the stack. In place of two retorts a single long one has been substituted, passing entirely through and having at each end an opening for charging and discharging. In large establishments as many as 600 or more retorts may be set, all of which may be kept employed in the winter season, when the consumption of gas is largest. The outer end of each retort projects a little way in front of the wall of the furnace, and is provided with a movable mouth-piece covering the entire end, which may be readily removed for admitting the charge of coal. Upon the top of this projecting end or neck stands the cast-iron pipe of about 4 inches in diameter, called the stand pipe, through which the volatile products pass from the retort. It rises a few feet, then curves over back, and passes down into a long horizontal pipe of large diameter, which is laid upon the outer edge of the brick-work, and extends the whole length of the furnace stacks. This is called the hydraulic main, and into it all the volatile products from the retorts beneath are discharged. It is kept about half filled with water or the liquid tarry matters, and the dip pipes terminate about three inches below this fluid surface. By this arrangement the retorts are kept entirely independent of each other, while their products all meet in one receptacle.

In manufacturing gas it is found necessary to introduce the charge into the retorts already at a full red heat, and bring it as rapidly as possible to the high temperature required for producing the richest gaseous hydrocarbons. A low and slowly increasing heat causes the ingredients of the charge to form a large proportion of liquid and oily substances, and little gas. It is only while the coal is approaching a vivid red heat that the best gaseous mixtures are obtained; and even these are deteriorated by change in the composition of the olefiant and other rich gases of which they are in part composed, if the mixture is exposed to too high temperature, or remains in contact with red hot surfaces of iron. The duration of the charge used formerly to be from 8 to 10 hours; but from the observations of the qualities of the gases evolved at different stages of the process, it has gradually been reduced to 4 to 6 hours, varying according to the character of the coal employed. The richest gases are obtained in the first hour, and after this the proportional quantity per hour steadily diminishes at the same time that the quality gradually deteriorates. The temptation, however, to obtain the largest amount of a commodity which is sold only by measure, and to consumers who have no means of assuring themselves of its real quality, no doubt often leads to extending the operation to the separation of gaseous mixtures having very little illuminating power. The manufacturers knowing their materials, and checking their operations by regular photometrical tests, can control the quality of the product as they see fit.

In order that the least loss may be incurred in bringing the charge up to the proper temperature, the retorts are kept at a full red heat; and when ready for a new charge the mouth-piece is partially removed, and the gas that escapes is ignited. When the danger of explosion by sudden admission of air has passed the lid is removed, and the red hot coke is raked out and quenched with water.

The new charge is then introduced by means of a long iron scoop bent up at the sides, which is pushed into the retort, and being turned over, discharges its contents. The mouth-piece is then replaced, and tightly secured with a luting of clay or lime. It is obvious that the more perfectly the coal is freed from moisture, the better must be the gas; and if it were also first somewhat heated, the result would be still more satisfactory. The coals employed at the different gas works of the United States are generally mixtures of the caking coals of the interior, or of those of Richmond, Virginia, and of Nova Scotia, with cannel coal, which for the cities near the coast is imported from Great Britain, and for those in the interior is obtained from the mines of this coal in western Virginia and in Kentucky. The larger the proportion of cannel, the better should be the gas, under the same method of manufacture. In the works in New York city, the proportion of cannel is generally from one third to one fourth of the whole. Other establishments generally use a less proportion of it. The amount of gas it may produce varies with the kind of cannel from 9500 cubic feet to the ton to 15,000 cubic feet. The last is the yield of the Boghead cannel. In general, the greater the yield the better also is the quality of the gas, as is indicated by its increased specific gravity, that of the cannel last named being .752, while the gas from other cannels yielding about 10,000 cubic feet may not exceed .500. The best Newcastle coals are not inferior, either in the amount or quality of the gas they afford, to most of the cannels. They produce about 12,000 cubic feet of gas to the ton, and of specific gravity sometimes exceeding .550 or even .600. The specific gravity is not depended upon as a certain test of the quality of the gas, the density of which may be increased by presence of impure heavy gases, or even of atmospheric air; but it is resorted to only as an indication in the absence of more exact tests.

The coke obtained from the retorts, amounting to about 40 bushels to the ton of coals, furnishes all the fuel required for the fires beneath, and three times as much more, which is sold for fuel. As the volatile products pass through the hydraulic main, the principal portions of the oily and ammoniacal compounds are deposited in it; but some of these pass on in vapors, and would, if not separated, cause obstructions in the pipes in which they might condense in liquids and solids. They are consequently passed through a succession of tall iron pipes standing in the open air, and sometimes kept cool by water trickling down their outside. A pipe from the bottom of each pair conveys the condensed tar and ammonia into a cistern in the ground. To still further separate the condensable portions, the gas at some works is next passed into the bottom of a tower filled with bricks, stones, etc., among the interstices of which it finds its way up, at the same time that water constantly sprinkled on the top is working down and keeping the whole cool. The water washes away the remaining ammonia; but it is to be feared that it also removes some of the richest hydrocarbons, and the use of the wet scrubber, as it is called, is already abandoned at some of the gas works for similar methods of condensing, except that the water is dispensed with. The gas makes its exit from the top of the scrubber; and its passage being already somewhat impeded so as to throw considerable pressure back into the retorts, thus effecting chemical changes in the gas, which impair its quality, it is found necessary to introduce a revolving exhauster, which takes off this pressure, and at the same time propels the gas forward into the succeeding apparatus. This is first a purifier, the object of which is to arrest the carbonic acid and sulphurous gases. Dry quicklime, and also the solution of this in water, known as milk of lime, have the property of absorbing these gases as they are made to pass among the particles of the one spread upon shelves, or interspersed among a porous substance such as dry moss; or to bubble up through the aqueous solution. The lime as it becomes saturated with the impure gases is replaced with fresh portions.

The cleansing process is now complete, and the gas is in proper condition to be delivered to the consumer. It must first, however, be measured, that a record may be kept of the quantity produced, and it is next conducted into the great gas-holders in which it is stored. The measurement is effected by means of a large station meter, constructed on the principle of the small service-meters, with one of which each consumer is supplied. A revolving drum with four compartments of equal capacity is made to rotate in a tight box by the gas entering and filling one of these compartments after another.

Their capacity being known, and the number of revolutions being recorded by a train of wheel-work outside the box, the quantity of gas which passes through is exactly indicated. The largest meters pass about 650 cubic feet by one revolution of the drum, or about 70,000 cubic feet in an hour.

The gas-holders are the large cylindrical vessels of plate iron, the most conspicuous objects at the gas works. Each one is set with its open end down, and immersed in a cistern of water of diameter a little exceeding its own. It is buoyed up by the water, and also counterbalanced by weights passing over pulleys. The gas admitted under the inverted cylinder lifts this up, and fills all the portion above the water. The weight of the cylinder when the influx is shut off, and the discharge pipes are opened presses the gas out and through the mains to the points where it is consumed. The gas-holders of the largest works are of immense size. In Philadelphia, there is one 160 feet in diameter and 95 feet high, holding 1,800,000 cubic feet of gas. Even this is exceeded by one at the Imperial Gas Company's works, London, which is 201 feet in diameter, 80 feet high, and of the capacity of 2,500,000 cubic feet. This cost upward of $200,000 ; and contains 1500 tons of iron, 5000 cubic feet of stone work, and 2,000,000 bricks. No advantage is gained in a single structure of this immense size over several smaller ones. On the contrary, this involves heavy expenditures to protect them against the force of the wind, and render them manageable. Those of great height are made in sections, which shut one within another in descending, like the parts of a telescope. As each section is lifted in turn out of the water, its lower edge, which is turned up in an outward direction, forming an annular cup, includes a portion of water, into which the upper edge of the next lower section catches, being turned over inward for this purpose. A gas-tight joint between the two sections is thus formed.

To insure uniformity of pressure, as the gas enters the mains it is first made to pass through the apparatus called a governor, in which, according to the force or slowness with which it moves, it causes a valve to rise and partially close an aperture within the machine through which the gas flows, or to descend and open this aperture. The increase of pressure as the gas is carried to higher levels, amounting to one fifth of an inch of water in every 30 feet, renders it important in hilly towns to have governors upon different levels. In high buildings a very sensible difference is perceived in the force with which the gas issues from the burners on the different stories. This involves a waste of gas where the pressure is great, for under such conditions a considerable portion of that consumed adds little to the illuminating effect. Various governors or regulators have been devised for the use of consumers with a view of producing an increase of light with reduced consumption of gas; and when judiciously applied, some of them, as Kidder's and Stirling's, have proved very successful. The latter has been introduced into some of the public buildings of New York city, controlled by the Street Department, and according to the report of the Street Commissioner, the saving has been in many instances very remarkable.

Each consumer of gas is supplied with a meter, which is under the control of the gas company; and from its indications the amount furnished is determined by inspection every month.

Though in the use of gas the consumer is in a great measure dependent on the manufacturer as regards the economy of the light, there are several points, by giving personal attention to which, he may more fully realize the saving it affords. In the first place, he must be aware that every one employing this source of light uses it more freely than that derived from lamps and candles. It is enjoyed with so little trouble and apparent cost, that much more light is soon regarded essential, than was perfectly satisfactory under the old methods of producing it. He should next see that the area of the delivery pipe bears such proportion to the quantity usually required, that there is no undue pressure upon the burners, as is evident when the gas "blows" through them as it burns. This should be checked by shutting off a part of the supply by means of the stop-cock at the meter; and this should be looked to after every visit of the gas man to the meter. The regulator also is intended to remedy this over supply, but it may still be necessary to keep part of the gas turned off, and by so doing the regulator may be dispensed with. Attention should next be directed to the burners, that those of largest size, such as consume with the ordinary pressure six feet or more of gas an hour, should be placed only where the greatest quantity of light is required, and that burners of four feet, three feet, two feet, or even one foot an hour, be placed where the light they give will be sufficient. The burners called Scotch tips, giving what is called the fish-tail flame, are in common use, but a great variety of others have been contrived, and some of them are highly recommended for affording more light with the same amount of gas. All, however, are liable to become foul after a time, and should be occasionally cleaned or replaced. The iron of which they are made is corroded by the ingredients of the gas, especially when not in use, and air entering its elements form acid compounds with those of the gas which remain in the open portion of the pipe. The argand burner is recommended for the powerful and steady light it gives, but it is far from being economical, and moreover produces great heat. For a steady light Gleason's "American gas-burner" combines the advantages of brilliant light, steadiness of flame, and moderate consumption.

The quality of gas is determined either by analysis, or more conveniently by testing with the photometer its comparative capacity of producing light. The standard adopted for comparison is spermaceti candles, each one burning 120 grains in an hour. An argand burner consuming five feet of gas an hour (the quantity carefully proved by the meter) is used in making the trial; and the number of candles required to produce an equal amount of light indicates the quality of the gas. At the points of consumption this is sometimes inferior to that of the gas at the works before it enters the gas-holders and passes through the mains; but in very cold weather, by the condensation of the richest hydrocarbon vapor in the pipes, the gas that reaches the burners is poorer than that which left the works. Consequently these facts should be taken into consideration in estimating the quality of gas furnished by any establishment. Again, after a period of excessive cold weather, when the gas has burned dimly by the condensation of its best portions in the pipes—it may be to the extent at times of obstructing the flow through them—and with the return of milder weather the vapors are released and mix with the new gas, they sometimes so overburden this with an undue proportion of the richest compounds, that with the ordinary burners the gas cannot be consumed, and the result is a smoky flame, of which the consumers make great complaint, believing it to be caused by inferior gas. Such are some of the causes, over which the manufacturers have no control, that involve more or less irregularity in the quality of the gas supplied.

The gas produced at different works is of various qualities. That of the Manhattan Gas Light Company is rated at sixteen candles, and is probably as good as any furnished in our cities. It is tested daily with the photometer at their office, at the corner of Irving Place and Fifteenth street, New York. In England, the gas of the London works varies from eleven to eighteen candles. That of Liverpool is much better, sometimes being equal to twenty-two candles.

Other materials than coal have been applied to some extent in the United States for producing gas, chiefly for small supplies for single buildings. The most successful of these processes is that with rosin oil. The apparatus is exceedingly simple, and is placed in an apartment in an out-building. It consists of a stove containing a chamber in the top, into which the rosin oil is allowed to drop slowly. It is decomposed by the heat of the surface upon which it falls, and the gaseous products pass immediately through the pipes into the gas-holder, whence they are distributed as at the large gas works. The supply for a week may be made in less than an hour with very little attention from the person in charge. The gas is superior to that from coal, and the expense, not reckoning the cost of the gas-holder and the apparatus, is less than the price ordinarily paid for gas.

In Philadelphia wood has been successfully used at the Market street bridge works. Six retorts have been kept in operation with it for some time, and the yield and quality of the gas have proved very satisfactory. As in the use of coal, it is found necessary to charge the material into retorts already at a high heat, otherwise the gaseous products have little illuminating power. Gas thus made from pine wood has been found to contain 10.57 per cent. of olefiant gas, and that from oak 6.46 per cent.

HYDROCARBON GAS.—What is known as the hydrocarbon or water gas manufacture was introduced into Philadelphia in 1858, and according to the published reports, its application to lighting a portion of the Girard House in that city, proved for several months perfectly satisfactory. It was introduced into the town of Aurora, Indiana, in January, 1861, and according to the statements published in the Cincinnati *Daily Commercial*, the operation had been very successful. The light is described as very brilliant, and the gas almost free from odor. The process appears to be similar to that of Mr. White, of Manchester, England, which consists in the generation of the non-illuminating gases by the action of steam upon charcoal highly heated in a retort, the aqueous vapor being thereby decomposed, and various gaseous compounds produced by its hydrogen and oxygen combining with the carbon of the charcoal. If the operation is properly conducted these compounds should be almost entirely carbonic oxide and free hydrogen; if carbonic acid is produced, as it may well be, even to the extent of one per cent., it may involve the expense of purification by means of a lime purifier. These gases are immediately passed through another retort, in which the illuminating gases are generated, and mixing with them the whole is immediately swept forward out of the reach of the high decomposing temperature. The material employed for furnishing the illuminating gas is either rosin or rosin oil gadually dropped into the heated retort; and it is stated that various other carbonaceous substances, as the tar from the gas works and cheap greasy compounds, may be economically applied.

Although this method of producing gas has been highly recommended by eminent English authorities, especially by Dr. Frankland, an account of whose experiments and conclusions is given in the recent edition of Ure's Dictionary (London, 1860), vol. i., p. 778, it has not been adopted by gas companies, whose first interest it would be to avail themselves of such improvements, and it is reasonable to suppose there are some insuperable objections to it. Indeed, in the last edition of Clegg's "Treatise upon the Manufacture and Use of Gas," the subject is passed by with scarcely any notice, although it had been in the previous edition treated in detail and with commendation. In the English *Gas Journal*, it is decidedly condemned. No analyses of the gas thus produced in this country have ever been published, nor any reports of photometrical experiments that might establish its light-giving capacity. As the subject has attracted so much interest of late, and has given rise to extravagant expectations of cheap production of gas, it is very desirable that such trials and reports should be made by some competent chemist. In Philadelphia, the subject has given rise to a newspaper controversy, and the publications were embodied, in 1860, in a pamphlet entitled "The Water Gas Correspondence." They contained nothing, however, to determine the real merits of the gas.

Gas for Steamboats and Railroad Cars.—Several methods have recently been put in practice of furnishing gas for the convenience of passengers in steam vessels, or upon railroads. One plan is to place in the boats or under the cars large cases of sheet iron, each one provided with a diaphragm or partition of india-rubber across its upper portion. A connection being made between the receptacle under the diaphragm and the street main, the gas fills this portion of the case and the connection is then shut off. When required for use, the gas is forced out by the pressure of air uniformly applied upon the upper surface of the india-rubber sheet by means of a meter running by clock work. This method has so far been successful; but danger is apprehended by some that atmospheric air may find its way through the flexible sheets, all of which are more or less permeable when used to separate different gaseous compounds, and that an explosive mixture may thus be introduced. By another plan of a New York company, the gas by means of force pumps is compressed into strong cylindrical gas-holders made like the boilers of steam engines. The gas is thus made to occupy a diminished space in proportion to the pressure used, that of 20 atmospheres placing 1000 cubic feet of gas in 50 feet space. In Jersey City, where this method has been applied to furnishing gas for railroad cars, the pressure employed is about 450 lbs. upon the square inch. Under this pressure the gas is conveyed through pipes to the points where the cars receive from them their supplies. The gas by its elasticity presses through the burners, and uniformity of discharge while this force is constantly diminishing is secured by a governor or regulator constructed on the principle already described.

Gas for Fuel.—Besides its use for producing light, gas has lately been applied to other domestic purposes for the sake of the heat it can be made to afford in burning. It was thus first used by chemists, and mechanics, as bookbinders, then applied it in suitable stoves to the heating of such tools as they required of a high temperature. After this stoves were contrived on different plans in which various culinary operations might be conducted, and some also for warming rooms. Though it would appear to be an expensive fuel, it has been found for many purposes, in which only a certain amount of heat is required, and this for a short time, not merely exceedingly convenient, but even economical. No more need be consumed than is required to effect the desired purpose, and it is moreover applied directly to the object to be heated with little dispersion or waste of heat. But for warming rooms, it is objectionable, not only on account of its cost, but also from its vitiating the atmosphere by the large amount of the noxious gases produced by its combustion. If these are conveyed away by ventilating flues, they carry with them a considerable portion of the caloric set free. No doubt when gas is afforded at lower rates, means will be devised of applying it more advantageously to this purpose.

CHAPTER XI.

HYDROCARBON OR COAL OILS.

NOTWITHSTANDING the substitution in the cities and most of the towns of considerable size throughout the country of gas for oils, the demand for the latter has increased much faster than the supply, as is shown by the price for sperm oil being now more than three times what it was in 1843, when it brought about fifty-five cents per gallon. Besides its use for illuminating purposes, the consumption of oil is enormous for lubricating machinery. The railroads and steamboats, and the increasing numbers of large factories, demand such quantities of it that all the ordinary sources of supply were overtasked, and the whaling business formerly so prosperous in New England, has fallen off in the face of advancing prices, or been forced to gather itself in fewer centres, where by concentration of its operations the business could be conducted with the greatest economy. From many seaports of New England this business has quite disappeared, and the following changes in others are reported to have taken place between the years 1843 and 1859. In the former period New Bedford had 214 whale ships, and in 1859 the number had increased to 316. In New London, Conn., the number had increased from 45 to 56, and in Mattapoiset from 11 to 19. In other towns the number of ships had fallen off as follows: Nantucket, to 33 from 85; Sag Harbor, to 20 from 43; Warren, R. I., to 15 from 21, etc. At Fairhaven, 46 ships were owned at both periods. The manufacture of lard oil, which of late years has been extensively carried on in the Western states, failed to meet the increasing demands, when at last attention began to be directed to the extraction of oils from the bituminous coals and shales, by processes of recent introduction in France and England. The success attained by Mr. James Young, of Glasgow, in his treatment of the "Torbane Hill mineral," or Boghead cannel of Scotland, served more than any thing else to give encouragement to this enterprise. In 1854, according to the testimony of this practical chemist, in a lawsuit in London, he was producing about 8000 gallons a week of an oil he called paraffine oil, which sold for 5s. a gallon, the sales amounting in all to about $500,000 per annum, of which the greater portion was profit. Operations of a similar character had for some time previously been conducted upon a large scale at Autun, Department of the Saone and Loire, in France; the materials employed being highly bituminous shales, probably not essentially different from the Torbane Hill mineral, except in producing much less oil to the ton.

The first factory for making coal oil in the United States was established on Newtown Creek, Long Island, opposite New York city, and commenced operations in June, 1854. This was known as the Kerosene Oil Works, and was designed to work the Boghead cannel, or coal of similar character from the province of New Brunswick, or from the West, by the patented process of Mr. Young. In Kentucky, Ohio, Virginia, and Pennsylvania cannel coals were found of suitable qualities for this manufacture; and in 1856 the Breckenridge Coal Oil Works were in successful operation at Cloverport, on the Ohio river, in Breckenridge county, Ky. The same year a factory was built in Perry county, Ohio, by Messrs. Dillie and Robinson, and others rapidly sprung up in the vicinity of Newark, which soon became an important centre of this new business. In 1858, several large factories were built in New England, one in Boston, and one in Portland, Maine. The following is an incomplete list of factories which have been put in operation, not including some which have been destroyed by fire:—

TABLE OF THE COAL OIL WORKS OF THE UNITED STATES.

State.	Town or county.	Name of works.	No. of factories.	Daily capacity in 1860. Gallons.
Maine,	Portland	Portland Company	1	4000
Massachusetts,	Boston	Downer Kerosene Co.	1	4000
"	"	Page & Co.	1	600
"	"	Suffolk Company	1	300
"	"	Pinkham	1	..
"	"	Peasley	1	..
"	East Cambridge	E. Cambridge Company	1	800
"	New Bedford	New Bedford Company	1	300
Connecticut,	Hartford	Hartford Company	1	200
"	Stamford	Stamford Company	1	..
New York,	Newtown Creek, L. I.	Kerosene Oil Company	1	4000
"	Hunter's Point, L. I.	Luther Atwood	1	2000
"	"	Carbon Company	1	300
"	South Brooklyn	Empire State Company	1	300
"	"	Franklin Company	1	500
"	Williamsburgh	Long Island Company	1	..
"	"	Knickerbocker Company	1	..
"	"	Fountain Oil Co.	1	400
"	Harlem	Beloni & Co.	1	50
"	"	Excelsior Company	1	..
Pennsylvania,	Darlington, Beaver Co.	Anderson & Co.	1	..
"	" "		1	..
"	Kiskiminitas	Aladdin Company	1	..
"	"	Lucesco Company	1	} 2000 (for the four works bracketed)
"	Freeport, Armstrong Co.	North American Company	1	
"	New Galilee	New Galilee	1	
"	Enon Valley	Enon Valley Company	1	..
Ohio,	E. Palestine, Columbiana Co.	Palestine Company	1	..
"	Canfield, Mahoning Co.	Cornell & Company	1	..
"	" "	Sherwood	1	..
"	" "	Phœnix	1	..
"	" "	Mystic	1	..
"	" "	Canfield	1	..
"	Cleveland	Dean	1	..
"	Zanesville	Brooks	1	..
"	"	Cox	1	..
	Newark, Licking Co.	Great Western	1	500
"	" "	Three others	3	..
"	Steubenville, Jefferson Co.		2	..
"	Coshocton Co.		7	..
"	Columbus, Franklin Co.		1	..
"	Cincinnati	Grasseli	1	..
"	"	Western Company	1	..
"	"	Phœnix Company	1	..
"	Perry Co.	Robinson & Co.	1	..
Virginia,	Kanawha region	Falling Rock Company	1	..
"	" "	Forest Hill Company	1	..
"	" "	Greers	1	..
"	" "	Great Kanawha Company	1	..
"	" "	Staunton Company	1	..
"	" "	Atlantic Company	1	..
"	" "	Union Company	1	..
"	" "	K. C. C. M. and O. M. Company	1	..
"	Preston Co.	Preston Company	1	..
"	Monongalia Co.	White Bay Company	1	..
"	Ritchie Co.	Ritchie Company	1	..
"	Wheeling	New York and Wheeling Company	1	..
"	Taylor Co.	Marion Company	1	..
Kentucky,	Maysville, Mason Co.	Union Company	1	..
"	" "	Ashland	1	..
	Carried forward		69	

State.	Town or county.	No. factories.
	Brought forward	69
Kentucky	Cloverport, Breckenridge Co.	1
"	Covington and Newport, opposite Cincinnati	2
"	Owsley Co.	1
Missouri,	St. Louis	1
	Total	74

Supposing these works to average 400 gallons of light oil daily, the total production would be 32,400 gallons, or for 300 days in the year, 9,720,000 gallons. The figures of capacity of production represent the amount of light oils only; besides these about half as much more heavy oils and paraffine are obtained, which are more or less converted to useful purposes. The quantities named are approximate averages of the production, which it is impossible to give with accuracy, as the factories are constantly varying in their capacity by the introduction of more retorts and stills. They are presented rather to show the rapid progress made in this branch of manufacture than to attempt to give its real extent. A correct list of all the works cannot yet be made out.

HISTORY AND METHOD OF THE MANUFACTURE.

The possibility of extracting oil from bituminous minerals appears to have been known since the year 1694, a patent having been granted in January of that year to Martin Eele, Thomas Hancock, and William Portlock, for "a way to extract and make great quantities of pitch, tarr, and oyle out of a sort of stone, of which there is a sufficient found within our dominions of England and Wales." This stone proved to be a bituminous shale; and in 1716 it was again applied to similar use under another patent, granted to M. & T. Belton, of Shrewsbury. In the course of the eighteenth century the oily product obtained was employed to some extent as a medicine, under the name of British or petroleum oil. Though from time to time other patents were granted in England for the same process, the business never became of importance there until the successful trials were made by Mr. James Young, of Glasgow, upon the Boghead cannel already referred to. On the continent the subject was brought before the public by the researches of Baron Von Reichenbach in 1829, '30, and '31, when he discovered and separated numerous new compounds from the products of the slow distillation of bituminous substances. The compound he named eupion is the same thing as the rectified oil now known as coal oil, paraffine oil, kerosene, photogenic, pyrogenic oil, and by other local or commercial names. He appreciated its useful properties, and recommended the prosecution of further trials with the object of establishing the best mode of separating it. In France its character was understood in 1824, when a patent was granted for its manufacture; and in 1833 factories were in operation for producing it. In 1834 the method adopted by Selligue was first published, and in the specification of the patent granted to him, March 19, 1845, is a full account of the process as conducted in the works at Autun. This is still the best treatise published upon the manufacture, and notwithstanding the numerous patents which have since been issued, the improvements are limited to comparatively unimportant modifications of the apparatus. In the United States the first patent granted in this manufacture was in March, 1852, to James Young for his process, which in this country was first introduced at the kerosene oil works on Newtown Creek. The next year two patents were granted, in 1854 and 1855 one each, in 1856 six, in 1858 seven, and in 1859 twenty-two.

As mentioned in the preceding chapter, the products obtained by the distillation of bituminous substances vary according to the amount of heat employed and the manner of its application, whether sudden or gradual. Coals thrown into red hot retorts are resolved into large quantities of gas, with the production of inconsiderable quantities of oily compounds heavier in the aggregate than water, and called coal tar. They consist of a variety of hydrocarbons, as the fluids designated by the name of naphtha, the white crystalline substance called naphthaline, the very volatile fluid benzole, besides carbolic acid and a great number of other curious and interesting compounds of hydrogen and carbon. In general they contain a less proportional amount of hydrogen than the products obtained by slow distillation, the fluids are denser, and their boiling points higher.

When the bituminous substances are gradually and moderately heated in retorts, the production of gas is small, the carbon and hydrogen separating chiefly in the form of oily compounds of a greenish color, the specific gravity of which is less than water. These compounds form what is called crude coal oil, and are similar in appearance and composition to the natural petroleum, or rock oil, obtained in some places from the earth, as will be described in the next chapter. Benzole and naphthaline, products of the other method of distillation, are found, if at all, as a result of the employment of too high heat, and instead of the latter the waxy or spermaceti-like substance called paraffine is generated and is held in solution in the oils, from which it may be separated by repeated distillations, and draining off through filters and pressing out the fluid portions of the concentrated residues, at the lowest available temperatures. The oily products are divisible into a great number of distinct compounds by means of repeated distillations, each one being carefully conducted at a certain degree of temperature, and the product which comes over at this degree being kept by itself. But in the large way they are separated into only three classes, which are distinguished as the light oils for lamps, the heavy oils which are suitable for lubricating purposes, and paraffine. Sometimes a mixture of the heaviest oils and paraffine is made use of and sold for wagon grease and such purposes; and the first products which come over in the distillation are kept by themselves, and sold under the name of naphtha (or incorrectly as benzole) to be used as a solvent for the resins, caoutchouc, etc., and for removing grease spots from fabrics.

The proportions obtained from a ton of coal or shale are very variable. The Boghead cannel yields, in well-conducted operations, about 117 gallons of crude oil, from which the product of refined oil is about 60 gallons. It can be made to produce even 130 gallons of crude oil, containing a larger proportion of refined oil than the 117 gallons ordinarily obtained. The Breckenridge coal yields from 90 to 100 gallons of crude oil, and this 50 to 60 of refined oil. The Cannelton coal of Virginia is of similar quality to the Breckenridge cannel. The coals of Ohio run from 55 to 87 gallons of crude oils to the ton, and those of Darlington, Penn., from 45 to 55 gallons. Besides the oils there also come over from the retorts, as in the gas manufacture, a quantity of water rendered alkaline by the ammonia it holds. This collects at the bottom of the reservoirs into which the products are received, and the oil that floats upon the surface being removed the ammoniacal liquors are allowed to escape.

While the general plan of the operations is the same in all the factories, the apparatus is variously modified. By Mr. Young's process the coal is distilled in cast-iron ⌓-shaped retorts, like those employed in making gas, and the volatile products are passed by a worm through a refrigerator kept at a temperature of about 55° F. The oils as they condense drop from the end of the worm into a receiver. Many patents have been granted in Europe and in this country for different kinds of retorts. Some are made of cylindrical form and set upright in the furnace; the charge is introduced at the top and drawn out, when exhausted, at the bottom; the volatile products making their exit either through pipes at the top or at different heights. Some have been constructed of fire clay instead of cast iron. In order that the charge may be uniformly heated, revolving cylindrical retorts have been contrived and patented, first in France many years ago, and recently in the United States. They are sometimes eight feet long and six feet diameter, suspended upon an axle at each end. They are charged through a manhole in the front end like the common horizontal retorts, and the vapors pass out through the axle at the opposite end, which is made hollow for this purpose. Retorts of the size named are charged with about a ton of cannel coal, and four such charges may be worked off in twenty-four hours. They revolve slowly, about twice in a minute, thus turning the charge over and causing it to be uniformly exposed to the fire beneath. At the Lucesco works, thirty miles above Pittsburg, on the Alleghany, ten large revolving retorts are stated to be in operation, each one of the capacity of two and a half tons. They are recommended for the rapidity with which the process is conducted, and the large amount of oil obtained to the ton of coal while they continue in good order; and on the other hand it is objected to them that the coal is apt to be ground to powder, and the dust is carried along with the vapors, obstructing the condensing worm and adding to the cost of purification. They are, moreover, expensive to construct and liable to get out of order.

By all these arrangements the fire which causes the expulsion of the volatile matters is outside of the retorts. But the same object is also attained by the use of ovens and pits similar to those used for producing charcoal and coke, in which the material operated upon is itself partially consumed, to generate the heat required to drive off so much of its volatile constituents as may escape combustion. Kilns thus designed for extracting coal oils have been in use in this country and in Europe; and in Virginia, near Wheeling, the plan has been adopted of distilling the coal or shale in large pits dug in the ground of capacity sufficient to contain 100 tons of the raw material. These are covered with earth, and the fire being started at one end, the heat spreads the volatile products forward, and they are drawn out at the opposite end by the exhausting action caused by a jet of steam, and received into suitable condensing apparatus. Some of the kilns are constructed to be fired at the bottom, and the vapors then pass upward through the charge, and are conveyed in pipes from the top to the condensers. The kilns of the Kerosene Oil Company, patented by Mr. Luther Atwood, are made open at the top, and a downward draught through the charge, which is fired on the upper surface, is produced by a steam jet thrown into the eduction pipe that passes out from the bottom of the kiln. A partial vacuum is thus produced, causing a current of air to flow in from the kiln. At the works of this company there are 18 of these kilns in shape like a circular lime kiln, built of ordinary brick and lined with fire brick. They are 20 feet high and 12 feet diameter inside, each one having a capacity of over 25 tons of coal. When this amount of Boghead cannel is introduced it is covered with about four tons of Cumberland coal and a quantity of pine wood. This is set on fire, and at the same time the steam jet is let on. The heated gases from the combustibles above pass through the bituminous materials below; but little air reaches these that is not already deprived of its power of sustaining further combustion. The volatile products are gradually expelled before the slowly increasing heat, and the operation is not completed till the expiration of four days. It is hastened or checked, as may be necessary, by means of the steam jet by which the draught is controlled. What is left in the kiln is unconsumed coal and ashes —no good coke is produced. The condensers at these works are tall cylinders of boiler-plate iron. Passing through a succession of these the vapors collect and trickle down their sides, and the mixed oily and aqueous products are received into iron vats placed in the ground. The uncondensable gases escape into the open air from the top of the last of the cylinders. From the vats the oil rising to the surface flows over into a conduit that leads to a large cistern in the ground of the capacity of 40,000 gallons. The water at the same time is discharged by a pipe, one end of which is at the bottom of the vat, and the other is bent over its upper edge, the flow being caused by the difference of an inch in the elevation of the surface of the two vats. Some oil is carried over into the second vat, and this is separated by a repetition of the same arrangement, and so on through several vats, till the ammoniacal waters are finally allowed to escape after being first received into a large cistern, where some oil still collects upon the surface, and is removed by occasional skimming.

Still another method of conducting the dry distillation is by the introduction of highly heated steam into the retorts, as patented by Mr. William Brown, in 1853, in England and in this country, though this seems also to have been used in the original operations of Selligue in France. The effect of the steam is to aid in heating the charge, while at the same time the vapors are taken up and carried along by it, and protected from being burned or decomposed by remaining in contact with the hot surfaces of the retort. In the subsequent distillation of the crude oil, high steam is similarly applied in the stills.

Nearly the same process of refining is practised at all the factories. The crude oil is pumped up into large stills of cast or boiler-plate iron, with cast-iron bottoms two inches thick. The capacity of these at the works above referred to is 1500 gallons each, and the time required for distilling off this amount of oil is 24 hours. They are heated by fires of anthracite and coke, the latter being itself a product of the distillation and obtained from the inside of the stills after each heat. It is deposited from the crude oil and forms a solid and extremely hard incrustation which is sometimes nearly a foot thick upon the bottom of the stills. It is a much superior coke to that obtained from the gas retorts, and in its structure is coarsely honey-combed in the upper or last formed portions, gradually growing closer and more compact toward the bottom upon which it adheres. The distillation should be conducted at a temperature not exceeding 800° F., and the process may be rendered continuous by admitting a small stream of oil into the stills. The vapors passing through the goose-neck are condensed in a long worm kept in the water condenser, which should be, in the latter part of the distillation, at a temperature of 80° or more. It is necessary to guard against so low temperature as might cause the paraffine to solidify in the worm, which by stopping the flow of the products might result in blowing up the still. The heat is carefully regulated so that the oil comes over uniformly, flowing from the end of the worm in a steady stream. It is still of a greenish color, with more or less of its peculiar, disagreeable odor. Yet it is evidently purified to a considerable extent by its separation from the free carbon and other impurities, usually amounting to 10 or 12 per cent., which are left behind in the stills. The oils are next pumped into large cylindrical cisterns called agitators, to undergo the chemical treatment, which is in general the same as that practised by Selligue. An addition is made to them of a quantity of sulphuric acid, it may be to the amount of 5 per cent. The mixture is then violently agitated or made to sweep rapidly round by stirrers in the cisterns, moved by machinery. The pure oil and paraffine are unaffected by the chemical agents, but the carbonaceous particles and coloring matters are more or less charred and oxidized, and their condition is so changed that when the mixture is left for some hours to repose, they subside in great part together with the acid, and these can then be drawn off leaving the partially purified oil in the upper portion of the cisterns. This is next washed with about one fifth its quantity of water, which removes the soluble impurities and a portion of the remaining acid. These, after subsiding, being drawn off, a strong lye of potash or soda is introduced into the oil, which neutralizes and fixes what acid remains, and causes the precipitation of further portions of the coloring and tarry matters. The mixture is again agitated and is then left six hours to repose, after which the sediment being drawn off, it is again washed with water, and this too, with the matters it has taken up, are drawn off. In some places chalk or lime has been employed instead of the alkaline lye to neutralize and fix the acid, and the chemical treatment, as it is called, is in other respects variously modified. Though this has been designated the "cold" treatment, the temperature should not be allowed to fall below 90° during these processes.

At last the oils freed from most of their impurities are introduced into stills like those of the first set. The product which first comes over is a very light oil somewhat discolored, which is soon followed by a clear oil having little odor. This gradually increases in density from 0.733 to 0.820, up to which point the mixture of oils is classed as illuminating, and is without further preparation sufficiently pure to be at once barrelled for the market. After this the increasing depth of the color and the greater density of the product indicate that the light oils have been nearly exhausted, and the remaining portions are hence kept by themselves to afford the heavy lubricating oils, and also it may be, by means of fractional distillation, the additional quantities of light oils they still contain, and finally the paraffine which is chiefly concentrated with the last portions. This substance when separated from the oils by filtration and pressure at low temperatures, is of a dark color and somewhat offensive odor; and to bleach and deodorize it have proved to be somewhat troublesome and expensive operations. Exposure to the sunlight has a bleaching effect; but the processes for this purpose have not yet been made public. When obtained perfectly pure and white, difficulties have been encountered in running it into candles, which are not common to other materials used for this purpose. When cooled in ordinary moulds the paraffine would crack in lines radiating from the wick, and the exterior would present a clouded, mottled surface. The method of obviating this difficulty, as described in the French work, "Le Technologiste," of 1859, is to use a mould in two parts, that part for the point of the candle working in the other like a piston. These moulds being brought to the temperature of melted paraffine are filled and then immediately plunged into water at nearly the freezing point. Having remained 3 or 4 minutes, they are taken out and exposed to a current of cool air for 15 or 20 minutes. The candles then come out, as the movable part of the mould is pushed in, free from defects. This method is successfully introduced into the United States. Paraffine candles have been made at some of the coal oil works, as at those of New York, New Bedford, and Portland. They are of beautiful appearance, resembling the best sperm candles, and at the same time are more economical for the amount of light they afford. The oil that is pressed out from the paraffine is useful chiefly as a lubricator, and from the low temperature at which it is obtained, if for no other reason, it is insured against chilling in cold weather. The residue in the stills, is a mixture of the tarry matters with the portion of the chemical ingredients that was introduced with the oils. For this no use is found. The heavy oils find their principal application in lubricating machinery, and large quantities are consumed for this purpose upon the Western railroads. The heavier natural oils of Ohio, when washed clean from the sand that comes up with them, are also very well adapted for this use; but it is found advantageous to mix either the crude or manufactured article with an equal quantity of lard oil. The petroleum corrects the tendency of this to gum and chill, while it receives additional body from the lard oil. Another use for the heavy oils is for cleansing wool in the woollen factories, and where they have been tried for this purpose, they have been preferred to other oils. In currying leather, also, they are said to have proved a good substitute for fish oil. Experiments have been made with them in Ohio, for mixing paints, and the crude heavier kinds, as those of Mecca, treated in the same manner as linseed oil, boiling them with dryers, etc., formed a good body, covered the wood well, dried rapidly and perfectly, and formed a smooth, hard surface, retaining no odor. The great abundance of the supply of petroleum at the West has led to some speculation as to the probability of the hydrocarbon oils being used for fuel for steamboats, locomotives, and wherever a highly concentrated, portable, and manageable fuel is required. For domestic uses, also, such as require a fire only a little while at a time, the petroleum might be conveniently used in suitable stoves in the same manner that gas is applied to the same purpose. But experiments are wanting to establish the rate per gallon at which it might enter into competition with other fuels upon a larger scale. Besides the heavy and light oils, no other valuable products result from the distillation of the coal oils. Benzole is not a product of this process. It belongs, together with a special class of hydrocarbons designated as the benzole series, to the tar of the gas works; and if ever obtained in the coal oil distillation, it must be by bad management and the use of excess of heat. Some of the light oils, which first come over in the distillation, are often sold as benzole, and are used for removing grease spots—a purpose they answer nearly as well as benzole itself.

The light oils are superior in many respects to any other portable materials employed for illumination. The light they give is exceedingly brilliant, and at the same time pleasant to the eye. They have not the disagreeable odor of sperm oil, nor when spilled upon articles of dress or furniture are the spots difficult to remove. At present prices, the cost of the light is less than half that produced by sperm oil. Coal oils are free from the danger of explosion, which all the so-called "burning fluids" are liable to; and on the score of prudence and humanity their use ought to be encouraged in the place of these dangerous preparations, the employment of which, in spite of the numerous and ingenious safety lamps and expedients to guard against explosion, is continually resulting in terrible accidents and loss of life. The only objection to the coal oils, and the only cause that checks their more general use in the place of all other portable means of producing light, is that the lamps in which they are burned are somewhat more expensive than other lamps, and are incumbered with a glass chimney, which is found necessary for producing a flame free from smoke. Possibly some lamps may yet be contrived in which thorough combustion and a clear flame may be obtained without this inconvenient appendage. In the use of the coal oils a very mistaken preference is given by consumers to the most highly rectified—such as are clear like water; and these are now selling freely at 75 cents a gallon, while the oils of a slightly yellow color hardly find a sale at 60 cents. As regards illuminating power, the latter are actually to be preferred to the former at the same cost, so that the preference given to the clear oils is merely for their appearance.

CHAPTER XII.

PETROLEUM, OR ROCK OIL.

THE occurrence of an oily fluid oozing in some regions from the surface of the earth, coming out with the springs of water, and forming a layer upon its surface, has been noticed from ancient times, and the oil has been collected by excavating pits and canals, and also by sinking deep wells. Bakoo, a town on the west side of the Caspian Sea in Georgia, has long been celebrated for its springs of a very pure variety of petroleum or naphtha, and the annual value of this product, according to M. Abich, is about 3,000,000 francs, and might easily be made as large again. Over a tract about 25 miles long and half a mile wide, the strata, which are chiefly argillaceous sandstones of loose texture, belonging to the medial tertiary formation, are saturated with the oil, and hold it like a sponge. To collect it large open wells are sunk to the depth of 16 to 20 feet, and in these the oil gathers and is occasionally taken out. That obtained near the centre of the tract is clear, slightly yellow, like Sauterne wine, and as pure as distilled oil. Toward the margins of the tract the oil is more colored, first a yellowish green, then reddish brown. In the environs of Bakoo are hills of volcanic rocks through which bituminous springs flow out. Jets of carburetted hydrogen are common in the district, and salt, which is almost always found with petroleum springs, abounds in the neighborhood.

Another famous locality of natural oils is in Burmah, on the banks of the Irrawaddy, near Prome. Fifty years ago it was reported there were about 520 wells in this region, and the oil from them was used for the supply of the whole empire and many parts of India. The town of Rainanghong is the centre of the oil district, and its inhabitants are chiefly employed in manufacturing earthen jars for the oil, immense numbers of which are stacked in pyramids outside the town, like shot in an arsenal. The formation containing the oil consists of sandy clays resting on sandstones and slates. The lowest bed reached by the open wells, which are sometimes 60 feet deep, is a pale blue argillaceous slate. Under this is said to be coal (tertiary ?) The oil drips from the slates into the wells, and is collected as at Bakoo. The annual product is variously stated at 412,000 hogsheads, and at 8,000,000 pounds.

The Burmese petroleum has recently been imported into Great Britain, and is employed at the great candle manufactory of Messrs. Price & Co., at Belmont and Sherwood. It is described as a semi-fluid naphtha, about the consistence of goose grease, of a greenish brown color, and a peculiar, but not disagreeable odor. It is used by the natives, in the condition in which they obtain it, as a lamp-fuel, as a preservative of timber against insects, and as a medicine. It is imported in hermetically closed metallic tanks, to prevent the loss of any of its constituents by evaporation. At the works it is distilled first with steam under ordinary pressure, and then by steam at successively increasing temperatures, with the following results:—

Temperature, Fahr.	Proportional product.	Character of product.
Below 212°	11	Mixture of fluid hydrocarbons free from paraffine.
230° to 293°	10	" " " containing a little paraffine.
293° to 320°	..	Distillate very small in quantity.
320° to 612°	20	Containing paraffine, but still fluid at 32°.
About 612°	31	Product which solidifies on cooling, and may be submitted to pressure.
Above 612°	21	Fluids with much paraffine.
	3	Pitchy matters.
	4	Residue of coke, and a little earthy matter in the still.

Nearly all the paraffine may be separated from the distillates by exposing these to freezing mixtures; and the total product of this solid hydrocarbon is estimated at 10 or 11 per cent.

Many other localities might be named which furnish the natural oils upon a less extensive scale, as in Italy, France, and Switzerland. In Cuba impure varieties of bitumen are met with flowing up through fissures in the rocks and spreading over the surface in a tarry incrustation, which sometimes solidifies on cooling. In the island of Trinidad, three fourths of a mile back from the coast, is a lake called the Tar Lake, a mile and a half in circumference, apparently filled with impure petroleum and asphaltum. The latter, more or less charged in its numerous cavities with liquid bitumen, forms a solid crust around the margin of the lake, and in the centre the materials appear to be in a liquid boiling condition. The varieties contain more or less oil, and methods have been devised of extracting this; but the chief useful application of the material seems to be for coating the timbers of ships to protect them from decay. By the patented process of Messrs. Atwood of New York, the crude tar of this locality having been twice subjected to distillation, and treated with sulphuric acid and afterward with an alkali, as in the method of purifying the coal oils, is then further purified by the use of permanganite of soda or of potash. Being again distilled it yields an oil of specific gravity 0.900, which is fluid at 32° F., and boils at 600° F.

In the United States the existence of petroleum has long been known, and the article has been collected and sold for medicinal purposes; chiefly for an external application, though sometimes administered internally. It was formerly procured by the Seneca Indians in western New York and Pennsylvania, and was hence known as Seneca or Genesee oil. At various places it was recognized along a belt of country passing from this portion of New York across the north-west part of Pennsylvania into Ohio. In the last-named state it was obtained in such quantity in the year 1819, by means of wells sunk for salt water, that it is a little remarkable the value of the material was not then appreciated, and the means perceived of obtaining it to any amount. The following description of the operations connected with the salt borings then in progress on the Little Muskingum, in the south-western part of the state, written in 1819, was first published in the *American Journal of Science* in 1826: "They have sunk two wells which are now more than 400 feet in depth; one of them affords a very strong and pure water, but not in great quantity. The other discharges such vast quantities of petroleum, or as it is vulgarly called, 'Seneka oil,' and besides is subject to such tremendous explosions of gas, as to force out all the water and afford nothing but gas for several days, that they make but little or no salt. Nevertheless, the petroleum affords considerable profit, and is beginning to be in demand for lamps in workshops and manufactories. It affords a clear bright light, when burnt in this way, and will be a valuable article for lighting the street lamps in the future cities of Ohio." Several coal-beds were penetrated in sinking these wells.

In north-western Pennsylvania the existence of oil in the soil along the valleys of some of the streams was known to the early settlers. One stream, in consequence of its appearance in the banks, was called Oil Creek. In other localities also it was noticed, and similar occurrences of oil were observed at some places in western Virginia and eastern Kentucky. At Tarentum above Pittsburg, oil was obtained by boring about the year 1845. Two springs were opened in boring for salt, and they have continued to yield small quantities of oil, sometimes a barrel a day. This has been used only for medicinal purposes. On Oil Creek two localities were especially noted, one close to the northern line of Venango county, half a mile below the village of Titusville, and one 14 miles further down the stream, a mile above its entrance into the Alleghany river. All the way below the upper locality through the narrow valley of the creek are ancient pits covering acres of ground, once dug and used for collecting oil after the method now practised in Asia. Cleared from the mud and rubbish with which they are mostly filled, some of them are found to be supported at the sides with logs notched at the ends as if done by whites, and it has been supposed by some that this is the work of the French who occupied that region the first half of the last century. Others think the Indians dug the pits, and in proof of this they cite the account given by Day, in his "History of Pennsylvania," of the use of the oil by the Seneca Indians as an unguent and in their religious worship. They mixed with it their paint with which they anointed themselves for war; and on occasions of their most important assemblages, as was graphically described by the commandant of Fort Duquesne in a letter to General Montcalm, they set fire to the scum of oil which had collected on the surface of the water, and at sight of the flames gave forth triumphant shouts which made the hills re-echo again. In this ceremony the commandant thought he saw revived the ancient fire worship, such as was once practised in Bakoo, the sacred city of the Guebres or Fire Worshippers.

The old maps of this portion of Pennsylvania indicate several places in Venango and Crawford counties where oil springs had been noted by the early settlers. They made some use of the oil, collecting it by spreading a woollen cloth upon the pools of water below the springs, and when the cloth was saturated with the oil wringing it out into vessels. The two springs referred to on Oil Creek furnished small quantities of oil as it was required, and from a third, twelve miles below Titusville in the middle of the creek, the owner has procured 20 barrels or more of oil in a year.* In 1854 Messrs Eveleth and Bissell of New York purchased the upper spring, and leased mineral rights over a portion of the valley. They then obtained from Prof. B. Silliman, jr., of New Haven a report upon the qualities of the oil, and in 1855 organized a company in New York called the "Pennsylvania Rock Oil Company," to engage in its exploration. The same year a new company under the same name, formed in New Haven and organized under the laws of Connecticut, succeeded to the rights of the old company; but for two years they made no progress in developing the resources of the property they had acquired. In December, 1857, they concluded an agreement with Messrs. Bowditch and Drake of New Haven to undertake the search for oil. To the enterprise of Col. E. L. Drake, who removed to Titusville and prosecuted the business in the face of serious obstacles, the region is indebted for the important results which followed. After a well had been sunk and curbed near the spring, ten feet square and sixteen feet deep, boring was commenced in the spring of 1859, and on the 26th of August, at the depth of seventy-one feet, the drill suddenly sank four inches, and when taken out the oil rose within five inches of the surface. At first a small pump threw up about 400 gallons daily. By introducing a larger one the flow was increased to 1000 gallons in the same time. Though the pumping was continued by steam power for months no diminution was experienced in the flow. The success of this enterprise produced great excitement, and the lands upon the creek were soon leased to parties, who undertook to bore for oil for a certain share of the product, sometimes advancing besides a moderate sum to the owner.

The country was overrun by explorers for favorable sites for new wells, and borings were undertaken along the valley of the Alleghany river, and up the French Creek above Franklin. The summer of 1860 witnessed unwonted activity and enterprise in this hitherto quiet portion of the state, where the population had before known no other pursuits than farming and lumbering. Every farm along the deep, narrow valleys, suddenly acquired an extraordinary value, and in the vicinity of the most successful wells villages sprung up as in California during the gold excitement, and new branches of manufacture were all at once introduced for supplying to the oil men the barrels required for the oil and the tools employed in boring the wells. From Titusville to the mouth of Oil Creek, about 15 miles, the derricks of the well borers were everywhere seen. On the Alleghany river the number below Tidioute in Warren county, south into Venango county, showed that this portion of the district was especially productive, and the same might be said of the vicinity of the town of Franklin, both up the Alleghany river and French Creek. The wells had amounted to several hundred, or according to one published statement, to full 2000 in number before the close of the year, and from an estimate published in the *Venango Spectator*, (Franklin) 74 of these on the 21st of November were producing the following daily yield:—

	No. of wells.	Prod. bbls.
On Oil Creek,	33	485
" Upper Alleghany river,	20	442
Franklin,	15	139
Two Mile Run,	3	64
French Creek,	3	35
Total,	74	1165

The capacity of the barrel is 40 gallons, and at the low estimate of only 20 cents the gallon the total value of the daily product is not far from $10,000. The depth of the wells is in a few instances less than 100 feet. The shallowest one reported, belonging to the Tidioute Island Oil Company, was 67 feet deep, and its product was 30 barrels a day. In general the depth is from 180 to 280 feet; one well in Franklin is 502 feet in depth, and one on Oil Creek 425 feet. The deepest wells are not the most productive, and the fact of their being extended beyond the ordinary depths may generally be considered an evidence of their failure to produce much oil. There are exceptions, however, to this, one of the deepest wells, that of Hoover and Stewart, three miles below Franklin, producing largely of excellent oil.

* See a pamphlet by Thomas A. Gale, published in Erie, Penn, 1860, entitled "Rock Oil in Pennsylvania and elsewhere."

The selection of localities for boring is very much a matter of chance. Proximity to productive wells is the first desideratum; but this, when attainable, is not always attended with success. The oil does not appear to be spread out, as the rocks lie in horizontal sheets, or if so there are many places where it does not find its way between the strata, and wells near together from which oil is pumped do not always draw upon each other. No doubt the system of crevices and pervious strata through which the oil flows in its subterranean currents, is very irregular and interrupted. The valleys to which the operations are limited are narrow, and are bounded on each side by hills, the summits of which, from 250 to 400 feet above the bottoms, are on the general level of the country. The increased expense that would be incurred in sinking from the upper surface and in afterward raising the oil to this height, as also the uncertainty of finding oil elsewhere than in the valleys, have so far prevented the explorations being extended beyond the creek and river bottoms; but it cannot be long before the capacity of the broad districts between the streams to produce oil is thoroughly tested. At present the most favorable sites are supposed to be near a break in the hills that form the margin of the valley, as where a branch comes into the main stream. An experiment is already undertaken to test the high grounds west of Tidioute branch.

As the bituminous coals are known as a source of hydrocarbon oils, it is natural to suppose that the springs of oil found near the coal region are fed from the coal-beds or bituminous shales of the coal formation. But it happens that only a few oil springs of western Pennsylvania have been struck in the coal-measures themselves, and that some of these are sunk into the underlying groups of rock to reach the supplies of oil. The oil districts are in general outside of the coal-field and upon the outcrop of lower formations which pass beneath the coal-measures, the whole having a general conformity of dip. Hence the slope of the strata is toward the coal, and an obstacle is thus presented to the flow of the oil from the coal-field toward its margin; and though under some circumstances the elastic pressure of the carburetted hydrogen gas might force the oil considerable distances from its source, it is hardly to be supposed that this should first find its way down into lower formations and then be carried many miles (30 to 50) and find its outlet in another district, rather than to the surface at some nearer point. The strata of north-western Pennsylvania lie nearly horizontally, their general inclination being toward the south. The highest rock upon the summits of the hills of the oil region is the conglomerate or pebbly rock (the floor of the coal-measures). Beneath this are series of thin bedded sandstones, slates, and shales, alternating with each other with frequent repetitions. The shales, often of an olive green color, are readily recognized as belonging to the Chemung and Portage groups of the New York geologists—a formation which overspreads this portion of the country, extending in New York two thirds of the way toward Lake Ontario and as far east as Binghamton. It is also continued through Ohio, crossing the Ohio river at Portsmouth, and in this state is known as the Waverley series. Under this is a heavy bed of bituminous shale, 200 or 300 feet thick, called in Ohio the black slate and in New York the Hamilton shales. This group contains an immense amount of carbonaceous matter, and oil is often disseminated through it. Sometimes it runs out in springs and finds an outlet by the occasional fissures in the beds. Dr. J. S. Newberry, who has given much attention to this subject, is of opinion that this formation contains sufficient carbonaceous material to be the source of the oil, and that the more porous and open shales and sandstones of higher formations are its reservoirs. Such is the geological formation of the Seneca oil region and of the oil springs of Canada West, which are the districts affording this product most remote from the coal-field. But from whatever source the oil may be derived, its origin is at the best very obscure, and little light can be thrown upon the probability of the supply long enduring the heavy drain made upon it by hundreds of wells worked by powerful steam pumps. But though actual experience alone must determine the extent of the quantities of oil stored up and the period they will last, there is certainly encouragement to be drawn from the never-failing yield of the oil districts of Asia, which for centuries have poured forth without stint their rivers of oil.

The sinking of wells is conducted after the usual method of boring artesian wells. After much uncertain consideration of the chances, a particular spot is selected, more, perhaps, from the hope of its being the right one than from any very practical grounds for the choice; but as the oil flows only in crevices among the strata, the location is frequently determined—other things being equal—by the prospect of reaching the rock at a few feet from the surface, and thereby avoiding the necessity of sinking an open well or driving pipes through unknown obstacles down to the rock. If the bed rock is found within ten or fifteen feet, the boring is begun at once. The derrick being raised, an elm, hickory, hemlock, or other elastic timber is cut down, some 25 or 30 feet in length. The larger end is fixed in a notch of a tree, or heavy post planted in the ground, and another post is set under it at a distance from the butt determined by the elasticity of the timber. The spring of the pole should be sufficient to raise the drill quickly, with its iron connecting rods, weighing often 300 pounds. The rods are suspended from the free end of the pole by a swivel or simple bolt-head, turning freely around. At the commencement of the boring, the rods being very short do not weigh more, including the drill, than 70 or 80 pounds. Two men, therefore, jerk them forcibly down, to increase the momentum of the drill; the spring of the pole immediately raises the drill for the next stroke, while at each blow a man gives it a slight turn so that it may cut a round hole. Several other methods are employed for making the pole spring; by one, which is conveniently worked without employing steam or horse power, a sort of double stirrup is suspended from the pole into which two men place each a foot, and pressing the stirrup suddenly down it immediately springs up again with the drill. This is much used, though some wells are sunk by horse-power machinery, and some by steam engines of four or five horse power.

As the well is constantly deepening, while the stroke of the spring-pole (about 30 inches) remains constant, a vertical adjusting screw about 18 inches in length is attached to the end of the spring-pole; the rope is clamped to the lower end or nut of this screw, and then extended to the pulley above. As the well deepens, a slight turn of the screw lowers the rope with the rods attached to it, and thus keeps the drill always free to fall to the bottom with an equal stroke. The work is continued, by a constant succession of strokes, to a depth of about fifty feet, successive lengths of iron rods being screwed on as the hole deepens—increasing the weight of the tools to about 300 pounds. The use of any additional rods is then dispensed with, and the upper rod is suspended by a rope attached to the spring-pole, and continued above the pole around a pulley and windlass, used to raise the boring tools when it is necessary to draw them out. They are drawn up in this manner at intervals of an hour or two, in order to sharpen and temper the drill, and to make room for the sand pump. This is a thin iron tube, a little more than half the diameter of the hole, with a simple valve at the bottom opening upward. It is lowered by a cord to the bottom of the well, then raised up with a jerk, and suffered to drop again by its own weight. This is repeated quickly eight or ten times; a whirl is thus produced in the water below which stirs up the mud and small pieces of broken stone; as the tube drops, the mud and small stones enter the open valve and are retained when the tube is drawn out.

The jarrers are employed to increase the force of the spring-pole when the drill happens to be wedged in the hole by broken pieces of stone or by other obstructions. They are two rectangular links about 18 inches in length, formed of stout bars of iron, and connecting the upper rods with the lower. When the drill descends to the bottom, the upper link, as it descends, slips down eight or ten inches in the lower link, and when the pole springs up the upper link has the advantage of moving through this space, and thereby giving a sudden upward jerk to the drill rod. The force of this upward jerk is greatly increased by a heavy rod introduced above the upper link, and which, as it moves up, lends its momentum to the stroke.

The hole is carried down by three men at different rates according to the nature of the strata encountered, varying from a foot or less to six feet in a day. In the hard sandstones of quartz pebbles firmly united together, two or three inches sinking in 12 hours may be all the progress practicable. The material brought up is carefully scanned for any oily appearance indicating the proximity of oil, and the well is watched to observe if any carburetted hydrogen gas escapes from it, which is considered a favorable sign.

The process of drilling in the rock is considered by all concerned in boring for petroleum, a very simple and even welcome operation, especially when contrasted with the uncertainties and apprehensions that surround the driving of pipes. At the outset, the cost of four iron pipes and bands long enough to reach a depth of forty feet, is equal to that of a complete set of boring tools with the rods and ropes sufficient to bore half a dozen wells of 300 feet each in depth. There is often great uncertainty of knowing how deep the pipes will have to be driven, and it is impossible to foresee the various obstacles through which they have to go. When the work has gone down successfully 70 or even 100 feet, the lowest pipe is often suddenly broken or takes an oblique direction. The pipes in the ground are then abandoned, and a new set driven in another place, although in several instances pipes reaching 60 feet in depth have been pulled up by a lever and axle, with chains or rods attached to a lewis wedge driven into the bottom pipe.

The pipes are of cast iron, generally ten or twelve feet long, about five inches bore, and the shell full an inch thick. The lower end of the first pipe is not sharpened, but is driven down blunt as it comes from the mould. The pipes are fastened together in the simplest manner possible, by wrought-iron bands, the ends being turned off, leaving a neck somewhat larger than the interior diameter of the bands, to receive them when expanded by heat.

Through common earth or gravel the pipes are forced down by the ordinary process of pile-driving; but when large stones are encountered, or round boulders as large as a man's head, there is great risk of breaking or turning the pipes. As soon, therefore, as the pipes meet with any great resistance the driving is suspended and the drill is applied to break up the stone or to bore a circular hole in it, which is afterward reamed out as large as the interior diameter of the pipes. The driving is then resumed, and in soft shales the pipes are often forced on, crushing down the sides of the hole, and making their way through to the depth of 12 or 15 inches in the rocky stratum.

The cost of boring a well 200 feet deep is generally estimated at from $1000 to $1500. The latter sum includes the cost of all the tools and materials, and also of a small steam engine, a large tank of pine plank, in which the product is collected for the oil and water to separate, and it also allows for such accidents and delays as are common to these operations.

When the oil is struck it often rises up in the well, sometimes flowing over the top, and in several instances it has burst forth in a jet and played like a fountain, throwing the oil mixed with water high up into the air. Such jets have rarely lasted long, and are usually interrupted by discharges of gas, the elasticity of which drives out with violence the fluids mixed with it, as champagne wine is projected from a bottle on removing the cork. Hundreds of barrels of oil have, however, been wasted at some of the wells for want of means to collect it or stop its flow in its sudden first appearance. At Williams' well, half a mile below Titusville, about 100 barrels of oil were collected the first night the oil was reached, and a large quantity besides was lost. A similar event occurred near Tidioute, the oil rushing up so violently as to knock over the laborer who held the drill and to pass through the derrick and over the trees around. After a time the spouting wells become quiet and the oil settles down, so that it has to be raised by pumping. The pumps are contrived to work at any depth, and by men, or by horse power, or the steam engine. For a time at some of the wells the product has been water alone or water mixed with a little oil; and after pumping several days this has given place to oil with a moderate proportion of water. If the pumping be suspended for a day water accumulates, and it may be several days before this is drawn out and the former yield of oil recovered. The water is generally salt. The flow of oil has rarely if ever been known to fail entirely except by reason of some obstruction in the wells, and in such cases it has usually returned after the hole has been bored out larger or made deeper. The supply is not, however, altogether regular in any of the wells, even after the flow has settled down to a moderate production of 10 or 15 barrels a day. The maximum yield of a well for a considerable time is about 50 barrels a day, and from this the production ranges down to 4 barrels, below which it is considered insufficient to pay expenses.

The oil and water are conducted from the pumps into the large receiving vats, and after the water has subsided the oil is barrelled for the market. From the upper Oil Creek it is mostly wagoned to the Union Mills station in Erie county, on the Erie and Sunbury railroad; and from Tidioute to Irvine, at the mouth of the Broken Straw, on the same road. But most of the oil along the Alleghany river and French Creek is taken by steamboats down the river to Pittsburg. New York city is at present the principal market, but the country refineries are already taking a considerable share of the oil.

The product of the different wells varies somewhat in quality and value. At Franklin the oil for the most part is heavy, marking as low as 33° Baumé, which corresponds to specific gravity 0.864. Some of the wells furnish oils of 35° or 36°—on Oil Creek the range is from 38° to 46°, at Tidioute 43°. The French Creek oils are heavy. It is not unlikely that the depth of the wells may have some effect upon the quality of the oil, as from very shallow wells those of the lighter varieties must be likely to escape by evaporation, leaving the heavier portions behind. The oils obtained at Mecca, Trumbull county, Ohio, are heavy oils, being thick like goose grease and marking 26° or 27°, which is equivalent to specific gravity 0.900. At Grafton, Lorain county, Ohio, the oil is even darker and thicker than this, marking about 25° B.

With the exception of some light, clear oils of reddish color, the petroleum is usually of a greenish hue, more or less deep and opaque. It has an offensive smell which is not entirely removed by the ordinary methods of deodorizing practised in the refineries. The process of purification is similar to that of the coal oil manufacture, as already described. The proportion of light oils separated by distillation varies with the crude petroleum employed. The largest product is about 90 per cent., and from this less amounts are obtained down to about 50 per cent. The properties and uses of these products have already been considered in treating of coal oil.

To complete this account of the petroleum of the United States more particular mention should be made of the extension of the district from north-western Pennsylvania into New York on one side, and Ohio on the other. In Chautauqua, Cattaraugus, and Allegany counties, N. Y., are many places where the appearace of small quantities of oil upon the surface, and the escape of jets of carburetted hydrogen, indicate the existence of petroleum below; and the names of Olean and another Oil creek, a branch of the Genesee river, suggest the probability of this proving another oil district. About a mile north-west from Cuba in Allegany county, is a pool about 20 feet across and 10 feet deep that has always been called an oil spring, its surface being covered with a coating of oil from which supplies have been obtained for medicinal purposes. A pipe was sunk into this, and on the 3d of January, 1861, when it had been driven down 20 or 30 feet, oil mixed with water suddenly gushed up with great force. Oil also appeared on the water drawn up from an artesian well sunk to the depth of 130 feet in the same vicinity. Arrangements are now in progress for thoroughly testing the capacity of this district.

In Ohio the oil-producing counties are Noble, Adams, Franklin, Medina, Lorain, Cuyahoga, Trumbull, Mahoning, and some others. Near Cleveland and in the valley of the Cuyahoga oil appears in many places, but it has not yet proved of much importance. The vicinity of Mecca, Trumbull county, is the most productive locality. Operations were commenced there in February, 1860, and in November it was stated that between 600 and 700 wells had been sunk, and 75 steam engines were in operation pumping oil. Two of the wells were yielding from 50 to 100 barrels a day each. This statement is probably much exaggerated, and while others report that several hundred wells have been sunk, a dozen or more are said to be working profitably. These wells pass through the same formation as those near Titusville, but for the most part they are shallow, ranging in depth from 30 to 100 feet, and the most of them not much exceeding 50 feet. About 30 miles south-east from Mecca, at Lowellville, Mahoning county, a well was sunk 157 feet which proved very successful, yielding 20 barrels of oil a day. This well was commenced in the conglomerate and ended in the Chemung strata. Duck Creek, Noble county, was formerly noted for the oil which appeared with the brine of the salt wells.

In Ritchie and Wirt counties, Virginia, near the Ohio river, some wells are producing oil, and this promises to be an important oil district. Canada West also contains an oil region, extending from London toward the St. Clair river, from which petroleum has been obtained the last two years. The value of the product, however, is considerably deteriorated by its insufferable odor. On the southern coast of California petroleum is said to be found in considerable quantities; and springs of it are described by Captain Stansbury in the report of his expedition to the Great Salt Lake, in 1849, as occurring about 83 miles east from Salt Lake City, in the vicinity of sulphur springs and beds of bituminous coal.

The works for refining petroleum (excepting some originally designed for manufacturing coal oil) were all constructed in 1860–61. Their localities and approximate capacity, as far as known, are given below:—

Localities.	No. factories.	Daily capacity. Bbls.	Remarks.
Pittsburg, Penn.	2	..	Built for coal oil.
Tidioute, Warren Co., Penn.	1	35	
Union, Erie Co., "	1	35	Destroyed by fire.
Meadville, Crawford Co., "	1	50	
Franklin, Venango Co., "	1	10	
Titusville, Crawford Co., "	2	30 & 40	Not completed.
Oil City, mouth of Oil Creek	1	..	" "
Buffalo, N. Y.	1	..	
Cleveland, Ohio	1	..	Built for coal oil, recently burnt.
Columbus, "	1	..	
Canfield, "	1	..	Built for coal oil.

LAND SETTLEMENT—INTERNAL TRADE.

CHAPTER I.

WESTERN SETTLEMENT AND TRADE.

PURCHASE OF LOUISIANA—POPULATION AND LAND SALES—AVENUES TO THE VALLEY—CANAL AND RAILROAD EXPENDITURES—LAKE CITIES AND TRADE—RECIPROCITY.

THE original colonies, settled as they were under different grants, circumstances, and powers, had many and conflicting claims to the then comparatively unknown land running back to the Mississippi river, bounded on the north by the chain of lakes, and on the south by the Spanish territories of Florida and Louisiana, when there was a question of union into a confederacy. These various claims were a matter of dispute, which, from being serious, was settled by a mutual cession of the lands to the federal government, in trust, for the common benefit of all the states then existing, or thereafter to become members of the Union. The federal government having thus become owner of the lands, the constitution conferred upon Congress the power "to dispose of and make all needful rules and regulations respecting the territory and other property belonging to the United States." The obvious policy of the government, like that of every other thrifty owner, was at once to attract settlers to these lands, thereby making them serviceable to the whole people as fast as possible. To do so, the lands were to be sold cheap, and as few formalities as possible placed in the way of the settlers. The domain was organized under the control of the Secretary of the Treasury, being administered under him by a commissioner of the land office. The whole domain is divided into districts, for each of which there is a surveyor general, under whom the territory is subdivided for survey into districts. For each district there is a land office, occupied by a register and a receiver. A plan is prepared of each district by the surveyors, with the utmost care, showing ranges, sections, and townships, with topographic characteristics. Of this plan there are three copies; one is retained at the land office, one by the surveyor, and the third is sent to the general office at Washington, where it serves to regulate all transactions. The land being all surveyed into sections of 640 acres each, is offered for sale by the government at auction, at a *minimum* price of $1.25 per acre. After the land has been on sale two weeks, it may be sold in 40 acre lots, at a less price. The actual occupant of any land offered has the pre-emption to it. The buyer of the land pays the money to the receiver, and gets for it a receipt, of which the register sends a duplicate, with a certificate of the sale, to Washington. On the verification of the sale there, the deed of the land, called a "patent," is made out, and sent to the local land office register, who gives it to the purchaser in exchange for the receipt he holds, and his title is then complete. In addition to the attractions of low prices and pre-emption rights, long credits were originally given, to enable the settler to pay for the land out of its proceeds. But these speedily led to abuses, and the cash plan was finally adopted. There have been, however, large grants of land for military purposes, to schools and universities, to states for internal improvements, for seats of government, public buildings, benefit of Indians, salines, swamp lands, and lastly, in aid of canals and railroads—the construction of which aided the settlement of those lands at a distance from large water courses, and therefore from markets. Some time elapsed before the organization of the department was effected, and the first land office was opened in 1800, at Chillicothe, Ohio. The first sales of land, however, took place in New York three years before, and in that year a triangle on the lake was sold to Pennsylvania, in order to give her a port on the lake. That port is Erie, and is famous for the building of Perry's fleet there in 1812, in seventy days from the time the wood stood in the forest until the stars and stripes floated to the breeze of the lake from the mast-head. That fleet was fatal to British supremacy on the lakes. Almost all the land sales took place in Ohio, until 1807, when offices were opened in Indiana and Mississippi. In 1809 an office was opened in Alabama, and in 1814 one in Illinois; in 1818 in Missouri, Louisiana, and Michigan. The sales of the lands proceeded with great activity in most of these states up to 1821, particularly after the embargo and war had turned attention from commerce and navigation to agriculture and manufacture. Nearly all the lands of the government were then in the great valley of the Mississippi. This is a vast basin, the sides of which are the eastern slopes of the Rocky Mountains on the west, and the western slopes of the Alleghany Mountains on the east. The chain of great lakes stretches across the northern end of the basin, and the Mississippi river flows through its centre to the Gulf of Mexico, receiving on its eastern side the Illinois, the Ohio with its affluents, and other large rivers which flow generally west from the water-shed of the Alleghanies; and on its western side the Missouri and other large rivers whose waters descend from the eastern slopes of the Rocky Mountains. The only outlets to this vast basin were by the St. Lawrence River (not then navigable, however) north to the ocean, and the Mississippi river south to the gulf. Hardy pioneers did penetrate across the mountains, by a perilous seven weeks' journey, to the Ohio; but once there, intercourse was but limited with the east. The fertile soil was, however, attractive, and the Indian trade profitable. In 1790 the whole population west of the mountains was 108,868 souls, or about 3 per cent of the whole population of the Union. In 1800 that population had increased to nearly 400,000, but the only outlet for their produce was down the Mississippi through the French territory of Louisiana. That circumstance led to great dissatisfaction, and being adroitly handled by the political adventurers of that day, threatened disunion, by dissolving the states east and west—the latter to form a new confederacy with the south-west and Mexico. The remedy was to purchase Louisiana. Fortunately, at the moment Napoleon had relinquished his projects of forming French colonies; also being determined on war with England, he feared the seizure of Louisiana by that power, and determined to sell it to the United States for $14,984,872. This money, in 1803, gave him the sinews of war, and also the hope that the transaction would embroil the United States with his enemy. England did at a later period attempt to take the territories. But the troops who had driven the French out of Spain, embarked from France for the enterprise only to encounter the bloodiest defeat before cotton bags and western rifles. Louisiana was then possessed of a certain amount of population and wealth, which, from being French, by annexation became American. A considerable commerce had grown up. The amount of trade then existing between the eastern and western states may be gathered from the official returns of exports to New Orleans, in the four years before it was annexed, as follows:—

States.	1799.	1800.	1801.	1802.
Atlantic,	3,504,092	2,035,789	1,907,998	1,224,710
Western,	———	———	1,124,842	1,596,640
Total,	$3,504,092	2,035,789	3,032,840	2,821,350

The exports from the Atlantic States were mostly foreign merchandise destined for export up the western rivers. The exports of the western states were the produce sent down for sale. Those exports were the productions of hardy adventurers, whom circumstances had induced to seek their fortunes in the west. As long as the commerce of the country was active, and the sales of the farm products of the Atlantic states profitable, there was less inducement to migrate west than there was after the embargo had wrought a change in that respect, and the means of communication *via* New Orleans had improved. When that port became an American city, and the mighty river to its mouth an American stream, a new attraction was added to the fair lands of the valley, and in 1810 its population had risen to 878,315. The impulse thus given to western settlement was strengthened by the effects of war upon the Atlantic states. The interruption of commerce and stagnation of exports threw out of employment large numbers, who now turned an inquiring gaze beyond the mountains. The capital of the east thrown out of commercial employment by the same circumstances, flowed eagerly into banking, in the hope of leriving large profits from the growing re-sources of the west; although inevitable disaster followed the erroneous principles on which that banking was conducted, the capital, so lost to stockholders, really promoted agriculture. Instead of confining hemselves to advances on produce shipped, he institutions loaned money to make improvements and build houses that the farm profits could not pay for. The result was uin to those accepting such advances, and nsolvency to the banks making them. From 1810 to 1820 six states grew into the Union, while in the fifteen years that followed 1821 none were admitted.

This is an instructive fact, and it indicates hat western land speculation, so much overdone at those periods, was a long time n recovering itself. The process of forming new states is mostly a speculative one. The hrewdest operators get possession of the eading "sites" of future cities, and by timulating and guiding the tide of migraion, become wealthy in the rise of prices that he tide creates around them. As the wealthest names of the eastern cities were men minent in commercial enterprise, so were hose of the western cities the earliest and nost extensive land-holders. The political nfluence which brings the government patonage upon the theatre of such locations, s a part of the machinery to guide the poplar movement. When in seasons of speculation, these operators become possessed of considerable tracts, a period of steady and ealthy migration is required to distribute ossession among settlers and clear the way or a new excitement. Yearly the trade grows y reason of the increasing surplus that the ettlers throw off for market, and which eing sold increases their ability to buy nerchandise in return.

There are no data by which to measure the rowth of trade in those western states after ne admission of Louisiana, up to within wenty years, since the accounts were kept nly for the foreign trade, and when Louisiana became a state, reports were no longer nade. The sales of lands, and population f the new states, progressed as follows, however :—

	1790 to 1800	1800 to 1810
Population, increase,	276,769	492,678
Sales of land, acres,	1,536,152	3,008,982
	1810 to 1820	Total, 1820
Population, increase,	1,201,248	2,079,563
Sales of land, acres,	8,499,673	13,044,807

So rapid had been the settlement from 1810 to 1820. The agricultural productions of that region, as a matter of course, followed this rapid settlement of lands, and the exchange of those productions created a large trade of which there is little record. The mines and manufactures sprung up in the several towns, following the wants of the people.

The cession of Louisiana to the United States had produced a dispute in relation to its boundaries between this country and Spain, which then owned Florida. This dispute became very warm in 1819, when it was settled through the mediation of the French minister, by a cession of east and west Florida by Spain to the United States, in consideration of being released from claims for spoliation of American property to the extent of $4,985,599, which the United States government undertook to pay its own citizens. The coast line of the United States thus became complete. There were now large interests west of the mountains, a population of over 2,000,000 souls, occupying fertile land, capable of any development, and great numbers were interested in the rapid appreciation of those lands by settlement. The want of communication was a great obstacle. It required seven weeks to reach the newly settled cities of the west; and when during the war it was necessary to send a gun from New York city to Buffalo for defense, it cost six weeks of time and $1,000 in money to do it. There could be little trade under such circumstances, and the question was to open communication. A canal from the lakes to tide water on the Hudson was commenced in 1817, and completed in 1825. This Erie canal cost $7,143,789, and soon paid for itself, being the most profitable, as it was the greatest of modern improvements. It opened the door for the great western valley to tide water, and by doing so wrought an immense change in the condition and prospects of all that region. In October, 1823, New York had also completed the Champlain canal, running 63 miles, from Albany to Lake Champlain, at a cost of $1,179,871. Pennsylvania, in 1825, passed an act for the connection of Pittsburg, on the Ohio, with Philadelphia, a distance of 394 miles. This line was not completed until 1834. In 1828, a company was chartered to connect the Ohio with Georgetown, on the Potomac, by the Chesapeake and Ohio canal. These works gave three outlets from the great basin to tide water. While yet they were in process of construction, however, a new power was being developed to supersede them for trade and light freights. In 1828, Massachusetts had three miles of railroad; from that nest-egg, capital has since hatched 28,270 miles, which cover the country like a network. The opening of the Erie canal was attended with great results, since it placed the produce of western lands cheaply in competition with that of the valley of the Hudson, and of the less productive states of the Atlantic coast. Commerce and manufactures increased, for the reason that agriculture paid less. The supply of labor changed direction, and the increasing numbers in manufacturing employments drew their subsistence from the west. The natural water courses that discharged themselves into the lakes were lined with settlers, and soon Ohio connected the lakes with the Ohio river, by a canal from Cleveland to Cincinnati, and also to Portsmouth. Indiana projected a canal from Toledo, on the lakes, to the Ohio river, cutting the state nearly longitudinally; and Illinois projected one from Chicago to the navigable waters of the Illinois river, thus connecting the lakes with the Mississippi river, nearly opposite the old French town of St. Louis—across the state. These works were not completed, some of them, until ten or fifteen years after they were undertaken. That of Ohio, however, gave a new impulse to trade, not only by Cleveland, on the lakes, but by way of Cincinnati, down the river to New Orleans. These circumstances gave a new impulse to the sales of land and the settlement of the west. The expenditure of money for the construction of canals, and by the federal government for the construction of the great national road running west from the seat of government to the Mississippi, inaugurated the speculative movement in that direction. The bank fever then raged once more in support of the land movement, as it had done in the six years ending with 1820, and with the same results. $200,000,000 of money went from east to west, feeding the flame, until all real capital was nearly consumed, and the speculation ran wild until it burst in 1837. At that time a large quantity of land had passed, under the credit sales of the federal government, into the hands of private speculators, and the western fever lay dormant up to the revival that it experienced in 1846–7, by reason of the famine abroad, and the growing strength of the migration. Attention was then again turned to the lands, and the railroad expenditure began to exert the same influence that canal and bank expenditure had exercised in 1836, and the movement was progressive until the revulsion of 1857.

The natural water courses of the country had been followed by early migrations, and the settlement of the land bordering them had been stimulated by the bank paper speculation of 1810 to 1820. Following the excitement came the construction of the artificial means of navigation, involving an expenditure of some $50,000,000 for canals through new lands opened up by their operation; and these enterprises were again attended with a great bank expansion, that, although ending disastrously, nevertheless had the effect of drawing capital from England and the wealthier Atlantic states to spread it upon the fertile lands of the west. The subsidence of that speculation left the west in comparative quiet, although of general progress, for some years, during which a new and more powerful element of internal development was coming into action. This was the railroad system.

The first railroad of the country was three miles, built in Quincy, Massachusetts, and in operation in 1828, about the time the success of the Manchester railroad in England astonished the world with the new phenomena of locomotion. The example was not slow of imitation in this country; and the Boston and Providence railroad, uniting those cities by forty miles of rail, to connect with the steamboats to New York, was soon in operation. Its success caused other works to be undertaken in New England, and when the Western road was projected, to connect Albany with Boston, it gave the city a direct connection with the Hudson river and the Erie canal. New York projected the Harlem railroad; and from Albany several roads extended west, connecting city after city, until the united lengths of 380 miles made a continuous route to Buffalo—afterward, in 1850, consolidated in the New York Central railroad. Another road—the Erie—to connect New York with Lake Erie at Dunkirk (459 miles), through the lower tier of counties, was commenced in 1842 and completed in 1853. Baltimore projected the connection with Wheeling, on the Ohio, 380 miles, by rail, and Philadelphia connected Pittsburg, on the Ohio, 329 miles, by a line of works which became subsequently a continuous railway.

The New York railroads were not allowed by law to carry freight until 1850, except on payment of the canal tolls. These four routes opened the western valley by rail to tide water. The Canada roads, connecting Detroit and Buffalo, and Detroit and Portland, make five routes, with distances as follows:—

N. York to Chicago, *via* Erie, Lake Shore, and Mich. Southern, - - - - - -	957
N. York to Chicago, *via* Central, Canada, and Mich. Central, - - - - - -	957
Philadelphia to Chicago, *via* Pittsburg and Fort Wayne, - - - - - - -	823
Baltimore to Chicago, *via* Ohio Central, -	942
Portland to " " Canada and Michigan Central, - - - - - - - -	1,133

There had been, meanwhile, many western roads built in important localities, which had much favored the export of food in answer to the foreign demand growing out of the famine of 1846–7. In the year 1850, the federal government made a grant of land of about 2,500,000 acres to the state of Illinois, in aid of the construction of the Central railroad, which was to connect Galena, on the Mississippi, and Chicago, on the lake, with Cairo, at the junction of the Ohio and Mississippi rivers. The two roads leaving respectively Galena and Chicago, run south, converging until they meet at a point 50 miles from Cairo, and thence proceed together. The state not being able to do this herself, made over the lands to a company, on condition that they should construct the road. This was commenced in 1852, and finished in 1857, at a cost of $35,000,000. The tract given by the government was in size equal to the whole state of Connecticut, and was a part of 11,000,000 acres that had been over fifteen years in the market without finding buyers. The fact that the railroad was to run through them, and spend $25,000,000, and employ 10,000 men in the building of the road, made the lands attractive, and excited speculation. At about the same time the state of Michigan sold the Michigan Central road and the Southern Michigan road to two companies, on the condition of their finishing them, which was done in 1852, establishing a connection between Detroit and Chicago. About the same time the Galena and Chicago railroad was commenced and finished in 1850, making a direct communication from the river at Galena to Chicago, prolonged by the Michigan roads to Detroit, and thence by the Lake Shore to New York, by the Erie or the Central railroads, or *via* the Canada route to Portland or to Boston. Subsequent connections have been made with the Pennsylvania and the Baltimore roads; and the western connections of Chicago and Milwaukee have been pushed under a vast expenditure of money. The inauguration of land grants by government, in the case of the Illinois Central, has been followed by grants to other states for the same object, until all the grants amount to 25,403,993 acres. These grants have rapidly developed southern connections, until the route is now complete between Chicago and New Orleans, shortening the river route by over 400 miles. While these "trunk lines" were in process of construction, cross roads were multiplied to an immense extent, and the connections of them form a continuous route from Bangor, Maine, to New Orleans, 1,996 miles. This vast chain of railways is composed of eighteen independent roads, costing in the aggregate, for 2,394 miles of road, $92,784,084, or nearly one-tenth of the whole railway system of the United States.

The progress of the construction by miles in each locality has been as follows, in periods of ten years:—

	East'rn.	Middle.	South'rn.	West'rn.	Total Miles.	Cost.
1828....	3				3	221,101
1830....	3	38	6	6	43	3,501,100
1840....	444	1,436	461	28	2,369	98,170,001
1850....	2,896	2,925	1,415	1,041	7,777	291,482,101
1860....	3,824	8,176	5,552	10,718	28,270	$1,009,172,000

A vast sum of money, amounting in all to $717,689,899, has been expended in the last ten years in the construction of 20,493 miles of road, of which rather more than one half has been built at the west. There are, in addition to these roads, some 16,000 miles of road incomplete. A considerable amount of this money was drawn from abroad. The iron was got in exchange for bonds, which have not in all cases been paid; but if the bonds were poor, the iron has not been of good quality. The quantity of railroad iron imported in ten years, to 1850, was 242,449 tons, at a cost of $9,603,587. In the nine years ending with 1857, the quantity imported was 1,765,693 tons, at a cost of $59,196,300. This number of tons suffices for about 15,000 miles of road, at 70lbs. to the yard. The money expended upon the roads in the employment of men and in the manufacture of superstructure, rolling stock, etc., of itself caused an immense activity and demand for produce, which, as a matter of course, became scarce and high upon the theatre of such expenditure. The manufacture of superstructure, cars, locomotives, stations, etc., were the means of employing great numbers of men. The railroad iron, of which the manufacture requires the investment of much capital, was alone imported to any great extent. The remaining portions of the railroads were manufactured at home. The first locomotives in the United States were imported from England in the fall of 1829 or spring of 1830. The first Stephenson locomotive ever imported was the "Robert Fulton," in 1831, for the Mohawk and Hudson railroad. The first locomotive built in this country was constructed at the West Point foundry in 1830, for the South Carolina railroad. Since then the improvement and manufacture of railroads has been so successful as to admit of the export of many American machines. As the roads were completed, and the hands, numbering at least 200,000 men so employed, were discharged, they naturally turned their attention to the agriculture of the neighborhood where they had been employed, and production thus succeeded to consumption. The effect of the railroad expenditure upon the grain crops is to some extent indicated in the following table of miles of roads in operation in the western states at the periods named, and the population and corn product of those states:—

1850.	Miles of Road.	Population.	Bushels of Corn.
Ohio	299	1,980,329	59,078,695
Indiana	86	982,405	52,964,363
Illinois	22	851,470	57,646,984
Iowa		192,214	8,656,799
Michigan	344	397,654	5,641,420
Wisconsin		305,391	1,988,379
Missouri		682,044	36,214,537
	751	5,391,507	222,191,177
1857.			
Ohio	2,988	2,580,011	82,555,186
Indiana	1,291	1,146,717	80,111,416
Illinois	2,714	1,358,960	119,186,921
Iowa	344	596,251	32,111,502
Michigan	1,032	637,514	8,322,756
Wisconsin	822	822,606	14,186,822
Missouri	547	1,023,888	98,712,561
Total	9,738	8,165,947	435,187,164
Increase	8,987	2,774,440	212,995,987

The corn crops had nearly doubled, and the wheat crop in the same states had risen from 43,840,637 to 107,275,641 bushels in 1857—an increase of 63,400,000 per annum, worth as many dollars; and estimating the corn at the same aggregate, there had been a sum of $126,000,000 per annum, or half the cost of the railroads built, extracted each year from the soil through their influence. We may now observe what had been the actual sales of the public lands by the government in the forty years ending with 1860, to June 30th, when the fiscal year ends, divided into periods of ten years each; the first, being that of recovery from the speculation that attended the close of the war; the second, embracing the period of bank and canal building excitement; the third, that of recovery from that excitement; and the fourth, that of the last great railroad building excitement. The quantity sold during the forty years was, it appears, 140,883,740 acres.

ANNUAL SALES OF LAND BY THE FEDERAL GOVERNMENT.

	Acres.		Acres.
1821,	822,185	1831,	2,804,745
1822,	763,811	1832,	2,411,952
1823,	638,749	1833,	3,856,227
1824,	723,038	1834,	4,658,218
1825,	871,619	1835,	12,564,478
1826,	839,263	1836,	20,074,870
1827,	905,937	1837,	5,601,103
1828,	946,650	1838,	3,414,907
1829,	1,236,445	1839,	4,976,382
1830,	1,880,019	1840,	2,236,889
Total	9,627,716		62,599,771
Population	2,233,880		3,707,299
1841,	1,164,796	1851,	1,846,847
1842,	1,129,217	1852,	1,553,071
1843,	1,605,264	1853,	1,083,495
1844,	1,754,763	1854,	7,035,735
1845,	1,843,527	1855,	15,729,524
1846,	2,263,730	1856,	9,227,878
1847,	2,521,305	1857,	4,142,744
1848,	1,887,553	1858,	3,804,908
1849,	1,329,902	1859,	3,961,580
1850,	769,364	1860,	4,000,000
Total	16,269,421		52,385,782
Population	10,454,245		15,081,894

The total sales of lands, from the opening of the land offices to 1860, were 153,928,547 acres. There had been issued land warrants to the soldiers of the Mexican war, and former wars, which have taken up large portions of the land. These warrants are for 160 acres, 120 acres, 80 acres, and 40 acres, and have been sold in the markets at $1 per acre for the smaller lots, and about 80 cts. the larger warrants, by which means the lands come less to the buyer. In addition to the lands sold, the government has donated 67,736,572 acres to schools; 10,897,313 to internal improvements; 279,972 to individuals; 50,060 to seats of government;

W. H. Bartlett. A. L. Dick.

THE HORSE SHOE FALL, NIAGARA.—WITH THE TOWER.

44,109,979 to military services; 432,325 salines to states; 3,400,725 Indian reserves; 8,923,908 private claims; 21,948,916 swamp lands, granted to states; 25,463,993 to railroads; and there remain unsold lands on hand, 1,088,732,498 acres, as a small supply for new comers.

The population of the land states had increased, it appears, from 2,233,880 in 1830, to about 15,000,000 in 1860, during which period of thirty years, 131,255,074 acres of land were sold by the Government. These land sales and population are the ground work of the national trade, which grows with the surplus produced by the land settlers. Those people at first make few purchases of goods, but increase them as their surplus produce sells and enables them to do so.

The people who seek new lands on which to rear their future homes and fortunes, are, for the most part, not possessed of much capital, and under ordinary circumstances much is required for a family to perform a distant journey, locate and prepare land and wait until the crops are grown. Nevertheless, pioneers have ceaselessly pushed forward into the wilderness and battled with nature in the shape of forests, animals and savages, until twenty new states and millions of wealth have been added to the Union. The great instrument of this progress, has, under Providence, and in the hands of skilful and determined men, been Indian corn. That grain has been the poor man's capital, enabling him to conquer the wilderness. It needed on his locating his future home but to drop the seed in the fertile soil, and while he busied himself with his new dwelling, a sure crop grew up, which in a few months became food for his family and his animals. The husks furnish his bed and the cobs his fuel. He is thus by the gift of nature furnished with capital for the coming year, until his other crops and young animals have grown. Indian corn has thus given the pioneer a hold upon the land and made his footing firm where otherwise he might have been compelled to succumb to hardships. With every such remove on to new land the circle of trade has increased. A few months only suffice for the settler to furnish a surplus of production in return for comforts that he desires. For this reason chiefly corn figures so largely in the agriculture of the west. The prolific soil throws out quantities far beyond the wants of the planter, and in a region where all are planters, the supply becomes superabundant and must find distant markets only at rates so low as to leave little to the grower. Two local demands are created for it. The most important of them is to feed hogs, and pork becomes a leading staple export; the other is for distillation, and whiskey is largely exported. The quantity of corn required to make a certain quantity of pork becomes accurately known, and the price of meat rises and falls with that of the grain, as does whiskey also. Thus out of the great staple grain Indian-corn come directly the three great articles of export, corn, pork and its manufacture, and whiskey. Lumber in most new countries is also an important export, As the settlements progress, beef, wool, wheat and other grains follow, and trade increases. While Indian corn has been the indispensable instrument of settlement at the west, the nature of the country and the fertility of machine inventions have been no less necessary in securing a surplus for sale. If the corn grows readily it could not under the old system be so readily harvested in a region where land belonged to every man, and every man's labor could be applied only to his own service. At the same time no man's labor more than suffices for the wants of his own family. Here machinery steps in, and favored by the level nature of the soil operates to a charm. A man who could with the scythe cut from one to one and a half acres of grass per day, may ride round a field and cut ten acres in a day without fatigue. Instead of a gang to rake and turn and cock, his horse and himself may with a patent rake perform all that labor and more effectually when driven by a shower of rain, than any gang. His grain is cut by the same means and light labor as his grass. It is threshed out by a similar process; his corn is husked and shelled by machines; and when drawn to the railroad depots it is elevated into vast receptacles to be transported rapidly and at small cost to the best market. All these machine aids enable the man whose own labor would scarcely supply the demands of his family to turn out a vast surplus. This surplus seeks the river and lake cities by rail, canal, and steam, to be transported to the Atlantic markets for consumption or export, or may now leave Chicago and Milwaukee on the lakes, or St. Louis and Cincinnati on the rivers for Liverpool direct without breaking bulk. The table of land sales above gives a very good indication of the accumulating force behind the forwarding cities to push forward the trade. As every bushel of grain they receive requires an equivalent from them in goods, each grows under the double demand. Their combined growth is the basis of lake and river trade, distributing the produce for consumption, and bearing back goods in return, while the foreign commerce of the country grows with the aggregate surplus to be exported and the consequent increase of the merchandise received in exchange. Having glanced at the settlement of the western lands, it becomes no matter of surprise that the cities which were the focus at which such large quantities of surplus products concentrated grew rapidly, and grew in proportion to the rapidity of settlement and the perfection of the means of internal communication. It may be worth while to sketch the leading ones, first those of the lakes.

Buffalo, on Lake Erie, was laid out originally in 1801, but was of small importance until in 1825 by the opening of the Erie canal, it became the gateway from the great valley to the Atlantic states. Its population was then 3,000. As the "great valley" at that time had, however, but little to spare, the importance of Buffalo was to swell with the growth of the west which was rapid indeed. In 1832, thirty-one years from its settlement, Buffalo became a city with 8,653 inhabitants. In the twenty-eight years that have since elapsed the population has risen to 81,131. In 1825, the tonnage belonging to the port was 200 tons. It has grown to 91,974, valued at $3,640,950, besides 600 canal boats. The steam tonnage running to Buffalo is 60,740 tons. The exports of Buffalo by canal are $20,000,000 and by railroad as much more. The opening of Dunkirk to New York over the Erie road created a rival to Buffalo, and the Welland canal round the falls permitted vessels to go to Oswego, where they take either canal or railroad on a shorter route to New York, also rivaling Buffalo. It is obvious that a few miles longer trip adds little to the cost of a loaded ship, and by reducing the canal and railroad transportation the cost is diminished. Hence Oswego has an advantage over Buffalo.

The imports into Buffalo by lake and railroad, showing the relative and aggregate values, indicate the gain of "rails" over "sails." They were, for a number of years, as follows:

	Lake.	Railroad.	Total.
1850,	$22,525,781		$22,525,781
1851,	31,889,951		31,889,951
1852,	34,943,855		34,943,855
1853,	36,881,230	2,234,273	39,115,503
1854,	42,030,931	6,397,923	48,428,854
1855,	50,346,819	10,968,384	61,313,203
1856,	42,684,079	16,422,505	59,106,584
1857,	36,913,166	15,020,580	51,933,746

Oswego, settled in 1820 on Lake Ontario has been mostly the creation of the Oswego canal and of the railroad communication since established, which makes its position on the lake with reference to the Canada and lake trade very desirable. The canal was completed in 1828, and the Oswego and Syracuse railroad in 1848, when Oswego, having 10,305 inhabitants, was incorporated as a city. The modification of the English colonial trade system, and the admission by the United States of goods in bond under the warehouse system, laid the foundation for a great development of the business of Oswego on the occasion of the famine of 1847, when the trade of the place took a sudden start, which it has since sustained. The Welland canal, connecting Lakes Erie and Ontario, gave Oswego a line of communication with the west, by which freight coming thence to the east, would have, *via* Oswego, less canal navigation than by other routes. In May, 1857, the Welland railway, running along the banks of the canal, was projected, and is now completed, thus giving a communication all the year round. By these means Oswego draws its supplies from every western state; Oswego also is a great salt depot, and has a large lumber trade with Canada. The imports from Canada in 1859 were $3,831,041, and the exports $1,918,798; the tonnage of the port amounts to 26,395. Pop. in 1860 16,817

Cleveland.—The place was settled by one family in 1799, but its population did not increase beyond 500 in 1825, when the Erie canal was opened. Its greatest impulse was derived from the construction of the Ohio canal, connecting it with Cincinnati, the Pennsylvania and Ohio canal, connecting it with Pittsburg, and the Welland canal in Canada, connecting Lake Erie with Lake Ontario. Since that event a considerable Canadian trade has sprung up in Cleveland. The canals of Ohio brought down the increasing quantities of produce that were then exported in exchange for the merchandise that was delivered by lake for the consumption of the interior. In 1832 there were 26 sail vessels and one steamer belonging to

Cleveland; there are now 14 steamers and 142 sail vessels, with an aggregate tonnage of 39,984 tons owned there. The multiplication of railroads has, however, added of late more to the city business than either canals or tonnage. There are six roads running into Cleveland, of an aggregate length of 754 miles, and their annual receipts are $4,520,452. These crossing Ohio in every direction, connect the city with Toledo, Columbus, Pittsburg, and New York. With these advantages, under the action of the reciprocity treaty with Canada, a large foreign trade sprung up. In 1858 the imports and exports were as follows:—

	Vessels.	Tons.	Coastwise.	Foreign.	Total.
Exports....	2,084	705,577	$13,166,256	$224,986	$13,391,242
Imports....	2,137	721,519	26,087,849	168,409	26,256,258

The trade between Cleveland and Lake Superior has also become important within four or five years, in which time it has risen to $3,000,000 in value, mostly in copper ore. The most remarkable development of trade is, however, the direct trade between Cleveland and Europe. In 1856 a vessel built in Cleveland, loaded wheat at Chicago for Liverpool, where she was sold to advantage, and now runs to Brazil. In the following year others were sent, and a vessel arrived from Liverpool at Chicago with hardware, etc. In the following year a fleet of ten vessels, 3,600 tons, owned by Cleveland merchants, sailed for Liverpool, and since run to the Mediterranean, South America, and elsewhere. The coal trade of Cleveland has become large for the supply of the steamers and factories on and around the lakes; the supply is about 250,000 tons per annum. Population in 1860, 36,054.

Detroit.—This is the oldest of the western cities, having been early occupied by the French, but its progress, like the others, was slow until the opening of the Erie canal. In 137 years, up to 1820, the population had risen only to 1,442 souls. The greatest impulse has been given to Detroit by the formation, in the last ten years, of the railroad system, which connects it with the interior country. The Great Western railway of Canada, coming 229 miles, has its terminus virtually in Detroit. From Detroit west run the Michigan Central road, 228 miles, to Chicago, and connecting with the whole western net-work of rails; the Detroit and Milwaukee railroad, crossing the Peninsula, 185 miles, to Grand Haven; the Michigan Southern road running also to Chicago. The earnings of the three roads last year were $5,700,000. Pop. in 1860, 45,619.

Chicago is probably the most remarkable of the western cities for its growth. The place in 1812 was but a garrison that was abandoned. Subsequently, and as an Indian trading post, it collected some sixty or seventy persons in 1823. Although situated at the bottom of the lake, with a fine harbor sufficient for any lake trade, it could not thrive until the back country supplied it with produce to sell, and required of it merchandise in exchange. To procure this the Illinois and Michigan canal, connecting the lake with the navigable waters of the Illinois, was commenced in 1836, 100 miles in length. In aid of this work the federal government donated alternate six mile sections of the public lands. The state had also projected a large system of railroad improvements on a scale far beyond its means, and it failed in 1840. Subsequently the means was raised to complete the canal, which was effected in 1850. Since that date numerous railroads have been constructed, leading to the Mississippi river in a fan-like form, having Chicago for the centre. The expenditure of some $150,000,000 for the construction of those roads, over a circle of country of which Chicago is the natural market, has had a prodigious effect upon its welfare. The effect of that expenditure attracted immigrants and speculators, whose outlay reflected prosperity upon the city. The means of communication thus formed by 2,900 miles of railroad diverging from the city, over a vast circle of fertile country, has made Chicago the first primary grain port in the world, shipping as it does more than 20,000,000 bushels of grain per annum. It has millions of tonnage yearly entered and cleared, importing and exporting to the amount of $50,000,000. Chicago is only six or eight feet above the level of the lake, but the harbor has a depth of thirteen feet of water, and will always be ample for the commerce of the lakes. The number of vessels arriving here in 1857 was 7,557. The new Canadian rules in relation to navigation enable Chicago vessels to clear direct for Europe, and there are a number in the trade by which produce and goods are shipped direct to Europe. The total value of produce exported in 1859 was $24,280,890. Inasmuch as breadstuffs are the principal product of the country between Chicago and the Mississippi, and furnish so important an item in the commerce of the place, the following table will best illustrate as well the development of agriculture as the chief element of trade:

SHIPMENTS OF FLOUR (REDUCED TO WHEAT) AND GRAIN FROM CHICAGO FOR TWENTY-THREE YEARS.

	Bushels.		Bushels.		Bushels.
1838,	78	1845,	1,024,620	1853,	6,412,181
1839,	3,678	1846,	1,599,819	1854,	12,932,320
1840,	10,000	1847,	2,243,201	1855,	16,633,700
1841,	40,000	1848,	3,001,740	1856,	21,583,221
1842,	586,907	1849,	2,769,111	1857,	18,032,678
1843,	688,907	1850,	1,830,930	1858,	20,035,166
1844,	923,494	1851,	4,646,291	1859,	16,753,795
		1852,	5,873,141	1860,	30,000,000

The famine abroad in 1845–6–7, consequent upon the failure of the potato crops, caused a demand for grain that was felt in Chicago. The development was not large, however, until 1852, when the Galena road pushed out on to the prairie, and since then the receipts have not ceased to increase by every line of road; the quantity that came in the first six months of 1860 is larger than ever before. These grain receipts are said to make Chicago the largest primary grain port in the world. Pop. in 1860, 109,263.

MILWAUKEE is one of the chief cities of the western shore of Lake Michigan. It was settled in 1834, and up to 1840 could boast of but 1,700 inhabitants. The population had grown to nearly 20,000 in 1850, to 30,000 in 1853, and to 45,254 in 1860. The growth has been most rapid under the settlement of the country west of it, by means of the large expenditures there made in the last four years for railroads. These in the state of Wisconsin, have an aggregate length of 2,403 miles, and have been constructed mostly in the last ten years at an expense of $36,742,063. The expenditure of this large sum of money, in addition to that laid out by speculators and emigrants, imparted an impulse to the prosperity of the city which is reflected in its population and valuation. The circle of fertile country poured into the city products which were exported from it to the value of $27,974,748 in 1856, and in return $20,274,000 worth of goods was imported. The manufactures of the city were also valued at $8,057,000. The quantity of grain shipped from Milwaukee in 1858 was 6,155,507 bushels, and from other lake ports of Wisconsin 1,561,881 bushels. The grain movement, which is the basis of the city's commerce, indicates the ratio of its growth, and this has been as follows:—

	Bushels.		Bushels.		Bushels.
1851,	576,580	1854,	2,534,617	1857,	3,727,468
1852,	1,029,379	1855,	3,758,965	1858,	6,155,507
1853,	1,476,993	1856,	3,720,103	1859,	6,438,038

We may recapitulate these lake cities in the following table, showing the date of settlement, of incorporation, and population at that date, with the population and valuation in 1850 and 1860:—

	Settled.	Incorporated.	Population.
Buffalo	1801	1832	8,653
Oswego	1820	1848	10,305
Cleveland	1799	1836	4,000
Detroit	1683	1802	700
Chicago	1823	1835	800
Milwaukee	1830	1840	9,655
Total			34,113

	Population in 1850.	Total Valuation.	Population in 1860.	Total Valuation.
Buffalo	49,764	$18,427,000	81,131	$37,487,061
Oswego	12,205	9,107,202	16,817	21,500,000
Cleveland	17,034	12,102,101	36,054	21,951,428
Detroit	21.057	10,741,657	45'619	28,141,591
Chicago	29,963	31,205,000	109.263	78,291,000
Milwaukee	31,077	18,421,000	45,254	35,458,130
Total	161,100	$100,003,960	334,138	$222,829,210

Thus these prominent cities have grown up, so to speak, in 25 years, as points where farm produce is received from the country for sale and where goods are furnished in exchange. The whole value of the lake trade has been estimated at $600,000,000 per annum, and the transaction of this business has, it appears, created six cities, with a population of 347,000 and a taxable valuation of $222,829,210. The manufactures have gradually increased in those cities in order to produce a local supply instead of importing, and new inventions in sewing and other machines have promoted that change, as machinery aided the development of surplus produce. The aggregate trade poured upon the lakes from all these sources has been increasingly large. The aggregate quantities of grain shipped from the grain regions are seen in the following table, which shows the routes taken to market:—

	1857.	1858.	1859.
Via Lake Ontario	18,044,354	11,872,995	14,874,961
Via Suspension Bridge	1,049,108	1,900,000	337,778
Via Lake Erie	22,031,164	29,432,121	24,730,582
From Ohio River eastward	4,352,036	6,242,441	4,446,281
Grand total	45,476,662	49,447,557	44,389,602

The totals were composed of these following grains:—

	Flour. barrels.	Wheat. bushels.	Corn. bushels.	Oth. Grain. bushels.	Total in bushels.
1856,	3,879,189	19,956,025	14,282,632	4,634,969	58.269,571
1857,	3,412,904	17,362,161	8,779,832	2,270,149	45,476,662
1858,	4,602,780	20,794,515	10,558,527	5,080,615	49,447,557
1859,	3,760,285	16,864,812	4,423,096	4,310,269	44,389,602

These fluctuations follow the course of western business. In 1857 there was a heavy decline under the influence of the panic of that year. In 1858 the speculative consumption of the interior having ceased, the quantities that sought market were less

Painted by J. C. Ward. Steel Plate. Engraved by Henry.

than in 1856. The railroads also delivered considerable quantities.

The rapid settlement of the west attracted the attention of the Canadians, and they began early with some energy to take measures that should give them their share of it. The St. Lawrence river was for them the only outlet, and to make that serviceable, extensive works were necessary to pass around the rapids, and make navigation practicable from the lakes to the sea. The Welland canal, passing around the Falls and connecting Lakes Erie and Ontario, was constructed, with other necessary works, completing, in 1846, a system, at a cost of $20,000,000. The tolls on these works were considerable, and duties on goods imported into Canada from the United States were so high as to check trade—the more so that similar duties were imposed in the United States on Canadian goods. In 1850 the navigation laws were repealed, opening the canals and rivers to foreign vessels. The difficulties in the way of navigating the St. Lawrence have since that date been, to a great extent, removed. Many light-houses have been constructed, the system of pilotage has been revised, a service of tug-boats, of great power, and working at moderate rates, has been organized, and the depth of water between Quebec and Montreal has been increased by dredging, so as to permit the passage of vessels drawing eighteen feet six inches. With these changes and improvements a new element has been introduced. The construction of railways had begun to occupy the attention of the public mind in Canada. In 1849 an act of the Colonial Legislature was passed guaranteeing 6 per cent. on half the cost of all the railways seventy-five miles in extent. Three years later the Grand Trunk line, from Montreal to Toronto, and from Quebec to Riviere-du-Loup, was incorporated as a part of the Main Trunk line, and the line from Quebec to Richmond had been commenced. In 1853 the amalgamation of all the companies forming the Main Trunk line was completed, under a Parliamentary sanction with powers to construct the Victoria Bridge across the St. Lawrence, and thereby connect the lines west of Montreal with those leading to Quebec and Portland.

By the aid of all these enterprises combined, there is now in operation in Canada 2,093 miles of railway, including 1,112 miles of the Grand Trunk, the whole connected with the great winter harbor of Portland, in the state of Maine.

To give effect to this great system of communication, the whole system of tolls upon inland navigation has been abandoned. The whole line of navigation from Chicago to the Atlantic is now free from tolls and lake dues, the ports of Sault Ste. Marie and Gaspe have been made free ports, and it is probable many more will be thrown open. While these measures have been in progress to facilitate trade, a most important measure was adopted in 1854. This was the reciprocity treaty of that year, which designated a number of articles that were to be free on both sides. The treaty went into operation in the latter part of 1854, and the trade has been affected by it as follows:—

	Domestic exports.	Total exports to Canada.	Total imports from Canada.
1852,	$6,655,097	$10,509,016	$6,110,299
1853,	7,404,087	13,140,642	7,550,718
1854,	15,204,144	24,566,860	8,927,560
1855,	15,806,642	27,806,020	15,136,734
1856,	22,714,697	29,029,349	21,310,421
1857,	19,936,113	24,262,482	22,124,296
1858,	19,638,959	23,651,727	15,806,519
1859,	21,769,627	28,154,174	19,727,551
	$129,129,366	$181,120,270	$116,694,098

The exports of United States produce to Canada have been in this period of eight years over $12,000,000 in excess of all the imports from Canada. In addition there have been exported to Canada fifty millions of foreign goods that have been imported on the seaboard. The domestic exports are composed of the produce shipped from the American lake ports, and entered at the Canadian ports. The freedom of navigation on the canals and rivers enjoyed by the American vessels has also opened a large trade from Cleveland, Chicago, and other ports, direct to Europe. Last year the number of vessels passing through the canals of Canada was 26,466, with a tonnage of 2,455,021. Of these 22,800 were Canadian, with a tonnage of 1,828,383. Deduct 300,000 tons for the traffic on the local canals, from which the tolls are not removed, and there is still a balance of Canadian over American tonnage of 926,638. The lake ports also enjoy more or less import trade on which duties are collected. Those duties at all lake ports for the last four years have amounted to $288,508.

The efforts of Canada to obtain the trade, and cause it to pass down the St. Lawrence, had to overcome, however, the climate, to be successful; for four months in the year that outlet is ice-bound, while the ports of Lake Ontario are never closed by the ice, and offer railroad connection with New York, Boston, and Philadelphia, the former for export and the latter for supplies of manufacture.

CHAPTER II.

RIVER CITIES—ATLANTIC CITIES.

The development given to the lake cities by the canal and railroad construction, was participated in to as great an extent by the river cities, the course of whose trade flowed downward toward New Orleans as an outlet.

Pittsburg is situated at the point where the junction of the Monongahela and Alleghany forms the Ohio river, which thence flows to the Gulf of Mexico. The origin of the place dates from its occupation by the French as a post, and its growth is due to its commanding position. It is 301 miles east by north from Philadelphia, and is 130 miles from Lake Erie. The traveller descends the river 450 miles to Cincinnati; 583 to Louisville, Kentucky; 977 to Cairo, where the Ohio pours into the Mississippi; 1,157 to St. Louis, and 2,004 miles to New Orleans. That vast valley collects in its course the produce coming right and left by streams, canals, and railroads, to deliver it at New Orleans, whence ascend the merchandise, tropical products, and materials of manufacture, to be distributed at the commercial and manufacturing ports. The position of Pittsburg was the most important, commercially, until the opening of the Erie canal. Its resources were highly favorable to ship-building, and it supplied the first boats that descended the Ohio. The commerce and ship-building prospered largely during the war of 1812, but after the peace it declined. Since that period manufacture has taken the place of commerce, and it ranks next to Philadelphia as a manufacturing town. The facilities and resources for manufacture are immense. The population in 1800 was 1,565, and in 1816 it was incorporated as a city with about 6,150 inhabitants. The population of Pittsburg in the present year is given at 130,000, but this includes Alleghany City and other suburbs; the city proper is stated at 49,220. The progress of the city has been as follows:—

	Population.	Value of manufactures.
1816,	6,182	$1,896,366
1836,	15,481	15,575,440
1850,	46,601	55,287,000
1860,	49,220	

Cincinnati was located at the mouth of the Licking river in 1788, in the centre of an area which commanded the commerce of the Miami, the Wabash, the Scioto, the Muskingum, and the Kanawha rivers. These streams delivered large quantities of produce to foster the trade of Cincinnati, which grew with great rapidity, corresponding mostly with New Orleans, to which its merchants sent the produce, and made purchases of goods in the eastern states, which came up the river from New Orleans by a long voyage, charged with heavy expenses for freight, insurance, etc. The exchanges ran on New Orleans against the produce sent down, and these credits were the means of payments for goods. The opening of the Ohio canal to the lakes, to correspond with the Erie canal to tide-water, gave a new outlet for produce of the northern part of Ohio by way of Cleveland, and also a better channel for the receipt of goods. The net-work of railroads has still further multiplied the means of communication. Portland, Boston, New York, Philadelphia, and Baltimore, are almost equidistant from Cincinnati, which by the same means has its markets extended in a broader circle west. The progress of the city has been as follows:—

	Population.	Imports.	Manufactures.	Exports.
1800,	750			
1810,	2,540			
1820,	9,644	$1,619,030	$1,059,459	$1,334,080
1830,	24,831	2,528,590	1,850,000	1,063,560
1836,	31,207	8,270,000	12,388,200	8,101,000
1840,	46,338	16,972,000	17,780,033	15,480,000
1850,	115,486	41,256,199	54,550,134	33,234,896
1860,	161,044	96,213,274	112,254,000	66,007,707

These figures give the rapid growth of the city since the railroads have opened a broader field from which to draw the materials of trade in exchange for merchandise demanded by the growers.

Louisville, Kentucky, was a port early in 1781, and it made little progress as a city. Its population grew but to 600 in 1800, and was only 4,012 in 1820. The difficulties of navigation were a drawback upon its commerce, until the Portland canal, two miles long, which had been authorized in 1804, around the falls of the Ohio, was opened in 1830. The cost of the work, $600,000, was paid, one-third by the United

States, and the balance mostly in eastern cities interested in getting goods up the river. A bridge over the Ohio was built in 1836, at a cost of $250,000. The city was incorporated in 1828, and its population was then 10,336. In 1836 the population was 19,967, and the annual amount of business transacted was $29,004,202. In 1840 the population was 21,210, and in 1850 it had again doubled, reaching 43,194.

St. Louis was occupied as a French trading post in 1763, and the town was laid out in the following year, with the name of St. Louis, in honor of that Louis XV. who had so little claim to saintship. The first impulse to its growth was, however, the annexation of Louisiana to the United States, when emigrants poured into the new country, bringing with them a spirit of enterprise which soon made visible effects upon St. Louis, the commerce of which struggled against the difficulties inherent in barge and keel boat navigation. In 1817 the General Pike, the first steamboat, arrived at St. Louis. That event marked a new era, and in 1822, the population being 4,598, the city was incorporated. It was not until the settlement of the north-western states, under the influence of the canals and railroads, that the prosperity of St. Louis became marked. In 1836 the sales of merchandise in St. Louis were given at $6,335,000; in 1858 the local insurance was $31,800,232. The population of the city, which had been 63,491 in 1848, rose to 151,780 in 1860, and the city valuation was $78,463,375. The settlements of the upper Mississippi, east and west, pour naturally an increasing trade into the city, and its railroad connections are now pushing out toward the Pacific. We may recapitulate the leading river cities as follows:—

	Settled.	Incorporated.		1840.	1850.		1860.	
	Date.	Date.	Populat'n.	Populat'n.	Population.	Valuation.	Population.	Valuation.
Pittsburg	1784,	1816,	6,150	21,115	46,601	$27,960,600	49,220	$46,866,600
Cincinnati	1788,	1802,	890	46,338	115,436	55,670,631	161,044	91.861,978
Louisville	1773,	1828,	10,336	21,210	43,194	17,277,600	69,740	30,042,800
St. Louis	1764,	1822,	4,598	16,469	77,860	38,921,201	151,780	78,463,375
Total			21,974	105,221	283,091	$139,830,032	431,784	$247,234,753

The numbers and wealth of the river cities have increased in a ratio, perhaps, larger than the lake cities. They divide with the latter the trade of country lying between the lakes and the Ohio river, drawing produce and shipping merchandise, while they have also a strong hold upon southern trade. The business of all those cities, as well lake as river, is but a reflection of the growth of the great seaports. The canals, streams, and railroads that pour forth their products in a southerly direction, and feed the river cities, combine with the other business points of the region to swell the trade of New Orleans, the common correspondent of all; the roads, rivers, and streams that deliver their trade in a northerly and easterly direction, glut the great trunk lines with the merchandise which they pour into Boston, New York, Philadelphia, and Baltimore.

The city of New Orleans, at the Delta of the Mississippi, is commercially the second city of the Union, and in respect to the exports of domestic produce, it ranks first. Its position is very advantageous, and its growth has been proportional to the development of the country, the resources of which supply it with produce and depend upon it for merchandise in return. The city itself was founded by the French in 1717, and passed into the hands of the Spanish in 1762. By them it was reconveyed to the French in 1800, and was sold by Napoleon to the United States in 1804. At that time its population, mostly French, was 8,056, and it was rapidly increased by the fact of annexation, which not only carried enterprising men thither, but settled the upper country, which was the source of trade. The city was chartered in 1805. In 1820 the population had increased to 27,176 persons, but the exports of the city still consisted mostly of the produce of the upper country, which a population, increased rapidly by the influence of war and speculation, had greatly developed, although the valley of the Mississippi had not yet attracted cotton planters. In 1830 the trade of the city marked a larger production of farm produce. In the succeeding ten years the migration from the Atlantic cotton states to the new lands of the valley produced a great change in the trade of New Orleans. The cotton receipts rose from 300,000 bales in 1830, to 954,000 in 1840, and tobacco from twenty-four to forty-three thousand hogsheads, and the sugar crop also had risen to 85,000 hhds. The exports were now swollen by the sales of cotton and tobacco, but, with the operation of the canals and railroads in the upper country, the supplies of home produce had again become important. The progress of New Orleans has been as follows. The figures for 1860 are not published, but the cotton is 30 per cent. higher, and the amount will be about $200,000,000 received from the interior.

	Population.	Imports.	Exports.	Receipts from Interior.	Receipts of Specie.	Valuation of Real Estate.
1804,	8,056	..	$1,392,093	..	..	..
1810,	17,242	..	1,753,974	..	..	..
1820,	27,176	$3,379,717	7,242,415	..	..	..
1830,	46,310	7,599,083	13,042,740	..	..	..
1840,	102,193	10,673,190	34,236,936	$45,761,045	..	..
1850,	116,375	10,760,499	38,105,350	96,897,873	$3,792,662	..
1851,	..	12,528,460	54,413,963	106,924,083	7,938,119	..
1852,	..	12,057,724	49,058,885	108,051,708	6,278,523	$66,350,260
1853,	..	13,654,113	67,768,724	134,233,731	7,865,226	..
1854,	..	14,402,150	60,172,628	115,336,798	6,967,056	..
1855,	..	12,923,608	55,688,552	117,106,823	3,746,037	..
1856,	..	17,183,327	80,547,963	144,256,081	4,913,540	..
1857,	..	24,981,150	91,514,286	158,061,369	6,500,015	..
1858,	..	19,586,013	88,382,438	167,155,546	13,268,013	108,651,135
1859,	168,472	18,349,516	101,734,952	172,952,664	15,627,016	111,193,802

This table embraces the official figures for population, trade, and valuation. The most marked feature is the small amount of imports as compared with exports. This we shall find to be the reverse with the trade of New York; the trade of the two cities for the past year having been as follows:—

	New York.	New Orleans.
Imports........	$220,247,307	$18,349,516
Exports........	106,604,097	101,734,952

The domestic exports from New York, exclusive of specie, were but 54,000,000, showing an excess of about $166,000,000 imported; while at New Orleans the excess is $83,385,436 exported. These figures represent the course of trade. The receipts from the interior at New Orleans rose from $96,897,873 in 1850, to $172,952,664 in 1859. This embraces sugar and molasses, of which the value was nearly $32,000,000, but which being sent up the western rivers and to the Atlantic ports, is not exported. Cotton was $92,037,794 of the amount, and tobacco $9,324,326. These sums together make $133,362,120, leaving $39,590,544 as the value of farm produce, which comes down the western rivers as the readiest conveyance. On the other hand, the lighter merchandise which forms the sum of imports into New York, instead of going round by way of New Orleans, goes across the country on railroads. It follows, that when the west sends forty millions of produce to New Orleans for sale, and has purchased an equal amount of goods in the east, that its money is in New Orleans and its debts in New York. It draws upon New Orleans then to pay New York. New Orleans being so large an exporter, has large sums due it, for which it draws to meet what it owes to the west for produce. This state of affairs is the basis of bill operations. Firms being connected, one at Liverpool, one at New Orleans, and one at New York, the New Orleans house buys cotton for shipment to England, and draws for it at sixty days on the New York firm; the bill being discounted, places him in funds to pay for the cotton, which will arrive in Liverpool in thirty days. The New York firm draws a sterling bill against it at sixty days, and, with the proceeds, meets the bill drawn on it from New Orleans. The sterling bill is then met by the sales of cotton four months after it was bought. In the mean time, the bill on New York passes into the hands of the western debtors of New York, who send it thither in payment of goods purchased. The sterling bill is sold to the New York importer, who remits it abroad in payment of goods imported. The receipts of cotton and sugar have been very large of late years, but the quantities of western produce resulting from the more rapid settlement of the land under the influence of the railroads, have also greatly increased. In 1840, the value of cotton, sugar, and tobacco received was $36,124,275, leaving but $9,591,770 for western produce. In the year of famine the aggregate receipts at New Orleans rose to $90,033,251, of which $42,599,361 was western produce. In 1857, those articles were valued at $49,009,976; flour and grain counting in that year for nearly $15,000,000. By means of time bills, New Orleans thus furnishes a large capital to dealers; and in years of economy and re-

Drawn & Engraved by J.W. Watts

VICTORIA BRIDGE.

renchment, when the purchases of goods are liminished, it shows a large inward current of specie. In 1851, California supplied a ood deal of gold at that point, but changed lirection after the establishment of a mint t San Francisco, and the receipts of specie vere small at New Orleans in 1855—a specuative year. They became large with the anic year, and have since so continued. The large sales of produce bring a balance n favor of that point, giving great stability o its banking institutions.

While New Orleans thus expanded its rade, and grew in wealth under the influnce of western production, the proportion hat it enjoyed was by no means the largest. Each Atlantic city had made efforts to obain a share, and, with more or less success, Canada sought to attract it down the St. Lawrence. New York built two railroads to aid the canals in connecting the lakes with ide water. Boston formed a connection vith the Hudson river, and another with the akes at Ogdensburgh. Philadelphia imroved its hold on Pittsburg. Baltimore hrust out its iron arm to Wheeling, and all hese offered inducements to trade. The onnage of these works shows the progress of trade:—

	Tons.	Tons.
Erie canal, 1840		1,416,046
New York canals, 1858, ...	3,344,061	
New York Central railroad, 1858, ..	838,791	
New York and Erie, 1858, ...	978,066	
Northern, Ogdensburgh to Boston,..	177,728	
Pennsylvania, to Philadelphia,......	530,420	
Baltimore and Ohio, to Baltimore, ..	876,239	6,745,105
Increase in tonnage, ...		5,329,059

The valuation of this tonnage is nearly $350,000,000 per annum, and this affords an ndication only of the wealth which has passed eastward. Thus, in 1840, the value of western produce, that found market by New Orleans and the Erie canal, was $51,000,000; in 1858, it was nearly $400,000,000, or an ncrease ten-fold, and on this mainly has the prosperity of the eastern cities depended. The exports of the southern ports have grown mostly with the direct export of coton, and those at the north have added gradually food and manufactures thereto. The general course of trade has been to centralize imports in New York.

Charleston owes its origin to a stock similar to that of New England, since a colony of French Huguenots, flying from persecution, settled there in 1690. It was not chartered as a city, however, until nearly a century later, viz.: in 1783, when its population was nearly 16,000. The commerce of Charleston is not extensive, but its facilities for internal communications are large, and enjoys the trade of the whole state, together with much of that of North Carolina and Georgia. A canal, twenty-two miles long, connects the Cooper with the Santee river. It has a fleet of steamboats that are running to the neighboring cities, and several lines of packets running to New York regularly. Its most important connection is, however, the South Carolina railroad, running 136 miles to Hamburg, on the Savannah river, opposite Augusta, Georgia. The population and business have been as follows:—

	Population.	Imports.	Exports.
1790,	16,359	$4,516,205	$2,693,268
1820,	24,480	3,007,113	8,882,940
1830,	30,289	1,054,619	7,627,031
1840,	29,261	2,318,791	11,042,070
1850,	42,985	1,933,785	11,447,800
1860,	51,210	2,070 249	16,888,262

The importations have not apparently increased, while the exports have grown in proportion to the improvement of means of intercourse with the interior, affording better freights outward from Charleston.

Baltimore was laid out as a town, by Roman Catholics, in 1729, and up to 1765 it contained but fifty houses. The persuasion of the founders still predominates. It is situated on the Patapsco river, fourteen miles from Chesapeake bay, and two hundred miles from the ocean. The harbor is a very fine one. The city enjoys great facilities for commerce, and possesses the trade of Maryland and part of Pennsylvania, while it has of late obtained a good share of that of the western states. It was the great tobacco market of the country, but Richmond now rivals it in that respect. As a flour market, it has few equals. The building of railroads to connect with the interior has greatly promoted the city trade, which has progressed as follows:—

	Population.	Imports.	Exports.
1790,	13,503	$6,018,500	$2,239,691
1800,	26,514		12,264,331
1810,	46,555		6,489,018
1820,	62,738	4,070,842	6,609,364
1830,	80,625	4,523,866	3,791,482
1840,	102,313	5,701,869	4,524,575
1850,	169,054	6,124,201	6,967,353
1860,	212,419	8,930,157	10,442,616

The importations have been mostly followed with increase in exports, that have been promoted since 1850 by the opening of the Baltimore and Ohio railroad.

PHILADELPHIA, at the close of the last century, was the first city of America, and since that period, although it has not ceased to expand in wealth and population in a ratio far beyond the examples of the old world, yet New York, by force of natural advantages, has come to exceed it as a commercial city. Its resources for manufacturing are such, however, as to have given it a high rank in the interior trade of the country. The water-power of the neighborhood is very important, and rails and canals give it command of limitless supplies of raw materials, coal and iron in particular. The position of the city was early improved by the construction of canals to the extent of 336 miles, at a cost of $24,000,000; and seven lines, composed of twelve railroads, of 567 miles in length, radiate to every point of the compass, having cost $53,716,201. The canals and roads have swollen the coal receipts of Philadelphia from 365 tons in 1820, to 7,781,100 tons in 1859, valued at nearly $35,000,000 per annum. The population and external trade of Philadelphia have been as follows:—

	Population.	Imports.	Exports.	Total valuation.
1684,	2,500			
1790,	42,520		$3,436,893	
1820,	108,116	$8,158,922	5,743,549	$40,487,289
1840,	258,037	11,680,111	3,841,599	99,321,881
1850,	408,762	12,066,154	4,501,606	
1858,	550,000	12,892,215	6,036,411	155,697,669

The city of Philadelphia was first settled in 1627 by the Swedes, but was regulated and laid out in 1682 according to the views of William Penn, and its population in 1684 was 2,500. The city is one hundred miles from the ocean, eighty-seven miles from New York, and 130 miles from Washington. It is five miles from the junction of the Schuylkill and Delaware rivers, extending from one to the other, and its harbor is on the Delaware, or eastern side. Vessels drawing more than twenty feet water cannot reach Philadelphia, and the navigation for large ships below is a little difficult. Pilots take inward bound ships at sea. These circumstances have aided to give Philadelphia less of a commercial character as compared with the commanding harbor of New York.

If the foreign commerce of Philadelphia does not show large, owing to physical difficulties, the internal commerce, from sales of manufactures and goods imported at New York, is very large—and the real growth of the city is indicated by her external trade less than that of, perhaps, any other city of the Union. The census of 1860 has been estimated at 650,000. The manufacturing industry of Philadelphia has increased in a remarkable ratio. In 1845 the capital employed in the city proper was $18,000,000, the production $21,000,000, and of the neighborhood $33,000,000.

In 1858 the capital invested in the various industries was given at $72,000,000, employing 132,000 hands, and producing $145,348,738 of annual value. In the vicinity the amount is $26,500,000 additional. These figures denote that Philadelphia is probably the greatest manufacturing city of the Union, and will continue to grow in that direction by the force of the same influences which tend to give New York the commercial preponderance. The trade of the city is on a grand scale, and second to none in the world for magnitude of operations, or successful method in conducting them. A leading store of that city is a model of mercantile method. Each department in the store is alphabetically designated. The shelves and rows of goods in each department are numbered, and upon the tag attached to the goods is marked the letter of the department, the number of the shelf, and row on that shelf to which such piece of goods belongs. The cashier receives a certain sum extra per week, and he is responsible for all worthless money received. Books are kept, in which the sales of each clerk are entered for the day, and the salary of the clerk cast, as a per-centage on each day, week, and year, and, at the foot of the page, the aggregate of the sales appears, and the per-centage that it has cost to effect these sales is easily calculated for each day, month, or year. The counters are designated by an imaginary color, as the blue, green, brown, etc., counter. The yard-sticks and counter-brush belonging to it are painted to correspond with the imaginary color of the counter; so by a very simple arrangement, each of these necessaries is kept where it belongs; and should any be missing, the faulty clerks are easily known.

All wrapping paper coming into the store is immediately taken to a counter in the basement, where a lad attends with a pair of shears, whose duty it is to cut the paper into pieces to correspond with the size of the parcels sold at the different departments, to which he sees that it is transferred. All pieces too small for this, even to the smallest scraps, are by him put into a sack, and what is usually thrown away by our merchants, yields to the systematic man some $20 per year. In one part of the establishment is a tool closet, with a work-bench attached; the closet occupies but little space, yet in it is seen almost every useful tool, and this is arranged with the hand-saw to form the centre, and the smaller tools radiating from it in sun form; behind each article is painted, with black paint, the shape of the tool belonging in that place.

It is, consequently, impossible that any thing should be out of place except through design, and if any tool is missing, the wall will show the shadow without the substance. The proprietor's desk stands at the further end of the store, raised on a platform facing the front, from which he can see all the operations in each section of the retail department. From this desk run tubes, connecting with each department of the store, from the garret to the cellar, so that if a person in any department, either porter, retail, or wholesale clerk, wishes to communicate with the employer, he can do so without leaving his station. Pages are kept in each department to take the bill of parcels, together with the money paid, and return the bill receipted, and change, if any, to the customer. So that the salesman is never obliged to leave the counter; he is at all times ready either to introduce a new article or watch that no goods are taken from his counter, excepting those accounted for.

By a peculiar method of casting the percentage of a clerk's salary on his sales, coupling it with the clerk's general conduct, and the style of goods he is selling, a just estimate may be formed of the relative value of the services of each, in proportion to his salary. By the alphabetic arrangement of departments, numbering of shelves, and form of the tools, any clerk, no matter if he has not been in the store more than an hour, can arrange every article in its proper place; and at any time, if inquired of respecting, or referred to by any clerk, the proprietor is able to speak understandingly of the capabilities and business qualities of any of his employees. Population in 1860, 565,531.

Boston was settled early in the seventeenth century, and in 1684 was the most populous of the Atlantic cities, having 6,300 inhabitants. It is 216 miles from New York, and although possessed of one of the finest harbors on the coast, it had no facilities for reaching the back country, which was for the most part rocky and mountainous, until railroads were constructed. Its early trade was in navigation and the fisheries. Its first adventure was in 1627, when a sloop, loaded with corn, was sent to Narraganset to trade, and made an encouraging voyage. Its inhabitants soon became rich by doing the trade of others in their celebrated ships, until manufacturing became possible. The energy and intelligence of the race, when turned in that direction, soon drew large profits from their industry, and more freight for their coasting tonnage, which increased as the numbers engaged in manufacture required more food and raw materials. The greatest start was given to the trade of the city when railroads had laid open even the remotest regions of the interior to its enterprise. The general course of its population, trade, and valuation has been as follows:—

	Population.	Imports.	Exports.	Valuation.
1684,	6,300			
1790,	18,038	$5,519,500	$2,517,651	$6,990,890
1820,	43,298	14,826,782	11,008,922	38,288,200
1830,	61,392	10,453,544	7,218,194	61,780,210
1840,	93,388	13,800,925	9,104,862	102,101,201
1850,	136,881	30,874,684	10,681,763	180,000,500
1855,	162,629	45,113,774	28,190,925	249,262,500
1858,	170.000	40,432,710	20,979,853	262,014,500

The exports of Boston have taken a great start since 1830, and since then there have been constructed nine lines of railroad, which radiate from Boston in every direction; placing every town in New England in connection with it, and by continuous lines, every city of the Union, from Bangor to New Orleans, St. Louis, Chicago, and St. Paul. The running of the line of Cunard steamers gives it a European connection more prompt and regular than any other. Its extensive trade shows the effect of these connections, and its taxable valuation the wealth that accumulates from its manufacturing industry. That valuation is this year (1860) $276,339-900, and the population 177,481.

CHAPTER III.

NEW YORK—TELEGRAPH—EXPRESS—GOLD.

The city of New York, at the close of the revolution, was the second city of the new world, taking rank after Philadelphia. Its internal trade was limited to the capacity of the Hudson river, but its traders pushed across to Lake Champlain, and even to Lake Ontario, whence they drew skins and furs from the Indians, and brought down some of the produce of Vermont and New Hampshire. At this date there was little trade west of Albany. The trade was mostly with the towns on the east side of the river, and with Rutland, Burlington, and other Vermont towns, as well as the western towns of Massachusetts. Remittances were made from these towns in ashes, wheat, etc., and during the embargo and war, smuggling was very extensively carried on, taking pay in specie. The goods went up the river in sloops. The New England cities had equal commercial advantages, and Philadelphia enjoyed many others in addition. The valley of the Hudson furnished, however, large supplies of farm produce during the wars of Europe, which gave a preponderance to the New York trade, and it began to gain strength. In 1807 the passage of Fulton's steamer to Albany gave a great impulse to the river trade. Her statesmen, however, soon saw the necessity of a more extended inland communication, and the canal, which had been projected before the peace, became a legal reality in 1817, and a physical fact in 1825. The capital of the New York merchants began to be invested in enterprises which resulted in centring trade in the city. The canal connection opened the vast circle of the lake trade to New York city, and poured into its basin the western farm produce at rates far below what the same articles could be raised for at the east. As a necessity, therefore, New York became the point of supply, not only for the foreign trade, but for the neighboring states. The growing manufactures of Philadelphia and Boston found cheaper food in New York than in their own neighborhood, and North river sloops and schooners continued the Erie canal to the Delaware and the Charles river. As new routes to the west, and more extended settlements in that region opened new sources for the supply of produce, and new markets for goods, the tendency was to New York. The capital engaged in commerce at that point being the largest, produce found readier advances and more prompt realization, while the large imports and consignments of foreign goods made the assortment larger and the average cost less there than elsewhere. The same circumstance that drew produce into New York bay, also drew eastern manufactures to the same point, and this increased the assortment which was to be found at the common centre. The fact that produce tended generally to New York, as a matter of course made it the centre of finance. The United States government, and bank, and mint had been established at Philadelphia. Those circumstances could not, however, control the currents of trade. The pork, and corn, and wheat of the west, the manufactures of the east, the tobacco, cotton, and rice of the south, being sent to New York to obtain advances, it followed that from all quarters bills drawn against produce ran on New York. Those bills found buyers among the country dealers, who, in all directions, wanted to remit to New York to pay for goods there purchased. Capital could not keep aloof from the focus of transactions, and all loans to be made or financial operations to be conducted, sought New York. For the same reason all funds seeking investments went there to find them. Produce, goods, raw material, capital, all operated in reference to New York, and the foreign trade was the motor which kept up the circulation. This tendency to a centre once commenced, cannot be turned, but it strengthens with the general increase of the country. The other cities strive to turn a portion of the current each in its own direction, but the result of those efforts is only to increase the aggregate trade of the whole.

If the amount of specie exported, and for the most part that is but a transit trade from California, is deducted from the New York account, New Orleans will be found to exceed it in exports by $32,000,000. The lines of communication with the interior, and the facilities for advancing on produce, drew to New York a considerable portion of the western produce, and operations are now there carried on which partake of a speculative character. Pork, flour, etc., are often sold largely for future delivery on the New York exchange; and much of the cotton shipped from southern ports direct to Europe, is resold in New York many times before it arrives out. When the cotton is put on board ship for Liverpool, samples and bills of lading are sent to New York, and the cotton sold "*in transitu*"—that is, during its passage to Europe. Should the ocean telegraph come into operation, this system could be carried to a much greater extent, since news from the Liverpool market could be received at least thirty days after a cargo is shipped before its arrival out; and in speculative times, other articles will be subject to the same operations. The export of corn first became a large business in the famine years of 1847–8, and the subdivisions of qualities, round and flat, yellow, white, etc., then manifested themselves. In the present year, the crops are greatly beyond any former experience, and every available means of transportation is taken up to convey it to market. The realization of them depends upon the quantities that Europe may require, and this depends upon the events of a few weeks. The steamers now give intelligence in ten days, when formerly thirty were required. If the ocean telegraph had worked, the price of corn in Liverpool would have been known simultaneously in Chicago, and water transportation pressed to its utmost before the frost closed it.

The proportion which each of the cities named enjoys of the aggregate export trade of the whole country, is seen in the following table:—

EXPORTS OF THE LEADING ARTICLES OF DOMESTIC PRODUCE FROM THE CHIEF ATLANTIC CITIES.

	Boston.	Philadelphia.	Baltimore.	New Orleans.	New York.	Total.
Beef	$79,427	$281,010	$52,219	$170,715	$1,312,957	$2,081,856
Pork	379,998	205,154	317,737	154,101	1,169,707	2,852,942
Lumber	368,597	46,901	49,753	13,425	751,334	3,428,530
Furniture	328,654	24,274	22,704	3,894	331,281	922,499
Stoves, &c.	5,140	2,749	53,983	395,550	960,390	1,975,852
Butter	61,836	83,289	74,043	36,048	236,928	541,863
Cheese	15,113	9,742	21,797	9,626	561,451	731,910
Hams, &c.	34,559	68,072	75,056	184,634	1,485,958	1,957,423
Lard	144,047	163,319	254,713	1,962,121	1,172,950	3,809,501
Tallow	42,813	176,258	9,286	149,206	258,226	829,970
Cotton	815,968	87,512	10,985	73,152,768	8,368,500	131,386,661
Tobacco, manufactured.	404,569	52,138	55,965	5,929	1,113,428	2,400,115
" leaf.	143,653	78,019	3,430,287	7,564,247	1,482,970	17,009,767
Rice	92,128	76,834	72,743	18,097	664,969	1,870,578
Naval stores	34,076	34,419	22,577	7,161	1,219,553	1,464,210
Brass manufactures	45,024	34,398	1,205	973	1,705,426	1,985,223
Iron "	402,228	755,403	75,661	40,719	1,922,734	4,059,528
Cotton "	1,860,885	62,642	442,863	169,011	2,113,225	5,651,504
Wood "	584,685	193,578	156.614	23,233	413,806	2,234,678
Gold and silver coin	3,679,027	124,887	62,050		14,917,585	19,474,040
" bullion.	917,395			1,009	12,456,256	22,933,206
Corn	30,112	439,017	334,576	682,839	1,331,570	3,259,039
Wheat	3,491	251,991	308,657	632,221	5,451,491	9,061,504
Flour	955,257	1,293,228	2,909,679	2,257,152	7,017,790	19,328,884
Spirits	753,693	18,385	43,169	65,135	729.220	1,993,845
Other articles	3,191,437	1,050,005	1,220,064	570,710	14,253,857	30,513,151
Total	$15,373,812	$5,613,224	$10,078,386	$88,270,524	$83,403,562	$293,758,279

The opening of the Erie canal, in 1825, gave the first decided impulse to the city business, and produced a powerful effect upon its prosperity. The impulse was prolonged under the bank excitement that exploded in 1837. The effect of railroad extension at the west has, in the last fifteen years, had a still more powerful influence upon its growth. The following table gives the population, imports, exports, and taxable valuation, for a long period:—

	Population.	Imports.	Exports.	Valuation.
1684,	2,600	$4,579	$10 093	
1750,	10,381	267,130	85,632	
1790,	83,181	10,739,250	2,505,415	
1800,	60,489	26,201,000	14,045,079	$25,645,867
1820.	123,706	23,629.246	13,160,918	69,530,753
1830,	203,007	36,624,070	19,697,983	125,288,518
1840,	312,710	60.440,750	34,264,080	252,233,515
1850,	515,547	111,123,524	52,712,789	286,061,816
1855,	629,904	164,776,511	113,731.238	486,998,278
1860,	813,668	233,718,718	138,036,550	577,230,656

Up to the year 1840, the business of the west depended mostly on the canal, and by way of New Orleans. The city held then a kind of monopoly, but, like all monopolies, it cramped the producers. The large expenditure at the west for bank capital, in the years 1836–37, caused a great credit demand for goods upon New York, which was generally met. The facilities granted in those years by the American bankers in London, for the purchase of goods on credit, placed these within the reach of any dealer who could make a fair show; and the goods obtained on credit required to be sold on the same terms. The rivalry thus produced among those who could command goods, was very great, and the utmost efforts were made to obtain paper in exchange for goods. The banks showed the same eagerness to discount the paper that the merchants did to obtain it, and the mass grew in a rapid ratio, from the small country dealers to city jobbers and importers, and London bankers, until the

Bank of England, in August, 1836, issued a warning to those houses to curtail their credits. This was the "hand writing on the wall"—settling day had come. The business south and west had then been eagerly sought after by the jobbing-houses, who employed drummers to haunt the New York hotels and beset every new-comer with temptations to buy. The drummers of the day had usually no limit placed upon their expenses, which were intended to cover the "attentions" shown to the country dealer. These revelled in the dissipations of the town at the apparent expense of their entertainer, and they could do no less than buy of such attentive friends, when the bill, whether they discovered it or not, would often cover their own and other people's expenses. The mode of business then in vogue, when banks were multiplying so rapidly all over the country, was to take the paper of the dealers, payable at their own local bank. It was supposed that the dealer would be sure to keep his credit good at home. The result showed that the dealer, in order to pay the New York bill, got an accommodation note done at his bank, which thus became the debtor of the New York collecting bank. By this means, although the New York merchant got his money, the west was still in debt to the east; and this continued as long as capital was sent from the east to the west to start banks. The whole system exploded in 1837, and the bank capitals were sunk in these credits. From that date there was to be "no more credit," a threat which has often been repeated without being put in practice. The only permanent change seemed to be to require notes payable in New York. Those are given at dates longer or shorter, but the system is an improvement on the old mode. With 1840 also began the railroad building, which brought stocks and bonds to New York for negotiation, and the money being expended west promoted consumption of goods, which caused a greater demand in New York. The exports of produce increased at higher prices, and the sales of these gave the producers the means of buying more goods. In 1838, thirty-one years after the first successful steamboat, arrived the first ocean steamer, the Sirius, at New York, marking a new era in foreign trade, since communication with Europe was now reduced to half the time, a circumstance which was equivalent to an increase of capital engaged in commerce, because it could be turned oftener. From that date ocean steam navigation rapidly increased. The electric telegraph of Morse began a few years later to exert its influence in facilitating intercourse, and the express system was also introduced. It is somewhat singular, that with the breakdown of the old credit system and the adoption of the plan of making notes payable in New York, four important elements, having the highest centralizing tendencies, began to operate. These were, first, ocean navigation; second, the more extended construction of railroads; third, the invention and construction of telegraphs—there are now 25,000 miles of wires, that have cost over $2,000,000, consolidated in one company, and New York is the centre for the whole: and, fourth, the express system of intercourse. All these, centring in New York, came into active operation at the moment when gold was discovered in California, to give them an extraordinary impetus. The express business is peculiarly American, and has grown with a vigor which places it among the most important trading facilities of the country. In the spring of 1839, a year after the arrival of the Sirius at New York, W. F. Harnden, then out of employ in Boston, was advised by his friends to get a valise and take small packages and parcels from his acquaintances in Boston to their correspondents in New York, and return with what they had to send, making a small charge for his services. He did so, and discovered that a great public want was to be supplied. He soon contracted with the railroad to send a car through with his goods, and with business tact he opened offices, employed messengers, pushing the business with American energy. In 1840 an opposition was started by Adams. In 1841 new fields were explored by Harnden, who ran an express between Albany and Boston, and one between Albany and New York. Route after route was then opened to express agents, penetrating further and further, and multiplying their lines in the densely settled portions of the country; not only between cities, but between different portions of the same city. In 1845, Buffalo was reached by Wells & Co. In 1849, the gold fever brought California within the scope of express operations, and from San Francisco as a centre, "pony" expresses ran to the diggings with great success, placing the solitary miners of the Sierra Nevada in direct connection with the mint and with Wall street. As these busy agents continued to increase, and lessen the difficulty of communication, trade multiplied as a consequence. The telegraph had also penetrated most direct routes between cities, and that instrument came in aid of the express, which executed an order transmitted by telegraph. Instead of waiting the slow course of the post for a reply, the telegraph gave an instantaneous order for goods that the express conveyed. Thus, the three months that would once have been consumed in coming from Cincinnati for goods and returning, was reduced to three days. All the cities of the union were brought within similar speaking distance. In 1850 it was estimated that the expresses travelled twenty thousand miles daily, in discharge of orders, and the service has since doubled. Steam, the telegraph, and the express, had thus greatly facilitated trade, by making the long semi-annual expeditions to the large cities, for the purchase of goods, unnecessary. The small dealers could now buy frequently in small parcels the goods they found most in demand, instead of buying a six months' stock, and taking the risk of the goods being well selected for the market. This also brought with it another change. It had been the case, that most of the goods sent to America formerly were the surplus stock of the British manufacturers. That is, where patterns had been got up for the home consumption and the regular trade supplied, there would remain a stock that had become comparatively dead by age. This dead stock was "good enough for the American market," and was sent out almost for what it would bring, and being transported into the interior for six months' sales, became a sort of Hobson's choice for the consumers. When, however, frequent arrivals of new goods came to be laid before the customers, they immediately displayed a taste and exercised a choice. Ill-assorted goods would now not sell at all. English refuse became of no value, because American taste was developing itself with considerable strength. The customer was no longer to take what was laid before him; but in order to sell, the dealer was now to exercise his sagacity as to what would please his taste in selecting it, and his judgment in buying it. The manufacturer of dry goods was obliged to follow in the same direction, and the employment of designers became important. It was now that the sagacity and taste of the factory agents were felt to be an indispensable element in the success of a concern. The production of a design was promptly followed by the judgment of the public, and manufacturing became, as it were, one of the fine arts.

The joint operation of these new agencies manifested itself in 1850, when the west had become enriched with the large sales it had made of its produce during the famine years, and the railroads and canals, then in operation, had profited largely by the high freights and tolls paid by produce on its way to market. The gold of California was now in its turn adding a new stimulus to the business of the city. In 1852 the Michigan roads had opened through to Chicago, and New York was now, by rail, within thirty-six hours of that city. The projection and construction of railroads went on rapidly, constantly adding to the business of New York—the common centre, whence the means to build were drawn, and to which these means returned in the purchase of goods. The Crystal Palace, in 1853, drew great numbers of persons to the city, and gave a start to retail trade, which had an important effect upon the value of real estate and the location of business. In the above table we find that the imports into the city from abroad rose fifty per cent. in the five years to 1855, and the total valuation two hundred millions. This valuation followed the changed location of business. In the speculative times of 1836-7, the old Pearl street house, in Hanover square, was the headquarters of country dealers, and that square the centre of the dry goods trade, around which all others agglomerated. The great fire of December, 1835, by which the lower part of the city and a value of $18,000,-000 was destroyed, broke up the location, which, however, was speedily rebuilt, and, with the rebuilding, the Merchants' Exchange was enlarged and reconstructed at an expense of $1,800,000. The usual fate overtook occupiers in the inordinate demands of landlords, and the leading firms pushed across Wall street and made Pine and Cedar streets the great centre. Gradually firm after firm ventured upon Broadway, which, in 1845, was visited by a fire that caused the rebuilding of the lower portion, no longer for dwellings, but for substantial stores. One firm went up to the corner of Rector street, one-quarter of a mile from the Battery, and took the site, long vacant, of the old Grace church, at a lease. "Too high up," said conservatism, as the crowd rushed by, and the great retail firm of Stewart & Co. took the old Washington hotel at the corner of Chambers, and occupied the block with a marble store which has no equal in any city. Here importing, jobbing, and retailing are carried on to the extent of $10,000,000 by one who, by his energy and enterprise, has increased a capital of a few hundreds to millions, and now employs two hundred and fifty clerks and others. There were handsome stores before this was built, but this may be said to have commenced the era of expensive structures. The demands of luxury have led to the erection on Broadway of elegant trade palaces of iron, marble, and freestone for the leading firms in the dry goods, jewelry, clothing, porcelain, and other branches of trade; while the wholesale dealers, invading the old college ground, have covered it with marble stores of great size and beauty. The centre of business which, twenty years since, was within a quarter of a mile of the Battery is now a mile distant, and the value of real estate has followed like a "ground swell," reaching incredible rates. A marble store on Broadway was rented in 1860 for $50,000 per annum, or nearly a thousand dollars per week. A lot on Broadway, near Broome, sold lately at private sale for $110,000; it had been bought at auction, in 1852, for $35,000. An elderly gentleman present remarked, "This lot was part of the old Colonel Bayard farm, and was given by the colonel to his barber for a hair-dressing bill. I have seen it sold at auction four times, and each time people decided the buyer crazy to give such a price." The "Central Park," to cover 800 acres, was projected, and has since been prosecuted, at a cost of $5,406,193, having employed, in the four years, over 10,000 men.

The city has spread toward the upper wards through the agency of railroads, which have enabled workmen and merchants to live further from their places of occupation than formerly. The importance of consuming as little time as possible in coming from and going to occupation made it requisite formerly, when roads were barely paved, and conveyances not to be thought of, that persons should live near their business. The old cities of Europe are thus built with narrow streets and very high houses, to accommodate many in a little space. Modern cities are built on a broader scale. Omnibusses first came into play to give a greater breadth to the dwellings of the people, and horse-railroads have still further expanded the area. The island of Manhattan, from the Battery, which forms a point, runs northerly between the North and East rivers. From the park the city spreads in a fan-like form east and west, and from that point radiate the railroads. Of these there are six, including the Harlem, which runs by the Fourth avenue to Albany. The five other roads run on as many avenues, and carry their passengers from three to eight miles, returning with them to a common centre every morning to business. These four roads cost $4,600,000, and the receipts for 1859 were $1,481,010. In 1858 they transported 27,900,388 people, and in 1859, 32,718,351. If the Brooklyn railroads are included, the receipts would be swollen to $1,978,340 for 1859, and the number of passengers to 39,560,000 per annum. The passengers on the Brooklyn roads are mostly coming to business in New York, and, therefore, are part of its trade. The telegraph also comes to play an important part in the city business. Many large firms, whose offices are in the lower part of the city, and warehouses and manufactories in the upper part, connect the two by telegraph, to transmit orders and for information. All the police stations connect by telegraph to give alarms of robbery, and fire alarms are also conveyed by the same means. The "time ball" also operates by telegraph. On the top of the Custom House, sixty feet high, is a mast on which slides a black ball some 20 feet in diameter. This can be seen from any part of the bay. It is hoisted to the top of the pole, and is so arranged, that the moment the sun reaches the zenith, by observation, at Albany, it is released by electricity and falls, marking twelve o'clock, by which every ship-master in the port may set his chronometer.

All the railroads, continually running night and day, aided by twenty-five stage routes, on which run four hundred and forty-four two-horse stages, bring the business and working population to their occupations, and back at night. By all these conveyances there travel in New York every year a number of persons equal to twice the population of the whole United States. This makes a much larger breadth of land possible to a great city than otherwise, and allows of the thorough concentration of business. The country dealer, in making his purchases of different goods, is prone to buy of those nearest to his most important bills. The dry goods are to be selected, and the hardware, earthenware, cutlery, millinery, and the thousand and one subdivisions into which business, formerly one, now branches, are also to be purchased to the best advantage, and much time spent in going from one to the other cannot be afforded. Hence the importance of concentration and the value of "business sites." Manufacturers of small wares also spring up in such locations. The transformation in trade itself is quite as noticeable as the change in its locality; and there are those whose heads are not yet silvered, who can remember when the mode of doing business bore less resemblance to its present fashions, than the pants now in vogue do to the knee breeches worn by our grandsires. Formerly, a young man engaged in business for himself only after a long course of training, and then usually by uniting himself with his seniors; now beardless clerks dash into trade as if it were a holiday sport, requiring only a full flow of animal spirits. Then the principals of every house were working men, who lived frugally, and waited until their fortunes were made before they spent them; now, a start in business gives sufficient warrant for a generous expenditure, and many are too impatient to wait for their income, but spend the fortune they have—in prospect. Then, the word of a merchant was as good as his bond, and, with a few exceptions, his honesty was proverbial; now, there is more finesse in the place of open dealing, and the exceptions almost balance the rule. Then, insolvency was a bitter word, and failures in business from recklessness brought overwhelming shame; now, the gazette has lost its terrors, and bankruptcy is to many but a slight annoyance. Perhaps, however, the greatest difference which purchasers who come to the New York market are called to observe, is in the division of the goods. Formerly, a dry goods jobber kept a full assortment of every thing in his line, and it required no little tact and exercise of memory to keep each line full. Now, one house confines itself to woolens, another to cottons, another to silks, and yet another to fancy articles; and even these are subdivided, as in woolens one will keep tailors' goods, another dress goods and women's wear; in cottons, one confines himself to prints, another to the plain goods; in silks, we have establishments for piece goods, and others for ribbons and smaller articles. The tendency is to a still more minute division, and thus we have a dealer in hosiery, a dealer in lace, a dealer in perfumery, a dealer in pocket handkerchiefs, a dealer in shawls, and one house keeps nothing but suspenders! Twenty years since the manufacture of clothing became a separate business, and it has since subdivided into many branches. In ten years more there may be an establishment for spool cotton, and another for corset-laces, if such instruments of torture shall then be in vogue. We are not prepared to say that the division of goods here noticed may not be a positive convenience, although it certainly increases the labor of the purchaser. It may, however, induce more method in the selection of goods, and we think it has already led to some change in this respect. Buyers now make, to a considerable extent, a corresponding division of their time, and one day is set apart for woolens, another for silks, and so on through the whole catalogue. Could some staid customer of the last century, awaking from a Rip Van Winkle sleep, be set down at this day in some of our thronged thorough-fares, he would get sorely jostled and footweary before he had made a black cross against all the articles upon his memorandum.

The supplies of goods for the country dealers are derived from various sources; small wares from city manufacturers; domestics from the mills or agents; foreign goods from importers or agents of foreign manufacturers. The local manufactures are generally purchased by the jobbers to make good their assortments, as is also the case with hardware, and most articles of domestic manufacture, except the productions of the large mills, which have agents in the city for their special sale. These grant more or less credits, and sell goods for paper to turn into money. The agents of foreign manufacturers tempt buyers by granting long credits for paper which may be converted into money at the banks. The regular importing houses remit for their goods when they give the order, and sell at six and eight months to the jobbers, the largest purchases being made in the spring and fall; sometimes through the auction houses, whose paper is a favorite means of raising money. The jobbers, in their turn, sell at eight and twelve months' credit, seeking custom in the country by means of agents, instead of the old system of drummers, and allure buyers by the liberality of credits, depending upon the mercantile agencies for information in relation to the reliability of the buyer. These agencies have ramifications in every town of the country, but their usefulness is not what was at one time expected from them. The jobbers grant credits far beyond their own capital, and when they buy at eight months and sell at twelve, their notes are to be discounted at the banks with the paper they have taken from their customers as collateral, to meet their own notes to the importers. In times of panic, like the fall of 1857, the banks refuse to do this, and then the importer must renew the paper or the bank grant the extension needed, to avoid absolute stoppage. The credits granted by foreign manufacturers at such times are not met. The lapse of time, with fair crops, generally brings up the payment of the country paper, and the "extensions" are gradually extinguished. The grocers who sell sugar, etc., do so generally at four months, and get their money before the dry goods people, who also come after the hardware and earthenware dealers. The supply of capital in the city, under these circumstances, brings to it the largest assortment of goods, and of course it is the best point at which to buy, the more so that at times there is an over-supply of goods, which being worked off at auction, realizes a loss sometimes of 25 to 30 per cent. to the importer and foreign owner, and of course to the advantage of the country buyer. The general attractions offered to buyers make it to the advantage of sellers elsewhere to send their merchandise to New York to meet the purchasers. Boston made recently an attempt to break up this, by establishing sales of her manufactures there, instead of sending them to New York. The force of centralization is, however, difficult to overcome, and the imports at New York show an increasing share of the arrivals into the whole country. Thus, in 1859, New York imported $220,000,000 out of an aggregate of $338,000,000; in 1840, $60,000,000 out of an aggregate of $121,000,000. The proportionate imports at the Atlantic ports, are as follows:—

IMPORTS OF CERTAIN GOODS INTO THE LEADING ATLANTIC PORTS, AND ALSO THE TOTAL IMPORTS INTO THE UNION.

	Boston.	Philadelphia.	Baltimore.	New Orleans	New York.	Tot'l into Union.
Gold bullion	$1,975,795	$1,115	$9,950	$275	$269,833	$2,286,099
" coin	306,113	76,785	..	424,542	8,096,651	9,279,969
Silver bullion	112,085	..	2,500	..	271,027	408,879
" coin	3,613	36,683	..	4,096,034	689,533	7,299,549
Coffee	1,091,146	2,163,947	2,766,095	4,360,432	6,730,168	18,341,081
Tea	142,889	..	..	..	6,414,700	6,777,297
Linseed	2,211,684	..	..	..	940,077	3,243,174
Guano	28,539	..	195,470	..	242,648	525,376
Wool, free	2,493,470	30,501	130,690	..	1,173,075	3,843,320
" dutiable	137,036	..	4,528	2,714	4,961	179,365
Watches	184,900	117	..	20,388	1,980,864	2,118,838
Coal	37,361	5,606	2,402	16,448	521,774	772,925
Woollens	1,453,519	1,547,052	263,320	514,020	21,987,784	26,489,091
Cotton hose	33,881	235,246	139,546	70,691	1,625,833	2,120,868
" goods	2,010,601	1,180,172	184,848	1,385,594	9,917,270	15,057,398
" laces	500,682	4,093	281	50,138	2,274,033	2,845,029
Silks	1,621,388	76,491	5,254	356,843	19,238,760	21,471,488
Linen	532,836	551,531	73,224	457,098	4,823,264	6,527,894
Gloves	36,777	11,709	4,005	19,127	1,362,096	1,449,672
Window glass	141,308	5,299	..	22,879	454,344	626,747
Gunny bags and cloth	1,108,730	31,847	..	57,118	147,571	1,437,767
Iron, bar	1,016,541	298,186	95,376	119,476	1,610,970	3,318,713
" pig	218,695	74,612	4,069	47,650	329,785	739,947
" railroad	8,862	7,397	35,743	340,699	1,556,538	2,987,576
Cutlery	85,920	42,609	15,475	142,456	1,155,761	1,489,054
Jute	1,294,026	5,009	..	8,738	970,723	2,298,708
Leather	46,338	2,495	1,953	..	1,205,714	1,259,711
Hides	2,784,442	377,635	422,466	55,670	5,629,029	9,884,358
Molasses	717,742	223,616	183,352	30,263	1,414,168	4,116,759
Sugar	3,154,026	1,955,243	1,712,744	761,708	13,514,098	23,317,435
Other articles	14,939,245	3,935,373	2,656,766	5,794,033	53,727,835	100,099,063
Total	$40,430,190	$12,880,369	$8,920,157	$19,155,034	$170,280,887	$282,613,150

The aggregate imports at these five ports are thus $251,666,637, which, deducted from $282,613,150, leaves $30,946,513, as the imports of all other ports of the Union. The imports of coffee at New Orleans from Brazil, to go up the river, are large; and at

Boston, coffee and hides, from the same source, figure high. But both Baltimore and Philadelphia receive much coffee direct; in fact, that is the largest item of import at those two cities. Boston imports many materials for her manufacture—linseed, free wool, jute, hides, etc. Philadelphia also imports similar articles. The great mass of the goods for the consumption of the interior passes into the port of New York. It is to be borne in mind, however, that many of the importations at New York are really for Philadelphia, Albany, and other cities, even western ones. They are entered at the custom-house by a broker, who pays the duty and forwards them by express to their destination, for a small commission. The express, the rails, and the telegraph, facilitate such operations.

The gold and silver imported at New York are from various sources, but in the last few years have consisted mostly of doubloons and Spanish gold from Europe, to re-export to Havana for the purchase of the sugar crop. In 1857, that movement was very large, early in the year, to the island, and subsequently, when the stock of sugar accumulated very largely in New York, the gold came back from Havana to prevent it from being sacrificed. The bulk of the gold that forms the amount exported, is direct from California, and has been annually since the discovery, in sums of nearly fifty millions.

The gold extracted from the earth by the miners of California has a considerable degree of purity, and before refining establishments were set up in the state, sold at from $16 to $20 per ounce. Much was used as a currency. It was carried in little leather pouches, and weighed out to shopmen in exchange for goods. A large portion of it was carried to New York, in the pockets of home-bound adventurers, and sold in New York at such rates as were possible. The buyers mostly had it sent to Philadelphia, by express, at an expense of 3-8 per cent. It was then assayed and coined at the public mint, and the proceeds returned to the owner. This expensive and round-about process led to the establishment of a mint in San Francisco and an assay office in New York, where the miners themselves could deposit the dust and get the full value in return. When the dust is deposited, a certificate of weight is given and the gold in bars returned. There are a number of private assaying houses in San Francisco, where the dust is cast into bars of large size. Most of these are connected with banking houses, and the bars are the basis of exchange. The express companies deal in this gold. The miner now having a lot of dust, sells it to an express agent, or sends it down to a banker in San Francisco, who has it assayed and cast into bars. The value is credited to the depositor, less the commissions. The bars are mostly shipped to New York, and the bankers draw bills against them in favor of those who have remittances to make to the bank. The competition among the bankers reduces the rate at which these bills can be sold to a point that leaves apparently no profit, and it is charged in some cases that they draw at a loss, in the view of monopolizing the business. The refining leaves a small profit. The cost of shipping the gold to New York may be thus stated: freight, etc., $1 57; state stamp on bill, 20 cents; insurance, $1 50—making $3 27 on $100. But the insurer gets from the Mutual companies scrip, worth on an average 35 cts., which reduces the cost to $2 92. The bars sometimes command a higher price in New York than in San Francisco. Thus, a bar of 100 ounces, 880 fine, is at this moment worth *par* in San Francisco, and 900 fine it is worth 87½ cts. premium in New York. This price has reference to the gold only of the bar. There is some silver in each. Thus, in the bar 880 fine there is 88 ounces of gold, 11½ of silver, and 1-2 oz. copper. In the other, 90 oz. gold, 9 1-2 silver, and a half copper. This makes the gold worth ½ per cent. more in New York than in San Francisco, and reduces the cost of the bill to $1 92 per cent. It is evident that he who sells his bills at 2 per cent, makes but 8-10 of 1 per cent, or, including other items, a small loss. If the house feels strong enough to insure itself, it saves the insurance; but this must be more or less a risk to those who take the bills. Thus the operation is one of mere cost of shipment of the gold; but the control of so much gold on paper issued is an object with large firms. The higher value of gold at New York arises from the fact that it is the financial centre of the Union. The exchanges of the country with Europe and with the interior of the states turn there. The south ships its cotton, and tobacco, and rice; the west its produce; and the Atlantic states their manufactures. These, as we have seen, give an aggregate value of over $300,000,000 sent abroad in a year. The shippers of these goods draw bills against them, and offer them for sale. The market of sale must be where the greatest demand for them for remittance exists. New York imports two-thirds of all the goods received into the country, consequently the demand is there the greatest for the bills, and they are sent there for sale. It happens that the great majority of bill-drawers are unknown to the buyers, hence there is hesitation in taking their bills. To obviate this, a number of large banking-houses connected abroad, and having great capital, buy the bills that have "bills lading" attached, and the goods are sent to their correspondents abroad. In the seasons of the year when shipments are most active, these bills are plenty and low. They are then purchased and endorsed, and sold with the endorsement at a higher rate when the season advances and the cotton-bills run short. If the demand is active, and the rate of money higher here than abroad, the bankers draw on their own resources, and lend them the proceeds of the bills they sell on stocks or other securities. They are also the buyers of the gold bars as they arrive from California, and pay such rates as the demand for exchange, or the rate of money, or the price of gold on the continent, present or prospective, will warrant. A demand for silver to go to Asia, causes a demand for gold with which to buy it on the continent, and this demand draws upon New York, and indirectly upon the whole country. It is obvious that the bill business is thus mostly in the hands of large bankers. This grows out of the fact that there is abroad no market for bills on New York. Thus, the New York importer of goods, in order to pay for them, buys a bill on ships' specie, instead of ordering his creditor abroad to draw upon him, which would be done if a bill on New York were saleable in the London market. It is understood, that when such amounts of bills from the south and elsewhere are sent to New York for sale, the proceeds of those sales form a large fund due by New York to those sections. These funds are deposited in the New York banks, and by them employed in loans upon stocks, or in such other ways as will pay an interest. Thus the whole country contributes to the supply of capital at that common centre. The New York banks, some fifteen years since, in order to encourage that centralization, allowed interest of 4 per cent. on the funds so deposited. This caused a greater sum to be so employed, and imposed on the banks the necessity of lending it, in order to make a profit. The amount of funds lying in New York varies from $16,000,000 to $35,000,000, according to the season of the year. The banks in all sections of the country that have such funds in New York do not draw against it directly in favor of those who want to remit to New York, but they use the funds to buy up their own or other paper cheap. The effect is to swell the supply of funds in New York, and at times foster speculation there.

The funds that accumulate in New York, make it also the mart for stock operations; and these are very large, as well for regular investments, as for merely gambling operations.

With the creation of any commodity whatever, there springs up almost simultaneously a class of persons to deal in it, and to appropriate more or less capital to its prosecution. This capital is most generally applied to the purchasing of it when it is thought to be cheap, in order to hold it until it can be disposed of to better advantage, or in advancing money to the needy seller. The persons so engaged, by devoting their time and attention to the subject of their traffic, reduce it to science, and soon determine and classify the kinds and qualities adapted to the markets and wants of the public. The dealing in stocks is comparatively of modern origin, and commenced with the credit system of the European governments, at the close of the seventeenth century, when William of Orange avoided the dangers that beset the throne of the Stuarts, by borrowing money instead of extorting it by illegal taxation like Charles I., or stealing it like Charles II. The moment that government stocks—or certificates of debt issued to the government creditors—made their appearance, they became subjects of traffic, and with the certificates of stock in corporate companies, formed the material for speculation, and the exchange markets, where the surplus wealth of communities seek investment, became the theatre for operations in securities. The American colonies had no stock debts or corporate companies, since little surplus capital existed for such investments. The paper money that they issued, however, afforded by its fluctuation many opportunities of jobbing at the expense of the public. When the revolutionary war broke out, the continental money of the federal government gave a larger field for these operations, which were based mostly on the rapid depreciation of their value. Thus, a person would borrow a sum, returnable in the same description in a fixed time. Its value in that time having fallen, he could return it at a profit. Supposing the money to be par, a person would pledge a bag of $1,000 for paper; a fall of eight or ten per cent. in sixty days would enable him to redeem his dollars with $100 profit. In the time of the revolution, a stage driver, having a talent that way, made money in the traffic, and subsequently became the head of the largest bank and stock house of his time in New York, ending a long and respected life by suicide. This paper soon perished, and was succeeded by the government stock, representing the public debt. This was soon accompanied by United States and other bank stock, insurance, canal, mining, railroad, etc., to an immense amount. Up to 1825 the majority of the stocks were banks and insurance, but there was no regular stock market. There were brokers who bought and sold stocks, but there was no concentration of operations. In that year the legislature of New York authorized the New York stock board, which has since continued to be the stock market. Within the last few years a board of brokers has been started in Philadelphia and also in Boston. Their operations are, however, to a very great extent, based upon those of New York, with which they communicate by telegraph. The board of brokers sits with closed doors from 10 1-2 A. M. to 12 M.; an irregular session is held about 2 1-2 P. M. There is a president, a treasurer, and a secretary; the latter keeps a list of all the stocks dealt in in the market; the members are admitted by ballot after notice of nomination by one of the board. He must have been at least a year a broker, and on his admission pays a fee of $450. When the members are assembled, the president proceeds to call the list, and as each stock is named in succession, those who have orders to buy or sell make their offers, and the transactions are recorded, when they become binding upon the members. If any of these defaults he loses his seat until he can pay or arrange the claim. The theory of the board is that it is the reservoir where all stocks held by the public are brought for sale, and where all buyers come, through brokers, to purchase. The number of brokers is some 150, and the commission charged is a quarter of one per cent., that is to say $25 on $10,000. The board requires each member to charge not less than a quarter, but as most of them sell again for their customers for nothing, the charge is practically one-eighth.

The quantities of stocks to be dealt in have rapidly increased of late years. A late report of the Secretary of the Treasury gives an approximation of the amount of stocks now in the country; to that return we have prefixed the amount of the same at a previous date:—

	1840.	1859.
United States stocks	$25,000,000	$55,155,977
State stocks	174,906,997	210,487,000
113 cities' and towns' stocks	13,107,000	85,382,201
350 counties' stocks	1,500,000	15,927,292
1562 bank stocks	290,772,091	421,880,095
150 insurance stocks	40,101,000	70,500,000
400 railroad stocks	45,102,208	506,746,898
" bonds	40,897,792	411,199,702
16 canal and navigation stocks	31,219,911	35,888,918
" " bonds	19,207,101	22,130,569
45 mining and other co.'s stocks	10,101,201	44,208,006
" " bonds	1,000,000	3,971,204
	$692,915,301	$1,888,477,862

This vast increase of stocks is manipulated mostly upon the New York stock board, and the stocks are to a considerable extent caused to float by the sums sent to brokers by their correspondents in the country and neighboring cities, with which to "operate." The speculative transactions far exceed those of other kinds. The actual investments of capital are not large at the board. Those who take stocks for income do so of the issuers when the proposals are put out, and they hold them like the United States and state stocks, which rarely come on the stock exchange. The mass of the transactions then are of non-dividend paying stocks, that are the foot-ball of speculation, and so pay the operators profits. The brokers are mostly cliques of operators, who, when the market is dull and prices are low, combine, as "bulls," to purchase, producing a rapid rise, in the hope, seldom disappointed, that the speculative community will be tempted by that rise to come in and buy; as they do so the brokers unload themselves upon the buyers, and then become "bears," combining to depress the market, and to compel a fall at least equal to the rise, skinning the outsiders in the process. The speculators generally buy on time, that is, to pay for the stock at their option, any day within thirty or sixty, as the case may be. In this way the buyer pays interest on the purchases. He may also sell to deliver at any day he pleases within a specified time, or "seller's option," or to deliver at the "buyer's option;" he may borrow stock and sell it in the hope of buying it back cheaper on delivery; he may buy a privilege to deliver a stock at a certain price at a specified time, or not, as it suits him; or he may sell or buy a privilege of taking and paying for a stock or not as it suits him; he may buy cash stock and sell on time. To produce a fall, cliques will sell for cash all the stock they have or can borrow, and then offer time contracts without limit, until other holders are frightened and sell. Confederates keeping up a clamor to alarm the public at such times, all offers to buy are smothered, and orders to purchase are suppressed. On the other hand, a combination for a rise is accompanied by the most astonishing prophecies of a "good time." Considerable quantities are bought on time, the sellers hoping to get them cheaper. Meanwhile the cash stock is bought up and pledged for more money to repeat the operation; the demand for the stock bought on time runs up the rate, and the public are expected to come in with sufficient strength to let the clique all sell out at a profit, when they will be ready for a bear operation. There are numberless modes of varying and combining speculative operations, which would fill a volume. All these time operations were illegal until 1859, when they were all legalized, and a stock debt may now be collected like any other.

The amount of the transactions is immense. In 1840, the aggregate of sales for the month of June was $3,684,460; of this one-half was bank stock and one-half Delaware and Hudson canal. In June, 1857, previous to the panic, the sales reached $250,000,000, mostly railroad stocks. In the present year the sales have been for June nearly $70,000,000, mostly non-dividend paying railroad stocks. In a speculative year the transactions will run to two or three thousand millions. Those transactions require a great deal of money to conduct them, and these funds come to New York to a considerable extent from neighboring cities, as well as from the west. They also employ a large portion of the funds of the banks put out "at call," and also the proceeds of bills sold by large exchange houses. Thus we may suppose a house sells on the departure of a steam-packet $500,000 of sterling bills. This money is paid into bank, and is loaned out on stock securities at 7 per cent. on call, until, by a succeeding packet, it may be called in and remitted in gold to Europe. This operation, on a large scale, will induce the banks to call in their loans to protect their specie, and the value of money will rise in the market. The rule in stock speculation is loss, and the experience of the most fortunate dealers is that the interest and commissions absorb the whole average profits. The funds sent to New York, therefore, for stock-dealing, only contribute to the central profits.

If we were to throw into a tabular form the new agencies of business centring in New York, we should have results as follows:—

			Cost.
Ocean navigation, 11 lines,	33 ships.		$22,000,000
Telegraphs.............	20,000	miles.	2,000,000
Express companies.......	30,000	"	3,000,000
Railroads..............	2,000	"	128,000,000
City railroads...........	19	"	5,364,360
Canals.................	395	"	26,000,000
			$186,364,360

The number of strangers that are drawn to the city in a year by ocean steamers is nearly 50,000, and they fill the hotels that have of late taken such splendid proportions, and have been carried up to Twenty-third street and Broadway, a distance of three miles from the old business centre. The march of hotels up-town has been steady. The Astor House was, in 1833, the up-town house. From the Astor House to Chambers street was a long remove, in 1849. In 1852 the St. Nicholas advanced a mile to Spring street, and became not only the up-town, but the "upper-crust" of all hotels. In 1854, Niblo's Garden, on Prince street, was occupied by the Metropolitan; and, soon following, the Everett House, taking ground a mile higher, opened on Sixteenth street; and last year, superior in distance, size, magnificence, and expense, the Fifth Avenue Hotel opened on Twenty-third street. These magnates were accompanied by a crowd of lesser note: the New York, St. Denis, St. Germain's, etc., etc., all followed, and with each new opening the visitors seemed to spring from the walls to people and to pay. Extravagance is only an allurement. Indeed, the hotel-keepers seem to have followed the advice of Boyden, when he first gave popularity to the Astor. His cracker-baker complained that the waiters were inattentive: "Kill me two of them, and put it in your bill," he briskly replied. And to his partner, who spoke of the exactions of guests, he replied, "Furnish a gold-dust pudding, with diamond plums, if they require, but charge accordingly." That is the secret of hotel-keeping in New York—let nothing be wanting, not even a sufficient charge. Immense waste, no doubt, attends the system, but it attracts. The splendid arrangements tempt many city families to take up their abode in them; and a small family, even at $2.50 per day per head, do better than to pay the extravagant rents demanded for fashionable houses, with the attendant expenses. That these things are not done cheaply, the bill of $91,000, presented to the city of New York by the Metropolitan Hotel for the entertainment of the Japanese ambassadors, is ample evidence. The numerous visitors to New York from the south and west, as well as the constant current of traders, better class of emigrants, and California passengers, fill the hotels of the lower parts of the city; and the whole mass, by their purchases for personal use, make an important part of the city retail trade, of which Broadway is the main locality. The records of arrivals show the average number per day at all the hotels is not far from 2,000, or the immense number of 730,000 per annum. This, at an average of $2, gives $1,460,000 for hotel-bills alone, but all the expenses cannot be estimated under $7,000,000. The facilities of railroads and ferries also induce a great deal of trade from surrounding cities and towns within a reasonable distance. Within an area of fifty miles there are few who do not do their shopping in New York, and very many of the small local shops send daily messages to the city to complete orders they may have received. On the other hand, a large quantity of manufactures that were formerly confined to the city are now sent long distances into the country, particularly in the winter, where they are done cheaply by those who are not dependent upon them for a living. The large circle of country thus loses its rural character, and partakes of the metropolitan nature. It follows that, as city localities become known for particular business, and visitors seek them to trade, all of that class of dealers seek business places there, and thus concentrate the business. The fixed population of the city is given by the census at 813,668, and, with the neighborhood more or less connected, the wants of 2,000,000 require to be met from the retail stores of the cities, in addition to the crowds of visitors from abroad. The retail trade is therefore a very important one, and its vigor, apart from the purchases of visitors, depends in some degree upon the cheapness of food. Where immigration has reached over 1,000 souls per day, composed of persons skilled in almost all employments, and all eager to obtain work, competing with those in the city who live by their occupation, and with those in the country, who are, so to speak, amateurs, it is evident the wages cannot be extravagant, and the amount that can be spared from them, after deducting house-rent and food, is not much in the average. Food is, however, the important item. When that is cheap, trade is more active. An indication may be afforded in flour. The quantity used in New York is 2,000,000 bbls. per annum. In some years the price has been as low as $4, in others as high as $15. The difference between these sums is $22,000,000 in one year. The tax, in years of dear food, thus thrown upon the city is enormous. It fortunately happens, that in years of dear food the food-sellers make more purchases. The influence of such times is very perceptible in the operations of the pawnbroker, whose business it is to lend small sums on the pledge of almost any conceivable article that may be offered. They charge 24 per cent. per annum, and the article, unredeemed at the end of a year, becomes forfeit by sale at auction. The amount of loans in one year was given at $3,000,000, and the number of pledges 4,875,000, which would give an average of about 68 cents each loan.

While cheap food is an important item in the ability to purchase, yet employment is the main consideration, and this depends upon the prosperity of those sources on which the city depends for its business. These in the long run are progressive, notwithstanding the reactions that sometimes take place, and the diffusion of employments which machine inventions tend to bring about.

The general prosperity of the whole country does not, however, depend upon any locality: all production and all business is constantly seeking the conditions under which it can best thrive. These cannot be dictated; but, being found, the general welfare is as a consequence the greater, and with the general prosperity the common centre must only become the more magnificent.

BANKS IN THE UNITED STATES.

CHAPTER I.

BILLS OF CREDIT—GOVERNMENT ISSUES—UNITED STATES BANK.

The use of paper money is a modern invention, and may yet be considered but as an experiment, since, from its first emission in the colonies to the present day, paper money has constantly changed its form and the conditions of its circulation. It is not to be inferred that paper money originated on this continent, since it was used long before in the countries of Europe. Its nature has, however, been more developed here, and every phase of it has had full scope of action. The circulating paper is of many forms, such as bills of exchange, promissory notes, government bonds bearing interest, government bonds bearing no interest and not convertible into coin, but receivable for taxes and dues, and lastly, corporation or bank promises to pay coin on demand. There are many other descriptions of circulating paper, but these are the chief that are used. The last two are those which have figured most as money. The intention of paper money is to supply the place of coin where that article is not sufficiently abundant, as was eminently the case with the early colonies. The colonies were none of them rich, and had not been able to import and keep as much of the precious metals as would serve for a currency, that being as much an instrument of commerce as a road or a ship. In substituting paper for coin there is no difficulty as long as the quantity emitted does not exceed the demands of business for a currency. If there is no trade—that is, if no one wants to exchange his commodities for others—there is no want of currency. As the desire to trade increases, a want of money to represent commodities is experienced, and the want is proportioned to the numbers, wealth, and activity of the traders up to a certain point; because when trade is very active, money itself changes hands rapidly and performs more transfers than when it is sluggish. There must be, however, great confidence in the value of the money, because doubt in that respect instantly checks traffic. The early colonists were in that position. They had commodities which they had raised and made, but they had no currency, or not enough. In this position, in 1690, it became necessary for Massachusetts to send a military expedition to Quebec to drive the French out of Canada. The expedition failed, and the troops came back clamorous for pay. The colony had no money to pay with, and it adopted the expedient of issuing promises in convenient amounts. The faith of the colony was pledged for the payment of these, and they would be received for taxes and dues. It will be observed, that these bore no interest, and were not convertible into coin. They were, in fact, mere orders of the government upon farmers and others for food, clothing, etc., in favor of the soldiers, to be called in by taxes, not to be paid in money. The paper was worth nothing to export. Its only value consisted in its being good to pay taxes with. It is at once obvious that no man wanted more than would suffice for that purpose. The aggregate amount that could be issued was then measured by the sum of the taxes. In order to increase the amount, the colonial government made it a legal tender, that is, compelled creditors to take it for private debts. This was so palpably unjust, and was productive of so many evils, that the home government suppressed it. Nevertheless, the same necessities produced similar devices, and other colonies followed the example of Massachusetts with similar results.

In 1745, Massachusetts, to defray the expense of an expedition to Louisburg, again issued bills of credit to the extent of £3,000,000. This paper speedily depreciated to 11 for 1: that is, £1 in silver was worth £11 in those bills. The English government then sent out £180,000 in silver, to pay the cost of the expedition, and with this the thrifty colony bought up its own paper at 11 for 1. New York, during the period 1709 to 1786, made thirty-four issues of bills of credit, amounting in the aggregate to £1,563,407, and the depreciation was about 2 to 1; in other colonies much more. The evils attending these issues were very great, but the cause continued to operate, and when the war broke out in 1775, the Congress of the Confederation was forced upon the issue of $3,000,000 worth of "continental money," as distinguished from the state issues; and to give these issues some firmness, they made them a legal tender. This supply of paper, in addition to the colonial emissions, increased the difficulties, and some of the colonies went a step further and made *personal property* a legal tender, according to appraisals to be made for the purpose. Notwithstanding the general discredit, Congress was obliged to push the issues. In 1779 the amount outstanding was $160,000,000, and by 1780 it reached $200,000,000, when the value fell so fast that before the end of the year the bills ceased to circulate. There are those still living who remember giving $100 for "a cake of gingerbread," or $10,000 for a hat cocked in the fashion of the day. The whole amount issued by Congress was $359,456,000, and on the formation of the new government they were purchased at the rate of 1 cent for $1. The state issues met with similar fate. The entire absence of money thus brought about, with the attendant evils, mainly induced the adoption of the federal constitution, which at once prohibited the states from ever again issuing "bills of credit," or making "any thing but gold and silver a tender for the payment of debts." That is, those prohibitions are a record of the experience derived from the colonial experiments in paper money.

The condemnation of "bills of credit" was a great good. The important question was, however, what to do next; and this engaged all minds. Specie had vanished, and government paper money was dead. Mercantile sagacity had, however, on the death of the continental money, devised a partial remedy in 1781. This consisted of the substitution of private corporate credit in place of government credit, and took shape in the chartering of the Bank of North America, at Philadelphia; the Bank of New York, in the city of New York; and the Bank of Massachusetts, in Boston.

It is an erroneous idea, that was entertained for a long time, that banks, by the issues of credit, create capital, and on this idea many new banks were started, imparting much activity to trade. The good effects of their operation were due, however, rather to the concentration and application of capital to mercantile uses, than to an increase in the quantity of capital. Before the establishment of banks, individuals kept the money they received in their own houses, tempting robberies, and subjecting themselves to loss of interest, and to risk and trouble in seeking small investments. The shopkeeper and merchant who received money in the course of business in small sums, kept it by him until he made his wholesale purchases, when he paid it out altogether. The aggregate sum thus lying entirely idle was very large. On the establishment of a bank, the owners of money deposited it in the vaults. The institution thus became the common receptacle for all idle funds. Inasmuch as that, although all the depositors were entitled to draw their money whenever they chose, yet but a small proportion did so, the banks might safely lend the money so deposited on notes at short dates, sixty to ninety days, and still have as much within their control as would meet the probable demand of the depositors for payment. It was necessary, however, that the notes discounted should be promptly paid at maturity, in order that the bank, itself subject to be called upon to pay on demand, might have control of the means of payment. The discount of mercantile notes with two good endorsers then became the business of banks; and we may here remark in passing, that this wrought a change in the mode of borrowing money in the community. Up to that period, good character, industry, and sobriety were security for loans. An illustration of this is afforded in a bequest of Dr. Franklin in trust to the city (then town) of Boston, of a sum of money from which young mechanics of the above characteristics were to be loaned two hundred dollars to start them in business. They were to repay the money with interest, and the sum, with its accumulation, was to continue a fund for the same purpose. The fund still continues to exist, but without accumulation. Under the newly established banking system, character was no longer an element of credit. A note with two good names became indispensable. The capitals of the banks were seldom paid in loanable money. They were notes of the subscriber, or real estate, and were mostly designed to inspire confidence. A portion of it was requisite to be kept on hand in specie to meet the calls of depositors and note-holders. The banks, in order to increase their loanable funds, were permitted to issue their own promises to pay specie on demand, these promises to circulate as money. The old colonial issues of credit bills did not pretend to be payable on demand, and the application of that principle, it was now supposed, would obviate the evils that had grown out of the old system. The bills were freely taken and circulated. The institutions were not limited in the amount that they might issue, and they increased the currency almost at pleasure. It became obvious, however, that if one bank issued a larger quantity in proportion than the other banks, its notes, paid into the rival institutions, would immediately be sent back to it for redemption, and it would have to pay in specie the balance above what it held of their notes. Hence the laws of trade compelled each bank to keep its credits within a safe ratio to those of other institutions. This, however, did not prevent all from increasing their issues to any extent as long as their mutual balances were adjusted. When, however, the whole of them increased their circulation, the mass of currency became cheap, a fact which manifests itself in a rise in prices of all commodities. The effect of this is, that the produce of the country ceases to be exported, because it is too high to pay a profit to the merchant, while, on the other hand, goods are imported to avail of the high prices. This state of affairs involves an export of specie, which drains the banks, and forces back upon them their bills for redemption. Hence, if the banks regulate each other by their balances, the foreign trade becomes the common regulator of all. Kept within a certain limit, governed by produce and business, the bank circulation is useful. Although it does not in any degree create capital, it supplies the place of the precious metals as currency. If we suppose a miller wishes to purchase grain; he gets a note or acceptance at sixty days, on New York, discounted at a local bank, which pays out to him circulating notes. With these he purchases wheat of the farmer, flours it, and forwards it to New York for sale, and the proceeds are applied to the taking up of his draft that the bank had discounted. In the mean time the farmer has paid away the notes he took for his wheat, probably to the storekeeper in discharge of his bill. The storekeeper has now to remit to New York to pay a note that falls due for merchandise previously purchased, and furnished to the farmer. To do so he goes to the bank, and buys of it the draft on New York that the institution had discounted for the miller. This he remits to his merchant, who gets it paid from the proceeds of the flour. The transaction is thus closed, and by it farm produce has been got to market, and merchandise, in return, has passed from the manufacturer to the consumer, effecting an exchange of commodities without the use of any money at all. The notes that the bank put out on a draft, after performing the functions of money, returned to it in exchange for the draft, and all obligations were cancelled. This is the operation of paper when confined to actual business transactions. The number and kinds of these are almost infinite, but the principle is the same when the paper is only issued on actual commodities, the exchange of which cancels the obligations that grow out of them. There is, in this, no creation of capital, only the facilitating the exchange of that already created. Under such circumstances, the quantity of currency rises and falls with the quantities of produce and merchandise. The moment the banks lend their notes to speculative operators, who seek to borrow capital itself, rather than credits with which to interchange capital, it becomes insolvent, because it lends what it has not got to spare. The early banks mostly confined themselves to sound rules, and with the rapid increase of business which followed the formation of the new government, their business being profitable, stimulated the increase of institutions, mostly in New England, where commerce was concentrated. The three original state banks were eminently successful, and they suggested a resource to the federal government. This was developed in the celebrated report of Alexander Hamilton, Secretary of the Treasury, in favor of a National Bank. The proposition at once called up the right of Congress to charter a bank under the constitution. After a warm congressional debate upon the subject, President Washington demanded written opinions of his four cabinet officers. The Attorney General and the Secretary of State declared the bank unconstitutional. The Secretary of War and the Secretary of the Treasury were of a contrary opinion, and the celebrated paper of the latter upon the subject decided Washington, who signed the bill, and the bank went into operation with a capital of $10,000,000, of which $2,000,000 was subscribed by the government, and $8,000,000 by individuals. Of this latter amount, $2,000,000 was to be paid in specie and $6,000,000 in six per cent. stock of the United States. The charter was to continue until March 4, 1811. Immediately on the organization of the bank, the shares rose 25 to 45 per cent. premium, and the institution paid 8 1-2 per cent. dividend. The creation of this bank was attended by the rapid multiplication of banks in the various states, becoming rivals to each other, and gradually consolidating an interest which was strong enough in 1811, with other interests, to defeat the recharter of the Bank of the United States. The recharter was opposed on the grounds: 1st, that it was unconstitutional; 2d, that too much of its stock was owned by foreigners; 3d, that state banks were better. It is singular that at a time when capital was scarce in the country, objections should have been made to its coming in from abroad. Nevertheless, the bank was closed, and on settlement paid $108 1-2 to each share of $100. From that date, gold and silver only were by law receivable for government dues. The winding up of the National Bank was the signal for creating state banks to fill the vacuum. The old bank and its business was purchased by Stephen Girard, who conducted with it a large private banking business with great success on a capital of $1,000,000. In four years, to 1815, 120 banks, with an aggregate capital of $40,000,000, went into operation. Pennsylvania alone, by act of March 21, 1814, created 41 banks. The amount of notes emitted by these institutions was never known with certainty, but was estimated by Mr. Jefferson, in 1814, as high as $200,000,000. A large portion of these, in the middle states, were issued as loans to the government; and the war pressure became such, that in September, 1814, all the banks out of New England stopped payment. The bills immediately depreciated 20 per cent. in Baltimore, and 15 per cent. in New York. The news of peace, in February 1815, caused some improvement, but in 1816 the difficulties were greater than ever. The discount in Baltimore was 20 per cent., Philadelphia 17, New York 12 1-2. This kind of paper being the only currency, the government was compelled to take it for dues, in violation of law. This caused the greatest injustice, since the funds received in one place were more depreciated than in another, and New England, where the currency was sound, had great cause of complaint. In such a state of affairs, although the state banks had multiplied to 246, with $89,822,422 capital, a new National Bank became inevitable, and Congress, by act of April, 1816, again chartered a National Bank, which went into operation January 1817. Its charter was to last until March 4, 1836; its capital was $35,000,000, of which the United States subscribed $7,000,000 in a 5 per cent. stock, and the remaining $28,000,000 was to be subscribed by individuals—one-fourth in gold and silver and three-fourths in the funded debt of the United States. The debts of the bank, in excess of its deposits, were not to exceed $35,000,000. The bank was to pay a bonus of $1,500,000, and perform the money business of the government free of charge. In return it received the public funds on deposit, and nothing was to be taken for public dues except specie, treasury notes, notes of specie paying banks, and the National Bank notes. When the bank went into operation it became necessary for the state banks to resume or wind up. Those of New York, Philadelphia, Baltimore, and Virginia resumed, and those which did not were gradually purged off. From 1811 to 1830, 165 banks, with a capital of $30,000,000, closed business. The loss of the government by these was estimated at $1,390,707, and the public lost much larger sums. The bank, in the first few years of its operation, encountered many perils, growing out of the foreign trade. Imports poured into the country in prodigious amounts, and an active demand for silver sprung up for Europe and Asia. The institution had, however, in the public stock and in its own stock, forming its capital, the means of drawing specie from Europe, which it did to an extent that subjected it to a loss of over half a million dollars.

The institution was of much service to the government, and enjoyed great facilities from the use of the public funds. The principal bank was at Philadelphia, with branches in most of the large cities. This organization of the bank made it very powerful as a means of exchange, and this power was likely to grow with the increasing wealth of the country, up to the time when railroads and telegraphs made communication more rapid. The power of the bank was based upon the federal finances, of which it was the agent, and it operated through the growing business of the country, which was conducted largely upon the credit system. As the country increased in prosperity, other banks, under state charters, sprung up, and these became the recipients of mercantile deposits, or, in other words, of the money which each merchant received in the course of his business, and also of private funds. The merchants who thus placed their funds with the banks were constantly debtors of the government for duties and taxes; these they paid by checks on their respective banks. The United States Bank, being the common recipient of all these checks, was thus always the creditor of the local banks, and could always force them to contract their loans by compelling them to pay, or could permit them to increase their loans by being indulgent in regard to balances. The government funds thus collected by the United States Bank were paid out by it wherever the government required. Thus the Boston and New York branches would collect the largest amounts, but the branches in Richmond and elsewhere, or the parent bank in Philadelphia, would pay the drafts of the government. In the first year of the old bank it received $3,652,000 of the public money. As business prospered, the amount rose annually, until it reached $17,038,859 in 1808, before the embargo. Thus the receipts and payments on government account were thirty-four millions in a year, when the whole population was 5,200,000 souls. The new bank in 1817 received $32,786,662 for accounts of the government. The sum declined year by year to $21,347,000 in the year of crisis, 1825, and subsequently continued at about twenty-four millions per annum, until 1833, when the deposits were removed by the government. These large sums annually flowed in and flowed out of the bank on account of the government, and a large proportion of the payments were on account of the public debt. This reached $127,334,934 in 1816, and was by annual payments extinguished in 1835, a period of nineteen years; the average amount paid off annually by the government was thus $6,700,000. The government bank, being furnished with such machinery, was necessarily the best medium of collecting bills; thus the New York merchants, as an instance, sold their goods to the shopkeepers all over the Union, and they took notes payable at the local banks. The credits thus granted could be collected by the United States Bank cheaper than by any other bank. Hence, in New York, the "branch" would be the receptacle for accounts to be collected in all other cities; the bank would forward these to its appropriate branch, say Richmond; the branch there would notify the local merchants of the notes it held against them; these would pay in checks upon the local banks where they kept their deposits, and all these checks collected by the United States branch would make it the common creditor of all the local banks, whose specie it thus controlled; it would notify the New York branch of what collections had been made, and these would credit the mercantile owners with the amounts. The power of the bank from this source, operating through all its branches, was much greater than from the use of the government funds, and the state banks complained loudly of the tyranny that they alleged it exerted over them. A stormy opposition was thus formed against it, while, on the other hand, a generation of merchants had grown up under its administration of the exchanges, and they feared the results of a change. Meanwhile, the question became political, and a great party, as early as 1829, gave indication that the recharter in 1836 would not be granted. A struggle between the bank and the government ensued, and in 1833 the President removed the public deposits from the bank and placed them with numerous state banks. These ran a race of expansion with the United States Bank; the consequence was an immense speculation, which resulted in general bankruptcy in 1837. The government, on removing the deposits to the state banks, enjoined them to be liberal to the merchants. This was done in the view of counteracting the stringency which the closing up of the United States Bank was expected to cause. This did not occur, however, since that institution also was liberal with its loans. A rapid expansion resulted from this rivalry, and speculation ran wild, particularly in public lands. In the midst of this excitement, the government issued the famous "specie circular," by which the lands were to be sold for cash, gold and silver only. The effect of this would be either to kill the speculation or to drain all the specie into the land offices;

it did the former. This was followed by a resolution of the Bank of England to cut off credits to American merchants, and the revulsion was precipitated. The charter of the United States Bank was not renewed by Congress, but the same institution obtained a charter from the State of Pennsylvania, February 18, 1836, under the name of the United States Bank of Philadelphia. The terms of this charter were very onerous, such as no institution could pay from profits; the bank consequently failed, in common with all others in the Union, in 1837. It resumed its payments, following those of New York, January, 1839, and struggled on until October 1839, when it finally failed. On going into liquidation, it was found that more than the whole of its large capital, $35,000,000, had been swallowed up, subjecting the stockholders to a total loss. This disaster was no doubt brought about by its abandonment of sound principles in the vain hope of compelling the government to recharter it. But the institution had outlived its usefulness; the country had outgrown the circumstances for which such a bank was fitted. We have thus sketched the outline of that bank before glancing at the progress of the state institutions, because, up to 1840, that bank was the controlling power. The progress of banking among the states has been step by step with the growing wealth, population, and commerce of the country. This growth was manifestly too vigorous to permit of the continued existence of any regulating power.

The relative growth of the state banks, and the business of the country proportional to the national bank, was as follows :—

	No.	State banks. Capital.	National bank. Capital.
1791,	3	2,000,000	10,000,000
1811,	89	52,601,601	10,000,000
1817,	246	89,822,422	35,000,000
1837,	634	290,772,091	35,000,000
1860,	1,562	421,880,095	

Thus the national bank, which began with a capital five times as large as all the state banks, was only one-fifth of their aggregate in 1811. In 1817 the state capital was two and a half times the new National Bank capital, and in 1836 it was eight times that capital. Had it then been rechartered, with the same amount, it would now have been but one-twelfth of the capital of the state banks.

CHAPTER II.

STATE BANKS—SUFFOLK SYSTEM—SAFETY FUNDS—FREE BANKS.

The growth of state banks has fluctuated from time to time, under different circumstances of local trade, and the general nature of banks has changed in obedience to similar conditions. The nature of the banking systems of each locality has, however, undergone repeated modifications, and the general tendency is to the circulation of less paper. We shall endeavor to give a sketch of each. The first attempt at banking in New England was the creation of a land bank in 1740. At that time about eight hundred persons subscribed a capital in real estate, and having appointed ten directors, agreed to issue one hundred and fifty thousand pounds in paper, to circulate as money. This was dissolved by Parliament, and the stockholders held individually liable for the bills. In 1784 a bank was chartered by the Massachusetts Legislature, and the other New England states followed the example from time to time. In 1805 there were in existence forty-seven banks in the six New England states, with an aggregate capital of $13,353,000. In 1815, at the close of the war, these had risen to sixty-three banks, and $19,053,902 of capital, and the circulation had become large. In 1860 the number of banks in those states had risen to five hundred and five, with a capital of $90,186,990. In the course of this increase, the system of banking there had undergone less changes than in other states.

The paper currency of New England was generally of small denominations, and emitted by a larger number of banks with small capitals than that of most other sections. These institutions were scattered over the six New England states, and the bills of each bank forming the currency of its neighborhood, would, in the course of trade, ultimately find their way to Boston, the common centre of business. There being no provision for their redemption, they circulated at a discount, and this discount was increased in proportion to the issues of each bank, inflicting loss upon the community. To remedy this, the Suffolk Bank of Boston, in 1825, undertook to receive all the bills and send them home by an agent to the issuing bank, requiring each to redeem in specie at its own counter. This compelled each bank to keep a large amount of specie on hand, at an expense which ate up the profits of the circulation. They all agreed, in consequence, to keep at the Suffolk about three thousand dollars deposited, to redeem any balance of notes that might be there found against them. To keep down that balance each was then compelled to restrict its circulation to the actual business wants of its locality, that there might be no surplus currency; in other words, that the course of trade might carry to Boston no more of its bills than would be paid by the produce of the locality sent thither for sale, and also to send promptly to the Suffolk any bills of other banks that might come into its hands, as an offset to its own balances. Thus all the banks in New England are actively engaged in running each other, and five hundred streams pour country money daily into the Suffolk receptacle, to be assorted and sent back to the issuers. This keeps down the volume of the currency in that section. Since the creation of railroads and telegraphs, the difficulty of keeping out an excess of circulation is the greater. To be "thrown out of the Suffolk," or, in other words, not be able to meet a balance there, is fatal to the reputation of a bank. The system has worked well to the present day. It has been the case, however, that although those institutions cannot put out an excessive circulation in New England, many of them lend their notes on securities, on condition that the notes shall be paid out at the far west, whence they will be very slow in returning for redemption. The Suffolk mode of regulation by the laws of trade has, upon the whole, been very successful.

In New York the same evils manifested themselves as in New England, and in 1829 a remedy was attempted in the shape of the "safety fund." This did not undertake to restrain the issues of the banks, but to protect the public from loss by failure. Under it all the banks doing business in the state were required to contribute one-half of one per cent of their aggregate circulation to a fund to be called the "Safety Fund," out of which the notes of a broken bank were to be paid in full. This worked very well during a number of years of prosperity, but in the revulsion of 1837 a number of banks failed under disastrous circumstances, and the fund was found to be entirely insufficient—besides being wrong in principle, since it called upon the honest and well-conducted banks to pay the debts of the dishonest ones. It is hardly worth while, in a short history like this, to enumerate all the restrictions as to discounts, specie on hand, and emission of bills, that the various states have incorporated in bank laws. It may suffice to say, that all are powerless to prevent evil. On the failure of the safety fund system of New York, however, a radical change took place in the policy in regard to banks. The privilege of issuing notes to circulate as money at their own will and pleasure, had been found to be dangerous to the public, and the law of April, 1838, called the "free banking law," was passed, by which the power to issue bills directly was taken from the banks. Under that law, the Comptroller of the state prepares the plates, and delivers the bills to the banks, upon their lodging with him such securities, mostly state stocks, as amply secure the redemption of the bills. The name, "free banking," is given to the law, because it removes from the banks the restrictions relative to discounts, and the necessity for a charter. This law has been altered in some respects almost every year of its existence, but its main features remain the same, and it has in New York become the sole law to regulate banking. All the old banks, as their charters expire, reorganize under it, since the state constitution provides that no new charters can be granted or old ones renewed. The working of this law has been so efficient and popular, that it has spread into most of the northern and western states. The progress of banking in New York has been as follows:—

NUMBER OF BANKS AND AGGREGATE CAPITAL.

	No.	Capital.	
1801,	5	4,720,000	
1811,	8	7,522,760	Expiration of first U. S. bank.
1816,	27	18,766,756	Recharter U. S. bank.
1886,	86	81,281,461	Expiration of U. S. bank; suspension.
1838,	94	36,401,460	Free banking law; resumption.
1857,	294	107,449,143	Suspension.
1860,	303	111,441,370	Recovery.

The New York law requires the banks to issue the bills at the place of their location, and to redeem them at not more than one-half per cent. discount in the city of New York. These institutions, however, have an arrangement with the Metropolitan Bank, in New York, by which they are redeemed at a less rate.

Pennsylvania, in the early part of the century, was slow to create banks, and it had but three up to 1814, in which year 41 new banks were incorporated. Subsequently, it created numbers, and has probably suffered more than any other state from its abused bank credits. The progress of affairs there was as follows, exclusive of the United States Bank, which was situated at Philadelphia:—

	No.	Capital.	
1801,	2	5,000,000	
1811,	4	6,153,000	Expiration of U. S. Bank.
1815,	42	15,068,000	Low credit; 41 new banks.
1820,	36	14,681,000	Twenty-two banks failed.
1836,	49	23,750,338	State charter of the U. S. Bank; supension.
1839,	49	25,255,783	Resumption.
1859,	87	24,565,805	

There was, up to 1830, a great number of unauthorized banks doing business in Pennsylvania, and they presented a constant succession of bankruptcies. The authorized capital down to the present time has not kept pace with that of other states, taking the wealth and population of Pennsylvania into consideration.

Maryland chartered its first bank in 1790, the Bank of Maryland, capital $300,000, and continued to increase them moderately up to the present time. The progress of capital there has been as follows:—

	No.	Capital.	
1801,	2	$1,600,000	
1811,	6	4,835,202	U. S. Bank expired.
1814,	17	7,882,000	Banks suspended.
1820,	14	6,708,180	
1837,	21	10,438,655	Suspension.
1859,	32	12,560,635	

New Jersey has been influenced to some extent in her banking operations, by the state of things in New York and Pennsylvania, and in 1850 it adopted the general banking law of New York. Its progress has been as follows:—

	No.	Capital.	
1805,	2	$1,000,000	
1811,	3	789,740	U. S. Bank expired.
1815,	11	2,121,933	Suspension.
1820,	14	2,130,949	
1837,	25	3,970,090	Suspension.
1850,	24	3,565,283	Free law.
1855,	32	5,314,885	
1857,	48	7,494,912	Suspension.
1859,	46	7,359,122	

The multiplication of banks in New Jersey, under the new law, was mostly for the benefit of circulating their issues in New York at a discount, and they were of but little service to New Jersey.

Delaware has created banks in proportion to its size, in the following ratio:—

	No.	Capital.	
1801,	1	$110,000	
1815,	5	966,000	Suspension.
1819,	6	974,000	
1837,	4	817,775	Suspension.
1849,	2	210,000	Gold discovery.
1859,	12	1,638,185	

Ohio has been, of all the states, the most diversified in its policy in regard to banks. Its first bank was chartered in 1803, but it did not increase charters much until migration set thither after the war of 1812, when the new United States Bank established two branches, one in Cincinnati and one in Chillicothe. The progress of banks was then rapid up to the explosion of 1837, when about 36 of the banks of that state failed, under disastrous circumstances, leaving but few in existence on the resumption of specie payments in 1840. In 1845, a new system of banking was introduced, designed to restore that confidence in banks which had been so rudely shaken by the previous failures. It was called the "safety fund system," being composed of some forty banks which, together, form the State Bank, under a board of control, composed of delegates from each bank, which furnishes the notes to all for circulation. Each bank must deposit with the board 10 per cent. of its circulation in securities. Of 42 banks started under this law, 36 remain, with capital of $4,034,525. The same law created the "independent system," by which the banks doing business under it must deposit Ohio or United States stock with the State Treasurer to secure the circulation. There are 12 of these banks. There remained the old chartered banks, of which the Ohio Life and Trust—whose disastrous explosion in 1857 precipitated the panic which had been prepared for the public mind—was the last. In 1851, the free banking law of New York was adopted in addition to the other systems, and under this 13 banks were started. In the same year, by the new constitution of the state, the legislature was deprived of the right to grant banking powers until the law for so doing should be approved by the people. The general progress in Ohio has been as follows:—

	No.	Capital.	
1805,	1	$200,000	
1811,	4	895,000	
1816,	21	2,061,927	New U. S. Bank.
1837,	32	10,870,089	Suspension.
1845,	8	2,171,807	State bank law.
1851,	56	7,129,227	Free law.
1854,	66	7,166,581	" "
1859,	53	6,701,151	Recovery.

Indiana became a state in 1816, and in 1819 there were two banks, with a capital of $202,857, and so continued until 1834, when the State Bank of Indiana was created, capital $1,600,000, and with ten branches, which were mutually liable for each other's debts, and notes under $5 were prohibited. The bank stopped, partially, in 1837, and resumed payment October, 1841. In 1852 the general banking law of New York was adopted, and under it ninety-four banks were speedily organized, and fifty-one of them soon failed. The charter of the State Bank of Indiana having expired, the legislature chartered a new one, with capital of $6,000,000, and twenty branches, which buys out the state interest in the old bank, the charter to be paid up January 1, 1857. The progress of the state has been as follows:—

	No.	Capital.	
1819,	2	$202,857	
1835,	10	800,000	State bank.
1837,	11	1,845,000	Suspension.
1839,	11	2,216,700	Resumption.
1841,	11		
1852,	44	5,554,552	Free banking law.
1854,	59	7,281,934	New state bank.
1859,	37	3,617,629	

There are of these 17 free banks, capital $1,236,070.

Illinois came into the union in 1818, and in 1819 there were two banks, capital $140,910—one of which had been chartered in 1813, under the territory. It stopped in 1815 and remained so until 1835, when the legislature revived it and increased its capital to $1,400,000. The constitution of the state in 1818 forbade the creation of any new banks except a state bank, which was chartered in 1819, with a capital of $4,000,000. This was repealed and a new bank chartered, which speedily failed. In 1835 a new bank was chartered, capital $1,500,000 to $2,500,000. These banks suspended in 1837, going into liquidation in 1842, and no banks existed in the state until the adoption of the free banking law in 1851. The general progress has been as follows:—

	No.	Capital.	
1819,	2	$140,910	
1835,	2	278,739	State bank charter.
1838,	2	5,473,050	Failure.
1843,			Liquidation.
1854,	29	2,513,790	Free banking law.
1857,	45	4,679,325	Suspension.
1859,	103	8,900,000	Recovery.

Michigan was admitted as a state in January, 1837, but there had been already a number of small banks authorized by the territorial legislature. These rapidly multiplied under the state, during the speculative year 1837. In the early part of that year there existed 20 banks, with a capital of $1,918,361. These were a total wreck, and in March, 1838, a general banking law was passed, in order, as was alleged, to throw the business open. In one year, 49 banks, with a capital of $3,915,000, were projected. Of these, 43 went into operation. Those banks were not required to redeem their issues on demand. The result was utter insolvency, inflicting a heavy loss upon the public. In 1849, the "free banking law" was adopted, with personal liabilities to stockholders. The progress was as follows:—

	No.	Capital.	
1835,	8	$658,980	Territorial gov'nment.
1837,	9	1,400,000	State and general law.
1838,	43	2,317,765	Revulsion.
1844,	3	202,650	Liquidation.
1849,	5	392,530	Free law.
1859,	4	755,461	

Iowa was admitted into the union in 1846. It had at Dubuque the Miners' Bank, chartered by Wisconsin before the erection of Iowa territory, in operation since 1838, but with little credit. In 1858, the free banking law was adopted, and also the State Bank of Iowa was authorized. The latter, with twelve branches, went into operation in 1859.

Wisconsin was admitted into the Union in 1848. It had, during some ten years, two banks, that of Mineral Point and the Bank of Wisconsin; these came to grief, and in 1851 a new bank was started at Milwaukee. In 1854 the free banking law was adopted; since that time the progress has been rapid, as follows:—

	No.	Capital.	
1837,	2	$119,625	
1839,	2	139,125	Suspension.
1848,			State admitted.
1854,	10	600,000	Free law.
1857,	38	2,635,000	Suspension.
1859,	98	7,995,000	Expansion.
1860,	108	7,620,000	Expansion.

The operation of the free law, by retarding the convertibility of the bills of the Wisconsin banks, causes, at a time when crops are short, the rate of exchange on the east to rule high, in other words depreciates the currency. The bank circulation is about $5,000,000.

Minnesota has made, as yet, little progress in banking. It adopted the free banking law in 1858, and two banks have been started under it; the Bank of the State, at

W. H. Bartlett. A. L. Dick.

CUSTOM HOUSE, PHILADELPHIA.

St. Paul, capital $25,000, and the Exchange Bank, at Glencoe, capital $25,000.

Nebraska has also two banks, the survivors of a number recently started, but they were swept down by the ruin of 1857; the capitals are $56,000.

	No.	Capital.
Jan. 1857,	4	$205,000
" 1858,	6	15,000
" 1859,	2	56,000

Kentucky was admitted into the Union in 1792, and in 1801 it authorized a bank, with a capital of $150,000, under the guise of an Insurance Company, authorized to issue notes. In 1804 it chartered the Bank of Kentucky, capital $1,000,000; this bank failed in 1814, but resumed in 1815. In 1817 a batch of forty banks, with $10,000,000 capital, was authorized to redeem their notes by paying out Kentucky bank-notes for them instead of specie. The result was a flood of irredeemable paper, which stimulated all kinds of speculation and jobbing, and ended in a general explosion and distress within the year. To "relieve" the people, the state chartered the Commonwealth Bank, capital $3,000,000, pledging lands south of the Tennessee river, in addition to the faith of the state, for the redemption of the bills, which creditors were required to take at par for their claims, or wait two years for their pay. The bills fell at once to fifty cents on the dollar, and which proportion of their debts creditors were thus required to lose. This gave rise to party strife, which, at the end of five years, resulted in the repeal of the law and the suppression of the paper. The United States Bank had two branches in the state, one at Lexington and one at Louisville. When, in 1833, it became evident that that institution would not be rechartered, three new banks, with branches, were authorized, capital $7,030,000; subsequently another was started. These went into operation, but suspended in 1837, resuming in 1839 with the United States Bank, and again suspended on the final failure of that concern. In 1842, the banks again resumed, and since then the number has gradually increased, as follows:

	No.	Capital.	
1819,	18	$4,307,431	Irredeemable.
1833,	2	792,427	New charter.
1835,	4	4,106,262	With ten branches.
1837,	4	8,499,094	Suspension.
1851,	26	7,536,927	
1857,	35	10,596,305	Suspension.
1859,	37	12,216,725	Recovery.
1860,	45	12,835,670	

Tennessee commenced banking in 1807, with the Bank of Nashville, which soon failed with great loss. In 1811 it again chartered ten banks, and a number of others were from time to time started, but failed disastrously. In 1852 the free banking law was adopted, and the progress of affairs has been as follows:—

	No.	Capital.	
1819,	3	$1,545,867	Disastrous failure.
1820,	1	737,817	State bank charter.
1835,	3	2,890,381	Four branches.
1837,	3	5,293,079	Suspension.
1852,	23	6,881,568	
1857,	45	9,083,693	Suspension.
1859,	39	8,361,357	

Arkansas had two banks that were started upon state bonds. These the state issued to the extent of $3,500,000 to the banks to form their capitals. The bonds were sold through the United States Bank, and the money obtained for them was loaned out pro rata to the stockholders, who became so by filing mortgages on their plantations and lands. Speedy ruin, of course, overtook both banks. These are now in liquidation, owing the state some $3,000,000 on the bonds, which are not paid. There have been no banks started since.

Mississippi is a state in which banking for a long time ran riot, but which has had but little in the last ten years. When the state came into the Union in 1817 it had one bank, which continued with an increased capital to 1830. In that year the state chartered the Planters' Bank, with a capital of $3,000,000, two-thirds to be subscribed by the state in stock, which was issued, and the bank went into operation. Other banks were then chartered, and in 1837 there were seventeen, with eighteen branches, and a capital of $16,760,951. In that year the Union Bank was chartered, with a capital of $15,000,000 in state stock; of this amount $5,000,000 was issued, and repudiated on the ground of illegality of sale, and in 1852 the people refused, by a large vote, to pay those bonds. All the banks of Mississippi failed, and there has since been but little movement, as follows:—

	No.	Capital.	
1820,	1	$900,000	
1830,	1	950,600	Capital increased.
1834,	1	2,666,805	
1837,	17	16,760,951	18 branches.
1838,	11	19,231,123	Suspension.
1840,	18	30,379,403	Failure.
1850,	0		Liquidation.
1851,	1	118,460	
1859,	2	1,110,000	

Missouri had one bank when it came into the Union in 1821, but it failed disastrously. The State Bank of Missouri and branches continued to be the only institution up to 1856, when a law was passed authorizing others, and the progress has been as follows:—

	No.	Branches.	Capital.	
1819,	1		$250,000	
1837,	1	1	533,350	State bank.
1839,	1	1	1,027,870	
1856,	1	5	2,215,405	
1857,	5	5	2,620,615	Suspension.
1859,	17	5	5,796,781	Expansion.
1860,	9	29	9,082,951	

Louisiana came into the Union in 1812, with one bank, having a capital of $500,000, This was increased to three banks in 1815, capital $1,432,000. The progress subsequently was not great until after 1830, when the speculative spirit of those years was largely developed in Louisiana, and the progress was as follows:—

	No.	Branches.	Capital.	
1830,	3		$4,665,980	
1837,	16	31	36,769,455	Suspension.
1840,	16	31	41,711,214	Failure.
1843,	6	22	20,929,340	Liquidation.
1851,	6	22	12,370,390	Free bank law.
1857,	6		22,800,830	Suspension.
1859,	12		24,215,689	

The free banking law was adopted in 1853, and four banks have been started under its provisions, which require the banks to keep one-third of their liabilities in specie on hand.

Alabama has had éxperience of a disastrous nature in state banking, and there has been little enterprise in that direction since the failure of the State Bank. When she came into the Union in 1819 she had one bank, with a capital of $321,112. In 1830 she had two banks. It was then supposed that by embarking in banking, the state might derive profits enough to pay all the state expenses and dispense with taxation. Accordingly, state bonds were issued to form the capital of the State Bank, which, however, soon failed, and the state was saddled with a debt of some $11,000,000. The progress was as follows:—

	No.	Capital.	
1819,	1	$321,112	
1830,	2	781,010	
1837,	3	10,141,806	Suspension.
1840,	3	14,379,255	Liquidation.
1843,	1	1,500,000	Bank of Mobile.
1851,	1	1,500,000	Free banking law.
1857,	4	2,297,800	Suspension.
1860,	8	4,901,000	

Virginia chartered a bank as early as 1804 for 53 years, the Bank of Virginia, capital $1,500,000, since enlarged. In 1830 there were four banks, and the change was not great down to 1851, when the free law was adopted, but the charters of the old banks are renewed as they expire. The course of events was as follows:—

	No.	Branches.	Capital.	
1819,	3		$5,112,192	
1830,	4	18	5,571,181	
1837,	5	18	6,732,500	Suspension.
1839,	5	20	7,458,248	
1840,	6		10,363,362	
1851,	6	20	9,731,370	Free banking law.
1857,	22	40	14,651,600	Suspension.
1860,	24	41	16,005,156	

North Carolina began her bank career in 1804, in granting a charter for $250,000 capital. From that time the number and amount of capital has been steadily increased, without any material deviations from a steady course, which has been as follows:—

	No.	Branches.	Capital.	
1819,	3		$2,964,887	
1830,	3		3,195,000	
1837,	3	7	2,880,590	Suspension.
1850,	3	12	3,789,250	
1859,	12	16	6,525,200	

South Carolina has been more variable in its banking movement. Its first institution was the State Bank, owned by the state, and had more the character of a loan office than a bank. In 1820 the capital of the bank was pledged as security for the state debt, and it became a regular bank. The progress of the state has been as follows:—

	No.	Capital.	
1792,	1	$675,000	
1811,	4	3,475,000	
1820,	3	2,475,000	
1836,	10	8,636,118	
1837,	4	4,100,000	Suspension.
1839,	11	9,153,498	Eight new charters.
1850,	14	13,179,131	
1859,	20	14,888,451	

Georgia has had a regular supply of banks since the expiration of the first United States Bank in 1811, when she chartered an institution with $215,000 capital. In 1820 this had increased to four banks, with a capital of $3,401,510, and the progress has been as follows:—

	No.	Capital.	
1811,	1	$215,000	Old U. S. Bank expired.
1816,	3	1,502,000	New " chartered.
1820,	4	3,401,510	
1833,	13	6,534,691	Deposits removed.
1837,	16	11,438,828	Suspension.
1840,	39	15,098,694	
1846,	22	8,970,789	
1857,	30	16,015,256	Suspension.
1860,	29	16,689,560	

District of Columbia banks were established as early as 1792, in the district, and increased pretty rapidly, as follows :—

	No.	Capital.
1792,	1	$500,000
1802,	2	1,500,000
1811,	4	2,341,395
1815,	10	4,078,295
1820,	13	5,525,319
1830,	9	3,879,574
1837,	7	2,204,445
1844,	6	1,649,280

Most of the charters expired, and not being renewed, the concerns are in process of liquidation.

Florida came into the union in 1845, with a load of five banks that had been chartered by the territory in 1838, with an aggregate capital of $2,113,000. These were mostly based upon $3,500,000 territorial bonds, issued to the banks for capital, and sold in London. The concerns failed almost as soon as they got the money, and went into liquidation, when the state repudiated the bonds, and there have since been no banks in Florida, until this year two are started, with $300,000 capital.

From this sketch of banking in each state, it is to be observed that the creation of banks has been due more to the desire to borrow money through their operation than to lend it. The mistaken idea that they could supply capital, has been the temptation to their creation, and disastrous failure has everywhere attended the experiment. Gradually a principle of sound banking vindicates itself amid numerous disasters, and actual capital has come to be employed in the business.

CHAPTER III.

BANKS OF THE UNITED STATES—CLEARING HOUSES—PRIVATE BANKING.

Having sketched the course of events in each state, we may recapitulate the leading features of all the state banks :—

BANKS OF ALL THE UNITED STATES—TOTAL OF IMPORTS AND EXPORTS—POPULATION.

	No.	Capital.	Loans.	Circulation.	Specie.	Deposits.	Imports & exports.	Population.
1791,	3	$2,000,000	..	..	..	..	$48,212,041	3,929,827
1800,	32	23,550,000	..	..	..	..	162,224,548	5,305,925
1811,	89	52,601,601	..	$28,100,000	$15,400,000	..	144,716,833	7,449,960
1815,	208	82,259,590	..	45,500,000	17,000,000	..	165,599,027	8,353,338
1816,	246	89,822,422	..	68,000,000	19,000,000	..	229,024,452	8,595,806
1820,	308	137,110,611	..	44,863,344	19,820,240	$35,950,470	144,141,669	9,638,131
1830,	330	145,192,268	200,451,214	61,323,898	22,114,917	55,559,928	144,726,428	12,866,020
1837,	634	290,772,091	525,115,702	149.185,890	37,915,340	127,397,185	258,408,593	15,681,467
1840,	901	358,442,692	462,896,523	106,968,572	33,105.155	75,686,857	239,227,465	17,069,453
1843,	691	228,861,948	254,544,937	58,563,608	33,515,806	56,168,628	149,100,279	18,713,479
1846,	707	196,894,309	312,114,404	105,552,427	42,012,095	96,913,070	235,180,313	20,515,871
1854,	1,208	301,376,071	557,397,779	204,689,207	59,410,253	188,188,744	582,803,445	26,051,890
1857,	1,416	370,834,686	684,456 889	214,778,822	58,349,838	230,351,352	723,850,823	28,406,974
1860,	1,562	421,880,095	691,945,580	207,102,477	83,594,537	253,802,129	854,500,000	31'429,891

This table shows the number of banks, with their aggregate capital, at important eras. As in 1791, when the national bank and mint went into operation; 1811, when the bank charter expired; 1815, when the numerous banks that had sprung into being on the dissolution of the National Bank, were all suspended; in 1816, when the peace, bringing with it large imports of goods, and a heavy drain of specie to Europe and Asia, increased the confusion and aided the re-establishment of a national bank; 1820, when that bank, in full operation, was staggering under adverse exchanges and the operation of local banks; 1830, when five years of successful working, after the revulsion of 1825, and under a high tariff, had given confidence to the public; 1837, when the rivalry between the state and the national banks had, aided by the state of affairs in Europe, stimulated speculation, which resulted in the revulsion of that year; 1840, when the number of banks had reached the highest point, under efforts to restore prosperity by paper credits; 1843, the lowest point of depression after the failure of those efforts, and the liquidation of the unsound banks; 1846, when the bank capital was at a low point, but bank credits had begun to multiply under the effects of the famine abroad; 1854, when the activity growing out of the gold discoveries was in full blast, and five hundred new banks were, through the medium of credit, urging the public toward the panic of 1857. In the last two years there has been a renewed movement.

The mere figures, showing the magnitude of the bank movement, do not indicate the changes in the manner of doing business, nor do they indicate any unsafe expansion, except as in connection with the business they represent. Thus, in 1837, the bank loans were $525,000,000, and their circulation $149,000,000. Events proved that those loans were of the most speculative and unsafe character. In 1860, the loans were $691,900,000, and the circulation $207,000,000. Yet these larger figures were very far from being excessive. They represent but $6 circulation per head of the people, while that of 1837 was nearly $10 per head. The business of the country, as represented by imports and exports, was, in 1837, but half the amount of bank loans. In 1860 they exceeded the amount of bank loans. It is thus evident, that the larger sum of bank loans represents actual business, while those of 1837 represented only speculative values. This fact of the nature of loans made is the key to sound banking. It is a matter which depends upon the judgment and skill of the banker, and it cannot be regulated by law. Hence the futility of all the laws that have been devised to prevent banks from breaking. It is to be remembered, that the bank loans form but a portion of the credits which are the great purchasing power in trade. Almost all the wholesale business of the country is done with the notes of individuals, running for a longer or less time. These are entirely independent of law or banks. In a time of great mercantile confidence and speculative activity, business men are disposed to buy on credit, and their competition for produce and merchandise causes a rise in prices. This rise stimulates greater activity, which reacts upon prices until revulsion is brought about. The agency which the banks have in this matter is to discount a portion of the notes which a dealer takes in exchange for the merchandise he sells. The bank in discounting does not actually lend any money. It merely operates a canceling of credits by book accounts. Thus, a merchant buys goods and gives his note at six months. He then deposits what money he receives in the course of business to await the maturity of the note. As the period approaches, he finds that he has not money enough, but he has in his pocket-book a number of notes that he has taken for goods. These he takes to the bank and offers as collateral security for his own note, that he offers for discount. The bank making the discount places the amount to his credit. He draws a check against that credit in favor of the note he has to pay, and the two entries cancel each other. There has been no money used, but one kind of promise has supplanted another. As the crops come forward from the country, the drafts drawn against them pay the notes held by the merchant and lodged as collateral. Dearness or scarcity of money in the market depends mainly upon the disposition of the banks to facilitate the canceling of credits, and in this the institution affects to be governed by the state of the foreign trade. If the disposition to buy goods has been very active and prices are consequently so high as to pay good profits on imports, the arrivals of merchandise will be large and the exports proportionably small. This involves a demand for specie which the banks avoid, by refusing to come under new obligations. A competition in curtailment sets in. The bank that curtails the most rapidly will have the balances in its favor from the other banks, and will command their specie. Each endeavors to attain such a position. The pressure becomes great, the public alarmed, and individual depositors draw their specie, which exhausts the banks, and they stop. This was the state of affairs in 1857.

The general tendency of the banks has been, under the teachings of experience, to equalize balances and to insist on prompt payment. In the case of circulation this is done in New England by the Suffolk system, and in New York and most other states by the free law, which requires a deposit of state stocks of dollar for dollar of the circulation. It is obvious, however, that these regulations in no degree affect discounts and those operations where circulation is not in question; as in the checks of individuals, by which a large portion of credits are transferred. In New York city there are some fifty banks, each of which receives checks on all the other banks, and has checks drawn upon it in favor of all others. There are also drafts and bills from abroad, constantly coming to each to be paid by others. Up to 1853, all the banks employed each a man to go round and collect all these checks and drafts each day, and each bank kept fifty accounts open. To obviate this and to enforce settlement, the "clearing house" was devised. By this system, each bank sends thither every day a clerk, with all the demands it has against all other banks. The fifty-four clerks thus assembled make a mutual exchange of all claims, and the balance, if any, is struck, and each bank pays in cash the amount of that balance. This occupies an hour, within which all accounts are adjusted. The amount of accounts depends upon the activity of business. The clearing house has been in operation since October, 1853, and its operations have been as follows:—

	Amount exchanged.	Balances paid.
1854,	5,750,455,987	297,411,493
1855,	5,362,912,098	289,694,137
1856,	6,906,213,328	334,714,489
1857,	8,333,226,718	365,313,901
1858,	4,756,664,386	314,238,910
1859,	6,448,005,956	363,984,682
1860,	7,180,000,000	351,000,000

The emergencies of the war required the issue of demand notes by the Government, of small denominations to serve for circulation, as well as the putting forth of bonds, treasury notes, and loans of various kinds. At first these demand notes were the equivalent of gold and silver, and were receivable in payment of customs duties, as well as all other moneys due to the United States; but the gradual advance in the price of gold made them so valuable as to take them out of the circulation, and cause them to be hoarded as gold. Congress then authorized the issue of legal-tender notes of small denominations, receivable for the payment of all dues to the United States except customs, which must be paid in gold, the coin being needed to pay the interest on that portion of the national debt upon which interest in gold was guaranteed. Of this currency, usually known as *greenbacks*, four hundred and fifty millions of dollars was authorized, but only about $431,000,000 was issued. Beside this, Congress authorized the issue of postal and fractional currency, to the extent of fifty millions of dollars, but there have never been more than thirty millions in circulation, and the amount Jan. 1, 1866, did not exceed twenty-three millions.

It was soon found, however, that to prevent financial disorders and panics, it was necessary that the Government should be able to control the banking operations of the country to some extent. For this purpose the National banking system was devised. The act providing for the National banks was based, with such modifications as the circumstances and experience required, upon the New York Free Banking system. The capital on which circulation was granted consisted of the bonds, treasury notes, &c., of the United States, and these being deposited with the Controller of the Currency, National bank notes of different denominations, having the name of the bank and the coat of arms of the state inserted, were delivered to an amount not exceeding ninety per cent. of the bonds. No banks could be organized with a less capital than $50,000, and in places of more than 6,000 inhabitants the capital must be $100,000, or more. The amount of circulation to be issued to these National banks must not exceed in the aggregate $300,000,000. The National banks in the larger cities were required to keep on hand at all times an amount of coin and legal tender equal to one-fourth of their circulation and deposits; the country banks an amount equal to fifteen per cent. The bills of the National banks were receivable, like the legal tenders, for all dues to the United States except customs, and such arrangements were made for their redemption as made them virtually at par in all parts of the country. At first they had, in some sections, a severe struggle with the state banks, but it was not of long duration, and in the autumn of 1864 the state and local banks began to come under the National banking law, and by July, 1866, there were not more than 500 of the old banks throughout the United States which had not either become National banks or closed up their affairs. On the 1st of January, 1866, the number of National banks was 1,579, their authorized capital $403,357,346, and their circulation $213,239,530. Of these, 218 banks, with an aggregate capital of $172,-498,545, and a circulation of $73,964,619, were located in the large cities. The average loans and discounts of the National banks for the last quarter of 1865 were nearly 500 millions of dollars, about four times the amount of the loans of all the banks in 1859. Their deposits in the last quarter of 1865 averaged 513 millions. The circulation of the state banks was, after August, 1866, taxed by the Government ten per cent.

Private banking, which, previous to the war, had attained to very considerable proportions, has since greatly increased. The private banks, having no circulation to take care of, and dealing with their customers at the market price of money, conducting at the same time large transactions in Government securities, railroad bonds, &c., have possessed remarkable facilities for a profitable traffic, and many of the bankers have realized gigantic fortunes.

UNITED STATES MINT.

CHAPTER I.

ESTABLISHMENT OF MINT—STANDARD OF COINS—LAWS REGULATING COINAGE—PROGRESS OF COINAGE—PRECIOUS METALS IN THE COUNTRY.

The currency, or circulating medium of a country, is of itself a very simple matter, although complicated at times by the theories of financiers, and the efforts to make promises of a thing pass for the thing itself. In the early stages of society the products of industry constitute the wealth of the people, after they have ceased to be merely herdsmen. These products being exchanged against each other, the transactions form barter trade. As wealth increases and wants become more diversified, as well as the products of industry, by being subdivided, some common medium of value becomes requisite to meet all the wants of interchange. The precious metals have generally been adopted as this medium, because the supply is the most steady, the equivalent value most generally known, and the transportation most convenient. Hence all trade comes to be represented by a weight of pure gold or its equivalent of pure silver, and all commodities come to be valued, or called equivalent, to certain quantities of these metals. To ascertain the purity and weight of the metal offered in payment at each transaction would, however, involve difficulties that would neutralize the value of the metals as a common medium of exchange. Every man would require to be an assayer, and to be provided with scales. To obviate this the government steps in, and by means of a mint assays the metals, and weighs them into convenient pieces, placing on each a stamp, which soon becomes universally known, and this is called "money." Every nation makes the pieces of different weights, and puts in more or less pure metal. To ascertain the "*par* of exchange" between two countries, the coin of each is assayed, and the quantity of pure metal in each being ascertained, the *par* of exchange is known. When this continent was discovered, its inhabitants were savages, who had no idea of property, and no trade beyond the mere exchange of, perhaps, a skin for a bow or a bunch of arrows. Money was unknown, and the value of the precious metals was not understood. The little gold and copper that they had was twisted into rude ornaments; but no man would work for a piece of these metals. When the first emigrants landed, they commenced the cultivation of the earth and the interchange of its products. The accumulation of industrial products formed wealth. Their first exchanges were mere barter. As late as 1652 the payment of taxes and other dues was made in cattle, skins, and other products in Massachusetts; and tobacco was a medium of trade in Virginia. Some money existed, but this was mostly the coins brought by the immigrants from the mother country, and did not suffice for the daily wants. Massachusetts, therefore, established a mint for the coinage of shillings, sixpences, and threepences of sterling silver, which were "two pence in the shilling of less valew than the English coyne." This "pine tree shilling," so called from a pine tree on the reverse, was worth about twenty cents. This coinage gave umbrage to the mother country, and when Governor Winslow was introduced to Charles II., that usually good-natured monarch took him roughly to task for the presumption of the colony in assuming to coin money, at the same time producing the coin with the pine tree upon it. The ready wit of the governor, however, turned the rebuke, by assuring his Majesty that it was an evidence of the devotion of the colony, which struck these medals in commemoration of the escape of his Majesty in the Royal Oak, which was executed as well as the poor state of the arts in the colony would permit. The coinage was nevertheless suppressed, and the example of Massachusets was followed by Maryland with the like results. Carolina and Virginia struck some copper coins, but without much effect. There being no mint, therefore, in any of the colonies, foreign coins were circulated freely as a legal tender. The country produced none of the precious metals, but as the trade of the colonies increased, and they began to have a surplus of fish, provisions, food, tobacco, etc., beyond their own wants, to sell, they built vessels, and carried these articles, mostly fish, to the West Indies and the catholic countries of Europe; and as the mother country did not allow the colonies to buy manufactures except from herself, money was mostly had in exchange for this produce. Guineas, joes, half joes, doubloons, and pistoles of various origin constituted the gold currency, while the silver was mostly the Spanish American dollar and its fractions: the half, quarter, eighth, and sixteenth, with the pistareen and half pistareen. This silver coin flowed into the colonies from the Spanish West Indies, in exchange for fish and food; and the Spanish dollar thus came to be the best known and most generally adopted unit of money. The coin had upon its reverse the pillars of Hercules, and was known as the pillar dollar; hence the dollar mark ($), which represents "S," for "Spanish," entwining the pillars. Inasmuch as the "balance of trade" was in favor of England, the largest portion of the coin that flowed in from other quarters was sent thither, and this tendency was increased by the pernicious issues of paper money by the colonies. This paper displaced the coin, and drove it all out of the country. The exigencies of the several colonial governments caused them to make excessive issues of this "paper" or "bills of credit," and it fell to a heavy discount as compared with coin. Not being convertible at the date of the Revolution the depreciation in the several colonies was nearly as follows:—

VALUE OF THE DOLLAR AND THE £ STERLING IN COLONIAL PAPER MONEY.

	£ sterling.			Dollar.	
	£.	s.	d.	s.	d.
New England and Virginia ...	1	6	8	6	0
New York and North-eastern .	1	15	6⅓	8	0
Middle states....................	1	13	4	7	6
South Carolina and Georgia...	1	0	8¾	4	8

On the formation of the new government, the terrible state of the currency first attracted attention. The country had been flooded with "continental money," which had been issued to the extent of three hundred and sixty millions for war expenses. The states had issued "bills of credit," which were depreciated as in the table; and the debased and diversified foreign coins that circulated were very few in number. Private credit hardly existed. Frightful jobbing took place in the government paper, and industry could with difficulty get its proper reward. The first effort was to give the federal government alone the right to coin money, to prohibit the states from issuing any more "bills of credit," and to get the continental money out of circulation by providing for its payment. Robert Morris had been directed to report upon the mint and a system of coinage, and he did so early in 1782. Many plans were based upon his report, and finally that of Mr. Jefferson was adopted. It conformed to the decimal notation, with the Spanish dollar as the unit: A gold piece of ten dollars, to be called the eagle, with its half and quarter; a dollar in silver; a tenth of a dollar in silver; a hundredth of a dollar in copper.

In accordance with the plan of Mr. Jefferson, a law of April 2, 1792, enacted regulations for a mint, located at Philadelphia, and the coinage proceeded. It was found that, owing to the rise in the value of copper, the cent had been made too heavy, and, January 14, 1790, it was reduced to two hundred and eight grains, and January 26, 1796, it was again reduced to one hundred and sixty-eight grains, at which rate it remained until the late introduction of nickle. The mint being established at Philadelphia, the work of coinage went on slowly, for two principal reasons. The first was that the material for coin—that is, gold and silver, no matter in what shape it may be—was obtained only, by the operation of trade, from abroad, and nearly all of it arrived at New York, the property of merchants. Now, although the government charged nothing for coining, yet, to send the metal from New York to Philadelphia during the first forty years of the government, when there was none but wagon conveyance, was expensive, and accompanied with some risk. It was not, therefore, to be expected that the merchants would undertake this without any benefit; the more so, as the same law, in the second place, still allowed the foreign coins to be legal tender. The merchant who received, say ten thousand dollars in gold coin at New York had only to lodge that coin in the local bank, and use the paper money issued by the bank. There was no necessity to send the coin to Philadelphia merely to be recoined without profit. It was also the case that in the course of the newly developed commerce between the United States and the countries of Europe, it was found that silver had been valued too high at the mint. It was coined in the ratio of fifteen to one of gold, when its real value was nearer sixteen to one. This relative value of the two metals depends upon the respective demand and supply in the markets of the world. At about the date of the discovery of America it was ten to one; that is, ten ounces of pure silver were equal to one ounce of pure gold. When Peru and Spanish America poured in their large supplies of silver, the rate gradually fell to fifteen to one. At the close of the eighteenth century, and with the greater freedom of commerce in the first half of the nineteenth century, it was found still to decline. The reason of this is obvious, since, in any locality, the relative value of the metals will be proportioned to the local supply of either, influenced by the expense of sending either to other localities. Thus, silver may have been really fourteen to one in one place, and sixteen to one in another, and the difficulties of transportation prevented an equalization. As soon as communication became prompt and cheap the equalization took place, and the general relative value was found to be somewhat changed. The effect of this was that silver came here and gold went away. Nearly all the coinage of the mint was silver. This evil attracted the attention of the government, and a remedy was sought. This was finally found in changing the relative value of the silver to gold in the coinage by simply putting less pure gold into the eagle, and letting the silver remain as it was. The quantity of pure gold in the eagle was, therefore, by the law of June 28, 1834, reduced from 247.5 grains to 232 grains, or rather more than six and five-eighths per cent, and the quantity of alloy was slightly increased, so as to make the fineness of the gold nine-tenths, or nine grains of fine gold to one of alloy in each piece.

This was found not to be exact, and in 1837 the pure gold was slightly increased, and this regulation remains. Under all the laws the gold coins have been as follows:—

	Pure gold. Grains.	Alloy. Silver.	Alloy. Copper.	Total Alloy.	Total weight. Grains.	Fineness.
1792,	247.5	5.62½	16.87½	22.5	270	916.7
1834,	232.0	6.50	19.50	26.0	258	899.2
1837,	232.2	6.45	19.35	25.8	258	900.0

These proportions remain now the same for gold. In order to bring the silver to the same standard, the law of 1837 reduced the alloy in dollars three and a half grains, making the dollar weigh 412 1-2 grains instead of 416.

In all this period, up to 1838, there had been but one mint, and that at Philadelphia. In 1831, under the desire of the government to enlarge the metallic basis of the national currency, three branches were authorized, one at New Orleans, one at Charlotte, North Carolina, and one at Dahlonega, Georgia. These two latter were in mining districts, where gold began to be produced to some extent, and all three went into operation in 1838. The coinage progressed down to 1853, when, in consequence of the change brought about by the gold discoveries in California, a new law in relation to the silver currency was enacted. Before giving an account of that change, we may take a table of the coinage at the mint since its organization for several periods.

UNITED STATES COINAGE.

	Gold.	Silver.	Copper and Nickel.	Total.
1793 to 1820,	7,431,545	10,980,431	421,795	18,833,771
1821 " 1834,	4,394,345	25,314,647	236,795	29,945,787
Total to 1834,	11,825,890	36,295,078	658,590	48,779,558
1834 to 1837,	11,424,450	12,560,115	137,323	24,121,888
1838 " 1848,	53,329,965	24,351,769	513,336	78,195,570
1849 " 1852,	60,211,315	6,014,509	341,207	166,567,031
1853 " 1860,	318,169,102	42,803,767	553,365	371,526,234
	$564,960,722	122,025,238	2,203,821	689,190,281

In the first twenty-seven years of the mint operation, the gold coinage was about seventy-five per cent. of the silver coinage. That whole period embraced the European war, and the first operations of the mint were to coin as much of the metals already in the country as came within their reach. In the second period, from 1821 to 1834, the effect of the change in the relative value of the metals of which we have spoken, became manifest, and the gold coinage was about one-sixth only of the silver coinage. In 1834 the new gold bill produced a change, and the gold coinage became nearly equal to that of silver. Soon after the passage of this law, the payment of the French indemnity, enforced under the administration of General Jackson, took place, and it was paid in the form of gold bars, of weight varying from twenty-five to six hundred and fifty ounces each. The first of them were received at the United States mint September, 1834, and from that date to September, 1838, six hundred of these bars were deposited at the mint; the value was $3,500,000. In 1838 the branches came into operation, and the coinage was increased by their operations and by 13,705,250 of gold of domestic production, to the close of 1848. In 1849 California gold began to make its appearance, and $7,079,144 worth of it was coined in that year. The great influx of gold bullion upon the mint by far exceeded its capacity to do the work, and Congress authorized, by the act of March 3d, 1849, the coinage of double eagles, or $20 pieces, and also one dollar pieces to supply the place of the silver coin, which had been drained off to California in exchange for the gold, which sold as low as $15 and $16 per ounce, although worth $20 and $21. The law of May, 1852, authorized the coinage of $3 pieces.

In ten years, to the close of 1848, the gold coinage had amounted to double the silver coinage, and the new influx of gold excited fears that the value of silver would rise rapidly as compared with gold. From 1848 to 1857 the coinage of silver was very small, while the demand for it was large. To avoid inconvenience from this cause, a new bill was passed, to take effect April 1st, 1853. By this bill it was enacted that gold or silver deposited with the mint, might be cast into bars or ingots of pure metal, or standard fineness, at the option of the depositor, with a stamp designating the weight and fineness; no pieces less than ten ounces shall be other than of standard fineness; the charge for this is one-half per cent. Inasmuch as most of the gold arrives at New York, efforts were made to procure the establishment of a mint at that point. Instead, however, of a mint, an assay office was established there, and a branch mint at San Francisco, in 1854. The law allows the depositor to draw either bars or coin in return, the description desired to be stated at the time of the deposit. The production of bars and coins under all these regulations has been large, for gold as well as silver.

Until the law of 1834, the quantity of gold coin in circulation was not large. The banks supplied so large a quantity of small bills as to fill the channels of circulation for sums above a dollar, and under that amount the circulation was almost altogether small Spanish coins, which, being much depreciated by wear and tear, passed for more than their intrinsic value, and consequently flooded the country, greatly influencing retail prices. This was particularly the case with the pistareens, which, up to 1827, were taken at twenty cents, or five to the dollar, although they were really worth but eighteen and a half cents, consequently there was little other change to be had. In consequence of a report of the Mint Director of that year, they were refused at more than seventeen cents, and they very speedily disappeared from circulation, and have not now been seen for a quarter of a century. The quarters continued to circulate at twenty-five cents, although the average value was twenty-three and a half cents; the eighths were taken at twelve and a half, although they were worth only eleven and one-eighth; the sixteenth was taken at six and a quarter, although worth but five cents. It resulted that these coins became very abundant, driving out the dimes and half dimes, and in 1843 the post-office and the banks refusing them altogether, they were supplanted by the American coin, until the gold discoveries of 1848. After that event, owing to the increased production of gold, and the fact that some of the European states changed their monetary policy, making silver the sole standard of value, the latter metal became worth more in market than its nominal value in United States coin, and was gradually withdrawn from the currency, until, in 1852, silver coin became very scarce, and there was not sufficient left in circulation for the purposes of change. A premium of four per cent. was paid for dollars and half dollars for export, and the smaller coins commanded, in many cases, a still higher price, for use among shop-keepers and small traders. It was easy to see that, unless the weight of our silver coin was reduced, there would soon be none left in the country. Already the eating-houses and drinking saloons had issued their tickets, or shinplaster tokens, in place of coin; and the poor, who purchased the necessaries of life in small amounts, were put to great inconvenience, or obliged to submit to ruinous shaves upon their paper money. To remedy these evils, Congress passed the act of February 21st, 1853 (to take effect the 1st of April following), authorizing the coinage of half dollars, quarter dollars, dimes, and half dimes, weighing about seven per cent. less than the old coin. The change will be better understood by comparing the weight of the several pieces under the old law, with the weight of the new coin:—

	Old coin.	New coin.
Half dollar, grains ...	206¼	192
Quarter dollar, do. ...	103⅛	96
Dime, do. ...	41¼	38 2-5
Half dime, do. ...	20⅝	19 1-5

The dollar was not changed, and the weight of that piece is 412 1-2 grains, the weight which it has borne since 1836; this reduction of weight being fourteen and a half grains in the half dollar, or nearly seven per cent. The silver currency was not *debased*, in the ordinary sense of the word, the same fineness (nine hundred parts pure silver, and one hundred of alloy) being retained, and the only change in the coin itself being in the weight. A very important provision, however, was made in regard to it; it is not a legal tender in payment of debts in sums exceeding five dollars. The old silver coins have been mostly taken out of circulation. A few dollars are kept to pay depositors at the mint, who are entitled to silver coin, but the silver extracted from California gold is paid for in gold coin at a premium to the depositor. To prevent the government from forcing this silver currency upon the people, the right to make payments in it was restricted as above noticed; but to go further, and to prevent the mints from coining more than was needed, the purchase and coinage of the silver was placed under the control of the Secretary of the United States Treasury. The law went into operation at the date fixed, and the supply of coin was very acceptable to the people.

The continued active operation of the mint is, however, producing an excess of these coins. The quantity of silver coined at the mint and branches, under the law of 1853, has been as follows:—

	Philadelphia. Pieces.	New Orleans. Pieces.	S. Francisco. Pieces.	Total pieces.	Value.
Dollars	335,250	200,000	15,000	550,250	$ 550,250
Half dollars	15,038,208	22,440,000	1,099,950	38,578,158	19,289,079
Quarter do.	55,685,220	5,940,000	961,400	62,586,620	13,146,655
Dimes	31,838,010	6,030,000	120,000	37,988,010	3,798,801
Half dimes	36,495,020	9,226,000		45,721,020	2,286,051
3-cent pieces	16,314,000	720,000		17,034,000	511,020
	155,705,708	44,556,000	2,196,350	202,458,058	$39,581,856

This is a curious table, inasmuch as that it indicates the large amount of silver money in the hands of the people. This coin, it will be borne in mind, is undervalued six per cent., and is a legal tender only to the extent of five dollars. These two conditions prevent its export, and also its retention by the banks. It appears, then, assuming the number of people to be thirty millions, that there are nearly seven pieces of silver coin for every soul, and in value, a dollar and thirty-three cents each person. There are more than two quarter dollars for each person; nearly three half dimes for every two persons. In addition to this small silver coin, there has been coined since 1849, $17,046,053 in one dollar gold pieces. These have not been a popular coin, however, and do not remain in circulation. The remaining coins are of a large amount, but the quantity that remains in circulation cannot be ascertained.

The main source of supply of the precious metals to the mint was, until the discovery of California gold, from abroad, through the operations of commerce. Since that event, the Pacific state has been the leading source. The Atlantic states had, however, previously supplied important sums. The quantity of domestic gold deposited at the mint, up to 1851 and since, has been as follows:—

DEPOSITS OF DOMESTIC GOLD AT MINT AND BRANCHES.

	To 1851.	1851 to 1859.	Total 1859.
Virginia	1,197,338	327,977	1,525,315
North Carolina.....	6,707,458	2,236,951	8,944,409
South Carolina	817,692	462,913	1,280,605
Georgia	6,018,603	782,270	6,800,873
Tennessee	76,574	4,337	80,911
Alabama	186,627	10,181	196,758
New Mexico.......	38,963	9,709	48,672
California..........	81.838,079	419,472,761	451,310,840
Kansas		4 172	4,172
Oregon		69,272	69,272
Other places	41,103	33,121	79,224
Total........	$46,922,437	$423,418,614	$470,841,151

This large amount, $423,418,437, of raw material of money, was supplied to the mint in the past nine years, but after supplying the money required for circulation, it flowed off to Europe as an export, in the shape of bars. The domestic silver which has been supplied to the mint, has been $23,398 received from North Carolina, for the first time, in 1859; $45,745 from Lake Superior, and $3,221,225 parted from California gold. In the past few months the Washoe mines begin to furnish supplies.

The amount of specie actually in the country cannot be ascertained with any great degree of accuracy. The amount coined, the quantity imported and exported, afford data by which to estimate it, and these estimates have been made from time to time. Taking the amounts coined, the amounts in bank, and other data, the officers in the treasury estimated the amount in the country in 1821 to be $37,000,000. The calculation, then, up to 1849, upon official figures, would be as follows:—

Specie in the country in 1821,		$37,000,000
Product of U. S. mines to 1849,		13,811,206
Imported 1821 to 1849,	242,239,061	50,811,206
Exported " "	180,596,664	61,642,397
Specie in the country in 1849,		$112,453,603

Of this amount, $43,619,000 was in the banks and $5,700,925 in the federal treasury. Of the remainder, $32,133,688 was estimated to be in circulation, and $31,000,000 in plate and ornaments. From 1849 to 1859 the amount has been as follows:—

In the country in 1849,		$112,453,603
Coinage, 1849 to 1859,		529,619,919
Supply to 1859,		$642,073,522
Import of the metals, 1849 to 1859,	78,838,864	
Export " " "	435,023,906	
Excess export,		356,185,042
In the country in 1859,		$285,888,480

This gives an increase of $173,434,877 of specie in the country in ten years, to the first of 1860. The distribution of this money was nearly as follows:—

Stock in the country,		$285,888,480
United States treasury,	$10,000,000	
In all the banks,	104,537,818	
In plate, ornaments, &c.,	50,000,000	
In general circulation,	121,350,662	
		$285,888,480

There are large sums of money and metals that come into the country in the hands of emigrants. As these are no longer a legal tender, they find their way either to the mint or to the broker for export. We may now, on this basis, ascertain the amount of money that circulates in the country, as follows:—

	1849.	1859.
Bank circulation....	$128,506,000	$193,306,818
Less notes on hand	16,427,000	18,858,289
Bank notes in circulat'n	112,079,000	174,448,529
Specie in circulation	32,133,688	121,350,662
Total mixed circulat'n	$144,212,688	$295,799,191

The specie, as we have seen, is one-third in small silver coins, and the mixed mass is largely of the precious metals. The country, as a whole, has had its specie capital, which is a "machine of trade," increased over $173,000,000 in the last ten years.

The mint operates upon the various forms of the metals brought to it, and these are of great variety, from the most delicate plates and ornaments down to base alloys, and these are all included under the general term bullion, except United States coins. The bullion is either unwrought or manufactured. The first description embraces gold dust, amalgamated cakes and balls, laminated gold, melted bars and cakes. The "dust" is the shape in which it is derived by washing in North Carolina, Georgia, South Carolina, Virginia, and various states, besides California. In South America, Russia, and elsewhere, amalgamated gold is that which has been procured by the use of quicksilver, which combines with it, forming a lump. Laminated gold is that which is combined with silver, and derived mostly from Central America. Bars and cakes of six inches in length, and from one-half to one inch in breadth and thickness, are the forms into which the metal is cast at the mines. A bar of fine gold, six inches long, three wide, and one and a half thick, would weigh two hundred and seventy-five ounces, and its value would be five thousand nine hundred dollars. These are mostly the forms of unwrought gold received at the mint. The manufactured is mostly jewelry, plate, and coin. The first mentioned is received at the mint in every variety of article into the manufacture of which gold enters. These are of every form and fashion and degree of fineness. The value of all depends upon the quantity of pure gold in them, and this requires to be extracted by the melters' and assayers' art. The range of fineness of most jewelry is 300 to 600, or from 1-3 to 2-3 the value of coin of the same weight. In other words, where coin is 94 cts. per dwt., jewelry is worth 31 to 60 cts. the dwt. A good deal of "fair" jewelry is found to be worth 4 to 10 cts. the dwt. All this mass of metal must, by the melters and refiners, be reduced to a uniform material, containing the exact proportion of alloy allowed by the law. They are then in the shape of bars, twelve inches long, half inch thick, and from one to one and a half in breadth, according to the size of the coin to be struck. They are subjected to a test to see if they are of the legal fineness. They are then annealed, or heated to a red heat. This is to soften them for rolling, which is done into long thin strips by the power of a steam engine. These strips are then passed through plates of the hardest steel, by which they are "drawn" to their proper thickness. This being done, they are by a steam press cut into "planchets" or pieces of the exact size of the coin wanted. This "press" cuts one hundred and sixty per minute. The strip remaining full of holes is rolled up and sent back to the melting pot to be reformed into a bar. The planchets are then cleaned, annealed and whitened, and their weights accurately adjusted. They are then placed in a tube, which slides them one by one into a steel collar, in which they fit. The piece is then instantly pressed on both sides by the dies, and is instantly pushed away with perfect impressions on both sides, to be followed as promptly by another piece. The "dies" that make these impressions are of alabaster work. The devices are first cut in soft steel, those parts being sunk which are raised on the coin. This "original die" is then hardened, and is used to impress a piece of soft steel, which is then like a coin with the figures raised, and is called a "nub." This being again hardened, is used to impress dies, with which the coining is done, and a pair of them will do two weeks' work. The coining presses are of sizes proportionate to the work. That which impresses a half dime is a toy compared with the massive structure required for a dollar. The dollar and half dollar are struck at the rate of sixty per minute, the quarter dollar seventy-five, and the dime and half dime ninety per minute.

INSURANCE.

CHAPTER I.

FIRE—MARINE—LIFE.

When industry and commerce began, in modern times, to develop themselves, after the "age of chivalry" was gone, capital augmented itself in the hands of individuals, for the prosecution of various enterprises. It soon became evident, however, that the capital in these employments was exposed to entire loss from the accidents of fire, storms, and other vicissitudes, over which the owner had no control, and which his utmost foresight or sagacity could not prevent. This fact was a drawback upon enterprise, since every undertaking involved the chance of total ruin to the projectors; but when the commercial spirit became more largely developed, in the fifteenth century, some of the inventive spirits of that age devised the principle of insurance, by which a possible loss would be divided among a great number of persons, in such a manner that each would feel it but in a small degree. The individual merchant would thus be enabled to embark in his adventures secure from ruinous accidents. The principle of insurance thus devised was that of "average," or an application of the law of chances, which, it was discovered, obey certain rules. Nothing is more uncertain than winds and weather, or the accidents of fire, which occur in the face of the utmost care to prevent them. Births and deaths, and many other contingencies, seem to obey no law whatever, yet, taken in great numbers, it is found that the average that occurs in a given time is almost certain. If we look at single families, we find that some are all boys, others all girls, and many are of both sexes, without any apparent proportion. Yet the census returns of all civilized countries show that there are twenty-two males for every twenty-one females; and that, notwithstanding the uncertainty of death, this proportion will hold good through the lives of generations. The number of houses burned in a year, in any given locality, obeys the same law of average as do all the accidents of life. The number of ships engaged in any trade, that are lost, comes under the same rule. To fix the rate of average, however, a very large scale of experience is necessary, and the rate of premium is adjusted on the basis of the average. Thus, if there are forty ships engaged in a particular trade, and of them one is lost every year, then the chance of loss is one to forty, and the owner of the ship insured should pay one-fortieth part, to cover his risk, exclusive of the sums required for the expenses and profits of the insurers. Upon this principle the whole community came, as it were, to be responsible for the losses of individuals, and commerce received an impulse in consequence, since enterprises could be undertaken with more confidence. Toward the close of the seventeenth century, the same principle was applied to fire risks, and any description of property came to be protected from loss by the payment of a rate of insurance which experience showed, properly improved, would cover the average losses. Some half a century later, the principle was applied to life insurance, by which a person, on the payment of a certain sum annually, at a rate fixed by the largest experience, will insure to his heirs the sum covered by the amount he pays.

These three descriptions of insurance have flourished greatly in the United States in the last fifty years—the marine and fire risks particularly. Before the formation of the present government, insurance in this country seems to have been confined to individual underwriters, who took risks in their own names. In 1792, their was however, incorporated in Philadelphia, the Insurance Company of North America; in 1799, the Providence Company, at Providence; in 1806, the Eagle Company, of New York, and some were chartered at Boston. All these companies were organized as stock companies, and are, with many more, still in existence. The fire insurance of the country has naturally grown more than either of the other branches, since every citizen in the country is more or less interested in protection against fire. The immense quantities of goods that are sent from the factories and merchants, to be distributed in the interior, and all the produce which seeks a market, require protection against the accidents of fire, as well as those of internal transportation. The multiplication of houses and stores, with their contents, in all parts of the country, involves a growing necessity for insurance; and this every prudent man effects, not only to protect his own property from loss, but as a means of credit. The credit system, on which so much of the business of the country is transacted, makes it necessary that the utmost security should be given to the goods sold, and insurance is insisted on very generally by the sellers. A man who does not keep his goods insured has far less standing than one who does. The object of being insured is, of course, safety. The premium is paid annually, in the hope of receiving back the amount of loss in case of fire. At the same time, the insurer seeks to get this done at as low a rate as possible; nevertheless, there is a point below which the premium cannot be reduced without involving the solvency of the company. The law of average fixes the rate which the company must charge, in order that its income, improved at compound interest, shall suffice to meet the liability it undertakes; but this charge is "loaded" with a sum to meet profit and expenses. The great competition among companies guarantees that the charges shall be kept at a low point, and inducements are sometimes held out, of lower rates, to attract business. There are three modes of organization of insurance companies; these are the stock companies, the mutual companies, and the mixed companies. The first mentioned have a capital subscribed by any number of persons, who become incorporated in a company. This capital is a guarantee that the company is able to pay if losses occur. The capital must be safely invested in such a manner that it can be called in, if wanted. They then issue policies on certain terms, at certain rates of premium, dividing all the profits of the business among the stockholders. The premiums paid in, if fixed on sound principles and well employed, will generally suffice to make good all the liabilities until the reserve, or surplus profits retained, have grown into a guarantee fund. Out of this fact, resulting from experience, grew the mutual system of insurance. This was contrived after the "great fire" in London, 1666, and was introduced in New York after the great fire of 1835. By this system the company has no capital—the premiums paid in become the fund from which all losses are paid. The rates are charged on a sound principle, and the aggregate improved at compound interest. After the expenses and losses are paid, a certain portion of the surplus remains to increase the assets of the company, and the balance is divided among the insured according to the amounts they have paid. Thus the profits, instead of going to stockholders, go back to those who paid them into the company. This system, on its face, is by far the most economical in its action and beneficial in its results. It has been objected to it, however, that in a new company, with the small business incident to beginners, before there has been any accumulation of profits, the security is insufficient. To meet this objection, among others, mixed companies are sometimes started. They have a capital paid in, and this draws dividends from their first profits, to a certain extent, the insured getting a share of the remainder of the profits. Where the business is skilfully conducted on sound principles, the mutual system seems to command the most advantages. The stock companies assert that nothing is gained by the insured paying in money, in the shape of a premium, for the chance of getting it back again as profits. The object is, however, security; while the funds are in the hands of the company, the liabilities are well covered, and they are not divided until replaced by new accumulation. In the case of the stock companies, the accumulations are paid over to stockholders, the insured getting nothing. In some of these companies, the stockholders get their whole capital back every four years! yet the means of the company do not grow. The funds of a company require to be invested in securities of the utmost safety, and these, for the most part, only give the lowest rates of interest. It is only when a sum sufficient to meet all incurred claims is set apart in the best securities that can be had, that a company is justified in seeking, for the remainder of its means, second-class securities that give a higher rate of interest. The mutual system has been a favorite in some states, but in New York its reputation has been sadly damaged by the explosions of fraudulent companies. Thus in 1849, a general law for the organization of insurance companies was passed, and under it, forty-two companies were organized and reported in 1853. Of these, thirty-three have gone down, under circumstances of outrage and wrong inflicted upon citizens, which have gone far to destroy the reputation of that class of companies.

In Massachusetts the mutual principle has been more successful than the stock organization. The amount at risk in the former is $214,725,821, and in the latter it is $132,854,841. The movement does not appear to be entirely safe, however. There are sixty-nine mutual fire companies in the interior of Massachusetts, most of them so small as to make the policies of little value, since to pay losses, assessments would be required, and these are fatal to the standing of the companies. The losses by fire in Massachusetts were, last year, $1,241,669; of this, two-thirds was borne by the stock companies, and it is a sum double the losses of the previous year.

The laws of New York, where the largest amount of insurance has been done, indicate the changes which have taken place in the course of business. Up to the revision of the state constitution in 1846, it was usual to grant special charters for the incorporation of companies, and fire, marine, and life powers were often granted to a single company. In 1849 a general insurance law was passed, by which any number of persons exceeding fifteen might organize into a company for fire and marine insurance, but it was expressly ordered that no company insuring lives should take any other kind of risks. In 1853 another act was passed, by which it was ordered that no fire company should be incorporated to take any risks but fire and internal navigation. In 1836, when the great fire in New York had swept down nearly, if not quite all the existing companies, there were started eleven mutual companies, that still exist. In 1837, four more were started, and the number was increased by four more up to 1849. Under the act of that year, forty-two were started, of which nine remain. The mutual fire companies now in New York state compare as follows:—

	No.	Assets.	Cash on hand.
1853,	62	$11,621,914	$766,284
1859,	28	4,793,506	161,802
1860,	27	4,128,101	

This shows the decline of the mutual principle in New York; and a number of those now existing show such returns as point to winding up. The stock companies, on the other hand, showing a rapid increase, are most of them in the city of New York, while the mutual companies are all in the interior. Of the existing stock companies, twenty-one were organized prior to 1838; under the act of 1849, thirty-eight; and under that of 1853, thirty-seven were organized, making ninety-six now in operation, with a capital of $20,007,000. Of these companies, eleven, with a capital of $1,900,000, were organized in 1859. In addition to the New York state companies doing business in New York, there are companies chartered in other states, and English companies, doing business within the state. Formerly, or up to 1836, foreign companies could do business in New York by paying a tax of ten per cent. of the premiums. This assessed them about $2,369 per annum. The tax was then reduced to two per cent., which, in the ten years ending in 1846, amounted to $3,183 per annum, being an increase in amount of $813 per annum arising from one-fifth of the tax. The capitals and premiums of the New York fire companies were as follows:—

	No.	Capital.	Premiums.	Risks.
1844,	20	$5,710,000	$837,000	$119,571,000
1859,	92	19,407,000	7,692,635	701,215,624
1860,	96	20,007,060	8,032,493	719,267,809

In the year 1845 again occurred a large fire, which, burning the lower end of Broadway, and a large amount of property, swept into bankruptcy many of the fire companies. The law of 1849 favored the establishment of new ones, causing great progress in the fire companies in New York in the last eleven years. This large and increasing business has been of great profit to the companies, as appears from the handsome dividends declared. In the last eight years, the twenty-one companies organized prior to 1838 have declared dividends ranging from 106 to 236 per cent. The average is 142 per cent., or 18 per cent. per annum on the stock. The dividends of the other companies are not so large, but they show a handsome investment. Some of the companies are mixed; these declare dividends in cash on the stock, perhaps 5 per cent. semi-annual, and 20 or 30 per cent. in scrip on the earned premiums of the participating policies. All the policies are not participating. The plans are much diversified. The policies participate to a greater or less extent, as declared upon their face. The principle is this: if the year's business is $100,000, and of this, $40,000 is found to be profits, one-fourth of this will go to the stockholders, and there remains $30,000 for the participating policies. These policies may compose a greater or less proportion of the business. Under the supposition that it is six-tenths, or $60,000, then the dividend is called 50 per cent.

The law of 1853 permitted companies of other states to do business if possessed of the *active* capital required of companies in New York, and on compliance with certain conditions prescribed. Under this permission, many companies of Rhode Island, Connecticut, Philadelphia, New Jersey, Massachusetts, and Georgia have transacted business to a considerable extent.

In New England the insurance business has taken dimensions second only to those of New York. The Ætna Company of Hartford is one of the most successful companies of the world. It was founded in 1819. It has a capital of $3,000,000, and its whole assets are 1867, $4,478,000; while its risks are $285,000,000 on fire, and $46,000,000 on inland navigation. This company, in the last year, added $500,000 to its capital from accumulated profits, and divided $200,000 cash.

The amount insured against fire by these companies, the annexed table gives at nearly $2,000,000,000. The companies of other states than those mentioned, and of which we have no returns, would add, probably, $500,000,000 to this amount; and there are some risks, probably $50,000,000, taken by the English companies doing business here. This vast sum of property insured against fire, is the growth of the last fifty years, and we may compare it with the insurances of some of the European countries. Thus, in Great Britain, the fire risks amounted to $3,905,432,665, or double those of the annexed table; in France, the fire risks are $6,500,000,000; in Germany, the fire risks are $4,075,000,000. Thus the United States have already a fair proportion of property covered by policies, and the system extends itself gradually.

In New York the company having the largest risks is the Home, of $51,045,691. If we bring together the returns of the leading companies of the several states, as far as returns are obtained, we have the following figures:—

CAPITAL, PREMIUM, AND RISKS, OF FIRE COMPANIES IN THE UNITED STATES.

	No.	Capital.	Assets, including capital.	Cash premiums.	Fire risks.
New York Stock	96	$20,007,000	$26,323,384	$6,421,342	$719,267,809
" Mutual	28	..	4,793,506	..	87,310,910
Massachusetts	99	6,353,100	..	1,266,183	347,580,662
New Hampshire	23	..	..	33,000	39,784,084
Providence	6	900,000	1,519,688	552,153	26,648,143
Connecticut	12	4,550,000	5,364,686	3,715,320	279,322,184
Philadelphia	10	2,908,181	6,510,601	1,913,417	139,229,374
Jersey City	1	150,000	179,713	36,109	5,231,061
Peoria, Ill	1	300,000	363,995	89,375	6,806,377
Augusta, Ga	1	375,000	952,588	194,407	7,000,000
Charleston	2	833,558	..	472,000	98,000,800
New Orleans	9	4,500,000	6,738,031	2,910,000	221,100,000
			$52,746,192	$17,603,306	$1,977,281,404

The Illinois company has $1,572,387 marine risks, in addition.

The losses by fire in the United States in 1859, where the damage was $20,000 and upward, amounted to $16,058,000, and the estimated total losses incurred by the underwriters was $22,000,000—burned up in a single year. The losses above $20,000 amounted in six years, ending with 1859, to $98,197,000; and the total estimate was $127,500,000—an enormous amount to be destroyed. This amount is apparently borne by the insurance offices, but it is really paid by all those who get insurances. It is their aggregate premium which forms the fund which pays not only this loss, but the large profits derived by the stockholders in insurance companies. The companies contribute nothing toward it. The extent of their services is to collect the premiums from the insured, and, after paying salaries and expenses, meet the losses and divide the surplus among the shareholders of the companies. This service is, of course, an indispensable one. It brings all the property of the community to guarantee individuals against serious losses.

Marine insurance differs from both fire and life insurance, both in the mode of transacting the business, and in the diversified nature of the risks against which security is sought. The great emporium of marine insurance for the commercial world is London, and it is there done through the medium of individual underwriters, who congregate at Lloyd's, which may be considered as the focus of the commerce of the world. There is not a seaport of any consequence, where it has not an agent to give intelligence of all departures and arrivals, ships spoken, wrecks, accidents, weather, and every item that affects navigation. In this way they are supplied with information from all quarters, and almost all vessels that float are registered, with every minute particular in regard to them; and vessels of all nations are more or less thus insured. In the United States, marine insurance was the first that engaged the attention of the eastern states, and it has, as a matter of course, been confined mostly to the great cities. In New York there are seven companies incorporated by special charters before 1849; one of these is at Buffalo. There are also seven which are organized under the act of 1849; of these, two were started in 1859. There are no companies organized in other states or foreign countries, that do business in New York, none having complied with the provisions of the law of 1859; and a fine of $500 each offence is imposed upon those who transact business without being authorized. The fourteen marine companies of New York have assets, $20,932,067, and received premiums during the year, $13,730,438; losses and expenditures during the year, $9,446,293. In the marine companies, after the profits of the year are made up, certificates are issued to each of the insured for his proportion of the profits; these bear interest, and have a market value. When the funds accumulate, these certificates are called in and paid off. As an example, the Atlantic Mutual was organized in 1842. The profits, as they were earned, were yearly paid to the insured in the shape of the certificates. Thus, a dividend of thirty-five per cent. was declared Dec. 31st, 1859, and, for this, certificates bearing interest were issued. It was then found, after paying all expenses and interest on the outstanding certificates, that the reserve fund of the company amounted to $3,809,250 after paying off the certificates issued previous to 1858; and it was resolved to pay off those of that year. The whole account stood thus:—

Profits, July 1, 1842, to June 1, 1860,	$10,428,470
Certificates redeemed previous to 1858,	6,619,220
Net earnings on hand, Jan. 1,	$3,809,250

The dividends of scrip of the marine insurance companies of New York, as shown by the official returns, were as follows:—

	Capital and assets.	Premiums marked off.	Scrip rate per cent. 1859	1860
Atlantic	$6,002,732	$4,497,468	40	35
Anchor	372,559	49,127	—	—
Commercial	928,783	603,571	40	15
Great Western	3,396,258	2,801,664	20	10
Mercantile	1,125,102	894,775	20	11
New York	1,002,637	812,519	35	12
Orient	1,316,552	566,092	21	20
Pacific	1,005,966	828,655	43	30
Union	1,647,181	581,544	45	36
Columbian	1,264,443	755,142	12	—
Sun	1,914,230	1,025,167	30	—
Neptune	268,161	(new) 48,133	—	—
Washington	150,201	(new) —	—	—
			264	169
Average			33	21⅛

The totals and average are exclusive of the Columbian and Sun, which have not yet issued scrip.

In Massachusetts, the marine risks for the past year were $101,972,974; of this, $45,545,105 was in stock companies. The marine losses reached $3,905,186.

A large proportion of the risks taken in the eastern cities, is for internal navigation, and the loss by steam and sail in 1859 was $1,020,100; about two-thirds sail. The aggregate marine losses are very nearly $40,000,000 for the year.

Life insurance has taken large proportions of late years, and the amounts now at risk involve many millions. In 1825, the first company chartered, the Massachusetts Hospital and Life Insurance Company, commenced its business. In 1829 the New York Life Insurance and Trust Company was chartered. Though of the highest standing, and possessing fully the public confidence, both of these institutions found the trust business authorized by their charter to be more attractive than life assurance; and for several years neither of these companies has made any effort to increase the number of its policies. Most of the remaining companies in this country are of recent date, and very few of the number have seen the period of half a generation, yet the magnitude of this business is such that the following facts appear in the reports: In New York there are twelve companies doing business. The oldest of these was organized in 1830; two in 1859; and two more were established in the present year, 1860. These companies have a capital, with accumulation, amounting to $12,090,815, and the outstanding risks are $72,147,436; the annual premiums are $2,762,366. There are a number of companies of other states doing a life business in New York, and three English companies. These are required to comply with the New York law of 1853 in relation to security. This requires that a sum of $100,000 shall be lodged with the insurance department for the security of the policy holders.

In life insurance the principle is based on the average continuance of life, than which nothing is more uncertain as regards individuals or a limited number of persons. Nevertheless, in a large number, the average of those who arrive at a certain age is ascertained with much precision. To ascertain this, Mr. Milson, of the Sun Life Office of England, constructed a table at Carlisle from observations made upon 10,000 persons born nearly at the same time; the number of these that were alive in each subsequent year, until the whole were extinct. These are called the "Carlisle tables," and are supposed to give pretty accurately the average English life, and they are used mostly in this country, although it is supposed that life here is really shorter than in England. The tables show that of 10,000 born at the same time, 4000 lived to be 56. The number of those who died at 66 was 124. Hence the probability that a person now 56 will die in his 66th year is as 124:4000. The probability of life being ascertained, it remains to find what sum per annum a person must pay in order to obtain a fixed sum, say $1,000, for his heirs at his death. It is to be borne in mind that insurance creates nothing; all that it does for the individual is to take his money, and improve it at compound interest into a sum that it agrees to pay his heirs. The time of payment is the uncertain part, and this in a company where great numbers are insured, is fixed by the principle of average. Suppose a person 35 years old wants to be insured for $1,000. The tables say his expectation of life is 31 years. The company assume that as a fact, and with them it is an agreement to pay $1,000 at the end of 31 years. What sum paid annually and improved at 4 per cent. compound interest will come to $1,000 in 31 years? This would be $17, but the company add to or load this with a certain per-centage to defray expenses and for profit, and the charge will probably be $27. This amount per annum for 31 years will, without interest, amount to $839, and improved at 6 per cent., will amount to $1,560 in 31 years. Thus, if the individual lives the whole time, and improves his own money, he will have 50 per cent. more than the company agrees to pay. The company have many sources of profit, however. The first is that they put the expectation of life lower than the fact. This is necessary in young companies. Thus, if among 10,000 persons, 4,000 live to be 56, it will not do to take that as the rule for 200 persons; but a less rate must be assumed, and a higher charge made. If the company's business increases, so that they get out 10,000 policies, they will have the full benefit of the average, or, in other words, the insured pay more than they ought. In the second place, the company calculates the premiums improved at 4 per cent., when they get really from 6 to 7. This makes the amount at the end of a year's time 50 per cent. more than the estimate. In the third place, the calculation of expectation of lives is for ordinary lives, whereas the lives taken are only those carefully selected. Those that are less likely to die are only chosen. Hence, this makes the rate of premium higher than the tables justify. In the fourth place, the profits of a company are increased by the forfeiting of policies by persons who do not pay up. There is also a profit when a policy is purchased from those who surrender. All those sources together tend to make the profits far larger than the simple compounding of the rates indicated in the tables would show. In the mutual system it is claimed that these profits are paid over with the amount insured at the end of the time, or at the death of the insured. There is no limit, however, on the expenses, which are an item in making up profits. It is apparent, from all these facts, that the money does not accumulate with the company faster than it would if the individual improved it himself, since the advantages of the company, in lapse of policies, etc., only offset the expenses they incur. The advantage is in the security offered for the repayment of the money. The idea that money will grow by the operation of interest any faster in the hands of a company than in those of an individual is a fallacy, which was some years since applied to building associations. These drew in large amounts of money in small payments from numbers of persons who were to obtain house lots, through some magical mode of making money grow. Disappointment generally attended them. In the case of the life companies, however, the contingency exists that the person insured may not live to accumulate his money. He *may* die as soon as he has made his first payment, in which case the operation is a good one for his family. This is the chance feature which is the great attraction, since the payment once made, there is the certainty that the family will not be destitute in case of death. It is only those in the best of health, however, that can avail themselves of this opportunity for security, since the lives in any degree doubtful are rejected.

In Massachusetts there are five life companies, which have issued 7,007 policies, and the risks are $17,408,713. The Mutual Benefit Company of New Jersey has outstanding risks, $22,559,177, and the Connecticut Mutual, $22,701,204.

The largest life company in the world is the Gotha, of Germany; it has 15,000 policy holders. The united German companies have insured for $35,000,000. The Equitable, of London, has the largest accumulated capital, having been in operation more than ninety years. It received, during a period of eighty-six years, premiums and dues to the amount of $95,338,180, which accumulated at compound interest to such an extent, that the company has been enabled to pay out $126,683,158 to families of deceased members and other policy holders; and for expenses, $2,091,180, retaining in hand an accumulated fund of $44,000,000 to meet running policies, and claims outstanding to the amount of $70,500,000. During one period of ten years, the Equitable paid out about $40,000,000. Its annual income is $2,850,000, and the number of policy holders about 5,200. The profits are divided among the oldest 5,000, in the order of their admission. The amount of life insurance effected in great Britain, is $750,-000,000.

The usual method adopted by the Life Insurance companies has been to base their estimates of the cost of insurance on the Carlisle tables, which are explained on a previous page, and taking their statement of the sum, which, placed at compound interest at four per cent., would, on the average of duration of human life, produce $1,000; add to that a "loading" of a per-centage sufficient to cover commissions, expenses of rent, salaries, &c., failures, depreciation of stocks, and the prevalence of any fatal epidemic. These several items are supposed to be fully covered by an addition of about thirty-one per cent. to the amount given by the Carlisle tables. Thus, by these tables, a healthy man of thirty years old could be insured safely at $17.50 per annum, that sum compounded at four per cent. producing $1,000 at the average duration of life. The additional "load" of thirty-one per cent. makes the amount $22.92; and, in order to be safe, the mutual companies charge from $23.02 to $23.60 per $1,000 for insurance to a man of thirty years.

But further and more careful observation has demonstrated that the Carlisle tables are inaccurate, the error being largely in favor of the companies; the average chances of life under forty-five years in selected lives being at the present day nearly forty per cent. better than those tables show. There is also no difficulty in this country in compounding the amount received for premiums at six per cent., and but little at seven per cent.; so that there is a gain of at least fifty per cent. from this source. Added to this, is the large per-centage of gain from the lapsing of policies. The Mutual Insurance companies might therefore make their terms considerably lower than they now are, and still, if they were managed judiciously, retain a sufficient reserve to reinsure all their patrons. But most of them pay very large commissions to their agents, the competition being very strong, and expend large sums in fitting up elegant offices, paying high salaries, &c. The joint-stock companies, which make dividends only to their stockholders, and none to the insured, insure at much lower rates, some of them even putting the rates of insurance to persons under forty-five years below those of the Carlisle tables. The following table shows the comparative rates of the two classes of companies:—

COMPARATIVE RATES OF DOMESTIC LIFE INSURANCE.

I.—PARTICIPATION, OR MUTUAL SCALE FOR INSURANCE OF ONE THOUSAND DOLLARS.

AGE.	Knickerbocker Mut. Life.	Manhattan.	New York Mutual.	Mutual Life of N. Y.	New England Mut., Boston	New York Life.	Connecticut Mutual.	Mutual Benefit, N.J.	Girard, Philadelphia	American Life & Trust, Philad'a.
20........	17.26	17.80	17.30	19.89	17.30	17.70	17.30	17.70	17.70	17.70
25........	19.85	20.40	19.89	19.89	19.80	20.40	20.40	20.40	20.40	20.40
30........	23.08	23.60	23.02	23.02	22.70	23.60	23.50	23.60	23.60	23.60
35........	26.82	27.30	26.87	26.87	26.50	27.50	27.50	27.50	27.50	27.50
40........	31.71	32.00	31.73	31.73	31.50	32.00	32.00	32.00	32.00	32.00
45........	37.76	37.40	38.04	38.04	38.00	37.30	38.00	37.30	37.30	37.30
50........	45.91	45.40	46.42	46.42	47.00	46.00	47.70	46.00	46.00	46.00
55........	57.75	57.80	57.58	57.58	59.40	57.80	59.40	57.80	57.80	57.80
60........	74.30	74.60	..	..	76.40	..	..	..	..	70.00

II.—NON-PARTICIPATION, OR JOINT-STOCK SCALE FOR INSURANCE OF ONE THOUSAND DOLLARS.

AGE.	Knickerbocker non-participation	Manhattan.	N. Y. Life.	N. Y. Life & Trust.	Ætna Life, Hartford.	American Life & Trust, Philad'a.	Baltimore Life.	Conn. General.	Universal Life, N. Y.	Travelers' Life & Acc'd't Hartford.
20........	15.54	16.00	14.14	16.50	14.80	14.70	16.50	13.70	..	12.16
25........	17 96	18.40	16.44	19.00	17.10	17.00	19.00	15.30	14.92	13.86
30........	20.77	21.30	19.20	21.90	19.90	19.60	21.90	17.42	17.02	16.06
35........	24.14	24.60	22.20	25.30	23.00	22.90	25.30	20.50	19.78	18.92
40........	28.54	28.80	26.28	29.70	27.30	26.70	29.60	23.98	23.47	22.75
45........	33.98	33.70	30.72	34.70	32.00	31.00	34.70	29.80	28.48	28.04
50........	41.32	40.90	37.68	42.10	39.10	38.40	42.10	37.51	35.38	35.18
55........	51.97	52.10	48.60	53.60	50.60	48.20	53.50	..	..	44.80
60........	66.87	67.20	..	67.50	66.20	58.40	66.80	..	..	57.74

Within the past four or five years most of the Life Insurance companies have granted what are termed *Ten years non-forfeitable policies*, in which the insurance premiums are paid in ten annual payments, and the policy is paid at death; and when, from any cause, the premiums are paid for only a portion of the time, the party, for whose benefit the insurance is effected, receives an amount proportioned to the number of payments which have been made. By this plan it is claimed that a man can effect an insurance for life, and bring the payments for it within the most active business portion of his life, when the premiums can be paid with least inconvenience to himself. The following table shows the rates of insurance on this plan of several Mutual and Joint-Stock companies.

TEN YEARS NON-FORFEITABLE PLAN FOR ONE THOUSAND DOLLARS INSURANCE.

Age.	Mutual System.			Joint-Stock System.			
	Mutual Life of N. Y.	Connecticut Mutual.	Mutual Benefit, N.J.	Ætna Life, of Hartford (without profits).	Connecticut General.	Universal Life, N. Y.	Travelers' of Harf'd, Life Department.
20............	41.95	42.00	42.10	30.00	29.02	. .	26.14
30............	46.51	52.65	52.34	38.40	36.22	36.44	32.66
40............	57.44	64.61	64.78	48.80	45.70	45.51	42.44
50............	72.31	82.35	79.72	62.00	61.73	59.19	57.90

Several new features have been adopted by the new companies organized during the past two or three years. One of these, adopted by the Universal Life Insurance Co., is the insurance of invalids, or persons of impaired health or constitution, on the payment of a larger premium than that of selected lives, the rate being fixed by the report of the medical examiner. Another, is the reduction of the rate in first-class cases to that of an age two, three, or five years younger, and the advance in doubtful cases to a corresponding degree, above the normal rate for their age.

Accident insurance, though no novelty in England—companies having been organized there in 1848 and 1849—had never been attempted here till 1864, when the Travelers' Insurance Company of Hartford was chartered by the Legislature of Conn. It had a capital of $500,000, and its surplus in October, 1866, was $242,000. At first it confined itself to insuring against death or disability from accidents, paying a weekly compensation to those totally disabled, or a sum agreed to the heirs, in case of the death from accident of the insured party, or both, where the policy was issued with that provision.

At the end of two years, it organized a department of general life insurance, on the joint-stock plan, and put its rates of premium lower than the other companies; which it was able to do by having lighter expenses, its accident business defraying the larger share of expenses, and by paying smaller commissions; while it scrutinized very carefully the chances of life of all applicants, and rejected many whom other companies received. It combined with this, when desired, at a small additional premium, weekly compensation for total disability caused by accident.

Other Accident Insurance companies have since been formed, one of them on the mutual plan; but none of the others have combined a general life policy with accident insurance. The Accident Insurance companies sell tickets of insurance from the danger of railroad and steamboat travel, viz., from accident or injury from the destruction or partial injury of the vehicle in which the passenger is travelling, at a given rate per day. The ordinary accident policy pays a weekly compensation for all injuries from any accident producing a temporary total disability, however it may have occurred, or a fixed sum on death induced by accident, or both, as may be provided in the policy, according to the premium paid.

The application of the insurance principle to other objects has recently been attempted. Thus we have one or more Live-Stock Insurance companies, protecting the owners of live-stock against losses by debt or theft, based on the experience of English companies, where this description of insurance has been conducted for fifty years; a company to insure the owners of steam boilers against their explosion; and a Fidelity Insurance company, to furnish bonds for men who are appointed to positions of trust and responsibility.

IMMIGRATION.

CHAPTER I.

GENERAL MIGRATION — COLONIES AND UNITED STATES.

At the date of the last national census, in 1850, more than one-tenth part of all the inhabitants of the United States were foreign born, that is, one soul in every ten had been born in a foreign land. Since that census, viz.: from 1850 to the close of 1859, two million five hundred and fifty thousand more aliens have arrived in this country, which, added to the number then reported as foreign born, would make very nearly one foreigner out of four citizens at the date of 1859. The natives have, however, since progressed in numbers, as have also the emigrants, and the progeny of these latter will class as "natives" in the forthcoming census.

The term "native" has been used to distinguish the born citizen from the newly arrived foreigner, as well as the former from the "red man," who was also an emigrant in the view of the lost races that preceded him, and of which monumental traces alone remain in evidence that they ever existed. The history of the human race, adopting the Mosaic account, is a history of migration. Twice has the race comprised only a single family, occupying a single point on the earth's surface, and twice has it spread in all directions, forming nations and founding empires. The antediluvian world was swept away by the deluge, and all traces of the race of Adam had been washed away by the obliterating waters from the earth's surface when the ark gave up its freight. From its door migration was resumed, and three continents owe their populations to the several sons of the patriarch. Asia, Africa, and Europe were settled by Shem, Ham, and Japhet and their descendants, who have stamped their characteristics upon each. From that day to the present the same recurring circumstances have from time to time produced the same results. As each locality became overcrowded by increase, the most adventurous sallied forth in quest of new homes, which, in their turn, filled, and overflowed into some more distant region. These successive waves rolling on until the remotest shores of each continent were occupied, were succeeded by more formidable hosts of armed invaders, who came, sword in hand, to dispossess occupiers and seize accumulated wealth. Successive empires have gone down before these barbarian hordes, and modern Europe has but lately recovered from the shock that attended the fall of the Roman empire amid a deluge of barbarians. With the growth of modern civilization migration has no longer a destructive character. It seeks to build up by bringing industry in aid of natural resources, rather than to destroy by seizing what others have produced. It is more steady, penetrating, and effective in its commercial character—having industry for a means and prosperity for an object—than in its old turbulent military form, plundering by force and leaving desolation in its train.

The British Islands were the last subjects of European incursions. The Britons, of mythic origin, were plundered by Norse enterprise, and the Saxons alternated with the Danes in dominating the nation on the withdrawal of the Romans, to be in their turn subjected to the Normans. Since then 800 years have been spent in amalgamating the races and in peopling the islands. Even at that date the adventurous Norsemen, in search of the whale, had discovered the new continent and formed a colony on what is now known as Newfoundland. It required long centuries, however, in that barbarous age, for the people to struggle successfully against the effects of feudal oppression, civil wars, and their consequences, famine and plague. Nevertheless, progress was made and commerce a good deal developed, when, at the close of the fifteenth century, the discovery of the West Indies by Columbus was followed by an influx of the precious metals into Europe, giving a renewed impetus to industry and enterprise. The Spanish were attracted by gold, and the commercial Dutch by the desire to found colonies, and their example was followed by the English and French. In both these cases, however, the desire of civil and religious freedom was a powerful incentive to the emigrants. These motives were more strongly developed when the English revolution began to operate in the first half of the 17th century. The new world was then looked upon as the place of refuge, and Cromwell himself, with his companions, were only prevented from migrating by the interposition of that government that they afterward overthrew. Of the four leading nations that planted colonies on this continent, the English alone became permanently successful. The Spaniards sought gold only. The French settlement of the Mississippi was more a financial bubble of Law than a movement of settlers. The Dutch had not sufficient breadth at home to sustain the undertaking; and the English necessarily absorbed the whole, with their steady industry and abiding religious faith. The numbers of the colonists were continually reinforced by new settlers, and a trade soon sprang up which gave prosperity and wealth to the provinces.

The disposition to emigrate to America gradually gained ground as the eighteenth century advanced, more particularly in Ireland and the north of Scotland, which already enjoyed the advantage of some intercourse with friends in America, and whose descriptions of it formed a strong contrast to the distress at home. Just before the Revolutionary war, this disposition to emigrate showed itself strongly. The linen weavers in the northern part of Ireland were, by the decline in that trade, induced to migrate. For the two years, 1771 and 1772, sixty-two vessels, of seventeen thousand three hundred and fifty tons, left with eighteen thousand passengers for America, paying passages seventeen dollars each. Most of these were linen weavers and farmers, possessed of property, and they carried with them so much money as to attract the notice of the government. The movement, however, continued in 1773 and extended itself to the north of Scotland, whence the highlanders migrated in great numbers. There were then no means of ascertaining the actual numbers, nor were there, as since, in existence any of those admirable arrangements by the government or private companies for the comfort and aid of emigrants. Knox, in his view of the British empire at that time, asserts that in the twelve years ending in 1775, above thirty thousand highlanders emigrated, exclusive of the lowlanders; and it was computed that there were sixty thousand highlanders citizens of the United States in 1799. In the report of the committee on the linen manufactures in the Irish Parliament in 1774, it is stated that the whole emigration from the province of Ulster was estimated at thirty thousand people, of whom ten thousand were weavers, who, with their tools and money, departed for America ; thus adding to the numbers and wealth in the new world, in the proportion that the British Islands lost from the same cause.

The breaking out of the War of Independence, naturally interrupted the communication between America and the old world; but with the return of peace, in 1783, the migration revived, notwithstanding the incredible hardships which at that time attended the transit. The shipping was little adapted to the trade, and no special laws protected the rights of the poor emigrant. As an instance of this, it is related that in September, 1784, a ship left Greenock with a large number of passengers, who had paid twenty-five dollars each for their passage. They were robbed of their chests and provisions by the master, and one hundred of them turned ashore on the Island of Rathlin, coast of Ireland. Another vessel rescued seventy-six emigrants from a desert island, where they had been turned adrift by the master of a brig, who had engaged to carry them from Dunleary, in Ireland, to Charlestown. In the same year there were great numbers landed at Baltimore, Philadelphia, and elsewhere. The movement continued with more or less vigor to the close of the century. Blodget's Statistical Manual, published in 1806, states that from 1784 to 1794, the arrivals were four thousand per annum. In the year 1794, ten thousand persons were estimated to have arrived in the United States. Adam Seybert, a member of the House of Representatives, in his "Statistical Annals," admitting the number for that year, states that so large a movement did not again occur until 1817.

When the colonies separated from the mother country, the population of the latter was, for England and Wales, 7,225,000, and about 2,000,000 for Ireland, making together 9,225,000 souls, or about one-third the number of whites now in the United States. The population of the newly formed United States in the year 1790 was 3,174,-167 whites, or about one-third the numbers in England and Wales. The founders of the nation were then not unmindful of the fact that these three millions of people, occupying 163,746,686 acres of land although possessed of a vast territory, had little else to depend upon. Capital was scarce, and manufactures had not been permitted under imperial rule, hence skilled artisans were not to be found. While all these things were indispensable to the new country, crowds of poorly paid and oppressed operatives on the other side of the Atlantic were impatient to enjoy the privileges that our new form of government held out to them. The French, German, and English troops, that returned home after the war, had not only left a portion of their numbers here as settlers, but had carried home favorable reports of the advantages to be here enjoyed. It was manifestly to the interest of the new government here to invite and encourage these settlers, at the same time to guard against possible political abuse of the privilege. The new Constitution therefore required Congress to pass uniform laws for naturalization. This was not done until April 14th, 1802, when the regulations that have since mainly continued were enacted. By that law, those aliens who were in the country prior to 1795 might be admitted to citizenship on proof of two years' continuous residence in the United States, sustaining a good moral character, and abjuring allegiance to foreign nations. Any alien arriving in the United States after the passage of the act was to comply with the following conditions:—

1. He shall, before some competent court, swear, at least three years before his admission, that it is his *bona fide* intention to renounce forever all allegiance to any sovereign state to which he was a subject.

2. He shall swear to support the Constitution of the United States.

3. Before he can be admitted he must show that he has resided within the United States five years, and within the jurisdiction of the court one year. He must also show that he has been of good moral character, and well disposed to the happiness of the United States.

4. He must renounce all titles of nobility.

The law of March 3, 1813, required that the residence of five years should have been continuous in the United States. This restriction was repealed Jan. 26, 1848. The law of May 26, 1824, reduced the term of notice of intentions from three to two years. These were the chief regulations of the federal government in relation to naturalization. Many of the states have, however, from time to time, passed laws relative to immigrants, importation of paupers, convicts, lunatics, etc. New-York and many other states have laws requiring of the owner, or master, or consignee of the passenger ship, a well secured bond to the people of the state against loss for the relief or support of such passengers. In lieu of this bond, commutation money may be paid.

The federal government having smoothed the way, the migration proceeded until unfriendly relations between the United States and Great Britain, growing out of the wars of Europe, checked intercourse. The claim enforced by Great Britain to the principle, "Once a subject always a subject," served to take from emigrants the security they sought under the American flag; and in 1806 Great Britain declared France in a state of blockade, and France retorted upon the British Isles. These proceedings being succeeded by others, compelled the United States, in 1809, to prohibit intercourse with France and Great Britain. In 1810 Napoleon annulled his decree, but Great Britain continued her vexations, seizing American seamen, and riding rough-shod over their rights. The embargo was then succeeded by the war of 1812, during which migration was very limited. In February, 1815, peace was concluded, and the stream of migration, long pent up, resumed its flow with greater force. The accommodation was, of course, limited, and the more restrained that a law of Parliament restricted the number that might be carried to the United States to one for every five tons, although one for every two tons might be carried to any other country. In the year 1817, 22,240 persons arrived in the United States, including Americans who returned home. This large migration, at a time when the business was not systematized, and when shipping was not built with a view to its accommodation, was attended with immense suffering. The attention of Congress was called to it, and a law was passed, March 2, 1819, to regulate the transportation of passengers. That act limited the number to two for every five tons of measurement, and provided for an ample allowance of food and fuel. When the famine of 1846–7 gave a new impulse to the movement, more complete laws were found requisite, and a number were passed: that of Feb. 22, 1847; March 2, 1847; May 17, 1848; March 3, 1849; and finally, March 3, 1857, the present passenger act was enacted, repealing all former laws upon the subject, and establishing the regulations now in force. This regulates the space for each passenger, the number and construction of the berths, requires a house upon deck, the ventilation of the ship, regulates the number and size of cooking-stoves, obliges the ship to furnish each passenger with food, viz.: twenty pounds bread, fifteen pounds rice, fifteen pounds oatmeal, fifteen pounds peas and beans, twenty pounds potatoes, one pint vinegar, sixty gallons water, ten pounds salt pork, ten pounds beef free of bones; this food is to be dealt out one-tenth part weekly, and if any passenger is put on short allowance, the master or owner shall pay him three dollars each day of short allowance; enforces perfect cleanliness. There are also a number of other rules in relation to the mode of carrying out and enforcing these requisitions. The laws and regulations in the United States have come in aid of the efforts of foreign governments in ameliorating the difficulties of the emigrant; and these laws have, no doubt, tended to swell the numbers of the passengers.

The first authentic accounts of the numbers of immigrants, therefore, commenced in 1820, under the law of 1819. These accounts have been continued down to the present moment with great regularity, and the aggregate results are seen in the following table, showing the birth-places of the emigrants that have arrived in forty years:—

NUMBER OF ALIENS ARRIVED IN THE UNITED STATES.

From	1820 to 1835.	1836 to 1845.	1846 to 1850.
England	21,595	10,327	23,608
Ireland	50,304	29,430	138,892
Scotland	5,658	680	3,221
Wales	347	115	1,154
United Kingdom	108,362	405,481	613,597
Great Britain	186,266	446,033	780,472
France	26,638	51,488	53,588
Spain	3,565	2,232	1,153
Portugal	891	202	466
Belgium	33	1,008	4,083
Prussia	433	13,321	2,771
Germany	52,868	197,729	326,667
Holland	1,757	2,631	6,402
Denmark	467	959	365
Sweden & Norway	509	5,521	9,168
Poland	164	310	21
Russia	325	263	329
Turkey	23	31	33
Switzerland	6,020	5,155	1,597
Greece	29	50	6
Italy, Malta, &c.	2,339	1,136	1,200
Europe	2	48	3
British America	6,677	20,735	30,421
South America	1,004	918	3,055
Central America	147	38	334
Mexico	9,033	4,232	1,423
West Indies	9,528	12,115	8,184
Asia	46	50	49
Africa and Australia	546	174	329
All other	87,707	10,388	50,796
Total	397,017	776,767	1,282,915

From	1851 to 1855.	1856 to 1859.	Total 40 years.
England	151,592	82,172	289,294
Ireland	529,304	170,799	918,729
Scotland	25,000	11,718	46,277
Wales	3,916	2,544	8,076
United Kingdom	221,242	61,823	1,410,505
Great Britain	931,054	329,056	2,672,881
France	57,020	15,377	204,511
Spain	4,301	4,065	15,316
Portugal	490	443	2,492
Belgium	1,867	2,818	9,809
Prussia	19,450	20,692	56,667
Germany	627,823	229,211	1,434,298
Holland	6,793	3,645	21,228
Denmark	1,268	1,939	4,998
Sweden & Norway	14,253	7,390	36,841
Poland	823	259	1,577
Russia	21	371	1,309
Turkey	36	43	166
Switzerland	13,349	5,749	31,870
Greece	23	7	115
Italy, Malta, &c.	3,670	3,249	11,594
Europe	473	10	536
British America	33,866	20,929	112,628
South America	463	553	5,993
Central America	121	320	960
Mexico	1,281	1,568	17,537
West Indies	5,490	3,786	39,103
Asia	16,693	19,296	36,134
Africa and Australia	1,074	1,843	3,966
All other	19,772	23,531	192,194
Total	1,761,474	696,150	4,914,723

The returns gave the number from Great Britain in many cases without distinguishing the particular divisions where all the passengers were born. A very large portion of the whole, however, came from Ireland. The return shows, then, that Ireland and Germany furnish the largest proportion of the emigrants. Other nations have supplied a greater or less number, but irregularly. Since 1850, or the era of gold discovery,

Asia—that is to say China—has sent a considerable number to California. Those do not, however, as a general thing, intend remaining. They are for the most part fitted out with small sums borrowed of friends and neighbors, who share in the profits of the adventurer on his return. Numbers of those who come from other countries, as France, West Indies, and Southern Europe, as well as to some extent from England, are merchants and travellers, who are not to be embraced in the aggregate of settlers in new homes. The great sources of migration are, then, British and German, and the latter are confined mostly to the valley of the Rhine. The people of the north of Europe do not migrate much. They seem to have lost the nomadic character of their ancestors. It is true that then they were led by chiefs and tempted by plunder to overrun the richer countries of the west, while at the present day migration has no object but to seek an honest living in countries where labor is in demand, and where hospitality and protection await the worker. The Russian, unless in charge of his master, cannot quit his native soil, of which he is, as it were, a portion. Whoever should penetrate into Russia for the purpose of recruiting emigrants, would be treated as a robber of property, and the Russians in the table are mostly merchants and travellers. The Swede and the Norwegian are more free in their choice, but the greater freedom they enjoy is an inducement to remain at home; nevertheless, they figure as high in the tables as the Swiss. These latter are to a considerable extent free and thrifty in their mountain homes, but great divisions exist in respect of religion as well as politics, and there is among them a want of nationality. The cantons of Vaud and Geneva are mostly French, and threaten to become quite so. On the side of the Tyrol the Swiss become Italians. The German Swiss are mostly connected with Baden, and are embraced in the German movement. Although the Swiss is attached to his country, he is enterprising, and is to be found in almost all countries. Every important city has Swiss firms among its most considerable merchants, and one of the early secretaries of the United States treasury, A. Gallatin, was a Swiss. The Hollanders migrate to some extent, and often from motives of religion. The Moravian Brethren thus founded colonies in Pennsylvania. Gold seems, since its discovery in California, to have stimulated Dutch enterprise. The Italians and Spanish do not migrate in the true sense of the word; they leave their homes to some extent for the countries that border the Mediterranean, but they do not, unless under the ban of exile, cross the Atlantic. The Sardinians and Basque Spaniards go to some extent to the La Plata in South America; they do not frankly abandon their country to adopt a new one. The French are more markedly attached to their native soil and national character, and colonise little; they migrate hardly at all. Even Algiers has grown but very slowly under thirty years of governmental fostering care, and there are now but 60,000 French in that colony. Of those French who arrived in the United States up to 1850, but 14 per cent. remained in the country according to the census.

The great continental movement is, then, on the part of the Germans, and of these the valley of the Rhine is the chief source.

CHAPTER II.

EUROPEAN MIGRATION—FRENCH AND GERMAN—NEW TRADE.

The peace of 1815, in re-establishing the liberty of the seas, so long suppressed, opened new countries to European commerce. On the other hand, many interests underwent adverse changes; numerous armies were newly disbanded, and great numbers of men were forced to leave home in search of a useful application of their talents and energies. America was to them the chief point of attraction; those who knew only the trade of arms, offered their swords to the Spanish colonies then fighting for emancipation. Of these a majority found early graves from excess, fatigue, and misery; many turned their attention to agriculture, and the wisest sought refuge in the United States, where services were well requited, and the broad territories offered a limitless field for activity. At first the emigrants were isolated individuals; soon entire families went in quest of new homes, and their success was a tempting example to other families, each of whom drew others in their train, until a regular and continuous movement was established from the valley of the Rhine to America.

This developed a new era in the international commerce. The cotton of the southern states had up to that time found a limited market in Havre, but being carried thither in American ships, there being little return freight for those vessels, the cotton was charged with freight both ways, out and home. The moment that considerable numbers of passengers offered themselves for the return, that trade of itself became an object, affording a profitable home freight. It was then apparent that the light and elegant models of the American ships, which had so well answered the purpose of speed and efficiency during the war, were not adapted to the transportation of passengers. A different style of construction was needed,allowing of greater stowage of cotton out, and better accommodation to passengers, in accordance with the provisions of the law prescribing the room to be allowed to each passenger. This change causing greater attractions to the American ships, drew increasing crowds from the valley of the Rhine across France to Havre. Many of these poor people could raise only the sum needful for the passage, and depended upon begging their way across France to the port. These crowds of beggars alarmed the government, and it took measures to stop them. It was ordered that no one should be admitted to cross France unless he had previously paid his passage in the ship, was possessed of $150 for every member of the family over eighteen years of age, and had his passport signed by the French embassador at Frankfort. The effect of these absurd regulations was to destroy the trade of Havre, and turn the migration down the Rhine to Antwerp, Bremen, and Hamburg. The Havre merchants made great efforts to remedy the evil by sending agents to aid the emigrants, lending them the money to pass the frontier, and to be returned immediately after. A great rivalry was thus engendered between the northern ports and Havre, which still had great advantages in respect of the number of American vessels that arrived with cotton, and finally the obstacles interposed by the government were removed. The city of Bremen was prompt to take advantage of the error of the French government, and used every effort to attract the emigrants to that port, by granting facilities and protecting them from imposition. A law was passed regulating in the most minute particular the accommodations to be given to emigrants on shipboard. They are not to be taken on board until the moment of departure. To accommodate them prior to shipment, an immense building was constructed to hold 2,000 people; it has a front of 200 feet, and is 100 in depth. It has public rooms, sleeping apartments, kitchens, baggage-rooms, etc., and is warmed by steam throughout. There are also chapels for catholic and protestant worship, and a hospital, with thirty-three beds. The price charged with board is fourteen cents per day. By these and other means Bremen has acquired a large share of the emigrant business. Hamburg did not make the same efforts; and it is only recently that societies for the protection of emigrants have been there formed.

One-third only of the Germans leave German ports. The expense of reaching there is about the same as to go to Havre. They, indeed, find in the language greater facilities, but the voyage thence is longer and the vessels are mostly German, whereas at Havre they find Americans, where the accommodations are better, and once on board of them, they feel as if they had already reached the country of their adoption. The passage across France is also greatly facilitated by the freight agents. The Bremen vessels have not the same facilities for return freight as the Americans at Havre. The Germans go nearly all to the United States, that is from Havre to New York or to New Orleans. There are numbers who go from Rotterdam, Ostend, or Hamburg, to England, and depart thence to their final destination. From Bremen the destinations are more numerous than from Havre. The United States is, however, the ultimate destination of nearly all.

The motives that impel German migration are variously understood. The reports of the numerous emigration societies give evidence of the highest traits of character. The German is described as a persevering worker, seeking to ameliorate his condition. He is always ready to go where his services will be the best paid, and certain professions have long been pursued by him in all countries. If his feeling of nativity is strong, his love of family is still stronger. And, moreover, the Teutonic race may now be said to be at home on half the entire globe. There are, however, other motives, and these are evidently the desire to find civil, political, and religious liberty, of which they have not the perfect enjoyment at home. The Germans have never succeeded in founding colonies of their own under good government, but they are a valuable acquisition where others have established liberty and order. They seek exemption from military service. They wish to contribute in just proportion to the public expenses, of which they enjoy the benefits, as equal citizens. They seek to escape the trammels of corporations. They wish also freely to dispose of the fruits of their own industry, and by so doing to avoid the misery of destitution. All this that they seek is evidently that which they have not got, or at least very imperfectly, at home.

The emigrants belong to many different states, and the same reproaches do not attach to all governments, neither in the same proportion to all. The very divisions of Germany are an injury to industry. They cause the proportion of the general expenses to be heavier for each individual, and destroy the spirit of nationality. The idea of "German unity" cannot be strongly impressed on the minds of people who leave the soil annually by tens of thousands.

The German governments have all, more or less, occupied themselves with the question of migration, and in some cases have sought to check it. Among these attempts was that by Prussia to found agricultural colonies. The king offered lands in the duchy of Posen, and agents were sent among the emigrants from the valley of the Rhine. The conditions were, that the settlers should not leave the country without permission, and never without having performed military service.

These, it may be supposed, were without success. Emigrant agents are, by some governments, required to submit to regulations; sometimes the number is limited, and sometimes they must give security. In Bavaria only two houses are authorized to treat with emigrants for their passages across France, and the contracts must be inspected by the consul at Havre. There results a large clandestine emigration to avoid these restrictions, and at the frontiers numerous agents are ready to assist—a sort of underground railroad. The governments of Wurtemberg, Baden, and the two Hesses, are less rigorous, but nowhere can passports be obtained until every effort has been made to dissuade the emigrant. In case he persists, he must renounce all rights of citizenship and nationality. On the other hand, measures are taken to aid the emigrant. When the cause of departure is destitution, the communes and the government subscribe, while stipulating that the emigrant shall renounce all right to ulterior aid. All the persons so aided go from one canton together. When the emigrants pay their own expenses and have a small capital, bands of numerous families from divers points assemble and depart together. Political exiles are very few, but these have generally considerable means.

It is melancholy, however, to reflect in how great a degree destitution becomes the cause of migration. Singularly enough, the valley of the Rhine, of which the German poets sing the beauty and the fertility, is precisely the spot, of all Europe, where the misery of Ireland is most nearly reproduced. From the Lake of Constance to the frontiers of Holland, that famous valley has so long felt the oppression of feudalism and been the battle-field of contending powers, as to have become completely impoverished. In the duchy of Baden the day's wages of a skilled workman is twenty-eight cents—a sum which may sustain life in a year of good harvest, but which is utterly insufficient in time of dearth, as in 1846, when potatoes became diseased. The insurrection of 1849 added to the calamities, and in 1852, of a population of 1,356,943 souls, 14,400 emigrated, or one per cent in one year. The thrift and endurance of the Germans are well developed in a land of such hardships, and on their arrival in the United States they are not slow in turning their persevering industry to account. It is singular that the distress and destitution which centuries of misrule have produced in Ireland, so famed for its natural advantages, should be reproduced in Europe only in the Rhine valley, the garden of Europe. The two localities best endowed by nature are precisely those where man is most anxious to escape by migration from an accumulation of miseries. The highest migration from Germany, by the four ports of Hamburg, Havre, Antwerp, and Bremen, rose to 203,537 in 1854. The movement has since declined, fluctuating with the harvests. There are, however, considerable numbers who go, by other conveyance from those ports than the emigrant ships, to Liverpool, and embark thence for America. This aggregate German movement has come of late years to rival, and in some cases to exceed the broad stream of British migration. The migration from Great Britain has always been largest in the years of dear food, and it has again subsided when good harvests have diminished the prices of bread. The number that went abroad in 1843 was 57,212, and it continued to augment year by year until it reached 368,764 in the year 1852. Several causes concurred to produce this increase. The first was the famine of 1845–46–47, and the consequent means adopted by the British government for the relief of Ireland; the second was the gold fever, which carried off thousands; and the third was the prosperity of the emigrants in the United States, where railroad building and other employments gave the means to send for friends in unusual numbers. The most important cause was, probably, the condition of Ireland. The conquest of that country, which was commenced seven centuries since, is but now being completed. We now see the insubmissive Celts quitting, with the aid of their conquerors, the disputed country, to seek new homes beyond the seas. They cannot assimilate to the conquering race, and not being able to defend themselves, they abandon the country rather than submit. During all the time of religious persecution, from the reign of Henry VIII. to George III., the economical condition of Ireland was deplorable, and misery made incessant progress. The landed population became involved in debt, and a fatal subdivision of the land was introduced in the mode of culture. Farms were subdivided as fast as the people multiplied, which was fully equal to the proverbial fecundity of a state of extreme poverty, and the potato came to be the sole dependence of all for food. The sudden destruction of that dependence by rot was an overwhelming calamity, that brought matters to a crisis. It was felt that migration could not remedy the evil, but that a radical change in a wrong system was become indispensable. The system pursued had been for the landlords, mostly in debt, to absent themselves altogether. The land was then taken by "middle men," at a rate which hardly met the interest on incumbrances. This land was then parcelled out to the poor cotters in lots down to one-fourth acre or less, mere patches, at rates which gave a large aggregate rent to the "middle man." Those patches were planted with potatoes, which were the sole dependence of the family for food in the year. They were gathered, when ripe, into a pile, and that pile diminished by daily consumption until an approaching new crop found it exhausted. The supply of food for the year depended entirely upon the amount of the crop. Its yield was the sole dependence of the family to sustain life. The cotter had no property or capital of any kind to be made available in case of emergency. His only means of paying rent was an annual migration to England in harvest time to earn the necessary sum. That done, the balance of the year was idly spent in watching the sinking pile of potatoes. It may well be imagined how great was the horror that seized such a people when the sole barrier between themselves and starvation was found rotten, suddenly perishing under their eyes. The scenes that followed were awful to contemplate. All that could, fled, and these were mostly the robust males, leaving the infirm, the old, and the young to encounter the slow death that was gradually approaching, and which overtook multitudes. The greatest efforts were made by the British government to purchase and distribute food, and to employ hands upon roads. At one time over 500,000 were so employed. The introduction of the Indian corn was attempted as a substitute; but it was nearly impossible amid a people entirely ignorant of its use. Hand-mills were furnished to grind it, and the priests and others used great exertions to teach them to cook it. It was frequently the case, however, that the grain did not agree with the people, but exhibited poisonous effects on being eaten. The body swelled, and severe illness ensued. Migration and famine did its work in spite of all efforts of humanity, and the census of 1851 showed how awful had been the havoc.

The population of Ireland has been as follows, per official reports:—

1821,	6,801,827	1851,	6,553,291
1831,	7.767,401	1859,	5,988,820
1841,	8,175,124		
	Decrease from 1841....		2,186,304

In the ten years ending with 1831, the increase was one and a half per cent. per annum. From that date to 1841 it was nine-tenths of one per cent, and that was a period of much comparative prosperity. The crops were still good, and the failure of the English wheat crops in 1837 raised the prices of Irish grain, and gave much employment to its agriculturists. If it had continued the same rate up to 1847, the famine year, the population would then have been 8,616,680 souls, when the migration took place in large numbers, and continued the succeeding thirteen years down to 1859. The same increase in that thirteen years would have made the population 9,651,678 persons, or as follows:—

Population in 1841	8,175,124
Ten years' increase at 9 per cent	735,761
The population should have been in 1851	8,910,885
Actual population	6,553,291
Loss by famine and migration	2,357,594
Number emigrated	1,422,000
Population in 1851	6,553,291
Ten years' increase at 9 per cent.	595,500
The population should have been in 1859	7,148,791
Actual population	5,988,820
Loss by migration, etc.	1,159,971
Number emigrated	1,742,260

In the famine years, up to 1851, 935,594 persons disappeared more than were accounted for by migration. From 1851 to 1859, there migrated 582,289 more persons than should have been lost by the census. This shows that there were numbers returned, and that the natural increase was large. The numbers who have returned have been, it is known, upwards of twenty thousand per annum, and these have carried back much larger sums than they brought with them. In this view the emigration reacts upon the northern states, the emigrants carrying off all that they have created. The whole operation above was as follows for thirteen years:—

Population in 1847	8,616,680
" 1859	5,988,820
Decrease	2,627,860
Emigrated	3,163,260
Excess	535,400

If this was all natural increase it would be in the ratio of one-half per cent. per annum. This year the failure of crops in Ireland has given a renewed impetus to the movement, and migration promises to be larger this year than for several previous ones.

The first reformatory efforts of the English government were to throw the support of the Irish poor upon the parishes, and as the tax became onerous the forced sale of the encumbered estates was authorized. The two measures have succeeded. The land has passed into thrifty hands; the bankrupt landlord is dispossessed, and the extortionate "middle man" is abolished; and the excessively poor population has been purged off by migration. The "clearing of the lands" was in many cases conducted with much barbarity. The little huts of the peasants were pulled or burned down, and the hapless people driven forth to seek homes beyond the seas as they best could. In other cases the landlords, the government, or societies furnished the means of shipments. The government soon found the necessity of interposing by law, as the United States had done, to protect them from the rapacity of shippers and their agents. The law of 1849 was passed with that object. By its provisions no ship shall carry more than one person for every two registered tons; nor shall there be more than one person for every twelve superficial feet on the main deck and below it. The size, number, and construction of the berths are regulated, and the captain is required to issue food as follows to each person twice a week:—

Bread	2½ lbs.
Wheat Flour	1 "
Oatmeal	5 "
Rice	2 "
Tea	2 oz.
Sugar	½ lb.
Molasses	½ "

A surgeon must be carried where there are one hundred or more passengers, and many other regulations that experience has pointed out as necessary, are enforced upon the carriers. The food is to be furnished entirely irrespective of the price of the passage, which fluctuates almost daily between $16 and $24 each adult, and half price for children. The starving and destitute race each year sends forth crowds from all parts of Ireland to embark at Liverpool. The means are mostly furnished by Irish in America, who consider it their duty to appropriate their first earnings in their new homes to the rescue of their relatives, and small remittances, aggregating millions in a year, find the way into every cabin and workhouse as messengers of life to the despairing. Those poor people, once started on their travels, encounter numerous perils before reaching their destination. As soon as a party of emigrants arrives in Liverpool, they are beset by a tribe of people, both male and female, who are known by the name of "man-catchers" and "runners." The business of these people is, in common parlance, to "fleece" the emigrant, and to draw from his pocket, by fair means or by foul, as much of his cash as he can be persuaded, inveigled, or bullied into parting with. The first division of the man-catching fraternity are those who trade in commissions on the passage money, and call themselves the "runners" or agents of the passenger brokers. The business of the passenger broker is a legitimate and necessary one. Under the passenger act of the 12th and 13th Victoria cap. 3, the licenses of all the passenger brokers expired on the 1st of February, 1850, subject to renewal after their being approved of by the government emigration agent, and to their entering into bonds, with two sureties, in the sum of $1,000, for the due fulfilment of all the requirements of the act of Parliament relating to the comfort and security of emigrants. The passenger brokers at Liverpool, in common with the unwary and unsuspecting emigrants, have suffered greatly from the malpractices of the "runners," who pretend to be their agents. These man-catchers procure whatever sums they can from emigrants as passage money—perhaps $25 or $30, or even more—and pay as little as they can to the passenger broker, whose business they thus assume—often as little as £3, or £3 5s. In addition to these large and knavish profits, they demand a commission of seven and a half per cent. from the passenger broker, and they have been often known to obtain and enforce this commission, although their whole concern in the matter may have been to watch the number of emigrants going into or coming out of the brokery office, and to put in a claim for having brought or "caught" them.

To form an idea of the sums paid in any one year as commission to the man-catchers, in the item of passage money, we have but to take the total steerage emigration of that year and multiply it by £3 10s., or seventeen dollars—the average amount of passage money—and calculate what a per-centage of seven and a half per cent. would amount to. The total steerage emigration of 1859 was one hundred and forty-six thousand one hundred and sixty-two souls, which, at seventeen dollars a head, would amount to no less than two million four hundred and eighty-four thousand seven hundred and fifty-four dollars, on which, taking the commission at the low rate of six per cent., they draw one hundred and forty-nine thousand and forty dollars, which is generally stated to be about the sum actually paid to this particular class of people, on the average of the last three years, by the passenger-brokers of Liverpool. But these are not the only class of the man-catching fraternity, nor do they confine their operations to an exorbitant profit upon passage money. The man-catchers keep lodging-houses for emigrants—wretched cellars and rooms, destitute of comfort and convenience, in which they cram them as thickly as the place can hold. The extra profits they draw from this source cannot be inferior in amount to their previously mentioned gains, and the cherished hoards of the poor pay a large per-centage to their unscrupulous rapacity.

In addition to this trade, some of them deal in the various articles composing the outfit of emigrants, such as bedding, clothes, food, cooking utensils, and the nick-nacks of all kinds which they can persuade them to purchase. Some of the store-keepers in this line of business pay their "runners" or "man-catchers" as much as ten per cent. commission on the purchases effected by the emigrants, from which the reader may form some estimate of the enormous plunder that must be drained from the poor ignorant people. As every emigrant must provide his own bedding, the sale of mattresses, blankets, and counterpanes, enters largely into this trade. After the bedding is provided, the man-catchers, who are principally Irishmen themselves, and know both the strength and weakness of the Irish character, fasten upon their countrymen—many of whom, poor and miserable as they look, have sovereigns securely stitched amid the patches of their tattered garments—and persuade them into the purchase of various articles, both useful and useless. Among these may be mentioned clothes of all kinds—shirts, trowsers, waistcoats, shawls, petticoats, south-westers, caps, boots and shoes, slippers, cooking utensils, cans for the daily allowance of water, and tins to hold their meal, rice, and sugar. Provisions, such as bacon, herrings, salt beef, and other articles not found them on board, and luxuries, in which whiskey and tobacco are generally included, come next on the list, after reiterated assurances from the man-catchers that no emigrant will be taken on board without them. These being provided, and an Irishman being easily squeezeable when a friend and a countryman is the man-catcher who has him in hand, and when he fears that his passage-money will be lost for non-compliance with the regulations, his attention is next directed to such articles as pocket-mirrors, razors, bowie-knives, pistols, telescopes, etc.

The stranger in Liverpool, who takes a walk in the immediate vicinity of the Waterloo Dock, whence the greater number of emigrant vessels take their departure, will see a profuse display of the various articles upon which the man-catcher makes his gains—articles generally of the most inferior quality, and sold at the most extravagant and ridiculous prices. The man-catching business, in all its various departments, has been reduced to a regular system, and no London sharper can be more sharp than the Liverpool runners. Perhaps the most complicated and ingenious trick is the following: When a steam-vessel laden with emigrants leaves an Irish port for Liverpool, one of the Liverpool fraternity, dressed up as a raw Irishman, with the usual long-tailed, ragged, and patched gray frieze coat, the battered and napless hat, the dirty unbuttoned knee-breeches, the black stockings, the shillelah, and the short pipe, takes his place among them, and pretends to be an emigrant. Before the vessel arrives at Liverpool he manages to make acquaintance with the greater portion of them, learns the parish they came from and the names of the relatives whom they have left behind, not forgetting those of the parish priest and the principal people of the neighborhood. He also ascertains the names of the friends in America whom they are going to join. He tells them of the roguery of Liverpool, and warns them against thieves and man-catchers, bidding them take especial care of their money. On arriving at the quay, in Liverpool, he jumps ashore among the first, where a gang of his co-partners are waiting to receive him. He speedily communicates to them all the information he has gained, and the poor people on stepping ashore are beset by affectionate inquiries about their friends in Ireland, and that good old man the parish priest. They imagine that they have fortunately dropped among old acquaintances, and their friend of the steamboat takes care to inform them that he is not going to be "done" by the man-catchers, but will lodge while at Liverpool at such and such a place, which he recommends. They cannot imagine that men who know all about the priest and their friends and relatives can mean them any harm, and numbers of them are usually led off in triumph to the most wretched but most expensive lodging-houses. Once in the power of the man-catchers, a regular siege of their pockets is made, and the poor emigrant is victimized in a thousand ways for his passage money, for his clothes and utensils, and for his food. Even after they have drained him as dry as they can, they are loth to part with him entirely, and they write out per next steamer a full, true, and particular account of him—his parish, his relations, his priest, and his estimated stock of money—to a similar gang in New York. Paddy—simple fellow—arrives in New York in due time, and is greeted on landing by the same affectionate inquiries. If his eyes have not been opened by woeful experience, he thinks once more that he has fallen among friends, and is led off by the "smart" man-catchers of the New York gang, to be robbed of the last farthing that he can be persuaded to part with; and he is possibly induced to spend the savings of years in the purchase of land, supposed to be in the far west, but having no other existence but such as paper and lies can give it.

It must not be supposed, from the statements in reference to the rogueries practised by runners and man-catchers upon the simple, emigrants themselves do not occasionally endeavor to commit frauds, both upon each other and upon the owners and captains of ships. The Irish emigrant, with the passion for hoarding which is so common among his countrymen, often hides money in his rags, and tells a piteous tale of utter destitution, in order to get a passage at a cheaper rate. The shameless beggary, which is perhaps the greatest vice of the lower classes of Irish, does not always forsake them, even when they have determined to bid farewell to the old country; and I have several times been accosted by men and women, on board emigrant ships in dock, and asked for contributions to help them when they got to New York. "Sure, yer honor, and may the Lord spare you to a long life; I've paid my last farden for my passage," said a sturdy Irish woman, with a child in her arms, when accosted on the quarter-deck of a fine ship, in the Waterloo Dock, "and when I get to New York I shall have to beg in the strates, unless yer honor will take pity on me." On being asked to show me her ticket, she said her husband had it; and her husband—a wretched-looking old man—making his appearance and repeating the same story, was pressed to show the document. He did so at last, when it was apparent that he had paid upwards of seventeen pounds—eighty-two dollars and twenty-five cents—for the passage of himself and wife and his family of five children. "And do you mean to say that you have no money left?" was inquired of him. "Not one blessed penny," said the man. "No, nor a fardin," said the woman, "and God knows what'll become of us." "Do you know nobody in New York?" "Not a living sowle, yer honor." "Have you no luggage?" "Not a stick or a stitch, but the clothes we wear." As the good ship was detained two days beyond her advertised time of sailing, all the emigrants, as usual, had liberty to pass to and from the ship to the streets, as caprice or convenience dictated. On the following day, this sturdy woman and her husband were seen entering the Waterloo Dock gates with a donkey-cart, tolerably well piled with boxes, bedding, and cooking utensils. When they were down in the steerage, and she was asked whether that was her luggage, she replied it was. "You said yesterday, however, when you were begging, that you had no luggage." "Sure, it's a hard world, yer honor, and we're poor people—God help us."

An incident of a kind not very dissimilar occurred on board of another American liner. When the passenger roll was called over, it was found that one man, from the county of Tipperary, had only paid an instalment upon his passage money, and that the sum of $6 each for three persons, or $18, was still due from him. On being called upon to pay the difference, he asserted vehemently that he had been told in the broker's office that there was no more to pay, and that to ask him for more was to attempt a robbery. The clerk insisted upon the money, and showed him the tickets of other passengers to prove the correctness of the charge. The man then changed his tone, and declared that he had not a single farthing left in the world, and that it was quite impossible he could pay any more. "Then you and your family will be put on shore," said the clerk, "and lose the money you have already paid." The intending emigrant swore lustily at the injustice, and declared that if put on shore he would "get an act of Parliament" to put an end to such a system of robbery. The clerk, however, was obdurate, and the man disappeared, muttering as he went that he would have his "act of Parliament to punish the broker, the clerk, and the captain." He returned in a few minutes from below, and, without saying a word of what had happened, and looking as unconcerned as a stranger, coolly presented a £5 note, or $24 25, and asked for his change. Such is a specimen of the rogueries attempted by those who have money. Those who really have none at all, or who possibly have not sufficient to pay their passage, resort to other schemes for crossing the Atlantic at a reduced rate, or free of charge altogether, and "stow away." This is a practice which is carried on to a great and increasing extent.

After encountering these perils of poverty and cheating, the crowd becomes finally located on board of ship, and assigned their quarters for the voyage. It is a strange place for the new-comers, and their admiration of the new life they have entered upon begins with the first day's issue of regulation food. The experience of most of them in the edible way, has hitherto been confined to "murphys" or, at most, Indian meal, which they heartily detest as "starvation porridge." They now come to the allowances, as above, handed them by law. The meal, the tea, the rice, the sugar, and molasses prove frequently a puzzler—tea in particular—and it is not unfrequently the case that a brawny Pat, who could do a good turn at Donnybrook fair, but whose knowledge of drinkables is confined to whisky, will, after gravely surveying the tea for a while, deliberately fill his pipe with a portion, and smoke it with much satisfaction. Others, with more expansive ideas, will at times mix the whole in a mass, and boil it into a thick soup or pudding, well specked with the expanded tea leaves. Information comes with experience, however, and the first serious experience is sea-sickness, which utterly prostrates them, mind and body, aggravating every dirty habit they may have formed. Then is exerted the utmost power of the captain to enforce cleanliness; he usually selects a dozen or two of the more intelligent, and investing them with authority, a general turn-out, and a thorough cleaning every morning, and in all weathers, is compelled.

By the rigid observance of this rule, much of the former sickness and mortality has been avoided. A voyage of some thirty days usually brings the human freight within sight of New York harbor. It almost invariably occurs that in the first delight of arrival every utensil and article of bedding is pitched overboard. No matter how poor are the people, or how hardly the things may have been come by, over they go; and cleaning for the landing takes place. How full of anxieties is that landing!

CHAPTER III.

LANDING IN NEW-YORK—FUTURE HOMES.

The Castle Garden, at New York, is allotted for the reception of the passengers under the Commission of Emigration, which was organized by law in 1847, and which charges a tax of two dollars per head on each immigrant, applying the proceeds to the support of the needy and destitute among them. The operations of this commission have become very extensive. It has charge of the Quarantine. Since its organization it has raised large hospitals on Ward's Island, where the sick are cared for. They are also sent to the Marine Hospital and the New York Hospital, and they reimburse the towns and counties of the state for the charges they incur for support of poor aliens, and advance money to immigrants on pledge of baggage, without interest. In the year 1859 $2,180 was so advanced to 162 families, and $2,031 was paid back. The operations of the commission in 1859 were:—

Receipts for commutation		$159,112
Other receipts		23,454
Total receipts		182,566
Balance in hand, January, 1859		5,656
		$188,222
Office	$16,486	
Hospitals	6,380	
Counties for support	23,555	
Castle Garden	34,727	
Agent at Rochester	1,087	
" Albany	2,160	
" Buffalo	2,601	
Ward's Island	54,890	
Marine Hospital	18,360	
Floating "	4,647	
Forwarding Immigrants, &c., &c.	32,130	
Incidental	721	
		$197,744

This account gives a general idea of the operations of the commission. The whole amount disbursed by the commission, May 5, 1847, to Jan. 1, 1860, was $834,786. The proportion who go into hospital appears to be about six per cent. of the arrivals.

A large majority of those who here land have their friends awaiting them to guide them to their future homes. Numbers have to seek their way amid numberless perils. But nearly all these have come provided with instructions more or less minute, derived from the numerous agents in Europe of the American land companies, who hold out inducements to settlers. The Germans are mostly inclined to agriculture, and they soon find their way, by the emigrant trains of the great trunk lines of railroads. Those lines have all exerted themselves to profit by the movement.

The following table, from official sources, gives the number of Germans and British under each head, and also the aggregate of all the aliens arrived since the returns have been regularly kept. Some of the passengers report themselves from Great Britain, without stating which portion. These are under the head "Great Britain." Thus, the total from Great Britain to 1859, is 2,670,059, of which, 1,415,399 are reported from Great Britain, 289,654 from England, 918,729 from Ireland, 46,277 from Scotland.

NUMBER OF PASSENGERS THAT ARRIVED IN EACH YEAR IN THE UNITED STATES FROM ENGLAND, IRELAND, SCOTLAND, GREAT BRITAIN, AND GERMANY, WITH THE TOTAL FROM ALL COUNTRIES.

	England.	Ireland.	Scotland.	Gt. Britain.	Germany.	Switzerland.	Prussia.	Total.
1820,	1,782	1,725	268	2,249	948	31	20	8,385
1821,	1,036	1,518	293	1,881	365	93	18	9,127
1822,	856	1,346	198	1,088	139	110	9	6,911
1823,	851	1,051	180	926	179	47	4	6,354
1824,	713	1,575	257	1,064	224	253	6	7,912
1825,	1,002	4,157	113	1,711	448	166	2	10,199
1826,	1,459	3,333	230	2,705	495	245	16	10,837
1827,	2,521	3,282	460	7,689	435	297	7	18,875
1828,	2,735	5,266	1,041	8,798	1,806	1,592	45	27,382
1829,	2,149	3,106	111	5,228	582	314	15	22,520
1830,	733	747	29	2,365	1,972	109	4	23,322
1831,	251	1,647	226	6,123	2,395	63	18	22,633
1832,	944	5,120	158	11,545	10,168	129	26	53,179
1833,	2,966	4,511	1,921	4,166	6,823	634	155	58,640
1834,	1,129	6,772	110	26,953	17,654	1,389	32	65,365
1835,	468	5,148	63	24,218	8,245	548	66	45,374
1836,	420	2,152	106	41,006	20,139	445	568	76,242
1837,	896	737	14	39,079	23,036	383	704	79,340
1838,	157	1,225	48	16,635	11,369	123	314	38,714
1839,	62	1,199	..	32,973	19,794	607	1,234	68,069
1840,	318	677	21	41,027	88,581	500	1,123	84,066
1841,	147	3,291	35	50,487	13,727	751	1,564	80,289

	England.	Ireland.	Scotland.	Gt. Britain.	Germany.	Switzerland.	Prussia.	Total.
1842,	1,743	4,844	24	66,736	18,287	483	2,083	104,565
1843,	3,517	1,173	41	23,369	11,432	553	3,009	52,496
1844,	1,357	5,491	23	40,972	19,226	839	1,505	78,615
1845,	1,710	8,641	368	53,312	33,138	471	1,217	114,371
1846,	2,854	12,949	305	57,824	57,010	698	551	154,416
1847,	3,476	29,640	337	95,385	73,444	192	837	234,968
1848,	4,445	24,802	659	118,277	58,014	319	451	226,527
1849,	6,036	31,321	1,060	175,841	60,062	13	173	297,024
1850,	6,797	40,180	860	167,242	78,137	375	759	369,980
1851,	5,306	55,874	966	210,594	71,322	427	1,160	379,466
1852,	30,007	159,548	8,148	2,544	143,575	2,788	2,343	371,603
1853,	28,867	162,649	6,006	2,703	140,653	2,748	1,293	368,645
1854,	48,901	101,606	4,605	5,141	206,054	2,953	8,955	427,883
1855,	38,871	49,627	5,275	1,176	66,219	4,433	5,699	200,877
1856,	25,904	54,349	3,297	15,457	63,807	1,780	7,221	200,436
1857,	27,804	54,361	4,182	26,493	83,798	2,080	7,983	251,306
1858,	14,638	26,873	1,946	12,372	42,291	1,056	3,019	123,126
1859,	13,826	35,216	2,293	10,045	39,315	833	2,469	121,282
	289,654	918,729	46,277	1,415,399	1,495,308	31,870	56,677	4,901,321

The returns give 1,495,308 Germans, mostly from the valley of the Rhine, a large portion of whom have arrived since the taking of the census of 1850. If we take the numbers of persons who had arrived from each country up to 1850, and compare them with the numbers reported by that census as living in the Union, we may be satisfied in how far two distinct official accounts correct each other.

STATEMENT OF THE NUMBER OF ALIENS ARRIVED IN THE UNITED STATES UP TO 1850, AND THE NUMBER OF EACH NATION RESIDENT IN THE UNION PER CENSUS OF 1850.

	Arrived 1820 to 1850.	Resident in 1850.	Excess of arrivals.
England........	55,530	278,675	
Ireland..........	218,626	961,719	
Scotland....... ..	9,559	70,550	
Wales..........	1,616	29,868	
Great Britain.....	1,127,440		
Total Gt. Britain..	1,412,771	1,340,812	71,959
Germany........	577,264	573,225	4,039
France..........	131,714	54,069	77,645
Spain...........	6,950	3,113	3,837
Portugal........	1,550	1,274	276
Belgium.........	5,724	1,313	4,411
Holland..........	10,790	9,848	942
Turkey....	87	106	
Italy............	4,675	3,645	1,030
Austria..........		946	
Switzerland......	12,772	13,358	
Russia..........	917	1,414	
Norway & Sweden.	15,198	{ 12,678 3,559	
Denmark.........	1,791	1,838	
Prussia......	16,525	10,549	5,976
Sardinia...	360	34	326
Greece..........	85	86	
China...........	386	758	
Asia............	145	377	
Africa...........	1,049	551	
British America...	57,833	147,711	
Mexico...... ...	14,689	13,317	1,372
Central America..	519	141	378
South America...	4,977	1,543	3,434
West Indies......	29,827	5,772	24,055
Sandwich Isles...	36	588	
Other............	1,171	8,214	
Total......	2,309,805	2,210,839	

These figures indicate the true currents of migration, as distinct from visitors. In thirty years there came from the British Islands 71,949 persons more than remained here. These represent those who returned home and those who died. Although a large number were reported as from Great Britain, their nativities, as reported by the census, inform us more than two-thirds were Irish. The French who arrived, it appears, did not remain in a proportion larger than forty per cent. The Belgians and Dutch returned to some extent. It is the case with these nations mentioned that the proportion of females is small, showing the character of the passengers to be more that of visitors than settlers. With some other nationalities more are reported resident than arrived. This may arise from the desire on the part of many, on arrival, to conceal their origin, because of some claims of the government upon them for military duty, such as we have seen exemplified in the correspondence of General Cass upon that point. In the case of British America, great numbers came over the lines not reported as emigrants in ships. With the West Indies, there are numbers come north in the summer season who return to their own homes in the winter. The aggregate results of arrivals and residences correspond pretty well.

Having traced these people from their various homes in Europe, and appreciated the motives that led them to migrate, and the difficulties that they encountered in so doing, we may now follow them to their final homes on this continent, as far as official returns permit. The French and English seem to cling to the sea coast, while the Germans push west into agricultural states, Ohio getting a large share of the whole. The "total" column includes all others, as well as English and German:—

LOCATION OF LEADING EMIGRANTS IN THE UNITED STATES.

	England.	Ireland.	Germany.	Switzerl'nd.	Prussia.	Total foreign.
Maine	1,949	13,871	290	11	27	31,456
New Hampshire	1,469	8,811	147	9	2	13,571
Vermont	1,546	15,377	218	2	6	32,831
Massachusetts	16,685	115,917	4,319	72	98	160,909
Rhode Island	4,490	15,944	230	8	5	23,111
Connecticut	5,091	26,689	1,671	55	42	37,473
New York	84,820	343,111	118,398	1,850	2,211	651,801
New Jersey	11,377	31,092	10,686	204	57	58,364
Pennsylvania	38,048	151,723	78,592	914	413	294,871
Delaware	952	3,513	343	22	28	5,211
Maryland	3,467	19,557	26,936	68	188	53,288
District of Columbia	682	2,373	1,404	36	11	4,967
Virginia	2,998	11,643	5,511	83	36	22,394
North Carolina	394	567	344	3	19	2,524
South Carolina	921	4,051	2,180	18	44	8,662
Georgia	679	3,202	947	38	25	5,907
Florida	300	878	307	7	17	2,757
Alabama	941	3,639	1,068	113	45	7,638
Mississippi	593	1,928	1,064	41	71	4,958
Louisiana	3,550	24,266	17,507	723	380	66,413
Texas	1,002	1,403	8,191	134	75	16,774
Arkansas	196	514	516	12	24	1,628
Tennessee	706	2,640	1,168	266	32	5,740
Kentucky	2.805	9,466	13,607	279	198	29,189
Ohio	25,660	51,562	111,257	3,291	765	218,512
Michigan	10,620	13,430	10,070	118	190	54,852
Indiana	5,550	12,787	28,584	724	740	54,426
Illinois	18,628	27,786	38,160	1,635	286	110,593
Missouri	5,379	14,734	44,352	984	697	72,474
Iowa	3,785	4,885	7,152	175	88	21,232
Wisconsin	18,952	21,043	34,519	1,244	3,545	106,695
California	3,050	2,452	2,926	177	158	22,358
TERRITORIES.						
Minnesota	84	271	141	22	5	2,048
Oregon	207	196	155	8	1	1,159
Utah	1,056	106	50	1	6	1,990
New Mexico	43	292	215	11	14	2,063
Total	278,675	961,719	573,225	13,358	10,549	2,210,839

In this manner were distributed in 1850 among the several states those of our citizens who were born abroad. In the aggregate, Wisconsin had the largest proportion of foreign citizens. Out of a population of 305,391, there were 106,691, or more than one out of three, born abroad. Of that number, nearly 40,000 were Germans. Next to Wisconsin, New York had the largest share of foreigners, these forming more than 1 out of 5 of the whole number. The New York state census of 1855 also reported the nativities, and these compare with 1850 as follows:

	English.	Irish.	Germans.	Total For'gn.	Native.
1850,	84,820	348,111	122,459	651,801	2,445,593
1855,	102,286	469,753	218,997	922,019	2,528,444
Increase	17,466	126,642	96,588	270,218	82,851

The foreign element, it appears, increased in these five years 270,218, while the native born only increased 82,851, showing how greatly the enterprise of those years sent people to the west. The natural increase of the white population in the United States is three per cent. per annum. Thus, on the 2,445,593 native whites in New York in 1850, the excess of births over deaths in one year would be 73,367; and for five years, to 1855, it would be 226,835 persons. But the census showed an increase of only 82,851, consequently 143,984 of the native population must have emigrated from the state during that period. Their places were more than supplied by the emigrants. The same movement is apparent in all the northern states. The number of persons born in the northern states and living at the time of the census, was 8,370,089. Of these, only 6,941,510 were living where they were born; the remainder, 1,428,579, were living in other states, south and west. But there were also living in the northern states, at the date of the census, 1,292,241 persons who were born abroad. These foreigners were mostly Irish—factory operatives, domestics, and artisans. It appears, then, that business enterprise had drawn 1,428,579 northern born men into other states, and their places had been supplied by 1,292,241 emigrants from abroad. This was up to 1850, and since then, as we have seen in the case of New York, the movement has been much more rapid; to how great an extent, the forthcoming census will show.

The amount of money or capital drawn from Europe by the emigrants is a question of much importance. The cost of preparation for the voyage in Europe, the cost of the passage, and the expenses incurred after arriving until the new home is finally reached, cannot, together, fall short of one hundred dollars each; and many have a small capital, in addition, with which to begin the world. The sums transported are often much larger. In 1854 the migration from the Palatinate, as stated in a Bremen report, was 8,908, and they carried $1,024,000. The reports of the New York commissioners of emigration, as the result of their investigation, show that the average of money brought is very near one hundred dollars per head—an amount which becomes formidable when taken in connection with the aggregate numbers arriving. This is exhibited in the following summary of arrivals:—

	Whole No. of Arrivals.	Number of Aliens.	Sums at $100 per head.
Ten years to Sept. 30, 1829.	151,636	128,502	12,850,200
" " 1839,	572,716	538,381	53,838,100
" " 1849,	1,479,478	1,427,337	142,733,700
" Dec. 31, 1859,	3,075,900	2,814,554	281,455,400
Total arrived......	5,279,730	4,908,774	$490,877,400

This is an immense sum, and poured forth even in small streams, has had an important effect upon the prosperity of the country at large, independent of the larger sums invested in land, stock, and utensils. On the other hand, very considerable sums are sent out of the country in aid of the emigrants, by their friends here, who have earned the money at service and otherwise. On this point, information has from time to time been gathered, of the houses through which remittances are made. These remittances are mostly small drafts, purchased in New York, for sums varying from five to one hundred dollars. The latter sum is seldom reached, however. The remittances of five of these houses, in one year, were as follows:—

			Average amount.
House A, number of drafts...	1,934	$32,125	$$16\frac{5}{8}$
" B, " "	6,198	123,290	$19\frac{7}{8}$
" C, " "	13,425	266,395	$19\frac{7}{8}$
" D, " "	18,175	363,140	$19\frac{9}{10}$
" E, " "	40,542	810,835	20
Total 5 houses 1 year..	80,274	$1,595,785	

These do not include the large banking-houses, of which there are no returns, but it is stated the Baring Brothers alone send $2,500,000. The British emigrant commissioners reported $2,160,000 so sent in 1848; $2,589,000 in 1849; $4,871,204 in 1850; $5,172,010 in 1851; $6,960,107 in 1852, and with the prosperous years during the great rail expenditures, up to 1857, large sums were remitted. It is to be remembered, however, that the sums so remitted come back mostly to American ship owners for passage money, so that, in fact, it does not all leave the country. In the same manner a good deal of the United States gold coin exported to Havre, Bremen, etc., is purchased there by emigrants in exchange for their native coin, and disbursed here on the arrival of the passengers. It results, then, that Europe sustained in the last ten years a drain of 2,814,554 souls, and at least $281,000,000 of money, which went to enrich the United States. This, without taking into account the productive value of the people after they arrived.

The legal rights of the emigrants, after they become naturalized, are the same in all respects as those of the native born citizens, with the single exception that they are not eligible to the office of president or vice-president of the United States. No law can be passed to abridge the freedom of their speech, or the free exercise of their religion, whatever that may be—even the enjoyment of Mormonism has been an attraction to some. Their right to hold real estate is perfect, as is the security afforded to persons, property, and papers, and they may be elected, or may elect to any office except those named.

Another very interesting feature of the passenger movement, although not strictly embraced within the emigration, is the number of United States citizens who annually arrive from abroad. There is no record of the number who go abroad each year, nor of the sums they expend in so doing; nevertheless, these are very considerable, and form an important element in the exchanges of the country. As a guide to the numbers who go, the returns of those who arrive each year become very interesting. These, distinguishing males and females, have been as follows:—

NUMBER OF NATIVE CITIZENS ARRIVED EACH YEAR FROM ABROAD.

	Males.	Females.	Not stated.	Total.
1820,	1,576	287	63	1,926
1821,	2,215	302	..	2,517
1822,	1,502	136	..	1,638
1823,	1,715	196	..	1,911
1824,	1,547	168	..	1,715
1825,	2,289	370	..	2,659
1826,	2,516	555	..	3,071
1827,	2,362	540	..	2,902
1828,	2,185	617	..	2,802
1829,	1,635	358	..	1,993
1830,	1,075	440	..	1,515
1831,	1,008	239	..	1,247
1832,	1,003	169	..	1,172
1833,	1,002	283	..	1,285
1834,	1,934	640	9	2,583
1835,	2,556	764	22	3,342
1836,	3,594	1,136	..	4,730
1837,	4,566	1,053	..	5,629
1838,	5,030	1,215	..	6,245
1839,	5,268	1,329	..	6,597
1840,	6,115	2,026	..	8,141
1841,	5,733	1,783	..	7,516
1842,	4,847	1,568	..	6,415
1843,	3,103	930	..	4,033
1844,	4,466	1,683	..	6,149
1845,	4,164	1,196	165	5,525
1846,	3,197	1,036	..	4,233
1847,	3,081	1,408	25	4,514
1848,	2,222	734	..	2,956
1849,	2,024	635	..	2,659
1850,	9,863	1,059	..	10,926
1851,	27,836	1,526	..	29,362
1852,	23,262	2,478	..	25,740
1853,	28,774	3,563	..	32,337
1854,	28,710	3,931	..	32,641
1855,	24,874	4,716	..	29,599
1856,	20,058	4,002	..	24,060
1857,	16,701	3,974	..	20,676
1858,	17,291	4,489	..	21,780
1859,	27,041	7,186	..	34,227
	309,940	60,710	284	370,968

At the era of the gold discoveries in 1849, a sudden movement in American travel took place, it appears. In the ten years ending with 1849, 51,951 persons arrived home; of these, one-fourth were females. In the ten years ending with 1859, 261,138 Americans arrived home. The amount of money spent by these persons abroad cannot be ascertained with precision, but it is known that the passage out and home, with a three months' expense, cannot be done inside of $600, at which rate the amount expended would be $156,682,800 for the ten years, or $15,000,000 per annum. The probability is that it is three times that amount; the passage-money alone would reach $52,227,000. This constitutes a very heavy drain upon the national resources, although the money paid for passages is mostly to American interests; as a whole it is doubtful whether the financial balance arising from migration is in favor of the country. The numbers of former emigrants who return home with accumulated means, added to the sums expended abroad by Americans, will probably at least cancel the amounts actually brought into the country by emigrants. But the vast amount of productive skill and labor that is brought into the country, and applied to the vast waste of land, develops more capital in a ratio which astonishes the observer. The number of persons who arrive in the United States in a single years equals the population of a whole state. Thus the numbers that arrived in 1857 were 427,883; the total white population of the state of Alabama was, in 1850, 428,779.

From 1859, the tide of immigration, which for two or three years previous had ebbed, began to flow again in something like its old abundance, and, though checked in 1861 and 1862 by the war and the presence of rebel privateers in the Atlantic, it soon increased again, and in 1863, '4, '5, and '6, has been very large. In 1860, the whole number of alien emigrants was 153,640. We have no returns from the whole country since that date, but the immigrants landed at New York since that time, which comprise about three-fourths of the whole number who enter the country, were, in 1861, 68,311; in 1862, 81,458; in 1863, 161,648; in 1864, 184,700; in 1865, 200,031; in ten months of 1866, 202,440. It is a noteworthy fact that the later immigrants, those of the last three or four years, are, socially and pecuniarily, of a much higher class than those of former years. A very large proportion of them are well, or at least tolerably educated, and many of them possessed sufficient means to enable them to go to the West and procure farms, or engage in other employments. Of the immigrants in 1865, 83,451 were from Germany, 70,462 from Ireland, 27,286 from England, and 15,153 from other countries.

SOCIAL AND DOMESTIC LIFE.

INTRODUCTORY.

Three quarters of a century ago, there were in the whole United States only about as many people as there are now in the state of New York; and now we have grown from less than four millions to thirty millions—having increased nearly eight-fold.

These large numbers will indistinctly represent the general progress of the nation; and the average social prosperity of each citizen has increased in a ratio materially larger. The actual amount of this increase in intelligence, wealth, and comfort, cannot be set down in figures, but will be understood as well as the case will permit, from an enumeration of details of improvements in social and domestic life.

There were sufficient reasons for a somewhat uncommonly low average of comfort at the end of the Revolution. The seven years' war had, of course, almost destroyed all industry, except farming and a few indispensable manufactures and trades. It had also drained all the specie out of the country, or frightened it into secret hoards; in consequence of which the currency was entirely disorganized. Government credit was at such a low ebb, that the bills of the United States (known as "continental money") would not purchase even such articles of comfort or luxury as existed, except at enormous nominal rates; nor was the paper money of the separate states in much better reputation. Thus, a hundred dollars in these depreciated bills was paid for a mug of cider; five hundred dollars for a bowl of punch; a thousand dollars for a pair of shoes; twenty-seven thousand dollars for an ordinary horse; and "part of an old shirt" was set in an inventory at fifteen dollars. The worthlessness of this money rendered it necessary to make payments, to a great extent, in barter—a mode of trading which always keeps the average of comfort and luxury down at a standard little above that of the better class of savages.

But even if this paper currency had been worth its face, or if specie had been plenty, it would have been possible to buy only a small share of comforts or luxuries compared with those now attainable, for the plain reason that they did not exist.

Beginning at this low period of average prosperity, we shall now rapidly sketch the progress of the country, up to the present time, under the general heads of

1. Domestic Architecture.
2. Furniture.
3. Food.
4. Dress.
5. Mental culture, intercourse, etc.

CHAPTER I.

DOMESTIC ARCHITECTURE.

Eighty years ago, houses were much more evenly distributed over the country than is now the case. There has ever since been a continual tendency to draw together into towns; and this tendency has been much assisted by the increased ease of travelling and transportation. At that time, therefore, there was much less difference between a country house and a city house than at present.

In the older parts of the northern states, the houses then built were often of the style called "lean-to," or "linter;" that is, with one side of the roof carried down so far as to cover an additional tier of rooms on the ground floor, or a wide shed. Another common style, rather later in use, was the "gambril roofed," where the roof rose at a very steep pitch from the eaves, about half the length of the rafters, and then fell in to the ridge-pole at a much flatter angle. This gave a very roomy garret. Dormer windows were very common, to light rooms finished off in the garrets.

Timber was plenty, and houses were built

almost exclusively of wood, and often with beams and rafters of dimensions that would now seem truly enormous. Brick was comparatively little used, until lumber grew scarcer in the older parts of the country, and "brick machines," first invented by Kinsley a little before 1800, had rendered the production of brick more rapid and cheaper than could be afforded by hand labor. Stone was scarcely used at all, except by a very few wealthy persons. Sometimes the spaces between the timbers of a frame house were filled in with brick, so as to make a sort of brick body to the house, with wooden bones, and with the clapboards put on over these.

A beam was very often left running across the ceiling of a room, six or eight inches below the plaster, and was a convenient place for driving nails or pegs on which to hang dried apples, seed-corn, peppers, hams, baskets, rope, etc., etc. In like manner the uprights often projected into the corner of the room, giving it a kind of coarse cornice. The centre of the house was usually occupied by the chimney stack—an immense pile of brick or stone, sometimes occupying almost a quarter of the ground plan. In the different sides of this huge mass opened the great old-fashioned fire-places, in many of which one could sit in the corner while the fire burned, and see the sky through the chimney-top. Half a cord of wood might burn at once in some of these great fireplaces, and yet, in the bitter cold of a northern winter, water would freeze at the other side of the room. This was by reason of the thinness of the walls, the imperfect fitting of doors and windows, and above all, the great proportion of heat that went off up chimney, and of cold that came down. Hinged to staples at the chimney-back was a crane, with its pot-hooks and hangers, or trammels, to accommodate the machinery of the cook. At one side of the fire-place was the oven—a cave in the masonry of the chimney-stack—and, usually, with an ash-hole underneath it. A great shovel, or "slice," with a handle five or six feet long, and a big pair of tongs to match, were for oven use; and to heat this affair thoroughly enough to bake bread, usually occupied an hour or an hour and a half, and consumed two or three good armfuls of dry wood.

Houses were commonly low "between joints," to economize heat. Roofs were shingled, with split shingles; the sawed shingles being little used until a little after 1800, from which time many patents for shingle sawing were taken out. A machine for getting out shingles was patented, however, as early as 1797. Slate roofs have never been much used, and tiles scarcely at all. Cypress wood is used for shingles at the south, instead of pine; exposure to the weather turns it to a quite distinct, but disagreeable black. Sheet tin has been quite extensively used for roofing during the last quarter of a century, being laid upon tongued and grooved boards; but most of such roofs leak vexatiously, from the alternate expansion or contraction of the tin from heat and cold. Since about 1840, quite a number of modes have been invented for covering roofs with oiled cloth, asphalt, mineral paints, etc., etc.; but no roof is better than a well made shingle roof.

A quite recent invention in domestic architecture is the plan of building what are called "gravel walls," by moulding gravel and loose stone with mortar into a kind of concrete wall on the spot, lifting up the moulding cases when the contents are firmly set, and moulding another section. This results in a house which may be said to be of one stone, for if the materials are good and well put together, they harden into an artificial breccia. This plan has not, however, been sufficiently proved; and a wrong choice of sand, or gravel, or lime might after a while cause the crumbling and ruin of the whole fabric.

Walls were usually finished inside with whitewash, paper, or paint; the use of stucco, or "hard finish," being quite rare until a late period. All house iron-work and trimmings of a better kind were imported from England, until within the present century. Wrought nails were used; cut nails having been invented, and their manufacture variously perfected by several Americans, from about 1791, when the earliest patent on the subject was issued, down to the present time. Jacob Perkins, of Newburyport, and Byington, of Connecticut, were two of the most prominent inventors in this line. Such latches, hinges, etc., as were then made in this country, were wrought iron, and clumsy and inconvenient. All such trimmings are, however, now manufactured to great perfection in our own workshops. Among the improvements of the last forty years in house trimmings, a very convenient one is the introduction of balance weights running over pullies, to facilitate opening and shutting windows. Before these were used, the practice was to use various kinds of catches, all of which made it necessary to lift the whole weight of the sash; and instead of which were often found merely a wooden button to turn under, and hold the sash open, or even nothing but a stick to hold it up.

The invention of the planing machine, first successfully introduced by William Woodworth in 1837, though many patents had preceded his, and of the circular saw, first patented by Cox, of Georgia, in 1795, were important improvements in dressing lumber, and cutting it; as the former could turn out boards smoothed, tongued and grooved, and fit for flooring, and the latter could cut thin work much more cheaply than a common saw movement. Another machine has been introduced within fifteen years, for boring auger holes, and others for cutting wooden mouldings, which save much time and labor in framing and in finishing respectively. During the last ten or twelve years, also, various new paints have been introduced, none of which, however, have entirely superseded the old-fashioned oil vehicle and ordinary mineral colors. Of these, the principal are preparations of zinc, to be used instead of lead, and also for a variety of browns and grays; and several "mineral paints," usually finely pulverized stone, which are recommended as good defences against fire.

The improvement of the last twenty years in architectural designs has been great. Up to that time, dwelling houses were built in the north most frequently on a plain parallelogram plan with the common ridge-pole roof. A style at that time quite frequently adopted for houses of a somewhat pretentious character was that of a Greek temple, usually with a row of pillars across one end. This absurd misapplication did not flourish long, and was succeeded by the Gothic cottage style; and this again, and with extensive and well-deserved success, by the very various and graceful modifications of the Italian villa style. In cities, where land is very expensive, a style called the "English basement house" is much used; with a front of brick, or stone, or both; a ground floor occupied by a library or dressing-room, and a dining-room; with the kitchen in the basement below, and the parlors and bedrooms on the floors above. This arrangement economizes land, but the great number of stories and stairs makes them very wearisome to the feeble frames of our American city housekeepers, unless they content themselves with sitting comfortably in the parlor, and letting Bridget govern, uncontrolled, in all the rest of the house. A modification of this house, known as the Boston style, has a front door sunk within a recess in the front, as a shelter from the weather.

A very common arrangement of old-fashioned houses was to set the house with the side toward the street, with the front door in the middle, opening into a little vestibule. From this the stairs passed up, often turning round three sides of the vestibule; and at each side a door led to two front rooms. These, often occupying all the ground floor of the two-story part, were parlors, or a parlor and a bed-room. Behind these, under the "lean-to" roof, was very probably one long room, used as kitchen, nursery, and sitting-room; for the parlor was used only for great occasions. The second floor was laid off as might be convenient.

The better houses of the southern states were built to suit the different demands of the climate—more airily, and usually with much piazza room, and not much provision for warmth. Early settlers in the south and west invariably put up log houses, whose chimneys were built outside against one end, of sticks laid in clay. A mode often used was to build two separate square rooms of logs, and then to throw one roof over both and the space between, thus securing an outdoor shelter. These log houses were floored with "puncheons," that is, small logs split once and hewed even. A standing table of puncheons, some three-legged stools, a rude bedstead, with a bed of leaves or cornhusks covered with buffalo-hide or bear-skins instead of sheet, blanket, and coverlet; a shelf, and a variety of pegs driven into the wall, completed almost the entire outside and inside of these rugged, but comfortable homes, the nurseries of so many brave and great men. In such houses were born and brought up Andrew Jackson, Henry Clay, and the numberless heroic Indian fighters and mighty hunters of the west. And such houses are still the homes of thousands of the bold pioneers who are advancing westward, carrying forward the limits of civilized society toward the Pacific ocean. As the newer states increase in population and wealth, the domestic architecture of the older ones is copied, and dwelling houses of the same general character are now commonly used in city and country.

Among the chief improvements in domestic architecture are those which have been applied to modes of warming houses. The earliest improvement on the ancient fireplace was the Franklin stove, invented by the great philosopher whose name it bears, and which was in use before the revolutionary war. These were only shallow iron fireplaces, with a draft which could be modified by a sort of valve, and were used only for wood. Large box-stoves, also for wood, were the first means used for warming churches. Even these were not introduced until within the memory of many persons now living, and, as is well known, were violently resisted by the conservatives, who fought hard to retain the privilege of mortifying the flesh by freezing fingers and toes all day Sunday.

The introduction of anthracite coal was the next step in this department. This had been known for years to the hunters and trappers of the wild interior of Pennsylvania, as a black stone sometimes found on the mountains, but was not thought combustible, any more than granite.

Some successful attempts had, however, been made to burn anthracite; one by Dr. C. T. James, in 1804; and one by Judge Jesse Fell, of Wilkesbarre, who burned it in a grate, in 1808. This brought it gradually into use in that vicinity. In 1814, White & Hazard, iron-masters in Carbon county, bituminous coal becoming scarce, resolved to try anthracite in their rolling mill. They got a cart-load, at a dollar a bushel, and wasted it all in vain endeavors to kindle it. Procuring another load, they tried again; but after fruitless endeavors for a whole night, the hands shut the furnace door in despair and left the mill. Half an hour afterward, one of them came back after his jacket, and to his surprise found the furnace door red-hot, and the inside at a strong white heat. The discovery was made; and with the use of a similar let-alone policy in kindling, anthracite was afterward used in furnaces with entire success, an improvement in quality of product, and a large saving of expense.

Thus introduced, the use of the new fuel gradually spread, although so slowly that in 1820, three hundred and sixty-five tons completely stocked the Philadelphia market for a year. Many patents were now taken out for grates, blowers, cooking-stoves, parlor and hall stoves, ranges, and hot-air furnaces. R. Trexler, of Berks county, manufactured stoves for anthracite in 1815; and the earliest patent for furnaces seems to have been that of Thomas Gregg, of Connellsville, Pa., in 1814. Three or four years now brought the new fuel into extensive use, and from the three hundred and sixty-five tons, which was all that was mined in 1820, the amount had risen in 1849, in thirty years, to three millions and a quarter of tons, and has been continually increasing ever since.

Nott's stoves were early much used for warming houses with anthracite; Olmsted's stove and Bushnell's were in fashion next; the first invented by a college president, the second by a college professor, and the third by an eminent clergyman. It would be vain to enumerate the numberless patents and designs that have since been introduced. About 1836, Isaac Orr, a man of great inventive talent, patented the air-tight stove for wood, which was for a time so extensively used as to cause a sort of interregnum in the reign of anthracite, and which is yet frequently seen. Grates, long used in England to burn the bituminous coal there, were early adapted to anthracite, and their cheerful open appearance has kept them to some extent in vogue. Hot-air furnaces were also invented, as early, at least, as 1813; but various faults, from the too great fierceness and dryness of the heat, imperfect defence against fire, etc., rendered them on the whole quite unsatisfactory, until about 1840, when great improvements began to be made; and many of the furnaces now employed afford a bountiful supply of air, almost fresh from out-doors, and not too warm and dry for health.

Apparatuses have also been devised for heating buildings by systems of hot-water pipes, and by systems of steam pipes; of which the latter, especially in manufacturing establishments, offices, public rooms, etc., succeed very well, though the heat would sometimes be somewhat too slowly diffused for private residences.

Until within twenty years, scarcely any care had been given to the ventilation of any buildings, whether public or private. At earlier periods, an abundant circulation of air was secured by the open chimney, through which a strong current of warm air continually rushed up, taking, as has been computed, at least nine-tenths of all the heat with it. With the introduction of stoves and furnaces, this ventilator was closed, and the air of warm rooms became unhealthily dry and hot, or vitiated by use, especially in schools, ball-rooms, court-rooms, public assemblies, etc. Many disorders were aggravated or made more common by this state of things; such as headaches, nervous affections, and lung complaints. Various plans of ventilation have been adopted to remedy these evils, but the principles of the science of pneumatics are even yet so imperfectly understood that no entirely satisfactory system of ventilation has yet been devised. The modes commonly used are, for large public buildings, such as churches, an opening at the ceiling, with a device outside for forming an upward current by the help of the wind; in private houses, openings at the sides of rooms, communicating indirectly with the external air; and where hot-air furnaces are used, a pipe supplying air from without, which is warmed by the furnace and passed on into the apartments. Stove-heat is, however, still not usually applied in such a manner as to promote health.

City residences are at present frequently furnished with two kinds of improvements rarely found elsewhere—gas and water.

The use of gas for lighting streets and houses was first invented by an Englishman named Murdoch, and tried at Redruth, in Cornwall, in 1792. It was first introduced in the city of New York by the old New York Gas Company, chartered in 1823. It is now used in most of our cities, and its deprivation would be thought a very serious misfortune.

An equally, and indeed much more labor-saving and convenient improvement in our modern domestic architectural arrangements, is the introduction of water from water works. Water works were commenced in New York before the Revolution, in 1774; but none were erected there until 1797, when the Manhattan Company put up a reservoir on what is now Chambers street. These small works were superseded by the Croton aqueduct, opened in 1842. Philadelphia was first supplied by a steam engine in 1799; and this was replaced by the celebrated Fairmount works, commenced in 1811. A number of our larger or more enterprising cities are now provided with aqueducts.

The fountains thus set flowing in our houses save all water-carrying, for bathing or cleaning purposes, either up or down stairs; for a proper connection with a sewerage system will admit of a sink as well as a water pipe in every story. The burdensome daily details of housework are thus very greatly lightened, and health, and time, and exertion very much economized by the various appliances of the modern city bathing-room.

Within about ten years, there have been introduced into one or two very luxurious city houses, hoistways, somewhat like those used in stores, but upholstered, and, in fact, fitted up like little rooms; these are raised and lowered so as to save the exertion of using the stairs, and are exceedingly convenient for the old and feeble.

This brief enumeration of improvements in domestic architecture could not properly include what may, however, in conclusion, be merely mentioned; that is, those large and splendidly finished houses which are erected by the great millionaires of the present day. The costly frescoes, the statues, the extravagant splendor of their fitting, the picture-galleries, conservatories, libraries, etc., etc., though good and beautiful in themselves, are exceptions, and not yet numerous enough to be considered domesticated in this country.

CHAPTER II.

FURNITURE—FURNISHING GOODS, ETC.

The furniture of country dwellings during the latter part of the last century was scantier than now, and, on the whole, of much cheaper quality and poorer make, although that of the wealthy was often handsomely designed, well and massively made, and heavily and tastefully ornamented. Little machinery was used in manufacturing furniture, which had, therefore, to be made by hand labor. This made patterns more numerous, as one design often served for a single side-board, set of chairs, etc., and for those made by one workman only; while now, one pattern may serve for thousands of sets. There was, therefore, greater variety, and often remarkably fine workmanship, and even artistic skill. The greater cheapness of wood, and the little use made of veneering, occasioned much furniture to be made of solid wood. Many pieces of this ancient, solid furniture now bring extravagant prices at auction, or from a second-hand store, where chance supplies a buyer with taste and means. As much as ten, or even twenty dollars each have been given for old-fashioned, carved, mahogany chairs; from twenty-five to forty dollars for a tall clock, etc., etc.

The increase in the supply of money, the decrease of any distinction between classes of society, and the general diffusion of wealth and comfort, render the difference between the furniture of the rich, and that of the poor, much less at the present day than formerly. Comparatively few luxuries of any kind are now accessible to the rich, which are not so to the farmer and the mechanic. This is not, of course, to be understood of the very poor, nor the very rich; nor of the most expensive luxuries; for Gobelin carpets an inch thick, marble statues by Powers, pictures by Church, Johannisberg wine, Strasburg pies, and the like, can never be possessed except by very few.

The bedsteads of our grandparents and great-grandparents were very commonly "four-posters;" that is, they consisted of four tall posts, into which were framed the side and end pieces. These posts often supported a wooden frame covered with cloth, somewhat like a roof, and called a "tester," from whose four sides hung down the curtains. Feather beds were universally used. Sheets were of linen; and coverlets of patchwork, marseilles, chintz, etc.

Carpets were comparatively little used; most people contenting themselves with a floor, washed clean, sanded, or, at most, painted. The carpets used eighty years ago were mostly English or Scotch ingrain, though a good many home-made rag-carpets were also used; and the price per yard was, perhaps, $1.50 to $1.75; not varying very much from the present price of a fair article, though the same sum represented more value then. There is a well-known anecdote of an honest old farmer who was one day introduced, for the first time, to a carpeted room. The carpet, as was usual in those days, was a sort of patch in the middle of the room, surrounded with a wide margin of bare floor. The visitor skirted cautiously along the sides of the room, and when invited by the lady of the house to walk across, excused himself with rustic politeness, because, he said, "his boots were too dirty to walk on the "*kiverlid.*"

Chairs were of hard wood—maple, oak, cherry, or mahogany—with seats of wood, basket-work, or cushion, covered with cloth, haircloth, or leather. Much skill and taste was expended on many of the costly solid mahogany parlor chairs, and they are even now much more stately than most of their modern successors. The rocking-chair—a truly American invention—dates back to a point not ascertained, but certainly not less than seventy or eighty years ago. No rocking-chairs of so antique a pattern as common chairs can, however, be found. An early improvement upon the old-fashioned wooden or wicker chair-seat was the straw-seat, of straw or rushes, woven together in four compartments, which converged to the middle of the seat. The cane-seat, woven like fine basket-work of slender strips of ratan, came afterward, and is still much used; it is strong, neat, light, and convenient. Many business and study chairs are now made with the seat pivoted on a stout iron pin—a very convenient invention, rendering it very easy to turn round from writing-desk to customer or client.

Tables were made of oak, pine, cherry, black walnut, and mahogany. In old-fashioned houses may sometimes still be seen a small table hinged to the wall at one side, so as to turn up flat against it, secured, when not in use, by a button. A leg hinged on beneath hung flat to the table when thus raised, and swung to its right place when lowered. Some old tables were enormously heavy, framed almost as strongly as a house, and with curiously complicated swinging legs to hold up the leaves. Such tables were often heirlooms, as was much household furniture. The substantial strength and solid materials used rendered it much more fit to serve generation after generation than the lighter and cheaper articles now made. The present "extension tables," which are frequently used in dining-rooms, were first patented in 1843; they draw out within certain limits to any length, when additional boards supply the top. Thus the same table accommodates either a large party or a small one.

The sideboard was an indispensable article in dining-rooms where it could be afforded, being used instead of a closet, to hold plate, wine, table-linen, cake, etc.

Bureaus, or chests of drawers, were made on a larger scale than now, sometimes towering far toward the ceiling, containing a great number of drawers, large and small, and often ornamented in a peculiar and striking manner at the handles and keyholes, with brass escutcheons elaborately and fancifully pierced or carved.

The movable wash-stands, still commonly used, have been replaced in some cases, where aqueduct water in pipes is used, by fixed stands, sometimes luxuriously topped with marble, having fixed basins sunk in them, faucets for water, and a hole below to let it off. A "water-back," or boiler, attached to the kitchen range or stove, is sometimes made to supply hot water through pipes, from which another faucet supplies hot water as desired to each basin—a most comfortable provision in cold weather.

China and glass ware were much more costly than at present; pressed glass, now so extensively used, having been introduced only within the present century. Pewter platters and plates were frequently the only dishes on a country table. Table crockery was most commonly of white stoneware, with blue edges, or of the "willow pattern." There was very little silver ware, and what there was, was much more solidly manufactured than is now usually the case. Block tin was much used, until to a great extent superseded by Britannia metal, which came into use about twenty-five years since; "albata," a sort of white metal, introduced within about ten years, and German silver, an invention dating back, in this country, about twice as far. A still later substitute for the precious metals is "oreide," a sort of brass, very closely resembling gold; and another, discovered within the last three years by a French chemist, is aluminium, a light, strong metal, resembling silver in appearance, which can be extracted from common clay, and other aluminous earths. It is by no means improbable that this last metal will come into very extensive use, for household as well as other purposes.

Silver forks were first brought into general use about twenty-five or thirty years since. Those previously used were the common three-pronged steel forks, or two-pronged ones, either of them sufficiently inconvenient for carrying loose food to the mouth. Another improvement, about as old, in table furniture, is the invention of balanced knife-handles, the weight in the handle keeping the blade off the table cloth when laid down; a little thing, but very promotive of cleanliness.

Instead of the modern Yankee clock, the first patent for which was taken out by Eli Terry, of Plymouth, Conn., in 1797, were used either small Dutch clocks, stuck up on the wall, like a swallow's nest, or the old-fashioned tall clocks, in cases seven feet high, which were sometimes very handsomely ornamented with carving, brass decorations, and richly painted dials. On the broad faces of these old clocks were sometimes given, besides the hour and the minute, a whole almanac of indications: the time of high tide, moon's age, day of the week and month, name of month, year, etc., etc. Occasionally, a wooden bird came out and was supposed to sing, or a tune was played when the hour struck. Quite a large number of these old clocks, most of the best of which were made during the first quarter of this century, are still in use, and are frequently excellent time-keepers.

These observations do not include the Mississippi valley, which was just beginning to be settled by Anglo-American pioneers at the close of the revolutionary war. In all that extensive region, the rudest substitutes for all the supposed indispensable instruments of civilized life were used. Furniture, indeed, scarcely existed. A bedstead and a table, rudely hewn out by the sharp axe of the master of the house, some stools of the same manufacture, a shelf, a row of pegs in the log wall, an iron kettle, which often served in its own proper person the various purposes of wash-basin, cooking-kettle, soup-tureen, slop-dish, dish-pan, swill-pail, and hog-trough; a few tins, or a little crockery, a chest or two, a stump hollowed at the top for a mortar to pound corn, and a stick for a pestle — such was the scanty furnishing of that day in that region. As the population has increased, it has brought with it from the older states all their improvements, and now no distinction can be found between the two sections—at least, so far as concerns those of moderate or liberal means.

Lamps, for oil, or candles of tallow, sperm, or wax, were the only means of lighting either rooms or streets, eighty years ago. The amount of ingenuity which has been exercised in this department of housekeeping is astonishing; a hundred and thirty-seven patents for lamps alone having been issued from 1798 to 1847. The variety of these, and of the substances to the use of which they are adapted, is remarkable. There are yet some families which make their own mould or dip tallow candles; but only a few. Those who still use candles mostly, either indulge in the costly luxury of wax or sperm, or use some of the various lately invented substitutes, introduced within ten or fifteen years, such as the so-called "margarine," "stearine," etc., made from lard, or the still more recent "paraffine" candles, of a material extracted from bituminous coal. The first innovation upon the old-fashioned custom of using oil lamps—not, however, including in this term the argand and similar modifications of it—was the introduction of lamps for the use of burning-fluid and of camphene, which are preparations of oil of turpentine and alcohol, and though neat and convenient to use, and giving a pleasant light, have, in careless hands, been the occasion of a terrible number of deaths and maimings by burning. These fluids have been in use during somewhat more than twenty years. The use of gas has been already referred to for the lighting of cities and dwellings. Not long after the introduction of camphene, a large number of lamps were invented for burning lard oil, just beginning to be manufactured, and also lard, tallow, and other gross animal fats. About thirty patents were issued for lard lamps alone, during 1842 and 1843, including lamps of the common standard style, argand and solar patterns, etc. These lamps, in some cases, gave a very good light, but it proved troublesome to light them during cold weather, and they required much greasy work in cleaning, etc.

During the last five years, another class of illuminators has come into use, and is at present spreading extensively. These are the various oils known as coal oil, kerosene, helion oil, etc., etc. They are all, or nearly all, distilled or purified from the crude coal oil of the wells of western Pennsylvania, or from the products of the more bituminous varieties of coal. It has thus far been found necessary to use a chimney in burning them, and they smoke very easily while burning; but the light they give is clear and pleasant, they are much more cleanly than any of the animal oils, and of an aromatic odor.

Improvements in furniture are gradually introduced, and in a manner which renders it peculiarly difficult to fix precise dates. It may be said in general, that the uniform tendency has been toward lightness and convenience of form. The artistic beauty of the designs has not materially improved.

CHAPTER III.

FOOD—COOKING, ETC.

The general character of the food, drink, and cooking of three quarters of a century ago, was very similar to that of to-day. Meats were the same, but less fresh meat was eaten; salt beef, salt pork, and bacon being the ordinary meat, and the beef and pork barrel being almost as universal and necessary in the household as the flour barrel. The common vegetables were potatoes, turnips, cabbages, and onions, with a few beets and parsnips. Carrots were scarcely used at all. At the south, sweet potatoes were, as at present, used in place of Irish potatoes, and okra, tomatoes, etc., were also cultivated as at present. Tomatoes were scarcely known at the north, until about 1820 or 1825, when they were occasionally brought from the south, and gradually began to be cultivated, under the name of "love-apples." The egg-plant, spinach, cauliflower, broccoli, and other kitchen-garden plants, have also been introduced since the beginning of the century, from abroad.

Bread of rye, "rye-and-Indian," or Indian meal alone, and Indian puddings, johnny-cake, and the like, were more used than at present; for most grinding was done at the small country mills; transportation was slow, difficult, and costly; neither the great wheat fields of the east, nor the greater ones of the west, were yielding their increase; and the great flouring mills that are supported by them had not grown up. Every farmer's family, therefore, commonly used breadstuff of its own raising; and but a very small share of that used in the towns was brought from any other than the immediate neighborhood.

All the labor of preparing the raw material for food was performed in the family. All the coffee had to be burnt and ground, spices pulverized, salt powdered, yeast made, soap manufactured, meat pickled, etc., etc., by each housekeeper for herself, or under her immediate supervision.

Throughout the extensive western forest frontier, a large proportion of the inhabitants lived in great part upon game; but this was, from the difficulty of transportation, even less accessible in the older settlements than now, when it must be brought from the distant lakes, and streams, and woods of Canada or Maine.

The use of spirituous and malt liquors was universal. It was thought no impropriety for distinguished clergymen to own a share in a distillery; and the meetings of ministers on religious business were made occasions of jollity, often even to such an extent that the reverend companions went home quite tipsy. Cider was drank in the country, and cider, rum, brandy, or wine in town, at every meal. Spirits were expected to be offered to every visitor, and if not, the host was thought mean and stingy.

Cooking was performed over an open wood fire; a mode in many respects more laborious and less convenient than the present use of stoves and ranges; but which, if skilfully conducted, gives the food a flavor more perfect and delicate than can be attained in any other manner.

As has been implied, the changes in food have thus been more in the treatment than in the materials of it. The chief of these changes, like those in warming houses, have arisen from the introduction of anthracite coal into use, which has caused the employment of cooking-stoves and ranges, instead of the open fire. Nearly four hundred patents for cooking-stoves and ranges were issued from 1812 to 1847, and great numbers of others have been granted since; the total number of such patents may safely be estimated at not less than six hundred.

An early style of cooking-stove, and quite a favorite one in its day, was the rotary, whose top could be swivelled round by a crank and cog-wheel geared to a ratchet underneath its edge, so as to bring any sauce pan or kettle forward to the cook. This variety is, however, now nearly obsolete, and innumerable later inventions have succeeded, each enjoying a brief reputation, usually conferred rather by diligent advertisement than by any real peculiar merits in the stove itself.

The cooking range may be described as a modified stove bricked into a fireplace, instead of standing out in the room. Its oven, instead of being back of the fireplace, as in a stove, is above it; and in most patterns, so far back as to render it very hot and inconvenient for use. Some late patterns, however, have brought the oven sufficiently far forward to remedy this objection.

The use of stoves and ranges has rendered cooking much more convenient, but has, in a great measure, substituted the baking of meats in the oven for the better old fashion of roasting. Their advantages, however, are greater than their disadvantages; they are far cheaper and easier in management than an open fire; and in all the older portions of the country are necessary, because wood could not be furnished to supply the kitchens.

CHAPTER IV.

DRESS.

In discussing the changes of costume since the revolutionary war, it will be more convenient to divide it with reference to female than to male costume. On this principle, the period from 1783 or thereabouts may be divided into five, thus:—

1. 1783 to French Revolution.
2. French Revolution to 1815.
3. 1815 to 1830.
4. 1830 to 1845.
5. 1845 to present time.

Speaking generally, the changes thus succeeding each other have been improvements; although almost all of them have been sufficiently absurd in themselves. These fashions have always come from England or France; since about 1815, almost entirely from France.

1. *Period first*, 1783 to French Revolution. At the close of the Revolution in 1783, the costume of gentlemen was in the English style of the day, viz.: a single-breasted low-collared coat of broadcloth, commonly of some gay color, often scarlet, bright blue, claret color, peach-blossom, with full skirts, and ample pocket-flaps, sleeves, and cuffs; a waistcoat, with long flaps; knee-breeches, often also of gay colors, fastened at the outer side of the knee with a buckle; long stockings, black, white, or colored; shoes with the well-known showy buckles, or boots with a broad piece of white or unstained leather turned down around the tops, and therefore called top-boots; a ruffled shirt, a lace cravat, powdered hair, a queue, not unfrequently a wig, and a three-cornered cocked hat. A very few aged men still wear or have worn this costume within the last ten years, even to the queue and the shirt-frill. The cocked

hat did not maintain its place so long, though quite often to be seen during the first quarter of the present century.

The formal stateliness of this old costume suited well the more careful manners and stiff politeness of the day; for even in our republican country, the distinctions of social rank and station prevailed to an extent which few people now realize. Old persons now living can remember when "Mr." was a title considered exclusively proper for the "gentry;" when a "gentleman's" son would have been reproved by his father for calling a farmer "Mr." A farmer or mechanic was called "goodman," and his wife not "Mrs." or "mistress," but "goody."

Female costume was on the whole, perhaps, less strikingly different from that now in vogue, except in head-dress. Its other most distinguishing characteristics were high-heeled shoes, often of bright red or other strong colors; sleeves to the elbows, with heavy lace ruffles; a tight, close, long waist, and a skirt stiffened out by hoops very nearly as much as by the "skeleton skirts" now used.

The head-dresses then fashionable were, however, most monstrous, and furnished an endless theme for satire and jest. The hair was greased, and powdered, and "craped," as it was called--that is, combed up over artificial hair, a mass of tow, or a cushion; artificial flowers were worked into it, broad ribbons hung around it, feathers three feet high stuck into it, all sorts of vegetable-looking leaves and even fruit and vegetables themselves (imitated) were piled on, and a mass constructed which it seemed totally impossible for a lady's neck to uphold or endure; which was often, literally and truly, quite as large as a bushel basket. A caricature of those days represents a lady sitting in a chair during her head-dressing, while one barber, mounted on a tall pair of steps, is frizzling a curl, and another stands off at one side, taking the altitude of the edifice he has helped to build, with a quadrant. Calashes, whose gig-top appearance almost every one may remember to have seen, were invented long before this time, as early as 1765, as the only contrivance in the nature of a bonnet which would cover these vast machines. Such head-dresses required great skill in preparation and adjustment, and could, of course, not be made up by the owner herself. It was the business of the barber, and often occupied two or three tedious hours. The idea of going through such an operation daily was out of the question, and these "heads," as they were called, were made to last sometimes for weeks together. Indeed, they were continually corrupting, even so that worms bred in them, among the flour used for hair-powder and the pomatum; and numerous recipes were in use for poisons to prevent vermin from breeding in them. Sleeping in the natural posture was, of course, impossible; ladies slept sitting up or with a carefully arranged support for the neck and head, adapted to the precious mass of absurdities that crowned it.

Period second, French Revolution to 1815. The French Revolution may be called the conclusion of the era of those strange fashions. The freedom of that period, so licentious in politics, was equally so in dress, and in this department, as in the other, caused many and great changes both at home and abroad. In this country, which had before that time followed the English fashions almost exclusively, those of France now began to take the lead, and the ancient caprices of dress to be replaced by others more modern, but not less absurd.

From about 1780, down to about 1800, women's skirts grew more and more scanty in circumference, until they were "gored," and cut so close as to almost impede walking. The waist was also carried up sometimes to one inch below the arm-pit, and the neck at the same time cut indecently low. The skirt was fitted closely to the figure, no wrinkles being admissible, and the fewest possible underclothes were worn; a fashion both abominably ugly and very unhealthy. These ungainly waists excited much deserved ridicule. A well-known song beginning—

> "Shepherds, I have lost my love—
> Have you seen my Anna?"

was parodied so as to apply to them, commencing with—

> "Shepherds, I have lost my waist—
> Have you seen my body?"

The variations in bonnets and head-dresses during this same period were many and wonderful. In 1786, women wore their hair frizzed and powdered; and for riding costume, a man's jacket with broad lapels, and a broad-brimmed hat. In 1789, the hair was frizzled out into an enormous bush, sometimes with a quantity of dangling curls besides; and bonnets, to hold this affair,

1776. EVENING DRESS. 1780. 1780. 1785.

EVENING DRESS. 1795. EVENING DRESS. 1797. 1800. 1805.

1805. 1812. 1812. 1812.

1815. 1818. 1820. 1825.

1828. WINTER DRESS. 1833. 1833. 1833.

1833. 1840. 1844. 1850.

were made like an upright bag stiffened out. In 1794 a fashion came in of finishing up the head-dress with feathers half a yard high. About 1795 these styles of expansive head-dress disappeared, and small bonnets came into use all at once, like a helmet or a straw cap, with a vizor such as is now worn on a boy's cap.

From 1805 to 1810, bare arms were much in fashion with women, and a singular mode of wearing gloves prevailed. The glove was worn with a long armlet attached, which was drawn on smoothly up to the elbow, and then pushed down again so as to lie in irregular wrinkles on the arm, which was reckoned remarkably pretty. These were termed "rucked gloves." About 1808 was introduced the "gunboat" style of bonnet, which consisted of a moderate-sized crown, and a wide expanse of brim, spreading out around the face, in a form fancied to resemble the peculiar shape of a gunboat, which is very wide toward the bows.

About 1810 appeared the plaid cloaks, used both by men and women, which may still sometimes be found hung up in an old closet; very wide and long, and for women having a great clumsy hood hanging at the back of the neck. In 1814 the bonnets all at once spread out into an immense crown, leaving very little brim.

Men's costume varied during this time no less. The reign of powder and pigtails may be said to have ended about 1793, immediately after the French Revolution; and about the same time the round hat took the place of the three-cornered cocked hat. A little later, perhaps about 1800, people began to leave off wearing wigs when they had hair of their own. It is hard to comprehend how people could submit so long to a custom so disfiguring, inconvenient, and cumbrous—for every wig-wearer had to have his whole head shaved every few days, and lived in constant peril of making a fantastic appearance if his clumsy and unsafe head-gear should be knocked off. Yet the mode prevailed for two hundred years; nearly from 1600 to 1800.

One of the early costumes which replaced the ante-revolutionary fashions for men, and which was the height of the *ton* in 1786, consisted of a very broad-brimmed hat; a powdered wig with a pig-tail; a coat with a very short waist, broad lapels, and tremendous swallow-tails; buckskin breeches, and top-boots.

During this period, and, indeed, down to about 1830, gentlemen's necks were often swathed with an enormous thickness of cravat; a fashion said to have been introduced by George IV., while a leader of fashion, to hide the scrofulous swelling of his neck. Two or three handkerchiefs, each a full yard square, were thus worn; giving the neck an appearance which now seems excessively dowdy and uncomfortable.

During the closing years of the last century, knee-breeches began to yield to the pantaloon, which came from France; and shoe-buckles disappeared to give place to a mere string or ribbon. The prince-regent of England, afterward George IV., first led this fashion, although he resumed buckles at the petition of the buckle-makers, who represented that the ruin of their trade would starve them. It was ruined, however, in spite of them and him, and notwithstanding that he was the inventor of a shoe-buckle.

This introduction of the pantaloon and the shoe-string, and the disuse of wigs, marks the era of the modern costume. The dress-coat, however, or a garment much like it, was worn at intervals, as early as 1750; although it did not definitely occupy the place of the old-fashioned broad skirts until about 1800. It should be observed that "pantaloon" means, in its first strict sense, a garment fitting quite tightly to the shape of the leg, and buttoning close around the ankles, as if a prolongation of the knee-breeches. The present pantaloons are in strictness "trowsers," having been introduced as such, and by that name, under the auspices of the Duke of Wellington, after the battle of Waterloo.

High-heeled shoes, for women, went out of use about 1789, and were replaced by something very like the present graceful, low-quartered shoe. Round toes, for men's shoes and boots, came in about the same time, and prevailed until about 1804 or 1806, when the first beginnings appeared of square toes.

Period third, 1815 to 1830. The last period may be characterized as that of tight, scant dresses. The present one may be described as that of big bonnets, puffed hair, and leg-of-mutton sleeves, which last, however, appeared only toward its end.

Knee breeches, which had continued to be "full dress," were now quite out of date. Frock-coats had been introduced by the Duke of Wellington and his officers after the peninsular war, together with the boot called after him. In 1815 trowsers began to be worn, being also introduced under his auspices; although the original pantaloon, with its tight, close fit and ankle-buttons, maintained itself for ten years or more before quite disappearing. In 1815, also, bonnets underwent a great revolution, shrinking to small dimensions in the crown, and spreading into a portentous brim.

Not far from 1820 began what may be called the modern era of tight lacing, which was adopted as the short waists began to be replaced by longer ones, and the modern type of female dress, viz., a long waist, bulging with a sudden angle into a voluminous skirt, became established. About 1825 was adopted a method of wearing the hair in great puffs at the sides and on the top of the head, dressed, also, with large bows of ribbon. To hold this array, an enormous bonnet was required, and was used. Skirts now began to be a very little fuller; two or three plaits at the waist being all that were at first admitted, and more being introduced from time to time. About 1828 began the "leg-of-mutton sleeves," which grew at once to enormous proportions. These ridiculous and most inconvenient appendages were stuffed out with down, or held out with reed, millinet, or whalebone; but they were continually becoming crushed, and were very troublesome. They had a certain absurd harmony with the big bonnets and puffed hair of the day, as well as with the broad-shouldered, stiffly-cut capes that were worn with them.

Period fourth, 1830 to 1845. The beginning of this period is marked by the introduction of the costume of the days of Jackson—the bell-crowned hat, long, swallow-tailed coat, with high collar and "bishop" sleeves, and loose trowsers. The bishop sleeves were distinguished by rising into a ridge where they were set in at the shoulder, as do the sleeves of the episcopal vestments; this ridge being in 1830-35, stuffed with cotton to hold them up. The big bonnets and puffed hair, wide capes and leg-of-muttons still prevailed. Boots and shoes were worn with very broad, square toes until about 1840, when narrow toes took their place; and the calash, invented almost a hundred years before, was still employed to cover the elaborate head-dress. The decrease in the size of women's sleeves is the chief feature of this period; the minor details of the successive changes of style were innumerable, as usual.

Period fifth, 1845 to 1860. This period, also, may be dismissed with brief consideration. Its first years were marked by the introduction of the sack coat, or, as it is called in France, the *paletot*. This easy, commodious, and cheap garment is infinitely more becoming than a dress-coat, and very much more convenient than either that or a frock coat. This garment, though introduced in the present century later than either the dress or frock coat, may be traced to a far greater antiquity; a very similar garment having been worn at the courts of France and England about the year 1450—nearly half a century before the discovery of America. At about the same time was introduced that most preposterous of all feminine fashions, the *bustle*, which was a sort of pad tied on behind to make the skirts stand out with the desirable degree of fulness. This was made of various materials: cloth stuffed with bran, hair, cotton, rags, old newspapers, etc., and sometimes of India-rubber, inflated with air. The bustle marked the beginning of the present period of expanded skirts. As this machine did not sufficiently spread out these garments, various other means were resorted to; the use of an enormous number of skirts—a habit most pernicious to health—and skirts fewer in number, of stiffly-starched cloth with cords sown on, or of grass cloth, or hair-cloth, or stiffened out with many cords of new manilla rope or common clothes-line, or with whalebone or coils of brass wire. All these having been tried and failed, the present fashion came up, of "skeleton-skirts," made of strips of iron somewhat similar to a watch-spring. These seem at present to be quite adequate to their purpose; although what the real reason of that purpose is, it would be impossible to say. Why women's skirts should constitute a great stiff, hollow cone about their lower limbs, within which they must wear an entire second suit of clothes for warmth and protection, is as unanswerable a riddle, as would be the inquiry why, during the first years of this century, they should be so scanty in dimensions, so thin, and clinging so closely to the figure.

Another fashion introduced during this period is that of wearing soft felt hats instead of the round hats, which last are now often described as "hard-shells," or "stove-pipe" hats; nick-names well applied, and which may aid in driving out this very uncomfortable and unreasonable fashion. The felt hat was not often seen among us until the enthusiasm which attended Kossuth's visit to the United States, in 1851 and 1852; after which it was brought out, at first with a feather, in close imitation of the national hat of the Hungarian hero, and called a "Kossuth hat." The feather was soon left off, being not much more suitable to our national characteristics than a nose-ring would be; but the hat itself, being found both comfortable and graceful, was retained, though many different patterns have since been used.

The size of bonnets, so large about 1830, gradually decreased until a minimum was reached in the very small ones worn during the last few years. These scarcely covered the back half of the head, and were, therefore, kept in place by a sort of skewer thrust through two holes in the back lining and the knotted back hair. The bonnets worn now are a very little larger, and we may, perhaps, be on the verge of a return to large ones. Among the latest styles of ladies' head-dress are two quite remarkable ones. One is a very homely hat, singularly like an inverted tin wash-basin in form; the other is as graceful as this is awkward; namely, the "Spanish hat," a small, low-crowned hat of black felt, velvet, etc., with a brim turned up at the sides, usually worn with a feather, and with a net for the hair.

Perhaps the very latest invention of the tailors is one for men, similar in purpose to the artificial means often used by women to remedy natural defects of form. This is a sort of pad, or frame of wire covered with cloth, to be worn under the shirt-bosom, to give the chest an appearance of manly fulness. No criticism is necessary upon such a trick; for no dandy so silly as to use it could be reached by any argument whatever.

In reviewing the whole series of fashions as thus briefly presented, it will appear that, on the whole, there has been a decided improvement. There are, doubtless, a sufficient number of not very wise fashions in dress now prevailing; but the preposterous, filthy head-dress of 1783, the indecent, scanty costume of 1800, the pudding-like cravat of the same period, the broad shadow of the gunboat bonnet, the balloon-like appendage of the leg-of-mutton sleeve, have each, in turn, been superseded by something, on the whole, less foolish; and it may be claimed with safety, that at this present writing, the fashions, both for men and women, are based upon something more like common-sense principles, and admit more freedom in adaptation, and, therefore, greater convenience and grace, than has ever before been the case. It is matter of congratulation, however, that an American taste is being developed, and our ladies becoming less dependent on fashions from abroad; and every year is yielding a larger liberty to our female population, in adopting such forms and colors as suit the peculiarities of each individual, without regard to any absolute or universal decree, and this is still more the case with men. Thus we seem to be approaching that condition of eclectic philosophy which, if it becomes actually a received law, will afford the utmost possible variety, comfort, and elegance.

CHAPTER V.

SOCIAL AND MENTAL CULTURE—INTERCOURSE—HEALTH—ART, ETC.

Nearly all the increase in comfort and happiness which is the pride of modern civilization is traceable to scientific discovery and to mechanical invention. These causes have supplied the means of the labor-saving machines and processes of the last three-quarters of a century. The use of these machines and processes has brought it to pass that men can earn their living by the labor of a less proportion of their time than formerly. And this power enables them to devote a correspondingly larger share of effort to the task of gaining knowledge, and of pressing forward in the path of moral and mental improvement. The amount of mental activity which has been devoted to these material processes is astonishing, and is only feebly indicated by the statistical fact that from 1801 to 1848, inclusive, the number of patents issued in the United States reached the large total of 15,844.

The readiest way to sketch the general progress of society at present sought to be described, will be to set forth briefly, in chronological succession, the periods or occurrences which have marked the commencement or maturity of any important influence upon the prosperity of the community, without attempting to classify them particularly.

In 1796 was taken out the first American patent for a pianoforte, by J. S. McLean, of New Jersey. The manufacture of these instruments has become very extensive; the larger manufactories sometimes turning out thousands a year. Many improvements have been made in their construction; and they are now so good and so numerous, as to be an important means in the increasing diffusion of musical knowledge.

In 1799 Dr. Waterhouse, of Harvard University, first introduced Jenner's discovery of vaccine inoculation; a measure which has substantially freed our community from the fear, the pain, and the disfigurement of the small-pox. This single discovery has had no inconsiderable influence in lengthening life, and increasing its happiness by dispelling the apprehensions, always felt before, of suffering and death.

The importance of regular, rapid, and cheap modes of travel and transportation, to the general improvement of society in wealth and intelligence, is exceedingly great. Distance of residence, difficulty of travelling, difficulty of carrying, has, through all the history of the world, been a chief means of keeping nations poor, because thus they could not exchange what they had for what they had not; and thus, however much they possessed of one thing, they were poor. For wealth does not consist in mass of possessions. Not mountains, even of gold, if unexchangeable, are wealth. Wealth is *mass and variety* of possessions together, and must therefore necessarily arise by exchange, that is, travel and transportation. The seacoast nations, commanding water-carriage, have thus always been the rich ones; it was not until steam destroyed the obstacles of river currents, and of wide plains and rugged mountains, that inland nations could be rich in any sufficient sense.

In the same way, speed and certainty of intercourse promotes exchange of mental wealth, by correspondence, visiting, etc.; maintains a sense of nationality, and keeps up acquaintance and good feeling. Were it not for ease of travel, there would be but slight hopes of keeping Maine and Georgia in the same republic with California and Oregon. As it is, they will remain.

In 1811 commenced a movement of a very different character from that of the inventor Fulton, but which has exerted an influence upon the health and morals of our nation, even more important than the benefits of cheap and rapid locomotion. This was the temperance reform.

The laxity of manners and morals which must attend war, had greatly increased the use of intoxicating liquor during the Revolution, and it continued to spread after the peace. Dr. Rush had published his "Inquiry into the Effects of Ardent Spirits," in 1804; but no decided movement against their use was made until 1811, when the Presbyterian General Assembly appointed a committee on the subject. That and other ecclesiastical bodies, at various times, passed different resolutions and recommendations intended to limit the use of liquor, but with no very great success. The first total abstinence society was formed in Boston in 1826, and during the following ten years, others multiplied with great rapidity, liquor-selling became disreputable, and the common use of ardent spirits was to a very great extent broken up. For the last quarter of a century it has been a generally received belief that the use of any intoxicating liquors as a beverage is hurtful, demoralizing, and an unmitigated evil in every respect; and the consequence has been perceptible improvement in health, diminution of crime, and saving of money both public and private. It must, however, be admitted that the temperance cause has stood still, if it has not actually retrograded, during the last few years; and that the so-called "Maine law," which its advocates hoped would prove a final bar to the folly and wretchedness of intemperance, has, in some cases at least, produced rather a reaction than a progress. Still, the practice of total abstinence, and the very great diminution in the quantity of liquors drank by those not total abstinents, has accomplished an inestimable amount of good, and immensely promoted the prosperity of the nation, both in material and in moral respects.

In 1832 the study of phrenology was introduced into this country by Spurzheim. This system, whatever the correctness of its doctrines as to indications by the shape and size of the head, which are certainly believed by many intelligent persons, is at any rate entitled to the merit of having furnished a new and very clear classification of the mental faculties, which has become the means of a great improvement in mental philosophy.

Two years later, viz., in 1834, the homœopathic system of medicine was introduced, which has since become very extensively believed. As in regard to phrenology, it may be said of this system, that whether all its peculiar doctrines are true or false, it has at least done good indirectly, by operating to reduce the quantity of medicines given by the old-fashioned practitioners, and to direct their attention more than before to the very important points of regimen, ventilation, and the other collateral departments of general hygiene.

About 1840 was introduced into this country the greatest improvement in pictorial art since the discovery of painting in oils by John Van Eyck in the fifteenth century; the greatest discovery ever made in that department of human knowledge; viz., the art of taking pictures by the chemical action of light, named, from its discoverer, daguerreotyping; and various modifications of which are known as the talbotype, photograph, ambrotype, crystalotype, etc. These methods render it both easy and cheap to procure an absolutely and necessarily perfect representation of a person or a thing. Besides the pleasure of thus being enabled, at a trifling cost, to possess a whole gallery of perfect portraits of friends—a privilege heretofore scarcely attainable, even at an immense price, by the great men of the earth—this new art has already been made exceedingly useful in securing diagrams of lunar and other astronomical phenomena, and in taking pictures of buildings, landscapes, statues, etc.; and promises in many ways to promote the progress of many other arts, by means of its wonderful power of perfect representation.

Not far from the same time, another system of medical treatment was introduced—the "water-cure," or "hydropathic" system, which has proved very useful in certain classes of diseases, and has, like homœopathy, done its part in relaxing the dogmatic and extreme severity of much of the old, or regular practice. This treatment, besides a very simple mode of life, consists only in the application of water, at various temperatures and in various ways; and it is successfully practised in many establishments devoted to it, which have been put in operation at places where water of the requisite purity could be had.

In 1845 the principle of cheap postage was established in this country by a law of Congress, and another step thus taken toward the entire release from tax or encumbrance of the intercourse of one mind with another. Cheap postage is one of the latest signs of a high civilization; it is one of the most promising indications of our own future.

Still one year later was discovered the medical process, since termed "anæsthesia," which consists in rendering persons insensible by the inhalation of certain gases (usually an ether, or chloroform), thus affording an opportunity of performing surgical operations quite without the knowledge of the patient. The agonies suffered in the dentist's chair, or under the hands of the surgeon, and the not less tormenting pain of many nervous diseases, may thus be much alleviated, and even entirely relieved.

In the same year was issued the first patent for sewing machines, to Elias Howe, jr. It is only necessary to allude to the very great saving of time, and strength, and health which these machines have effected; their effects are before the eyes of all. They are performing in a day the work of weeks, and doing very much to relieve women of a species of labor which was principally confined to them, but which consumed, in the merest petty drudgery, a wretchedly great proportion of their time, and often ruined health and destroyed life.

An important outgrowth of one of the departments of improvement which have been described, is the modern hotel. The American first-class hotel is an institution quite peculiar to this country, and includes within itself many of the various inventions which have just been catalogued: splendid furniture, elaborate food, economical and yet liberal housekeeping, labor-saving machinery; in short, an unrivalled combination of the applications of human ingenuity to the improvement of domestic life.

To recapitulate: It has thus been shown, though briefly and with many imperfections, that the course of our nation during the seventy-seven years since the Revolution has been one of steadfast, and essential, and solid improvement in things material and immaterial, physical and mental, practical and ornamental; in business, travel, dress, homes and home comforts, wealth, morals, intellect—in short, in every department of human activity.

BOOKS.

CHAPTER I.

BOOK TRADE—PUBLISHING—JOBBING—RETAILING.

"Yankee curiosity" is frequently a subject of remark with the flippant writers and travellers of the old world, and if not always urged as a reproach, it is not seldom referred to in a deprecating sense by those who do not appreciate the immense activity of intellect of which it is one manifestation. There is no doubt either of the existence of the alleged curiosity, or that it sometimes exhibits itself in a ludicrous light; but it also manifests itself in the indefatigable investigations to which nature and art are continually subjected by the ever inquiring American mind. There result from those investigations, not the dreary metaphysical theories that are evolved from German contemplation, but those countless inventions, improvements, and applications of mechanical principles that are every year recorded in the patent office, and the effects of which are seen in every department of industry. The religious and political assemblies; the amusing, instructive, and scientific addresses of the lecture-room; and the marvellous circulation of the public press, all reflect that thirst for knowledge which is a part of Yankee curiosity. This, however, gives a still stronger evidence of its vigor in the book trade, which, in the United States, shows an extent of sales that no other country can hope to approach. It is based on the universal ability of the people to read, and on that "curiosity," or thirst for knowledge, which induces them to do so, accompanied by means to purchase books. The word "means" comprehends not only greater wealth on the part of the purchaser, but reduced prices for the books. The existence of 20,000,000 of people who can all read, composes an immense market for books, that must be supplied; and happily, busy intellects have written, while the mechanical processes of publishing have been developed in a manner to supply the demand. In order to compare the book market of the United States with that of Europe, we may refer to the census returns of 1850. That informs us that in that year there were 19,553,068 white persons in the country. Of these, 9,421,557 were over 20 years of age, and of these, 962,898 could neither read nor write, of whom 195,114 were aliens. We now turn to France, and we find that there were 17,000,000 persons over 20 years of age; and of these, 3,400,000 only could read and write, and the remainder, 13,600,000, could not. In other words, there were, in the United States, 8,458,000 readers of books, against 3,400,000 in France. But there were, also, in the United States, 4,530,845 persons between 10 and 20. Of these, 4,063,046 attended school, and, as a consequence, bought and read school-books. The ratio of these scholars to the whole number who can read and write must be the same in France. Hence there are, in fact, three times as many readers in the United States as in France.

The making of books has kept pace with the increasing demand for them. If we look back to the library of King Alfred, we find that he gave 8 hydes of land for a book on cosmography, brought from Italy by Bishop Biscop. At such rates, none but a king could afford to buy a book; but, on the other hand, there were few, even among nobles, who could read if they had them! There was no market, and no manufacture. As the art of reading became so far progressive that the old barons could sign their names, instead of punching the seals of instruments with their sword pummels, some little demand for books sprung up, but at enormous rates. The state of the book market, when literature began to dawn in those iron ages, Scott makes old Douglas describe in terse phrase:—

> "Thanks be to God! no son of mine,
> Save Gawain, e'er could pen a line."

A modern canvasser would not have gotten

his name in advance for numbers to be left. Louis XI., of France, in 1471, was obliged to give security and a responsible endorser to the Paris faculty of medicine, in order to obtain the loan of the works of an Arabian physician. The art of printing, which was introduced into England in 1474, had an important influence upon the production of books, and this, probably, was the cause of a greater spread of learning, that reacted upon the demand. The Bible was the most commonly used, and these, in noble houses, with heavy covers and clasps, were chained to shelves and reading-desks. In the sixteenth and seventeenth centuries, books were mostly folio and quarto. But the dimensions of books decreased as they became popularized, and this was in proportion to the spread of learning among the people. This went on gradually, until both the market and supply were considerable, up to the eighteenth century. With the colonies of America—among whom both religious and political views were based upon general education—schools became an institution, and in New England the use of them an obligation. From that time the market for books increased with the numbers of the people. The first bookseller mentioned is Hezekiah Usher, of Boston, in 1652; and his son, John Usher, is mentioned by a writer in 1686, as very rich, and as having "got his estate by bookselling." That books, in the early part of the century, were by no means abundant, or easy to be got at, is evident from what Franklin tells us of the difficulties he encountered, and the great advantage he enjoyed, in having access to the library of a merchant. The most of them were imported at, no doubt, such expense as confined their general use to the better classes. Some years after, viz., in 1732, at the time Franklin commenced the publication of "Poor Richard's Almanac," in Philadelphia, a Boston bookseller advertised as follows:—

"Whereas it has been the common method of the most curious merchants of Boston to procure their books from London, this is to acquaint those gentlemen that I, the said Fry, will sell all sorts of account books, done after the most acute manner, for 20 per cent. cheaper than they can have them from London.

"For the pleasing entertainment of the polite parts of mankind, I have printed the most beautiful poems of Mr. Stephen Duck, the famous Wiltshire poet. It is a full demonstration to me that the people of New England have a fine taste for good sense and polite learning, having already sold 1,200 of those poems."

This was pretty well for Richard Fry, and we hope he had not then introduced the art of magnifying his sales on paper. That there were a number of booksellers then doing well, is evident from the fact that Mr. John Usher had made his fortune at it 50 years before; and in 1724 there was held a convention of Boston booksellers, to regulate the trade, and raise the price of some descriptions of books. The publication and sale of books increased slowly, until the events of the war began to excite the minds of the public, and works on those subjects were eagerly taken up. The practice was, to some extent, to sell books in sheets, to be bound as the purchaser might fancy—perhaps to be uniform with his library. This is now done only where the work is sold in numbers by subscription. There was then less capital in the trade, and few were disposed to risk the amount required to get out large works of a standard character. The cost was then more than it now is, and the time required much longer to complete and dispose of it. There was then formed, in 1801, the American company of booksellers, and these generally subscribed together in the publication of a work, to guarantee the outlay. There was a sort of union, that regulated the principles of publication, and those who did not conform to these regulations were repudiated. School-books were, as a matter of course, as having the largest and steadiest market, the first that were extensively published. A type of this class of books is Webster's Spelling-Book, which has grown with the country in a remarkable manner. In 1783, with the advent of the peace, Mr. Noah Webster published his elementary spelling-book. The work became a manual for all schools, and its influence has been immense, in giving uniformity to the language throughout the whole country. The "Yankee schoolmaster," who was raised upon that book, has gone forth into every section of the Union, spreading the fruits of that seed of knowledge, as writes Fitz-Greene Halleck:—

"Wandering through the southern countries, teaching
The A, B, C, from Webster's spelling-book."

When it was first published, there were 3,000,000 people in the United States; there are now 30,000,000, and there have been sold 32,000,000 copies of the work, or one for every soul in the Union. The spelling-book was enlarged into a dictionary in 1806, and immediately Dr. Webster went on with preparations for a still larger work. This occupied him 20 years of unremitting research, during which the sales of his spelling-book supported his family; and in 1828 the work was published in two quarto volumes. Twelve years after, viz., in 1840, a new edition made its appearance, greatly improved; and the last edition contains a vocabulary of more than 80,000 words. These works have exerted a wonderful influence in giving uniformity to the use and pronunciation of the language. There have been sold more than 200,000 copies of the large dictionary; and the sales of the spelling-book are 1,500,000 per annum by D. Appleton & Co., New York. During 70 years the spelling-book grew into a dictionary superior to what any other nation could boast of in its language, and with its growth, its sales spread in proportion. It is a type of the country itself, and its future is still before it.

The publication of religious works was greatly promoted by the societies formed, particularly the American Bible Society, which was formed in 1816; the Bible Society of Philadelphia in 1808; one in Connecticut in 1809; and also one in Massachusetts. The American Society in New York published, in its first year, 6,410 volumes, mostly Bibles and Testaments. In 1854, the issues were 815,399, and the whole number during 42 years, was 12,804,083 volumes of the Bible. A good copy of the Bible is sold for 45 cents, and a cheaper edition at 25 cents; Testaments as low as 6¼ cents. Contrast this with the Bible copied in 22 years by Alcuin for Charlemagne about 800, and which was sold in modern times to the British Museum for $3,750, and the distance we have gone appears great.

The American Bible Union was organized in 1850, and it has since issued 59,748,804 pages of matter, including Bibles. The publications by other societies have been considerable.

These societies were not a portion of the regular book trade, which continued to be mostly under the association, until the appearance of the Waverley Novels in 1820 to 1830. The competition to which the large demand for these works gave rise, broke down old arrangements of the trade. The publishers thenceforth acted independently. At the same time, the supply of desirable books from abroad, upon which there was no charge for copyright, was much increased; and as all the publishers were upon the same footing in respect to those books, the competition extended only to the mechanical process, reducing its cost to the lowest rates. The capitals of the publishing houses gradually increased, but there was still great difficulty in getting an American book printed. Cooper tells us, in the preface to his Pilot, that so great was the difficulty he encountered in getting a printer to undertake it, that he was obliged to write the last page of the story first, and have it set up and paged, to insure the extent to which the matter would run.

About the period of the establishment of the American Bible House, a number of firms commenced business, some of which have reached great eminence in the trade, such as Harper Bros., and Appleton & Co.

In the publication of books, the expenses are of various kinds, and may be classed under general heads as follows: First, as in the case of Mrs. Glass's recipe for cooking, catch your fish. This is done in various ways. Among the American publishers, until lately, the works to be printed were supplied from abroad, without cost, and the publisher only selected and printed according to his judgment. To decide upon these, readers are employed to read manuscripts, as well as books; but the difficulty of deciding what will "take" with the public is very great. At other times the written matter is purchased for a sum of money of the author, who offers it for sale. Again, an author may have the publishing done at his own risk and expense. Sometimes this is done only to the extent of a few copies to present to his friends. At another time the work is printed at the expense of the publisher, who allows the author a certain sum for every copy sold—the author retaining the copyright. At other times a work may be gotten up by the publisher, employing a number of writers, and paying them by the page for their labor. After any or all these plans have been adopted, and the "matter" is in hand, the expenses are, first, "composition," or setting up the types, from which proofs are taken to be read by the author. When all corrections are made, the type is sent to the stereotyper, who casts therefrom plates, each one containing a page of the book. These plates are sent to the press-room, where they are "worked off," generally on an "Adams press." The paper is purchased according to the size of the proposed book; sent to the press-room; and "wet down," by being opened and sprinkled with clean water. Standing in piles for a number of hours, the dampness diffuses itself through the paper, and it is ready for the press, whence it goes to the binder, leaving his hands ready for sale. Thus the composition and stereotyping, the press-work, the paper, and the binding, are the chief expenditures, requiring large capital. If the work is illustrated, the expense of designs, of engraving and printing, swells the amount considerably. When in the hands of the publisher, there are a number—perhaps from 100 to 200—appropriated to the press, a copy to each editor. Two copies are deposited with the copyright clerk, with his fee. The expense of advertising is then added, and this is according to circumstances. Sometimes large sums are so spent, particularly when the author is himself interested, and has not the means of spreading the book possessed by the large publishers. There are two distinct prices to all books. These are the trade price, charged to those who sell again, and the retail price, charged to the public. This, however, sometimes depends upon circumstances. The city publishers have correspondence with all the booksellers throughout the Union, and to them they send numbers of the books published to sell, and with them show-bills, and means of making the work known. In such cases, the works, if not sold, are returned in a certain time at the expense of the publisher; but, if sold, the trade price is charged.

The number of book publishers in the United States is about 400. There were 385 in 1857, mostly in New York, Boston, and Philadelphia. About thirty years since, a practice sprung up of holding semi-annual sales by auction, called trade sales, which are now regularly held in the cities of New York, Philadelphia, and Cincinnati. These sales are made up by contribution from all the leading publishers, and are attended by retailers as well as wholesale buyers. That opened in New York, September 4, for the fall sales this year (1860), was very full. The catalogue comprised 522 pages, and probably cost $1,500 to get out. The sales reached over $500,000. It did not comprise, however, the books of Harper & Brothers, that firm holding a sale on their own account. This mode of selling diffuses the publications through all branches of the regular trade. This is divided into publishers, jobbers, and retailers. The number of regular booksellers who distribute the productions of the publishers is about 6,500; but the number of those who keep books as one item of a general assortment of goods is very large, and cannot be ascertained exactly. The jobbers buy in quantities of the publishers, and consequently obtain them at rates which allow them to supply retailers at the publisher's, or trade price, and still realize a profit. The retailers are to be found in every town and hamlet of the country; almost every country store has some books among its wares. Through these regular channels the books descend, from the great reservoir of the publishers to the little lots that are brought to the view of the reader. Although the large publishing houses issue any description of work that will pay, yet the increasing extent of the trade has led to subdivision in bookselling; such as those who keep foreign books only, and import any work in any language to order. These are, again, divided into French, German, and English. There are also sellers of medical books, of law books, of religious books, of scientific works, and miscellaneous productions.

It is obvious that this "regular trade" depends upon the demand from the public; that the readers shall come to the book. To do this, it is necessary that the public shall know, first, that the book exists, and second, that it is one in which they have an interest. To spread this information is the most difficult problem; and it is done by the regular trade through advertising in the papers, by means of the editorial notices in exchange for the presentation copy, and by means of placards spread plentifully in public places, particularly in all the stores where the books are for sale. These are means which are applicable only to the first appearance of the book, since the notices and placards are promptly succeeded by others, and the announcement forgotten by the public. If the work takes, and creates a sensation, the sale continues large. This sensation is sometimes artfully brought about by means of political or other organization, according to the nature of the work. Sometimes an immense number of copies of most worthless matter is thus put upon the public.

The enormous difficulty of making any work known to the public, can be appreciated only by those who have tried it; and this difficulty increases in proportion to the number of people and the extent of the country. The fame of a really good work spreads among those only who are interested in the matter of which it treats, and not at all among those who are either not interested or opposed to its teaching. Hence religious, scientific, and political publications form, as it were, parishes within which the work may circulate. From these circumstances arise the thousand and one modes adopted by publishers to arouse public curiosity, and sometimes with very great success. The publication of school books has at times assumed an extraordinary character. The object of the publishers is, of course, to create for them a popularity with the schools, and to have them introduced by any means. This desire has induced many to send agents to various schools, and substitute new books for the old, without charging for the difference in value. A system so ruinous cannot, of course, last long. The competition in school books by many ways, direct and indirect, greatly enhances the cost of education, by causing children, who cannot always afford it, to buy new sets frequently.

Another mode of selling, recently introduced with some success, is the "gift-book" system. By this plan, the books are sold at the regular retail price; but with each and every book sold, some article of jewelry is presented to the buyer. Every book in the store being numbered when the buyer selects, he receives the jewelry which bears a corresponding number. This numbering, of course, takes place preparatory to the sales, and is so arranged that the jewelry is apparently of greater or less value, according to the work. The actual value of the jewelry is really very small, not so much as if a small sum were deducted from the price of the book, as a commission on its sale. There seems to be nothing objectionable in the mode of selling beyond the sort of chance which the buyer is led to suppose he plays for jewelry in making a purchase. The book is generally worth the money. It has in a few cases been very successful, so much so as to have broken down the old-fashioned barriers of legitimacy, and taken rank with the elder magnates of the trade; Prof. Ingraham's "Pillar of Fire," "Throne of David," etc., which were thus introduced to the world, being among the largest selling books of the day.

The sale of old or second-hand books is also a very extensive branch of business in the great cities. It is obvious, that where book-buying and book-reading are so prevalent, as is the case among all classes of the people here in the United States, there must exist a large number both of public and private libraries, and that these, through death, and the continual vicissitudes that attend families, are being constantly broken up. If every family has a library of greater or less magnitude, sooner or later there is a sale, and it generally comes to the hammer in one or more of the large book auctions that are held almost nightly. These auctions are attended by the public, but mostly by the second-hand booksellers. Of these there are numbers in those parts of the city frequented most by strangers. They are the same as the "book-stalls," so familiar a feature in the literature of England and the countries of western Europe, as they are in fact a necessity everywhere. In New York, the stall-keeper generally procures, for a rent of $50 to $150 per annum, according to circumstances, the privilege of putting up a set of shelves against the outside of some store corner. These shelves shut up at night, like a large window, and the shutters are fastened by iron bars that have padlocks. These shelves contain a small stock, from $300 to $400 value, of the most saleable books that can be picked up cheap at the auctions of books, or of household furniture of families breaking up, or purchased of needy persons who offer them. It follows that the stalls, or stands, become the receptacles of all old books, and sometimes very rare and valuable ones that have gone out of print, and can be found nowhere else. A great many valuable foreign books are found here, having been disposed of by immigrants who become necessitous. A large number of books are sold from these stalls, which also keep much of the current new literature. The keepers—some of them—soon become possessed of sufficient capital to open whole stores; and there are now in New York, and most cities, some quite large stores that have rare collections of old books. This business has also extended across the water, so that persons of more scholarly tastes have, through these agencies, access to the reservoirs of old books to be found in the cities of Europe.

A distinct class of publishers are those who issue books by subscription, or send the books to the reader, instead of waiting for him to come to the book. These are of two classes—those who issue books in numbers, and those who issue complete works. We have spoken of the great difficulty in bringing the existence of a work to the knowledge of the individual reader. The regular trade seek to do this by general appeals through the public press. The publishers by subscription take the more direct and energetic method of appealing personally to each individual, showing him the work, stating its merits, and enlisting his judgment. Harper's "Illustrated Bible" was published in this way, the number of issues being known in advance, and the edition reached 25,000 copies, at $20 each, or $500,000. The mode of publishing by numbers involves the employment of a great number of agents, and the success of the enterprise depends in a great measure upon these. Much dissatisfaction has grown out of this plan of sales, arising from the nature of it. The numbers will sometimes far exceed what the agent promised to complete the work; and many other contingencies arise, not anticipated by the buyer. The contracts made with the agents are various, according to the expense of the publisher. The numbers are delivered at uncertain times; and, when completed, the expense is generally much more than was looked for by the subscriber. The numbers, if then all preserved, are to be bound at greater outlay of trouble and expense. It not unfrequently happens in this class of publications, that the subscribers drop off so fast, from disappointment and dissatisfaction, that the work is abandoned, unfinished, by the publisher.

The plan of combining the two systems is now coming into favor. It is to publish a complete work of a high character, and sell it by agents. This is found to be far the most satisfactory. The agent accosts the individual reader with the complete work in his hand; the buyer inspects it, and pays the price, at once completing the transaction on the spot. A well-organized system of canvassers will thus gradually bring a deserving work to the notice of the whole people by personal appeal. The work does not fall still-born because the first notices have failed to attract readers; but its sale grows steadily with its increasing reputation, since the publisher, looking to a continued sale, takes care that it shall be of such a character that its reputation will grow as the work spreads. This plan is so obviously useful and proper, that many important works, published originally on the trade plan, are now being withdrawn and placed in the hands of agents, who, being responsible and intelligent men, bring the book to the notice of the reader directly. This system, which had met with considerbale success, previous to the war, has, since that time, been pushed with great energy, and the amount of sales of popular works has been enormous. Of histories of the war, sold by subscription, the sales of three considerably exceeded one hundred thousand copies each, and three others approached that figure, while several others sold 30,000, 40,000, or 50,000 copies. Of other books, "The Nurse and Spy" sold over 160,000 copies; "Life and Death in Rebel Prisons" about 75,000; "Raymond's Life of Lincoln" 70,000; Richardson's "Field, Dungeon, and Escape," over 100,000; and Junius Browne's "Four Years in Secessia," above 60,000. Many other books, having a more or less direct connection with the war, sold very largely.

In the period from 1848 to 1857, works of fiction, both from known and unknown authors, had an immense sale. Mrs. H. B. Stowe led the way in this matter, her "Uncle Tom's Cabin" selling to the extent of 310,000 copies here, and nearly a million and a half copies in England; of "The Lamplighter," by Miss Cummins, 90,000 copies were sold; of "Fern Leaves," 70,000; "Alone," by "Marion Harland," over 50,000; "Fashion and Famine," by Mrs. Ann S. Stephens, 30,000; "Wide, Wide World," and "Queechy," by Miss Warner, nearly 100,000 each, &c., &c.

The circulation attained at times by sterling and standard works is very large, as follows:—

Irving's Works	1,100,000	copies.
Irving's Sketch Book	98,000	"
Longfellow's Hiawatha	43,000	"
Hugh Miller's Works	50,000	"
Grace Aguilar's Works	157,000	"
Amer. Cyclopædia, Appleton's, 16 vols., 8vo.	33,000	sets.
Benton's Thirty Years' View, 2 vols., 8vo.	98,500	copies.
Kane's Arctic Voyages, 2 vols., 8vo	65,00	"
Harper's Pictorial Bible, $20	25,000	"
Goodrich's History of all Nations, $7	30,000	"
Dana's Household Book of Poetry	100,000	"

Kane's Voyages paid $65,000 copyright. The sale of Prescott's Histories was very large, giving, it is said, 50 cts. copyright. The sales of school books surpass in quantity those of all other books.

We have referred to the very large sales of Webster's Spelling-books and Dictionaries. The aggregate of these to the close of 1865 exceeds fifty millions of volumes. For several years before Messrs. Cooledge & Brother relinquished the business (in 1857), their sales of Webster's Speller were very nearly one million copies per annum. Messrs. Appleton became the publishers in 1857, and though for several reasons their sales have, a portion of the time, been smaller than Cooledge's, yet their aggregate sales, to the close of 1865, were 6,390,000 copies, and their present rate of issue is about 1,300,000 per annum. This house have also sold about one and a half millions of Cornell's Geographies, and nearly 700,000 copies of Quackenbos' Series of Text-books.

Messrs. E. H. Butler & Co., of Philadelphia, the present publishers of Mitchell's Geographies, sell about half a million copies annually, and the aggregate sale in the twenty-five years since their first publication has been about 7,500,000 copies. Smith's Grammar, also published by this house, sells at the rate of 100,000 copies a year. Two and a half millions of copies of it have been sold.

Messrs. Ivison, Phinney, Blakeman & Co., one of the largest houses in the school-book trade, sell annually of their Sanders' Readers and Spellers over one million copies, and of their other text-books about 1,300,000 more. The Sanders' Spellers and Readers had been sold up to the close of 1865 to the extent of more than twenty millions of copies; Robinson's Mathematics, two millions of copies; Colton's Geographies, over one million; Fasquelle's French, and Woodbury's German Series, half a million copies.

Messrs. A. S. Barnes & Co., also largely engaged in the school-book trade, have sold over five millions of volumes of Davies' Mathematical works, one work (the old "School Arithmetic") having sold to the extent of 1,250,000 copies. They have sold of Mrs. Willard's Histories 350,000 volumes, and over 400,000 of Clark's Grammars, a still larger number of Parker and Watson's Readers and Spellers, and of Monteith and McNally's Series of Geographies; and the entire annual sales of text-books by this house reach nearly two millions of volumes.

Messrs. Sargent, Wilson & Hinkle, of Cincinnati, the publishers of McGuffey's Readers and the Eclectic Educational Series, sell annually about 2,000,000 volumes of these books.

The sales of Comstock's text-books of Philosophy, Chemistry, &c., Olney's Geographies, and Bullions' Latin and Greek text books, now published by Messrs. Sheldon & Co., has been very large. Of Comstock's Philosophy over 1,100,000 copies have been sold, and about 2,200,000 of Olney's Geographies.

Messrs. Harper & Brothers have combined with the largest list of miscellaneous publications in the country a very extensive issue of school text-books of all kinds, to which they are constantly making additions. They also publish two of the most widely-circulating periodicals in the United States. They employ an active capital of about one million dollars in stock and machinery, expending more than $600,000 per annum for paper alone. They run forty-one power presses, thirty-five of them Adams presses, and many of them night and day. They have published 2,200 works, in over three thousand volumes, about equally divided between original works and reprints. Their issues of bound books amount to more than three millions of volumes per annum.

Messrs. Lippincott & Co., of Philadelphia, publish a large list of books, but their most important business is the jobbing of books to booksellers throughout the country. Their business in favorable years amounts to from five to seven millions of dollars. It is estimated that, on an average, ten tons of books are sent out of their establishment daily.

The sale of music books is very large. Some of the smaller music books for schools and Sunday-schools have sold to the extent of more than a million of copies, and the "Carmina Sacra," a popular collection of church music, has had a sale of over 500,000 copies. A single house, Messrs. Mason Brothers, with whom the sale of music books is but one department of their business, sell over 300,000 volumes per annum.

The publication of agricultural books has been made a specialty by one or two houses, and one of these, Messrs. Orange Judd & Co., who are also the publishers of the agricultural paper of largest circulation, sell very large quantities.

The following table gives the number of works of the different classes specified, published in each year or period mentioned.

	1855. Works.	Jan., 1856, to Mar., 1858. Works.	1864. Works.	1865. Works.
Educational	139	748	47	67
Natural History, Agriculture, and Science	65	160	241	189
Biography	124	213	104	150
Essays, Poetry, and Fiction	776	1,667	407	465
Theology and Religion	531	842	165	129
History	76	231	143	191
Juveniles	92	117	428	312
Music	42	154	65	37
Voyages and Travels	29	157	80	25
Medicine	29	138	54	55
Drama	29	28	..	..
Classics	13	61	10	10
Mechanical Sciences	23	80	36	42
Miscellaneous	94	290	112	116
	2,162	4,886	2,028	1,802
Of which were Reprints	649	1,492	301	276

Mr. S. G. Goodrich (Peter Parley), in his "Recollections of a Life-time," gave a table of the value of books manufactured and sold at different periods in the United States. We add to that table an estimate of the values of each class of books sold in 1860, based upon the census returns for that year:—

	1820.	1830.	1840.	1850.	1856.	1860.
School Books	$750,000	1,100,000	2,000,000	5,500,000	7,500,000	10,100,000
Classical Text-Books	250,000	350,000	550,000	1,000,000	1,600,000	2,000,000
Theological and Religious	150,000	250,000	300,000	500,000	650,000	1,000,000
Law	200,000	300,000	400,000	700,000	800,000	900,000
Medical	150,000	200,000	250,000	400,000	550,000	700,000
All others	1,000,000	1,300,000	2,000,000	4,400,000	4,900,000	6,500,000
	2,500,000	3,500,000	5,500,000	12,500,000	16,000,000	21,200,000

The aggregate of 1865 was probably four or five millions of dollars beyond this, not because there had been any very considerable increase in the number of books manufactured and sold, but that, owing to the expansion of the currency and the consequent advance in the cost of labor and material, the cost of production and the market price of books was from 33 to 50 per cent. higher than in 1860.

The reading portion of the population of the country is increasing at present in a ratio somewhat more rapid than the general growth of numbers in the nation. According to the census of 1860, there were 1,126,575 whites and 91,736 free colored persons over twenty years of age who could not read or write. There were also probably not less than 3,500,000 slaves who could not read or write. Since the emancipation proclamation of January, 1863, large numbers of the freedmen have been earnestly engaged in acquiring a rudimentary education, and before 1870 it may safely be calculated that nearly two millions of this class will be able to read. Great efforts are making all over the country to bring into the schools the very large class of children who have hitherto not received instruction; and the census of 1870 will doubtless show full thirty millions of people in the United States capable of reading intelligently. All this creates a larger demand for books, and makes a market for instructive reading probably unequalled in any country on the globe.

BOOK-BINDING.

CHAPTER I.

BOOK-BINDING.

The binding of books is an art probably older than the art of book printing itself, since there existed a necessity for confining the manuscripts and scrolls that were the medium of preserving thought in ancient days. Even that was a progress, however; since the slabs of stone that bore the divine commandments could not have needed binding, nor could the rocks and bricks, on which the Babylonians traced their ideas, have well been bound. The different modes of conveying and preserving ideas, that were adopted in different ages and nations, caused recourse to be had to almost all materials according to exigencies, and these were preserved according to the exigency.

The books of wood, or metal, were bound

PATENT BOOK AND PAPER TRIMMING MACHINE.

BOOK ROLLING MACHINE.

EMBOSSING MACHINE.

by fastening the sheets of which they were composed at the backs by hinges. When parchment and paper succeeded, the backs of the sheets were sewed together, and the covering varied as the arts progressed and materials were adopted. The art itself has made material progress only of recent years. It came to be a separate art only when the discovery of printing, by multiplying books, made the binding of them too laborious for those who did it when years were spent in copying one book. In 778, Alcuin, a monk, native of England, commenced to copy the Bible, and finished it 800, for the Emperor Charlemagne. When twenty-two years was required to make one copy, there was not much business for the binder, whose labors commenced with those of the printing press. While books were still comparatively dear, the binding bore a small proportion to the cost. Of late years, the tendency has been toward neatness and durability. The requisites of a well-bound book are solidity, elasticity, and elegance. Among the nations of Europe, the French take the lead in artistic taste, but the English excel in the expensive finish of the more costly editions. In the United States, machinery is employed, more than elsewhere, to attain the desirable result at less cost.

Books are printed upon paper of various sizes, which formerly were three, called royal, demy, and crown. The book took the size indicated by the paper used. The demy size was mostly used, and the sheets were folded a greater or less number of times. Thus, folded once in the middle, gives two leaves, or four pages, and is called folio. When the sheet is again folded, it gives four leaves, or eight pages, and is called quarto; folded again, the result is eight leaves, or sixteen pages, and is octavo. By folding into twelve leaves, or twenty-four pages, we make a duodecimo; and if into eighteen leaves, or thirty-six pages, it forms octodecimo. Of a size less than this, the books are pocket editions. The sizes of books thus formed are generally designated as 4to, 8vo, 12mo, 18mo, 24mo, 32mo, 48mo, etc. The size of the printed page corresponds with the size of this fold. Thus, the size of this volume is royal octavo, being printed on paper a size larger than demy, or ordinary octavo. Each sheet of paper contains eight leaves, or sixteen pages; and there are fifty of these sheets in the book. Thus, the type is composed of sixteen pages in one "form," and one side of a double sheet receives the impression of those sixteen pages by one movement of the press, and then, being reversed, receives an impression on the other side from the same type. As the sheets leave the press they are hung up to dry, when they are placed under a hydraulic press of great power. They are then counted out into quires of twenty-four sheets each, and sent to the binders. There, in the folding room, the sheets are folded by girls. The object is to fold down the pages, so as to fall one upon the other with perfect accuracy, since upon this the proper binding of the book depends. The whole edition of sheets is folded with great rapidity by one girl. Some of these will fold 400 in an hour, but the average may be 300. A folding machine has lately been introduced, by which, it is said, two girls will do as much as eighteen by hand. Each sheet folded is a signature, and generally these are designated by some figure at the bottom of the first page of each sheet. The folded sheets are laid in piles, in the order of these signatures. The "gatherer" then, with the right hand, takes them, one by one, and places them in the left, until a complete set, or full book, is collected. This is performed so rapidly, that it is said an active girl will gather 25,000 in a day. After this, the sheets are "knocked up" evenly, and pressed in a hydraulic press; but recently, a machine has been introduced, by which time is economized. The engraving, on another page, shows the figure of that by Hoe & Company, which is the favorite for embossing, as well as compressing. The machine runs slower for smashing. The size, 15 by 17, weighs half a ton, and is sold at $400. The book is now examined by the collector, in order to detect any error of arrangement in the signatures. The books then go to the sawing machine, where, being properly arranged, fine circular saws cut fine indentations in the books, to admit as many pieces of twine, to each of which each sheet is sewed. This is performed by girls, at a table appropriated for that purpose. When the sewing is complete, the "end papers" are pasted on the book.

The books next are trimmed by having the edges cut by a machine. To effect this they are piled upon a platform, under a large knife, which, being worked by a crank, descends, like a guillotine, cutting a large number at once. The figure of the trimming machine is given on another page. The knife used in this machine is 21 inches long, and has a short, vibratory movement; thus combining the advantages of the long stationary knife with those of the ordinary plough. The work to be trimmed is placed against the adjustable guide on the bed of the press, in front of the knife, and is compressed by the wheel and screw. The table, on which the press stands, is adjustable in all directions, and is also self-acting, so that, when thrown into gear, it rises to the required height and disengages itself—thus preventing injury to the knife—and then drops down to its original position. Three sides of the work can be successively presented to the action of the knife, by simply turning the press to the quarter and half-turn stops. The machine can be worked either by hand or steam power, and can be easily adjusted to cut any size from 3 to 18 inches long, and from 1 to 15 inches wide. This machine has been in operation some twenty-five years. The backs now receive a coat of glue, to impart firmness. They are then, by the "backing machine"—which is an improvement of some ten years' standing—rounded on the back, and receive a groove for the boards. They are then cut on the ends. A piece of muslin, nearly as long as the book, and extending an inch over the sides, is then pasted on, and the book is ready to receive the boards, or cases. These consist of mill-boards cut a little larger than the book, and cloth cut large enough to turn over all. The cloth is glued, and one board is placed upon it. The corners of the cloth are then cut, and the edges turned down and rolled smooth. It is then dressed, when it goes into the hands of the stamper. The stamping, or embossing, is done in a press, from dies previously prepared. When the sides are lettered, the letters are engraved in metal, and impressed upon the cloth. Gold leaf is placed upon the cloth, and the heat of the stamp causes it to adhere in the desired places. The book is then pasted on the sides, placed in the covers, and pressed, when it is a book bound in cloth. The stamping, or, as it is sometimes called, the arming press, will perform, almost instantaneously, what formerly would have required a week. This has been brought about by a combination of the arts —designing, die-sinking, and application of machinery. When a particular design is required upon a book, the artist draws it upon paper; it is then cut in brass, or steel, and this block in the press embosses a great many covers at a blow.

With books bound in leather, the process is not so expeditious. In order to insure solidity, the books were formerly beaten upon a stone with a broad-faced hammer. They are now squeezed between steel rollers, to effect the same object. The engraving of the rolling machine, in another column, will give a good idea of the one that is now used by bookbinders, in place of screw and hydraulic presses, for pressing folded sheets. The work is placed on an iron table in front of the rollers, between plates of iron, pasteboard, or leather, and passed through the machine as often as necessary. The adjusting screws are geared together, so that the rollers are always parallel to each other. It is strongly geared, and may be run by either hand or steam power. The sewing is done in a more substantial manner. The volume, placed in the laying press, has its back hammered very carefully, so as to spread the sheets on each side of the boards without wrinkling the inside, and the work proceeds until it leaves the hands of the finisher a perfect model. It opens easily, and lies flat out without any strain, and its hinges are without crease.

In gilding the edges of a book, they are scraped smooth and covered with a preparation of red chalk, as a groundwork for the size, which is formed of one egg to half a pint of water. The gold is laid on the size, and then burnished with a bloodstone.

The embellishment of book covers is called "tooling," and, when plain, blind tooling. By this latter, sometimes glossy black indentations are made to contrast tastefully with the rich color of the morocco. This is performed by wetting the morocco, and applying the tool in a heated state.

There has been a method invented by which the leaves of a book are fixed together with India-rubber instead of sewing. The sheets being cut evenly, receive a solution of the material; as each leaf is held only by the rubber, the book is made to lie very flat. This does not appear to have come into much favor. The fashion of imitating antique styles of binding has led to the use of wood instead of pasteboard, in some fancy styles of costly books. It is only a passing caprice, since wood cannot supplant the pasteboard.

WRITERS OF AMERICA.

CHAPTER I.

THEOLOGIANS—STATESMEN—NOVELISTS—HISTORIANS.

With the settlement of the colonies, there were necessarily but few attempts at literary productions. The Pilgrim Fathers brought with them many books from their native land, but these were mostly bibles and theological works. They were persons whose minds bore the strongest religious impressions. In them the sentiment of piety approached austerity; and they were not unfrequently charged with fanaticism. The time they had to devote to literature was wholly absorbed in the perusal of those devotional works that sustained and illustrated that faith which they had made their rule of action under all circumstances, and which they lived up to with all the sternness of their bold and decided characters. They had encountered the perils of the wilderness to rear free homes; and they were determined, also, to make them temples to the Lord. It is not to be inferred that literature and the finer arts of life were, even at that remote period, foreign to the people of the country. The founders of all the colonies were among the most elegant writers and accomplished scholars of the time. Such men as Raleigh, Baltimore, Penn, Oglethorpe, Smith, Winthrop, and a crowd of others, would have been ornaments to the most brilliant circles of any country: with them and their successors, education and religion were the foremost objects of attention. But among men so busy with the work in hand, as to declare "that the laws of God should govern until they had time to make others," much general literature could not find cultivation. Theological works were the staple, and these were produced with an independence of thought and a vigor of argument which enchained their adherents and astonished the opponents they had left at home. As the laws of God were the models of government, so were the inspired writers the only guides for the faith of that steadfast people. Those original and strong thinkers were also powerful and prolific writers; and some of them won the first place, in the estimation of the learned, as theologians. Cotton Mather, who had no equal as a scholar, wrote 382 works, of one of which, "Essays to do Good," Dr. Franklin remarks: "It perhaps gave me a tone of thinking that had an influence upon some of the principal future events of my life." Thus was one of the most powerful minds of the eighteenth, or, indeed, any century, impressed with the vigorous style of a colonial author. The simple missionary, Jonathan Edwards, a large portion of whose useful life was spent on the confines of civilization, produced works which, according to Dr. Chalmers, a century afterward, stamped him as "the greatest of theologians," and called from Sir James Mackintosh the remark that, "in power of subtle reasoning he was, perhaps, unmatched among men." Mr. Edwards succeeded to the presidency of the New Jersey College, and died in 1758. He was the type of the theological age of the country. His work became the standard of orthodoxy for enlightened Protestant Europe. That voice, which was indeed "one crying in the wilderness," became the textbook of the most learned divines of the old world.

As the colonies advanced in wealth and numbers, more diversified views naturally sprung up, but the books of amusement and instruction were mostly imported from England. There was little in the rude struggle with the wilderness to foster an independent school of literature, which flourished much better in England, where existed all the resources of libraries and information. That bold and strong natural intellects, like that of Dr. Franklin, should grow up, was almost a necessity of the vigorous race that produced him; and his works were at once appreciated, because they reflected the genius of the people. The clear, strong sense of "Poor Richard" struck a responsive chord in every heart, and there was little reason to be surprised that the almanac reached a circulation of 10,000 in 1735. The school system that had been early established by the colonists, laid a broad foundation for future literature. To make all classes of persons readers, was to create a demand for books that must sooner or later be gratified; and writers and speakers were sure to find the avenue to the public mind when the occasion offered. This presented itself when the disputes with the mother country began to take a serious form. Those events stirred the depths of feeling in all ranks and classes, and an army of orators rose into public view at once, to fan the flames of discontent into a conflagration that ultimately consumed the loyalty of the colonists, and left their original sturdy independence of character to assert itself in political separation. The eloquence of Otis, of John Adams, Patrick Henry, Samuel Adams, of Pinckney, of Rutledge, and others, live for us only in the effects they produced, and of which our institutions are the manifestation. Unhappily there were then no means of reporting by which those soul-stirring speeches could be preserved, and we have but a few sketches of Fisher Ames and Patrick Henry. While those illustrious men roused the nation with their voices, numbers aided with their pens; among these, Thomas Paine's pamphlet, "Common Sense," and his series of tracts entitled "The Crisis," produced a marvellous effect. The papers in themselves, at the present day, give no evidence of great ability, but they were fitted to the epoch with extraordinary aptness; and tradition assures us that each, on its appearance, produced a *furore* difficult to conceive. The epoch was one of intense excitement; and those papers held up clearly the dark side of kingcraft to a people in whose minds republicanism was making rapid growth. The pamphlets and papers that circulated at that period were, some of them, marked with great learning and power. The correspondence then carried on among public men, and which has since been collected and given to the public, surpasses in learning, political sagacity, grace of diction, vigor of thought, and power of expression, any thing of the kind that ever before appeared in any country. We, that read those papers by the light of seventy years of subsequent history, are better able to appreciate the extraordinary ability they evince. The letters of Franklin, Jefferson, Jay, Adams, Washington, Morris, and others, will, while the nation lasts, be preserved as models of literary excellence. The publication of the "Federalist" was an era in political writing; the work was the joint production of Alexander Hamilton, James Madison, and John Jay. The papers were signed "Publius," and their object was to urge the importance of union in the adoption of the constitution. The statesmen of Europe regarded the work with admiration; and the *Edinburgh Review* remarked: "It exhibits an extent and precision of information, a profundity of research, and an acuteness of understanding which would have done honor to the most illustrious statesmen of ancient or modern times." In his work on "Democracy in America," De Tocqueville remarks that "it ought to be familiar to the statesmen of every nation." If the reader of the present day is struck with the clear-sighted sagacity that the papers evince, how much greater is our admiration when we reflect that those statesmen were reared in our colonial state, without any of that experience which has shed its light upon us. The wisdom they displayed was the result of their own profound deliberation. The writings were an interchange of views between a race of intellectual giants who were giving birth to a nation. The works of James Madison comprise fifteen octavo volumes of 600 pages each, and are distinguished for soundness of reasoning, and great sagacity. The report of Hamilton, as secretary of the treasury, on banks and manufactures, was of great celebrity; and, as far as it described the existing state of affairs, was valuable. It is to be borne in mind that he was one of a race of Titans who were organizing a nation of a kind that never before existed; and if the views he advocated have not been justified by the experience that the nation has wrought out in the last seventy years, it is not surprising; nor can his great wisdom be taxed on that account any more than the vast ability of Patrick Henry be questioned because he opposed the new constitution. The writings of Jefferson, the statesman and patriot, were of a nature more durable and statesmanlike than the effusions of Hamilton, which were more the products of a subordinate executive officer than a directing head. The pen which wrote the Declaration of Independence and the state papers, wrote, also, the "Notes on Virginia," the autobiography, correspondence, and Anas, included in the four volumes of his works published after his death by Mr. Randolph. Of the same age as these eminent statesmen, was John Marshall, the celebrated chief justice of the United States. Judge Marshall appeared as an author in 1805, when he published his "Life of Washington." The introductory volume, being a "History of the Colonies planted by the English on the Continent of North America," was published separately in 1824. In 1832 an abridgment of his "Life of Washington" appeared. Mr. Marshall occupied the posts of minister to France and secretary of state, and his state papers commanded admiration as of the very highest order. His appointment and career as chief justice seems to have been one of those special providences that have so often manifested themselves on behalf of the United States as a nation. The powers of the Supreme Court are such as were never before, by any people, confided to a judicial tribunal. It determines, without appeal, its own jurisdiction, and that of the legislature and the executive. It is not merely the highest court in the whole country, but the constitution of the country is in its hands. This tribunal was to decide upon every question that should arise under the new constitution, in relation to all the rights and powers of each department of government, and also those of all the states. A want of ability or of integrity upon the part of the court, possessed of such power, might, by vicious interpretation, have destroyed the whole fair fabric that had been raised with so much care and wisdom. This immense responsibility devolved upon John Marshall, and nobly did his great capacity and sterling integrity meet the occasion. During thirty-four years, that great man decided every question that arose; and, so to speak, fairly launched the constitution and government upon the stream of time.

Cotemporary with Judge Marshall, upon the supreme bench, was Joseph Story, who, born in Massachusetts in 1779, was appointed in 1811, and held the office until his death in 1845, a period of thirty-four years, during twenty-four of which he was associated with Judge Marshall, and displayed talents worthy of such a colleague. His literary writings were published in 1835, comprising sketches of eminent men, and other papers.

The eminent statesmen who have adorned the literature of their country, have been many. Henry Wheaton, Esq., who was born in 1785, served the country in many capacities. He published the most complete work on international law, in 1835. John Quincy Adams, one of the most remarkable men of the country, was born in Braintree, July, 1767, while his great-grandfather, who was born in the reign of Charles II, yet lived. Mr. Adams graduated at Harvard College in 1787, just 100 years after the birth of his great-grandfather. He chose the law as a profession, and began to write for publication over the signature of "Publicola." He replied to some portions of Paine's "Rights of Man." Washington appointed him minister to the Netherlands from 1794 to 1801. He had, also, appointed him to Portugal, but while on his way, his destination was changed to Berlin by the accession of his father to the presidential chair. While in Berlin, Mr. Adams became acquainted with German literature. A series of letters at this period to his brother in Philadelphia, was afterward published. They were of high interest. Subsequently, he was a member of the Massachusetts legislature, and professor of oratory at Harvard University. He was appointed minister to Russia by President Madison. From thence he was transferred to Ghent, to negotiate peace in company with Messrs. Bayard, Clay, and Gallatin. Afterward, he was appointed minister to St. James. He was eight years in the cabinet, and four years president. In 1831, he was sent to the House of Representatives, where he remained until his death, in 1848. He filled more of the high offices of government, than any other man in the country. The largest portion of his published writings consists of orations and miscellaneous discourses of a high character. He gave to the world some essays upon Shakspeare; also, translations from the German of Wieland. In 1832 he published "Dermot Mac Morrogh; A Tale of the Twelfth Century," with some shorter poems, chiefly lyrical. All the writings of Mr. Adams display the most mature scholarship, but the statesman seems to have overshadowed the man, since it is probable that from a less eminent person they would have been more highly considered.

William Wirt was born in 1772, at Bladensburg, Maryland, and became a lawyer in 1792, in which profession he was eminently successful. In 1802, he wrote the

"British Spy," which had a great success. In 1807, he earned a great reputation by his famous speech in favor of Blennerhasset. He produced many works before he gave to the world his extraordinary "Life of Patrick Henry" in 1817. That work has an enduring reputation.

Daniel Webster, that type of New England intellect, was born in 1782, in the same year with Audubon, the great American naturalist. He was a New England farmer's son, of Salisbury, N. H., and pursued learning with the indomitable energy of his race—teaching school as he himself acquired learning—forcing his way to notice, until he acquired a world-wide reputation. His earliest literary performance was in 1806, when 24 years of age, being a Fourth of July oration. He was a contributor to the *North American Review*, and his orations on different occasions were eagerly read in every section of the country. No speeches were more fraught with wisdom and eloquence, or had greater influence upon the public mind, since, being models of their kind, many are daily read in the public schools. He is so thoroughly American, and so in earnest in his expositions of the constitution, that his name, to use his own expression, must ever have an "odor of nationality." He speaks always to the understanding, and always with effect.

In the same year in which Webster was born, South Carolina gave birth to her great statesman, John C. Calhoun. He was born in Abbeville district, in March, 1782. He graduated at Yale College in 1804, and began the study of law, in which he attained great success. In 1809, he was elected to the state legislature. In 1811, he was elected to the House of Representatives, immediately taking a foremost post, until 1817, when he became secretary of war under Mr. Madison, and so continued eight years. Subsequently, he was twice elected vice-president, the last time in 1828. He soon resigned for the Senate, where he continued until his death, in 1850. Mr. Calhoun was one of the most extraordinary men of the country, and one of those whose works will live far into posterity. His eloquence was of a most refined cast, and distinguished for its compact reasoning. He was possessed of that quickness of perception and subtleness of argument, which made Jonathan Edwards the first of theologians. His works have been collected since his death, in six volumes.

Cotemporary with Webster and Calhoun, were the great orators, Clay, Mangum, and others, whose speeches belong to the standard literature of the country, but who have not contributed to it directly by writing. Thomas H. Benton, the great Missouri senator, was born in North Carolina in 1782, and pursued the study of law. In his "Thirty Years' View" of the American government, he has contributed a work of great value to the historical literature of the country. That great work is not only a faithful record of the political history of the country for the thirty years, but the clear Saxon style in which it is composed, gives it a charm seldom found in similar productions. When this work was completed, he commenced the task of condensing, reviewing, and abridging the debates of Congress, from the foundation of the government, which he lived to bring down to the compromise measures of 1850. With a strong intellect and bold character, Col. Benton was well calculated to dominate in the western states. In Missouri, at one time, his power was boundless.

The brothers Everett have deservedly occupied a high place among the literary men of the country. The elder, Alexander, was born in 1790, in Boston. He graduated at Harvard in 1806, and pursued the profession of law, but filled many offices of public trust, being minister to China at the time of his death, in 1847. During his life, his attention was never long diverted from literature, and his writings were numerous in the *North American Review*, of which his brother, Edward, was editor, and elsewhere. Edward Everett was born in 1794, and graduated at Harvard in 1811. He began the study of law, but adopted theology, and at 19 years was called to the Brattle street church, Boston, to fill the vacancy caused by the death of Mr. Buckminster, one of the most remarkable orators of modern times. He soon after was elected Greek professor at Harvard. While filling that office, he published some school books. In 1820, he became the editor of the *North American Review*, to which he largely contributed. He became member of Congress, and afterward governor of Massachusetts. He was minister to England, president of Harvard College, and United States senator. Like his brother of opposite politics, he has enjoyed a succession of offices, and was, in 1860, the candidate of a large party for the vice-presidency. When Lord

Macaulay, from over occupation, declined to add a memoir of Washington to the many brilliant biographical papers he prepared for the new edition of the "Encyclopædia Britannica," he suggested to the publishers of that work, that his friend Edward Everett would be the very man to execute the task; the counsel was adopted, and Sheldon & Co., of New York, obtained permission to bring out this memoir in a separate volume, which has just been accomplished. It may be said of Mr. Everett, that he has been perfectly successful in every thing he has undertaken, and his reputation is world wide.

John P. Kennedy, of Baltimore, was born in 1795. He pursued the law as a profession, until he entered Congress. He is one of the most genial and popular of writers. He is, perhaps, best known as the author of "Horse Shoe Robinson," in 1835, and "Rob of the Bowl," published in 1838, followed by "Annals of Quodlibet," in 1840. His delineations of nature are truthful, and his character drawing marked with great delicacy and freedom.

Hugh S. Legaré was born in South Carolina, in 1797, and graduated at the South Carolina College, following the law as a profession. In 1820, he was sent to the state legislature, and subsequently was appointed attorney-general of the state, was made chargé d'affaires at Brussels, and chosen to Congress in 1836. His contributions to the *New York Review* gave him a high literary reputation. In 1846, a collection of his writings was published in Charleston, establishing his high reputation as of the first class of intellects.

There are a number of others of our statesmen and political men, who have contributed by their writings to the literary capital of the country, but we have here selected only the most prominent of them.

Of those who have made literature a profession, Charles B. Brown seems to have been the first. He was born in 1771, in Philadelphia, and was of very early promise. In New York, in 1793, he was introduced to a literary society, which numbered among its members James Kent, afterward chancellor, Dr. Mitchill, Dunlap, Bleecker, and others. In 1797, he published a work on the rights of women, which then found less favor than some writers on the same subject have more recently experienced. He published, subsequently, a number of works that met with no very great success.

A year younger than Daniel Webster was Washington Irving, he having been born in 1783. Mr. Irving, "the prince of story tellers," is the admitted leader of American literature. His first publications were in 1802, over the signature of Jonathan Oldstyle, Gent., in the *Morning Chronicle*, of which his brother was editor. In 1806, in connection with James K. Paulding, he began writing "Salmagundi." This created a great sensation. It attacked, with amusing ridicule, the ignorance, presumption, and vulgarity of the British tourists, and satirized pretenders at home and abroad in a most effective manner. He soon after commenced the "History of New York, by Diedrich Knickerbocker," which must ever remain the finest monument of his genius. He was connected in business with his brothers, and upon the failure of the firm, he was, happily for the public, forced to depend upon literature for support. His next production was the "Sketch Book," published in New York and in London, in 1819-20. Its success was great at home and abroad, fully establishing the fame of the author. From that date, his works appeared at pretty regular intervals, although he was absent from the country seventeen years, up to 1832. Soon after, he purchased the old mansion of the Van Tassels, on the Hudson, near "Sleepy Hollow." He then resumed his literary labors until his appointment as minister to Spain, in 1841. He returned, in 1846, to his residence, and remained there until his death, still continuing, at times, to add to the list of his productions, the last of which was the "Life of Washington," which has had a sale probably as extensive as all the rest of his works, and the aggregate of which will exceed half a million volumes. It may be said that he has been one of the most successful of authors.

James K. Paulding, the colleague of Irving in "Salmagundi," was four years his senior, having been born in 1779, in the town of Pawling, on the Hudson. Notwithstanding the great success of "Salmagundi," the publisher refused to remunerate the writers, and it was brought suddenly to a close. In 1813, Mr. Paulding published a satirical poem, called "The Lay of a Scotch Fiddle," and in 1816 the most humorous of his satires, "The Diverting History of John Bull and Brother Jonathan," was published. His works were numerous up to 1831, when the "Dutchman's Fireside" appeared, meeting with great success. It is called the best of his novels. This was followed by "Westward, Ho!" in which his characters are drawn with great truth and vigor. His sketch of the Kentucky hunter in his comedy of "Nimrod Wildfire," has met with great popularity. In 1837, Mr. Paulding became secretary of the navy under Mr. Van Buren. On his retirement he resumed his pen, and some of his later productions were contributions to the *Democratic Review*. All the works of Mr. Paulding would probably reach some thirty volumes. His works evince great descriptive power, skill in character drawing, with much humor and a strong natural feeling running through them all.

James Fenimore Cooper, the most widely known of American novelists, as well as the most distinguished, was born in 1789, at Burlington, New Jersey. He became a student in Yale College in 1802, in the same year with John C. Calhoun. On quitting college, in 1805, he entered the navy as a midshipman, for which position his daring and open-hearted nature seemed to fit him. He was very popular in the service, and a most promising officer, when, after six years of sea service—more than many old officers see in a whole life-time—he resigned, married, and finally retired to Cooperstown, N.Y. His first work was "Precaution," which had success, but not that eminent success that attended his subsequent works. His next work was the "Spy." This was decidedly the best historical romance ever written by an American, and its success was immense. Notwithstanding many attempts of the press to speak slightly of it, it created a *furore* in the public mind, and imparted an immense impulse to literature. The work was immediately republished in all parts of Europe, and it demonstrated the fact that everybody read "an American book," since even in England it rivalled the Waverley Novels in popularity. A few years before his death, Mr. Cooper received information that it had been translated into the Persian, Arabic, and some other oriental languages. When it is remembered that this story was a life picture of the struggle for independence, the effect of such a wide-spread circulation among readers under every form of government, may be estimated.

In 1823, the "Pioneers" made its appearance, commencing that series of Leather-stocking tales that will last while the country stands. The next work of Mr. Cooper's opened the series of his sea tales, in which he stands confessedly without a rival. Those two lines of romance, the American forest and the domain of Neptune, Mr. Cooper made peculiarly his own, and they both illustrate scenes peculiarly American. The "Pilot," it is said, originated in the fact that the "Pirate" of Sir Walter Scott having recently appeared, the conversation turned upon the faultiness of the sea delineation, and Cooper undertook to write a sea story in which the seamanship could not be criticised, and the "Pilot" resulted. Its success was unbounded. The next work was "Lionel Lincoln," a story of the war during the British occupation of Boston, and although it was quite equal to the "Spy," yet for some reason did not take with the public in so great a degree. In 1826, the "Last of the Mohicans" was produced, and it had a success from the first, greater than any novel had ever before had. It was purely original, introducing for the first time upon the field of literature, that race of men of whom but a few years will leave only the tradition. In the "Pilot," a real seaman for the first time came upon the stage, in the person of Paul Jones; and in the "Mohicans," the red man made his *début* in the person of Uncas. Mr. Cooper immediately took rank in England as one of the first romance writers of this, or any other age. Like the "Spy," it was reproduced in every language of Europe. The "Prairie" appeared next, while Mr. Cooper was in Europe, and it carried the reputation of the writer to a still higher point. That work was succeeded by the "Red Rover," which was followed by the "Water Witch." The labors of Mr. Cooper continued up to 1839, when his "History of the American Navy" appeared. It had a great and deserved success. It is a noble monument to the gallant service which, springing from the bosom of a newly formed country, successfully grappled with the tyrant of the seas, and demonstrated to the world that a new power had arisen to redress the balance of the old upon the ocean. There followed this work a continuation of the Leather-stocking tales, in the "Pathfinder" and the "Deerslayer," both of which sustained the high reputation of the series. The complete works of Mr. Cooper embrace a great number of volumes. Not all of them are of the high grade of those which have given him a world-wide character. There is not a language in Europe into which they were not all translated as soon as they appeared in London. The readers of books in South America, in India, throughout England, and in Russia, are familiar with the name of Cooper, even where America is only known as his home. The world has no author whose fame, while living, was so universal as Cooper's. This fact is the conclusive answer to the sneering English critic, who asked, "Who reads an American book?"

James Hall, born in Philadelphia in 1793, has made many contributions to the national literature. He is the author of "Legends of the West," "A History of the Indian Tribes of North America," "The Wilderness and the War Path." The works are creditable.

The years 1804 to 1810 were prolific in the production of authors. No less than ten distinguished writers were born in those years: Theodore S. Fay, Geo. B. Cheever, Chas. F. Hoffman, C. M. Kirkland, Nathaniel Hawthorne, N. P. Willis, H. W. Longfellow, W. G. Simms, Joseph C. Neal, S. M. Fuller. Mr. Fay was educated for the New York bar, and published first, in 1832, "Dreams and Reveries of a Quiet Man," and essays written for the *New York Mirror*, in which he was associated with Willis, Gen. Morris, Rufus Dawes, etc. His novel of "Norman Leslie" is better known. In 1837 he produced the "Countess Ida;" subsequently, "Hoboken; a Tale of New York." He has spent most of his life abroad, under government appointments.

Rev. Dr. Cheever was born in Maine, and now presides over a Congregational church in New York. He has twice visited Europe, and on each occasion has published some works, and made other contributions to literature.

Charles F. Hoffman was born in New York, where he graduated at Columbia College, and commenced the study of the law. He began his literary career as editor of the *New York American*, associated with Charles King, Esq., since president of Columbia College; and in 1835 he published "A Winter in the West," which met great success, as well in London, where it was published, as in New York. This was followed by "Wild Scenes in the Forest and the Prairie," and subsequently by "Greyslaer."

Mr. Hoffman was the first editor of the *Knickerbocker*. In 1843 he published "The Vigil of Faith;" and many songs and essays appeared afterward.

Nathaniel Hawthorne was born in Salem, and graduated at Bowdoin College, in Maine, in the class with Longfellow, in 1825. Franklin Pierce graduated a year before him. In 1837 he published "Twice Told Tales," that had previously appeared in periodicals, in book form. In 1846 a new collection of his magazine papers was published, under the name of "Mosses from an Old Manse." He had a custom-house appointment in Boston, under Collector Bancroft; and subsequently joined the Fourierite community at "Brook Farm," Roxbury. Afterward appeared "The Scarlet Letter," and "The House of Seven Gables," which confirmed his rank as one of the great masters of romance. He is one of the most distinguished of American writers; and was appointed consul to Liverpool by President Pierce. In 1851 he published "True Stories from History and Biography;" in 1852, "The Snow Image;" in 1853, "The Wonder Book;" and in 1859 "The Marble Faun."

N. P. Willis is a native of Portland, but went early to Boston; whence he went to Yale College, where he graduated in 1827. He was then engaged by S. G. Goodrich, since known as "Peter Parley," to edit "The Token." About the year 1830 he was appointed *attaché* of the American legation at Paris; in which capacity he collected the materials for "Pencillings by the Way," which was first published in the *New York Mirror*. In 1839 he was one of the editors of the *Corsair*, which was short-lived. In 1840 an illustrated edition of his poems was published, and his "Letters from under a Bridge." In 1843, he, in connection with Geo. P. Morris, revived the *Mirror*, which lived but a few months. In 1846, he, with Mr. Morris, commenced the *Home Journal*, which continues to flourish. Mr. Willis has a wide reputation at home and abroad. While he wins the admiration of the most refined taste, he enjoys the widest popularity. He commands more of the public sympathy than, perhaps, any other writer.

Henry W. Longfellow is also a native of Portland. He graduated at Bowdoin College, and commenced the study of the law; but abandoned it for a professorship of modern languages in Bowdoin College, which office he assumed in 1829. He speedily won the reputation of a most graceful poet, as well as of an accomplished scholar. In 1836 he was called to the professorship of modern languages at Harvard

College, which he has since retained. In 1833 he published his translation from the Spanish of the *Coplas* of Don Jorge Manrique. In 1835 he published "Outre-Mer," and in 1838 "Hyperion; a Romance," followed by other poems. The merits of Mr. Longfellow as a poet are of the highest order. Some of his poems have had an unusual success. "Hiawatha" circulated to the extent of 45,000 copies, and the "Courtship of Miles Standish" acquired great popularity.

William G. Simms is a native of Charleston, South Carolina, and became a lawyer in that city. When only eighteen years of age, he published his first poems, lyrical and others. These were followed, successively, by "Early Lays," "The Vision of Cortes," and, in 1830, by the "Tri-color." In 1832, while travelling at the north, he wrote, at Hingham, Massachusetts, his chief poem—"Atalantis; a Story of the Sea." This was followed by the stories of "Martin Faber;" "Guy Rivers; A Tale of Georgia;" "The Yemassee; A Tale of South Carolina;" and these by a great number of poems, historical romances, revolutionary stories, histories and biographies, essays, and reviews—making in all fifty volumes in twenty years.

John Greenleaf Whittier was born in Haverhill, Mass., in 1807. His parents were members of the Society of Friends. Receiving a very thorough English education, at the age of twenty-two he became editor of the *American Manufacturer* at Boston, and in 1830 succeeded George D. Prentice in the *New England Weekly Review* at Hartford. In 1831 he published "Legends of New England," and in 1833 returned to his early home, where he published an essay entitled "Justice and Expediency; or, Slavery Considered with a View to its Abolition." In 1836, he became secretary of the American Anti-Slavery Society, and soon after removed to Philadelphia, where he edited for some years the *Pennsylvania Freeman*. Meantime he had been writing some stirring poems, afterward collected under the title of "Voices of Freedom." In 1840 he settled at Amesbury, Mass., and since that time he has been a prolific writer of both prose and poetry. His poems have been collected in several forms, and entitle him to rank among the best of American poets.

Joseph C. Neal, born in Greenland, N. H., in 1807, became editor of the Philadelphia *Pennsylvanian* in 1831, and, after ten years' conection with it, started the *Saturday Gazette*. He is best known by a humorous volume—"Charcoal Sketches." He died in 1848.

Fitz-Greene Halleck (born 1795) belongs rather to the period of Cooper and Irving than to the more recent class of poetical writers. He has written but little, but his "Marco Bozzaris" and "Alnwick Castle" will live.

Edgar A. Poe (born 1811—died 1849) was, both as a poet and prose writer, a man of extraordinary genius.

James Russell Lowell (born 1819), editor of *Atlantic Monthly*, and later of *North American Review*, is, perhaps, the ablest of our younger poets, possessing both humor and pathos. He is also a vigorous prose writer.

Oliver Wendell Holmes (born 1809) has distinguished himself both in prose and poetry. His humor is both delicate and pungent, and his pathetic pieces full of feeling. J. G. Saxe (born 1816) has a high reputation as a humorous poet. Alfred B. Street (born 1811) is a poet of great descriptive power. Of the younger literary men, Bayard Taylor, as traveller, poet, and novelist, occupies the foremost rank. T. B. Aldrich, J. R. Thompson, G. H. Boker, T. B. Read, R. H. Stoddard, W. Allen Butler, and E. C. Stedman, have all won a high reputation.

Among the clerical contributors to general literature, Rev. Timothy Dwight, D. D. (born 1753—died 1817), deserves the first place. In 1774 he published an epic poem, "The Conquest of Canaan," which was followed by numerous lyric pieces. After his accession to the presidency of Yale College in 1795, he published "Travels in New England and New York" in four volumes, the best picture of the life and manners of those times now extant.

Timothy Flint was born in Reading, Mass., in 1780, and graduated at Harvard College, after which he was settled as a minister, but soon departed for the west, where he collected the materials for his "Recollections of Ten Years in the Valley of the Mississippi," which were published in 1826. The success of this work was so great as to induce him to make literature his profession. His next work was "Francis Berrian; or, The Mexican Patriot," followed by the "Geography and History of the Mississippi," in 1827. These works were followed by many others, and, in 1833, Mr. Flint had charge of the *Knickerbocker Magazine* for some time, after which he removed to Cincinnati, and continued there until his death.

William E. Channing was born at Newport in 1780. He graduated at Harvard in 1798, Judge Story being his classmate. On leaving college, he became a tutor in a family of Virginia. He was ordained pastor of the Federal street church in Boston in 1803, and he continued there until his death in 1842. His earliest publications were theological, particularly one on the "Unitarian Belief," in 1819, which excited great attention. In 1823, he published an essay upon "National Literature." This was followed by "Remarks on the Life and Character of Napoleon Bonaparte." The address delivered in Boston, on "Self-Culture," in 1838, was regarded as one of his best efforts. These were followed by many others.

Joseph S. Buckminster was born at Portsmouth in 1784. He graduated at Harvard in 1800, and became the pastor of Brattle street church in 1805, and, after much illness, died in 1812, with a great reputation for eloquence and literary genius.

Andrews Norton was born in Hingham in 1786, graduated at Harvard in 1804, and became a tutor in Bowdoin College. He published many able works, with some poems.

Horace Bushnell was born in Connecticut in 1802, and graduated at Yale College in 1824. At one time, he was literary editor of the *New York Journal of Commerce;* from 1833 to 1856 he was pastor of a Congregational church in Hartford. The first of his theological works was published in 1847, and he has since written many others, which have attracted great attention.

Orville Dewey was born in 1794, in Sheffield, Mass. He graduated at Williams College in 1814. He supplied the pulpit of Dr. Channing when that gentleman went to England. After being settled ten years in New Bedford, he became pastor of the Church of the Messiah in New York, but has for some years past resided in Boston. He has published many volumes at different times on various subjects; among others, in 1836, "The Old World and the New;" in 1838, "Moral Views of Commerce, Society, and Politics." He is one of the most popular pulpit orators that the country has produced.

Among the other clergymen who have attained a high reputation for scholarship and literary ability, we should name George Bush, a critical Hebrew scholar, Moses Stuart, Thomas J. Conant, Horatio B. Hackett, all eminent Hebraists; Bennet Tyler, Nathaniel W. Taylor, Lyman Beecher, Edward Beecher, Mark Hopkins, Leonard Woods, George P. Fisher, theological writers; T. C. Upham, J. Torrey, W. G. T. Shedd, Leonard Bacon, Henry B. Smith, Bishop C. P. McIlvaine, W. B. Sprague, J. W. and J. A. Alexander, G. W. Bethune, S. H. Tyng, Francis Wayland and Bishop Brownell, as religious and ecclesiastical writers; and Nehemiah and Wm. Adams, Richard S. Storrs, Jr., George B. Cheever, Joseph P. Thompson, R. D. Hitchcock, H. W. Beecher, A. L. Stone, Bishops Potter, Burgess, Coxe, Doane, and Kip, Richard Fuller, William R. Williams, William Hague, Robert Turnbull, Abel Stevens, J. P. Durbin, W. P. Strickland, Daniel Curry, Stephen Olin, and James Floy, as eloquent preachers and writers. The two Roman Catholic Archbishops Kenrick, Archbishop Hughes, Archbishop McCloskey, and Bishops Fitzpatrick and Rosecrans, have all acquired distinction as preachers and authors, mostly on controversial topics.

Francis Wayland was born in the city of New York in 1796, and graduated at Union College. He was first settled over a Baptist church in Boston, but ultimately succeeded to the presidency of Brown University, in 1827. His publications have been numerous on moral and scientific subjects, and he has contributed largely to the periodical press. The editions of some of his works have been very large: 12,000 were sold of his "Political Economy," and nearly 30,000 of his "Moral Science."

William Ware was born in 1797, at Hingham, Mass., and graduated at Harvard in 1816. He was soon after settled in a Unitarian church in New York. He commenced, in the *Knickerbocker Magazine*, in 1836, a series of papers, which were subsequently published together, as "Zenobia; or, The Fall of Palmyra: an historical romance." Then followed "Probus; or, Rome in the Third Century;" "Julian; or, Scenes in Judea," appeared in 1841. The writings of Mr. Ware are graceful, pure, and brilliant in style.

Herman Hooker was born in Poultney, Vt., in 1807. Graduating at Middlebury College, he took orders in the Episcopal church, but, abandoning the pulpit, he removed to Philadelphia. He has given several works to the public, which have met with great success.

Orestes A. Brownson was born in Vermont in 1802. The early life of Mr. Brownson was obscure. He seems, however, to have been very erratic, but published several works, until, in 1838, he began the *Boston Quarterly*, and in 1840 he published a metaphysical novel called "Charles Ellwood." He continued to write for many reviews, until, in 1844, he began *Brownson's Quarterly Review*, after having united with the Roman Catholic church. Since then he has met with success.

John James Audubon, the great ornithologist, was born in Louisiana in 1782. He was educated in Paris. On his return he immediately commenced the series of drawings, which, with the lapse of time, grew into "The Birds of America"—of which work Baron Cuvier remarked: "If ever it be completed it will have to be confessed that, in magnificence of execution, the old world is surpassed by the new." After encountering many vexations and disappointments, he succeeded in publishing, in 1830, his first volume, containing one hundred plates, representing ninety-nine species of birds; every figure of the size and color of life. The kings of France and England headed the subscription list; he was made a member of the Royal Societies of London, Edinburgh, and Paris, and the scientific world were enthusiastic in his praise. The second volume was published in 1834; in 1840 the fourth and last volume was completed. The whole comprises 435 plates, containing 1065 figures, from the bird of Washington to the humming-bird, of the size of life, and a great variety of land and marine views, carefully drawn and colored from nature. He had spent half a century in completing this marvellous work, and well might he say: "I look up with gratitude to the Supreme Being, and feel that I am happy."

After the completion of this work, he began the "Quadrupeds of America," which was also a marvellous production. His drawings exhibit a perfection never before attempted, and his pen is scarcely inferior to his pencil. When Buffon had completed the ornithological portion of his history, he supposed that he had described all the birds in the world, and remarked that the list "would admit of no material augmentation!" Yet his list comprised but one-sixteenth of those now known to exist. Mr. Audubon died in 1851.

Gulian C. Verplanck was born in 1785, in New York—a true representative of the Knickerbocker race. He graduated at Columbia College, and soon after obtained admission to the bar. In 1818 he came before the public in a literary character, in an address before the New York Historical Society. He became professor of the evidences of Christianity in the theological seminary of the Episcopal church, in 1820. Subsequently Mr. Verplanck, in connection with Mr. Bryant and others, formed a literary confederacy, contributing to the literary magazines and daily journals. At this time was published "The Talisman," mostly by Mr. Verplanck. He was for some years a member of Congress. In 1844–46, he edited a pictorial edition of Shakspeare, in which he fully sustained his high reputation.

Henry R. Schoolcraft was born in 1793, near Albany, and was early distinguished for his literary and scientific acquirements. He has contributed largely to the preservation of the history of the fast disappearing red races of the continent, and is a high authority on all that concerns their customs.

In the range of history, American writers have won the foremost position among historians of the present century; and Europeans admit the high reputation of American histories.

Jared Sparks was born in 1797, and graduated at Harvard College in 1815. He became then a tutor, and was subsequently ordained in the Unitarian church in Baltimore. His first historical work was the "Life of John Ledyard, the American Traveller." This met with some success, and in 1831, he published, under an order of Congress, the "Diplomatic Correspondence of the American Revolution," in twelve volumes. In 1832, he published the "Life of Gouverneur Morris," who was the American minister to France during the reign of terror. Between the years 1833 and 1840, he published in twelve octavo volumes the "Life and Writings of Washington." The memoir, by Mr. Sparks, contained in the first volume, was translated into French by Guizot, the minister of Louis Philippe. The whole work was translated into German, and published at Leipsic. In 1835, he published the complete works of Franklin. In this the autobiography of Franklin is continued to his death. Mr. Sparks also published two series in 10 and 12 volumes of the "Library of American Biography." In the preparation of these he was aided by the brothers Everett, Prescott, Wheaton, and others. He also published a history of the American Revolution. In 1849, he succeeded Mr. Everett as president of Harvard College, but resigned in 1853.

William H. Prescott was born in 1796, at Salem. He was grandson of that Prescott who commanded at Bunker Hill. In 1814, he graduated at Harvard College, and entered upon the study of the law. At college, by an accident, one of his eyes was destroyed, and the sight of the other much injured. He was possessed of a handsome income, $12,000 per annum, and he devoted himself to the study of the languages and literature of Europe, and contributed largely to the *North American Review.* Ten years thus passed in a kind of preparation for historical studies; ten years more were occupied with investigation, and then his "Ferdinand and Isabella" was published. The materials for this had been sent him by Alexander Everett, when minister to Spain. The work of acquiring the contents of books and writing without the use of eyes was a severe labor, but was overcome by ingenuity and patience. The work was everywhere hailed with enthusiasm. Mr. Prescott was made a member of the Royal Academy of Madrid, and its rich collections, with those of the archives of Seville, placed at his disposal, and every reservoir of Spanish history laid open to him. The "History of the Conquest of Mexico" followed, and was succeeded by the "Conquest of Peru," and the "History of Philip the Second," which appeared successively, added to the high fame of Mr. Prescott. He died in the midst of his honors and usefulness.

George Bancroft was born in Worcester in 1800, and graduated at Harvard in 1817. He commenced the study of divinity, but adopted literature as a profession. In 1834, he published the first volume of the "History of Colonization in the United States." He was subsequently appointed collector of Boston, and in 1844 secretary of the navy, which post he resigned to represent this country at the Court of St. James. During more than thirty years his great "History of the United States" has been in progress, and the tenth volume has appeared the present year (1867).

William C. Bryant was born in Massachusetts in 1794. He contributed lines to the county gazette when ten years old, and four years later he published two poems; when nineteen years old, he wrote his "Thanatopsis." He graduated at Williams College, and studied law. In 1825 he edited the *New York Review,* and in 1826 he became editor of the *Evening Post,* with which he is still connected. His works have been many, in both poetry and prose. His prose is remarkable for the purity and elegance of its style.

John Lothrop Motley, who at once took rank with Prescott and Bancroft as a historian, was born in Dorchester, Mass., in 1814, educated at Harvard University, and subsequently at Gottingen and Berlin, studied law, and was admitted to the bar in 1836, but did not practice. He wrote two historical novels, published in 1839 and 1849, was secretary of legation to Russia in 1840, became interested in the history of Holland in 1845, and after collecting material for a history here, went to Europe in 1851, and spent five years at Berlin, Dresden, and the Hague in investigations, and the composition of his "Rise of the Dutch Republic," published in 1856. This was followed, in 1860, by three volumes of a history of "The United Netherlands," and in 1866 he published two more volumes of this history. In 1861 he was appointed U. S. minister to Austria.

Richard Hildreth (born at Deerfield, Mass., 1807—died 1865) was an able political writer, novelist, and historian. He will be longest remembered for his valuable "History of the United States," in six volumes. He was also author of a work on Japan. He was, at the time of his death, U. S. Consul at Trieste.

Benson J. Lossing (born in Beekman, N. Y., in 1813) has attained a high reputation as a historian and historical biographer. His "Pictorial Field Book of the Revolution," his works on Washington and Mount Vernon, his life of "Philip Schuyler," his "History of the United States," his "War of 1812," and his "Pictorial History of the Rebellion," are all works of interest and value, and their illustrations are from his own skilful pencil.

James T. Headley, Jacob and John S. C. Abbott, John Foster Kirk, Francis Parkman, John G. Palfrey, J. Romeyn Brodhead, E. B. O'Callaghan, Parke Godwin, Charles Gayarre, Francis L. Hawks, have all published historical works of some reputation.

The female writers of America have been numerous, and many of them have achieved great distinction. Mrs. Emma Willard has written extensively on history and educational topics, and her sister, Mrs. Almira H. Phelps, has not only contributed several text-books to physical science, but has a fair reputation as a novelist. Hannah Adams, the pioneer of female writers in America, born 1756, wrote a "History of New England," "Vienna," &c. Mrs. Eliza Leslie (1787–1857) wrote several excellent novels, and some works of great value, in the domain of the culinary art. Mrs. Lydia H. Sigourney (1791–1865) was alike remarkable for her poetical and her prose works; many of the latter were prepared for the young. Miss Catharine M. Sedgwick, one of our oldest living female writers, is the author of "The Linwoods," "Redwood," "Hope Leslie," &c., novels of great merit. Mrs. Harriet Beecher Stowe (born in 1812) has been the most successful of novelists. Her "Uncle Tom's Cabin" sold to the extent of about 320,000 copies in the United States, and over a million and a half in Great Britain, and her subsequent novels, "Dred," "The Minister's Wooing," "Agnes of Sorrento," and "The Pearl of Orr's Island," have had a very large sale. She has also written several prose works of the essay class, a volume of "Travels in Europe," and some occasional poems of great merit. Her sister, Miss Catharine E. Beecher, has written numerous works, educational and controversial, which have been very popular. Miss Emily Warner achieved a high reputation (under her *nom de plume* of Elizabeth Wetherell) by her novels, "The Wide, Wide World," "Queechy," "The Hills of the Shatemuc," and "Say and Seal." Mrs. S. P. W. Parton (Fanny Fern) has been very successful, not only as a novelist, in her "Ruth Hall," but as a light essayist, in her "Fern Leaves," &c. Miss M. J. Mackintosh, the author of "Charms and Counter-Charms," and numerous other novels, has a high reputation. Mrs. E. D. E. N. Southworth (born in 1818) commenced her career as an author in 1843, and since that time has published over one hundred novels, all of them of considerable merit. Mrs. Ann S. Stephens (born in 1813) has attained distinction as a novelist, as a writer of historical and practical works, and as editor of a ladies' magazine. Mrs. E. Oakes Smith has written largely and well on the most diverse subjects—metaphysics, literature, household matters, criticism, the drama, poetry, and fiction have been alike the topics of her works.

Mrs. Lydia Maria Child (born 1802) has been a very popular writer. Her "Hobomok" and "The Rebels" were her earlier efforts, and brought her reputation, which was increased by her subsequent works. Mrs. Caroline M. Kirkland (1801–1864) was a graceful and elegant writer. Her "New Home—Who'll Follow?" first introduced her to the public, and her subsequent works enhanced her reputation. Mrs. Alice B. (Neal) Haven (1828–1863) edited the *Saturday Gazette* after the death of her husband (Joseph C. Neal) for some years, and subsequently published a volume of poems of great merit, and a number of admirable juvenile books.

Mrs. Mary J. Holmes, Mrs. Virginia Terhune (Marion Harland), Mrs. Anna C. (Mowatt) Ritchie, Miss A. J. Evans, Miss Alice Cary, Mrs. E. F. Ellet, Mrs. E. C. Embury, Miss Maria Cummins, Miss Caroline Chesebro, Miss H. E. Prescott, Mrs. E. Robinson (Talvi), Mrs. Catharine A. Warfield, Mrs. Harriet Stuart Phelps, and her daughter, Miss E. Stuart Phelps, Mrs. Elizabeth Stoddard, Mrs. Mary A. Denison, Mrs. M. A. Sadlier, Mrs. Margaret C. Lawrence, Mrs. Madeline Leslie, Miss Caroline Kelley, Mrs. M. E. Hewitt, Miss Virginia F. Townsend, Mrs. L. C. Tuthill, Mrs. Emily C. Judson (Fanny Forrester, 1817–1854), Mrs. Helen C. Knight, and Mrs. Hubbell (author of "Shady Side," &c.), have all written works of fiction, or light literature, which have had a very considerable and many of them a very large sale.

Miss S. Margaret Fuller, afterwards Countess D'Ossoli, one of the most vigorous and thoughtful writers of any age (1810–1850) was for some years in charge of the literary department of the *N. Y. Tribune*, and published, beside some translations and many essays, a work entitled "Woman in the Nineteenth Century."

Several of the ladies named above have distinguished themselves as poets, particularly Mrs. Sigourney, whose religious and elegiac poems have given her a high reputation; Mrs. Stowe, Mrs. E. Oakes Smith, Mrs. Alice B. Haven, Mrs. Emily C. Judson, Miss Alice Cary, and her sister, Miss Phœbe Cary. But there are other American female writers, whose poetry alone has won them high distinction. Among these we may name Mrs. Maria Brooks (Maria del Occident, 1795–1845), whose principal poem, "Zophiël," attracted attention in Europe from its remarkable creative power; the Davidson sisters, remarkable instances of precocious talent; Mrs. Frances Sargent Osgood (1812 – 1850), remarkable for her playfulness of fancy and felicity of expression; Miss Hannah F. Gould, a poet of rare ability and vigor; Mrs. Julia Ward Howe, perhaps the most gifted of our living female poets; Mrs. Frances Anne Kemble (born 1811); Mrs. Caroline Gilman; Mrs. Sarah J. Lippincott (Grace Greenwood), whose "Ariadne a Naxos" attracted great attention from its intensity of passion; Mrs. Amelia B. Welby, remarkable for the exquisite rhythm of of her poetry; Mrs. Sarah Helen Whitman, Mrs. Anne C. (Lynch) Botta, Mrs. Estelle Anna Lewis, Mrs. Sarah J. Hale, Miss Caroline May, Mrs. Maria Lowell, Mrs. Mary H. C. Booth, Miss Edna Dean Proctor, Mrs. Rosa V. Johnson, Miss Rose Terry, and Mrs. M. S. B. Dana. There are, very possibly, yet others who deserve a place in this record, but these have all gained a prominent position as poets.

PRINTING-PRESS.

CHAPTER I.

PRINTING PRESS—HANDPOWER—LIGHTNING.

If a middle-aged man now visits the press-room of a "crack" daily, and observes a huge machine, some twenty feet high, driven by a steam engine, delivering seven large newspapers, nicely printed, at every tick of a clock, and watches the piles of paper growing at the rate of 420 per minute, or at that of 20,500 per hour, weighing over one ton, and reflects that the utmost power of the best machines of his youth would require an active man and a boy two long hours to do what this whizzing monster does in a minute, he will form some idea of the progress made in paper printing, and also of what is required to meet a daily demand. In the days of Franklin, the press-work of a paper was a very laborious affair. The machines of that day were very imperfect, and, if reference is had to the illustration on another page, contrasting the actual machine which Franklin used, and which is still preserved in the patent office at Washington, with the fast press now in use, a good idea will be formed of the progress in press-building. In that press, it will be observed, the bed is a platform about three feet high, between two uprights. In the cross-piece at the top is a female screw in which works the screw attached to the wooden platen. This screw being turned by the pressman, causes the platen to ascend and descend. There is, in front, a table, which slides over the platform at the will of the operator, who, to effect this, turns a crank. On this table was laid the type. Over the type was a frame, which encircled the type, or form, and crossed it in those places where the white margin appears in a printed paper. On this frame the paper of proper size was laid, after being "wet down;" another fold of the frame confined the paper; the whole was then slid on to the platform. The screw being turned, caused the platen to descend, and the impression was made. The screw was then raised, the form slid back, the frame raised, and the paper lifted and examined by the pressman to see if his impression was "good." If it satisfied him, he proceeded to ink his types for a new impression. The ink employed in printing is very different from that employed for writing, and much skill is required in the manufacture. It must be soft, adhesive, and easily transferred; it must dry quickly, and be durable, and not liable to spread. The usual materials are linseed oil, rosin, and coloring matters, lamp-black being used for black ink. The peculiar mode of the best makers is somewhat of a secret. The old mode of applying it was by two ink balls, about the size of a man's hat, made of soft leather, and stuffed with cotton, the leather being nailed round a wooden handle. The pressman, taking one in each hand, daubed them with ink, and worked them together until he had spread the ink. He then applied them to the types as evenly as possible; then, laying them aside, he proceeded, as before, to lay his paper evenly upon the frames, slide it up, work the screw, etc. By this process, an active man could work fifty sheets in an hour; by ten hours steady industry, he could get off an edition of 500 copies for the carriers in the morning. There was little room for much expansion under such a state of printing. The first great advance in the direction of speed, was when the lever was substituted for the screw in making the impression. This was introduced by Mr. John Clymer, and called the Columbian, or Clymer press, in which there was no screw, but the head itself was a large and powerful lever, acted on by proportionate levers, thus bringing to perfection, for presses of a large size, certain principles of leverage which had previously been patented in England, and used in presses of a small size, such as foolscap. The platen was, in fact, a fulcrum for the head, or great lever. Thus the fulcrum and lever superseded the inclined plane, or screw. Mr. Clymer went to England in 1817, and, at that time, the famous "Cobbett's Register" was printed on an "American press," a circumstance that was regarded as a great joke at the time. By this invention, two levers, one affixed at the cross-piece above, and one to the platen, were brought together by a joint, like the bent knee of a man's leg. At this joint was applied a lever, by which the pressman, with one pull, brought the joint into a perpendicular line, by so doing giving an instantaneous and powerful impression. The platen being suspended by spiral springs, instantly rose when the lever was released. The saving in time was immense, one pull of the workman being sufficient for all the old screwing and unscrewing. Improvements in the Clymer press were made by Peter Smith and Samuel Rust, and these improvements are combined in Hoe's Washington press, of which a cut will be found on another page. Inventions of a similar character were made by Mr. John Wells, of Connecticut. The principle of the lever has been applied in various ways, and contains the chief feature in press power. The form of lever now generally used, will be seen in the engraving of Hoe and Smith's printing press, which is the favorite for all work where power presses are not required. Next to the introduction of the lever, was the substitution of the inking machine for the old ink balls. This was constructed of a cylinder which revolved, by hand, against an ink trough, and, by so doing, received evenly over its surface the ink. The smaller rollers were constructed on a light frame, to which a handle was attached. These, laid upon the ink roller, received from it the ink, and then being pushed forward over the type, imparted it to them with one movement of the hand. This, worked by a boy, is seen in the engraving. The pressman was now relieved of the inking, and, working with a lever, he could print, with active industry, 250 sheets in an hour. The next movement was to make this inking machine self-acting, by attaching it to the press in such a manner that lifting the paper frame would cause it to act. The boy was now dispensed with.

In 1839, the Ruggles Job press was introduced, and is now extensively manufactured in Boston, on the site of the house where Franklin was born. The Combination press was introduced in 1854, and is manufactured by the Power Press Co. on a very large scale.

The next important improvement in the machines, was the introduction of the cylinder, or Napier press. In this machine, of which an engraving is presented in another column, the form of type is locked upon a strong iron table, which moves forward and backward, passing in its course under a cylinder, which, made of iron, is covered with a soft blanket, and provided with a set of fingers to seize the sheet as it is presented. Against this is inclined the feeding bench, on which is laid the paper. On the bench is a small brass peg, or pointer, against which the feeder brings the paper accurately, in order that the sheets may "register"—that is, each receive the type at the same distance from the margin. When the cylinder revolves, it raises with its fingers the edge of the paper, draws it round itself, and presses it against the type, which, at the same instant, passes under it. The paper then released by the cylinder, is carried by ribbons to the rear, while the type vibrates back, to return as soon as the cylinder has again drawn forward a sheet of paper. At first, a boy was required to fly the papers, or catch them as they were thrown back from the cylinder, and pile them up. This, by the self-acting flyer, as seen in the engraving, is now dispensed with. This machine raised the number that might be printed to between 2,000 and 3,000 per hour. The bed is made of a size to take a paper from 25x33 inches, to one 40x60 inches. The cost of the former size is $1,390, and of the latter, $2,600. An obvious improvement suggested itself soon. The type, in moving forward and backward, made only one impression. It was easy to introduce another cylinder, in order to take an impression from the type on its return. This was the double cylinder, which delivers a paper at each end. The cost of these is, for the large size, $4,250, and it will give 3,500 to 6,400 impressions per hour. In this operation, the vibration of the type bed was the great difficulty. The type and bed will weigh over 1,000 lbs. This mass, moving backward and forward with great momentum, produced a great concussion, although it was met by strong springs which stopped its progress and aided its return. Many improvements were made in these springs. The noise and annoyance occasioned by the concussion of the bed against the springs, which are placed at each end of the machine to overcome the momentum of the bed, was removed by means of adjustable India-rubber buffers placed at the points of contact, which in no way interfere with the lively and certain action of the spiral springs. The same object is also effected by air springs, by which the head of the bed, plunging into a receiver, condenses the air, causing it to act as a spring.

It was obvious, however, that the weight and concussion of this bed were a bar to further progress in this direction, and it was felt that greater speed could be attained only by causing the type itself to revolve. This was no new idea. It had been patented in England in 1790, but the inventor could not succeed in holding the types, since the rapid revolution of such a weight gives a powerful centrifugal motion. What they could not do in England, Richard M. Hoe did in New York, in 1847, after many attempts had been made to accomplish the desired result. In this machine, as will be seen in the illustration, the form of type is placed on the surface of a horizontal revolving cylinder of about four and a half feet in diameter. The form occupies a segment of only about one-fourth of the surface of the cylinder, and the remainder is used as an ink-distributing surface. Around this main cylinder, and parallel with it, are placed smaller impression cylinders, varying in number from four to ten, according to the size of the machine. The engraving represents three. The large cylinder being put in motion, the form of types is carried successively to all the impression cylinders, at each of which a sheet is introduced, and receives the impression of the types as the form passes. Thus, as many sheets are printed at each revolution of the main cylinder, as there are impression cylinders around it. One person is required at each impression cylinder to supply the sheets of paper, which are taken at the proper moment by fingers or grippers, and, after being printed, are conveyed out by tapes and laid in heaps by means of self-acting flyers, thereby dispensing with the hands required in ordinary machines to receive and pile the sheets. The grippers hold the sheet securely, so that the thinnest newspaper may be printed without waste.

The ink is contained in a fountain placed beneath the main cylinder, and is conveyed by means of distributing rollers to the distributing surface on the main cylinder. This surface being lower, or less in diameter than the form of types, passes by the impression cylinder without touching. For each impression, there are two inking rollers, which receive their supply of ink from the distributing surface of the main cylinder, which rise and ink the form as it passes under them, after which, they again fall to the distributing surface.

Each page of the paper is locked up on a detached segment of the large cylinder which constitutes its bed and chase. The column rules run parallel with the shaft of the cylinder, and are, consequently, straight, while the head, advertising, and dash rules, are in the form of segments of a circle. The column rules are in the form of a wedge, with the thin part directed toward the axis of the cylinder, so as to bind the types securely. These wedge-shaped column rules are held down to the bed by tongues projecting at intervals along their length, which slide in rebated grooves cut crosswise in the face of the bed. The spaces in the grooves between the column rules are accurately fitted with sliding blocks of metal even with the surface of the bed, the ends of which blocks are cut away underneath to receive a projection on the sides of the tongues of the column rules. The form of type is locked up in the bed by means of screws at the foot and sides, by which the type is held as securely as in the ordinary manner upon a flat bed—if not even more so. The speed of these machines is limited

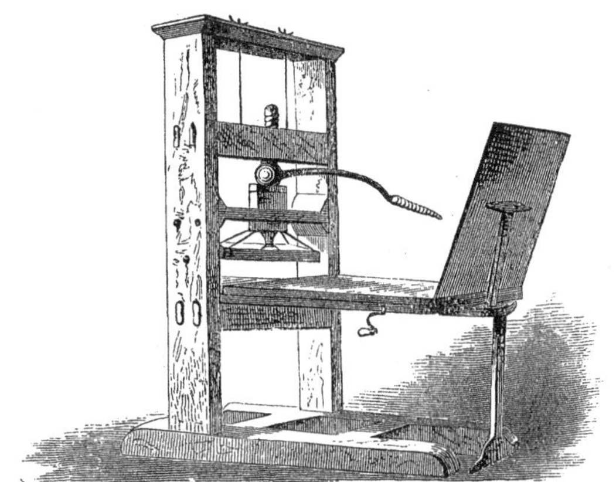

FRANKLIN PRESS.

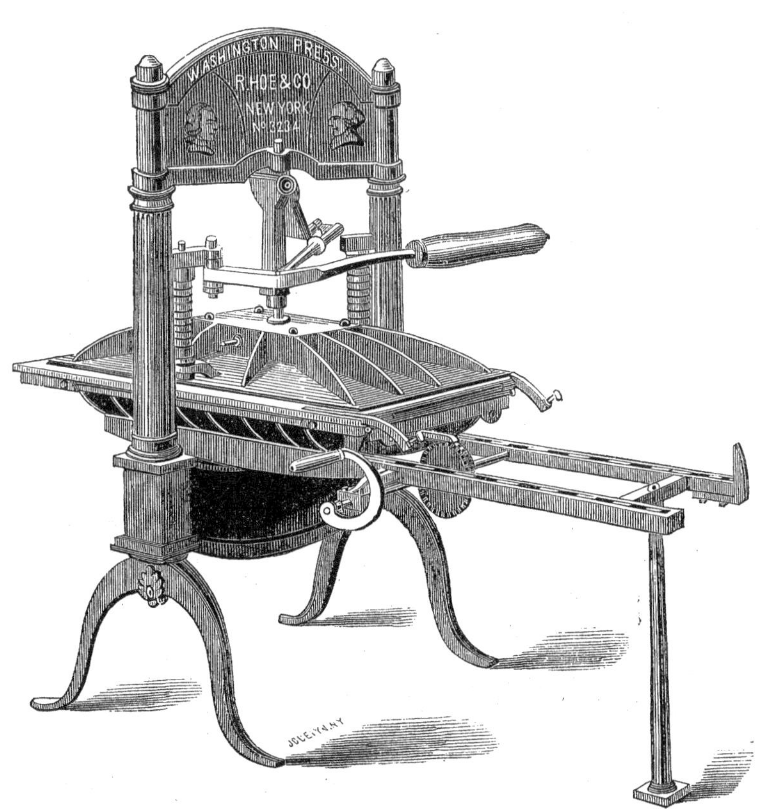

PATENT WASHINGTON PRINTING PRESS.

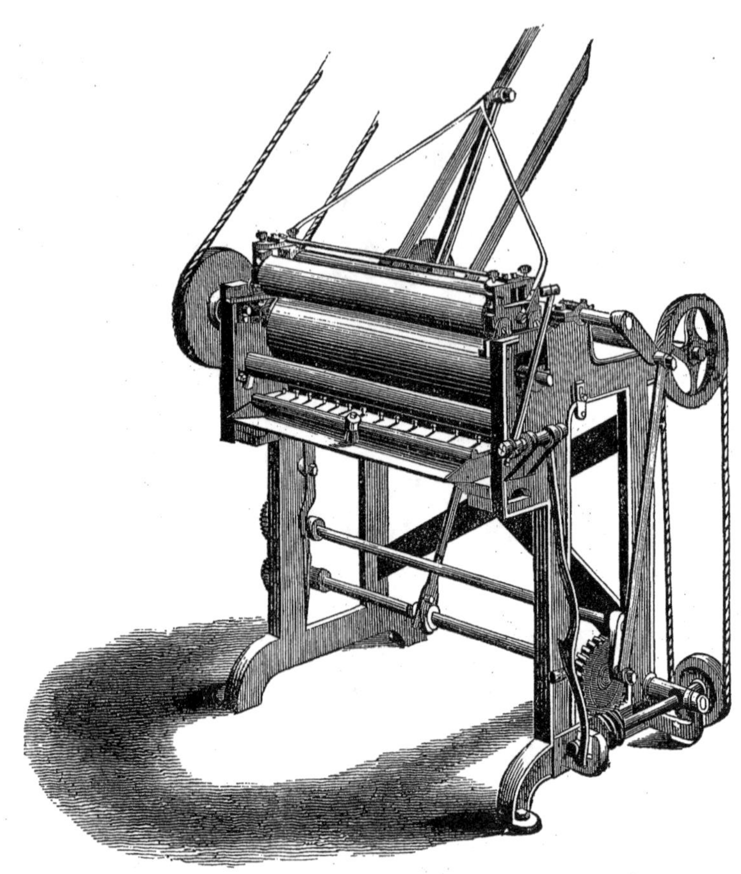

PATENT HAND-PRESS STEAM INKING MACHINE.

IMPROVED INKING APPARATUS FOR THE HAND-PRESS

PATENT SINGLE SMALL CYLINDER PRINTING MACHINE.

EIGHT CYLINDER TYPE-REVOLVING PRINTING MACHINE.

TEN CYLINDER TYPE-REVOLVING PRINTING MACHINE.

FOUR COLOR PRINTING MACHINE.

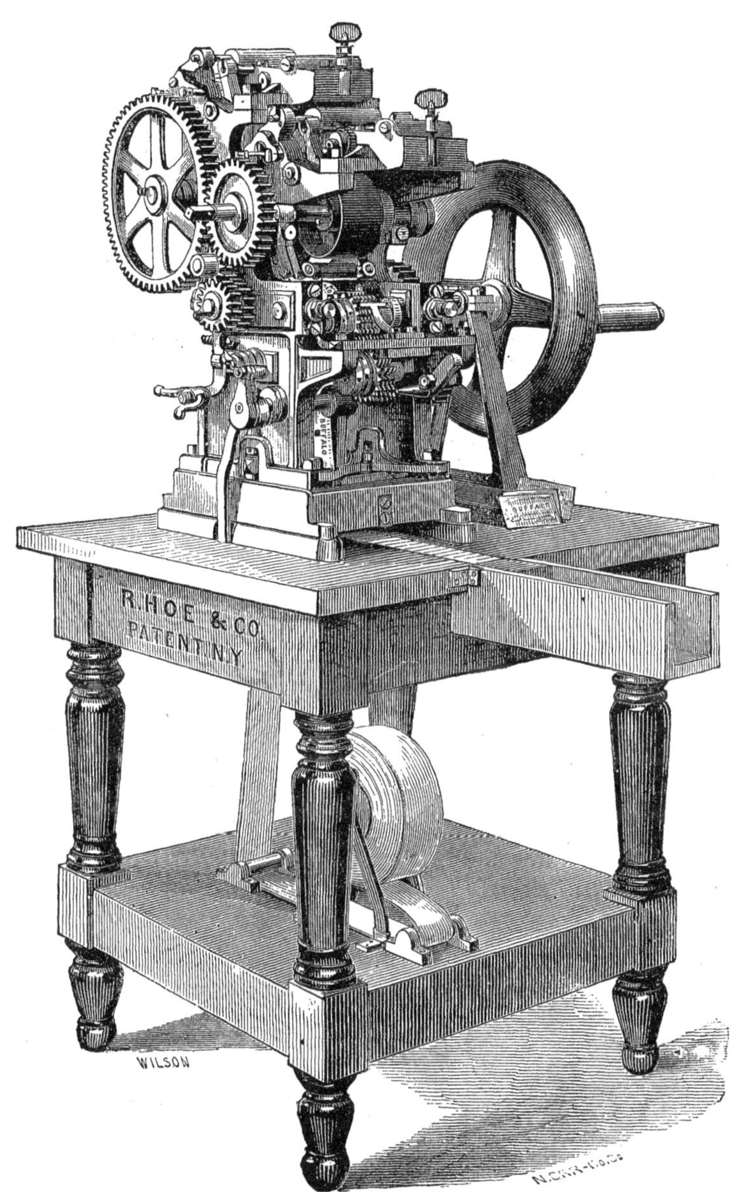

PATENT RAILROAD TICKET MACHINE.

In this machine the forms are placed on a cylinder which enables it to run with a continuous rotary movement. The tickets are worked from a roll of paper, and are printed, numbered, cut, and deposited in a receptacle in numerical order in a single operation. The numbering apparatus prints the number in a different color from the body of the ticket, and can be set at 0 or any required number with great facility. The machine will print from 10,000 to 12,000 tickets per hour, and occupies a space of about two feet square.

BED AND PLATEN POWER PRINTING MACHINE.

only by the ability of the feeders to supply the sheets. The four-cylinder machine is run at a speed of over 10,000 per hour; the six-cylinder machine, 15,000 an hour; the eight-cylinder machine, 20,000; and the ten-cylinder machine, 25,000. This system combines the greatest speed in printing, durability of the machinery, and economy of labor. As we have said, this great machine delivers seven sheets per second, or 420 per minute. It does in one minute what Franklin required ten hours to do, and the papers contain ten times as much matter, and are eight times as large. Thus, to print as much reading would have required 100 hours in the last century, against one minute now. In other words, 6,000 men with 6,000 presses, would have done very badly what this machine does very well.

The next attempted improvement in the speed of machines has been, to do for the revolving cylinder what was done before with the Napier press. In the case of the latter, another cylinder was introduced to take the type on its return vibration, thus getting two impressions from one movement. In the case of the revolving type, something similar has been attempted. It has been stated that the form of type occupies but a segment of the cylinder. It was conceived that by placing the other form on the vacant space of the cylinder, that both would be printed with one revolution, thus doubling the amount of work done by the same number of revolutions. The mechanical part the Messrs. Hoe succeeded in perfecting, but the difficulty encountered was in the paper. It will be conceived that when the paper is printed with such inconceivable rapidity, that the ink has no time to "set," and to impress it on the other side in almost the same instant of time is more than the nature of the operation will permit, and the type "takes off," so to speak, or will not produce a perfect impression. Some other persons made the same attempt, with similar results. Progress in that direction has, therefore, been given up, but the efforts of genius are being directed anew, and the experience of the past has warned us not to be surprised at what may yet be done. There have been attempts made to simplify the process by fitting stereotype plates to cylinders, and with some success; but the necessary delay in stereotyping defeats the object required, which is to save time. The adaptation of electrotype plates to cylinders in printing presses, has also been made with success, but these also require time in perfecting, and are, therefore, not adapted to the daily press.

The work of the weeklies of large circulation, is done on Hoe's large single-cylinder press. In these cases, where time is not so much an object, the forms are multiplied by the electrotypes and worked on a large number of presses. In some cases, the circulation running up to 400,000 weekly, a press running 1,500 per hour, or 20,000 in a day, will require 10 presses four days to perfect the edition on both sides, and for this purpose, ten separate forms will be required. These machines will take a form 19x23½ inches, and up to 40x57 inches. The cost of the former is $960, and of the latter size, $2,650.

The press most used for book work, differs in principle from either the Napier or the revolving type. It was the invention of Isaac Adams, of Massachusetts, and it bears his name. The type in the press has no movement except slightly up and down. It receives the ink from a self-acting machine, and the paper is fed to it from an inclined plane, when, the impression being made, it is lifted off by the fly and deposited in the rear. It is the most perfect of all presses. The prices of these vary from $600 to $2,980, according to size. The engraving on another page will give a good idea of this machine, of which the patent is secured by the Messrs. Hoe.

The printing on all the machines described admits of but one colored ink, but for fancy work of various kinds, more colors are at times desirable, and for this purpose, Hoe & Co. have devised a machine by which four colors can be printed. It is simply the ordinary single small cylinder press, having the bed sufficiently long to receive four forms (when four colors are to be printed), and provided with four ink fountains, each one of which inks its appropriate form. The sheet is fed from a feed board and taken by fingers in the usual manner, but after receiving an impression from the first form, instead of being thrown off, it is held by the fingers and continues to revolve with the cylinder, and thus receives an impression from the second, third, and fourth forms, as they successively pass under it. The fingers then open, and the sheet is thrown off and down by the sheet-flyer in the ordinary manner. It is thus seen that the sheet is printed in four colors at one operation, and in perfect register, without any pointing being required. These machines are made to print two, three, or four colors, as ordered. An idea of its action may be gathered from the illustration.

TYPES.

CHAPTER I.

TYPE FOUNDING—STEREOTYPING—ELECTROTYPING.

There has been little change in the general form of metal types used in printing, but much improvement in the quality of the metal used, in the style of the letters, and in the process of casting. There are many sizes of type used, but the ten following are those most used in books and newspapers. They are mentioned in the order of the sizes, the smallest being first:—Diamond; Pearl; Agate; Nonpareil; Minion; Brevier; Bourgeois; Long Primer; Small Pica; Pica. The size of the type employed in this page is Long Primer.

There are some combinations of these sizes; but these are the leading ones most in use. These have not varied much for a long period of time, although the competition among the type founders has led to the introduction of many styles.

In 1812, on the publication of "The Columbiad," by Joel Barlow, a size of type, known as Columbian, was cut for the work, which was designed to be very perfect. It was embellished by Robert Fulton; and it was the first ever printed upon Clymer's newly invented press, which press took the name of the Columbian in consequence.

The casting of the type was, until within fifteen years, done by hand for each separate letter. The matrix of the type is of copper, $1\frac{1}{4}$ inches long, $\frac{1}{8}$ of an inch deep, and of the breadth of the type to be cast. The form of the letter is made in the end of the copper matrix by a steel die. The copper matrix is then inclosed in a wooden box, which has a hopper to admit the melted metal. There is a spring attached, by which the matrix may be opened to release the letter when cast. The caster, holding this in his left hand, takes from the furnace, with a very small iron ladle or spoon, about as much of the metal as will form one letter. This he pours in, and at the same time gives the matrix a smart upward jerk, which settles the metal into the finest cuts of the letter. He then presses the spring, hooks out the letter, closes the matrix, and proceeds as before. A skilful man will in this way cast 500 types in an hour. In 1811, Mr. David Bruce received a patent for an improvement in the mould, by which 25 per cent. more work was done. This system has changed since the introduction of machinery.

About 15 years since, Mr. Geo. Bruce, Jr., of New York, invented a very beautiful machine for casting type, and it is the best in the world. The patent has been renewed at the last session of Congress for seven years, and the right, title, and interest, have been purchased by Messrs. J. Conner & Sons. By this machine a man can cast three times as much in a day as by the old plan. The wages are less than half, per thousand, what they were before, but the caster, nevertheless, earns more. In these machines the type metal—which is a mixture of lead, tin, and antimony—is contained in a state of fusion in a small iron reservoir, about 5 inches square, and into which it is forced with great power. This is tapped by a nipple, which holds as much melted metal as will cast a type. The mould is of steel, in a small machine which is worked by a crank. It is simply for the body of the type, and is so placed that the lower end, by a movement of the machine, will fit exactly over the orifice of the nipple. Against the other end is applied a copper matrix of the letter, and firmly held by a spring. The operator then causes the metal to jet into the mould. Then, as soon as it is "set," he releases it, opens the mould, and allows the type to drop into a box. In this process, the matrix of the letter is separated from the body of the type. It is formed on a steel die, and impressed into the copper previously prepared, with great force. The adjustment of this matrix to the mould is a work of great care and nicety. After the type is cast, by whatever process—whether by machinery or the ancient spoon method—it has to undergo a smoothing operation. This is performed by young people, principally girls; three or four sitting around tables surmounted with properly prepared stone slabs, and by the fingers rubbing the roughness off each individual type. At this work they earn from $5 to $7 per week. The type goes then into the hands of the dresser. He cuts out what is called the jet end, by which process all the types are made of the exact height. On the nicety of this operation depends the ability to use the type. It may be here remarked that American type comes nearly always perfect into the hands of the dresser, while in England nearly one-fourth is rejected as imperfect.

The types have upon one side a "nick." As the types are perfected, a boy sets them on a "galley," with all the nicks out. They are then assorted into small "fonts," and are then ready for the printer. The proportions in which the different letters are cast to a font of type, and in which they occur in print, are as follows: Letter e, 1500; t, 900; a, 850; n, o, s, i, 800; h, 640; r, 620; d, 440; l, 400; u, 340; c, m, 300; f, 250; w, y, 200; g, p, 170; b, 160; v, 120; k, 80; q, 50; j, x, 40; z, 20. Besides these, are the combined letters: fi, 50; ff, 40; fl, 20; ffi, 15; ffl, 10; æ, 10; œ, 5. The proportion for capitals and small capitals differs from the small letters. In those, I takes the first place, then T, then A and E, etc. The "cases" in which the types are put for use, are arranged in the manner seen in the engraving on another page. The little square boxes in which the type is laid are not arranged in the regular order of the alphabet, but in the order which experience has shown is the most convenient for the compositor. Those letters which occur the oftenest—as e, for instance—occupy the largest squares nearest his hand, and the others in the order of their relative importance; the capitals, small capitals, and marks, each in its proper place, in the upper case. The workman does not look at the type. He reads his copy only, and that frequently tasks his ingenuity to make out. He knows the types from the boxes they occupy, and the "nick" enables him to place them right side up by sense of feeling only. He is paid by the thousand ems when working by the piece. An em is about the space of a letter M, and 2,200 ems go to one of the pages of this book. A good workman will set 5,000 to 6,000 ems in a day. Sometimes they are paid by the week, $12 per week, which is about the amount that an expert workman will earn by the thousand. The type he places in a small iron frame, held in his left hand, and called a "stick," which is adjusted to the breadth of the column or page. When this is full, it is deposited on a "galley," in a long column. From this galley a proof impression is taken to be read by the author and proof-reader. The inaccuracies are marked on this, and when corrected in the type, the foreman "makes up his form." If for a daily paper, this is done by screwing the columns into the "turtle," which is fastened upon the revolving cylinder of the press. When the type has been printed from or worked off, it is immediately washed in a strong alkali, to clear it from the ink. If this is not done thoroughly, it will not print clear. Formerly this washing was done with urine, but of late an alkali is substituted. The clean type has now to be "distributed," or put back into the cases. For this purpose the compositor takes the "matter" in his left hand, reads a line, and drops each letter into its appropriate place. This occupies a good deal of time.

All this type-setting and distributing is done, letter by letter, by hand up to the present time, although the greatest efforts have been made to introduce machinery. A number of type-setting machines have been invented, and many of them work well in the setting of the type—the operator working upon keys, like those of a piano, with the copy before him. The arrangement is such that, by touching the proper key, the appropriate letter falls into line, and the work goes on rapidly and well, even to the punctuation. The difficulty not yet overcome, and which is an obstacle to its usefulness, is that no means of "justifying" have been discovered—that is, of breaking the lines into the suitable length, and "spacing" them out so that each line shall have the exact length of all the rest. This is done by the hand compositor, with great nicety, in his iron stick, as his work progresses. As this must still be done by hand, after the machine has set up the type, no great advantage is derived from its action. In type distributing more success has been obtained. The machine is so constructed that it will distribute 12,000 ems per hour with unerring accuracy, and one man may tend three machines; hence he will distribute, by its aid, 36,000 ems per hour, while a good workman by hand will only distribute 3,000 ems. This seems very desirable, but a new difficulty presents itself. The machine cannot read, so as to distinguish one letter from another, and it is guided in its selection by the "nicks." It follows, that no two of the twenty-four letters of the alphabet should have the same "nicks;" consequently, a special kind of type must be cast for the machine. They are then put into it in a mass, and present themselves alternately until the proper "nick" goes through. The advantages of the machine do not overcome its disadvantages.

In book work the type is not hurried from the compositor to the pressman, as in the case of the daily papers. There is more time, and the type itself is, therefore, not usually printed from, but it is stereotyped. This was introduced in America about the year 1817, by Mr. G. Bruce, the father of the inventor of the type-casting machine.

In this process, the type being locked up in the form, which usually contains 2 to 6 pages, and carefully revised and corrected, is sent to the stereotyper.

Stereotyping is the mode of casting perfect fac-similes, in metal, of the face of movable types. The plan is simple. After arranging the type in pages, and getting it perfectly smooth and clean, it is placed in a frame, the surface being thoroughly oiled, to prevent the mould from adhering, when liquid gypsum, or plaster-of-Paris, is poured over the page. The mould, thus taken, if found perfect, is dressed with a sharp instrument, and is then ready to receive the metal. It is then put into an iron casting-box, and the whole immersed in liquid type metal. Twenty to thirty minutes usually suffice for casting. The box is then swung out of the molten mass into a cooling-trough, in which the under side is exposed to the water. When hard, the caster breaks off the superfluous metal, and separates the plaster mould from the plate. It is then picked, the edges trimmed, the back shaved to a proper thickness, and made ready for the press.

The process of electrotyping has, of late, become an important element, and is generally preferred to the old system of stereotyping. It results from the disposition of copper, held in solution, to deposit itself on a metal surface, when under the influence of magnetism.

This art has a very extended application, since a very small quantity of the metal held in solution will suffice to change the apparent character of that galvanized. A copper pencil, for instance, of elaborate ornamentation by pressure, will require 20 cents worth of gold galvanized upon it, to become solid "gold;" a thimble becomes "gold" for 5 cents worth of that metal; and the most astonishing jewelry can, for a few cents, be made gold. The art of the transmutation of the metals, so long sought after with such assiduity and perseverance by the alchemists of old, seems to have been discovered. It is not altogether a seeming, since the operators have, in many cases, realized fortunes at the expense of the credulous.

Stereotyping by the Electrotype process is conducted as follows: An impression is taken from the corrected forms or engraved block upon a plate of wax, and finely pulverized plumbago is then dusted thinly over the surface of the wax. The excess is blown away in a machine contrived for this purpose, and the fine dust remains uniformly in contact with the wax in every little depression and line, without filling these up. The object of the plumbago is to act as the conducting medium for the galvanic current, until a film of copper is deposited. But by a recent modification of the process, this film is also produced before the article is put into the trough, by the application of a wash of sulphate of copper, (solution of blue vitriol), and dusting over it fine iron filings. The solution is decomposed by the iron, and metallic copper is immediately precipitated, forming a delicate film which uniformly covers the whole surface. The wax plate retaining this film is well washed, and is then ready for the galvanic trough. In this it is left over night under the influence of the electric current, and in the morning when taken out the coating of copper is found to be sufficiently thick for handling. The wax is removed, and the copper sheet, first tinned on the back, is placed face down in an apparatus in which it is covered with melted type metal. Thus backed a plate is obtained, which, after being dressed by planing and squaring, is screwed down upon a mahogany block, the height of the whole being the same as that of type.

Plates for use upon the cylinders of printing machines are made with the curve of the cylinders, the forms themselves in which the type are paged having a convex surface, which gives them the name of "turtles."

In making copper-faced type, ordinary types are set in a frame so arranged as to let only the letter end in the copper solution of the battery. The deposit of copper adheres to this end, which it completely covers. Such type are now extensively used in large establishments, and are very durable.

NEWSPAPERS.

CHAPTER I.

NEWSPAPERS—DAILIES—WEEKLIES—PERIODICALS.

The power and circulation of the daily press are among the marvels of the present day, and they are features peculiarly American. No country presents such a number of news publications, and none such a universal popular demand for them. This result has been obtained mostly in the last twenty-five years, by a combination of causes. The two leading ones, are the introduction of the cheap press and the invention of the means of so multiplying numbers, that much interesting matter can be sold for a little money. Take a leading morning daily. This is equal to a book of more than 100 solid octavo pages, sold to the retailer for one and a half cents every morning, no profit being derived from the sale. This has become possible only through the ability to produce a vast number on one hand, and through the immense receipts for advertising on the other. By the introduction of a cheap press, is not to be understood the mere printing of a mass of matter for a small price, but the introduction of such matter as attracts the attention of persons not previously habitual readers, and exciting in them so strong an interest as to make papers for the future a necessity. It is this which has been done by the cheap press.

The first newspapers of the country were hardly worth the name. In the colonies there was little of interest to draw public attention, and such papers as the *Spectator* and *Tattler* came across the water to meet the literary taste of the more wealthy, while the jealous care of the mother country watched over the colonial papers, lest they should breed sedition. Dr. Franklin informs us that the first start he got in life was through the misfortune of his brother, who owned the paper on which he was an apprentice, in incurring the displeasure of the government for disrespectful remarks. The paper was suspended, as Paris papers are at the present day, and Benjamin's indentures were cancelled in order that he might become the nominal owner. The editor of the *Boston Courant*, in 1732, made his valedictory to the public, because he found it too vexatious to be running with his proof in his pocket to the government house, and the new editor promised to do the best he could under the circumstances. There were few subjects then to interest the general reader, and the restricted state of industry allowed but little range for advertising. The paper was poor, and mostly imported at a high price from England, while the laborious work of a man through the live-long night on the presses of the day, gave but a few hundred to circulate in the morning, and these few were to be sold at a rate that must cover all the expenses—that is to say, for more than they were worth.

The first daily paper published in the United States, was the *Pennsylvania Packet or General Advertiser*, started as a weekly, by John Dunlap, in 1771, and merged into a daily in 1784, at the peace. To one of the conductors of the paper, Washington gave the manuscript of his "Farewell Address, and which, at a recent sale of his executors, was purchased by Mr. Lennox, of New York, for $2,000. The first form in which printed news appeared in England was that of doggerel ballads, which were issued as early as the reign of Queen Mary. These were followed by occasional sheets, or pamphlets, of news; but the first approach to a regular newspaper was the *Weekly Newes from Italy, Germanie, &c.*, May 23, 1622, which was continued, with some variations of title and occasional intermissions, until 1640. The earliest specimen of parliamentary reporting is entitled, *The Diurnal Occurrences or Daily Proceedings of Both Houses in this Great and Happy Parliament, from 3d November*, 1640, *to 3d November*, 1641. More than one hundred newspapers, with different titles, appear to have been published between this date and the death of Charles I., and upward of eighty others between that event and the Restoration. Occasional papers were issued after the civil war began, limited to local or special occurrences, as *News from Hull, Truths from York, Tidings from Ireland.* The more regular newspapers were published weekly at first, then twice or thrice in a week. The impatience of the people soon led to the publication of daily papers; and Spalding, the Aberdeen annalist, mentions that in December, 1642, daily papers came from London, called *Diurnal Occurrences*, declaring what was done in Parliament. In the Scottish campaign of 1650, the army of Charles and that of Oliver Cromwell each carried its printer along with it to report progress, and, of course, to exaggerate successes. It is from this circumstance that the first introduction of newspapers into Scotland has been attributed to Oliver Cromwell.

The stirring events of the American Revolution in like manner gave a great impulse to printing; but that took the form of pamphlets and circulars more than that of the periodical press. The event made the press free, and it began a new career; but the habits of the people had not been overcome, nor were the means of popularizing the press yet in existence. Nevertheless, politics became the staple of newspapers, which were started in most sections as the organs of parties and to support candidates for office; as a matter of course these were read mostly by those who were of the same way of thinking. The circulation could never reach a point that would make it profitable of itself, because the limit was the power of the press to work the papers. In the great cities the chief support of the press was the advertising patronage, bestowed in some degree in the light of political support. The foreign news and domestic items of intelligence made up the general interests, with ship news, that began after the war of 1812 to have a more extended character. These papers, published at $10 per annum, did not much interest the mass of people, beyond whose reach the price for the most part placed them; advertising patronage and government "pap" were therefore the sources looked to for profit. These papers were seldom left in families, but were carried home by those who took them at their places of business. The papers of the early part of the century were very meagre. The oldest existing papers of New York are the *Commercial Advertiser*, founded in 1797, and the *Evening Post*, in 1801. The rivalry among the papers of the day was not so much to interest the general reading public, as to conciliate those commercial interests on the patronage of which the means of the paper mostly depended. The *Commercial Gazette*, of New York, became a leading journal through the enterprise of its editor in collecting ship news. He himself rowed a boat, boarding vessels coming up the bay, to collect reports with which he enriched his columns. The other papers of New York and neighboring cities followed the example, and competition was mostly in that direction. In 1827, the *New York Journal of Commerce* was started, chiefly by Arthur Tappan, Esq., of Boston, and David Hale, then an auctioneer in Boston, was made joint editor with Mr. Hallock, of New Haven. About the same time, two papers were united in the *New York Courier and Enquirer*, under James Watson Webb. These two papers employed news schooners to furnish ship news at great expense. This enterprise was promoted by the introduction of a Napier press, which allowed of an increased circulation of larger sized papers, and these became filled with advertising as the speculative years that exploded with 1837 came on. The success of these two rival papers, however, so absorbed the newspaper business, that it was fatal to the other old papers. The *Mercantile Advertiser*, by Butler; the *Daily Advertiser*, by Dwight and Townsend, and the *Commercial Gazette*, by Lang, which had long flourished, died out. There are many who still remember the old gilt head of Franklin, which for so many years surmounted the door of the *Gazette* publication office, and which still looks out upon Wall street from another office, with the inscription, "Old Lang's Sign." Several other papers followed, among which was the *New York American*, evening paper, edited by Charles King, Esq. At that period cheap newspapers, fast presses, telegraph and express companies made their appearance all together, to work out by mutual aid the marvels that we have since witnessed. The first penny paper was published by Benjamin H. Day, in 1833. It was about ten inches square, and sold for one cent, or to the newsboys for sixty-two and a half cents per hundred. It was without editorials, but was filled with news items. It grew rapidly to a large circulation, and acquiring advertisements, swelled into a larger sheet, which got into the hands of Mr. Beach. This was hardly known out of New York, and being confined mostly to local news and without marked character, never became an influential paper, although its circulation ran up to 60,000, and it was one of the first to use Hoe's fast press. This large circulation was obtained at first through the notoriety that the publication of the celebrated Moon Hoax imparted to it. A great number of other penny papers were started as the result of the success of the *Sun*. That paper, however, occupied the ground, and none succeeded, until in 1835 the *New York Herald* was started by James Gordon Bennett, a veteran editor.

From that time really dates the new era of newspapers. The *Herald* was sold at one cent, and Mr. Bennett, with great industry and genius, wrote the whole of it himself. The first week's expenses were $56, and from that time they have not ceased to increase up to the present time, when they are several thousand dollars per week, and the profits probably $150,000 per annum. The principle of the cash press was radically different from that of the old papers. Of the latter, politics had been the staple; every paper was the organ of some clique, and the commercial community the patrons. The new press explored every possible topic of interest, making politics secondary. It excited in the public mind an interest in topics that had been before dormant, and satisfied that interest by selling a very cheap paper. The *Herald* began systematic reports of the money and commercial markets, maintaining them with a vigor that gave it a world-wide reputation, and soon made such reports a necessity for all papers. It sent efficient reporters to the courts, to public meetings, to give graphic descriptions of what actually occurred, instead of (as in the old style) printing the proceedings from manuscript prepared before they took place. It reported religious anniversaries, and opened every avenue of interest with the most persevering industry and in a style that attracted readers. The proprietor was ever on the alert for more efficient means of obtaining news, and spared no expense to be the first in the field. Expresses by railroad were frequently run at great cost, and reporters were sent to any part of the country where events were of an interest to justify it. The appearance of the telegraph was the signal for new enterprises. These, on the part of the *Herald*, have done more to extend the telegraph than all other means together. Its enterprise did for the telegraph what before it had done for the press. In 1847, Mr. Clay spoke in Lexington, eighty miles from Cincinnati, on the Mexican war. There was no telegraph nearer than Cincinnati. The *Herald* reporters took down the speech, and by horses relayed every ten miles, carried it to Cincinnati in eight hours, whence it was sent by telegraph and issued in the *Herald* next morning, at an expense of $500. This is one instance of many by which the *Herald* has impelled enterprise.

The Associated Press, which embraces the New York papers and those of the neighboring cities, together with many of those of the interior cities, pays $200,000 per annum for the daily reports. The *Herald's* proportion of this forms, however, but a small portion of its outlay for telegraph. In two weeks in September, 1860, when the Prince of Wales was in Canada, and the political events of the presidential campaign to be gathered, it expended $2,301 for extra telegraphic reports, and its whole expense for that item will average $1,000 per week during the year. It is such enterprise as this that makes telegraphs possible and the paper indispensable. That the circulation swelled beyond the capacity of the press is, under such circumstances, no matter of surprise. The result was an affluence of circulation that could have been met only by the opportune appearance of the fast presses of Hoe & Co. The first *Heralds* were printed by hand; a single-cylinder turned by hand followed, and was succeeded by the double-cylinder, turned at first by hand and then by steam. In 1848 the four-cylinder press came hardly in time to meet the *Herald's* wants. The six-cylinder, the eight-cylinder, and the ten-cylinder succeeded each other, carrying the printing per hour from 250 to 2,000, to 3,500, to 10,000, to 15,000, to 18,000, and to 25,000, even at which last figure the tardy press still lingers behind the public demand for *Heralds*.

In all this time other papers have followed on the same general plan. The *Ledger* of Philadelphia has as large a circulation as any in the world. It employs two eight-cylinder presses. Baltimore, Boston, and other and distant cities have seen the growth of flourishing papers. In 1841 the *New York Tribune* was started by Horace Greeley. The paper soon reached a paying stage, since when it has been highly successful. The circulation of all its editions reaches nearly 500,000 copies per week.

The *New York Times* was started in 1850, H. J. Raymond, Esq., editor. He had been connected with the *Tribune* and the *New York Courier*. The paper has attained a great success, after struggling a long time to win a paying position. In 1860 the *World* was started on the same principle, with a large capital, subscribed by a company of gentlemen. These three papers are joint-stock concerns. The *Tribune* was divided into shares, which are held by those who are connected with the editorial and publishing departments. The *Times* is owned in a similar manner, and the shares of both are at a high premium. The *Herald* is the only one owned by an individual.

The circulation of the New York dailies is now (1866) about 350,000 against about 10,000 in 1835. The greater part of this is divided among six papers, viz., the *Tribune*, *Herald*, *Times*, *Sun*, *Staats Zeitung* and *Evening Post*. The following items from the census of 1860 show the extent of newspaper publishing in New York city at that time: it has more than doubled since in value, and greatly increased in the number of issues. There were, in 1860, in the city, 51 newspaper establishments, with a capital of $2,941,200, and employing 2,486 hands, which printed newspapers and periodicals annually to the value of $6,182,946. In the second ward of New York, 134,116,800 newspapers were printed annually, of an estimated value of $3,574,493; and in the fourth ward, 83,541,960 papers and periodicals were printed, having an aggregate value of $2,143,613. We give elsewhere the aggregate numbers of newspapers and periodicals printed in the United States in 1860. These statistics, like all those of manufacturing in the United States, are confessedly far below the truth.

Every family, and almost every individual has his paper, and is interested in its success. The advertising columns of a morning paper contain, in a remarkable degree, the wants, desires, occupations of our people—a photograph, as it were, of their daily life.

The advertisements of one day in the daily *Herald* numbered 1,191, a large number of them being very short, 341, for instance, being comprised under the four headings, Situations Wanted, Males and Females, and Help Wanted, Males and Females, and 308 more under the heads of Houses and Rooms Wanted, To Let and For Sale, and Boarding and Lodging, or thirteen-twenty-fourths of the whole in these items. The *Herald* has a much larger number of these advertisements than any other of the dailies, the *Tribune* having in a single issue only 119 advertisements of these classes, while of all others it had 458, against 542 in the *Herald*, and its advertisements being longer, occupied somewhat more space than those of the *Herald*. The *Times* is about midway in the number of its advertisements between the *Tribune* and the *Herald*, having more short advertisements than the former, and more long ones than the latter. There is very little difference in the actual space occupied by advertisements in the three papers.

The procuring these long advertisements is now a business of itself, employing numerous canvassers, and making large fortunes for the managers. Enterprising men, publishers of newspapers, principals of business colleges, proprietors of sewing and other machines adapted for general use, or of popular articles of food or medicine, have availed themselves of the opportunities afforded by the large circulation of these papers to give one, two, or even four pages of advertising in a single number, and this lavish expenditure, amounting in some instances to $200,000 or $300,000 per annum, has proved immensely profitable in the end.

The *Evening Post* and the *Commercial Advertiser*, though printed as folios, and not as quarto sheets, have a very large advertising patronage, mostly from the shipping and wholesale merchants, book publishers, &c. The advertisements in the morning papers are, to a large extent, fresh advertisements daily, received and paid for the previous day. Those of the evening papers are, many of them, less frequently changed. The advertisements of the morning papers belong to the day on which they appear, and compose a part of the life and the news thereof, like any other matter in the paper—to many people more interesting and more important. No portion of a great metropolitan journal, then, is dead matter; even the advertising columns, which many suppose to be dull and tedious, are full of life and interest, and fresh every day. It is amusing to contrast such a paper with the *Philadelphia Gazette* of 1750, then conducted by Benjamin Franklin. Its dimensions are about eight by ten. The news and reading matter which it contains, could all be put into one of the pages of this book. *It has not a single line of editorial.* Its latest foreign news was about three or four months old. Its domestic news principally related to the Indians. Among its advertisements were several notices of the sale of negroes in Pennsylvania. The progress of the newspaper art is well illustrated by comparing this sheet with those issued in our large cities at the present day.

It is to be remarked that, since the era of the cheap cash press, there have been no papers started on the old or credit system. The *New York Express* was started in 1837, and it has maintained its position only by adopting the cash plan for its evening edition. By the old system of publication, the subscription was taken for the year at generally $10, which was collected at the end of six months by the collector employed. These were served at the houses or offices by carriers, employed by the paper at a weekly salary. The subscriptions from the country were paid the first year in advance, but when the papers are continued on trust, enormous sums accrue in arrear subscriptions—from $10,000 to $50,000 bad debts sometimes accumulating. These being scattered in small sums all over the country, and that at a time when communication was not so prompt as now, did not pay to collect. The advertising was generally $40 per square per annum. A square was twenty lines. This was mostly commercial advertising; the public and retail trade did not advertise much. The system involved much expense in collecting, and inevitable losses in bad debts.

The system with the cheap press is entirely different. The papers were started only by sales to the newsboys, who paid the money when they took the papers. There are no subscriptions taken at the office, and, consequently, no carriers employed. The penny papers sell to the boys at 62½ cents per hundred, and the two cent papers at $1.50 per hundred.

When the city circulation of the papers extended itself, many persons wished to get them regularly at their houses every morning. Thus some of the newsboys got regular subscribers, and became carriers on their own account. Although they were obliged to pay cash every morning for the papers when they took them, they soon acquired as much means as enabled them to leave the papers with their patrons, and collect the twelve cents at the end of the week. This promoted circulation, because the customers could not always have the two cents early in the morning to pay with. The carriers then extended their routes, and became proprietors of them, independent of the newspapers. A carrier who succeeded in getting 1,000 subscribers to serve every morning, paid out to the office every morning $15 for the papers. At the end of the week he collected $120 from the subscribers, which gave him $30 a week profit. This was a good business, and many came to employ boys to serve under them, and serve several different papers on their routes. These routes have been sold by the carriers, according to value, from $200 to $2,000 each. There also arose the publishing agencies, which took large numbers to sell at stations and small shops in the city, and to send to other cities by express, in bundles to be served there.

The country subscriptions are taken for a year in advance. Their subscriptions are all written in "mail books," which are classified North, East, South, West, according to the direction in which they are to be sent. The books are laid off into states, counties, and towns, and the name of the subscriber is written under the appropriate town, with the date up to which he has paid. The wrapping paper being prepared, a number of boys are employed copying the names upon the wrappers, which are then laid in order ready to receive the papers when printed and folded. When the date to which a subscriber has paid is expired, the mail boy crosses it off, unless it has been renewed by a new date. This simplifies the accounts very much, any number of subscribers requiring no other account than these simple mail books, and no one gets a paper that is not paid for. Thus there were grown up four chief avenues for the sale of papers—the mail, the carriers, the newsboys, and the agencies. Each of these wanted their papers *first* in the morning, and the rush of all at once made so great a pressure that it was difficult to count the small sums of money that each offered, and count the papers also. Hence it became the rule for all to go the evening before to the office, pay in their money, and take a ticket for the number wanted. The matter of precedence was settled by the necessities of the case, and the decision of the "cutter," like those of a chief justice, are open to "influences." It is now to be borne in mind that 50,000 daily papers, and in some cases, on the day of publication, 200,000 weekly papers are to be distributed to all these persons at once. There must be no delay. The mail is to swallow its share; the express have its allowance; and the community must not be disappointed at breakfast by either newsboys or carriers. Thirteen tons weight of paper is to be divided up into quantities of from five ounces to thousands of pounds without mistake or delay. Let any one undertake to fold up a wet paper that has never been folded, and he will estimate the difficulty of getting 200,000 folded, wrapped up, and mailed in an hour's time. To facilitate the folding, a machine has been invented, which does the work rapidly and well. A machine has also been invented to direct papers; this does not do so well. The cylinder machine is flinging off the copies seven per second, and newsboys, mail boys, carriers, and agents, are vieing with each other in the rapidity and skill of the operation. Within a short time after the huge machine begins to relax its speed, the whole mass is gone, in bags and bundles, in carts and wagons, while fifty carriers, with lots under their arms, are on their routes, and the newsboys are seeking the ferries and landings, with their shrill cries. Contrast this with the solemn grunting of a hand press thirty years ago, through the live-long night, to work off its seven reams of paper that were to furnish 3,500 copies, as the immense edition of a "crack" daily, to sleepy carriers and a mail clerk!

The operation of the express companies greatly facilitated the sending of the papers to the publication agencies in other cities. These are sent in bundles as they come from the press, and are opened, folded, and served after their arrival. There has been a growing demand in this way for city papers, and an individual recently conceived the magnificent idea of extending, as it were, a carrier's route 300 miles, and ensuring those distant readers their paper at the breakfast-table. He ascertained by calculating time, that if he could procure all the daily papers at a certain time in the morning of each day, he could run a special express up the North River in time to catch the early train going west, and by so doing deliver the papers in all the cities of the North River and on the line of the Central road, to the readers at the same time the readers in New York city get them. To do this, it was necessary for the daily papers to get to press at a certain hour, and deliver to this express the first numbers worked. This they agreed to; at the stated hour the wagon receives the papers in sheets, drives rapidly to the car waiting with steam up at the Hudson River railroad, tosses in the papers, when they are immediately seized by folders and wrappers, and made up into bundles, in the order of the nearest towns first. The locomotive starting the moment the papers reach it, whirls on like a thunderbolt, and as it passes each town and village, the package that belongs there is thrown out to be picked up by expectant hands for distribution. The first towns reached get these before they are wanted, but even with the terrific pace of the iron horse, daylight gradually breaks upon the rapid folding, wrapping, and tossing, as each successive town comes as it were out of the gloom of night, to brighten into gray and catch the gilding of the rising sun as well as the intellectual light emitted from the passing meteor. The race is sustained until the papers are all delivered and the early morning spent. The limit to this enterprise is the rate of speed only, since if that could be doubled, a radius of 600 miles around New York might feel the morning's rays of the press as well as one of 300 miles. The tendency of this is to centralize the power of the press, since, if all the readers of papers within a circle of 300 miles can get the New York papers as early and as cheap as in the city itself, and these papers contain the news of all those cities conveyed by telegraph to be printed and returned, why the carriers' routes of the city press are only extended, and the papers so conveyed will look down, or read down all competition. This enterprise was suspended after a few weeks' operation, as not yet paying sufficiently.

The sale of papers at the steamboats and in the cars has become a large business, and the privilege of doing so is now farmed out by the companies. The privilege is paid for at rates sometimes as high as $5,000 per annum on good routes, say some of the best travelled into New York. The conductor employs boys who start with the out-trains in the morning, supplying all who go. These trains meet others, in an hour's ride, coming in, filled not only with passengers from a distance, but with persons who, doing business in the city, commute on the road, and come in every day; all of them are anxious for the papers, and they are sold at 50 per cent. advance, say 3 cents for the 2 cent papers; a sale of 2,000 papers at this rate gives a profit of $30 per day, or $8,000 per annum.

The Sunday press has become a feature in New York within twenty years. The first Sunday paper was the *Sunday Morning News*, published in 1835, by Samuel Jenks Smith. It had a considerable success, but stopped on the death of Mr. Smith. In 1840, the *Atlas* was started by Herrick, Ropes & West. The last-named had been a reporter on the *Herald*. The paper had a great success, and is still flourishing. The *Sunday Mercury* was next started, and received a great impulse from the "Patent Sermons" of Dow, jr. Then followed the *Sunday Times*, the *Dispatch*, and others, which have attained much success.

The illustrated weekly papers have also become successful in the last ten years. The first was started with a good deal of capital and spirit in 1845, but lived only a short time. Then followed many which did not succeed, until Mr. Barnum and others started the *Illustrated News* in 1853, which failed in a year, although Mr. Barnum had declared that he would carry it on if he had "but one subscription, and paid that himself." A number of papers were started in imitation of the London *Punch*, but without success. The vein of American humor could not be reached until the *Yankee Notions*, a collection of grotesque wood-engravings, cheaply got up, had a success that has earned a fortune for the proprietor. The *New York Journal*, a literary paper without much circulation, introduced a few pictures. It was purchased by Frank Leslie, who, after Barnum's failure, started his successful *Illustrated Newspaper*, having of late a rival in the *New York Illustrated News*. The Messrs. Harper started, in January, 1857, *Harper's Weekly*, which was at first partially illustrated. It gradually, however, acquired the pictorial character, and attained an immense circulation, supported, as it is, by the highest talent at home and abroad. Stories by Dickens, Bulwer, Wilkie Collins, and original tales by American authors appear in it. Hence it is a work of a high character, of which the illustrations are a feature, and not the sole dependence. There were issued in 1865 over 6,000,000 copies of the *Weekly*. The largest circulation of the secular weeklies is perhaps the *Ledger*, which is partly illustrated, and is an instance of singular success. It was, at first, as its name indicates, a commercial paper, struggling to live. During the popularity of Fanny Fern as a writer, it suddenly changed character, gave that lady $100 per week to write for it exclusively, advertised freely, and obtained a circulation of about 400,000 copies weekly, which it still maintains.

We have spoken mostly of the city press, the general features of which apply to the press of most large cities, numerous examples being found in the papers of western and southern cities. The papers which have the most enduring influence upon the public mind are, probably, the country weeklies. These are, from the circumstances of the case, not endowed with the flash and energy of city papers, but their enterprise being confined to their localities, their teachings are concentrated in a manner that is read and makes an abiding impression upon the understanding of the readers. The number of these precludes any attempt at particular description, and some idea of their extent may be formed from the aggregate number as reported by the census of 1860.

		Number of copies.
Daily	387	1,478,435
Tri-weekly	86	107,170
Semi-weekly	79	175,165
Weekly	3,173	7,581,930
Monthly	280	3,411,959
Quarterly	30	101,000
Annual	16	807,750
Total	4,051	13,663,409

The census of 1860 omitted all notice of semi-monthly, or fortnightly periodicals, of which there are a considerable number, and some of them of large circulation.

The aggregate *annual* circulation of these newspapers and periodicals was 927,951,548 copies, an increase of 118 per cent. over 1850, when it was 426,409,000.

TELEGRAPHS—THEIR ORIGIN AND PROGRESS.

CHAPTER I.

TELEGRAPHS—THEIR ORIGIN AND PROGRESS.

"Canst thou send lightnings, that they may go, and say unto thee, 'Here we are'?"—JOB.

THE invention and use of electric telegraphs are among the most important of modern improvements; and it is somewhat remarkable that the invention justifies the trite observation, that great inventions are made always at the moment they are wanted. Telegraphs have been used from the remotest antiquity, by signals of various kinds; and one by flags, to signal the arrival of vessels below, has been used during the present century in Boston; and, in New York, one operating by arms has been used for the same purpose from the Narrows to the roof of the Merchants' Exchange in New York. The electric telegraph applied lightning to intelligence as steam was applied to motion, and came into being to exceed, by its rapidity of intelligence, the means just invented to convey more rapidly by rail. Indeed, its action is necessary to the latter, since it would be very difficult to operate long lines of railroad, like the New York Erie and Central, without the aid of the electric telegraph. The patent of Morse, who was the originator of the modern telegraph, was taken out in the year 1840; since then, numerous modes of recording have been invented, and improvements adopted, and there are now three instruments in use—House, Hughes, and Morse—with a fourth, which is a combination of the two former.

It is curious, that just ninety years after Dr. Franklin identified lightning with electricity, by means of his kite, Morse should have schooled electricity to do messages instantaneously, over wire, at limitless distances. We say instantaneously, because the ascertained speed is 288,000 miles per second, which is scarcely perceptible, although, at that rate, it would take six minutes to send a despatch to the sun.

This all-pervading element manifests itself in countless ways—in the sparkling of animal hair; in the rustling of silk, which "betrays your poor heart to woman;" in the aurora that illumines the north; in the meteor that startles the astonished observer; it flashes in the lightning-bolt that rives the oak, without, while it gently penetrates into the lady's parlor and fills her form, as she glides over her warm, thick carpet, until the metal tube of the gas burner will attract enough from her finger to ignite the gas, or from her lips to startle a newly-entered friend. It will also convey to her the thoughts of distant minds with more than the assiduity of Puck, by means of the invention of Morse.

Morse was by no means the discoverer of the analogy between magnetism and electricity, but he was the first who made practicable all former discoveries and improvements. The three leading properties of electricity that make telegraphs possible, are, first, its constant desire to seek an equilibrium, always going where there is less; second, that the production of electricity is always in two currents, one *positive* and the other *negative*, having different tendencies; third, that different substances have very different conducting powers—over some it passes with the utmost freedom, while over others it will not pass at all. On this depends the possibility of telegraphing, since by it the current of electricity may be arrested or conveyed at the will of the operator. It was known that a current of electricity would render steel magnetic, and that to wind wire, in a certain way, round the steel, would greatly increase the effect. This magnet would then attract soft iron, and would remain magnetic as long as the current of electricity ran on it. The telegraph, then, consisted in connecting two of these magnets by a wire of any number of miles in length, and directing through it a current from an electric battery. By cutting off

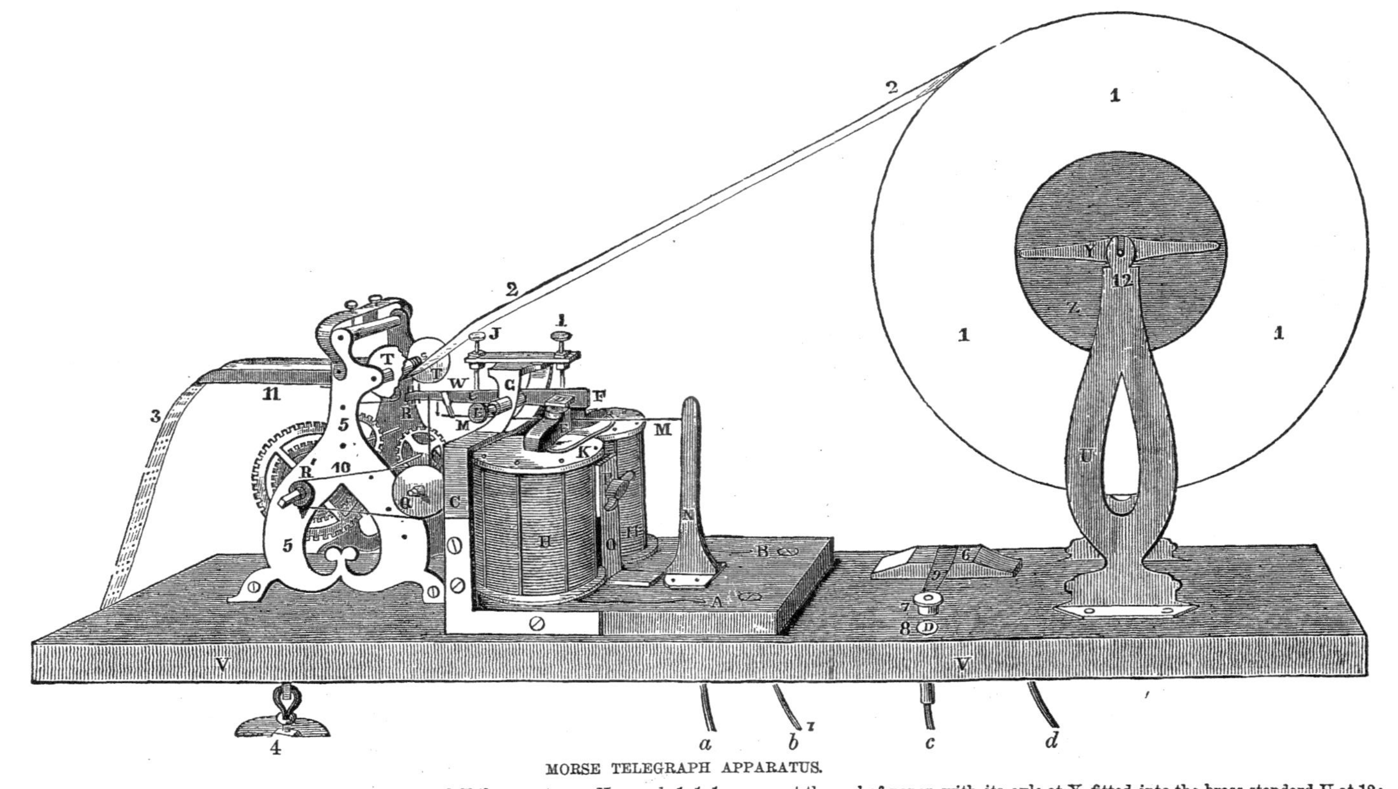

MORSE TELEGRAPH APPARATUS.

H H represents the electro-magnet, L the pen-lever, and F the armature. Numerals 1, 1, 1, represent the reel of paper, with its axle at Y, fitted into the brass standard U at 12; 2, 2, is the paper coming from the reel; 11 is a metallic trough; and 3 is the paper after it has been marked by the pen points R; 4 is the weight that puts in motion the clockwork revolving wheel, to which is fastened the pulley R', with an endless band 10, which puts in motion the wheel Q. The letters *a*, *b*, are the line wires, one running to the battery, and the other to the telegraph poles. When the current passes through the coils H H, the armature F is attracted, and the lever W attached is elevated in the direction of the arrow, causing the small steel points, R, to puncture the paper passing between them and the roller T T. 6, 7, 8, and 9 represent the key. V V is the platform; 8 is a metallic anvil, with its smaller end appearing below, to which is fastened the wire *c*; 7 is the metallic hammer attached to the brass spring 9, which is secured to the block 6, and the whole to the platform. The copper wire *d* is fastened to the brass spring 9, and the other end to the line wire; *c* to *b*, and *a* runs to the voltaic battery.

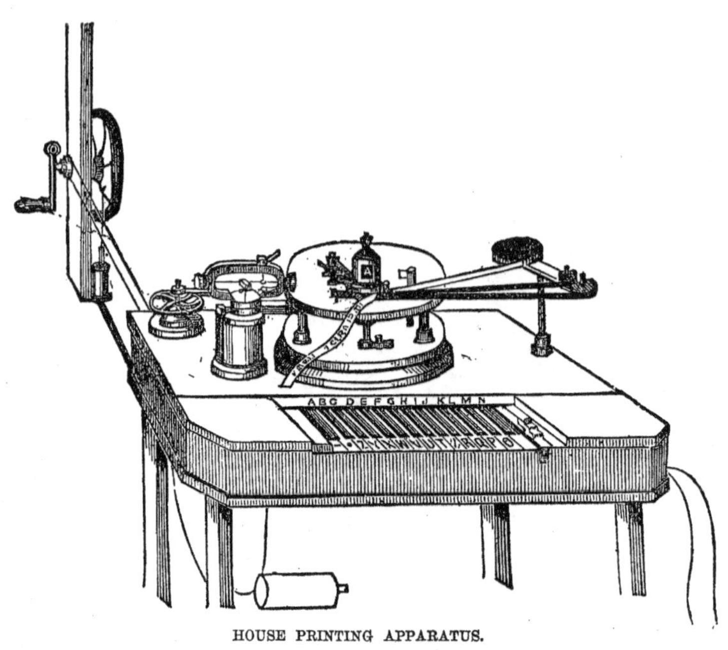

HOUSE PRINTING APPARATUS.

BAIN'S ELECTRO-CHEMICAL TELEGRAPH.

the current, the steel becomes alternately charged and at rest with great rapidity. To form the current, it is necessary that each end of the wire should communicate with the ground. The interruption is caused by stopping this communication. The first invention of Morse was to place a small, soft iron bar across the end of a rod supported on pivots, in such a manner that the iron bar should be near the magnet. The moment the electricity excites the latter it attracts the iron, and, by bringing it down, causes the other end of the rod on which it rests to rise. That end is armed with a pen, which, as it rises, is pressed against a slip of paper, making a dot upon it. The distant operator, by making his connections longer or shorter, causes the pen to make marks more or less long, and these marks convey words or ideas. This instrument is called the register. This was improved by a clock-work accompaniment, by which the slip of paper is moved from a spool steadily under the pen in operation, thus receiving the impression conveyed.

The transmitting apparatus is very simple, being designed only for the opening and closing of the circuit in a manner more easy than by holding the ends of the wire in the hands, as is done where there is no apparatus. The two ends of wire are separated by two pieces of metal, on one of which is an ivory button, and on the other piece a steel knob, or "anvil." The operator, by depressing the button, brings the two together, completing the circuit, which is instantly broken by releasing the button; this may be done with great rapidity. To this system, at a later period, was added the "sounder," a simple contrivance, by which signals are conveyed by sound at the will of the operator, when the electric current is weak. Up to 1842 the operator read the despatch from slips of paper to the copyist, who wrote it down. It was soon found, however, that the despatch could be read by the "click" of the instruments, and the operator now copies, himself, from the sound. If a line is well insulated, a despatch may be sent 1,000 miles with as much ease as a shorter one; but variable weather, and other causes, prevent proper insulation, and "repeaters" are used. By this, the breaks and connections of one circuit are transmitted to another for the purpose of renewing the power. These are the chief features of Morse's system.

In 1846, a patent for a printing telegraph was applied for by Mr. House. By this, seventy strokes, or breaks, may be made in a second. A key-board, similar to that of the piano, has the twenty-six letters of the alphabet, and a dot or a dash painted over them. Under the key-board there is a wheel with fourteen cogs and as many spaces. Over all is a spring, which, when it presses against a cog, closes the circuit, and when over a space, opens it; a man turning a crank causes this to revolve, and at each revolution the circuit is opened and closed twenty-eight times. The paper receives its impression from the steel type cut in the surface of the type-wheel, by a press, which forces, by an ingenious contrivance, a blackened silk ribbon upon the type-wheel with sufficient force to make an impression. The type-wheel can make just as many revolutions as the circuit-wheel, and no more, and it has equally as many cogs. The press can only work when the type-wheel is at rest, and that is controlled by the keys. These are leading features of the House system. The first line that used this was the New York and Philadelphia, in 1849, and in the same year it was adopted on the New York and Boston, and others have since adopted it.

The system of Hughes was the most extraordinary of all in point of mechanism, and, in fact, was proved to be too perfect for the state of the other apparatus used. The instrument is not worked by a crank, like that of House, but by clock-work, with weights. Inasmuch, however, as the ordinary pendulum would be far too slow in its movements, he invented a vibrating spring called the "governor." This depends upon a law of acoustics, by which a certain number of vibrations per second produces a certain musical tone, and, per contra, two springs at the same tone will give the same number of vibrations. These springs control the speed of the instrument; hence, if all the instruments on a line of telegraphs are set to the same tone, they will run with the utmost accuracy. So great is this, that Mr. Hughes has run his instruments 140 revolutions per minute, through an entire day, without a perceptible variation—a result of the most surprising character, enabling the type-wheel to present the same letter in the same place all along the line at the same moment. The type-wheel of Mr. Hughes' system is the same nearly as that of House, with the important difference, that it does not stop to print, but imparts an impression with ink on the paper itself while revolving at the rate of 130 revolutions per minute, or, it prints a letter at every pulsation of the telegraph; while that of House requires seven, and Morse three and a half. The sensibility of the combination of Hughes is so great, that the simple contact of zinc with copper wire gives sufficient power to work it. The operating of the type-wheel is very simple and effective. The key-board contains twenty-eight keys, and is operated like that of House. Suppose there are twenty-eight spaces on the circumference of a cylinder, at equal distances, and a peg upon the end of each key, so arranged that, upon being depressed, it enters into an allotted space once during each revolution; upon entering the space it completes the circuit; by so doing it causes the type-wheel to make the impression of a letter; nothing could be more perfect. In practical operation, however, the movement by weights required such a complication as to lead to continual breakage. It was also found that the high degree of sensitiveness, which was to cause the machine to operate longer distances without relays, was a serious objection, since no insulation being perfect, any change in the weather disconcerted it. To obviate these difficulties, a combination of the Hughes and House has been perfected, and is now used by the American Telegraph Company. The combination is so perfect, that six letters may be printed at every revolution, and as the machine runs 140 revolutions per minute, it gives the enormous result of 50,400 letters, or 10,080 words, per hour. This number is, however, far beyond practicability, since no operator could manipulate with such rapidity. The ordinary speed with the electro-magnetic governor of Mr. Phelps is 2,000 words per hour. The usual rate on the Morse line is 1,000 per hour, and on the House, 1,800 per hour.

These are the principal inventions that have brought the telegraph system to its present perfection. It is but fifteen years since the first line was constructed, and there are now 50,000 miles in operation on this continent, having 1,400 stations, and employing 10,000 operators and clerks. The messages are estimated at 5,000,000 per annum, paying $2,000,000; in addition to which, the press pays $200,000 for despatches.

The wire used for the telegraph is of iron, No. 9. This metal conducts only about one-seventh as well as if of copper; but it is preferred for its superior strength and cheapness. The best prepared is coated with zinc. Without such coating, especially near the sea, it would rust off in a very few years. With the coating, it may have been in use ten years, and will still be in good preservation. When the distance between the supports is necessarily great, as river crossings, and the like, steel wire is used. The most important point in the construction of the lines is insulation; and this is very defective. The materials mostly used are glass; glass protected by iron; glass inserted in pine-wood, soaked with shellac; baked clay; white flint; and bone-rubber. All these are very imperfect; and yet, upon every 500 miles of wire, there are 15,000 of these imperfect insulators mostly affixed to chestnut posts, that are green. There is little matter of surprise, therefore, that constant interruptions occur, and that in wet weather most lines are unmanageable. The cost of a line is $61 per mile. The stations, or relays, are at certain distances from each other; and when a break occurs in the line, the operator ascertains on which side of him it has occurred, east or west. If east, he sends out a repairer to search until he comes to the next station. The operator there, meanwhile, has ascertained that the break is west of him, and he sends out a repairer to search until he meets the other repairer coming east, and the two repair the broken wire in a very simple manner.

The Bain system was completed in 1849, and is one of the simplest construction. There is no magnetism used; only the chemical effects of the current are necessary. A metallic disc, moved by clock-work, receives a sheet of prepared paper. Upon the paper rests a screw-plate, which serves to guide a pen in regular spiral lines from the inner to the outer edge of the disc. The current passes through this paper to the earth, and a very small battery will cause the pen to leave a blue mark upon the paper at 250 miles distant. This system was set up on the Boston line, and was afterward united with the Morse system. This adoption of the chemical effects of electricity has led to various modes, by which *fac-similes* of handwriting may be transmitted to long distances with the greatest rapidity, say 19,500 words per hour!

This system it is which excited much interest in the public mind some time since, from the idea that it could transmit signatures; that a person in New York might, supposing the Atlantic cable in operation, sign his name to a bill in London. This was invented by M. Caselli, of Florence. The despatch is written upon tin-foil, and the copy is blue, upon white ground. The ingenuity of the system consists in the fact that the resistance of the ink to the passage of the electricity reverses the polarity in the point of the receiver. From negative it becomes positive, producing upon paper a colored and perfect image of the original despatch. The chemical effect is so delicate, that the minutest traces of writing or drawing are accurately reproduced. The method by which this is done remains a secret with M. Caselli. The commercial world were much interested in the idea of writing to any distance by telegraph, but it is not likely to come speedily into general use.

The first line constructed in the United States was from Washington to Baltimore, in May, 1844, a distance of forty miles. It was then extended to New York, a distance of 250 miles. In 1845 it reached Boston. From this great northern line branched one of 1,000 miles, from Philadelphia to St. Louis; another, of 1,300 miles, *via* Albany and the lake cities, to Milwaukee; a fourth, of 1,395 miles, from Buffalo to Halifax. A line was constructed of 1,200 miles, from Cleveland to New Orleans; and one of 1,700 miles, from Washington *via* Charleston, S. C., and Savannah, Georgia. In 1851 there were seven Bain lines in operation, over 2,000 miles; eight House lines, having 3,000 miles of wire; and 67 Morse lines, having 20,000 miles. In the autumn of that year, the Magnetic Telegraph Company, having lines extending from New York to Washington, and the Bain Company, having lines over the same route, were consolidated. In the following spring, the Morse and Bain lines, Boston and New York, were united under one company. This was followed by the union of the Morse, Bain, and House lines, New York to Buffalo. The Rhode Island Telegraph Company, having lines between Worcester, Providence, Fall River, Taunton, New Bedford, Warren, and Bristol, were sold in 1853 to the Morse and Bain line, called the New York and New England, for $5,000. Their cost was $10,000. In the fall of that year, all the leading lines west, south, and north-west, were united in interest. There then remained in that year only the House lines between New York and Washington, and New York and Boston; all others having been sold out to rival lines. The receipts of the Magnetic Telegraph Company, which was the first organized, were in 1847, $32,810; in 1848, $52,252; in 1849, $63,367; in 1850, $61,383; in 1851, $67,737; in 1852, $103,232. The most profitable of all lines was the Maine Telegraph Company, from Portland to Calais, Maine, 306 miles. This company paid about 20 per cent. per annum up to 1855, when it was leased to the American Company. In 1853 it bought the Portland and Boston lines out of its earnings, and divided 50 per cent. in stock. In 1855 the American Telegraph Company leased that line at a rate that gives 10 per cent. on the stock. It leased many other lines, until, in the beginning of the present year, it had consolidated all the lines from New Brunswick to New Orleans; thus acquiring the exclusive use of all the patents of the various telegraphic apparatus in use. The company has 25,000 miles of wire in operation, and a capital of $1,500,000. The receipts of the company for the six months ending May, 1860, were $485,395, giving net profits of $123,400. This process of consolidation, however, marks an immense loss of money on the part of those who have subscribed for telegraph lines, mostly arising from the severity of the competition. The use of the telegraph by the daily press is such, that the Associated Press pay to the various lines $200,000 per annum, a sum sufficient to maintain a line from New Orleans to Halifax; and it may at any time become the sole director of the whole. The New York press pays one-half this amount, and the remainder is divided among the papers of other sections; the country papers paying about $30 to $40 per month. The great impulse to telegraphing west was given by the *Herald*, in 1847. In that year Mr. Clay was to speak in Lexington, eighty miles from Cincinnati, on the Mexican war. Horses were relayed every ten miles. When the speech was taken down by the short-hand writers, it was carried to Cincinnati in eight hours, and was issued by the *Herald* next morning. The expense was $500.

At the commencement of 1848 there were 3,000 miles in operation in the United States; in 1850, 22,000; in 1853, they had increased to 26,375; and at the present time there are 50,000 miles on the continent.

The number of messages sent each year is estimated at 5,000,000; giving a revenue of $2,000,000, and employing 10,000 operatives and clerks.

A message throughout the United States and British provinces is scaled to ten words; beyond which, the price for each word is generally about 20 per cent. less. On the line from Savannah to New Orleans it is 50 per cent. less for each added word; from Boston to New York, 25 per cent. less; and from St. Louis, westward, 16 per cent. less. The average may be considered at 20 per cent. discount on all words over the first ten. No charge is made for signature or address. Thus, a message may be transmitted:—

"Tremont House, Boston, Massachusetts, January 1st, 1859.

"To John James Doe, Esq., No. 500 William street, 3rd story, room No. 25, New York city.

"Purchase for me 1,000 bbls. of flour, and ship to me at New Orleans, immediately. 44.33.

"WILLIAM RICHARD ROE."

The above is the form of a message, usual on the American lines. There are fifteen words. According to the tariff hereinbefore mentioned, for the first ten words the charge is 40 cents, and the five added words 3 cents each, or 15 cents: total, 55 cents. The figures 44 mean, "Answer immediately by telegraph," and the figures 33 mean, "Answer paid here." These figures are free. Each number is counted as a word. The telegraph companies in the United States and the British provinces solicit particulars as to address, and the policy is good. In Europe, many men locate and remain a lifetime in the same building and in the same business. Like cases rarely occur in America. In the former country, a brief address is sufficient; but in the latter, particulars are necessary. In the regular form, forty-four words are transmitted in one despatch for 55 cents. There is no charge for delivery.

ATLANTIC TELEGRAPH.

Prof. Morse had, in 1843, predicted that there would be, within a few years, an Atlantic telegraph, and Mr. F. N. Gisborne, a practical telegraphic engineer, conceived the project of uniting St. John's, Newfoundland, with the main continent in New Brunswick, by telegraph wires. In 1851 he obtained an appropriation from the Colonial Legislature, and having made a survey for 350 miles through the forest, attempted the prosecution of his work, but met with misfortunes and financial disaster, which ruined him, and postponed the completion of his project. Early in 1854 he came to New York, and attempted to find parties who would renew the enterprise; and, in so doing, was brought into the company of Cyrus W. Field. This gentleman, though willing to hear what he had to say, was not in favor of his enterprise, but in conversation with him conceived the possibility of laying a submarine cable across the Atlantic, and the next day wrote to Lieutenant Maury, to enquire in regard to the possibility of laying such a cable, and to Prof. Morse, to ascertain whether it would serve the purpose designed, if it were laid. Encouraged by cordial and satisfactory letters from both of these gentlemen in reply, Mr. Field resolved to make the effort to form a telegraph company, which should unite New York, by way of Newfoundland, with London. He enlisted four gentlemen of large wealth with him in the enterprise, and obtained from the Colonial Government of Newfoundland a new charter, securing to them, as the New York, Newfoundland, and London Telegraph Co., for fifty years, the exclusive right of laying cables across the Atlantic, which should terminate in the colony or its dependencies; and also to connect St. John's, Newfoundland, with the lines in the United States. This line was completed after two years, and at an expenditure of about a million dollars. Meantime Mr. Field and his associates had been busily making preparations for their greater enterprise. The United States Government, and that of Great Britain, at their request, sent, in 1856 and 1857, vessels to make soundings anew over the proposed route. Both guaranteed the use of their ships of war to aid in laying the cable, and a subsidy of $70,000 premium was granted by each, to cover the cost of transmitting their own messages. The Atlantic Telegraph Company was formed near the close of 1856, in England, with a capital of £350,000 ($1,750,000), of which Mr. Field took for American stockholders, £88,000 ($440,000). This company had a submarine cable prepared, which was to be laid by the *Niagara*, an American steam frigate of the largest size, and the *Agamemnon*, an English steamship of the line; the *Niagara* beginning at Valentia Bay, on the Irish coast, and laying it to mid-ocean, where the *Agamemnon*, uniting the end of the *Niagara's* coil to her own, should proceed with it toward the coast of Newfoundland. Partly by the fault of the engineer, and partly for the want of proper machinery for paying out the cable, it was broken on board the *Niagara* when about three hundred miles from Valentia. The season was so far advanced, that it was deemed inexpedient to make another attempt to lay it that year. About six hundred miles of new cable was made to replace that lost, and the portion remaining on the *Niagara*, and that on the *Agamemnon*, having been landed, were kept in coil on shore.

In 1858 the experiment of laying the cable was again made, beginning this time in mid-ocean. After three failures, from the breaking of the cable, the last of which caused the return of the two war ships to England, they again set sail, and, though not without several alarms from the cessation of continuity, the cable was at length laid, and messages sent through its whole extent on the 5th of August, 1858. Owing to delay in the completion of the connections, Queen Victoria's congratulation to the President was not received till August 16, and President Buchanan's reply was returned the same day. Great was the rejoicing throughout the United States at this wonderful success. In the midst of this universal rejoicing, and on the very day when hundreds of thousands were assembled in New York, to do Mr. Field honor, the public were stunned by the intelligence that the ATLANTIC CABLE WAS DEAD; that there was an absolute cessation of all transmission of telegraphic signals through it. For a time it was hoped that this cessation might be temporary, as several previous ones had been, but no efforts were availing to resuscitate it. Prostrated for the time, but not utterly overwhelmed, by this sudden wreck of four years of intense labor, Mr. Field again crossed the Atlantic, and for two or three years he and his associates, together with a commission appointed by Parliament, were engaged in experiments upon the best modes of construction and insulation of electric cables, the most effective means of operating them without destroying them, and the best methods of laying them. On all these points much valuable light was gained. His next effort was to obtain the necessary capital and guarantees for the construction and laying of a new and better cable. After almost superhuman efforts, he succeeded in obtaining from both Governments fresh guarantees, and from English capitalists (Thomas Brassey, Esq., a merchant of immense wealth, taking the lead) the needed resources to enable him to procure a new cable, the manufacturers, Messrs. Glass, Elliot & Co., taking one-half the stock for the new enterprise, and the *Great Eastern* being purchased by the Telegraph Construction and Maintenance Company, to lay it. On the 15th of July, 1865, the *Great Eastern* set sail with her vast cargo on board, paying out from Valentia, where the shore-end had been landed and secured. They paid out over twelve hundred miles of the cable, and, though they had met with two or three mishaps, were proceeding well, when, in consequence of an accident, it suddenly broke, at a point where the water was about two and a half miles deep. The attempt was made to grapple for it, and three times it was caught and raised nearly a mile; but the grappling apparatus broke each time, and they were compelled to return to England. In 1866, a new cable having been manufactured, and the external protecting wire galvanized, and the remainder of the cable of 1865 also taken on board, the attempt was repeated, the *Great Eastern* leaving Valentia on the 13th of July, and landing the western end of the cable without mishap at Heart's Content, Trinity Bay, Newfoundland, on the 27th of July. The great work was at last completely successful. All the details being completed, the *Great Eastern* next proceeded to the point where the cable of 1865 was broken, and, after some grappling, secured and spliced that cable, and, steaming slowly, laid the remainder of that also. The cables have now been for more than four months (Dec., 1866) in operation, and their power of transmitting signals has constantly improved.

Another telegraphic line is now in course of construction, from St. Petersburg, east, through Siberia, to the mouth of the Amoor (and with a branch connecting with the principal cities of China), and thence through Kamtchatka, across Behring's Straits, and down the interior of Russian America, to British Columbia, Washington Territory, and Oregon, where it connects with the telegraph from San Francisco, across the continent to New York; and a company has been formed to lay a cable by way of the West Indies and Azores to Spain.

THE ARTS OF DESIGN IN AMERICA,

FROM 1780 TO THE PRESENT TIME.

CHAPTER I.

PAINTING, SCULPTURE, AND ENGRAVING.

Horace Walpole says, in his "Anecdotes of Painting in England" (writing in 1762): "As our disputes and politics have travelled to America, is it not probable that poetry and painting, too, will revive amidst those extensive tracts, as they increase in opulence and empire, and where the stores of nature are so various, so magnificent, and so new?"

These lines were penned, perchance, in grave prophetic faith, but it may be that they were only idle speculations—a play of fancy, meaning nothing. Certain it is, that were the critic ever so much in earnest, very little could he have expected the full and noble response which so short a period would make to his query.

Little could he or any one have foreseen the rapid growth of these "extensive tracts" in population and in every phase of material life; still less the wonderful strides which they have made in all branches of mechanical and industrial art; and least of all, their achievements in the higher and æsthetic arts of design. Little could he have dreamed that within a period seemingly insufficient for the construction even of the rude foundations of empire, our country would have reached that point of refinement and intellectual development which gives it, in ample store, its own literature and its own arts—both with a strong and peculiar individuality of character and life.

The only artists in America in Walpole's time were a few strangers—Englishmen for the most part—who had wandered hither in quest of a fortune which their very humble talents had failed to win at home. They did little or nothing toward the development of the public taste, and left no works to honor the future; though they may, perhaps, have served, in some measure, to open the path for the distinguished group of *native* painters who, quickly succeeding them, fairly and surely lighted the lamp of art which now burns with such pure and ever-growing brightness.

The earliest of these pioneers, whose name has been preserved, was John Watson, a native of Scotland. He crossed the seas and set up his easel in Perth Amboy, in New Jersey, in the year 1715. In this little port, which was then thought destined to be what the city of New York is now—the commercial emporium of the country—Watson painted portraits, such as they were, through a long life. He appears to have had plenty of "sitters," and to have grown rich upon the fruits of well-employed industry; but we can gather no intimations of the state of the popular taste at that time through the medium of his works, inasmuch as none of them now remain for our inspection. Watson was buried about the 22d of August, 1768, in the old church-yard of his adopted village, at the venerable age of eighty-three years.

Our next pioneer was John Smybert, a stronger man, much, than Watson, and one who, though he painted no pictures to be treasured in our galleries, yet left footprints of good incentive and example, which we may clearly trace beneath the subsequent march of greater gifts. Copley, though but thirteen years of age at the time of Smybert's death, confesses indebtedness to him and his works. So also does Trumbull, who at one time painted in the apartments he had occupied, and in which many of his pictures still remained; while Allston is thankful for the advantage he enjoyed in the permission to copy a head which Smybert had executed after Vandyke. Smybert accompanied Bishop Berkeley to America in the year 1728, at the age of forty-two. Like Watson, he was a Scotchman, and like him, again, he pursued his craft in the colonies with gratifying financial success. He lived in Boston in high public favor until 1751, leaving behind him many portraits of the distinguished characters of his time.

Nathaniel Smybert, a son of John Smybert, followed his father's profession worthily in Boston for a short time, and, according to the opinion of cotemporary critics, gave promise of more than ordinary talents. No record of him remains beyond the meagre facts here mentioned, and the additional one that he died early.

While the Smyberts were planting the seeds of art in Boston, there was in Philadelphia a Mr. Williams, an Englishman, remembered gratefully by West as the man who awakened his love of pictures by lending him books and by showing him the first works in oil which he had ever looked upon. During the same period, Woolaston and Taylor were also in Philadelphia; a Mr. Hesselius was at Annapolis in Maryland; a Mr. Theus in Charleston, and other laborers were in Virginia.

Besides the foreign adventurers here spoken of, there were a few native artists scattered over the country during the ante-revolutionary period of our history. It is hardly desirable to recall even their names, or to add to our list of the yet earlier strangers; since, despite the service their little light may have done, in the then deep darkness, not one of them all possessed more than the most moderate talent, and not one will be remembered excepting in the way in which they are now so briefly referred to—that is, in consideration of the *initial* times in which they chanced to live.

The birth of American art was not in any portion of our colonial epoch, but singularly and felicitously enough, was in that day of happy augury when our country itself sprang into life, and started upon its conquering course of national development and power; and with equal strangeness and equal felicity, the very beginning of our individual existence as a people produced, on a sudden, full-grown artists of first-rate genius, as it did Minerva-born statesmen, soldiers, and philosophers.

During the progress of our great revolutionary struggle with the mother land, and at the time of our successful emergence from that trial, Benjamin West, born in the forests of Pennsylvania, was reaching the highest honors in the art world of London, surpassing all native competitors, becoming the successor of Reynolds in the presidental chair of the English Academy, and enjoying the most distinguished consideration, the patronage, and the personal friendship of the very monarch against whom his countrymen were waging angry war.

It is, then, with Benjamin West, and with the birth of our country as an independent nation—about eighty years ago, as we now write—that our story of American art properly and prosperously begins. We shall, however, say but little of West, since the space that has been allotted to this subject does not afford room for an extended notice of any one. Though we may rightfully honor him as the father of American painters, and may write his name first on the long catalogue of eminent laborers in the noble field of art which we now possess, yet, the fact that the greater part of his professional life was spent in England, and that his chief success was won there, places him, in one sense, among the painters of that country, rather than of this; just as the life-long residence among us of a foreign-born artist may make him ours, instead of his own countrymen's.

West was born in 1738, in Pennsylvania, as we have already said, near Springfield, Chester county. His parents were Quakers, and their habits of life, together with all surrounding circumstances, were such as to discourage rather than foster a predisposition toward the study of art. The bent of the boy's mind was, nevertheless, early and powerfully manifested. The sight of Williams' pictures inflamed his youthful predilections to such a degree that, in want of better pencils, he manufactured a supply from the stolen fur of his mother's favorite cat; in want of subjects, he, while yet a child, seized upon his infant sister sleeping, all unconscious, in her cradle; and in want of pigments, he borrowed ochres of the Delaware and Mohawk Indians, and indigo from the maternal laundry! He studied after a while in Philadelphia, and subsequently painted portraits in New York. At the age of twenty-one he went abroad, and after a tour through the art cities of the continent, he established himself in London, where he afterward chiefly resided, rising rapidly into popular favor, until, upon the death of Sir Joshua Reynolds, the first president of the Royal Academy, his position as the head of the English school was affirmed by the high honor of his election to the vacant chair. This distinguished position he filled with great dignity until his death, on the 11th of March, 1820, at the advanced age of nearly eighty-two years.

West's fame was won chiefly in the noble field of historical painting—a department which his brother artists of America have not continued fittingly to cultivate; though one in which they cannot, in due time, yet fail to distinguish themselves no less honorably than they have already done in landscape and portraiture; so rich and boundless are the themes at their command, and growing with every passing year yet more beautiful and noble in aspect.

Among the chief productions of his skilful and most industrious pencil, we may mention the Battles of the Hague and the Boyne; the Death of General Wolfe; the Return of Regulus to Carthage; Agrippina Bearing the Ashes of Germanicus; the Young Hannibal Swearing Eternal Enmity to the Romans; the Death of Epaminondas; the Death of Chevalier Bayard; Penn's Treaty with the Indians; Death on the Pale Horse; and Christ Healing the Sick. Many of his works are now in America; among others, Death on the Pale Horse, which is in the galleries of the Pennsylvania Academy of Fine Arts in Philadelphia; and Christ Healing the Sick, also in Philadelphia, in the Pennsylvania Hospital, to which it was given with noble generosity by the artist himself.

In the same year in which West was born in Pennsylvania, John Singleton Copley, another distinguished man in the earlier days of American art, appeared in the city of Boston. The one, like the other, after following his profession at home for some time, went to London, and there continued to live and labor for the rest of his days. The simultaneous appearance of these two gifted men, at this early period of our country's progress, and in sections of the Union then so far separated, was, as Cunningham says, when alluding to the circumstance—most "noteworthy." Copley was occupied for the most part with portraits, though he made successful incursions at intervals into the domains of history. One of his best works in this department of the art, and that to which he first owed his fame, was the large canvas representing the Death of the Earl of Chatham. Copley died in 1815, five years earlier than his *confrère*, Benjamin West. Many of his pictures are now treasured in the galleries and in the private collections of Boston, and in other parts of the Union. Lord Lyndhurst, of England, was a son of this artist.

In 1754, just sixteen years after the birth of West and Copley, Gilbert Stuart, of Rhode Island, came upon the stage, the earliest of that gifted line of portrait painters whose works have placed this branch of the art as high in America as in any part of the old world. Stuart, with Trumbull as a companion, studied under West in London, where he afterward painted successfully, and in due time rose to great eminence. Unlike his distinguished predecessors, West and Copley, he returned after a time, to his native land, and after some years practice of his art in Philadelphia, Washington, and Boston, he died in the latter city in July, 1828, in his seventy-fifth year. His name is familiar to the public at large, through his great picture of Washington, which he repeated for various societies and state legislatures, and which is spread over our land in every style of the graver's art. He painted noble portraits of many other of the distinguished people of his time—from presidents to private gentlemen. His works are cherished among us as master-pieces and models, exerting still, as they have ever done, a marked influence upon the character of American portraiture. The especial characteristics of his style were a marvellous freedom and boldness of touch, a wonderful freshness and fulness of color, and a truth of character which placed the very soul of his sitter before you in the most striking individuality. "He seemed," says a cotemporary writer, "to dive into the thoughts of men—for they are made to rise and speak on the surface;" and Sully is reported to have remarked of one of his portraits: "*It is a living man looking directly at you!*"

Stuart was a man of eminent social disposition and abilities, a famous wag and humorist, fond of a jest, and overflowing with anecdote. Innumerable amusing illustrations of this trait in his character, sprinkle and enliven the recorded and remembered records of his life.

Another pupil of West's, at this period, was Robert Fulton, who was born in Little Britain, in the county of Lancaster, Pa., in 1765. Fulton commenced the practice of art in 1782, at the age of seventeen, but continued it only a few years, being more powerfully led toward those scientific studies to which his genius was, as the end proved, better adapted; and from which sprang that glory of our time, the practical and permanent application of steam to navigation. Fulton's short career as an artist left no legible mark; what might have been his achievements had he continued in the guild, we cannot say, and are, indeed, careless to inquire, in view of his immortal labors otherwise. American art is willing to spare him, as it has since spared the illustrious Morse, to its graver sister, Science; and is no less proud of the practical blessings he has bestowed upon his country, than it would be of the highest æsthetic success. Fulton died upon the 24th of February, 1815.

Next among the men of service and influence in the cause of art in America was William Dunlap, who was born in Perth Amboy, N.J., February 19th, 1766, and who commenced the profession of portrait painter about 1782. Dunlap will be remembered as an artist more for his long life of reverent and persistent devotion to the craft, and for the respect and estimation which his character gained for it, than for his success at the easel; though he both attempted and achieved works which were commended at a less brilliant period than the present. He was also an author of considerable ability. Among his works is a "History of the American Theatre," published in 1832, and another of the New Netherlands, which appeared in 1840; a memoir of Charles Brockden Brown, and various plays of considerable interest. But the most important of his literary labors is the only record we possess of the early story of American art, an invaluable work under the circumstances, and one for which he will be ever remembered, although clumsily constructed and injured by a most wearisome medley of irrelevant matter. In this "History of the Arts of Design," Dunlap gives us his own biography with great discursiveness and fulness, though with humble and characteristic reverence, exhibiting his own career as one to be shunned rather than followed. 'I look back," he says in mournful reflection, "upon a long life, with the persuasion that what is called misfortune in common parlance is caused generally by our own folly, ignorance, mistakes, or vices." To read his story as recorded in his "History of the Arts of Design," is to read a sad record of untoward circumstances, varied effort, and ever-following failure; but, withal, a praiseworthy and even exalted longing to be of use to his fellows and his country. His pictures were generally of a very ambitious character, scriptural themes on canvas twenty feet long. Among these productions of high art were Christ Rejected; Bearing the Cross; Calvary; and Death on the Pale Horse; the first of which was made up in part, and the last wholly, from West's pictures of the same names.

Besides thus remembering Dunlap for the art records which he has preserved with so much honesty and industry, and for what he would have done, and sought to lead others to do at the easel, he must be honored as one of the founders and the first vice-president of our leading art society, the National Academy of Design in New York. Dunlap died on the 28th of September, 1839.

To the life and works of Colonel John Trumbull our early art owes great obligations, though it is much the fashion at this day to disparage and deny his genius. Trumbull's name is familiar to the people through his grand pictures of revolutionary story which decorate the walls of the national capitol. He was the son of the first governor Trumbull of Connecticut, and was born at Lebanon on the 6th of June, 1756. To high birth he added, through life, high character and learning, and great culture and dignity of manners. His early studies were, as was the case with all the artists of his time, pursued abroad and under Benjamin West. He entered the American army at the commencement of the Revolution, and was an eye-witness of, and participant in, some of its most stirring scenes, of which the subsequent delineation won for him his fame as a painter. The four large works executed for the government, are: the Declaration of Independence; the Surrender of Cornwallis; the Surrender of Burgoyne; and Washington's Resignation. An appropriation of thirty-two thousand dollars was made for these pictures, besides which, the artist received considerable emolument from their public exhibition through the country. Among his other historical works may be mentioned the Battle of Bunker Hill; the Death of General Montgomery; Capture of the Hessians at Trenton; and the Death of General Mercer at the Battle of Princeton. In addition, he executed various scriptural subjects, and many portraits, among which was a full-length of Washington, painted in 1792, in the artist's best days. A few years before his death, he presented his collected works to Yale

College, upon the condition that they should be suitably housed, and that he should receive an annuity of one thousand dollars. The college erected a gallery on its grounds in New Haven, where the pictures were placed, and where they now may be seen.

Colonel Trumbull was president of the American Academy of Fine Arts, in New York, until that effete organization was superseded in 1826 by the establishment of the National Academy of Design. Trumbull did not, at any period of his life, possess much of that genial fellowship and social habit so characteristic of artists, and so essential to personal popularity in the profession. He died in 1843, at the venerable age of eighty-seven years, leaving behind him a name unspotted, and a claim to distinguished remembrance in the history of art in America, despite all the faults of his works, and however much they have since been or yet may be surpassed.

Charles W. Peale, born at Chesterton, on the eastern shore of Maryland, April 16th, 1741, was an active colaborer with Trumbull and his fellows, but was not eminently successful at the easel. He was a man of versatile gifts, and at various times dabbled in all sorts of crafts. He made his brothers, sisters, sons, and daughters all artists. He died in 1827, at the age of eighty-five years.

John Vanderlyn was born in Kingston, in the state of New York, in October, 1776, where he died at the age of seventy-six years, in 1852. Aaron Burr was struck with his boyish performances in art while he was a blacksmith's apprentice in his native village, and befriended him at the commencement of his career. At the age of twenty he made the foreign tour, so customary at the time, studying in Paris and other cities of the continent of Europe. In the year 1817, the corporation of New York having given him the lease of the ground, he erected the building in the north-east corner of the City Hall park in New York, afterward used as the Post Office, and always known as the Rotunda. Here he exhibited in succession a series of panoramas, the first seen in this country, of Paris, Athens, Mexico, and Versailles, with his own pictures—Marius, Ariadne, and other subjects. The unexpected cost of the building, and the resumption of the lease by the city before the artist had fairly tried his speculation, made it a matter of serious pecuniary loss to him. Among his chief pictures are the Landing of Columbus, which fills one of the panels of the rotunda of the Capitol in Washington—one of the pendants of those already mentioned by Trumbull; his fine picture of Marius Musing over the Ruins of Carthage, painted in 1808; and his superb full-length figure of Ariadne, so beautifully engraved by Durand; portraits of Presidents Madison, Monroe, and Jackson; of Calhoun, De Witt Clinton, and other distinguished men. He exerted a most healthy influence upon his fellow artists, and his works remain as models for future study.

Edward G. Malbone was born in Newport, Rhode Island, in 1777, and died in Savannah, in May, 1807, in his thirty-second year. During his short life he won high reputation as a miniature painter; and his works in this department are still preserved in various parts of the country as masterpieces of art. One of his most successful productions—a picture of three half-length female figures, called The Hours—is now in the possession of the Athenæum in Providence.

Rembrandt Peale, whose history belongs to this period, though but so recently deceased, was born of a family of artists in Pennsylvania, on the 22d of February, 1778. He was an active, earnest man in his time, and did much in the service of art, by his own works, and the incentive which his example gave to others. His picture of Washington, painted in the artist's boyhood, and afterward often repeated by him, is well known; as also his grand work called the Court of Death. His long and honored career, which embraced nearly the whole period of our art history, was closed on the 3d of October, 1860.

John Wesley Jarvis, one of the most distinguished portrait painters of this era, was born in England in 1780, and brought to America at the age of five years. He painted innumerable pictures, many of them of great merit; and did good service as the instructor of Henry Inman, and other distinguished artists. He was a man of eminently social disposition, with a great turn for humor—traits of character pleasant enough when well employed, but which he unhappily permitted to lead him into low and ruinous dissipation, which impaired his artistic powers, and brought a life begun under the happiest promise to the dreariest end.

Charles B. King, born in Newport, Rhode Island, 1785; Alvan Fisher, born in Needham, Massachusetts, 1792; William E. West, and William James Bennet, born in London, 1787, may be mentioned in this part of our story as men of mark and influence in their day, though they left no works behind them of great excellence. Mr. King, indeed, still lives at an advanced age in the city of Washington, where he for many years virtually filled the fashionable position of court painter, preserving to posterity the likenesses of presidents, ministers, statesmen, and the chiefs of the Indian deputations who came to see their great white father at the capital.

The life of Thomas Sully fills a delightful page in the history of American art. Born in England in June, 1783, he came hither at the age of nine years, struggled bravely through an indigent youth and a laborious manhood to a position of high honor and usefulness. He is still pursuing, at his residence in Philadelphia, the profession which he has through many years so effectually contributed to advance. His pictures are characterized by grace and beauty of feeling, and a daintiness and freshness of color well deserving of most careful study. He has painted many full-length pictures of distinguished personages, among them one of Queen Victoria, which was exhibited with great success in all the Atlantic cities, and numerous fancy heads of great poetic beauty.

Charles Fraser, who was born in Charleston, South Carolina, August 20th, 1782, was an intimate and esteemed associate of the best men of the days of which we write. His works have materially advanced the standard of public taste in his native state. After obtaining a competency by the industrious pursuit of legal studies, he began the profession of artist in earnest at the age of thirty-six. Following the successful lead of his friend Malbone, he turned his attention especially to miniature painting, in which style he executed a picture of Lafayette, and of nearly all of the prominent men of his region. An exhibition of his collected works in 1857, included 313 miniatures, 139 landscapes, and other works in oil.

Chester Harding, a veteran still on the stage, was born in Conway, Mass., September 1st, 1792. His humble parentage sent him at first to farm work and chair-making. After the war of 1812, in which he served, he engaged in cabinet-making in Caledonia, New York. He subsequently went to the head waters of the Alleghany, and thence on a raft to Pittsburg, where he worked at house-painting; he returned home through the forest, two hundred miles, on foot, with no guide but blazed trees. Again visiting the west with his family, he worked from sign painting into portraiture; thenceforth gradually rising in his profession, until he numbered among his sitters such men as Madison, Monroe, Marshall, Wirt, Clay, Webster, Calhoun, and Allston, in America; and the dukes of Norfolk, Hamilton, and Sussex, Lord Aberdeen, and Samuel Rogers, in England.

Washington Allston, one of the most illustrious of our artists, was a native of South Carolina, having been born on his father's plantation at Waccamaw, in that state, on the 5th of November, 1779. He was a high-toned man, of poetic temperament and scholarly tastes, and was eminent as a poet as well as an artist. He was a student of the Royal Academy in London in 1801, and an exhibitor on the walls of that institution the following year. At this early period of his life he became an intimate friend of Coleridge and Thorwaldsen, West and Fuseli, and other distinguished men. In a second visit to Europe, about 1810, he exhibited his famous picture of the Dead Man Revived, which is now in the Pennsylvania Academy at Philadelphia. For this work a prize of 200 guineas was awarded to him by the British Institution. His next considerable works were: St. Peter Liberated by the Angel; Uriel in the Sun, which was painted for the duke of Sutherland; and Jacob's Dream. In 1818 he returned home, with his picture of Elijah in the Wilderness, which afterward went back to England. Within the next twelve years he produced in Boston his Prophet Jeremiah, now in the possession of Miss Gibbs, of Newport; Saul and the Witch of Endor; Miriam Singing the Song of Triumph, and other justly celebrated works. Among his smaller pictures, the Valentine and Beatrice, female ideal heads, are remarkable for their power of expression and strength of color. In the studio in which he finally settled himself at Cambridge, he painted Spalatro's Vision of the Bloody Hand; Rosalie; and his grand unfinished subject, Belshazzar's Feast. In his early life he was an intimate friend of Washington Irving, whom he almost won over to his own studies, as the author's profession may have attracted him, for during his life he made frequent incursions into the literary arena, publishing in London, in 1813, a poem entitled "The

Sylphs of the Season," and afterward the metrical satire entitled, "The Two Painters," the weird story of the "Paint King," "Monaldi, a Tale of Passion in Italy," followed after his death by a volume of "Lectures on Art." He was twice married, first in 1809 to a sister of Dr. Channing, and again in 1830. He died at Cambridge on the 9th of July, 1843.

Thomas Birch, a marine painter, and Joshua Shaw, a landscape painter, were born in England about the time of the Revolution, the latter in the year of the Declaration of our Independence. They became residents of the United States in childhood, and gained a reputation in their respective departments.

Among the popular painters of this time were Samuel L. Waldo and William Jewett. These gentlemen painted an immense number of portraits together, under the famous firm of Waldo & Jewett.

Our narrative now passes the line, as nearly as such a line may be drawn, between the artists of the revolutionary and immediately following years, and the earlier part of the present century. Already have we seen the arts firmly rooted in the love of the people and the genius of their professors; seen native artists grow up, and by their labors reflect high and imperishable honor on their country. In the continuation and the sequel of our history it will be our pleasure to see this glory ever brightening, and the public taste and artistic skill still more rapidly advancing hand in hand. This progress cannot, however, be better understood than by following, step by step, the lives of those from whose genius and works it alone springs. We therefore continue as we have begun, the chronological mention of the men to whom we are the most indebted for it.

We have already seen how our country had no sooner come of age than its early indebtedness to the mother-land for the humble aid of her Smybert and others, was promptly and nobly repaid by the fame which we sent her of a West and a Copley. Not content with this ample acknowledgment, we added to these high names at a later day those of Leslie and Newton, which she has inscribed upon the brightest tablet of her art achievement. Both these eminent artists were Americans by their parentage, though, through the chances of the moment, the former first saw the light in London. The latter was born in Halifax, in Nova Scotia, during a temporary visit of his parents thither from Boston. They established themselves in London, where they passed their lives in such successful labors as to leave a name and fame cherished zealously both by their native and their adopted homes.

The men most distinguished and the most serviceable in the cause of art in America, who came upon the stage at or near the beginning of the present century, are nearly all yet living to see the happy fruits of their toil, in the general diffusion of an appreciative and enduring love of art throughout the land, in the growing up of a community of artists, large and influential enough to have become an acknowledged and revered power in society, and in the firm foundation of a strongly individualized and healthful national school.

Among these great men, we should, perhaps, first of all, mention Samuel Findley Breese Morse, to whom (though he was drawn out of the profession as Fulton was before him, by the allurements of science) we owe much for the excellent labors of his pencil and the yet more excellent effects of his earnest sympathy with his art brethren throughout his long and illustrious life. It is to this strong and indefatigable love that we are, more than to any other agency, indebted for the foundation and success of our chief art society, the National Academy of Design. Morse was the leading spirit in this great enterprise. He was its first president; an office which he continued to fill with high honor for a score of years, and which, only that other duties required him to resign, he would have filled to this day. Prof. Morse was born in Charlestown, Mass., April 29th, 1791. His father was the famous geographer, the Rev. Jedidiah Morse. He was educated at Yale College under Dr. Dwight. In his twentieth year he went to England, and yet two years later successfully exhibited a large picture of the Dying Hercules at the Royal Academy. He had previously executed a plaster model of the Hercules, which he also displayed, and for which, greatly to his own surprise, he received the *gold medal* from the Society of Arts. From this happy commencement of his life as an artist, and from the portraits and other works which he subsequently produced, until other studies drew his mind away from the easel, we may fairly suppose that he would have reached the highest position as a painter had he continued to seek it, and some regret at his loss to the arts may be permitted, even in view of what the world at large owes to his scientific studies in the priceless gift of the Magnetic Telegraph.

Charles C. Ingham, born in Dublin, 1796, is one of the bright lights of this epoch yet shining brightly among us. He was an earnest colaborer with Morse in the establishment of our National Academy, which has always owed and still owes much in its exhibitions to the productions of his easel—his exquisite pictures of fair women and brave men. He at this time fills the office of vice-president of the academy.

Robert W. Weir, who has been for many years, as now, professor of drawing at the Military Academy at West Point, holds a distinguished place among the older of our living artists. He was born on the 18th of January, 1803, at New Rochelle, in the state of New York. It is to his pencil that we owe that best of the pictures in the Capitol at Washington, the Embarkation of the Pilgrims, a work eminently illustrative of the thoughtfulness and conscientiousness of his genius. He has painted numerous historical compositions, *genre* subjects, landscapes, and portraits of great excellence.

Thomas S. Cummings, another of the founders of the academy, and always one of its officers, held high rank at this period in the department of miniature painting. Mr. Cummings was born in Bath, England, in 1804, and became a resident of the United States in early childhood.

John G. Chapman, born in Alexandria, Virginia, on the 11th of August, 1808, now residing in Italy, is well known as the painter of the Baptism of Pocahontas, in the Capitol at Washington, and as the author of innumerable designs in our illustrated books.

William S. Mount, born in Setauket, L. I., November, 1807, was the first American artist who achieved high success in subjects of a purely national character, in a series of happy pictures of the humbler features of our country life. His Bargaining for a Horse, Haymaker's Dance, the Power of Music, and other light themes, have been often engraved, and are familiar to everybody.

Francis W. Edmonds has produced many pleasant pictures in the same vein of quiet humor with Mount.

William Page, born in Albany, January, 1811, has distinguished himself, at home and abroad, in the field of portraiture. He has painted, also, many excellent classic themes, among them the Venus, recently exhibited through the Union with so much applause.

Henry Inman, born in Utica, N. Y., October 20th, 1801, was one of the most eminent artists of the time. He was a pupil of Jarvis, whom he soon surpassed, excellent as Jarvis was. He was a man of remarkable versatility, and worked with equal facility in portraiture, landscape, and history. He was the guest of Wordsworth, during a visit to England in 1844, at which time he painted a characteristic picture of the great poet, and that charming illustration of the scenery of his region, the Rydal Water. While in England, he painted, also, portraits of Dr. Chalmers, Macaulay, and other eminent people. The exhibition which was made, after his death, of his works, was one of the most interesting and varied ever seen in New York. Inman died on the 17th of January, 1846.

In coming now to the life and works of Asher B. Durand, we enter the great field of landscape art, in which our painters are so pre-eminently distinguishing themselves—that field first explored with such brilliant success by Durand, and his fellow-laborers Cole and Doughty, and which is now being brought to such high culture by the present host of younger men. Durand was the first of our landscapists to pursue that course of severe and earnest study of Nature herself, in all her details of form, character, and color, which is now universal among us, and to which (following the richness and variety of our scenery) our wonderful progress in this department of the art may, in a great measure, be ascribed.

Mr. Durand is president of the National Academy, in which office he succeeded Prof. Morse. Though now in the autumn of life (having been born as long ago as 1796), he is still as active and as efficient a worker, in his special field, as he was when he first entered its untrodden paths long years ago. Everybody loves Durand's landscapes, for they appeal to and satisfy the dearest emotions of the soul, in their deep-thoughtedness, their quiet and serene beauty, and their sweet poetic suggestion. No artist has more truly rendered the characteristics of our American scenery, or under a greater variety of aspects. Besides innumerable landscapes, many of them of great size, he has painted a large number of excellent portraits, and various successful figure pieces. He was, too, before he became a landscape painter professionally, perhaps the best of our engravers upon steel; in which art, his skill is well attested by the fine print of Ariadne, after Vanderlyn. He is a native of Jefferson, in New Jersey.

Side by side with Durand—for they worked together through many fruitful years—was Thomas Cole, born on the 1st of February, 1801. He was a native of Bolton-le-Moor, in England, and was eighteen years of age when his father emigrated to America; yet so thoroughly did he acquire the spirit of American landscape, in all its most peculiar idioms, that never would he, of all our artists, be thought of foreign origin. While Durand painted our hills, and valleys, and waters in their more calm and contemplative mood, and in the bright, yet quiet garb of summer green, Cole loved to watch their more stirring and active humors, and to depict them in the gorgeous parti-colored vesture of varied autumn. The one, with delicate and dainty touch, records the gentle whisperings of the meadows, and lakes, and rivulets, while the other, with his freer and bolder pencil, transcribes the grander language of the cloud, or the snow-capped mountain crest, and of the turbulent and roaring torrent.

Cole's earlier professional life was passed among scenes of hardship, trials, and poverty, which only the most persistent spirit and the truest genius could have conquered. It is a pleasant thing to record that the first real encouragement which he met with, the first recognition of his great merit, came from brother artists, when Durand, Trumbull, and Dunlap took him generously by the hand, and led his steps into the pathway of success and fame. His later years sped happily, in a beautiful home on the Hudson, in the midst of that charming mountain and river scenery, which his pencil has done so much to endear to us. His earnest, poetic temperament did not permit him to rest content with the literal delineations of natural beauty, but led him to embody them in imaginative conceptions, with high moral meanings. To this noble ambition, we owe that great series of works representing the rise, progress, and fall of Empire, now in the gallery of the Historical Society in New York; that famous epic, in four parts, familiar to the world under the name of the Voyage of Life, in the possession of the Rev. G. D. Abbott, of New York; and the third group, left unfinished at his death, and now, we think, in the possession of his family, at Catskill, called the Cross and the World. Apart from these great serials, his principal productions are the Allegro and the Penseroso, the Home in the Woods, the Mountain Ford, the Hunter's Return, the Mount Etna, the Dream of Arcadia, the Cross in the Wilderness, and the Departure and the Return.

Cole died at his home, in Catskill, on the 11th of February, 1848, universally lamented, scarcely less as an artist than as a man of exalted principle, singular kindness of heart, and rare literary tastes and ability.

With the name of Thomas Doughty, we end our mention of the trio of which we have spoken, as the founders of our American school of landscape art. If his works, with all their poetical beauty, were, even in his best days, behind those of his *confrères*, and do not preserve the place they once had in the public esteem, it may be set down, probably, to the fact that, at the earlier period at which he commenced his studies, it was not the custom, as it soon after came to be, to go directly and implicitly to Nature for instruction. Doughty was born in Philadelphia, July 19th, 1793, and died in New York, July 24th, 1856. In his youth, he was apprenticed to a leather manufacturer, and afterward became a leather dealer on his own account. It was not until he was nearly twenty-eight years of age that he turned painter, and then against the counsels of good friends. He practised his art for many years in New York, and also in London and Paris.

Daniel Huntington was born in New York, October 14th, 1816. No pencil has contributed more to the healthful progress of our art, in elevation of theme, and refinement of treatment, than that of Huntington. Every thing he does is, in all the higher æsthetic qualities of art, a lesson to both artists and the public. His genius is of the greatest versatility, being equally at home in portrait, landscape, or history, sacred and profane.

Charles L. Elliott, born in Scipio, N. Y., in 1812, and now pursuing his art in the city of New York, sustains, in his vigorous style of portraiture, the fame early reflected upon this department of American art by Stuart and his cotemporaries. He is pre-eminent for the bold execution of male heads.

George A. Baker, of New York, is equally distinguished for his heads of women and children. Henry Peters Gray, also of New York, holds a high position as a painter of portraits, and of small pictures of *genre* and history. Of the latter class of works, his Pride of the Village, from Irving, is a most charming example. Thomas P. Rossiter is familiarly known by numerous large works, chiefly from scripture history, which have been exhibited to admiring throngs throughout the country. He has recently established himself in a pleasant home, at Cold Spring, on the Hudson. Arthur F. Tait is particularly happy in pictures of game and sporting life, a branch successfully followed by the late William Ranney. Thomas Hicks is among the most popular of the present group of portrait painters in New York. Hicks is now engaged upon a large picture of the living authors of America. Edwin White's great picture of Washington Resigning his Commission, painted for the legislature of Maryland, is a fair example of this artist's style and class of subjects.

Emanuel Leutze stands at the head of the living historical painters of the country. Much of his life has been passed in Dusseldorf, but he has lately returned home, and is pursuing his art in New York. A large picture of Washington Crossing the Delaware, is an excellent example of his vigorous and effective style.

P. F. Rothermel is one of the leading artists of Philadelphia, in historical subjects. The Lambdins, of Philadelphia, father and son, hold a distinguished place in the art, the elder as portrait painter, and the latter as painter of poetical and dramatic scenes.

F. O. C. Darley has achieved a world-wide fame, by his designs and book illustrations. Nothing can surpass, in beauty of conception, his charming outline drawings from Irving's "Rip Van Winkle" and "Sleepy Hollow," or his compositions from Judd's novel, "Margaret." He is now illustrating an edition of Cooper's works in thirty-two volumes, containing upward of five hundred designs. John W. Ehninger has been most successful in the same walk with Darley, besides which he has made many happy *genre* pictures in oil. E. D. E. Greene is justly famous for the classic beauty of his female heads; J. T. Peele for his dainty pictures of childhood; Rowse and Colyer for their charming heads in crayon; W. J. Hays for his animal subjects; Eastman Johnson for his domestic passages of negro and other humble life; Healy and Lang for brilliant portraiture; Wenzler and Stone for their female heads, and May in historical subjects.

Nearly all our landscape painters, after the trio already mentioned as the first who entered the field, are young men, many of them giving promise of a success even beyond that of their gifted fathers in art. The pictures of Church, who has not yet reached the middle of man's three-score years and ten, are famous the world over. Everybody has seen his wonderful picture of Niagara, and his still more popular Heart of the Andes. No works have done so much as those of Church to increase the foreign estimate of American art. Cropsey is now extending in London a fame fairly won at home. Kensett's pictures of our forest scenery are admired and loved by all. Mignot and the brothers Hart are among the best landscapists of this or any land, which may be said also in brief of Casilear, Gignoux, Gifford, Hubbard, Weber, Gay, Bierstadt, Brown, Shattuck, Colman, and Inness.

Our catalogue of bright names might run on almost forever, now that we have fully entered among the artists of our own day; but of them, great as is their genius—greater, indeed, in many instances, than that of any of their predecessors of whom we have said so much—it was not our intention to speak at length. Their name and fame is still rising; we meet them in our daily life, and gain of them that cotemporary knowledge which is better than all historic record; besides, our only desire was to gather up the fast fading mementoes of the early condition of art among us, and of the steps by which it has risen to its present noble state. This present is before us all, to delight our eyes, and encourage our hearts for the future.

We pass now to a brief glance at the remarkable performance of our young land in the noble art of Sculpture, a performance confessedly surpassed by no modern school.

Sculpture, as the more costly art, and as the less intelligible to the popular eye, of course *followed* painting in its progress among us as elsewhere. The surprise is that it should have followed so speedily and with such grand strides. It is possible that this happy result may have sprung in a measure from the circumstance that our first foreign visitors and instructors in marble art were men of the highest genius, instead of the third-rate talent only which our early *painters* brought to us. It is seldom amiss to make a good start, and much is saved where there is nothing left to be *un*learned.

One of our first heralds of the chisel appeared in 1791, when Ceracchi, an eminent Italian sculptor, arrived at Philadelphia. He was scarcely less celebrated as a revolutionist than as an artist, and leaving France when the dangers there grew too thick around him, he marched over to the New World, with a scheme for building us a grand marble monument to Liberty. His project was submitted to Congress, which was then in session, but that body supposed that the public funds could be employed, at the moment, more advantageously in the cause of Liberty, than in honoring her with sculptured shrines. Washington, however, gave his personal assent to the idea, and headed a private subscription, by means of which it was hoped the required thirty thousand dollars could be procured. Not an inch, though, of the proposed hundred feet of stone ever rose from the ground. Instead of the monument, the sculptor employed his chisel upon busts; and, among others, executed fine portraits of the commander-in-chief, of Alexander Hamilton, of Thomas Jefferson, Geo. Clinton, John Jay, and Paul Jones.

On returning to France, Ceracchi's red republicanism reappeared in a madder form than ever, and he plotted to take the hated life of Napoleon, then first consul, even in the sanctity of his own studio, and while he should be sitting for his bust. He was afterward guillotined on a charge of complicity in the famous scheme of the "infernal machine."

Yet earlier than the time of Ceracchi's residence in the United States, Houdon, a celebrated French sculptor, was invited to visit this country for the express purpose of perpetuating in marble the form and features of Washington. The result of his visit was the full-length statue which now adorns the vestibule of the Capitol at Richmond, in Virginia. The sculptor's legend on this work reads thus: "*Fait par Houdon, Citoyen Français*, 1788." The Father of his country is here represented of life size, and in the military style of the Revolution. The figure stands, resting on the right foot, having the left somewhat advanced, with the knee bent. The left hand rests on a bundle of fasces, on which hang a military cloak and a small sword, a plough leaning near.

Another noble statue of Washington, by Canova, adorned the Capitol of North Carolina, at Raleigh, until that edifice was unhappily destroyed, and the statue with it, by fire, in 1831.

Of our native sculptors, perhaps the first who gave indications of talent above the humblest mediocrity, was John Frasee, born in Rockaway, in New Jersey, July 18th, 1790. A bust which he executed in 1824 of John Wells, now in Grace Church, in New York, was, says Dunlap in his "Arts of Design," the first portrait in marble ever attempted in the United States. Ceracchi's works were probably only modelled here, and were afterward put into stone at home. Frasee made excellent busts of Chief Justice Marshall, of Daniel Webster, and others. "He had advanced," adds Dunlap in 1834, "to a perfection which leaves him without a rival at present in this country." To those who know any thing of our sculptors of *this* day we hardly need say, that Dunlap lived too long ago to witness the real beginning of its brilliant history, and that the talent of Frasee, excellent as it was, did not even indicate the high rank the art now holds.

Shobal Vail Clevenger, who was born at Middleton, Ohio, in 1812, and died at sea in 1843, left behind him admirable busts of Webster, Clay, Allston, Van Buren, and others. His early death interrupted a progress which might have extended far toward the point which our sculptors have since reached.

In the year 1805, on the 6th of September, Horatio Greenough was born in Boston, to fill a distinguished place in the annals of American sculpture. He received his earliest instruction from a resident French artist named Binon, and at the age of twenty went abroad. After modelling busts of John Quincy Adams, Chief Justice Marshall, and many others, he executed, at the order of Fenimore Cooper, the novelist, his Chanting Cherubs, which was the first original group from the chisel of an American artist. This work was made in Florence, where he had permanently established his studio at this time. In 1831 he went to Paris to model the bust of Lafayette, and thenceforward received liberal commissions, especially from his countrymen abroad.

Through the influence of his generous friend, Cooper, he received a commission from Congress for the colossal statue of Washington, which now stands so grandly on the great lawn opposite the east front of the national Capitol. This work was completed in 1843, after many years of industrious toil. Among others of Greenough's works at this period, were the Medora, commissioned by Mr. Robert Gilmor, of Baltimore; the Venus Victrix, in the Boston Athenæum; and the Angel Abdiel. In 1856 he returned to the United States to superintend the placing at Washington of his group of the Rescue, symbolizing the triumph of civilization, which he had executed in fulfilment of an order from Congress. It is supposed that the vexatious delays in the arrival of this work from Italy, together with the hurly-burly of American life, to which his long residence abroad had unaccustomed him, contributed to induce the attack of brain fever, from the effects of which he died, December 18th, 1852.

Greenough was educated at Harvard, and was a man of elegant attainments and accomplished manners. He was engaged in the delivery of a course of art lectures in Boston at the time of his last illness. An interesting memorial of Greenough was published by the poet Tuckerman in 1853.

The first general and popular acknowledgment, at home and abroad, of our success in sculpture, was won for us by the genius of Hiram Powers, and dated from the time of the exhibition of his Greek Slave. Not that this is by any means the best performance our artists have reached—for other men have followed with yet greater works; and among these others, one, of whom we shall speak, who has cast off the conventionalities of old art, and has, upon his own native soil, not that of Europe, gone beyond mere classic beauty, to the higher attainment of individual and national character and truth. Yet, as we have said, it was from the popular success of this statue of the Greek Slave that the world picked up and recognized the fact of the genius of American sculptors.

Powers is a native of Vermont; but, like most of our men of marble, resides and works abroad. He established himself long years ago in Florence, since which time we do not know that he has even visited his native land. He is an industrious worker, and has made innumerable busts, in addition to his more ambitious ventures into the field of poetry and the imagination. It is, indeed, in portraiture that his strength lies—with a temperament more practical than fanciful, and with a sympathy more with the real than with the ideal. His colossal figure of Eve, and his full-length statue of Calhoun, are preserved in South Carolina.

In the lamented Crawford, who was born in New York, March 22d, 1814, and who died in London, October 10th, 1857, we possessed a man of stronger and nobler grasp than any of his predecessors; a man, who not only *could* have done great things had he lived, but who did them even without living to the full years of ripe experience. Crawford was a poor boy, and began his art life in the humble occupation of a wood-carver. At the age of nineteen he was promoted to a place in the studio of Frasee and Launitz, in New York; and, when about twenty-one, he went to Rome, and became a pupil of the Danish sculptor Thorwaldsen. Here he toiled so unremittingly that he is said to have modelled no fewer than seventeen busts in the space of ten weeks, besides copying, in marble, the figure of Demosthenes in the Vatican. In 1839, when in his twenty-fifth year, he exhibited his Orpheus, with the warm congratulations of his master, Thorwaldsen, and other sculptors, and with the hearty approval of the public. From that period his fame continued to increase up to the hour of his untimely death. The Orpheus—which is now in the Athenæum in Boston—was followed by numerous admirable subjects from classical and scriptural history. Among his greater and later works, was the remarkable statue, in bronze, of Beethoven, executed for the Boston Music Hall; and the completion of which, at the foundry in Munich, was celebrated by a musical festival, at which the royal family of Bavaria, and a grand concourse of people, assisted. Afterward came the equestrian statue of Washington, which now adorns the Capitol hill at Richmond; where it was placed by the patriotism and liberality of the people of Virginia. This great work was cast in bronze in Munich, and sent home in 1857. Its pedestal rests upon a star-shaped elevation, with six points, upon which statues of Jefferson, Henry, Lee, and other illustrious sons of Virginia are to be placed. He executed orders from Congress for various works for the new Capitol, some of the most successful of which were his designs for the pediment and the great bronze doors. His grandest effort is, perhaps, the model for the colossal statue of the Genius of America, which is to be cast in bronze, and placed upon the pinnacle of the

Capitol dome. This statue represents a female figure, fully draped, and posed with marvellous grace and dignity. During his brief career, Crawford finished more than sixty works, many of them of the grand size; besides which, he left nearly as many sketches in plaster, and numerous designs, which his assistants are to complete. In 1844, he married Miss Louisa Ward, daughter of the late Samuel Ward, of New York. Soon after his return from his last visit to his native land, in 1856, he was afflicted with a cancerous tumor on the brain, from the effects of which he died, after many months of acute suffering, borne with heroic patience.

Henry Kirke Brown, another of the most eminent of our American sculptors, was born at Leyden, Massachusetts, in 1814. He began the study of portrait painting in Boston, when eighteen years of age; and afterward he became a railroad engineer in Illinois, much to the injury of his health, and at length repaired to Italy to pursue the grave art of the statuary. Among his more famous works, are the well-known marbles of Hope; the Pleiades; the Four Seasons; the bronze statue of De Witt Clinton at Greenwood Cemetery, and the noble equestrian statue of Washington, which stands in Union square in the city of New York. Most, if not all of these works, were executed in Brooklyn, New York; though, of late years, the artist has established himself in a pleasant cottage at Newburgh, on the Hudson. Brown's Washington was the first statue ever cast in bronze in this country.

Palmer, who is, perhaps, the most popular of American sculptors at the present day, was born in the interior of the state of New York. His noble character—no less personal than professional—is seen in all the interesting incidents of his career, from the humblest boyhood to his present high position, social and artistic. In his younger days he toiled hard at the carpenter's craft; afterward he rose to the dignity of a carver in wood, of models and moulds for stove and other iron castings; and at length he became a cutter of cameos. He was a married man, with a young family growing up around him, before he finally made that venture in marble which has brought such high honor to himself and his country. His works are marked with singular simplicity, truth, and naturalness of treatment, and with a finish and delicacy of execution rarely obtained in obdurate stone. Among his chief and best known productions, are the full-length, life-like figures of the Indian Girl, and the White Captive; the Moses, and many beautiful bas-reliefs and female heads, both portrait and ideal. An exhibition of his collected works was made a few years ago, with great advantage to his own fame and fortune, and to the public pleasure and profit.

Launt Thompson, a young pupil of the eminent sculptor above named, is pursuing his art in New York with a success which promises the most enviable results.

Clark Mills, a self-educated man, in the proper sense of the phrase, is known by his popular equestrian statues of Jackson and Washington, executed by the order of Congress, for the embellishment of the national Capitol.

Harriet Hosmer, of Watertown, Massachusetts, is achieving a fair fame in this difficult field of art as we now write. She is scarcely thirty years of age, yet is already intrusted with important public commissions. The approval which followed her first original work—a bust of Hesper—induced her father to send her to Rome, where she at present resides. She began her studies in the eternal city, as a pupil of Gibson, in 1852. Her first works abroad were the busts of Daphne and Medusa, and a statue of Œnone. Afterward came the well-known reclining figure of Beatrice Cenci; and, in 1855, the charming statue of Puck, and a pendant thereto, entitled Will-o'-the-Wisp. In 1859, she completed her statue of Zenobia in Chains, which is of colossal size, and is said to be, thus far, her best work.

Mosier, Rogers, Story, Akers, Bartholomew, Ball, Hart, Ball Hughes, and Stone, with many others whom it would be pleasant and profitable for us to name, did our opportunity allow, have each won most honorable distinction by their admirable creations in the sculptor's art. They are all well employed either with public or private orders. Such orders, from states and from individuals, are now, happily, no longer things of rare occurrence. They come numerously and generously from all quarters, and always, by preference, to our native artists; not at rare intervals, and then to foreign *ateliers*, as at the commencement of the period of which we are writing—a com-

The above engravings, representing the Seasons, are from the *Farmer's Almanac*, showing the Anderson style of engraving; the opposite page, engraved from sketches about Newport, R. I. by A. H. Jocelyn, illustrates the improvement in the art.

mencement lying back, by our rapid reckoning, eighty long years in the remote past.

The love of pictures, so general among our people of all grades, has been greatly fostered and cultivated, of late years, by the universal diffusion of engravings. Besides the best of this class of works, more accessible examples, in the form of book illustrations, and especially in illustrated magazines and newspapers, have been scattered, through a cheap press, broadcast over the land, and have penetrated its remotest corners, doing the labors of the missionary in the great cause of art. It is true that these heralds—the pictorial papers, at least—are not always the best possible teachers; yet have they cleared the way for greater things to follow, and it is gratifying to know that they are themselves every day reaching toward a higher standard. It would, indeed, be quite beyond the power of our mathematics, to cipher out the good effect upon the art progress of the nation, of even one of our best pictorial magazines, with the immense audience which they are wont to address; such a magazine, for example, as that of the Harpers—read, or at least seen, every month, by millions of people.

This grand aggregate of the good influence of the graver, is gained through the agency, not of the ambitious steel-plate, but the humble wood-cut. The art of working on wood—which has thus of late become the chief medium of the engraver, and has almost superseded all other mediums—has, though an old art, so greatly improved during the eighty years life of our republic, that it may fairly be said to have grown up with it, and in a great degree *from* it.

The general demand among us for cheap art, and the general ability to buy, at least, such cheap art, obviously required the wood-cut; and so the wood-cut—which had kept its humble place from a period even far beyond the invention of types—was brought from its obscurity, and made—in our own hands, as much as in those of any people—to fill its present exalted office.

The art was, really, almost reinvented in America, and soon after the great Revolution, when Dr. Anderson, in 1794, left his *materia medica*, and set up in New York as a wood-engraver. Anderson's first considerable performance was the repetition, in a work called the "Looking-Glass," of some cuts by Bewick. Some of these pictures he executed on type metal, and only a portion of them on the wood-block. For these he had to invent his own tools, and then manufacture them. He continued to improve, and all through his professional career he contributed greatly to develop the resources of the art, and to put it upon the track of its present mature power. In 1812, the art was introduced and successfully practised in Boston by Abel Brown, and in Philadelphia by William Mason.

About the year 1826, Mr. Adams entered the profession, and by his industry and skill gave it a great impetus toward the perfection to which it has since been brought. The innumerable illustrations which he produced in his superb pictorial edition of the Bible, published by the Harpers, called forth all the talent which the country possessed in this direction, and exercised it to yet greater excellence. This great work served, also, no doubt, to promote the popular appreciation of the art, now so universally manifested in the demand for illustrated books and pictorial papers of all kinds. From the time of Mr. Adams, the number of our engravers on wood has steadily and rapidly increased; and so, too, has the quality of their work, until the present day shows us pictures on wood which are, in many respects—as in delicacy of finish, softness of texture, and vigor of expression—quite equal, if not superior to the best examples of work on copper or steel. The greater cheapness of the wood-block; its capacity of use, in printing *with* the type (which metal plates do not possess); and the ease with which it may be duplicated by stereotyping or by electrotyping—have caused it to supersede copper and steel-plates in a great measure, except for very large and costly subjects, and for bank note engraving. The invention, in recent times, of Lowry's "ruling machine;" of improved methods of printing, as in the process called "overlaying," by means of which the nearer parts of the picture are made to receive a stronger pressure than the more distant portions; and various mechanical aids—have contributed to the present wonderful perfection of the art among us. The country now possesses a host of excellent wood engravers, who find full and remunerative employment.

For the finer class of wood-engravings, box-wood (imported chiefly from Germany) is used; while, for coarser and larger work, that of the pear-tree will answer, and sometimes even that of the apple-tree, beech, and even mahogany and pine. The wood is cut across the ends of the fibre, of the thickness of type; and after being smoothly planed, a thin covering of white is rubbed over the surface; after which the drawing to be engraved is made upon it with a lead pencil, or with India-ink, or both combined. The block is then cut away with the graver, in such manner as to leave the lines of the drawing all in *relief*, like type. On copper or steel, on the contrary, the drawing is *sunk* into the plate, and is necessarily printed with greater slowness and care, and at a greater cost. In engravings printed in colors, a separate block is made for each tint.

Copper-plate engraving is an art as old, almost, as xylography or wood-cutting. A picture upon this metal is preserved in Germany of as ancient a date as 1461. Instead of the simple wooden blocks of other days, our cotton manufacturers now print their calicoes from copper plates of cylindrical form, by which improvement the fabrics are made infinitely more beautiful and greatly cheaper. Most of the larger print-works employ skilful artists and engravers to produce their designs, paying them large salaries for their labors. In some establishments thousands of dollars are thus profitably expended each year. Copper-plate engraving, after reaching the highest degree of excellence, both at home and abroad, has, within the present century, given way in a great measure to the superior capacity of the steel plate, a capacity revealed to the world and developed in the highest degree by Jacob Perkins, of Newburyport, in Massachusetts. Mr. Perkins, who began his experiments about 1805, may, indeed, almost be said to have invented steel engraving, since the metal had been used only once before his time, in an English print in Smith's "Topographical Illustrations of Westminster." Mr. Perkins discovered the present invaluable processes by which the steel plate is so hardened after being engraved, that by the pressure upon it of other soft plates, the picture can be transferred in relief and again repeated so as to duplicate the work to any extent. The first impression in *relief*, from which duplicates of the original engraving are made, is taken upon a soft steel cylinder by repeated rollings over the hardened plate. By this process any bank note vignettes can be transferred, in *combination*, at will, from the separate original plates to the steel cylinder, and from that to other plates for the printer. The product is thus greatly cheapened, inasmuch as all the pictures, the central vignette, the end scene or portrait, and the bottom or tail piece, usually put upon a bank note, can be furnished for the cost of a special engraving of one of them. Mr. Perkins' system is employed throughout England and the continent of Europe, no less than all over the United States. By it the art of bank note engraving has been so perfected among us that only the highest skill and the costliest machinery can now produce successful counterfeits. Nothing remains but to insure the bank note against the wonderful power of the art of photography, and this security our engravers will no doubt soon effectually provide. In 1858-9 the principal bank note engravers of the country formed themselves into two associations, the American and the National Bank Note Companies, and these companies furnish nearly all the engraving and printing required on the western continent, and thus give employment to the best talent of the land in this department of art. Among the most successful of American steel engravers of bank notes and other works, are Durand, Smillie, Cheney, Sartain, Danforth, Deck, Casilear, and Alfred Jones. All these eminent men have worked in the greatest perfection upon steel in the several styles of line, stipple, mezzotint, aquatint, etc. Engraving on copper or steel is practised in its most simple form, called line engraving, by covering the face of the polished metal with a thin surface of melted white wax; on this the sketch is transferred by laying, face down, a tracing of the design in black lead pencil upon the wax, and subjecting it to a heavy pressure; the lines are then seen distinctly upon the wax when the paper is removed. The workman then with a fine graver makes the lines through upon the metal; after which the wax is melted off and the engraver proceeds to complete the work by cutting the lines to the proper depth and shade. The graver, when in use, is pressed forward, cutting a furrow and raising burrs on each side. The burr, pushed up by the graver in its progress, is removed by the scraper. Lines are softened by rubbing over with a smoothly pointed burnisher. In some instances the burrs made by the finest etching needles being allowed to remain, produce a pleasing effect, seen in some of Rembrandt's engravings. The parallel lines that are sometimes required in series are cut by a ruling machine. The fainter shades, too delicate for the graver, are scratched in with a needle.

In the stippling or dotted style, the effect is produced by dots made in curved lines, with the graver. The more closely the dots are grouped together, the darker the shade, and the whole effect is more like painting than the line engraving. In the shadows of the limbs of the human figure it is much used, and sometimes in portraits the line and stipple are combined with good effect.

The style called etching is practised upon other metals, also upon glass. By this process the coating of wax is formed of white wax, Burgundy pitch, and asphaltum, and is applied in silk bags, through which the composition oozes. When the plate is covered it is held over a smoking lamp until the wax is covered with lamp-black. The lead pencil design is then laid upon this lamp-black and pressed. The lines are then drawn through the wax, and nitric acid with four parts water is poured upon the plate. This remains until the fainter portions of the sketch are corroded. The acid is then poured off and the plate washed with water. An application of lamp-black and turpentine, called stopping, is applied with a camel's hair brush to those portions sufficiently corroded; a reapplication of the acid eats deeper into those parts that require deeper lines. This process of stopping is repeated until the work is complete. Being then cleaned of the wax, those portions of the plate that require it are gone over with the graver, and not unfrequently the shades are stippled.

Aquatinta is a French invention of 1662, and takes its name from the resemblance it has to water colors on India-ink drawings. After the design is etched in outline and the wax removed, a solution of Burgundy pitch in alcohol is poured over the plate as it lies in an inclined position. The alcohol evaporating, the pitch remains. The design is then drawn with a gummy syrup called the bursting-ground, which is applied only wherever a shade is wanted. The whole is then covered with a turpentine varnish; water being left on it for fifteen minutes, the bursting-ground cracks open and exposes the copper. The etching process is then pursued. Sometimes colors are applied and printed from the plate; but when there are different tints, it is customary to use a distinct plate for each one.

The mezzotinto, or half-painted style, was introduced into England by Prince Rupert. The invention has been ascribed to Sir Christopher Wren. The plate is roughed up by running over its surface little toothed wheels of different degrees of fineness, called cradles, which by a rocking motion are caused to raise little burrs, pointing in different directions. The whole plate being thus made rough, the burrs are rubbed off with scrapers, wherever light shades are required, and the shades are deepened by increasing the burrs. The effect is fine where dark grounds are desired. This method combined with etching, produces an improved style. Some mezzotints are now prepared for the trade by a machine. The prints wear much better on steel than on copper.

Admirable examples of these branches of the art may be seen in the superb landscape works of Smillie, especially those from the four pictures of Cole's Voyage of Life, in Durand's works after Vanderlyn's, in our many beautiful illustrated books, in the publications of the late American Art Union, and, as already intimated, in the dainty vignettes which embellish our myriad bank notes.

In the art of die sinking—a process conducted in a similar manner to that already described of the transfer in relief of the impression from a hardened plate or plug of steel to a soft plate, and from that again, when hardened, to yet another—many admirable works have been produced. Excellent examples may be seen in the medals of Allston, Stuart, and other subjects executed for the American Art Union by the late C. C. Wright.

By the assistance of the electrotype process, the work of the engraver is now repeated, in as many copies as may be desired, each of the copper transcripts thus produced being an absolute duplicate of the original plate or block. It is these electrotyped copies which are now used by the printer, the same picture sometimes on several presses at once, while the original wood block is preserved untouched, except to form the mould for other copies in metal when they may be required. The effect of this power of perfect and inexpensive repetition of engraved blocks has been to reduce the cost of pictorial illustrations to a point within the compass of the most unpretending purse, and thus to send good examples of the engraver's art to the remotest and humblest corners of the land.

What may be the consequences of the many processes, now more or less perfected, for the mechanical production of engraving by the aid of photography, it is hardly possible to imagine: not other than advantageous, however, even to the engravers themselves, since their field of labor will be higher, if not broader, when their pictures shall be, as they promise to be, not only drawn for them on their plates and blocks by photography, but even etched and engraved besides!

In the art of lithography, or drawing upon stone, a steady advance may be witnessed; though our works of this class cannot yet claim comparison with those of the continent of Europe.

The introduction of the daguerreotype, the perfection to which the art has been brought in the skilful hands of American operators, and the immense extent to which it is used among us (apart from its share in the work of other arts), have had, no doubt, a most wonderful influence upon our art progress. Furnishing pictures which are, through their cheapness, accessible to all classes, it has worked, like the engraving, as an elementary instructor, while its truthfulness has been a constant lesson to the artist himself. Better pictures have, unquestionably, been painted through the hints of the daguerreotype and photograph; and many people who, but for them, would never have dreamed of pictures, have become intelligent lovers and liberal patrons of the arts.

We must not, in ever so cursory a glance at the history of the arts, forget the service of our academies and schools of painting, little as some affect to think of art academies—so far, at least, as their *honorary* character is concerned.

The first attempt to found an institution of this nature in the United States, was made in Philadelphia, in 1791, by Charles Wilson Peale, the father of the painter Rembrandt Peale. The elder Peale was a very energetic laborer in the cause of art, all through his long life. This first attempt of his to found an academy, was seconded by the Italian sculptor Ceracchi, who was in the country at the time. The attempt failed, however, from some cause or other, and a second and rather more fortunate venture was made in 1794, when the Columbianum was established. This society lived a year, held one exhibition, and was forgotten.

In 1802, some art-loving citizens of New York, headed by Edward Livingston, founded the New York, afterward the American Academy of Fine Arts. There were so few artists in this society, and the governing influence was so little of a professional character, that it was an academy of art only in name, and quite failed in its office of an academy. The necessary result was an inefficient life, until it was, in due time, superseded by a better organized establishment. This result followed in 1826, in the institution of the present National Academy of Design.

The National Academy, thus founded by Morse, and his brother artists of the period, has steadily advanced to this day in position and usefulness, and now numbers among its academicians and associates nearly all the leading painters of the land. Its annual exhibitions have been prepared, without interruption, from 1826 until now, with a catalogue of works extended gradually from less than two hundred, to over eight hundred, and with an aggregate of receipts from less than nothing up to six or seven thousand dollars annually. The academy has always supported free (evening) schools for the study of the antique statuary, and the living model-schools, to which any student has access, when coming with the required preparatory knowledge of the use of the crayon. Membership in the academy, except in the grade of "student," is awarded only to professional artists, and then by ballot, as a mark of honorary distinction. The progress of art in America during the last thirty or forty years cannot be better seen than in the continued growth of the National Academy, and in its present large and varied exhibitions as compared with those of days gone by.

The Pennsylvania Academy of Fine Arts in Philadelphia is doing a good work, though it is not so fully an association of artists only as is the National Academy at New York. Conducted in part by laymen, it labors under some of the disadvantages of the old superseded American Academy. It was founded as early as 1807, and is now a flourishing and most useful institution, keeping a valuable permanent gallery always open to the public view, and providing besides an annual display of the current productions of our artists. It possesses also a fine collection of casts from the antique, gratuitously accessible to all students.

The art gallery of the Athenæum in Boston, serves, in a measure, the purposes of an academy in that city. Of late years Academies of Art have sprung up in some form, and with more or less success, in many other of our chief cities, as in Baltimore, Charleston, St. Louis, Cincinnati, and elsewhere, giving us a fair promise of picture galleries and facilities for art study, as general and as liberal as our wants demand.

Besides these institutions for the use of the profession itself, there is happily a rapid extension throughout the Union of drawing schools for all classes of the population. Professorships of drawing are being introduced into our universities and colleges, and a higher standard is being everywhere set up in our seminaries of all grades. Schools of Design for women are springing up in our larger cities, and such an institution has been recently incorporated with the Cooper Union of New York, under the highest promise of successful result. When the principles of art become universally known to us, as we have good cause to believe they soon will be, we shall realize the fact not only in the increased excellence and fame of our pictures and our sculptures, but in the higher beauty, utility, and value of our manufactures and fabrics of all kinds, from the rarest luxury to the simplest article of necessary use. In another and less material sense we shall feel it and enjoy it, in breathing the air of a more refined and more beautiful social and national life.

EDUCATION AND EDUCATIONAL INSTITUTIONS.

CHAPTER I.

EDUCATIONAL DEVELOPMENT IN THE COLONIAL PERIOD.

INTRODUCTION.

The origin, nomenclature, and early peculiarities of the systems, institutions, and methods of instruction adopted in the original colonies, which now constitute a portion of the United States of America, will be found in the educational institutions and practices of the countries from which these colonies were settled—modified by the education, character, motives of emigration, and necessities of the settlers themselves.

The earliest effort to establish an educational institution in the English dominions in America, was made under the auspices of King James I, and by contributions of members of the Church of England from 1618 to 1623. In a letter addressed to the Archbishops, he authorizes them to invite the members of the Church throughout the kingdom to assist "those undertakers of that Plantation [Virginia], with the erecting of some churches and schools for the education of the children of those barbarians" [the Aborigines] and of the colonists. Under these instructions, a sum of £1500 was collected for the erection of a building for a college at Henrico—a town whose foundations, or site even, cannot now be certainly determined, but which according to the best authorities was situated near Varina on Cox's Island, about fifty miles above Jamestown. Authority was given by the Company to the Governor to set apart 10,000 acres of land for the support of the college, and one hundred colonists were sent from England to occupy and cultivate the same, who were to receive a moiety of the produce as the profit of their labor, and to pay the other moiety toward the maintenance of the college. In 1620, George Thorpe was sent out as superintendent, and 300 acres of land was set apart for his sustenance. Other donations and legacies were made for the endowment of this institution of learning.

In 1619, the Governor for the time being was instructed by the company to see "that each town, borough, and hundred procured by just means a certain number of their children to be brought up in the first elements of literature; that the most towardly of them should be fitted for college, in the building which they purposed to proceed as soon as any profit arose from the estate appropriated to that use; and they earnestly required their help in that pious and important work." In 1621, Rev. Mr. Copeland, chaplain of the Royal James, on her arrival from the East Indies, prevailed on the ship's company to subscribe £100 toward a "free schoole" in the colony of Virginia, and collected other donations in money and books for the same purpose. The school was located in Charles City, as being most central for the colony, and was called the "*East India School.*" The company allotted one thousand acres of land, with five servants and an overseer, for the maintenance of the master and usher. The inhabitants made a contribution of £1500 to build a house, for which workmen were sent out in 1622.

The "college" and "free school" thus projected and partially endowed were in the style of the "college" and "free school" and the "free grammar school" of England, and were intended to be of the same character as the college afterward established at Cambridge, and the institution for which "the richer inhabitants" of Boston in 1636 subscribed toward "the maintenance of a free schoolmaster," and the same as, according to Governor Winthrop, in his journal, was erected in Roxbury in 1645, and other towns, and for which every inhabitant bound some house or land for a yearly allowance forever, and many benevolently disposed persons left legacies in their last wills, and the towns made "an allowance out of the common stock," or set apart a portion of land "to be improved forever, for the maintenance of a free schoole forever."

The same leading idea can be traced in the educational policy of the Dutch West India Company—which bound itself, in receiving its charter of colonization, "to maintain good and fit preachers, schoolmasters, and comforters of the sick." The company recognized the authority of the established Church of Holland, and the establishment of schools and the appointment of schoolmasters rested conjointly with the company and the classis (ecclesiastical authorities) of Amsterdam. When the company granted a special "Charter of Freedom and Exemptions" to the "Patroons," for the purpose of agricultural colonization, they were not only to satisfy the Indians for the lands upon which they should settle, but were to make prompt provision for the support of a minister and schoolmaster, that thus the service of God and zeal for religion might not grow cold, and be neglected among them. In 1633, in the enumeration of the company's officials at Manhattan, Adam Roelandsen is mentioned as the schoolmaster, and that school, it is claimed, is still in existence in connection with the Reformed Dutch Church of New York. In the projected settlement at New Amstel on the Delaware, the first settlers were encouraged to proceed by certain conditions, one of which was that the city of Amsterdam should send thither "a proper person for a schoolmaster;" and we find among the colonists who embarked, "Evert Pietersen, who had been approved, after examination before the classis, as schoolmaster." In these early efforts to establish schools, we trace the educational policy of the Reformed Church of Holland as indicated by the synod of Wesel in 1568, and matured at the synod of Dort in 1618, by which the training of Christian youth was to be provided for—"I. *In the house, by parents.* II. *In the schools, by schoolmasters.* III. *In the churches, by ministers, elders, and the catechists especially appointed for this purpose.*" Owing in part to the commercial purposes entertained by the companies having charge of the colonization of New York, Virginia, and some other portions of the country, and to the educational and religious institutions of the colonists being not so much a matter of domestic as of foreign policy, these institutions never commanded the regular and constant attention of the local authorities, or of the settlers themselves.

The outline and most of the essential features of the system of common schools now in operation in the New England states, and the states which have since avowedly adopted the same policy, will be found in the practice of the first settlers of the several towns which composed the original colonies of Massachusetts, Connecticut, and New Haven. The first law on the subject did but little more than declare the motive, and make more widely obligatory the practice which already existed in the several neighborhoods and towns, which had grown up out of the education of these colonists at home, and the circumstances in which they were placed. They did not come here as isolated individuals, drawn together from widely separated homes, entertaining broad differences of opinion on all matters of civil and religious concernment, and kept together by the necessity of self-defence in the eager prosecution of some temporary but profitable adventure. They came after God had set them in families, and they brought with them the best pledges of good behavior, in the relations which father and mother, husband and wife, parents and children, neighbors and friends, establish. They came with a foregone conclusion of permanence, and with all the elements of the social state combined in vigorous activity—every man expecting to find or make occupation in the way in which he had been already trained. They came with earnest religious convictions, made more earnest by the trials of persecution; and the enjoyment of these convictions was a leading motive in their emigration hither. The fundamental articles of their religious creed, that the Bible was the only authoritative expression of the divine will, and that every man was able to judge for himself in its interpretation, made schools necessary, to bring all persons "to a knowledge of the Scriptures," and an understanding "of the main grounds and principles of the Christian religion necessary to salvation." The constitution of civil government adopted by them from the outset, which declared all civil officers elective, and gave to every inhabitant who would take the oath of allegiance the right to vote and to be voted for, and which practically converted political society into a partnership, in which each member had the right to bind the whole firm, made universal education identical with self-preservation. But aside from these considerations, the natural and acknowledged leaders in this enterprise—the men who, by their religious character, wealth, social position, and previous experience in conducting large business operations, commanded public confidence in church and commonwealth, were educated men—as highly and thoroughly educated as they could be at the best endowed free and grammar schools in England at that period; and not a few of them had enjoyed the advantages of her great universities. These men would naturally seek for their own children the best opportunities of education which could be provided; and it is the crowning glory of these men, that, instead of sending their own children back to England to be educated in grammar schools and colleges, these institutions were established here amid the stumps of the primeval forests; that, instead of setting up "family schools" and "select schools" for the ministers' sons and magistrates' sons, the ministers and magistrates were found, not only in town-meeting, pleading for an allowance out of the common treasury for the support of a public or common school, and in some instances for a "free school," but among the families, entreating parents of all classes to send their children to the same school with their own. All this was done in advance of any legislation on the subject, as will be seen from the following facts gleaned from the early records of several of the towns first planted.

TOWN ACTION IN BEHALF OF SCHOOLS.

The earliest records of most of the towns of New England are either obliterated or lost, but among the oldest entries which can now be recovered, the school is mentioned not as a new thing, but as one of the established interests of society, to be looked after and provided for as much as roads and bridges and protection from the Indians. In the first book of records of the town of Boston, under date of April 13, 1634, after providing by ordinance for the keeping of the cattle by "brother Cheesbrough," "it was then generally agreed upon that our brother Philemon Purmont shall be entreated to become schoolmaster for the teaching and nurturing of children with us." This was doubtless an elementary school, for in 1636 we find a subscription entered on the records of the town "by the richer inhabitants," "for the maintenance of a free schoolmaster, for the youth with us—Mr. Daniel Maude being now also chosen thereunto." Mr. Maude was a clergyman, a title at that day and in that community which was evidence of his being an educated man. This "free school" was, in the opinion of the writer, not necessarily a school of gratuitous instruction for all, but an endowed school of a higher grade, of the class of the English grammar school, in which many of the first settlers of New England had received their own education at home. Toward the maintenance of this school, the town, in 1642, in advance of any legislation by the General Court, ordered "Deer Island to be improved," and several persons made bequests in their last wills. Similar provision can be cited from the early records of Salem, Cambridge, Dorchester, and other towns of Massachusetts Bay.

The early records of the town of Hartford are obliterated, but within seven years after the first log-house was erected, thirty pounds are appropriated to the schools, and in April, 1643, it is ordered "that Mr. Andrews shall teach the children in the school one year," and "he shall have for his pains £16, and therefore the townsmen shall go and inquire who will engage themselves to send their children; and all that do so, shall pay for one quarter, at the least, and for more if they do send them, after the proportion of twenty shillings the year; and if they go any week more than one quarter, they shall pay sixpence a week; and if any would send their children and are not able to pay for their teaching, they shall give notice of it to the townsmen, and they shall pay it at the town's charge." Mention is also made of one "Goody Betts," who kept a "Dame School" after the fashion of Shenstone's "schoolmistress" at Leasower, in England. Similar entries are found in the town records of Windsor and Wethersfield in advance of any school code by the colony of Connecticut.

The records of the town of New Haven are full of evidence of the interest taken by the leading spirits of the colony, particularly by Governor Theophilus Eaton and Rev. John Davenport, in behalf of schools of every grade, and of the education of every class, from the apprentice boy to those who filled the high places in church and state. The first settlement of the colony was in 1638, and within a year a transaction is recorded, which, while it proves the existence of a school at that early period, also proclaims the protection which the first settlers extended to the indigent, and their desire to make elementary education universal. In 1639, Thomas Fugill is required by the court to keep Charles Higinson, an indentured apprentice, "at school one year;" or else to advantage him as much in his education as a year's learning comes to. In 1641, the town orders "that a Free School be set up," and "our pastor, Mr. Davenport, together with the magistrates, shall consider what yearly allowance is meet to be given to it out of the common stock of the town, and also what rules and orders are meet to be observed in and about the same." To this school "that famous schoolmaster," Ezekiel Cheever,* "was appointed," "for the better training up of youth in this town, that, through God's blessing, they may be fitted for public service hereafter, in church or commonwealth." Not content with a Grammar School, provision was early made for "the relief of poor scholars at the college at Cambridge," and in 1645 forty bushels of wheat were sent forward for this purpose, and this was followed by other donations, and by a richer consignment of young men to enjoy the advantages of the institution. In 1647, in the distribution of home lots, it was ordered in town meeting, that the magistrates "consider and reserve what lot they shall see meet, and most commodious for a college, which they desire may be set up so soon as their ability will reach thereunto." Among the active promoters of education and schools, the name of Governor Eaton, in connection with Mr. Davenport, is particularly prominent. In 1652, he calls a meeting of the magistrates and elders "to let them know what he has done for a schoolmaster;" that he had written a letter to one Mr. Bower, a schoolmaster of Plymouth, and another to Rev. Mr. Landron, a scholar; and many of the town thought there would be need of two schoolmasters—"one to teach boys to read and write," as well as the "Latin schoolmaster." At another time he reports his correspondence with a teacher in Wethersfield, then with one at old Plymouth, and again with one at Norwalk, "so that the town might never be without a sufficient schoolmaster." He seems to have been considerate of the health of the teachers, and proposes to excuse one "whose health would not allow him to go on with the work of teaching," which he seems to regard as more laborious than that of the ministry. On another occasion he introduces to the committee a schoolmaster who has come to treat about the school. He is allowed £20 a year, and 30 shillings for his expenses in travel, besides his board and lodgings. He wished to have liberty to visit his friends, "which he proposed to be in harvest time, and that his pay be such as wherewith he may buy books." These particulars show the considerate interest taken by men in local authority in the school and the teacher, in advance of any directory or compulsory legislation of the colony of New Haven. It was owing, in part, to the timely suggestions of Rev. Mr. Davenport, that Gov. Edward Hopkins, of Connecticut, by his will, dated London, March 7, 1657, bequeathed the residue of his estate (after disposing of much of his estate in New England) to trustees residing in New Haven and Hartford, "in full assurance of their trust and faithfulness" in disposing of it, "to give some encouragement in those foreign plantations for the breeding up of hopeful youths both at the grammar school and college, for the public service of the country in future times." By the final disposition and distribution of this estate three grammar schools were established at New Haven, Hartford, and Hadley, which are in existence at this day, among the oldest institutions of this class in America.

The early records of the several towns which subsequently constituted a portion of the colony of New Hampshire, exhibit evidence of a different character and spirit in the first settlers. The plantations on the Piscataqua river were made by proprietors from mere commercial motives, and the settlers were selected in reference to immediate success in that direction; and in these settlements we find no trace of any individual or town action in behalf of education until after their union with the colony of Massachusetts, whose laws made the establishment of schools obligatory.

In the early records of the Rhode Island and Providence Plantations, we find traces of the same educational policy which marked the early history of towns in Massachusetts and Connecticut. According to Callender, in Newport, "so early as 1640, Mr. Lenthal was by vote called to keep a public school for the learning of youth, and for

*See Barnard's *American Teachers and Educators*, vol. i., art. "Ezekiel Cheever."

his encouragement there were granted to him and his heirs, one hundred acres of land, and four more for a house lot. It was also voted that one hundred acres should be appropriated for a school for encouragement of the poorer sort to train up their youth in learning. And Mr. Robert Lenthal, while he continues to keep school, is to have the benefit thereof." The proprietors of other plantations reserved a portion of land for the maintenance of schools, and generally of a "free schoole;" and "Mr. Schoolmaster Turpin," petitions the town of Providence, that he and his heirs, so long as any of them should maintain the worthy art of learning, may be invested in the lands set apart for a school.

These citations show the action of the towns independent of any general legislation by the several colonies of New England—action prompted by their own consciousness of the advantages of education in "Dame Schools," in "Free Schools," in "Grammar Schools" and in "Colleges" at home—aided by the presence among them of "masters" and "ushers," and also of "schoolmasters" and "schoolma'ams" willing to engage in the same vocations in the new townships and villages—stimulated by magistrates and ministers, who had themselves received the best education that such schools could give in England, who inculcated the reading of the Scriptures as of daily obligation, and who believed that the foundations of the state should be laid in the virtue and intelligence of the whole people.

COLONIAL LEGISLATION AND ACTION.

We shall now notice briefly the legislation respecting children and schools of each of the colonies, in the order of their settlement.

VIRGINIA.—Although several attempts were made to establish "Free Schools" and a "College" in Virginia, by the Virginia Company and benevolent individuals, at an earlier day, the first general legislation respecting the education of children by the Colonial Assembly was in 1631, when it was enacted: "It is also thought fit, that upon every Sunday the mynister* shall, halfe an hour or more before evening prayer, examine, catechise, and instruct the youths and ignorant persons of his parish in the ten commandments, the articles of the beliefe, and in the Lord's prayer; and shall diligentlie heere, instruct, and teach the catechisme, sett forth in the book of Common Prayer. And all fathers, mothers, maysters, and mistrisses, shall cause their children, servants, or apprentices, which have not learned their catechisme, to come to church at the time appoynted, obedientlie to heare, and to be ordered by the mynister untill they have learned the same. And yf any of sayd fathers, mothers, maysters & mistresses, children, servants, or apprentices, shall neglect their duties, as the one sorte in not causinge them to come, and the other in refusinge to learne as aforesayd, they shall be censured by the corts in these places holden." To secure the execution of this last clause, it is provided in the oath of the warden, taken before "the justices for the monthlie corts"—"they shall present such mastyrs and mistresses as shall be delinquent in the catechisinge the youth and ignorant persons. So help you God."

In 1660 an attempt was made to found a college for the supply of educated clergymen. "Whereas the want of able and faithful ministers in this country deprives us of those great blessings and mercies that always attend upon the service of God; which want, by reason of the great distance from our native country, cannot in all probability be always supplied from thence: *Be it enacted*, that for the advance of learning, education of youth, supply of the ministry, and promotion of piety, there be land taken for a college and free school with as much speed as may be convenient, houses erected thereon for entertainment of students and scholars." In the same year it was ordered that a petition be drawn up by the General Assembly to the king for a college and free school; and that there be his letters patent "to collect the charity of well disposed persons in England, for the erecting of colledges & schools in this countrye," and also to bestow universities "to furnish the church here with ministers for the present." And this petition was recommended to the right honorable Governor, Sir William Berkeley. Sir William does not appear, in his reply to the Lords Commissioners of Foreign Plantations, dated 1670, to have been very kindly disposed to public schools of high or low degree.

"Question 23. What course is taken about the instructing the people within your government in the Christian religion;

* In this and some other quotations we have followed the orthography of the original.

and what provision is there made for the payment of your ministry?"

"*Answer.* The same course that is taken in England out of towns; every man according to his ability instructing his children. We have forty-eight parishes, and our ministers are well paid, and by my consent should be better if they would pray oftener and preach less. But of all other commodities, so of this, the worst are sent us, and we had few that we could boast of, since the persecution in Cromwell's tyranny drove divers worthy men hither. But I thank God there are no free schools, nor printing, and I hope we shall not have these hundred years; for learning has brought disobedience and heresy and sects into the world, and printing has divulged them, and libels against the best government. God keep us from both!"

In 1691, "the good design of building a free school and college for the encouragement of learning," was recognized, but it was not till 1693 that an act was passed locating the college, for which a royal charter had been obtained April 8, 1692, with the title of William and Mary, at Middle Plantation, afterward Williamsburgh. Toward its endowment the royal founders granted £2000 in money, land, and a revenue duty on tobacco; and the Assembly enacted an export duty on skins and furs. The money grant of £2000 did not meet with much encouragement from the English Attorney General (Seymour) who was instructed to prepare the charter, who remarked to the Rev. James Blair, the agent of the colony for this purpose, that the money was wanted for other purposes, and that he did not see the slightest occasion for a college in Virginia. The agent represented that the intention of the colony was to educate and qualify young men to be ministers of the Gospel, and begged Mr. Attorney would consider that the people of Virginia had souls to be saved as well as the people of England. "Souls!" said he; "damn your souls! make tobacco." The plan of the building was designed by Sir Christopher Wren. The first commencement was held in 1700, at which, according to Oldmixon, "there was a great concourse of people; several planters came thither in their coaches, and several sloops from New York, Pennsylvania and Maryland; it being a new thing in America to hear graduates perform their academical exercises. The Indians themselves had the curiosity to come to Williamsburgh on this occasion; and the whole country rejoiced as if they had some relish of learning." After the English fashion, the college had a representative in the General Assembly. As a quitrent for the land granted by the Crown, the students and professors every year marched to the residence of the royal Governor, and presented, and sometimes recited, some Latin verses. On the breaking out of the Revolution the endowments of the college were cut off, and its constitution was somewhat changed.

No general school law was established in Virginia until 1796, although a plan was proposed by Mr. Jefferson in 1779, which recognized three degrees of public instruction, viz.: 1. Elementary schools for all children. 2. Colleges for an extension of instruction suitable for the common purposes of life. 3. A university, an extension of the means of higher culture on the basis of the college at Williamsburgh.

Scattered through the colony were schools in connection with churches, both Episcopal and Presbyterian, and in many families private teachers were employed, and in some cases sons were sent out to England to complete their education.

MASSACHUSETTS.—In 1636, six years after the first settlement of Boston, the General Court of the colony of Massachusetts Bay, which met in Boston on the 8th of September, passed an act appropriating £400 toward the establishment of a college. The sum thus appropriated was more than the whole tax levied on the colony at that time in a single year, and the population scattered through ten or twelve villages did not exceed five thousand persons; but among them were eminent graduates of the university of Cambridge, in England, and all were here for purposes of permanent settlement. In 1638, John Harvard left by will the sum of £779 in money, and a library of over three hundred books. In 1640 the General Court granted to the college the income of the Charlestown ferry; and in 1642 the Governor, with the magistrates and teachers and elders, were empowered to establish statutes and constitutions for the infant institution, and in 1650 granted a charter which still remains the fundamental law of the oldest literary institution in this country.

In 1642 the attention of the General Court was turned to the subject of family instruction in the following enactment:—

"Forasmuch as the good education of hildren is of singular behoof and benefit to ny commonwealth; and whereas many arents and masters are too indulgent and egligent of their duty in this kind:

"*It is therefore ordered by this Court and he authority thereof*, That the selectmen of very town, in the several precincts and uarters where they dwell, shall have a vigi- ant eye over their brethren and neighbors, o see, first, that none of them shall suffer so uch barbarism in any of their families, as ot to endeavor to teach, by themselves or thers, their children and apprentices so uch learning as may enable them perfectly o read the English tongue, and knowledge f the capital laws, upon penalty of twenty hillings for each neglect therein; also, that ll masters of families do, once a week, at ast, catechise their children and servants the grounds and principles of religion, and any be unable to do so much, that then, the least, they procure such children or pprentices to learn some short orthodox atechism, without book, that they may be ble to answer to the questions that shall be ropounded to them out of such catechisms y their parents or masters, or any of the electmen, where they shall call them to a ial of what they have learned in this kind; d further, that all parents and masters do reed and bring up their children and ap- rentices in some honest lawful calling, labor employment, either in husbandry or some her trade profitable for themselves and the mmonwealth, if they will not nor cannot ain them up in learning to fit them for igher employments; and if any of the select- en, after admonition by them given to such asters of families, shall find them still neg- gent of their duty in the particulars afore- entioned, whereby children and servants ecome rude, stubborn and unruly, the said lectmen, with the help of two magistrates, all take such children or apprentices from em, and place them with some masters for ars, boys till they come to twenty-one, d girls eighteen years of age complete, hich will more strictly look unto and force em to submit unto government, according the rules of this order, if by fair means d former instructions they will not be awn unto it."

In the same year the following general hool law was enacted:—"It being one ief project of that old deluder, Satan, to ep men from the knowledge of the Scriptures, as in former times, keeping them in an unknown tongue, so in these latter times, by persuading from the use of tongues, so that at least the true sense and meaning of the original might be clouded and corrupted with false glosses of deceivers; and to the end that learning may not be buried in the grave of our forefathers, in church and commonwealth, the Lord assisting our endeavors:

"*It is therefore ordered by this Court and authority thereof*, That every township within this jurisdiction, after the Lord hath increased them to the number of fifty householders, shall then forthwith appoint one within their town to teach all such children, as shall resort to him, to write and read, whose wages shall be paid, either by the parents or masters of such children, or by the inhabitants in general, by way of supply, as the major part of those who order the prudentials of the town shall appoint; provided, that those who send their children be not oppressed by paying much more than they can have them taught for in other towns.

"*And it is further ordered*, That where any town shall increase to the number of one hundred families or householders, they shall set up a grammar school, the masters thereof being able to instruct youths so far as they may be fitted for the university, and if any other town neglect the performance hereof above one year, then every such town shall pay five pounds per annum to the next such school, till they shall perform this order."

With various modifications as to details, but with the same objects steadily in view, viz., the exclusion of "barbarism" from every family, by preventing its having even one untaught and idle child or apprentice, the maintenance of an elementary school in every neighborhood where there were children enough to constitute a school, and of a Latin school in every large town, and of a college for higher culture for the whole colony, the colonial legislature, and the people in the several towns of Massachusetts, maintained an educational system, which, although not as early or as thorough as the school code of Saxony and Wirtemberg, has expanded with the growth of the community in population, wealth, and industrial development, and stimulated and shaped the legislation and efforts of other states in behalf of universal education.

The early records of the colony of Plymouth contain no trace of the zeal for schools which characterized the colonies of Massachusetts Bay, Connecticut, and New Haven. In 1662 the profits of the codfishery were appropriated to the maintenance of grammar schools in such towns as would make arrangements for the same; and in 1669 towns having fifty families were authorized to raise by rate on all the inhabitants the sum of twelve pounds for this class of schools, "for as much as the maintenance of good literature doth much tend to the advancement of the weal and flourishing state of societies and republics." After the union of the two colonies under one charter, several towns in the old colony were fined for not complying with the provisions of the law of 1647 respecting children and schools.

In addition to the grammar school which each town having one hundred families was obliged by law to maintain, to enable young men to fit for college, in several counties endowed schools were set up; and in 1763 the first of that class of institutions, known and incorporated as academies, was established in the parish of Byfield in the town of Newbury, on a legacy left by Gov. William Dummer. Its objects were the same as those of the town grammar school, but its benefits were not confined to one town, nor was it supported in any degree by taxation.

Rhode Island.—In this colony education was left to individual and parental care, no trace of any legislation on the subject being found in the proceedings of the General Assembly, except to incorporate in 1747 the "Society for the Promotion of Knowledge and Virtue," which was established in Newport in 1730 by the name of the "Company of the Redwood Library;" and in 1764 to grant the charter to the College of Rhode Island, which was first located in Warren, and in 1770 removed to Providence, and in 1804 called, after its most liberal benefactor, Brown University.

Connecticut.—In 1646, Mr. Roger Ludlow was requested to compile "a body of laws for the government of this commonwealth," which was not completed till May, 1650, and is known as the code of 1650. The provisions for the family instruction of children and the maintenance of schools are identically the same as in Massachusetts, and remained on the statute-book, with but slight modifications to give them more efficiency, for one hundred and fifty years. In the chapter on "capital" offences, it is enacted that if any child above sixteen years of age, and of sufficient understanding, shall curse or smite his father or mother, he shall be put to death, "unless it can be sufficiently testified that the parents have been unchristianly negligent in the education of such children." In the chapter respecting schools, the proposition made by the "Commissioners of the United Colonies," that it be commended to every family which "is able and willing to give yearly but the fourth part of a bushel of corn, or something equivalent thereto," "for the advancement of learning," was approved, and two men were appointed in every town to receive and forward the contributions. This was done in the larger towns of the colonies of Connecticut and New Haven, from time to time, until ten of the principal ministers, in 1700, at Branford, brought each a number of books, and as they laid them on the table, declared—"*I give these books for founding a College in Connecticut*;" and on that foundation rose Yale College. To fit young men for the college at Cambridge, and subsequently for Yale, in 1672 it was ordered by the General Court, "that in every county there shall be set up a grammar school for the use of the county, the master thereof being able to instruct youths so far as they may be fitted for college;" and to aid the county towns in maintaining their schools, six hundred acres of land were appropriated by the General Court to each, "to be improved in the best manner that may be for the benefit of a grammar school in said towns, and to no other use or end whatsoever;" and in 1677 a fine of ten pounds annually is imposed on any county town neglecting to keep the Latin school. In 1690, the county Latin schools of Hartford and New Haven are denominated "Free Schools," probably in reference to the partial endowment of schools of this class by the trustees of the legacy of Governor Hopkins.

As early as 1700, the system of public instruction in Connecticut embraced the following particulars:

1. An obligation on every parent and guardian of children, "not to suffer so much barbarism in any of their families as to have a single child or apprentice unable to read the holy word of God, and the good laws of the colony;" and also, "to bring them up to some lawful calling or employment," under a penalty for each offence.

2. A tax of forty shillings on every thousand pounds of the lists of estates, was collected in every town with the annual state tax, and payable proportionably to those towns only which should keep their schools according to law.

3. A common school in every town having over seventy families, kept for at least six months in the year.

4. A grammar school in each of the four head county towns to fit youth for college, two of which grammar schools were free or endowed.

5. A collegiate school, toward which the General Court made an annual appropriation of £120.

6. Provision for the religious instruction of the Indians.

The system, therefore, embraced every family and town, all classes of children and youth, and all the then recognized grades of schools. There were no select or sectarian schools to classify society at the roots, but all children were regarded with equal favor, and all brought under the assimilating influence of early associations and similar school privileges. Here was the foundation laid, not only for universal education, but for a practical, political, and social equality, which has never been surpassed in the history of any other community.

New Hampshire.—From 1623 to 1641, the early records of the first settlements within the present limits of New Hampshire exhibit no trace of educational enactments; from 1641 to 1680, the school laws of Massachusetts prevailed, and the presence of such men as Philemon Purmont and Daniel Maude, who were the first schoolmasters of that colony, must have contributed to inaugurate the policy of local and endowed schools. When the necessities of the college at Cambridge were made known, the people of Portsmouth, in town meeting, made a collection of sixty pounds, with a pledge to continue the same amount for seven years, "for the perpetuating of knowledge both religious and civil among us and our posterity after us." In the original grants for towns one lot was reserved for the support of schools.

In 1680 New Hampshire became a separate colony, and in 1693 the Colonial Assembly enacted "that for the building and repairing of meeting houses, ministers' houses, and allowing a salary to a schoolmaster in each town within this province, the selectmen shall raise by an equal rate an assessment upon the inhabitants;" and in 1719 it was ordained that every town having fifty householders should be constantly provided with a schoolmaster to teach children to read and write; and those having one hundred should maintain a grammar school, to be kept by some decent person, of good conversation, well instructed in the tongues. In 1721 it was ordered that not only each town but each parish of one hundred families should be constantly provided with a grammar school, or forfeit the sum of twenty pounds to the treasury of the province. This system of elementary and secondary instruction continued substantially until the adoption of the state constitution in 1792.

In 1770 Dr. Wheelock removed a school which he had established in Lebanon, Connecticut, under the name of "Moor's Indian Charity School," to the depths of the forests in the western part of New Hampshire. Here, side by side with the school for Indians, he organized another institution, termed a college in the charter granted by Governor Wentworth in 1769, and which held its first commencement in 1771, with four graduates, one of whom was John Wheelock, the second president of the institution, which was called Dartmouth College after Lord Dartmouth, one of the largest benefactors of the Charity School.

At the close of the colonial period of our history, according to Noah Webster, the condition of the educational system in Connecticut and New England was as follows:

"The law of Connecticut ordains that every town or parish containing seventy householders, shall keep an English school, at least eleven months in the year; and towns containing a less number, at least six months in the year. Every town keeping a public school is entitled to draw from the treasury of the state a certain sum of money, proportioned to its census in the list of property which furnishes the rule of taxation. This sum might have been originally sufficient to support one school in each town or parish, but in modern times is divided among a number, and the deficiency of money to support the schools is raised upon the estates of the people, in the manner the public taxes are assessed. To extend the benefits of this establishment to all the inhabitants, large towns and parishes are divided into districts, each of which is supposed able to furnish a competent number of scholars for one school. In each district a house is erected for the purpose by the inhabitants of that district, who hire a master, furnish wood, and tax themselves to pay all expenses not provided for by the public money. The school is kept during the winter months, when every farmer can spare his sons. In this manner, every child in the state has access to a school. In the summer, a woman is hired to teach small children, who are not fit for any kind of labor. In the large towns, schools, either public or private, are kept the whole year; and in every county town, a grammar school is established by law.

"The beneficial effects of these institutions will be experienced for ages. Next to the establishments in favor of religion, they have been the nurseries of well-informed citizens, brave soldiers and wise legislators. A people thus informed are capable of understanding their rights and of discovering the means to secure them. In the next place, our forefathers took measures to preserve the reputation of schools and the morals of youth, by making the teaching them an honorable employment. Every town or district has a committee, whose duty is to procure a master of talents and character; and the practice is to procure a man of the best character in the town or neighborhood. The wealthy towns apply to young men of liberal education, who, after taking the bachelor's degree, usually keep school a year or two before they enter upon a profession. One of the most unfortunate circumstances to education in the Middle and Southern states, is an opinion that school-keeping is a mean employment, fit only for persons of low character. The wretches who keep the schools in those states very frequently degrade the employment; but the misfortune is, public opinion supposes the employment degrades the man: of course no gentleman will undertake to teach children while in popular estimation he must forfeit his rank and character by the employment. Until public opinion is corrected by some great examples, the common schools, what few there are in those states, must continue in the hands of such vagabonds as wander about the country."

"Nearly connected with the establishment of schools is the circulation of newspapers in New England. This is both a consequence and a cause of a general diffusion of letters. In Connecticut, almost every man reads a paper every week. In the year 1785, I took some pains to ascertain the number of papers printed weekly in Connecticut and in the Southern states. I found the number in Connecticut to be nearly eight thousand; which was equal to that published in the whole territory south of Pennsylvania. By means of this general circulation of public papers, the people are informed of all political affairs; and their representatives are often prepared to deliberate on propositions made to the legislature.

"Another institution favorable to knowledge is the establishment of parish libraries. These are procured by subscription, but they are numerous, the expense not being considerable, and the desire of reading universal. One hundred volumes of books, selected from the best writers, on ethics, divinity, and history, and read by the principal inhabitants of a town or village, will have an amazing influence in spreading knowledge, correcting the morals, and softening the manners of a nation. I am acquainted with parishes where almost every householder has read the works of Addison, Sherlock, Atterbury, Watts, Young, and other similar writings; and will converse well on the subjects of which they treat."

New York.—In the early history of the settlements of the New Netherlands, the school was regarded as an appendage of the church, and the schoolmaster was paid in part out of the funds of the government. Down to its organization as a royal province of England, a parochial school existed in every parish. In 1658 a petition of the burgomasters and schepens of New Amsterdam was forwarded to the West India Company, in which "it is represented that the youth of this place and the neighborhood are increasing in number gradually, and that most of them can read and write, but that some of the citizens and inhabitants would like to send their children to a school the principal of which understands Latin, but are not able to do so without sending them to New England; furthermore, they have not the means to hire a Latin schoolmaster, expressly for themselves, from New England, and therefore they ask that the West India Company will send out a fit person as Latin schoolmaster, not doubting that the number of persons who will send their children to such teacher will from year to year increase, until an academy shall be formed whereby this place to great splendor will have attained, for which, next to God, the honorable company which shall have sent such teacher here shall have laud and praise." In compliance with this petition, Dr. Alexander Carolus Curtius, a Latin master of Lithuania, was sent out by the company. The burgomasters proposed to give him five hundred guilders annually out of the city treasury, with the use of a house and garden, and the privilege of collecting a tuition of six guilders per quarter of each scholar. Dr. Curtius proved not to be a good disciplinarian, and parents complained to the authorities that "his pupils beat each other, and tore the clothes from each other's backs." The doctor retorted that he could not interfere, "as his hands were tied, as some of the parents forbade him punishing their children." He accordingly gave up his place and returned to Holland, and was succeeded in the mastership by Rev. Ægidius Luyck in 1662. His school had a high reputation, and was resorted to by pupils from Virginia, Fort Orange, and the Delaware.

After the establishment of the English authority, the governor claimed the privilege of licensing teachers even for the church schools, but no general school policy was established. In 1702 a free grammar school was founded and built on the King's Farm, and in 1732 a "Free School," for teaching the Latin and Greek and practical branches of mathematics, was incorporated by law. The preamble of the act of incorporation opens as follows: "Whereas the youth of this colony are found by manifold experience to be not inferior in their natural genius to the youth of any other country in the world, therefore be it enacted," etc. In 1710, the Society for the Propagation of the Gospel in Foreign Parts established a charity school in connection with the Episcopal church, which is still in existence, and is now known as the Trinity School. In 1750, Charles Dutens announced to the public "that he taught a school for the use of young ladies and gentlemen, whose love of learning might incline them to take lessons from him in French, at his house on Broad street, near the Long Bridge, where he also makes and vends finger and ear rings, solitaires, stay-hooks and lockets, and sets diamonds, rubies, and other stones. Science and virtue are two sisters, which the most part of the New York ladies possess," etc.

Judge Smith, in his "History of the Province of New York," when speaking of the action of the legislature for founding a college in 1746, says: "To the disgrace of our first planters, who beyond comparison surpassed their eastern neighbors in opulence, Mr. Delancy, a graduate of the University of Cambridge (England), and Mr. Smith, were for many years the only academics in this province, except such as were in holy orders; and so late as the period we are now examining (1750), the author did not recollect above thirteen men, the youngest of whom had his bachelor's degree at the age of seventeen, but two months before the passing of the above law, the first toward erecting a college in this colony, though at a distance of above one hundred and twenty years after its discovery and settlement of the capital by Dutch progenitors from Amsterdam."

In 1754 a royal charter was obtained for a college in New York, with the style of King's College, which came into possession of a fund raised by a lottery authorized for this purpose by the Assembly in 1746, and of a grant of land conveyed to its governors by Trinity Church in 1755. Out of this grant, Columbia College is now (1860) realizing an income of $60,000 a year. The first commencement was celebrated in 1758.

"For the advantage of our new intended college" (King's), "and the use and ornament of the city," a number of eminent citizens of New York, in 1754, united in an association to form a library, which in 1772 was incorporated with the title of the "New York Society Library."

MARYLAND.—The first settlement was effected within the present limits of Maryland in 1634; and in the years immediately following, we find no record of any marked individual or legislative effort to establish institutions of learning. The first act of the colonial Assembly is entitled a "Supplicatory Act to their sacred majesties for erecting of schools," which was passed in 1694, and repealed or superseded by an act entitled a "Petitionary Act" for the same purpose. Appealing to the royal liberality, which had been extended to the neighboring colony of Virginia in the institution of the college, "a place of universal study," the Assembly ask, "that for the propagation of the Gospel, and the education of the youth of this province in good letters and manners, that a certain place or places for a free school or schools, or place of study of Latin, Greek, writing and the like, consisting of one master, one usher, and one writing-master or scribe to a school, and 100 scholars," be established in Arundel County, of which the Archbishop of Canterbury should be chancellor, and to be called "King William's School;" and a similar free school is asked for in each county, to be established from time to time as the resources of the several counties may suffice. To increase the educational resources of the counties, in 1717 it was enacted that an additional duty of twenty shillings current money per poll should be levied on all Irish servants, being papists, to prevent the growth of popery by the importation of too great a number of them into this province, and also an additional duty of twenty shillings current money per poll on all negroes, for raising a fund for the use of public schools. In 1723, "an act for the encouragement of learning, and erecting schools in the several counties," was passed, with a preamble setting forth that preceding Assemblies have had it much at heart, "to provide for the liberal and pious education of the youth of the province, and improving their natural abilities and acuteness (which seem not to be inferior to any), so as to be fitted for the discharge of their duties in the several stations and employments in it, either in regard to church or state." By this act seven visitors are appointed in each county, with corporate powers to receive and hold estate to the value of £100 per annum; and they are authorized with all convenient speed to purchase, out of funds realized from revenues already set apart for this purpose, one hundred acres more or less, one moiety of which is to serve for making corn, grain, and pasturage for the benefit and use of the master, who is prohibited growing tobacco, or permitting it by others on said farm. The visitors are directed to employ good schoolmasters, members of the Church of England, and of pious and exemplary lives and conversation, and capable of teaching well the grammar, good writing, and the mathematics, if such can be conveniently got, on a salary of £20 per annum, and the use of the plantation. In 1728 the master of each public school is directed "to teach as many poor children gratis as the majority of the visitors should order."

Up to the establishment of the state government in 1777, there was no system of common schools for elementary instruction in operation in Maryland. "A free school," like the free endowed grammar school of England, was established in a majority of counties, two of which were subsequently converted into colleges, that of Charlestown in Kent county, into Washington College in 1782, and the second at Annapolis into St. John's College in 1784—the former "in honorable and perpetual memory of his excellency General Washington, the illustrious and virtuous commander-in-chief of the armies of the United States."

In 1696, Rev. Thomas Bray, then residing in the parish of Sheldon, England, was made commissary of Maryland, to establish the Church of England in the colony. His first act was to inaugurate a plan of parochial libraries for the use of ministers in each parish. Through his influence, Princess Anne made a benefaction for this purpose, and in acknowledgment of the honor of having the capital of the province called after her name (Annapolis), donated books to the value of four hundred pounds to the parish library, which he called "the Annapolitan Library." By his influence in England a plan of "lending-libraries" was projected in every deanery throughout the kingdom, and carried out.

New Jersey.—In the history of New Jersey as a colony we find no trace of any general legislation or governmental action in behalf of schools. Scattered at wide intervals over the state were schools kept by clergymen in connection with their churches.

In 1748 a charter of incorporation for the College of New Jersey was obtained from George II., during the administration of Governor Belcher, "for the instruction of youth in the learned languages and liberal arts and sciences." During the administration of Governor Franklin in 1770, a second college was chartered, with the name of Queen's (now Rutger's) College, as a school of theology for the Reformed Dutch Church. Neither of the institutions received any aid from the government.

Pennsylvania.—The frame of government of the province of Pennsylvania, dated April 25th, 1682, drawn up by William Penn before leaving England, contains the following provision: "The governor and provincial council shall erect and order all public schools and reward the authors of useful sciences and laudable inventions in said province." In the laws agreed upon a few months later in the same year by the governor and divers freemen of the province in England, it is provided "that all children within this province of the age of twelve years shall be taught some useful trade, or skill, to the end that none be idle, but that the poor may work to live, and the rich, if they become poor, may not want." In 1683 the governor and council in Philadelphia, "having taken into their serious consideration the great necessity there is of a schoolmaster in the town of Philadelphia, sent for Enoch Flower, an inhabitant of said town, who for twenty years past hath been exercised in that care and employment in England, to whom having communicated their minds, he embraced it upon the following terms: to learn to read English, 4s. by the quarter;" to learn to read and write, 6s.; read, write and cast accounts, 8s.; for boarding a scholar, £10 per year. In 1689 the Society of Friends established a Latin school of which George Keith was the first teacher. In 1725 Rev. Francis Alison, a native of Ireland, but educated at Glasgow, became pastor of the Presbyterian church in New London, in Chester county, and opened a school there, which had great reputation. He at one time resided at Thunder Hill, in Maryland, where he educated many young men who were afterward distinguished in the Revolutionary struggle. He was subsequently Provost of the college at Philadelphia.

In 1749 Benjamin Franklin published his "*Proposals relating to the Education of Youth in Pennsylvania*," out of which originated subsequently an academy and charity school, and ultimately the University of Pennsylvania. At the head of the English department of the academy in 1751 was Mr. Dove, who was then engaged in giving public lectures in experimental philosophy with apparatus—an early lyceum or popular lecturer.

In 1743 the American Philosophical Society originated in a "Proposal for Promoting Useful Knowledge," published by Benjamin Franklin, which, after various forms of organization, took its present name and shape on the 2d of January, 1769.

In 1765 the Medical School originated with the appointment of Dr. Morgan to the professorship of the theory and practice of physic; in 1767 it was fully organized, and in 1768 degrees in medicine were for the first time conferred.

Among the denominational schools which grew up in the absence of any general legislation on the subject, was a Moravian school for boys at Nazareth in 1747, and for girls at Bethlehem 1749, both of which are still in existence, and the latter, especially, since 1789, has been one of the most flourishing female seminaries in this country.

DELAWARE.—In the early settlements of the Swedes and Dutch in Delaware, the policy of connecting a school with the church was probably imperfectly carried out, but there is no historical trace of its existence. The only school legislation of the colony extant, is an act incorporating "the Trustees of the Grammar School in the borough of Wilmington, and county of New Castle," dated April 10, 1773.

NORTH CAROLINA.—In North Carolina for fifty years, the policy of the provincial authorities was to discourage all forms of religious and educational activity outside of the Church of England, to the extent of forbidding expressly the establishment of printing presses. The first act on record relating to schools, in 1764, was "for the building of a house for a school, and the residence of a schoolmaster in the town of Newbern"—appropriating the half of two lots, before set apart for a church, for this purpose. In 1766 another act was passed incorporating trustees for this school, with the preamble "that a number of well-disposed persons, taking into consideration the great necessity of having a proper school, or public seminary of learning established, whereby the present generation may be brought up and instructed in the principles of the Christian religion, and fitted for the several offices and purposes of life, have at great expense erected a school-house for this purpose;" and providing that the master of the school shall be "of the established Church of England, and licensed by the governor." Similar acts were passed in 1770 and 1779 for schools at Edenton and Hillsborough. In 1770 an act, reciting that a very promising experiment had been made in the town of Charlotte in the county of Mecklenburg, with a seminary of learning "a number of youths there taught making great advancement in the knowledge of the learned languages, and in the rudiments of the arts and sciences, having gone to various colleges in distant parts of America," incorporates the same with the name of Queen's College. This act was repealed by proclamation in the next year, but in 1777 it was reincorporated by name of "Liberty Hall." With the downfall of the royal authority, and the religious party which had swayed the colony, a new educational policy was inaugurated.

South Carolina.—In the early history of the colony of South Carolina, as of several other colonies, the first efforts to establish schools were in connection with the predominant church of the settlers, *i. e.*, of the Church of England, through the aid of the "Venerable Society for Propagating the Gospel in Foreign Parts." By the missionaries of that society charity schools were established in several parishes, some of which were afterward endowed by individuals, and incorporated by act of the legislature, and called "Free Schools." In 1710 a free school of this character was established at Goosecreek, and in 1712 in Charleston; and by the general act of February 22, 1722, the justices of the county courts were authorized to erect a free school in each county and precinct, to be supported by assessment on land and negroes. These schools were bound to teach ten poor children each, if sent by said justices. In 1724, a memorial to the "Venerable Society" from the parish of Dorchester sets forth—"The chief source of irreligion here is the want of schools; and we may justly be apprehensive, that if our children continue longer to be deprived of opportunities of being instructed, Christianity will of course decay insensibly, and we shall have a generation of our own as ignorant as the native Indians." The society sent out schoolmasters to this and other parishes, and about 2000 volumes of bound books. In 1721 Mr. Richard Beresford bequeathed to the parish of St. Thomas and St. Dennis, in trust, for the purpose of educating the poor, £6500; and in 1732 Mr. Richard Harris, for the same object, £1000. In 1728 Rev. Richard Ludlam bequeathed his whole estate to the parish of St. James, which in 1778 amounted to £15,272. Other bequests for the same objects were made at different times before the Revolution. In 1743 Rev. Alexander Garden wrote to the society that the negro school consisted of thirty children, and in 1750 that it was going on with all desirable success. In 1748 a library was founded in Charleston by an association of seventeen young men, whose first object was to collect new pamphlets and magazines published in Great Britain, but in the course of a year embraced the purchase of books. After many delays and refusals, an act of incorporation was obtained in 1754. There is but one older library in this country.

Georgia.—The earliest effort to establish schools in Georgia was made by the Rev. George Whitefield. Before leaving England in 1737, he had projected an Orphan House, after the plan of that of Dr. Franké, at Halle, of which an account about that time appeared in English. His first visit to Savannah in 1738 satisfied him of the necessity of a charity school for poor and neglected children, and in the course of that year he returned to England to obtain his ordination as priest and collect funds for his educational enterprise. The trustees of the colony gave him five hundred acres of land upon which to erect his buildings. These were selected about ten miles out of Savannah, and on the 25th of March, 1740, he laid the first brick of the house, which he called Bethesda, or House of Mercy, and opened his school in temporary shelters with forty children. In the fall of the same year he made a collection and preaching tour in New England, during which he collected over £800 for his charity. After disasters by fire, etc., the Orphan House property was bequeathed to Selina, Countess of Huntingdon, in trust for the purposes originally designed, and subsequently incorporated for this purpose. On her death, and after the Revolution, the legislature transferred the property to thirteen trustees, to manage the estate and make regulations for an academy in the county of Chatham. Schools were established by the missionaries sent out by the Society for the Propagation of the Gospel at Savannah, Augusta, and Frederica, and by the Moravians and Huguenots in their respective settlements.

RESULTS AT THE CLOSE OF OUR COLONIAL HISTORY.

The educational systems and provisions of the colonial period of the United States were, especially in its earlier portion, closely connected with the ecclesiastical systems of the colonies. Schools were maintained by individual youth trained up in very many cases, because it was a duty to prepare useful future members of the church, which in some of the colonies was also the state.

In three states, Massachusetts, Connecticut, and New Hampshire, it was very early made the legal duty of parents and towns to make provision for the education of youth. Elsewhere, such efforts as were made, aside from the natural desire of parents to afford their children such an education as was suitable to their rank in life, or such as would aid their subsequent progress and prosperity, were, generally speaking, put forth by clergymen, ecclesiastical bodies, or pious laymen, for colonial institutions for secondary education were not very numerous, including the town grammar schools of New England, and a small number of endowed or free schools. In these two classes of institutions, a small number of pupils were prepared to enter college. A far greater number of college students, more especially in the middle and southern states, were prepared by clergymen, who received each a small number of pupils into his family, as a means of securing some additional income. There were also a few private schools of considerable reputation and value.

In connection with these educational agencies, the small parochial and social libraries, and the two or three associations for the increase and dissemination of science, should also be referred to.

The institutions of superior education, established during the colonial period, were seven in number; namely, Harvard, William and Mary, Yale, Nassau Hall, Rutgers, Brown, and Columbia. From these came forth nearly all the liberally educated men of that day, though it was a custom of a few of the wealthiest families of the day to graduate their sons at a European university, Oxford or Cambridge being commonly selected. The colonial colleges, like the schools preparatory to them, were substantially church institutions, their pupils being the stock from which the clerical body was reinforced.

It was not until the very close of the colonial period that a few special or professional schools were established. A school of medicine, sufficiently entitled to the name, gave degrees in New York in 1769; a sort of theological seminary was founded in Pennsylvania in 1778; while the first law school only arose the year after the peace of 1783. Professorships, however, in these departments, had afforded a certain amount of instruction in all of them as part of the college course, long before; indeed, from the foundation of the earliest colleges.

Female education was comparatively neglected in the colonial period. Girls were taught housewifely duties far more assiduously than learning, and often depended upon home instruction for whatever education they received; neither the common schools nor those for secondary education affording or being designed to afford accommodation for them.

That special supplementary training which at the present day does so much to alleviate the misfortunes of the blind, the deaf and dumb, and the feeble minded, was quite unknown, nor was the idea entertained that such a training was practicable.

CHAPTER II.

REVOLUTIONARY AND TRANSITIONAL PERIOD.

The immediate effects of the war of the Revolution were adverse, and, in certain aspects, disastrous to the interests of education. Dangers so great and imminent almost engrossed all thought and absorbed all exertion and resources. Children, indeed, were not left without the instruction of the family and the local elementary school, and they were, thank God, everywhere surrounded with the most stirring exhibitions of heroic patriotism and the self-sacrificing virtues. But too generally the elementary school and the teacher, never properly appreciated, gave way to more pressing and universally-felt necessities. Higher education for a time experienced a severe shock. The calls of patriotism withdrew many young men from the colleges and the preparatory schools, and prevented many more from resorting thither. The impoverishment of the country, and the demand for immediate action, compelled others to relinquish an extended course of professional study. In some cases the presence of armies caused a suspension of college instruction and the dispersion of faculty and students, and even converted the college buildings into barracks. But the action and influence of this period were not wholly adverse or disastrous to schools and higher education. The public mind was stimulated into greatly increased activity—now, for the first time, assuming a collective existence and national characteristics. The heart of the people was thoroughly penetrated by the spirit of self-sacrifice, in cheerfully bearing the burdens of society with diminished resources, and in repairing the waste and destruction of the war. The examples of wisdom and eloquence in council, and courage and heroism in the field, and of patient endurance of privation and hardship, and towering above all and outshining all, the colossal greatness and transparent purity of the character of Washington—these were lessons for the head and the heart of a young nation, which amply compensated for the partial and temporary suspension of schools. In the discussion and reconstruction of political society, in framing constitutions and organic legislation, and in the disposition of unsettled territory, the importance of the elementary school, the academy, and the college, was recognized and provided for.

Among the earliest to do justice to this great subject was Noah Webster, who, in a series of essays, first published in a New York paper, and copied extensively by the press in other parts of the country, and afterward embodied in a volume with other fugitive pieces, advocated a liberal policy by the national and local governments in favor of a broad system of education. "Here every class of people should know and love the laws. This knowledge should be diffused by means of schools and newspapers; and an attachment to the laws may be formed by early impression upon the mind. Two regulations are essential to the continuance of republican governments: 1. Such a distribution of lands and such principles of descent and alienation as shall give every citizen a power of acquiring what his industry merits. 2. Such a system of education as shall give every citizen an opportunity of acquiring knowledge, and fitting himself for places of trust." "Education should be the first care of a legislature; not merely the institution of schools, but the furnishing them with the best men for teachers. A good system of schools should be the first article in a code of political regulations; for it is much easier to introduce and establish an effectual system for preserving morals, than to correct by penal statutes the ill effects of a bad system. I am so fully persuaded of this, that I should almost adore that great man who shall change our practice and opinions, and make it respectable for the first and best men to superintend the education of youth." As specimens of the utterances of eminent public men on this subject, we cite the following:

"Promote, as an object of primary importance, institutions for the general diffusion of knowledge. In proportion as the structure of a government gives force to public opinion, it is essential that public opinion should be enlightened." George Washington.

"The wisdom and generosity of the legislature in making liberal appropriations in money for the benefit of schools, academies and colleges, is an equal honor to them and their constituents, a proof of their veneration for letters and science, and a portent of great and lasting good to North and South America, and to the world. Great is truth—great is liberty—great is humanity—and they must and will prevail." John Adams.

"I look to the diffusion of light and education as the resources most to be relied on for ameliorating the condition, promoting the virtue, and advancing the happiness of man. And I do hope, in the present spirit of extending to the great mass of mankind the blessings of instruction, I see a prospect of great advancement in the happiness of the human race, and this may proceed to an indefinite, although not an infinite, degree. A system of general instruction, which shall reach every description of our citizens, from the richest to the poorest, as it was the earliest, so shall it be the latest of all the public concerns in which I shall permit myself to take an interest. Give it to us, in any shape, and receive for the inestimable boon the thanks of the young, and the blessings of the old, who are past all other services but prayers for the prosperity of their country, and blessings to those who promote it."

Thomas Jefferson.

"Learned institutions ought to be the favorite objects with every free people; they throw that light over the public mind which is the best security against crafty and dangerous encroachments on the public liberty. They multiply the educated individuals, from among whom the people may elect a due portion of their public agents of every description, more especially of those who are to frame the laws: by the perspicuity, the consistency, and the stability, as well as by the justice and equal spirit of which, the great social purposes are to be answered."

James Madison.

"Moral, political and intellectual improvement, are duties assigned by the Author of our existence to social, no less than to individual man. For the fulfilment of these duties, governments are invested with power, and to the attainment of these ends, the exercise of this power is a duty sacred and indispensable." John Quincy Adams.

"For the purpose of promoting the happiness of the State, it is absolutely necessary that our government, which unites into one all the minds of the State, should possess in an eminent degree not only the understanding, the passions, and the will, but above all, the moral faculty and the conscience of an individual. Nothing can be politically right that is morally wrong; and no necessity can ever sanctify a law that is contrary to equity. Virtue is the soul of a Republic. To promote this, laws for the suppression of vice and immorality will be as ineffectual as the increase and enlargement of jails. There is but one method of preventing crime and of rendering a republican form of government durable; and that is, by disseminating the seeds of virtue and knowledge through every part of the State, by means of proper modes and places of education; and this can be done effectually only by the interference and aid of the legislature. I am so deeply impressed with this opinion, that were this the last evening of my life, I would not only say to the asylum of my ancestors and my beloved native country, with the patriot of Venice, '*Esto perpetua*,' but I would add, as the best proof of my affection for her, my parting advice to the guardians of her liberties, establish and support PUBLIC SCHOOLS in every part of the State." Benjamin Rush.

"There is one object which I earnestly recommend to your notice and patronage—I mean our institutions for the education of youth. The importance of common schools is best estimated by the good effects of them where they most abound and are best regulated. Our ancestors have transmitted to us many excellent institutions, matured by the wisdom and experience of ages. Let them descend to posterity, accompanied with others, which, by promoting useful knowledge, and multiplying the blessings of social order, diffusing the influence of moral obligations, may be reputable to us, and beneficial to them." John Jay.

"The first duty of government, and the surest evidence of good government, is the encouragement of education. A general diffusion of knowledge is the precursor and protector of republican institutions, and in it we must confide as the conservative power that will watch over our liberties and guard them against fraud, intrigue, corruption and violence. I consider the system of our Common Schools as the palladium of our freedom, for no reasonable apprehension can be entertained of its subversion, as long as the great body of the people are enlightened by education. To increase the funds, to extend the benefits, and to remedy the defects of this excellent system, is worthy of your most deliberate attention. I can not recommend in terms too strong and impressive, as munificent appropriations as the faculties of the State will authorize for all establishments connected with the interests of education, the exaltation of literature and science, and the improvement of the human mind."

De Witt Clinton.

"The parent who sends his son into the world uneducated, defrauds the community of a lawful citizen, and bequeaths to it a nuisance." Chancellor Kent.

In the discussions which have taken place in the press and in the halls of legislation on the subject, the experience of the New England States is constantly cited as an irrefutable argument in favor of public schools and universal education. The character and value of this example are admirably set forth by Daniel Webster:

"In this particular, New England may be allowed to claim, I think, a merit of a peculiar character. She early adopted and has constantly maintained the principle, that it is the undoubted right, and the bounden duty of government, to provide for the instruction of all youth. That which is elsewhere left to chance, or to charity, we secure by law. For the purpose of public instruction, we hold every man subject to taxation in proportion to his property, and we look not to the question, whether he himself have, or have not, children to be benefited by the education for which he pays. We regard it as a wise and liberal system of police, by which property, and life, and the peace of society are secured. We seek to prevent in some measure the extension of the penal code, by inspiring a salutary and conservative principle of virtue and of knowledge in an early age. We hope to excite a feeling of respectability, and a sense of character, by enlarging the capacity, and increasing the sphere of intellectual enjoyment. By general instruction, we seek, as far as possible, to purify the whole moral atmosphere; to keep good sentiments uppermost, and to turn the strong current of feeling and opinion, as well as the censures of the law, and the denunciations of religion, against immorality and crime. We hope for a security, beyond the law, and above the law, in the prevalence of enlightened and well-principled moral sentiment. We hope to continue and prolong the time when, in the villages and farmhouses of New England, there may be undisturbed sleep within unbarred doors. And knowing that our government rests directly on the public will, that we may preserve it, we endeavor to give a safe and proper direction to that public will. We do not, indeed, expect all men to be philosophers or statesmen; but we confidently trust, and our expectation of the duration of our system of government rests on that trust, that by the diffusion of general knowledge and good and virtuous sentiments, the political fabric may be secure, as well against open violence and overthrow, as against the slow but sure undermining of licentiousness."

The action of Congress, and of the early constitutional conventions of the several states, shows how nobly the public mind responded to these appeals.

On the 17th of May, 1784, Mr. Jefferson, as chairman of a committee for that purpose, introduced into the old Congress an ordinance respecting the disposition of the public lands; but this contained no reference to schools or education. On the 4th of March, 1785, another ordinance was introduced—by whom does not appear on the journal—and on the 16th of the same month was recommitted to a committee consisting of Pierce Long of New Hampshire, Rufus King of Massachusetts, David Howell of Rhode Island, Wm. S. Johnson of Connecticut, R. R. Livingston of New York, Charles Stewart of New Jersey, Joseph Gardner of Pennsylvania, John Henry of Maryland, William Grayson of Virginia, Hugh Williamson of North Carolina, John Bull of South Carolina, and William Houston of Georgia. On the 14th of April following, this committee reported the ordinance—by whom drawn up no clue is given—which, after being perfected, was passed the 20th of May following, and became the foundation of the existing land system of the United States.

By one of its provisions, the sixteenth section of every township was reserved "*for the maintenance of public schools;*" or, in other words, one section out of the thirty-six composing each township. The same provision was incorporated in the large land sale, in 1786, to the Ohio Company, and the following year in Judge Symmes' purchase. The celebrated ordinance of 1787, for the government of the territory north-west of the River Ohio, and which confirmed the provisions of the land ordinance of 1785, provides further, that, "RELIGION, MORALITY and KNOWLEDGE being necessary to good government and the happiness of mankind, SCHOOLS, AND THE MEANS OF EDUCATION, SHALL BE FOREVER ENCOURAGED." From that day to the present, this noble policy has been confirmed and extended, till its blessings now reach even the distant shores of the Pacific, and FIFTY MILLIONS OF ACRES of the public domain have been set apart and consecrated to the high and ennobling purposes of education, together with five per cent. of the net proceeds of the sales of all public lands in each of the states and territories in which they are situated.

During this period individual beneficence and associated enterprise began to be directed to the building up, furnishing, and maintaining libraries, colleges, academies, and scientific institutions. Societies for the promotion of science and literature, and schools for professional training, were founded and incorporated, and men of even moderate fortune began to feel the luxury of doing good, and to see that a wise endowment for the relief of suffering, the diffusion of knowledge, the discovery of the laws of nature, the application of the principles of science to the useful arts, the conservation of good morals, and the spread of religious truth, is, in the best sense of the term, a good investment—an investment productive of the greatest amount of the highest good both to the donor and his posterity, and which makes the residue of the property from which it is taken both more secure and more valuable.

CHAPTER III.

'ROGRESS OF COMMON OR ELEMENTARY SCHOOLS.

To understand the real progress which has een made in the organization, administra- ion, and instruction of institutions of learn- ıg in this country, and at the same time to ppreciate the importance of many agencies nd means of popular education besides chools, books and teachers, we must, as far s we can, look into the schools themselves, s they were fifty and sixty years ago, and ealize the circumstances under which some f the noblest characters of our history have een developed. As a contribution to our nowledge of the early history of education ı the United States, we bring together the estimony of several eminent men who were upils or teachers in these schools, and who ssisted in various ways in achieving their nprovement.

LETTER FROM NOAH WEBSTER, LL.D.

"NEW HAVEN, March 10th, 1840.

"MR. BARNARD: *Dear Sir*—You desire e to give you some information as to the ode of instruction in common schools when was young, or before the Revolution. I be- eve you to be better acquainted with the ethods of managing common schools, at e present time, than I am; and I am not ble to institute a very exact comparison etween the old modes and the present. rom what I know of the present schools in e country, I believe the principal difference etween the schools of former times and at resent consists in the books and instruments sed in the modern schools.

"When I was young, the books used were ıiefly or wholly Dilworth's Spelling Books, e Psalter, Testament and Bible. No ge- graphy was studied before the publication f Dr. Morse's small books on that subject, out the year 1786 or 1787. No history as read, as far as my knowledge extends, r there was no abridged history of the nited States. Except the books above entioned, no book for reading was used efore the publication of the Third Part of y Institute, in 1785. In some of the early itions of that book, I introduced short tices of the geography and history of the nited States, and these led to more en- rged descriptions of the country. In 1788, the request of Dr. Morse, I wrote an account of the transactions in the United States, after the Revolution; which account fills nearly twenty pages in the first volume of his octavo editions.

"Before the Revolution, and for some years after, no slates were used in common schools; all writing and the operations in arithmetic were on paper. The teacher wrote the copies and gave the sums in arithmetic; few or none of the pupils having any books as a guide. Such was the condition of the schools in which I received my early education.

"The introduction of my Spelling Book, first published in 1783, produced a great change in the department of spelling; and from the information I can gain, spelling was taught with more care and accuracy for twenty years or more after that period, than it has been since the introduction of multiplied books and studies.*

"No English grammar was generally taught in common schools when I was young, except that in Dilworth, and that to no good purpose. In short, the instruction in schools was very imperfect, in every branch; and if I am not misinformed, it is so to this day, in many branches. Indeed there is danger of running from one extreme to another, and instead of having too few books in our schools, we shall have too many.

"I am, sir, with much respect, your friend and obedient servant, N. WEBSTER."

Dr. Webster, in an essay published in a New York paper in 1788, "On the Education of Youth in America," and in another essay published in Hartford, Ct., in 1790, "On Property, Government, Education, Religion, Agriculture, etc., in the United States,"† while setting forth some of the cardinal doctrines of American education as now held, throws light on the condition of schools and colleges in different parts of the country at that date.

"The first error that I would mention is a

* "The general use of my Spelling Book in the United States has had a most extensive effect in correcting the pronunciation of words, and giving uniformity to the language. Of this change, the present generation can have a very imperfect idea."

† These essays were afterwards collected with others in a volume entitled "A Collection of Essays and Fugitive Writings, etc." By Noah Webster, Jr. Boston: 1790.

too general attention to the dead languages, with a neglect of our own. . . . This neglect is so general that there is scarcely an institution to be found in the country where the English tongue is taught regularly from its elements to its pure and regular construction in prose and verse. Perhaps in most schools boys are taught the definition of the parts of speech, and a few hard names which they do not understand, and which the teacher seldom attempts to explain; this is called learning grammar. . . . The principles of any science afford pleasure to the student who comprehends them. In order to render the study of language agreeable, the distinctions between words should be illustrated by the difference in visible objects. Examples should be presented to the senses which are the inlets of all our knowledge.

"Another error which is frequent in America, is that a master undertakes to teach many different branches in the same school. In new settlements, where the people are poor, and live in scattered situations, the practice is often unavoidable. But in populous towns it must be considered as a defective plan of education. For suppose the teacher to be equally master of all the branches which he attempts to teach, which seldom happens, yet his attention must be distracted with a multiplicity of objects, and consequently painful to himself, and not useful to his pupils. Add to this the continual interruptions which the students of one branch suffer from those of another, which must retard the progress of the whole school. It is a much more eligible plan to appropriate an apartment to each branch of education, with a teacher who makes that branch his sole employment. . . . Indeed what is now called a liberal education disqualifies a man for business. Habits are formed in youth and by practice; and as business is in some measure mechanical, every person should be exercised in his employment in an early period of life, that his habits may be formed by the time his apprenticeship expires. An education in a university interferes with the forming of these habits, and perhaps forms opposite habits; the mind may contract a fondness for ease, for pleasure, or for books, which no efforts can overcome. An academic education, which should furnish the youth with some ideas of men and things, and leave time for an apprenticeship before the age of twenty-one years, would be the most eligible for young men who are designed for active employments.

* * * * * *

"But the principal defect in our plan of education in America is the want of good teachers in the academies and common schools. By good teachers I mean men of unblemished reputation, and possessed of abilities competent to their station. That a man should be master of what he undertakes to teach is a point that will not be disputed; and yet it is certain that abilities are often dispensed with, either through inattention or fear of expense. To those who employ ignorant men to instruct their children, let me say, it is better for youth to have no education than to have a bad one; for it is more difficult to eradicate habits than to impress new ideas. The tender shrub is easily bent to any figure; but the tree which has acquired its full growth resists all impressions. Yet abilities are not the sole requisites. The instructors of youth ought, of all men, to be the most prudent, accomplished, agreeable, and respectable. What avail a man's parts, if, while he is 'the wisest and brightest,' he is the 'meanest of mankind?' The pernicious effects of bad example on the minds of youth will probably be acknowledged; but, with a view to improvement, it is indispensably necessary that the teachers should possess good breeding and agreeable manners. In order to give full effect to instructions it is requisite that they should proceed from a man who is loved and respected. But a low-bred clown or morose tyrant can command neither love nor respect; and that pupil who has no motive for application to books but the fear of the rod, will not make a scholar."

LETTER FROM REV. HEMAN HUMPHREY, D.D.

"PITTSFIELD, Dec. 12th, 1860.

"HON. HENRY BARNARD: *Dear Sir*—I am glad to hear from you, still engaged in the educational cause, and that you are intending to 'give a picturesque survey of the progress of our common schools, their equipment, studies and character.' If my early recollections and experience will give you any little aid, I shall esteem myself happy in affording it.

"The first school I remember was kept a few weeks by a maiden lady, called Miss Faithy, in a barn. I was very young, as were most of the children. What I learned then, if any thing, I have forgotten. This was in the summer, of course. The next was a school, so called, kept a month or two by a neighbor of ours, who was the best *trout fisher*, with his horse-hair line, in all those parts. He wrote a fair hand, as I remember, on birch bark. What he taught us, but to say *tue* and *due*, has escaped my recollection. We had no school-house then in our district, and we met as much for play as any thing, where we could find shelter. The next winter, another neighbor took us a few weeks into one of the rooms of his own house, where every thing but learning was going on. His speech bewrayed him of Rhode Island origin, and whatever he knew, he certainly could never have had much if any chance of being whipped in school when he was a boy. I remember his tremendous *stamp* when we got noisy in school-time, and that is all. This, however, is not a fair sample of school accommodations in my boyhood; and I had a better chance for two or three winters afterward.

"School Houses.—Most of the other districts in the town had school-houses, but not all. The first winter that I kept school myself, was in a room next to the kitchen in a small private house. Some of the school-houses were better than others; but none of them in that or the adjoining towns were convenient or even comfortable. They were rather *juvenile penitentiaries*, than attractive accommodations for study. They were too small, and low from the ceiling to the floor, and the calculation of the builders seemed to have been, to decide into how small a space the children could be crowded, from the fire-place till the room was well packed. Not unfrequently sixty or seventy scholars were daily shut up six hours, where there was hardly room for thirty. The school-houses were square, with a very narrow entry, and a large fire-place on the side near the door. There were no stoves then. They were generally roughly clapboarded, but never painted. They had writing-desks, or rather, long boards for writing, on two or three sides, next to the wall. The benches were all loose; some of them boards, with slabs from the saw-mill, standing on four legs, two at each end. Some were a little lower than the rest, but many of the smaller children had to sit all day with their legs dangling between the bench and the floor. Poor little things! nodding and trying to keep their balance on the slabs, without any backs to lean against, how I pity them to this day. In the coldest weather, it was hard to tell which was the most difficult, to keep from roasting or freezing. For those nearest to the fire it was sweltering hot, while the ink was freezing in the pens on the back side of the room. '*Master*, I am too hot'—'Master, may I go to the fire?' That was the style of address in those days, and we did our best to be *masters*, anyhow.

"All the school-houses that I remember stood close by the travelled road, without any play-grounds or enclosures whatever. If there were any shade trees planted, or left of spontaneous growth, I have forgotten them. And in most cases, there were no outside accommodations, even the most necessary for a moment's occasion. I now marvel at it, but so it was. In that respect, certainly, the days of the children are better than the days of their fathers were.

"For the most part, the winter schools were miserably supplied with wood. I kept school myself in three towns, and in but one of the schools was there any wood-shed whatever; and no wood was got up and seasoned in summer against winter. Most of what we used was standing in the forests when the school began, and was cut and brought sled length by the farmers in proportion to the number of scholars which they sent. Not exactly that, either; for sometimes, when we went to the school-house in a cold morning, there was *no wood* there. Somebody had neglected to bring his load, and we were obliged to adjourn over to the next day. In many cases, the understanding was, that the larger boys must cut the wood as it was wanted. It always lay in the snow, and sometimes the boys were sent to dig it out in school-time, and bring it in, all wet and green as it was, to keep us from freezing. That was the fuel to make fires with in the morning, when the thermometer was below zero, and how the little children cried with the cold, when they came almost frozen, and found no fire burning; nothing but one or two boys blowing and keeping themselves warm as well as they could, by exercise, in trying to kindle it. Such were our school-houses and their disaccommodations.

"Branches Taught in the Schools.—They were reading, spelling, and writing, besides the A B C's to children scarcely four years old, who ought to have been at home with their mothers. They were called up twice a day by the master pointing with his penknife 'What's that?' 'A.' 'What's that?' 'D.' 'No, it's B.' 'What's that?' 'N.' 'No, you careless boy, it's C;' and so down to *ezand.* 'Go to your seat, you will never learn your lesson in the world, at this rate.' Our school-books were the Bible, 'Webster's Spelling Book,' and 'Third Part,' mainly. One or two others were found in some schools for the reading classes. Grammar was hardly taught at all in any of them, and that little was confined almost entirely to committing and reciting the rules. Parsing was one of the occult sciences in my day. We had some few lessons in geography, by questions and answers, but no maps, no globes; and as for *black-boards,* such a thing was never thought of till long after. Children's reading and picture books, we had none; the fables in Webster's Spelling Book came nearest to it. Arithmetic was hardly taught at all in the day schools. As a substitute, there were some evening schools in most of the districts. Spelling was one of the leading daily exercises in all the classes, and it was better, a good deal, I think, than it is now.

"The winter schools were commonly kept about three months; in some favored districts *four*, but rarely as long. As none of what are now called the higher branches were taught beyond the merest elements, parents generally thought that three or four months was enough. There were no winter *select* schools for the young above the age of sixteen or seventeen, as I remember, till after I retired from the profession, such as it then was. There may have been here and there an academy, in some parts of the state; but not one within the range of my acquaintance.

"Our Spring Exhibitions.—At the close of the winter schools we had what we used to call our *Quarter-days*, when the schools came together in the meeting-house, with a large congregation of parents and friends. The public exercises were reading, spelling, and speaking single pieces, and dialogues. Some of the dialogues we wrote ourselves, for our own schools. Most of them were certainly very flat; but they brought down the house, and answered the purpose as well as any we could pick up. We thought then, as I think now, that those quarter-days were of great advantage to the schools. The anticipation of them kept up an interest all winter, and stimulated both teachers and scholars to do their best in the way of preparation. As the time approached, we had evening schools for reading and rehearsing the dialogues, so as to be sure not to fall behind in the exhibitions. None of our college commencements are now looked forward to with greater interest than were those vernal anniversaries.

"Another thing that helped us a good deal was the occasional afternoon visits of the parents and other friends of the schools. They came in by invitation, or whenever they chose, and their visits always did us good.

"Still another practice we found to be quite stimulating and useful. We had a mutual understanding that, without giving any notice, any teacher might dismiss his own school for an afternoon, and, taking along with him some of the older boys, call in to see how his brother teacher got along in the next or some other district. The arrangement worked well. We made speeches, complimented one another as politely as circumstances would allow, and went home resolved not to fall behind the best of them.

"In the school, we made up our minds to be masters, in *fact* as well as in name. Though of late years I have not had very good advantages for making the comparison, I believe the schools were quite as well governed sixty years ago as they are now. Among other things which we did to maintain our authority, was to go out now and then and have a snowball skirmish with the boys, and though we commonly got beat, nothing we could do was more effectual.

"*Corporal* punishments, I believe, were sparingly resorted to in most of our schools. Though I myself believed in Solomon fully, I never flogged but one scholar in my life, though I shook the mischief out of a great many. I think Sam was of the opinion, in the premises, that the rod was laid on rather smartly, for I understood he promised, some day, to pay me in kind, which, however, I suppose he never found it quite convenient to undertake.

"We schoolmasters within convenient distances used to meet in the winter evenings for mutual improvement, which, to own the truth, we needed a good deal. Our regular exercises were reading for criticisms, reporting how we were getting along, and conversing upon the best method of managing our schools. This was very profitable, as we thought, to us all.

"In those ancient times, it was an almost universal custom in the rural towns of Connecticut, for the teachers to *board round*, and upon the whole I liked it. It was a good school for us. By going into all the families we learned a great deal. We were looked upon as having more in our heads than we could fairly claim, and they always kept us on the best they had. It is true, the cooking was not always the best, nor sheets always so clean as to guard against infection; and if, perchance, it sometimes broke out, we knew how to cure it.

"Our wages were generally screwed down to the lowest notch by the school committees, under the instruction of the districts. For my first campaign I received *seven* dollars a month and board; for the next, *nine;* for the third, *ten;* and I think I never went above thirteen till quite the last of my teaching before I went to college. As I had some reputation in that line, I suppose I was as well paid as my brethren.

"With regard to the summer schools of that period, I have very little to say. They were kept by females upon very low wages, about as much a week as they could earn in families by spinning or weaving. They took good care of the little children, and taught them as well as they could.

"As we had no grammar schools in which the languages were taught, we most of us fitted for college with our ministers, who, though not very fresh from their classics, did what they could to help us.

"Finally, you ask me whether there were any schools for young ladies in those old times? There may possibly have been in two or three of the largest towns, but the only one of which I had any knowledge was in Litchfield, kept by Miss Pierce, and I am not quite sure that her school was established as early as your question contemplates.

"These, dear sir, are some of my old remembrances, which you may make such use of as you please.

"Respectfully yours,

"H. HUMPHREY."

LETTER FROM HON. JOSEPH T. BUCKINGHAM.

"CAMBRIDGE, Dec. 10th, 1860.

"HENRY BARNARD, ESQ.: *My Dear Sir*—I cheerfully comply with your request to give you some account of the schools and the educational books that were in use about the close of the last century. I never had the privilege of attending any higher institution of learning than the common district schools of Connecticut, in the town of Windham; but I have no doubt that those of that town were a fair type of many others, probably most of them, except such as were kept in the larger towns or thickly populated villages.

"According to the best of my remembrance, my school-days began in the spring of 1783. The school to which I was admitted was kept by a lady, and, like most of the district schools, was kept only for the younger pupils, and was open for two months during the summer season. The upper class in the school was formed entirely of females—such as could read in the Bible. The lower classes read in spelling books and the New England Primer. The spelling books, of which there were not, probably, more than three or four in the school, I believe were all by Dilworth, and were much worn and defaced, having been a sort of heir-loom in the families of the pupils. The teacher of this school was the daughter of the minister of the parish. She kept a rod hanging on the wall behind her chair and a ferule on the table by her side; but I do not recollect that she used either of them. The girls who constituted the first class were required, every Monday morning, to repeat the text or texts of the preceding day's discourse, stating the book, chapter, and verse whence it was taken. The next summer, 1784, the same lady, or one of her sisters, kept school in the same district. The same books were in use, and there was the same routine of exercises. It was kept on the first floor of the steeple. The lower end of the bell-rope lay in a coil in the centre of the floor. The discipline was so strict, that no one, however mischievously disposed, I believe ever thought of taking hold of it, though it was something of an incumbrance. I was then four years and a half old, and had learned *by heart* nearly all the reading lessons in the Primer, and much of the Westminster Catechism, which was taught as the closing exercise every Saturday. But justice to one of the best of mothers requires that I should say that much the greater part of the improvement I had made was acquired from her careful instruction.

"In December, 1784, the month in which I was five years old, I attended, for a few days, the school kept by a master—I do not remember his name. When asked up for examination, he asked me if I could read without spelling? I said I could read in the Bible. He hesitated a moment, and then placed me on one of the benches, opened a Bible at the fifth chapter of Acts, and asked me to read. I read ten or a dozen verses—being the account of Ananias and his wife falling dead before Peter for telling a lie. Whether he had any suspicion that I had told a falsehood, and took this method to reprove me, I know not; but he dismissed me with approbation. He used his ferule on the hands of some of the elder boys; but the severest punishment that he inflicted for any violation of order, was compelling a boy who had brought into the school the breast-bone of a chicken, (commonly called the *wishing-bone*,) and with which he had excited some noise among the pupils, to stand on one of the benches and wear the bone on his nose till the school was dismissed. I am strongly impressed with the belief that Webster's spelling book made its first appearance in the schools during this winter. The following summer I attended, but very irregularly, a school kept as before in the steeple of the meeting-house,* and had a copy of Webster. Whether there were any other copies in the school or not I am not able to say. The next two winters, circumstances which I have no desire to recall, and which you would not care to be acquainted with, prevented my attending any school. In the summer of 1786, these same circumstances caused me to be removed to another district three miles distant from the central village. The farmer with whom I lived thought I could read well enough, and as the district school-house was a mile or more distant, he considered it unnecessary to send me that distance in the winter, merely *to read;* and consequently for two or three winters I went to school not more than eight or ten days in each. At length, in 1790 or 1791, it was thought I was old enough to learn to *cipher*, and accordingly was permitted to go to school more constantly. I told the master I wanted to learn to cipher. He set me a *sum* in simple addition—*five columns* of figures, and *six figures* in each column. All the instruction he gave me was—add the figures in the first column, carry one for every ten, and set the overplus down under the column. I supposed he meant by the *first* column the left hand column; but what he meant by carrying one for every ten was as much a mystery as Samson's riddle was to the Philistines. I worried my brains an hour or two, and showed the master the figures I had made. You may judge what the amount was, when the columns were added from left to right. The master frowned and repeated his former instruction—add up the column *on the right*, carry one for every ten, and set down the remainder. Two or three afternoons (I did not go to school in the morning) were spent in this way, when I begged to be excused from learning to cipher, and the old gentleman with whom I lived thought it was time wasted; and if I attended the school any further at that time, reading and spelling, and a little writing were all that was taught. The next winter there was a teacher more communicative and better fitted for his place, and under him some progress was made in arithmetic, and I made a tolerable acquisition in the first four rules, according to Dilworth's Schoolmaster's Assistant, of which the teacher and one of the eldest boys had each a copy. The two following winters, 1794 and 1795, I mastered all the rules and examples in the first part of Dilworth; that is, through the various chapters of Rule of Three, Practice, Fellowship, Interest, etc. etc., to Geometrical Progression and Permutation.

"In our district, the books were of rather a miscellaneous character, such as had been in families perhaps half a century or more. My belief is that Webster's Spelling Book was not in general use before 1790 or 1791. The Bible was read by the first class in the morning, always, and generally in the afternoon before the closing exercise, which was always a lesson in spelling, and this was performed by all the pupils who were sufficiently advanced to pronounce distinctly words of more than one syllable. It was the custom for all such pupils to stand together as one class, and with *one voice* to read a column or two of the tables for spelling. The master gave the signal to begin, and all united to read, letter by letter, pronouncing each syllable by itself, and adding it to the preceding one till the word was complete. Thus, a-d *ad*, m-i *mi*, *admi*, r-a *ra*, *admira*, t-i-o-n *shun*, *admiration*. This mode of reading was exceedingly exciting, and, in my humble judgment, exceedingly useful; as it required and taught deliberate and distinct articulation, and inspired the youngest with a desire

* This was the last time I went to a *summer* school.

to equal the older ones. It is true the voices would not all be in perfect unison; but after a little practice they began to assimilate. I have heard a class of thirty or more read column after column in this manner, with scarcely a perceptible variation from the proper pitch of voice. When the lesson had been thus read, the books were closed, and the words given out for spelling. If one was misspelt, it passed on to the next, and the next pupil in order, and so on till it was spelt correctly. Then the pupil who had spelt correctly went up in the class *above* the one who had misspelt. It was also a practice, when one was absent from this exercise in spelling, that he should stand at the foot of the class when he returned. Another of our customs was to choose sides to spell once or twice a week. The words to be spelt went from side to side; and at the conclusion, the side which *beat* (spelt the most words) were permitted to leave the schoolroom, preceding the other side, who had to sweep the room and build the fires the next morning. These customs prevalent sixty and seventy years ago excited emulation, and emulation produced improvement. A revival of them, I have no doubt, would be advantageous in the common schools, especially where pupils are required to spell words given out indiscriminately from a reading book or dictionary. There was not, to my knowledge, any *reading book* proper, except the Bible, till Webster's Third Book, so called, came out about 1793 or 1794. A new edition of his spelling book furnished some new matter for reading—selections from the New Testament, a chapter of Proverbs, and a set of Tables, etc.; but none of these operated to the exclusion of the Bible.

"In the family in which I lived there were three or four old spelling books, which I presume had been used in schools before the period of my remembrance. One of these was a book of less than a hundred pages, printed in London, I think in 1690. The words were arranged in tables according to syllables. The terminations tion, sion, cial, tial, etc., were all divided and printed as two distinct syllables. (And I believe this mode of printing is still continued in England. It was in the time of Lindley Murray, as may be seen in his spelling book, printed about forty years ago.) This spelling book contained a numeration table which, from a singular feature, early attracted my attention. Every figure was 9, and the whole formed a curious triangle. Thus:

9
99
999 and so on to
the last, 999,999,999

"Another spelling book in our farmer's library was by Daniel Fenning, printed in London. It contained a short treatise on grammar, on which I sometimes exercised my memory, but understood not one of its principles. We had also a Dilworth, containing certain fables—such as Jupiter and the Frogs, the Romish Priest and the Jester, Hercules and the Wagoner, etc., etc. Another still we had, the author of which I never knew, as several pages had been lost from the beginning. It had a page of proverbs, one of which—'a cat may look upon a king'—occasioned me much thoughtful exercise. It also had an appropriate collection of couplets for writing-copies, of which the only one I recollect was this:

> "'X things a penman should have near at hand—
> Paper, pounce, pen, ink, knife, hone, rule, plummet, wax, sand.'

But that which rendered the book so memorable as never to be forgotten, was the astonishing, if not terrific, word of fourteen syllables — 'Ho-no-ri-fi-ca-bi-li-tu-di-ni-tu-ti-bus-que'—asserted to be the longest word in the English language.

"In the winter of 1793–4, we had for a teacher Erastus Ripley, who was an under-graduate of Yale College. I mention his name, because I cannot look back upon the time when I had the advantage of his instruction without a feeling of reverence for the man and respect for the teacher. I learned more from him than all the schoolmasters I had been under. He took more pains to instruct us in reading than all his predecessors within my knowledge. He opened the school every morning with prayer—which had not been practised in our district. He was preparing for the ministry, and was afterwards settled at Canterbury, I think. He was highly esteemed by all the people of the district, and gave such an *impetus* to the ambition of the pupils, that a subscription was made to employ him an extra month after the usual term of the school had expired.

"Mr. Ripley was succeeded in the winter of 1794–5 by a young man from Lebanon by the name of Tisdale, under whom my school days were finished; and here I may bring this long and, I fear, very uninteresting letter to a close. Hoping this may serve the purpose for which you suggested the writing of it, and wishing you all the success you can desire in the noble cause in which you are engaged,

"I am, very respectfully
"And truly yours,
"JOSEPH T. BUCKINGHAM."

LETTER FROM REV. ELIPHALET NOTT, D.D., DATED JAN., 1861.

"When I was a boy, seventy-five or eighty years ago, in good old Puritan Connecticut, it was *felt* as a practical maxim 'that to spare the rod was to spoil the child;' and on this maxim the pedagogue acted in the school-room, and applied it for every offence, real or imaginary; and for having been whipped at school by the relentless master, the unfortunate tyro was often whipped at home by his no less relentless father; so that between the two relentless executors of justice among the Puritan fathers, few children, I believe, were spoiled by the withholding of this orthodox discipline. For myself, I can say (and I do not think I was wayward beyond the average of district school-boys) that, in addition to warnings, and admonitions daily, if I was not whipped more than three times a week, I considered myself for the time peculiarly fortunate.

"Being of a contemplative and forbearing disposition, this discipline of the rod became peculiarly irksome to me, and, as I thought, unjustifiable; and I formed a resolution, if I lived to be a man, I would not be like other men in regard to their treatment of children.

"Through the mercy of God I did live to be a man, and when at the age of eighteen I became installed as master of a district school in the eastern part of Franklin, Connecticut—a school where rebellious spirits had previously asserted their rights, and been subdued or driven from the school by the use of the rod—nothing daunted, I made up my mind to substitute in my school moral motives in the place of the rod; and I frankly told my assembled pupils so, and that if they would have the generosity to second my efforts, they would secure to themselves and furnish me and their parents the happiness which is the heaven-appointed reward of well-doing.

"The school responded to my appeal, and thereafter, though we played and gambolled together as equals in play-hours, and on Saturday afternoons, which were also devoted to play, the moment we entered the school-room, a subordination and application to study was observable, that became matter of remark and admiration among the inhabitants of the district, the fame of which success extended to other districts, and even to adjoining towns, so that the examination and exhibition with which the school closed the ensuing spring, called together clergymen and other officials from places quite remote.

"This success brought me to the knowledge of the trustees of the Plainfield Academy, one of the most important, if not at the time the most important academy in the state, and I was by a unanimous vote appointed principal of said academy—an institution in which several hundred children of both sexes were in the same building successfully taught and governed, for years, without the use of the rod, it being at that time the prevailing usage, both in district schools and academies, for the two sexes to be taught in the same room, and subjected to the same form of government.

"This successful experiment in the use of moral suasion, and other kindred and kindly influences, in place of the rod, led to other and kindred experiments, until, whether for the better or the worse, the rod at length came to occupy a very subordinate place in the system of school education.

"In those days, education in common schools was not so diffusive as at the present day; but quite as thorough, if not more so. The same remark may be applied to the higher schools or academies—the whole field of natural science being at that time, for the most part, unexplored; but mathematics and classics were zealously taught. In evidence of this, though inferior in attainments to some of my classmates, I published successfully myself an almanac when about twenty-one years of age.

"As the rod in those days was the principal instrument in common school education, so when I was afterward called to Union College, fines, suspensions, and expulsions were the principal instruments of collegiate government. The faculty sat in their robes as a court, caused offenders to be brought before them, examined witnesses, heard defences, and pronounced sentences with the solemnity of other courts of justice; and though Union College had on its catalogue but a very diminutive number of students, the sitting of the faculty as a court occupied no inconsiderable part of the time of its president and professors.

"Soon after I became connected with the college as its president, a case of discipline occurred which led to the trial and issued in the expulsion of a student belonging to a very respectable family in the city of Albany. According to the charter of Union College, the sentence of the faculty is not final. An appeal can be taken to the board of trustees, and in the case in question an appeal was taken, and, after keeping college in confusion for months, by the different hearings of the case, the board reversed the decision of the faculty, and restored the young man. On the event of this restoration, I informed them that they should never, during my administration, have occasion to review another case of discipline by the faculty; and during the fifty-six years which have since passed away, I have kept my word; and though we have been less successful in our system of parental government than could be wished, we have had no rebellions, and it is conceded, I believe generally, that quite as large a proportion of our young men have succeeded in after life as of any other collegiate institution in the Union."

RECOLLECTIONS OF PETER PARLEY.

The following picture of the District School as it was a few years later, in the town of Ridgefield,* one of the most advanced agricultural communities of Connecticut, is from the pen of Peter Parley, in his "*Recollections of a Lifetime.*"

"About three fourths of a mile from my father's house, on the winding road to Lower Salem, which bore the name of West Lane, was the school-house where I took my first lessons, and received the foundations of my very slender education. I have since been sometimes asked where I graduated: my reply has always been, 'At West Lane.' Generally speaking, this has ended the inquiry, whether because my interlocutors have confounded this venerable institution with 'Lane Seminary,' or have not thought it worth while to risk an exposure of their ignorance as to the college in which I was educated, I am unable to say.

"The site of the school-house was a triangular piece of land, measuring perhaps a rood in extent, and lying, according to the custom of those days, at the meeting of four roads. The ground hereabouts—as everywhere else in Ridgefield—was exceedingly stony, and in making the pathway the stones had been thrown out right and left, and there remained in heaps on either side, from generation to generation. All round was bleak and desolate. Loose, squat stone walls, with innumerable breaches, inclosed adjacent fields. A few tufts of elder, with here and there a patch of briers and pokeweed, flourished in the gravelly soil. Not a tree, however, remained, save an aged chestnut, at the western angle of the space. This certainly had not been spared for shade or ornament, but probably because it would have cost too much labor to cut it down, for it was of ample girth. At all events it was the oasis in our desert during summer; and in autumn, as the burrs disclosed its fruit, it resembled a besieged city. The boys, like so many catapults, hurled at it stones and sticks, until every nut had capitulated.

"Two houses only were at hand: one, surrounded by an ample barn, a teeming orchard, and an enormous wood-pile, belonged to Granther Baldwin; the other was the property of 'Old Chich-es-ter,' an uncouth, unsocial being, whom everybody for some reason or other seemed to despise and shun. His house was of stone and of one story. He had a cow, which every year had a calf. He had a wife—filthy, uncombed, and vaguely reported to have been brought from the old country. This is about the whole history of the man, so far as it is written in the authentic traditions of the parish. His

* "Nearly all the inhabitants of Ridgefield were farmers, with the few mechanics that were necessary to carry on society in a somewhat primeval state. Even the persons not professionally devoted to agriculture, had each his farm, or at least his garden and home lot, with his pigs, poultry, and cattle. The population might have been 1200, comprising 200 families. All could read and write, but in point of fact, beyond the Almanac and Watts' Psalms and Hymns, their literary acquirements had little scope. There were, I think, four newspapers, all weekly, published in the state: one at Hartford, one at New London, one at New Haven, and one at Litchfield. There were, however, not more than three subscribers to all these in our village. We had, however, a public library of some 200 volumes, and what was of equal consequence—the town was on the road which was then the great thoroughfare, connecting Boston with New York, and hence it had means of intelligence from travellers constantly passing through the place, which kept it up with the march of events."

premises, an acre in extent, consisted of a tongue of land between two of the converging roads. No boy, that I ever heard of, ventured to cast a stone or to make an incursion into this territory, though it lay close to the school-house. I have often, in passing, peeped timidly over the walls, and caught glimpses of a stout man with a drab coat, drab breeches, and drab gaiters, glazed with ancient grease and long abrasion, prowling about the house; but never did I discover him outside of his own dominion. I know it was darkly intimated that he had been a tory, and was tarred and feathered in the revolutionary war, but as to the rest he was a perfect myth. Granther Baldwin was a character no less marked, but I must reserve his picture for a subsequent letter.

"The school-house itself consisted of rough, unpainted clapboards, upon a wooden frame. It was plastered within, and contained two apartments—a little entry, taken out of a corner for a wardrobe, and the school-room proper. The chimney was of stone, and pointed with mortar, which, by the way, had been dug into a honeycomb by uneasy and enterprising penknives. The fireplace was six feet wide and four feet deep. The flue was so ample and so perpendicular, that the rain, sleet, and snow fell direct to the hearth. In winter, the battle for life with green fizzling fuel, which was brought in sled lengths and cut up by the scholars, was a stern one. Not unfrequently, the wood, gushing with sap as it was, chanced to be out, and as there was no living without fire, the thermometer being ten or twenty degrees below zero, the school was dismissed, whereat all the scholars rejoiced aloud, not having the fear of the schoolmaster before their eyes.

"It was the custom at this place to have a woman's school in the summer months, and this was attended only by young children. It was, in fact, what we now call a primary or infant school. In winter, a man was employed as teacher, and then the girls and boys of the neighborhood, up to the age of eighteen, or even twenty, were among the pupils. It was not uncommon, at this season, to have forty scholars crowded into this little building.

"I was about six years old when I first went to school. My teacher was Aunt Delight, that is, Delight Benedict, a maiden lady of fifty, short and bent, of sallow complexion and solemn aspect. I remember the first day with perfect distinctness. I went alone—for I was familiar with the road, it being that which passed by our old house. I carried a little basket, with bread and butter within, for my dinner, the same being covered over with a white cloth. When I had proceeded about half way, I lifted the cover, and debated whether I would not eat my dinner then. I believe it was a sense of duty only that prevented my doing so, for in those happy days I always had a keen appetite. Bread and butter were then infinitely superior to *paté de foie gras* now; but still, thanks to my training, I had also a conscience. As my mother had given me the food for dinner, I did not think it right to convert it into lunch, even though I was strongly tempted.

"I think we had seventeen scholars—boys and girls—mostly of my own age. Among them were some of my after companions. I have since met several of them—one at Savannah, and two at Mobile, respectably established, and with families around them. Some remain, and are now among the gray old men of the town; the names of others I have seen inscribed on the tombstones of their native village. And the rest—where are they?

"The school being organized, we were all seated upon benches, made of what were called *slabs*—that is, boards having the exterior or rounded part of the log on one side: as they were useless for other purposes, these were converted into school-benches, the rounded part down. They had each four supports, consisting of straddling wooden legs, set into auger holes. Our own legs swayed in the air, for they were too short to touch the floor. Oh, what an awe fell over me, when we were all seated and silence reigned around!

"The children were called up, one by one, to Aunt Delight, who sat on a low chair, and required each, as a preliminary, to make his manners, consisting of a small sudden nod or jerk of the head. She then placed the spelling-book—which was Dilworth's—before the pupil, and with a buck-handled penknife pointed, one by one, to the letters of the alphabet, saying, 'What's that?' If the child knew his letters the 'What's that?' very soon ran on thus:

"'What's that?'

"'A.'

"''Stha-a-t?'

"'B.'

"'Sna-a-a-t?'
"'C.'
"'Sna-a-a-t?'
"'D.'
"'Sna-a-a-t?'
"'E.' &c.

"I looked upon these operations with intense curiosity and no small respect, until my own turn came. I went up to the school-mistress with some emotion, and when she said, rather spitefully, as I thought, 'Make your obeisance!' my little intellects all fled away, and I did nothing. Having waited a second, gazing at me with indignation, she laid her hand on the top of my head, and gave it a jerk which made my teeth clash. I believe I bit my tongue a little; at all events, my sense of dignity was offended, and when she pointed to A, and asked what it was, it swam before me dim and hazy, and as big as a full moon. She repeated the question, but I was doggedly silent. Again, a third time, she said, 'What's that?' I replied: 'Why don't you tell me what it is? I didn't come here to learn you your letters!' I have not the slightest remembrance of this, for my brains were all a-wool-gathering; but as Aunt Delight affirmed it to be a fact, and it passed into tradition, I put it in. I may have told this story some years ago in one of my books, imputing it to a fictitious hero, yet this is its true origin, according to my recollection.

"What immediately followed I do not clearly remember, but one result is distinctly traced in my memory. In the evening of this eventful day, the school-mistress paid my parents a visit, and recounted to their astonished ears this, my awful contempt of authority. My father, after hearing the story, got up and went away; but my mother, who was a careful disciplinarian, told me not to do so again! I always had a suspicion that both of them smiled on one side of their faces, even while they seemed to sympathize with the old petticoat and penknife pedagogue, on the other; still I do not affirm it, for I am bound to say, of both my parents, that I never knew them, even in trifles, say one thing while they meant another.

"I believe I achieved the alphabet that summer, but my after progress, for a long time, I do not remember. Two years later I went to the winter-school at the same place, kept by Lewis Olmstead—a man who had a call for plowing, mowing, carting manure, etc., in summer, and for teaching school in the winter, with a talent for music at all seasons, wherefore he became chorister upon occasion, when, peradventure, Deacon Hawley could not officiate. He was a celebrity in ciphering, and 'Squire Seymour declared that he was the greatest 'arithmeticker' in Fairfield county. All I remember of his person is his hand, which seemed to me as big as Goliah's, judging by the claps of thunder it made in my ears on one or two occasions.

"The next step of my progress which is marked in my memory, is the spelling of words of two syllables. I did not go very regularly to school, but by the time I was ten years old I had learned to write, and had made a little progress in arithmetic. There was not a grammar, a geography, or a history of any kind in the school. Reading, writing, and arithmetic were the only things taught, and these very indifferently—not wholly from the stupidity of the teacher, but because he had forty scholars, and the standards of the age required no more than he performed. I did as well as the other scholars, certainly no better. I had excellent health and joyous spirits; in leaping, running, and wrestling, I had but one superior of my age, and that was Stephen Olmstead, a snug-built fellow, smaller than myself, and who, despite our rivalry, was my chosen friend and companion. I seemed to live for play: alas! how the world has changed since I have discovered that we live to agonize over study, work, care, ambition, disappointment, and then ——?

"As I shall not have occasion again, formally, to introduce this seminary into my narrative, I may as well close my account of it now. After I had left my native town for some twenty years, I returned and paid it a visit. Among the monuments that stood high in my memory was the West Lane school-house. Unconsciously carrying with me the measures of childhood, I had supposed it to be at least thirty feet square; how had it dwindled when I came to estimate it by the new standards I had formed! It was in all things the same, yet wholly changed to me. What I had deemed a respectable edifice, as it now stood before me was only a weather-beaten little shed, which, upon being measured, I found to be less than twenty feet square. It happened to be a warm, summer day, and I ventured to enter the place. I found a girl, some eighteen years old, keeping 'a ma'am school' for about twenty scholars, some of whom were studying Parley's Geography. The mistress was the daughter of one of my schoolmates, and some of the boys and girls were grandchildren of the little brood which gathered under the wing of Aunt Delight, when I was an a-b-c-darian. None of them, not even the school-mistress, had ever heard of me. The name of my father, as having ministered unto the people of Ridgefield in some bygone age, was faintly traced in their recollection. As to Peter Parley, whose Geography they were learning—they supposed him some decrepit old gentleman hobbling about on a crutch, a long way off, for whom, nevertheless, they had a certain affection, inasmuch as he had made geography into a story-book. The frontispiece-picture of the old fellow, with his gouty foot in a chair, threatening the boys that if they touched his tender toe, he would tell them no more stories, secured their respect, and placed him among the saints in the calendar of their young hearts. Well, thought I, if this goes on I may yet rival Mother Goose!

"At the age of ten years I was sent to the up-town school, the leading seminary of the village, for at this period it had not arrived at the honor of an academy, the institution being then, and many years after, under the charge of Master Stebbins. He was a man with a conciliating stoop in the shoulders, a long body, short legs, and a swaying walk. He was, at this period, some fifty years old, his hair being thin and silvery, and always falling in well-combed rolls over his coat-collar. His eye was blue, and his dress invariably of the same color. Breeches and knee-buckles, blue-mixed stockings, and shoes with bright buckles, seemed as much a part of the man as his head and shoulders. On the whole, his appearance was that of the middle-class gentleman of the olden time, and he was in fact what he seemed.

"This seminary of learning for the rising aristocracy of Ridgefield was a wooden edifice, thirty by twenty feet, covered with brown clapboards, and, except an entry, consisted of a single room. Around and against the walls ran a continuous line of seats, fronted by a continuous writing-desk. Beneath, were depositories for books and writing materials. The centre was occupied by slab seats, similar to those of West Lane. The larger scholars were ranged on the outer sides, at the desks; the smaller fry of a-b-c-darians were seated in the centre. The master was enshrined on the east side of the room, contrary, be it remembered, to the law of the French savans, which places dominion invariably in the west. Regular as the sun, Master Stebbins was in his seat at nine o'clock, and the performances of the school began.

"According to the Catechism—which, by the way, we learned and recited on Saturday—the chief end of man was to glorify God and keep his commandments: according to the routine of this school, one would have thought it to be reading, writing, and arithmetic, to which we may add spelling. From morning to night, in all weathers, through every season of the year, these exercises were carried on with the energy, patience, and perseverance of a manufactory.

"Master Stebbins respected his calling: his heart was in his work; and so, what he pretended to teach, he taught well. When I entered the school, I found that a huge stride had been achieved in the march of mind since I had left West Lane. Webster's Spelling Book had taken the place of Dilworth, which was a great improvement. The drill in spelling was very thorough, and applied every day to the whole school. I imagine that the exercises might have been amusing to a stranger, especially as one scholar would sometimes go off in a voice as grum as that of a bull-frog, while another would follow in tones as fine and piping as a peet-weet. The blunders, too, were often ineffably ludicrous; even we children would sometimes have tittered, had not such an enormity been certain to have brought out the birch. As to rewards and punishments, the system was this: whoever missed went down; so that perfection mounted to the top. Here was the beginning of the up and down of life.

"Reading was performed in classes, which generally plodded on without a hint from the master. Nevertheless, when Zeek Sanford—who was said to have a streak of lightning in him—in his haste to be smart, read the 37th verse of the 2d chapter of the Acts—'Now when they heard this, they were *pickled* in their heart'—the birch stick on Master Stebbins's table seemed to quiver and peel at the little end, as if to give warning of the wrath to come. When Orry Keeler—Orry was a girl, you know, and not a boy—drawled out in spelling: k—o—n, *kon*, s—h—u—n—t—s, *shunts*, konshunts—the bristles in the master's eyebrows fidgeted like Aunt Delight's knitting-needles. Occasionally, when the reading was insupportably bad, he took a book and read himself, as an example.

"We were taught arithmetic in Daboll, then a new book, and which, being adapted to our measures of length, weight, and currency, was a prodigious leap over the head of poor old Dilworth, whose rules and examples were modelled upon English customs. In consequence of the general use of Dilworth in our schools, for perhaps a century—pounds, shillings, and pence were classical, and dollars and cents vulgar, for several succeeding generations. 'I would not give a penny for it,' was genteel; 'I would not give a cent for it,' was plebeian. We have not yet got over this: we sometimes say *red cent* in familiar parlance, but it can hardly be put in print without offence.

"Master Stebbins was a great man with a slate and pencil, and I have an idea that we were a generation after his own heart. We certainly achieved wonders according to our own conceptions, some of us going even beyond the Rule of Three, and making forays into the mysterious region of Vulgar Fractions. Several daring geniuses actually entered and took possession.

"But after all, penmanship was Master Stebbins's great accomplishment. He had no magniloquent system; no pompous lessons upon single lines and bifid lines, and the like. The revelations of inspired copy-book makers had not then been vouchsafed to man. He could not cut an American eagle with a single flourish of a goose-quill. He was guided by good taste and native instinct, and wrote a smooth round hand, like copper-plate. His lessons from A to &, all written by himself, consisted of pithy proverbs and useful moral lessons. On every page of our writing-books he wrote the first line himself. The effect was what might have been expected—with such models, patiently enforced, nearly all became good writers.

"Beyond these simple elements, the Uptown school made few pretensions. When I was there, two Webster's Grammars and one or two Dwight's Geographies were in use. The latter was without maps or illustrations, and was in fact little more than an expanded table of contents, taken from Morse's Universal Geography—the mammoth monument of American learning and genius of that age and generation. The grammar was a clever book; but I have an idea that neither Master Stebbins nor his pupils ever fathomed its depths. They floundered about in it, as if in a quagmire, and after some time came out pretty nearly where they went in, though perhaps a little obfuscated by the dim and dusky atmosphere of these labyrinths.

"The fact undoubtedly is, that the art of teaching, as now understood, beyond the simplest elements, was neither known nor deemed necessary in our country schools in their day of small things. Repetition, drilling, line upon line, and precept upon precept, with here and there a little of the birch—constituted the entire system.

"Let me here repeat an anecdote, which I have indeed told before, but which I had from the lips of its hero, G . . . H . . ., a clergyman of some note thirty years ago, and which well illustrates this part of my story. At a village school, not many miles from Ridgefield, he was put into Webster's Grammar. Here he read, '*A noun is the name of a thing—as horse, hair, justice.*' Now in his innocence, he read it thus: '*A noun is the name of a thing—as horse-hair justice.*'

"'What then,' said he, ruminating deeply, 'is a noun? But first I must find out what a horse-hair justice is.'

"Upon this he meditated for some days, but still he was as far as ever from the solution. Now his father was a man of authority in those parts, and moreover he was a justice of the peace. Withal, he was of respectable ancestry, and so there had descended to him a somewhat stately high-backed settee, covered with horse-hair. One day, as the youth came from school, pondering upon the great grammatical problem, he entered the front door of the house, and there he saw before him, his father, officiating in his legal capacity, and seated upon the old horse-hair settee. 'I have found it!' said the boy to himself, as greatly delighted as was Archimedes when he exclaimed *Eureka*—'my father is a horse-hair justice, and therefore a noun!'

"Nevertheless, it must be admitted that the world got on remarkably well in spite of this narrowness of the country schools. The elements of an English education were pretty well taught throughout the village seminaries of Connecticut, and I may add, of New England. The teachers were heartily devoted to their profession: they respected their calling, and were respected and encouraged by the community. They had this merit, that while they attempted but little, that, at least, was thoroughly performed.

"As to the country at large, it was a day of quiet, though earnest action: Franklin's spirit was the great 'schoolmaster abroad'—teaching industry, perseverance, frugality, and thrift, as the end and aim of ambition. The education of youth was suited to what was expected of them. With the simple lessons of the country schools, they moved the world immediately around them. Though I can recollect only a single case—that already alluded to of Ezekiel Sanford—in which one of Master Stebbins's scholars attained any degree of literary distinction, still, quite a number of them, with no school learning beyond what he gave them, rose to a certain degree of eminence. His three sons obtained situations in New York as accountants, and became distinguished in their career. At one period there were three graduates of his school, who were cashiers of banks in that city. My mind adverts now with great satisfaction to several names among the wealthy, honorable, and still active merchants of the great metropolis, who were my fellow-students of the Up-town school, and who there began and completed their education."

To the advantages, such as they were, of the district school, Mr. Goodrich adds an account of his experience on the farm, and his juvenile sports, as well as his early attempts at *whittling* and other mechanical arts, and adds the following reflections:—

"Now all these things may seem trifles, yet in a review of my life, I deem them of some significance. This homely familiarity with the more mechanical arts was a material part of my education; this communion with nature gave me instructive and important lessons from nature's open book of knowledge. My technical education, as will be seen hereafter, was extremely narrow and irregular. This defect was at last partially supplied by the commonplace incidents I have mentioned. The teaching, or rather the training of the senses, in the country—ear and eye, foot and hand, by running, leaping, climbing over hill and mountain, by occasional labor in the garden and on the farm, and by the use of tools—and all this in youth, is sowing seed which is repaid largely and readily to the hand of after cultivation, however unskilful it may be. This is not so much because of the amount of knowledge available in after-life, which is thus obtained—though this is not to be despised—as it is that healthful, vigorous, manly habits and associations—physical, moral, and intellectual—are thus established and developed.

"It is a riddle to many people that the emigrants from the country into the city, in all ages, outstrip the natives, and become their masters. The reason is obvious: country education and country life are practical, and invigorating to body and mind, and hence those who are thus qualified triumph in the race of life. It has always been, it will always be so; the rustic Goths and Vandals will march in and conquer Rome, in the future, as they have done in the past. I say this, by no means insisting that my own life furnishes any very striking proof of the truth of my remarks; still, I may say that but for the country training and experience I have alluded to, and which served as a foothold for subsequent progress, I should have lingered in my career far behind the humble advances I have actually made.

"Let me illustrate and verify my meaning by specific examples. In my youth I became familiar with every bird common to the country: I knew his call, his song, his hue, his food, his habits; in short, his natural history. I could detect him by his flight, as far as the eye could reach. I knew all the quadrupeds—wild as well as tame. I was acquainted with almost every tree, shrub, bush, and flower, indigenous to the country; not botanically, but according to popular ideas. I recognized them instantly, wherever I saw them; I knew their forms, hues, leaves, blossoms, and fruit. I could tell their characteristics, their uses, the legends and traditions that belonged to them. All this I learned by familiarity with these objects; meeting with them in all my walks and rambles, and taking note of them with the emphasis and vigor of early experience and observation. In after days, I have never had time to make natural history a systematic study; yet my knowledge as to these things has constantly accumulated, and that without special effort. When I have travelled in other countries, the birds, the animals, the vegetation, have interested me as well by their resemblances as their differences, when compared with our own.

In looking over the pages of scientific works on natural history, I have always read with eagerness and intelligence of preparation; indeed, of vivid and pleasing associations. Every idea I had touching these matters was living and sympathetic, and beckoned other ideas to it, and these again originated still others. Thus it is that in the race of a busy life, by means of a homely, hearty start at the beginning, I have, as to these subjects, easily and naturally supplied, in some humble degree, the defects of my irregular education, and that too, not by a process of repulsive toil, but with a relish superior to all the seductions of romance. I am therefore a believer in the benefits accruing from simple country life and simple country habits, as here illustrated, and am, therefore, on all occasions anxious to recommend them to my friends and countrymen. To city people, I would say, educate your children, at least partially, in the country, so as to imbue them with the love of nature, and that knowledge and training which spring from simple rustic sports, exercises, and employments. To country people, I would remark, be not envious of the city, for in the general balance of good and evil, you have your full portion of the first, with a diminished share of the last."

THE HOMESPUN ERA OF COMMON SCHOOLS.
BY HORACE BUSHNELL, D.D.

"But the schools—we must not pass by these, if we are to form a truthful and sufficient picture of the homespun days. The schoolmaster did not exactly go round the district to fit out the children's minds with learning, as the shoemaker often did to fit their feet with shoes, or the tailor to measure and cut for their bodies; but, to come as near it as possible, he boarded round, (a custom not yet gone by,) and the wood for the common fire was supplied in a way equally primitive, viz., by a contribution of loads from the several families, according to their several quantities of childhood. The children were all clothed alike in homespun; and the only signs of aristocracy were, that some were clean and some a degree less so, some in fine white and striped linen, some in brown tow crash; and, in particular, as I remember, with a certain feeling of quality I do not like to express, the good fathers of some testified the opinion they had of their children, by bringing fine round loads of hickory wood to warm them, while some others, I regret to say, brought only scanty, scraggy, ill-looking heaps of green oak, white birch, and hemlock. Indeed, about all the bickerings of quality among the children, centered in the quality of the wood pile. There was no complaint, in those days, of the want of ventilation; for the large open fire-place held a considerable fraction of a cord of wood, and the windows took in just enough air to supply the combustion. Besides, the bigger lads were occasionally ventilated, by being sent out to cut wood enough to keep the fire in action. The seats were made of the outer slabs from the saw-mill, supported by slant legs driven into and a proper distance through auger holes, and planed smooth on the top by the rather tardy process of friction. But the spelling went on bravely, and we ciphered away again and again, always till we got through Loss and Gain. The more advanced of us, too, made light work of Lindley Murray, and went on to the parsing, finally, of extracts from Shakspeare and Milton, till some of us began to think we had mastered their tough sentences in a more consequential sense of the term than was exactly true. O, I remember (about the remotest thing I can remember) that low seat, too high, nevertheless, to allow the feet to touch the floor, and that friendly teacher who had the address to start a first feeling of enthusiasm and awaken the first sense of power. He is living still, and whenever I think of him, he rises up to me in the far background of memory, as bright as if he had worn the seven stars in his hair. (I said he is living; yes, he is here to-day, God bless him!) How many others of you that are here assembled, recall these little primitive universities of homespun, where your mind was born, with a similar feeling of reverence and homely satisfaction. Perhaps you remember, too, with a pleasure not less genuine, that you received the classic discipline of the university proper, under a dress of homespun, to be graduated, at the close, in the joint honors of broadcloth and the parchment."

We might add other lights and shades to the picture of school life as it was down to a very recent period in New England and New York, but we must refer our readers to that amusing and instructive volume of Rev. Warren Burton, "The District School as it was." We must pass to the elementary schools of Pennsylvania and the Southern States.

LETTER FROM WILLIAM DARLINGTON, M.D., LL.D.

"At your request, I propose to attempt a brief and hasty sketch of my acquaintance with, and reminiscences of the *Country Schools*, and their condition, some sixty-five or seventy years since, in the south-eastern corner of the state of Pennsylvania; more particularly the school at Birmingham, Chester county, where the limited instruction of my youthful days was chiefly acquired.

"My earliest recollections of the school to which I was sent go back to that trying period of loose government, rusticity, and scarcity experienced in the interval between the War of Independence and the adoption of the Federal Constitution; and if it were given me to wield the pen of *Tom Brown of Rugby*, I might peradventure furnish some graphic details of our rural seminaries of learning in those days of general destitution. But, under present circumstances, I can only offer the imperfect narrative of incidents and observations, as retained in an almost octogenarian memory.

"At the time when I was first sent to school—say in 1787–8—school-houses were rare; and there was little or no organization for their maintenance. The country round, having been recently ravaged by a hostile army, was scantily supplied with teachers, who occasionally obtained schools by going among the principal families of the vicinage, and procuring subscribers for a quarter's tuition of the children on hand. Those who were too young to be serviceable on the farm were allowed to go to school in the summer season; but the larger ones (*expertus loquor*) could only be spared for that purpose during winter. The extent of rural instruction was then considered to be properly limited to what a worthy London alderman designated as the *three R's*, viz., 'Reading, Riting, and Rithmetic.' To cipher beyond the *Rule of Three* was deemed a notable achievement and mere surplusage among the average of country scholars. The business of teaching, at that day, was disdainfully regarded as among the humblest and most unprofitable of callings; and the *teachers*—often low-bred, intemperate adventurers from the old world—were generally about on a *par* with the prevalent estimate of the profession. Whenever a thriftless vagabond was found to be good for nothing else, he would resort to *school-keeping*, and teaching young American ideas how to shoot! It was my good fortune, however, to have a teacher who was a distinguished exception to the sorry rule referred to. JOHN FORSYTHE was a native of the Emerald Isle, born in 1754, received a good English education at home, and while yet a young man, migrated to the county of *Chester*, in the land of PENN, where he became an excellent schoolmaster. When he arrived in our quakerly settlement, he was a gay young Presbyterian, dressed in the fashionable apparel of the world's people; and being withal musical in his taste, was an expert performer on the violin. He soon, however, adopted the views and principles of the 'Friends,' among whom he remained, married one of the society, and was ever recognized as an exemplary and valuable member.

"As the head and master-spirit of the school, at Birmingham meeting-house, established under the auspices of the Quaker society, he taught for a number of years, and always applied himself *con amore* to his arduous duties. He accomplished more in exciting a taste for knowledge and developing young intellects, than any teacher who had theretofore labored in that hopeful vineyard. He effectually routed the lingering old superstitions, prejudices, and benighted notions of preceding generations, and ever took delight in introducing youthful genius to the bright fields of literature and science. The young men of his day, who have since figured in the world, were deeply indebted to John Forsythe for the aid which he afforded them in their studies, as well as for the sound doctrines which he inculcated; and some few of them yet survive to make the grateful acknowledgment.

"When the noble Quaker institution at *West-town* was erected, near the close of the last century, the skill and experience of John Forsythe were put in requisition, until it was fairly inaugurated; after which he retired to his comfortable farm, in East Bradford, where he passed a venerable old age, until his 87th year, in superintending agricultural employments and in manifesting a lively interest in the progress of education among our people. No instructor has labored in this community more faithfully, nor with better effect. None has left a memory more worthy to be kindly cherished.

"The old *school-house* at Birmingham was a one story stone building, erected by men who did not understand the subject; and was badly lighted and ventilated. The *discipline* of that day (adopted from the mother country) was pretty severe. The real *birch* of the botanists not being indigenous in the immediate vicinity of the school, an efficient substitute was found in young apple tree sprouts, as unruly boys were abundantly able to testify.

"The *school books* of my earliest recollection were a cheap English spelling book, the Bible for the reading classes, and when we got to ciphering, the 'Schoolmasters' Assistant.' The 'Spelling Book' and 'Assistant' were by Thomas Dilworth, an English schoolmaster at Wapping. The 'Assistant' was a useful work, but has long since disappeared. The 'counterfeit presentment' of the worthy author faced the title-page, and was familiarly known to every schoolboy of my time. The Spelling Book contained a little elementary grammar, in which the English substantives were declined through all the cases (genitive, dative, etc.) of the Latin. But *grammar* was then an unknown study among us. Dilworth's 'Spelling Book,' however, was soon superseded by a greatly improved one, compiled by John Pierce, a respectable teacher of Delaware county, Pennsylvania. This comprised a tolerable English grammar, for that period, and John Forsythe introduced the study into his school with much zeal and earnestness. Intelligent employers were made to comprehend its advantages, and were pleased with the prospect of a hopeful advance in that direction; but dull boys and illiterate parents could not appreciate the benefit. Great boobies often got permission, at home, to evade the study, but they could not get round John Forsythe in that way. They would come into school with this promised indulgence, and loudly announce, 'Daddy says I needn't *larn grammar;* it's no use:' when the energetic response from the desk was, 'I don't care what daddy says. He knows nothing about it; and I say thou shalt learn it!' and so some general notion of the subject was impressed upon the minds even of the stupid; while many of the brighter youths became excellent grammarians.

"In this *Friendly* seminary we were all required to use the *plain language* in conversation, being assured that it was wrong, both morally and grammatically, to say *you* to one person. Our teacher contrived a method of his own for mending our cacology, even while at our noonday sports. He prepared a small piece of board or shingle, which he termed a *paddle;* and whenever a boy was heard uttering bad grammar, he had to take the paddle, step aside, and refrain from play, until he detected some other unlucky urchin trespassing upon syntax; when he was authorized to transfer the badge of interdiction to the last offender, and resume his amusements. It was really curious to observe how critical we soon became, and how much improvement was effected by this whimsical and simple device.

"Pierce's 'Spelling Book' kept its position in our school for several years, but was at length superseded, in the grammatical department, by a useful little volume, prepared by *John Comly*, of Bucks county, Pennsylvania. *Lindley Murray* and others prepared elaborate grammars, which were successively introduced, as our schools improved or created a demand; and so rapidly have the bookmaking competitors in that department multiplied that their name is now legion, and the respective value of their works is known only to experts in the art of teaching.

"Excellent works in *Reading* and *Elocution* are now so abundant and well known in all our respectable seminaries, that they need not to be here enumerated. One of the best and most popular of those works, some half century or more since, was a volume entitled 'The Art of Speaking,' compiled, I think, by a Mr. Rice, in England.

"But, as we have now reached the age of academies, normal institutes, and schools for the people, I presume you will gladly forego a further extension of this prosy narrative, so little calculated to interest a veteran in the great cause of education. I have ever been a sincere friend and advocate of the blessing; but, unfortunately, my acquaintance with it has been mainly limited to a humbling consciousness of my deficiencies in the ennobling attainment.

"Very respectfully,

"WM. DARLINGTON.

"WEST CHESTER, PA., Dec. 21, 1860."

SCHOOLS IN PHILADELPHIA.

The following picture of the internal economy of one of the best schools of Philadelphia, is taken from Watson's "Annals of Philadelphia and Pennsylvania."

"My facetious friend, Lang Syne, has presented a lively picture of the 'schoolmasters' in those days, when 'preceptors,' and 'principals,' and 'professors' were yet unnamed. What is now known as 'Friends' Academy,' in Fourth street, was at that time occupied by four different masters. The best room down-stairs by Robert Proud, Latin master; the one above him, by William Waring, teacher of astronomy and mathematics; the east room, up-stairs, by Jeremiah Paul, and the one below, 'last not least' in our remembrance, by J. Todd, and severe he was. The State House clock, being at the time visible from the school pavement, gave to the eye full notice when to break off marble and plug top, hastily collect the 'stakes,' and bundle in, pell-mell, to the school-room, where, until the arrival of the 'master of scholars,' John Todd, they were busily employed, every one in finding his place, under the control for the time of a short Irishman, usher, named Jimmy M'Cue. On the entrance of the master, all shuffling of the feet, 'scrouging,' hitting of elbows, and whispering disputes, were hastily adjusted, leaving a silence which might be felt, 'not a mouse stirring.' He, Todd, dressed after the plainest manner of Friends, but of the richest material, with looped cocked hat, was at all times remarkably clean and nice in his person, a man of about sixty years, square built, and well sustained by bone and muscle.

"After an hour, maybe, of quiet time, every thing going smoothly on—no sound, but from the master's voice, while hearing the one standing near him, a dead calm, when suddenly a brisk slap on the ear or face, for something or for nothing, gave 'dreadful note' that an eruption of the lava was now about to take place. Next thing to be seen was 'strap in full play over the head and shoulders of Pilgarlic.' The passion of the master 'growing by what it fed on,' and wanting elbow room, the chair would be quickly thrust on one side, when, with sudden gripe, he was to be seen dragging his struggling suppliant to the flogging ground, in the centre of the room; having placed his left foot upon the end of a bench, he then, with a patent jerk, peculiar to himself, would have the boy completely horsed across his knee, with his left elbow on the back of his neck, to keep him securely on. In the hurry of the moment he would bring his long pen with him, griped between his strong teeth (visible the while), causing both ends to descend to a parallel with his chin, and adding much to the terror of the scene. His face would assume a deep claret color—his little bob of hair would disengage itself, and stand out, each 'particular hair' as it were, 'up in arms and eager for the fray.' Having his victim thus completely at command, and all useless drapery drawn up to a bunch above the waistband, and the rotundity and the nankeen in the closest affinity possible for them to be, then once more to the 'staring crew' would be exhibited the dexterity of master and strap. By long practice he had arrived at such perfection in the exercise, that, moving in quick time, the fifteen inches of bridle rein (*alias* strap) would be seen after every cut, elevated to a perpendicular above his head; from whence it descended like a flail on the stretched nankeen, leaving 'on the place beneath' a fiery red streak, at every slash. It was customary with him to address the sufferer at intervals, as follows: 'Does it hurt?' 'Oh! yes, master; oh! don't, master.' 'Then I'll make it hurt thee more. I'll make thy flesh creep—thou shan't want a warming pan to-night. Intolerable being! Nothing in nature is able to prevail upon thee but my strap.' He had one boy named George Fudge, who usually wore leather breeches, with which he put strap and its master at defiance. He would never acknowledge pain—he would not 'sing out.' Todd seized him one day, and having gone through the evolutions of strapping (as useless, in effect, as if he had been thrashing a flour-bag), almost breathless with rage, he once more appealed to the feelings of the 'reprobate,' by saying: 'Does it not hurt?' The astonishment of the school and the master was completed, on hearing him sing out, 'No! Hurray for leather crackers!' He was thrown off immediately, sprawling on the floor, with the benediction as follows: 'Intolerable being! Get out of my school. Nothing in nature is able to prevail upon thee—not even my strap!'

"'Twas not 'his love of learning was in fault,' so much as the old British system of introducing learning and discipline into the brains of boys and soldiers by dint of punishment. The system of flogging on all occasions in schools, for something or for nothing, being protected by law, gives free play to the passions of the master, which he, for one, exercised with great severity.

The writer has, at this moment, in his memory, a schoolmaster *then* of this city, who, a few years ago, went deliberately out of his school to purchase a cow-skin, with which, on his return, he extinguished his bitter revenge on a boy who had offended him. The age of chivalry preferred ignorance in ts sons, to having them subjected to the 'ear of a pedagogue—believing that a boy who had quailed under the eye of the schoolmaster, would never face the enemy with boldness on the field of battle; which t must be allowed is 'a swing of the pendulum' too far the other way. A good writer says: 'We do not *harden* the wax o receive the impression—wherefore, the eacher seems himself most in need of *cor-ection*—for he, unfit to teach, is making hem unfit to be taught!'

"I have been told by an aged gentleman, hat in the days of his boyhood, sixty-five ears ago, when boys and girls were together, it was a common practice to make he boys strip off their jackets, and loose heir trowsers' band, preparatory to hoisting hem upon a boy's back so as to get his whipping, with only the linen between the lesh and the strap. The girls too—we ity them—were obliged to take off their tays to receive their floggings with equal ensibility. He named one distinguished ady, *since*, who was so treated among oth-rs, in his school. All the teachers then were from England and Ireland, and brought with them the rigorous principles which ad before been whipped into themselves at ome."

Robert Coram, in a pamphlet devoted in art to a "Plan for the General Establish-nent of Schools throughout the United tates," printed in Wilmington, Delaware, 1 1791, characterizes the state of education s follows: "The country schools, through nost of the United States, whether we con-ider the buildings, the teachers, or the reg-lations, are in every respect completely des-icable, wretched, and contemptible. The uildings are in general sorry hovels, neither ind-tight nor water-tight; a few stools erving in the double capacity of bench and esk, and the old leaves of copy books ma-ing a miserable substitute for glass win-ows. The teachers are generally foreign-rs, shamefully deficient in every qualifica-on necessary to convey instruction to outh, and not seldom addicted to gross vices. Absolute in his own opinion, and proud of introducing what he calls his European method, one calls the first letter of the alphabet, *aw*. The school is modified upon this plan, and the children who are advanced are beat and cuffed to forget the former mode they have been taught, which irritates their minds and retards their progress. The quarter being finished, the children lie idle until another master offers, few remaining in one place more than a quarter. When the next schoolmaster is introduced, he calls the first letter *a*, as in mat; the school undergoes another reform, and is equally vexed and retarded. At his removal a third is introduced, who calls the first letter *hay*. All these blockheads are equally absolute in their own notions, and will by no means suffer the children to pronounce the letter as they were first taught; but every three months the school goes through a reform—error succeeds error, and dunce the second reigns like dunce the first. I will venture to pronounce, that however seaport towns, from local circumstances, may have good schools, the country schools will remain in their present state of despicable wretchedness, unless incorporated with government. * * * The necessity of a reformation in the country schools is too obvious to be insisted on; and the first step to such a reformation will be by turning private schools into public ones. The schools should be public, for several reasons—1st. Because, as has been before said, every citizen has an equal right to subsistence, and ought to have an equal opportunity of acquiring knowledge. 2d. Because public schools are easiest maintained, as the burthen falls upon all the citizens. The man who is too squeamish or lazy to get married, contributes to the support of public schools, as well as the man who is burthened with a large family. But private schools are supported only by heads of families, and by those only while they are interested; for as soon as the children are grown up, their support is withdrawn; which makes the employment so precarious, that men of ability and merit will not submit to the trifling salaries allowed in most country schools, and which, by their partial support, cannot afford a better."

SCHOOL HOLIDAY IN GEORGIA.

We have not been very successful in gathering the printed testimony of the dead, or the vivid reminiscences of the living, respecting the internal economy of schools, public or family, in any of the Southern states prior to 1800. The following graphic sketch of "the turn out" of the schoolmaster, from Judge Longstreet's "Georgia Scenes," is said to be "literally true:"

"In the good old days of *fescues*, *abisselfas* and *anpersants*,* terms which used to be familiar in this country during the Revolutionary war, and which lingered in some of our country schools for a few years afterward, I visited my friend Captain Griffen, who resided about seven miles to the eastward of Wrightsborough, then in Richmond, but now in Columbia county. I reached the captain's hospitable home on Easter, and was received by him and his good lady with a *Georgia welcome* of 1790.

"The day was consumed in the interchange of news between the captain and myself (though, I confess, it might have been better employed), and the night found us seated round a temporary fire, which the captain's sons had kindled up for the purpose of dyeing eggs. It was a common custom of those days with boys to dye and peck eggs on Easter Sunday, and for a few days afterward. They were colored according to the fancy of the dyer; some yellow, some green, some purple, and some with a variety of colors, borrowed from a piece of calico. They were not unfrequently beautified with a taste and skill which would have extorted a compliment from Hezekiah Niles, if he had seen them a year ago, in the hands of the '*young operatives*,' in some of the northern manufactories. No sooner was the work of dyeing finished, than our 'young operatives' sallied forth to stake the whole proceeds of their '*domestic industry*' upon a peck. Egg was struck against egg, point to point, and the egg that was broken was given up as lost to the owner of the one which came whole from the shock.

"While the boys were busily employed in the manner just mentioned, the captain's youngest son, George, gave us an anecdote highly descriptive of the Yankee and Georgia character, even in their buddings, and at this early date. 'What you think, pa,' said he, 'Zeph Pettibone went and got his uncle Zach to turn him a wooden egg; and he won a whole hatful o' eggs from all us boys 'fore we found it out; but, when we found it out, maybe John Brown didn't smoke him for it, and took away all his eggs, and give 'em back to us boys; and you think he didn't go then and git a guinea egg, and win most as many more, and John Brown would o' give it to him agin if all we boys hadn't said we thought it was fair. I never see such a boy as that Zeph Pettibone in all my life. He don't mind whipping no more 'an nothing at all, if he can win eggs.'

"This anecdote, however, only fell in by accident, for there was an all-absorbing subject which occupied the minds of the boys during the whole evening, of which I could occasionally catch distant hints, in under tones and whispers, but of which I could make nothing, until they were afterward explained by the captain himself. 'Such as 'I'll be bound Pete Jones and Bill Smith stretches him.' 'By Jockey, soon as they seize him, you'll see me down upon him like a duck upon a June-bug.' 'By the time he touches the ground, he'll think he's got into a hornet's nest,' etc.

"'The boys,' said the captain, as they retired, 'are going to turn out the schoolmaster to-morrow, and you can perceive they think of nothing else. We must go over to the schoolhouse and witness the contest, in order to prevent injury to preceptor or pupils; for, though the master is always, upon such occasions, glad to be turned out, and only struggles long enough to present his patrons a fair apology for giving the children a holiday, which he desires as much as they do, the boys always conceive a holiday gained by a 'turn out' as the sole achievement of their valor; and in their zeal to distinguish themselves upon such memorable occasions, they sometimes become too rough, provoke the master to wrath, and a very serious conflict ensues. To prevent these consequences, to bear witness that the master was *forced* to yield before he would withhold a day of his promised labor from his

* The *fescue* was a sharpened wire or other instrument used by the preceptor to point out the letters to the children.

Abisselfa is a contraction of the words "a by itself, a." It was usual, when either of the vowels constituted a syllable of a word, to pronounce it, and denote its independent character by the words just mentioned, thus: "a by itself, *a*, c-o-r-n corn, *acorn*;" "e by itself, *e*, v-i-l, *evil*," etc.

The character which stands for the word "*and*" (&) was probably pronounced with the same accompaniment, but in terms borrowed from the Latin language, thus: "*& per se*" (by itself) *and*. Hence, "anpersant."

employers, and to act as a mediator between him and the boys in settling the articles of peace, I always attend; and you must accompany me to-morrow.' I cheerfully promised to do so.

"The captain and I rose before the sun, but the boys had risen and were off to the school-house before the dawn. After an early breakfast, hurried by Mrs. G. for our accommodation, my host and myself took up our line of march toward the school-house. We reached it about half an hour before the master arrived, but not before the boys had completed its fortifications. It was a simple log pen, about twenty feet square, with a doorway cut out of the logs, to which was fitted a rude door, made of clapboards, and swung on wooden hinges. The roof was covered with clapboards also, and retained in their places by heavy logs placed on them. The chimney was built of logs, diminishing in size from the ground to the top, and overspread inside and out with red clay mortar. The classic hut occupied a lovely spot, overshadowed by majestic hickories, towering poplars, and strong-armed oaks. The little plain on which it stood was terminated, at the distance of about fifty paces from its door, by the brow of a hill, which descended rather abruptly to a noble spring that gushed joyously forth among the roots of a stately beech at its foot.

"The boys had strongly fortified the school-house, of which they had taken possession. The door was barricaded with logs, which I should have supposed would have defied the combined powers of the whole school. The chimney, too, was nearly filled with logs of goodly size; and these were the only passways to the interior. I concluded, if a *turn out* was all that was necessary to decide the contest in favor of the boys, they had already gained the victory. They had, however, not as much confidence in their outworks as I had, and therefore had armed themselves with long sticks, not for the purpose of using them upon the master if the battle should come to close quarters, for this was considered unlawful warfare, but for the purpose of guarding their *works* from his approaches, which it was considered perfectly lawful to protect by all manner of jabs and punches through the cracks. From the early assembling of the girls, it was very obvious that they had been let into the conspiracy, though they took no part in the active operations. They would, however, occasionally drop a word of encouragement to the boys, such as 'I wouldn't turn out the master; but if I did turn him out, I'd die before I'd give up.'

"At length Mr. Michael St. John, the schoolmaster made his appearance. Though some of the girls had met him a quarter of a mile from the school-house, and told him all that had happened, he gave signs of sudden astonishment and indignation when he advanced to the door, and was assailed by a whole platoon of sticks from the cracks: 'Why, what does all this mean?' said he, as he approached the captain and myself, with a countenance of two or three varying expressions.

"'Why,' said the captain, 'the boys have turned you out, because you have refused to give them an Easter holiday.'

"'Oh,' returned Michael, 'that's it, is it? Well, I'll see whether their parents are to pay me for letting their children play when they please.' So saying, he advanced to the school-house, and demanded, in a lofty tone, of its inmates, an unconditional surrender.

"'Well, give us a holiday, then,' said twenty little urchins within, 'and we'll let you in.'

"'Open the door of the *academy*'—(Michael would allow nobody to call it a school-house)—'Open the door of the academy this instant,' said Michael, 'or I'll break it down.'

"'Break it down,' said Pete Jones and Bill Smith, 'and we'll break you down.'

"During this colloquy I took a peep into the fortress, to see how the garrison were affected by the parley. The little ones were obviously panic-struck at the first words of command; but their fears were all chased away by the bold determined reply of Pete Jones and Bill Smith, and they raised a whoop of defiance.

"Michael now walked round the academy three times, examining all its weak points with great care. He then paused, reflected for a moment, and wheeled off suddenly toward the woods, as though a bright thought had just struck him. He passed twenty things which I supposed he might be in quest of, such as huge stones, fence rails, portable logs, and the like, without bestowing the least attention upon them. He went to one old log, searched it thoroughly, then to another, then to a hollow stump, peeped into it with great care, then to a hollow log, into which he looked with equal caution, and so on.

"'What is he after?' inquired I.

"'I'm sure I don't know,' said the captain, 'but the boys do. Don't you notice the breathless silence which prevails in the school-house, and the intense anxiety with which they are eyeing him through the cracks?'

"At this moment Michael had reached a little excavation at the root of a dogwood, and was in the act of putting his hand into it, when a voice from the garrison exclaimed, with most touching pathos, 'Lo'd o' messy, he's found my eggs! boys, let's give up.'

"'I won't give up,' was the reply from many voices at once.

"'Rot your cowardly skin, Zeph Pettibone, you wouldn't give a wooden egg for all the holydays in the world.'

"If these replies did not reconcile Zephaniah to his apprehended loss, it at least silenced his complaints. In the mean time Michael was employed in relieving Zeph's storehouse of its provisions; and, truly, its contents told well for Zeph's skill in egg-pecking. However, Michael took out the eggs with great care, and brought them within a few paces of the schoolhouse, and laid them down with equal care in full view of the besieged. He revisited the places which he had searched, and to which he seemed to have been led by intuition; for from nearly all of them did he draw eggs, in greater or less numbers. These he treated as he had done Zeph's, keeping each pile separate. Having arranged the eggs in double files before the door, he marched between them with an air of triumph, and once more demanded a surrender, under pain of an entire destruction of the garrison's provisions.

"'Break 'em just as quick as you please,' said George Griffin; 'our mothers 'll give us a plenty more, won't they, pa?'

"'I can answer for yours, my son,' said the captain; 'she would rather give up every egg upon the farm than to see you play the coward or traitor to save your property.'

"Michael, finding that he could make no impression upon the fears or the avarice of the boys, determined to carry their fortifications by storm. Accordingly he procured a heavy fence-rail, and commenced the assault upon the door. It soon came to pieces, and the upper logs fell out, leaving a space of about three feet at the top. Michael boldly entered the breach, when, by the articles of war, sticks were thrown aside as no longer lawful weapons. He was resolutely met on the half-demolished rampart by Peter Jones and William Smith, supported by James Griffin. These were the three largest boys in the school; the first about sixteen years of age, the second about fifteen, and the third just eleven. Twice was Michael repulsed by these young champions; but the third effort carried him fairly into the fortress. Hostilities now ceased for a while, and the captain and I, having levelled the remaining logs at the door, followed Michael into the house. A large three inch plank (if it deserve that name, for it was wrought from the half of a tree's trunk entirely with the axe), attached to the logs by means of wooden pins, served the whole school for a writing desk. At a convenient distance below it, and on a line with it, stretched a smooth log, resting upon the logs of the house, which answered for the writers' seat. Michael took his seat upon the desk, placed his feet on the seat, and was sitting very composedly, when with a simultaneous movement, Pete and Bill seized each a leg, and marched off with it in quick time. The consequence is obvious; Michael's head first took the desk, then the seat, and finally the ground (for the house was not floored), with three sonorous thumps of most doleful portent. No sooner did he touch the ground than he was completely buried with boys. The three elder laid themselves across his head, neck and breast, the rest arranging themselves *ad libitum*. Michael's equanimity was considerably disturbed by the first thump, became restive with the second, and took flight with the third. His first effort was to disengage his legs, for without them he could not rise, and to lie in his present position was extremely inconvenient and undignified. Accordingly he drew up his right, and kicked at random. This movement laid out about six in various directions upon the floor. Two rose crying: 'Ding his old red-headed skin,' said one of them, 'to go and kick me right in my sore belly, where I fell down and raked it, running after that fellow that cried "school butter."'*

---

* "I have never been able to satisfy myself clearly as to the literal meaning of these terms. They were

" 'Drot his old snaggle-tooth picture,' said the other, 'to go and hurt my sore toe, where I knocked the nail off going to the spring to fetch a gourd of *warter* for him, and not for myself n'other.'

" 'Hut!' said Captain Griffin, 'young Washingtons mind these trifles! At him again.'

"The name of Washington cured their wounds and dried up their tears in an instant, and they legged him *de novo*. The left leg treated six more as unceremoniously as the right had those just mentioned; but the talismanic name had just fallen upon their ears before the kick, so they were invulnerable. They therefore returned to the attack without loss of time. The struggle seemed to wax hotter and hotter for some time after Michael came to the ground, and he threw the children about in all directions and postures, giving some of them thrusts which would have placed the *ruffle-shirted* little darlings of the present day under the discipline of paregoric and opodeldoc for a week; but these hardy sons of the south seemed not to feel them. As Michael's head grew easy, his limbs, by a natural sympathy, became more quiet, and he offered one day's holiday as the price. The boys demanded a week; but here the captain interposed, and after the common but often unjust custom of arbitrators, split the difference. In this instance the terms were equitable enough, and were immediately acceded to by both parties. Michael rose in a good humor, and the boys were of course. Loud was their talking of their deeds of valor as they retired. One little fellow about seven years old, and about three feet and a half high, jumped up, cracked his feet together, and exclaimed, 'By jingo, Pete Jones, Bill Smith and *me* can hold any *Sinjin* [St. John] that ever trod Georgy grit.' "

---

considered an unpardonable insult to a country school, and always justified an attack by the whole fraternity upon the person who used them in their hearing. I have known the scholars pursue a traveller two miles to be revenged of the insult. Probably they are a corruption of 'The school's better.' '*Better*' was the term commonly used of old to denote a *superior*, as it sometimes is in our day: 'Wait till your betters are served,' for example. I conjecture, therefore, the expression just alluded to was one of challenge, contempt, and defiance, by which the person who used it avowed himself the *superior* in all respects of the whole school, from the preceptor down. If any one can give a better account of it, I shall be pleased to receive it."

AN OLD FIELD SCHOOL, OR ACADEMY, IN VIRGINIA.

THE experience of one of that class of teachers, who found temporary occupation in teaching the children of one or more families of planters in Virginia and other southern states, will be found in the "Travels of Four Years and a Half in the United States (in 1798, 1799, 1800, 1801 and 1802), by John Davis." Mr. Davis was an Englishman of more than ordinary education and of social address, and while in this country numbered among his friends such men as Aaron Burr, President Jefferson, and other men of high political standing. He was a private tutor in New York, South Carolina and Virginia, and his graphic sketches of men and manners show some of the deficiencies in the means of education which even wealthy planters in the southern states experienced. With letters of introduction from President Jefferson he proceeds to the plantation of a Mr. Ball, and is engaged to teach his and his neighbors' children:

"The following day every farmer came from the neighborhood to the house, who had any children to send to my Academy, for such they did me the honor to term the log-hut in which I was to teach. Each man brought his son, or his daughter, and rejoiced that the day was arrived when their little ones could light their tapers at the torch of knowledge! I was confounded at the encomiums they heaped upon a man whom they had never seen before, and was at a loss what construction to put upon their speech. No price was too great for the services I was to render their children; and they all expressed an eagerness to exchange perishable coin for lasting knowledge. If I would continue with them seven years! only seven years! they would erect for me a brick seminary on a hill not far off; but for the present I was to occupy a log-house, which, however homely, would soon vie with the sublime college of William and Mary, and consign to oblivion the renowned academy in the vicinity of Fauquier Court-House. I thought Englishmen sanguine; but these Virginians were infatuated.

"I now opened what some called an academy,* and others an Old Field School;

---

* "It is worth the while to describe the academy I occupied on Mr. Ball's plantation. It had one room and a half. It stood on blocks about two feet

and, however it may be thought that content was never felt within the walls of a seminary, I, for my part, experienced an exemption from care, and was not such a fool as to measure the happiness of my condition by what others thought of it.

"It was pleasurable to behold my pupils enter the school over which I presided; for they were not composed only of truant boys, but some of the fairest damsels in the country. Two sisters generally rode on one horse to the school-door, and I was not so great a pedagogue as to refuse them my assistance to dismount from their steeds. A running-footman of the negro tribe, who followed with their food in a basket, took care of the beast; and after being saluted by the young ladies with the courtesies of the morning, I proceeded to instruct them, with gentle exhortations to diligence of study.

"Common books were only designed for common minds. The unconnected lessons of Scot, the tasteless selections of Bingham, the florid harangues of Noah Webster, and the somniferous compilation of Alexander, were either thrown aside, or suffered to gather dust on the shelf; while the charming essays of Goldsmith, and his not less delectable Novel, together with the impressive work of Defoe, and the mild productions of Addison, conspired to enchant the fancy, and kindle a love of reading. The thoughts of these writers became engrafted on the minds, and the combinations of their diction on the language of the pupils.

"Of the boys I cannot speak in very encomiastic terms; but they were perhaps like all other school-boys, that is, more disposed to play truant than enlighten their minds. The most important knowledge to an American, after that of himself, is the geography of his country. I, therefore, put into the hands of my boys a proper book, and initiated them by an attentive reading of the discoveries of the Genoese; I was even so minute as to impress on their minds the man who first descried land on board the ship of Columbus. That man was Roderic Triana, and on my exercising the memory of a boy by asking him the name, he very gravely made answer, Roderic Random.

"Among my male students was a New Jersey gentleman of thirty, whose object was to be initiated in the language of Cicero and Virgil. He had before studied the Latin grammar at an academy school (I use his own words) in his native state; but the academy school being burnt down, his grammar, alas! was lost in the conflagration, and he had neglected the pursuit of literature since the destruction of his book. When I asked him if he did not think it was some Goth who had set fire to his academy school, he made answer, 'So, it is like enough.'

"Mr. Dye did not study Latin to refine his taste, direct his judgment, or enlarge his imagination; but merely that he might be enabled to teach it when he opened school, which was his serious design. He had been bred a carpenter, but he panted for the honors of literature."

Mr. Davis accounts for his fidelity in teaching more hours than he was required to do by his contract, by his interest in the lessons of one of his female pupils:

"Hence I frequently protracted the studies of the children till one, or half past one o'clock; a practice that did not fail to call forth the exclamations both of the white and the black people. Upon my word, Mr. Ball would say, this gentleman is diligent; and Aunt Patty the negro cook would remark, 'He good cool-mossa that; he not like old Hodgkinson and old Harris, who let the boys out before twelve. He deserve good wages!"

"Having sent the young ladies to the family mansion, I told the boys to break up, and in a few minutes they who had even breathed with circumspection, now gave loose to the most riotous merriment, and betook themselves to the woods, followed by all the dogs on the plantation."

"There was a carpenter on the plantation, whom Mr. Ball had hired by the year.

---

and a half above the ground, where there was free access to the hogs, the dogs, and the poultry. It had no ceiling, nor was the roof lathed or plastered, but covered with shingles. Hence, when it rained, like the nephew of old Elwes, I moved my bed (for I slept in my academy) to the most comfortable corner. It had one window, but no glass, nor shutter. In the night, to remedy this, the mulatto wench who waited on me, contrived very ingeniously to place a square board against the window with one hand, and fix the rail of a broken down fence against it with the other. In the morning, when I returned from breakfasting in the 'great big house,' (my scholars being collected,) I gave the rail a forcible kick with my foot, and down tumbled the board with an awful roar. 'Is not my window,' said I to Virginia, 'of a very curious construction?' 'Indeed, indeed, sir,' replied my fair disciple, 'I think it is a mighty noisy one.'"

He had tools of all kinds, and the recreation of Mr. Dye, after the labor of study, was to get under the shade of an oak, and make tables, or benches, or stools for the academy. So true is the assertion of Horace, that the cask will always retain the flavor of the liquor with which it is first impregnated.

"'Well, Mr. Dye, what are you doing?'

"'I am making a table for the academy school.'

"'What wood is that?'

"'It is white oak, sir.'

"'What, then you are skilled in trees, you can tell oak from hickory, and ash from fir?'

"'Like enough, sir. (A broad grin.) I ought to know those things; I served my time to it.'

"'*Carpenter.*—I find, sir, Mr. Dye has done with his old trade; he is above employing his hands; he wants work for the brain. Well! larning is a fine thing; there's nothing like larning. I have a son only five years old, that, with proper larning, I should not despair of seeing a member of Congress. He is a boy of genus; he could play on the Jews-harp from only seeing Sambo tune it once.'

"'*Mr. Dye.*—I guess that's Billy; he is a right clever child.'

"'*Carpenter.*—How long, sir, will it take you to learn Mr. Dye Latin?'

"'*Schoolmaster.*—How long, sir, would it take me to ride from Mr. Ball's plantation to the plantation of Mr. Wormley Carter?'

"'*Carpenter.*—Why that, sir, I suppose, would depend upon your horse.'

"'*Schoolmaster.*—Well, then, sir, you solve your own interrogation. But here comes Dick. What has he got in his hand?'

"'*Mr. Dye.*—A mole like enough. Who are you bringing that to, Dick?'

"'*Dick.*—Not to you. You never gave me the taste of a dram since I first know'd you. Worse luck to me; you New Jersey men are close shavers; I believe you would skin a louse. This is a mole. I have brought it for the gentleman who came from beyond sea. He never refuses Dick a dram; I would walk through the wilderness of Kentucky to serve him. Lord! how quiet he keeps his school. It is not now as it was; the boys don't go clack, clack, clack, like 'Squire Pendleton's mill upon Catharpin Run!'

"'*Schoolmaster.*—You have brought that mole, Dick, for me.'

"'*Dick.*—Yes, master, but first let me tell you the history of it. This mole was once a man; see, master (Dick exhibits the mole), it has got hands and feet just like you and me. It was once a man, but so proud, so lofty, so puffed-up, that God, to punish his insolence, condemned him to crawl under the earth.'

"'*Schoolmaster.*—A good fable, and not unhappily moralized. Did you ever hear or read of this before, Mr. Dye?'

"'*Mr. Dye.*—Nay (a broad grin), I am right certain it does not belong to Æsop. I am certain sure Dick did not find it there.'

"'*Dick.*—Find it where? I would not wrong a man of the value of a grain of corn. I came across the mole as I was hoeing the potato-patch. Master, shall I take it to the school-house? If you are fond of birds, I know now for a mocking-bird's nest; I am only afeared those young rogues, the school-boys, will find out the tree. They play the mischief with every thing, they be full of devilment. I saw Jack Lockhart throw a stone at the old bird, as she was returning to feed her young; and if I had not coaxed him away to look at my young puppies, he would have found out the nest.'

"I had been three months invested in the first executive office of pedagogue, when a cunning old fox of a New Jersey planter (a Mr. Lee) discovered that his eldest boy wrote a better hand than I. Fame is swift-footed; *vires acquirit eundo;* the discovery spread far and wide; and whithersoever I went, I was an object for the hand of scorn to point his slow unmoving finger at, as a schoolmaster that could not write. Virginia gave me for the persecutions I underwent a world of sighs, her swelling heavens rose and fell with indignation at old Lee and his abettors. But the boys caught spirit from the discovery. I could perceive a mutiny breaking out among them; and had I not in time broke down a few branches from an apple tree before my door, it is probable they would have displayed their gratitude for my instructions by throwing me out of my school-window. But by arguing with one over the shoulders, and another over the back, I maintained with dignity the first executive office of pedagogue.

"I revenged myself amply on old Lee. It was the custom of his son (a lengthy fellow of about twenty) to come to the academy with a couple of huge mastiffs at his heels. Attached to their master (*par nobile fratrum*) they entered without ceremony Pohoke Academy, bringing with them myriads of fleas, wood-lice, and ticks. Nay, they would often annoy Virginia, by throwing themselves at her feet, and inflaming the choler of a little lap-dog, which I had bought because of his diminutive size, and which Virginia delighted to nurse for me. I could perceive the eye of Virginia rebuke me for suffering the dogs to annoy her; and there lay more peril in her eye than in the jaws of all the mastiffs in Prince William County.

"'Mr. Lee,' said I, 'this is the third time I have told you not to convert the academy into a kennel, and bring your dogs to school.' Lee was mending his pen 'judgmatically.' He made no reply, but smiled.

"I knew old Dick the negro had a bitch, and that his bitch was proud. I walked down to Dick's log-house. Dick was beating flax.

"'Dick,' said I, 'old Farmer Lee has done me much evil—(I don't like the old man myself, master, said Dick)—and his son, repugnant to my express commands, has brought his father's two plantation dogs to the academy. Revenge is sweet—'

"'Right, master,' said Dick. 'I never felt so happy as when I bit off Cuffey's great toe and swallowed it—

"'Do you, Dick,' said I, 'walk past the school-house with your bitch. Lee's dogs will come out after her. Go round with them to your log-house; and when you have once secured them, hang both of them up by the neck.'

"'Leave it to me, master,' said Dick. 'I'll fix the business for you in a few minutes. I have a few fadoms of rope in my house—that will do it.'

"I returned to the academy. The dogs were stretched at their ease on the floor. 'Oh! I am glad you are come,' exclaimed Virginia; 'those great big dogs have quite scared me.'

"In a few minutes Dick passed the door with his slut. Quick from the floor rose Mr. Lee's two dogs, and followed the female. The rest may be supplied by the imagination of the reader. Dick hung up both the dogs to the branch of a pine-tree; old Lee lost the guards to his plantation; the negroes broke open his barn, pilfered his sacks of Indian corn, rode his horses in the night—and thus was I revenged on Alexander the coppersmith.

"Three months had now elapsed, and I was commanded officially to resign my sovereign authority to Mr. Dye, who was in every respect better qualified to discharge its sacred functions. He understood tare and tret, wrote a copper-plate hand, and, balancing himself upon one leg, could flourish angels and corkscrews. I, therefore, gave up the 'academy school' to Mr. Dye, to the joy of the boys, but the sorrow of Virginia."

Whilst schools were thus poorly equipped and the instruction given was thus defective in its methods and meagre in its extent, it becomes of interest to inquire whence such a measure of general intelligence and so many individual cases of attaining to an eminent position in society. This was the result of no single cause alone, but of a variety in combination.

The first of these that may be named, both in its influence upon childhood and upon manhood, was the necessity of a hard fought battle for existence, but relieved by the assurance that victory would be the reward of persistent exertion. Its results were robustness, patience of toil, resoluteness and perseverance in encountering difficulties, and fertility of resources. The rustic lad,—and making the necessary variations, we include the female sex with the representative male,—the rustic lad who had been trained to help his parents from the moment he had acquired strength to steady his steps, to toil on all the same whether the bright sun cheered him or the chill air benumbed his limbs; whether his tasks were varied, pleasant and light, or, on the contrary, he had learned patience, marching beside the patient ox all the long hours of a long spring day, the animals only alternating with others which served as relays; and had been no stranger to such discipline as picking stones in the stubble whilst the sad heavens distilled a drizzly rain, they condensing all their gloom in his soul, but withheld those large and frequent drops which would have been the signal of his release; and among the least severe of whose lessons in acquiring hardihood had been, in gathering the fruits of autumn, to face its frosts without mittens or shoes; this lad found nothing in the difficulties of the school-room to appall him, and storms and deep drifts rather added zest to his daily walks. No unintelligible jargon of the spelling book, no abstruse section in his reader, was an overmatch for his industry.

True, he did not understand all he studied, but he learned to spell and to read and to commit to memory what was assigned him. And when he took his arithmetic, which contained only definitions, rules and examples, although his teacher vouchsafed him little explanation, he had perseverance enough to ponder every dark process till light broke through. And there were instances of boys who worked for consecutive hours and days at problems confessedly some of the most knotty that could be found, till at last their unaided exertions were rewarded with success, which brought more exquisite joy than ever thrilled the finder of a rare gem. These exceptional cases stimulated the more dull, and most became possessed of at least the rudiments of the science, quite sufficient for practical life, or which under the stimulus of necessity became subsequently enlarged to that extent. In manhood no blind adherence to traditional methods was or could be observed. Emergencies were constantly arising which taxed ingenuity to the utmost in devising the fitting expedients to meet them. It was a daily study to make the narrowest means serve the same ends as the amplest. Hard thought was expended without stint upon labor-saving processes, improvements and inventions. Thus was gained a discipline of mind beyond what the higher college mathematics usually imparts, and ofttimes a readiness in applying mechanical principles, of which many an engineer trained in the schools is utterly devoid, however prompt he may be in the routine to which he is accustomed.

The family training, aside from the inuring of children to patient industry, contributed greatly to their profiting from their school privileges. To do or not to do was not then left so generally to the child's pleasure. He was made to obey before he had experienced the delight of carrying into effect his own will in opposition to that of others; and thus was formed the habit of unquestioning compliance with the requirements of parents. When the child could understand the subject, he was taught that however irksome at times were the tasks imposed upon him, it was only in virtue of the allotment that man was to eat bread by the sweat of his brow, and that only by a cheerful performance of what was within his power could he make a return for the care he was continually receiving. Thus from a sense of religious and filial obligation the rigor of their early discipline was the more easily sustained. Self-control and a certain measure of self-reliance were results of the discipline of infancy even ; and in advancing childhood it was inculcated in the house and in the field, that each must depend upon himself for whatever he was to be and to possess in life. And knowledge, knowledge that was not the mere blind recipient of instruction, intelligent knowledge which perceived relations, and reasoning knowledge which could make the practical application as opportunity served, was set forth as the condition indispensable to render exertion successful. Hence it was a prized privilege to go to school, as well as a pleasant exchange for physical toil for a brief period, an exchange of work at home for another variety of work in the school-room, not of one manner of busy idleness and mischief for another. Also in many cases the home was itself a school, and either that knowledge was there gained which others acquired at school, or study was further pursued under the guidance of parent, or brother or sister, who by some happy gift of Providence had required little tuition. Often also, winter evenings or other hours, when the labor of one pair of hands might be spared, were passed in the social reading of instructive books.

The listening every seventh day to two discourses, wherein were discussed the deepest theories which can be proposed to man, may be named as an additional item in the answer to our inquiry. The clergymen of that day had received the best education that the country afforded, and were daily cultivating intimacy with the profoundest theologians. Thus they had ever thoughts which they had originated or had made their own to present. And these thoughts were inwardly digested by a goodly number of their hearers, and becoming a part of their being, they too

> "reasoned high
> Of Providence, foreknowledge, will and fate,
> Fixed fate, free will, foreknowledge absolute;"

and if they "found no end," they were not "in wandering mazes lost," for, unlike the lost angels, they ruled their discussions by the infallible word of inspiration. It cannot be said that serious thought then bored, or that the sparkle of the unsubstantial poem chiefly drew, or that triviality was the characteristic of the multitude.

The study of one book, and that the Bible, simple enough in parts to meet the understanding of the little child, and of interest enough to absorb his attention, and in other parts of depths which no finite intellect can sound, and everywhere wise above the wisdom of men, and without any alloy of error, was one of the most efficacious means of raising the mass of the people in intelligence, and in educating a few, who made it their constant meditation, to a nicety of discrimination and a profundity of thought truly wonderful. Take as an example one silvery haired man whose memory is cherished with veneration. His school privileges had been less even than the scanty amount of most of his contemporaries, hardly amounting to three winter schools in all. Moreover, weakness of the eyes almost cut him off from reading books and papers throughout his life. But he was able to read daily a few verses, sometimes several chapters, in his large quarto Bible, and when he read aloud, all untaught as he was, he read with a naturalness and gave the sense, so that the hearer marvelled. Comparing scripture with scripture, he had attained to a skill in interpreting which seldom erred. His quickness in detecting a fallacy or in observing a doctrine which harmonized not with the living oracles was surpassed by very few of even the most highly educated of schoolmen. He was exceedingly retiring, but to the few who knew him, his life and his language seemed as correct as the words of that book on which both, with perfect naturalness, without any tinge of formality or quaintness, were modeled. Who will venture to say that this man's education was not incomparably superior to that of him who has delved a whole life in conflicting systems, who has sought to know the thoughts of all reported as great, but who has settled nothing for himself?

The political principles which found their expression in the declaration of independence, and which were a cherished inheritance from the fathers, leading to a general participation in the government of the country, and producing the habit of earnestly debating every question of public concern, had no small share of influence in exciting intensity and energy of mental action. By the fireside, in the field, at the corners of the streets, in the shops and stores, those powers were developed which had further exercise in the town meeting, and carried their possessor to some humble position of trust or authority; and when here trained and shown to be capable of sustaining higher responsibilities, advanced him again, so that he who had forged iron chains, was chosen to fashion the more efficacious restraints of laws; he who had occupied the cobbler's seat, was promoted to the bench of justice; and he who had been wont to rule oxen was thought worthy to govern men.

The newspaper, and the family, and the village library contributed largely to the general intelligence. The weekly paper furnished no small part of the topics of conversation in the family and among neighbors, and, in particular, supplied the pabulum for political discussions. The few books owned or borrowed were carefully read again and again. The small proprietary libraries furnished some of the most valuable histories and the choicest works in belles-lettres. It was not of rare occurrence to find persons who showed familiarity with Rollin, Ferguson, Gibbon, Robertson, and Hume; and sometimes one might even be met, who could give an orderly account of an entire work of these authors; and there were many who could repeat favorite poems, peradventure even the entire *Night Thoughts* of Dr. Young, if that was the chosen *vade mecum.* Even some children of twelve or fifteen years of age,—barefoot boys who had only "noonings" and the time they might gain by manual dexterity in accomplishing their "stents,"—had perused several of the voluminous historians named above. How will such lads compare in mental strength and vigor with children who willingly read nothing but the most exciting tales or the most intellectual pap made toothsome?

The observation of men and of nature, pursued to good advantage where no unbending usages restrained free development of character, no wrappings of conventionalities gave a uniform semblance to all, where the woods and the waters and the inhabitants thereof had only begun to recognize the dominion of man, quickened too by the necessity of turning to account every item of knowledge that could be gained, was an ample equivalent for the more comprehensive speculations of mental philosophy and the scientific nomenclatures and descriptions of natural history to be learned from the mouth of the lecturer.

Finally, those defective schools of the past generation did place the key of knowledge in the hands of the inquisitive; which is nearly all that the schools of the present day accomplish, or at least is their most valuable result. With reading, writing, and the elements of arithmetic, and the stimulus of necessity and emulation, and perhaps religious principle added, he who felt any of the inspiration of genius, or who became conscious of a talent that had been improved, might advance with a speedier flight or a slower and more toilsome step up the steep ascent to the temple of knowledge, and sit a crowned king on one of her numberless thrones. Books procured and mastered one at a time, moments of leisure seized and improved, oneness of aim and unfaltering perseverance, wrought the result.

It is a plain inference that school education, as the correlate of the professional teacher's labors, usually receives credit to which it is not entitled. As we have elsewhere remarked, with all the agencies for the education and improvement of teachers, the public schools of Europe, with their institutions of government and society, do not turn out such practical and efficient men as our own common schools, acting in concert with our religious, social and political institutions. A boy educated in a district school of New England, taught for a few months in the winter, by a rough, half-educated, but live teacher, who is earning his way by his winter's work in the school-room out of the profession into something which will pay better, and in the summer by a young female, just out of the eldest class of the winter school, and with no other knowledge of teaching than what she may have gathered by observation of the diverse practices of some ten or twelve instructors who must have taught the school under the intermittent and itinerating system which prevails universally in the country districts of New England—a boy thus taught through his school-life, but subjected at home and abroad to the stirring influences of a free press, of town and school district meetings, of constant intercourse with those who are mingling in the world, and in the affairs of public life, and beyond all these influences, subjected early to the wholesome discipline, both moral and intellectual, of taking care of himself, and the affairs of the house and the farm, will have more capacity for business, and exhibit more intellectual activity and versatility than the best scholar who ever graduated from a Prussian school, but whose school-life, and especially the years which immediately follow, are subjected to the depressing and repressing influences of a despotic government, and to a state of society in which every thing is fixed both by law and the iron rule of custom. But this superiority is not due to the school, but is gained in spite of the school.

Now when the causes which conduced to this superiority are less operative and less general, the improvement of schools becomes doubly important. This can be effected only as the moulders of educational institutions intelligently apprehend their proper aim, or, in other words, the due relation of school education to education in its enlarged sense, and as they succeed in leading teachers to a judicious direction of their efforts, and to the employment of methods adapted to the end in view. Omitting the consideration of the last topic suggested as not embraced in the design of this article, we shall have before us a practical aim, in addition to supplying the criterion for estimating the excellences and the defects of the education of the past and the present, if we consider as well as we may the question,

WHAT IS EDUCATION?

To facilitate the attainment of definiteness and accuracy of the conception, we shall attempt to distinguish the related ideas. And,

1. *Formation of character*, which is the most comprehensive of these related ideas, represents the combined result of human, natural and supernatural agencies in fashioning every lineament of the man in every department of his inner being. The human agency embraces parent, brother, sister, nurse, playmate, teacher, chosen companion, casual acquaintance, in short, all of his kind, contemporaries or predecessors, who have directly or indirectly contributed to the moulding of the man. The natural agency is the external world or physical universe, which in its influence upon persons similarly situated varies with their susceptibility. The supernatural agency comprehends that exercise of the sovereign power of the great First Cause, which places the individual in the special condition and relations that attend him on his introduction into existence and throughout his life, with whatever of direct operations there may be upon the mind, experienced consciously or unconsciously, of divine, angelic or demoniacal origin. The estimate of this last influence will de-

pend upon the theological views entertained. Character is raised to its highest elevation when the prevailing motive in the conduct of life is regard for the perfect will of God; and it is then called *piety*. Education viewed actively is not the correlative of formation of character, neither, viewed as a result, is it identical therewith. However we may employ sensible objects or those only conceived of, it proceeds by human agency alone. Whilst the disorganization of the human constitution has proved beyond the ability of mere education to rectify, on the supposition that perfection of character was attained, education might go on indefinitely. Formation of character gives a certain combination of features or qualities; education presents cultivated susceptibilities and stores of gathered treasures. Strictly, education is always immediate. We may employ another, or assist in preparing him, to educate a third person; but if this is all, we are not ourselves with him educators of that person.

2. *The development of the faculties* is the second related idea. Development is the unfolding of something which had existed only in embryo, by exciting its dormant vital energy or inherent force to activity. The result of the development of the mental faculties is *power*, power, intellectual, moral, and voluntary; power of instigating and power of controlling action. When the moral faculty or conscience controls action in all the relations of a man to his fellow-men, *rectitude* or uprightness is the result. It is the function of education to superintend the development of the faculties, accelerating that of some, circumscribing or restraining that of others, and to regulate them in their exercise. Development, even when regulated by education, must fail to give to man perfection of character, for it neither gives nor takes away, and hence original imperfection must remain, though it may be partially concealed. In an unregulated but stimulated development the proportions of what is fair would be outgrown and obscured by all forms of ugliness.

3. *Training*, of which the third related idea is the conception, is directed specifically to the forming of habits. Thus from the earliest mental training there may proceed the habits of obedience, order, neatness, trust, gentleness, kindness, self-denial, &c.; from corporeal training habits of motion, and physical action in general. Education is not, like training, directed exclusively to the forming of habits. This is rather its preliminary work.

4. *Instruction* is the communication of knowledge which may be of value to the recipient, either in itself or as a means to a remoter end. Education gives the discipline which turns knowledge to account. Instruction calls into exercise a sort of passive activity, a reception of facts and a perception of relations as presented. Education trains the pupil to discover relations, and to make deductions from facts, and thus excites an independent activity. Teachers and books instruct when they convey thoughts and explain processes; they educate in so far as they lead the pupil or reader to think for himself and to institute new processes. Instruct a man, and he will become well informed in regard to the subject of the instruction; educate a man, and his mind will be not only furnished, but also disciplined and cultivated in proportion to its capacity and the extent of the process. Precisely the same process may be instruction in one respect and education in another. Often, however, their methods are essentially different, for instruction may simply labor to facilitate to the utmost the acquisition of knowledge, but education, whilst careful to adapt its requirements to the strength of the learner, introducing its severer methods gradually, and never prematurely assigning the abstruser branches of study, only directs the learner how to encounter the difficulties of his path, and leaves him to take every step for himself, aiming to bring him as soon as possible to the condition where he may dispense with all aid. Thus, although instruction and education are inseparable, there may be much instruction where there is very little education, and very little instruction where there is much education. Instruction is limited to what the teacher does; education is measured by what the pupil is rendered competent to perform.

5. *Tuition*, distinctively regarded, has for its end simply advancement in specific branches of study. It is related to education in its restricted sense as a part to a whole. Also, it is objective only.

Education, in its enlarged sense, is the disciplining, cultivating, and furnishing of the mind of man, as a man, and for the particular position which he is to hold. It is thus general and special; general, so far as it seeks to advance man towards the perfection of his being; special, so far as it is directed to preparation for a particular sphere of activity. Discipline gives trained strength, the ability to exercise developed power at will. Culture brings the mind into the condition, relative to its capacity, to produce what is useful and beautiful and good and true. The furniture of the mind is its general stores. Incidental to the principal objects of education is physical culture. Education regards the body as a casket which must be guarded well, that the contents receive no injury; as a servant to be kept in good condition for the master's benefit.

Education in its restricted sense is that extent of mental discipline, culture and furniture, to be systematically gained under the direction of a teacher, which is requisite to the indefinite improvement of the pupil by himself, or to his independent completion of his preparation for his business in life. It is thus, like education in its enlarged sense, general and special.

This last definition determines the sphere to which the teacher is limited, and which he must occupy as completely as possible. It dictates no uniform course or method. These must be varied to suit the character and circumstances of pupils. It prescribes for each simply the text that is practicable, not every thing which is desirable. Beyond the mere fundamental branches of knowledge it makes the furnishing of the mind a secondary end. It utterly forbids the striving to make every pupil the recipient of all the sciences. In the most extended course of study it marks out the pupil's becoming an adequate self-educator as the limit of the teacher's duties, and the aim for the attainment of which he must strive. It countenances no forcing processes, which generate mere hot-bed developments, and prevent all possibility of the solid growth requisite to convert the tender plant into the majestic tree; and least of all, no measure tending to blunt the sensibilities or sour the disposition. It admits that the most valuable part of education is what is superadded to the labors of the teacher, or goes on independently of him, but it requires of him unceasing watchfulness over his pupils, and consummate wisdom and skill in directing their studies and guiding their efforts. Finally, if it permits time and effort to be devoted chiefly to literary attainments, it implies that all intellectual acquisitions must be made subordinate to moral culture.

We will close this chapter by marking some of the successive steps, agencies, and results, in the development of our present system of public elementary education.

1. As has been already remarked, in the reconstruction of civil society which followed the change from colonies to independent states in confederated and afterward national union, the necessity and wisdom of making some provision for the education of children was generally recognized, and in some instances thoroughly and liberally provided for in the fundamental laws.

The constitution of Massachusetts adopted in 1780 has this provision: "Wisdom and knowledge as well as virtue diffused generally among the body of the people, being necessary for the preservation of their rights and liberties, and as these depend on spreading the opportunities and advantages of education in the various parts of the country, and among the different orders of the people, it shall be the duty of legislatures and magistrates in all future periods of this commonwealth, to cherish the interests of literature and the sciences, and all seminaries, especially the University of Cambridge, public schools, and grammar schools in the towns; to encourage private societies and public institutions, rewards and immunities for the promotion of agriculture, arts, sciences, commerce, trades, manufactures, and a natural history of the country; to countenance and inculcate the principles of humanity and general benevolence, public and private charity, industry and frugality, honesty and punctuality in their dealings; sincerity, good humor, and all social affections and generous sentiments among the people." In the revision of the school laws in 1789, it is provided that "towns of fifty families are required to sustain schools wherein children are taught to read and write, and instructed in the English language, arithmetic, orthography, and decent behavior, for a term equal to one school of six months in each year; every town of one hundred families, twelve months; every town of one hundred and fifty families, eighteen months; and every town of two hundred families twelve months, and in addition thereto sustain a school wherein is taught the Latin, Greek and English languages for twelve months in each year." It is also "made the duty of the president, professors and tutors of the University at Cambridge, preceptors and teachers of academies, and all other instructors of youth, to take diligent care, and to exert their best endeavors to impress on the minds of children and youth committed to their care and instruction the principles of piety, justice and a sacred regard to truth, love to their country, humanity and universal benevolence, sobriety, industry and frugality, chastity, moderation and temperance, and those other virtues which are the ornament of human society, and the basis upon which the republican constitution is structured; and it shall be the duty of such instructors to endeavor to lead those under their care into a particular understanding of the tendency of the before-mentioned virtues to preserve and perfect a republican constitution, and to secure the blessings of liberty as well as to promote their future happiness, and the tendency of the opposite vices to slavery and ruin."

Vermont in the constitution adopted in 1793 ordains "that a competent number of schools shall be maintained in each town for the convenient instruction of youth, and one or more grammar schools to be incorporated and properly supported in each county," and by subsequent legislation imposed the necessary tax for their support.

New Hampshire in 1789 empowers and requires the selectmen of the several towns to assess an annual tax upon the inhabitants for the support of a school or schools for teaching, reading, writing and arithmetic, and in each county town a grammar school for the purpose of teaching the Greek and Latin languages in addition to the other studies.

Connecticut in 1795, in addition to a special tax for the support of common schools, collectable with the other public taxes, appropriated the avails of the sales of three millions of acres of land belonging to the state and situated in Ohio—since known as the Western Reserve—as a perpetual fund for the same object.

New York in 1795 appropriated $50,000 annually for the purpose of encouraging and maintaining common schools in the several cities and towns, which were required to raise by tax for the same purpose a sum equal to one-half the amount received from the state.

Pennsylvania in the constitution adopted in 1790 ordains "that the legislature shall provide by law for the establishment of schools throughout the state in such manner that the poor may be taught gratis;" "and that the arts and sciences shall be promoted in one or more seminaries of learning." The peculiar feature in the constitution and laws of Pennsylvania providing for the free education of the poor instead of common schools, was unfortunately adopted by New Jersey, Delaware, Maryland, and most of the southern states which had not enjoyed from their first beginnings the inestimable advantages of public schools "good enough for the rich and cheap enough for the poor." Owing to the sparseness of their population, their "peculiar institution," and difficulty of establishing good school habits in any community, public schools have never flourished in the southern and south-western states.

Virginia in 1796 passed a general school law, a portion of the preamble of which is as follows: "Whereas, upon a review of the history of mankind, it seemeth that, however favorable a republican government founded on the principles of equal liberty, justice and order may be to human happiness, no real stability or lasting permanency thereof can be rationally hoped for, if the minds of the citizens be not rendered liberal and humane, and be not fully impressed with the importance of those principles from whence these blessings proceed; with a view, therefore, to lay the first foundations of a system of education which may tend to produce those desirable purposes," etc. Georgia, Kentucky and Tennessee passed school laws with aims as generous as those of the above preamble; but the institutions established were for higher learning and the few, and not for the great masses of the community.

Ohio, Indiana, and all of the states formed out of the north-western and Louisiana territories, as they were admitted into the Union, adopted in their organic and early laws provisions for the appropriation of the funds created out of the educational land grants of Congress, before spoken of, to the support of common schools and colleges, on the plan of the eastern states. But it was soon found that it was not sufficient to pass laws, or even appropriate money liberally for the support of schools; those laws must be efficiently and uniformly administered, and the condition of the schools be brought constantly to the attention of the legislature and the people.

2. New York was the first state to create an officer to look after the operations of the school law, and to advise and assist local

school officers in its administration. The appointment by the legislature in 1813 of Gideon Hawley as superintendent of common schools, and his annual reports to the legislature on the working of the system, constitute an important era in the history of public instruction in the United States. Other states created the office, but devolved its administration on some other department already burdened with other and dissimilar duties. In 1826 Massachusetts required returns to be made of the condition of the public schools of each town, and in 1836 instituted a state board of education, with a salaried secretary whose business it was made "to collect information of the actual condition and efficiency of the common schools and other means of popular education, and diffuse as widely as possible throughout every part of the state information of the most approved methods of conducting the education of the young, that they may have the best education that common schools can be made to impart." This example was followed by Connecticut in 1838, and in less than ten years this great interest of public instruction, so far as covered by elementary schools, was recognized as a legitimate department of the government, in all the northern and western states.

Under the able and enthusiastic leadership of Horace Mann, the first secretary of the board of education in Massachusetts, the various plans and suggestions which had been proposed for ten or fifteen years previous, for the improvement of common schools, were matured and applied in the most efficient manner. Conventions of teachers, parents and friends of popular education were held for addresses and discussions, in every state, and in almost every county in every state which had appointed either a single officer, or a board with a paid secretary, to look after this interest. The regular and punctual attendance of all the children of a suitable age at school, the advantages of a gradation of schools, of parental visits to the schools, of an association of the teachers for mutual improvement, and the visiting of each other's schools; the evils arising from an improper location, construction and furniture of school houses, from a diversity of text books in the same study, from a multiplicity of studies in the same school, from the neglect of the young pupils and the primary studies, from a constant change of teachers, from the employment of teachers not properly qualified, from severe and unnatural punishments, from the want of suitable apparatus, from the mechanical processes of teaching reading, arithmetic, and other studies, from the neglect of moral education, these and other subjects were discussed in official reports, in the public press, and in professional school journals. Out of the more enlightened and interested public opinion of the country, in neighborhoods, villages, and cities, have resulted wise legislation, efficient organization, vigorous administration, and liberal appropriations, in respect to the material outfit of schools; and with these, but not as rapidly or as widely, have grown up better school attendance, more philosophical arrangement of studies, and improved methods of instruction and discipline.

3. Since 1840 the most marked improvement in the organization, administration and instruction of public schools, has been made in the larger cities of the several states, sometimes under the general school law of the state, but generally under special legislation. With the exception of Boston and a few of the other large cities of New England, the system of public schools was altogether inadequate to the educational wants of large communities. Expensive private schools were the main reliance for the education of the children of professional and wealthy families, while a large number of those whose means were inadequate, were left without provision for their instruction. The establishment of schools of different grades for children of different ages and studies, and especially of primary schools for young children under female teachers, and of a high school for the older boys and girls in studies heretofore pursued only in expensive private schools, has greatly increased the attendance and elevated the character of the public schools of our cities. By means of evening schools which have been established in many of our cities, the defective education of many young men has been remedied, and their various employments have been converted into more efficient instruments of self-culture.

4. With the improvement of schools in cities and large villages, the establishment of normal schools, teachers' associations, teachers' institutes, and educational journals, and state and local supervision, the country schools throughout the northern and western states are now in a good and hopeful condition.

CHAPTER IV.

ACADEMIES, HIGH SCHOOLS, AND OTHER INSTITUTIONS OF SECONDARY EDUCATION.

The first public schools of the American colonies were the free endowed grammar schools and subscription grammar schools; schools for secondary education. Public primary or elementary common schools were of later date, both in chronological order, and as being a logical result of their predecessors of higher grade.

The first school laws, those of Connecticut and Massachusetts, which were subsequent to the establishment by individuals or towns of the classes of schools they referred to, recognized all three grades of educational institutions, both what are at present termed common or elementary, and also secondary or superior; that is to say, common or neighborhood schools, grammar schools, and colleges.

The class of secondary schools, since the very earliest period of their establishment, has been far less cherished and supported, either by public opinion or by legal provisions, than either of the other two classes. Almost universally, the academy, the endowed school, the grammar school, has been wholly left to the support of those wealthier or more learned classes who have been tacitly assumed to have the only use for them; and where any state assistance has been extended to them, it has usually been in the exceptional form of individual acts of incorporation or individual grants of money or land.

It may be observed that such a co-equal public recognition, if extended to the class of secondary schools, would at once produce a definite and important result, in throwing probably half of what may be termed the present secondary course of study back within the course of the elementary grade of schools, and also in bringing back a large number of what are termed colleges into their appropriate grade of secondary institutions.

The noticeable and important fact is moreover thus brought out, that public opinion in the United States has never, up to the present time, demanded or recognized any universal privilege of education beyond that in the merest rudiments of it.

This neglect has of course caused the existing almost entire deficiency of recorded statistics of schools of this class. Such statistics are not accessible at all, except in the single state of New York, and even there, only from such secondary institutions as are obliged to furnish them as a condition of their receipt of a portion of the literature fund. This remark is not applicable to the grade of schools known as public high schools, for boys or girls, or both, in several of our larger cities; but these schools, few in number and of modern origin, are not so much the outgrowth of popular feelling, as the creations of a few intelligent friends of public education, in advance of any general demand for this class of institutions. Although not recognized generally as part of our systems of public instruction, schools of the former class have increased rapidly, and now exist in almost every village in the land, and their aggregate number in 1850, according to the census of that year, will be seen in the table on page 451.

The progress of this class of schools, in respect to studies, books, and equipment generally, and methods of instruction and discipline, can be readily measured by any one who will look into the best academy or public high school in his neighborhood, and then read the following communications—the first by the Hon. Josiah Quincy, respecting one of the earliest institutions of the class known as academies; and the other two by eminent public men, respecting the public schools, and particularly the Latin school of Boston, as it was prior to or about the beginning of the present century, and at that time pronounced "the best on the American continent."

"Mr. Barnard: *Dear Sir*—You ask briefly the position of Phillips Academy as to studies, text-books, methods, and discipline. That academy was founded in the year 1778, in the midst of the war of the Revolution, by the united contributions of three brothers—Samuel, John, and William Phillips—all of them men of property according to the scale of that day, and all of a liberal spirit toward every object, religious, moral, or educational. But the real author and instigator of that foundation was the only son of the first of the above-named, who was known during the early period of his life by the name of *Samuel Phillips, Junior*. He was, during his whole life, one of the most distinguished, exemplary, and popular men in Massachusetts; active, spirited, influential, and ready, and a leader in every good work;

and he had the control of the hearts of his father and two uncles, and was undoubtedly the influential spirit giving vitality to the plan of that institution. There was only one academy in the state at that time—Dummer Academy at Newbury—which, although it had sent forth many good scholars, was then going to decay; and the beautiful and commanding site in the south parish of Andover which that institution now occupies, was unquestionably one of the causes of the idea of the institution as well as of its locality. Eliphalet Pearson had been educated at Dummer Academy, was distinguished for his scholarship and zeal in the cause of classical learning; Samuel Phillips, jr., had formed an intimacy with him at college, though in different classes, and entertained a high opinion both of his literary attainments and spirit of discipline. Phillips Academy was projected with reference to his becoming its first master; and his aid was joined with that of his friend Phillips in forming the constitution of the academy.

"The time of its foundation was unquestionably most inauspicious to its success, but young Phillips was of a spirit that quailed before no obstacles. It was designed to be a model institution of the kind, and no pains were omitted to secure its success; and notwithstanding the uncertainties of the political aspect of the time and the perpetually increasing depreciation of paper money, it was sustained in great usefulness and prosperity. I was sent to that academy within a month after its opening, in May, 1778, being the seventh admission on its catalogue. I had just then entered upon my seventh year, and was thrust at once into my Latin at a period of life when noun, pronoun, and participle were terms of mysterious meaning which all the explanations of my grammars and my masters for a long time vainly attempted to make me comprehend. But the laws of the school were imperious. They had no regard for my age, and I was for years submitted to the studies and discipline of the seminary, which, though I could repeat the former, through want of comprehension of their meaning, I could not possibly understand. I was sent to the academy two years at least before I ought to have been. But William Phillips was my grandfather; it was deemed desirable that the founders of the academy should show confidence in its advantages; I was, therefore, sent at once, upon its first opening, and I have always regarded the severe discipline to which I was subjected, in consequence of the inadequacy of my years to my studies, as a humble contribution toward the success of the academy.

"The course of studies and text-books I do not believe I can from memory exactly recapitulate; I cannot, however, be far out of the way in stating that 'Cheever's Accidence' was our first book; the second, 'Corderius;' the third, 'Nepos;' then, if I mistake not, came 'Virgil.' There may have been some intermediate author which has escaped my memory, but besides Virgil I have no recollection of any higher author.

"Our grammar was 'Ward's,' in which all the rules and explanations are in Latin, and we were drilled sedulously in writing this language far enough to get into the university. Our studies in Greek were very slight and superficial. Gloucester's Greek Grammar was our guide in that language, and a thorough ability to construe the four Gospels was all required of us to enter the college.

"These are the best answers I can give to your inquiries on the subject of 'studies and text-books,' but I am not confident that my memory serves me with exactness. Our preparation was limited enough, but sufficient for the poverty and distracted state of the period.

"Of 'methods and discipline,' for which you inquire, I can only say that the former was strict and exact, and the latter severe. Pearson was a convert to thorough discipline; monitors kept an account of all of a student's failures, idleness, inattention, whispering, and like deviations from order, and at the end of the week were bestowed substantial rewards for such self-indulgences, distributed upon the head and hand with no lack of strength or fidelity.

"In that day arithmetic was begun at the university. The degree of preparation for college and the amount of the studies within it are not worthy of remembrance when compared with the means of acquirement now presented to the aspiring student.

"Your other inquiries I should be happy to make the subject of reply, but long cessation of familiarity with the objects to which they relate makes me dubious of my power to add any thing important to their history. My knowledge of the common schools of Boston was obtained only during the vacations of the academy, and had chief reference to improvement in my writing. Their advantages were few enough and humble enough; the education of females very slight, and limited to reading, writing, and the earlier branches of arithmetic.

"The interests of schools and of education were, thirty years ago, subjects of my thought and writing; but the lapse of time and the interposition of other objects and new duties deprive me of the power of aiding your researches on these subjects, which are, however, easily and far better satisfied by the active men of the day. Wishing you all success in these wise and noble pursuits,

"I am, very truly,
"Your friend and servant,
"JOSIAH QUINCY."

"BOSTON, Dec. 1st, 1860."

The following "Memorandum of an eminent clergyman, who was educated in the best schools of Boston just before the Revolution," we copy from a volume of the "Massachusetts Common School Journal," vol. xii., pp. 311, 312. The notes are by the editor of the Journal, Wm. B. Fowle:

"At the age of six and a half years, I was sent to Master John Lovell's Latin school. The only requirement was reading well; but, though fully qualified, I was sent away to Master Griffith, a private teacher, to learn to read, write and spell. I learned the English Grammar in Dilworth's Spelling Book by heart. Griffith traced letters with a pencil, and the pupils inked them.

"Entered Lovell's school at seven years. Lovell was a tyrant, and his system one of terror. Trouncing* was common in the school. Dr. Cooper was one of his early scholars, and he told Dr. Jackson, the minister of Brookline, that he had dreams of school till he died. The boys were so afraid they could not study. Sam. Bradford, afterward sheriff, pronounced the *P* in *Ptolemy*, and the younger Lovell rapped him over the head with a heavy ferule.*

"We studied Latin from 8 o'clock till 11, and from 1 till dark. After one or two years, I went to the town school, to Master Holbrook, at the corner of West street, to learn to write; and to Master Proctor, on Pemberton's Hill, in the south-east part of Scollay's Building. My second, third, and fourth year, I wrote there, and did nothing else. The English boys alone were taught to make pens. Griffith was gentle, but his being a private teacher accounts for it.

"The course of study was, grammar; Esop, with a translation; Clarke's Introduction to writing Latin; Eutropius, with a translation; Corderius; Ovid's Metamorphoses; Virgil's Georgics; Æneid; Cæsar; Cicero. In the sixth year I began Greek, and for the first time attempted English composition, by translating Cæsar's Commentaries. The master allowed us to read poetical translations, such as Trappe's and Dryden's Virgil. I was half way through Virgil when I began Greek with Ward's Greek Grammar.

"After Cheever's Latin Accidence, we took Ward's Lily's Latin Grammer. After the Greek Grammar, we read the Greek Testament, and were allowed to use Beza's Latin translation. Then came Homer's Iliad, five or six books, using Clarke's translation with notes, and this was all my Greek education at school. Then we took Horace, and composed Latin verses, using the Gradus ad Parnassum. Daniel Jones was the first Latin scholar in 1771 or 1772,

* "Trouncing was performed by stripping the boy, mounting him on another's back, and whipping him with birch rods, before the whole school. James Lovell, the grandson of John, once related to us the following anecdote, which shows the *utility* of corporal punishment! It seems that a boy had played truant, and Master John had publicly declared that the offender should be trounced. When such a sentence was pronounced, it was understood that the other boys might seize the criminal, and take him to school by force. The culprit was soon seized by one party, and hurried to the master, who inflicted the punishment without delay. On his way home, the culprit met another party, who cried out, 'Ah, John Brown,' or whatever his name was, 'you'll get it when you go to school!' 'No, I shan't,' said the victorious boy, who felt that he had got the start of them, 'No, I shan't, for *I've got it*,' and, as he said this, he slapped his hand upon the part that had paid the penalty, thus, as the poet says, 'suiting the action to the word.'"

* "We saw this done by another Boston teacher, about thirty years ago, and when we remonstrated with him upon the danger of inflicting such a blow, upon such a spot, 'O, the caitiffs,' said he, 'it is good for them!' About the same time, another teacher, who used to strike his pupils upon the hand so that the marks and bruises were visible, was waited upon by a committee of mothers, who lived near the school, and had been annoyed by the outcries of the sufferers. The teacher promised not to strike the boys any more on the *hand*, and the women went away satisfied. But, instead of inflicting blows upon the hand, he inflicted them upon the soles of the feet, and made the punishment more severe."

and he was brother to Thomas Kilby Jones, who was no scholar, though a distinguished merchant afterward.

"I entered college at the age of fourteen years and three months, and was equal in Latin and Greek to the best in the senior class. Xenophon and Sallust were the only books used in college that I had not studied. I went to the private school from 11 to 12 A. M., and to the public from 3 to 5 P. M.

"The last two years of my school life, nobody taught English Grammar or Geography, but Col. Joseph Ward (son of Deacon Joseph Ward, of Newton, West Parish, blacksmith,) who was self-taught, and set up a school in Boston. He became aid to General Ward when the war commenced, and did not teach after the war.

"I never saw a map, except in Cæsar's Commentaries, and did not know what that meant. Our class studied Lowth's English Grammar at college. At Master Proctor's school, reading and writing were taught in the same room, to girls and boys, from 7 to 14 years of age, and the Bible was the only reading book. Dilworth's Spelling Book was used, and the New England Primer. The master set sums in our MSS. but did not go farther than the Rule of Three.

"Master Griffith was a thin man, and wore a wig, as did Masters Lovell and Proctor, but they wore a cap when not in full dress. James Lovell was so beaten by his grandfather John, that James the father rose and said, 'Sir, you have flogged that boy enough.' The boy went off determined to leave school, and go to Master Proctor's; but he met one of Master Proctor's boys, who asked whither he was going, and when informed, warned him not to go, for he would fare worse."

Hon. Edward Everett, in an address at the Annual School Festival in Faneuil Hall in 1852, gives the following account of the educational advantages he enjoyed in early life:—

"It was fifty-two years last April since I began, at the age of nine years, to attend the reading and writing schools in North Bennett street. The reading school was under Master Little, (for 'Young America' had not yet repudiated that title,) and the writing school was kept by Master Tileston. Master Little, in spite of his name, was a giant in stature—six feet four, at least—and somewhat wedded to the past. He struggled earnestly against the change then taking place in the pronunciation of *u*, and insisted on saying *monooment* and *natur*. But I acquired, under his tuition, what was thought in those days a very tolerable knowledge of Lindley Murray's abridgment of English grammar, and at the end of the year could parse almost any sentence in the 'American Preceptor.' Master Tileston was a writing master of the old school. He set the copies himself, and taught that beautiful old Boston handwriting, which, if I do not mistake, has, in the march of innovation, (which is not always the same thing as improvement,) been changed very little for the better. Master Tileston was advanced in years, and had found a qualification for his calling as a writing master, in what might have seemed at first to threaten to be an obstruction. The fingers of his right hand had been contracted and stiffened in early life, by a burn, but were fixed in just the position to hold a pen and a penknife—and nothing else. As they were also considerably indurated, they served as a convenient instrument of discipline. A copy badly written, or a blotted page, was sometimes visited with an infliction which would have done no discredit to the beak of a bald eagle. His long, deep desk was a perfect curiosity-shop of confiscated balls, tops, penknives, marbles and Jews-harps—the accumulation of forty years. I desire, however, to speak of him with gratitude, for he put me on the track of an acquisition which has been extremely useful to me in after life—that of a plain, legible hand. I remained at these schools about sixteen months, and had the good fortune in 1804 to receive the Franklin medal in the English department. After an interval of about a year, during which I attended a private school kept by Mr. Ezekiel Webster, of New Hampshire, and on an occasion of his absence, by his ever memorable brother, Daniel Webster, at that time a student of law in Boston, I went to the Latin school, then slowly emerging from a state of extreme depression. It was kept in School street, where the Horticultural Hall now stands. The standard of scholastic attainment was certainly not higher than that of material comfort in those days. We read pretty much the same books—or of the same class—in Latin and Greek, as are read now, but in a very cursory and superficial manner. There was no attention paid to the philosophy of the languages—to the deduction of words from their radical elements—to the niceties of construction—still less to prosody. I never made a hexameter or pentameter verse, till, years afterward, I had a son at school in London, who occasionally required a little aid in that way. The subsidiary and illustrative branches were wholly unknown in the Latin school in 1805. Such a thing as a school library, a book of reference, a critical edition of a classic, a map, a blackboard, an engraving of an ancient building, or a copy of a work of ancient art, such as now adorn the walls of our schools, was as little known as the electric telegraph. If our children, who possess all these appliances and aids to learning, do not greatly excel their parents, they will be much to blame."

CHAPTER V.

COLLEGES.

The colleges of the United States were, at the close of the Revolutionary war, seven in number. They had been founded with the design of providing for the new commonwealths the means of a training for the young men, substantially similar to that afforded by the universities at home. Their course of study was four years in length, and was at first decidedly theological in character, and subsequently more and more secularized. The average age of those entering was somewhat less than now; and they conferred, as at present, degrees in arts in course, and honorary ones in arts, law, and divinity.

With the growth of the United States they have rapidly increased in number, being supported, beyond the receipts for tuition, either by endowments raised for each among the denomination to which it belongs, or by the proceeds of state gifts of lands or money. The number of this class of institutions incorporated with power to confer academic honors, exceeds two hundred. The length of their course of study remains the same, and indeed this is the case in all their essential characteristics. Although there has been a gradual elevation of the standard of acquirements made requisite for entrance, this preliminary examination has not been sufficiently exacting and uniform. As their funds and the number of their students have enlarged, they have shown a tendency, not to increase the length and completeness of their course of study, but rather to multiply the number of studies attempted to be taught, by adding them to the undergraduate course; and in a few instances also to annex special schools in one or another department, such as law, medicine, theology, and the application of science to industrial occupations.

Mr. Everett gives the following picture of college life at Harvard as it was fifty years ago:—

"But short as the time is since I entered college (only half as long as that which has elapsed since the close of the seven years' war), it has made me the witness of wonderful changes, both materially and intellectually, in all that concerns our *Alma Mater.* Let me sketch you the outlines of the picture, fresh to my mind's eye as the image in the *camera*, which the precincts of the college exhibited in 1807. The Common was then uninclosed. It was not so much traversed by roads in all directions; it was at once all road and no road at all,—a waste of mud and of dust, according to the season, without grass, trees, or fences. As to the streets in those days, the 'Appian Way' existed then as now; and I must allow that it bore the same resemblance then as now to the *Regina Viarum*, by which the consuls and proconsuls of Rome went forth to the conquest of Epirus, Macedonia, and the East.

"As to public buildings in the neighborhood of the university, with the exception of the Episcopal church, no one of the churches now standing was then in existence. The old parish church has disappeared, with its square pews, and galleries from which you might almost jump into the pulpit. It occupied a portion of the space between Dane Hall and the old Presidential House. I planted a row of elm and oak trees a few years ago on the spot where it stood, for which, if for nothing else, I hope to be kindly remembered by posterity. The wooden building now used as a gymnasium, and, I believe, for some other purposes, then stood where Lyceum Hall now stands. It was the county court-house; and there I often heard the voice of the venerable Chief Justice Parsons. Graduates' Hall did not exist; but on a part of the site, and behind the beautiful linden trees still flourishing, was an old black wooden house, the residence of the professor of mathematics. A little further to the north, and just at the corner of Church street, which was not then opened, stood what was dignified in the annual college catalogue (which was printed on one side of a sheet of paper, and was a novelty) as 'The College House.' The cellar is still visible. By the students this edifice was disrespectfully called 'Wiswall's Den,' or, for brevity, 'the Den.' I lived in it in my freshman year. Whence the name of 'Wiswall's Den' was derived, I hardly dare say; there was something worse than 'old fogy' about it. There was a dismal tradition that, at some former period, it had been the scene of a murder. A brutal husband had dragged his wife by the hair up and down the stairs, and then killed her. On the anniversary of the murder—and what day that was no one knew—there were sights and sounds—flitting garments draggled in blood, plaintive screams, *stridor ferri tractæque catenæ*—enough to appall the stoutest sophomore. But, for myself, I can truly say, that I got through my freshman year without having seen the ghost of Mr. Wiswall or his lamented lady. I was not, however, sorry when the twelvemonth was up, and I was transferred to the light, airy, well-ventilated room, No. 20 Hollis; being the inner room, ground-floor, north entry of that ancient and respectable edifice."

The tables on pages 451-3 exhibit the number, date of foundation, and statistics of our American colleges in several important particulars.

CHAPTER VI.

PROFESSIONAL, SCIENTIFIC, AND SPECIAL SCHOOLS.

As the body of human knowledge increased in extent, and filled out in detail, it subdivided by a natural process into a greater and greater number of sciences, as did the industrial side of life into a greater and greater number of employments. A subdivision and increase in the number of schools, preparatory to the business of life, naturally accompanied this process.

The colleges of the United States, according to this law of development, were in their early day designed primarily to train future clergymen, and secondarily to train those intending to enter the public service. For a long time college graduates had no means of enjoying further instruction in either of the then recognized learned professions, but by residing near or in the family of some eminent clergyman, lawyer, or physician, acting as his assistant and receiving his instructions. Then, when they considered themselves fit, or an invitation came, they took their place in the ranks of their profession. Gradually the necessity of special opportunities of instruction in the principles, and their diverse and complicated applications, led to the establishment of schools of theology, medicine, and law; and still later, of special courses of instruction, and finally, of special schools for the practical chemist, geologist, civil and military engineer, agriculturist and teacher. This department of education is not yet aided systematically in any state, and is hardly recognized by a majority of the states in their systems of public instruction. Most of this class of institutions have been established by denominational or professional associations, or by the liberality of individuals in advance of or as the inducement to legislative aid.

CHAPTER VII.

THEOLOGICAL SCHOOLS.

The future clergyman, in the American colonies, had already studied theology in his college course. It was probably common for graduates to serve what may be well enough termed an apprenticeship under some eminent clergyman, after leaving college. During the first half of the eighteenth century, the custom grew up of subjecting the candidate for the ministry to examination by a number of ministers, and licensing him to preach as candidate. Dr. Bellamy first introduced at his house at Bethlem, Connecticut, the plan of giving something like a regular course of instruction to students in theology. A little later the practice became quite general, and was confirmed by the gradual elimination of its theological character from the course of study in the colleges.

The first separate theological school in the United States was that at Andover, founded and opened in 1807. The thorough three years' course of study here established soon did away with the comparatively inefficient and superficial apprenticeship scheme, which afforded a professional training of twelve, six, or even only three months.

Of previous departmental or imperfect provisions for specific ministerial training, should be mentioned the academy known as "Log College," of Rev. William Tennent, at

Neshaminy, Bucks county, Pa., opened about 1728; the preparatory school opened by Rev. John Smith in the west of Pennsylvania in 1778, afterward under Rev. J. Anderson, D. D.; William and Mary College, which included a professorship of divinity in 1693; the foundation of the Hollis professorship of divinity at Harvard College in 1721; and that of the Livingston professorship of divinity at Yale College in 1746.

The table, altered into chronological succession from the American Almanac, 1861, gives the growth of this class of special schools.

CHAPTER VIII.

LAW SCHOOLS.

The professional education of colonial lawyers was equally unscientific, with the exception of the few who obtained a legal education at the Middle or Inner Temple in London, those inns of court being the favorite resorts of American students. Law, indeed, was then scarcely considered a liberal science in this country, and the profession was in more than one instance discouraged or actually forbidden by colonial constitutions or laws. Thus, in 1660, Virginia, by her house of burgesses, voted for "the total ejection of mercenary attorneys;" Massachusetts, in 1663, prohibited "usual and common attorneys in any inferior court," from being members of the legislature; and Locke's constitution for Carolina permitted "no one to plead another man's cause." The only professional training between the college course and actual practice was in the office of some practitioner already established, where the aspirant served for an indefinite period as an attorney's clerk, usually learning to draw instruments, and obtaining a desultory knowledge of forms, technics and special pleading, but very seldom pursuing any regulated course of study or systematically mastering his subject.

The first separate institution for legal instruction was the celebrated law school at Litchfield, Connecticut, established by Judge Reeve in 1784, taught by him alone until 1798, then together with Judge Gould until a little before Judge Reeve's death in 1823, and afterward by Judge Gould alone until 1827. Seven hundred and fifty students in all studied law in this school; who, scattered over the whole country, carried with them and instilled into the profession at large the idea of a special and systematic training for the practice of law.

We append a table, altered from the American Almanac for 1861, of the existing law schools or collegiate departments in the United States, in the order of their foundation. It should, however, be observed that some legal studies were included in the original scheme of William and Mary College, founded 1693, and the law course became of some positive value by improvements about 1730. Also, that a law professorship was founded in the College of Philadelphia in 1790; a professor of law appointed at Yale College in 1801; and the Royall Professorship of Law at Harvard, founded in 1815.

CHAPTER IX.

MEDICAL SCHOOLS.

Medical schools are of quite recent date; and the training of the young physician was of a very irregular character during the colonial period. Degrees of Doctor of Medicine were possessed by a very few practising physicians, who had studied at Edinburgh, Leyden, or other European schools. The few eminent physicians who were trained exclusively in the colonies, were to a great extent followers of a natural gift and tendency, which went far to supply their lack of school learning. Young men proposing to become physicians, practised in the offices and under the instruction of established physicians. Down to the middle of the 18th century, it was the frequent practice, in Connecticut, at least, to obtain a formal license from the general court, which was commonly granted on petition of the aspirant, reinforced by testimonials from the freemen of his town, the town officers, or practising physicians. Sometimes the only credentials of the beginner, were the certificate of the physician with whom he had studied. After college courses of medical lectures were established, a license from the faculty was given, which served instead of the subsequent diploma.

The earliest collegiate medical department in the United States was that of the University of Pennsylvania in 1765. Dr. Shippen had lectured on anatomy in 1762.

We add a chronological table, altered from the American Almanac for 1861, of the medical schools of the United States.

CHAPTER X.

MILITARY AND NAVAL SCHOOLS.

The experience of the Revolutionary war occasioned a very general conviction among the officers of the American army, of the necessity for such a provision for the military education of native officers as would relieve the United States from a dependence upon professionally trained soldiers of foreign birth. The idea of a military school of some kind, to be connected with each United States arsenal, was entertained at the close of the war among the officers.

In the spring of 1783, General Washington requested from a number of leading officers, statements of their views on all subjects connected with the peace establishment of the United States army. In reply to this request, Colonel Timothy Pickering, then quartermaster-general, drew up an able and interesting memoir, which contains, it is believed, the first suggestion of a single central government military academy, and he also suggested West Point as a proper location for it.

President Washington's annual address to Congress of December 3, 1793, asks "whether a material feature in the improvement of a system of national defence ought not to be to afford an opportunity for the study of those branches of the military art, which can scarcely ever be attained by practice alone."

An act of Congress of May 9, 1794, authorized a corps of four battalions of artillerists and engineers, to each of which were to be attached eight cadets. This was the first introduction into the military service of the United States of this term, which may be defined to signify a grade of officers between the highest non-commissioned officer, a sergeant, and the lowest commissioned one, an ensign. For the use of this corps and cadets, the secretary of war, Colonel Pickering, was authorized to procure the necessary books and apparatus. The secretary, in 1796, reports that this organization is important, and should be as stationary as practicable, with a view to instruction.

President Washington's last annual speech to Congress, December, 1796, again urged strongly the establishment of a military academy. In April, 1798, the corps of artillerists and engineers was increased by an additional regiment, and the number of cadets enlarged to fifty-six. In July following, four teachers were by Congress authorized to be employed in that regiment for instruction in science and art. Some officers and men were collected at West Point, and a sort of military school opened, which, however, acted with little efficiency, owing to the want of preparatory training, and of organization.

Secretary of War McHenry, in a report on the organization of the army, made during the expectation of a war with France, dated December 24, 1798, lamented the want of engineers and artillerists trained at home. In January, 1800, the same officer laid before the President, who transmitted it to Congress, a plan for establishing a military academy. After referring to the imperfect steps already taken in this direction, he proceeds to suggest that the proposed academy shall consist of a "fundamental school," to instruct in such departments of science as are necessary in common in all the arms of the military force; and three special schools, one of engineers and artillerists, one of cavalry and infantry, and one of the navy. The institution was to be in charge of a director-general, four directors, twelve professors, and nine other instructors. This school, so far as Secretary McHenry recommended its immediate establishment, was to accommodate annual classes of one hundred pupils each, for courses of four and five years.

The Military Academy at West Point, according to Colonel Williams' report in 1808, was first opened in 1801, as a "mathematical school for the few cadets that were then in service," and under a private citizen. In 1802, an act of Congress separated the artillerists and engineers, distributing the cadets of the former class among the twenty companies of that arm, and constituted the engineers the Military Academy, making it consist of seven officers and ten cadets.

The operations of the school continued to be deficient in order and efficiency for some years, still for want of proper and energetic administration, and a well adjusted course of study. In 1812, it was much enlarged, and its organization quite changed. The period from 1817 to 1824, however, during which a thorough course of theoretical and practical studies, properly adapted to the military profession, was for the first time introduced, marks the establishment of the academy as a military and scientific school of high grade and value.

The academy, in 1860, was organized under a superintendent, who is commandant of the post, and a corps of forty-six instructors and officers. Its course of study is of five years, and is intended to train the pupils in military science and art as applicable to all arms of the service. The number of pupils is by law fixed at one from each congressional and territorial representative district, together with ten appointed at large; being at present a total limit of 252.

OTHER MILITARY SCHOOLS.

In 1839, the state of Virginia established in connection with Washington College, at Lexington, Va., the "Virginia Military Institute," intended to instruct young men in tactics and civil engineering. There were in 1858 eleven instructors. The pupils are divided into state cadets and pay cadets; the latter class paying their expenses, and the former supported out of a state appropriation of $6000 a year, and an additional sum of $1,500 from the literary fund.

Two similar schools were established by South Carolina in 1842—the Arsenal Academy at Columbia, and the Citadel Academy at Charleston. These contemplate a similar course, and are aided by a state appropriation, which was in 1859 $30,000. A military academy at Lexington, Kentucky, is aided by the state, and is under a board of nine members, appointed by the state. Louisiana has a military school of the same character. These institutions have been found well adapted to the character of southern pupils, and are flourishing and useful.

Of the various private schools which have or have had an infusion of the military element, one of the most prominent was that of Captain Alden Partridge. Captain Partridge was a native of Norwich, Vt., where he died, aged 70, in 1854. He was a military instructor during nearly fifty years, being principal of the West Point Academy from 1812 to 1816; and afterward conducting a private military school, successively at Norwich, Vt., Middletown, Ct., Portsmouth, Va., and Brandywine Springs, Del., nearly or quite down to the time of his death.

A number of private schools and other institutions in various parts of the country have adopted more or less of a military organization, as a means of securing physical exercise, amusement, and mental and moral discipline. A military drill, for instance, is part of the regular exercises of the University of Nashville, Tennessee; and the pupils of the well-known school of Professor William Russell, of New Haven, Connecticut, are regularly and thoroughly drilled as an infantry company.

THE NAVAL ACADEMY.

The Naval Academy at Annapolis, Maryland (in 1861 removed to Newport, R. I.), was founded in October, 1845, by the efforts of the Hon. George Bancroft, then secretary of the navy. All the efforts which had previously been made on board of our national cruisers, in the navy yards of Boston, New York, and Norfolk, and in the Naval Asylum of Philadelphia, were found to be insufficient for the proper training and education of midshipmen.

During the infancy of the academy, several plans of an experimental character were tried, which led gradually to the adoption of the admirable system of education now in operation. Midshipmen who had made a cruise at sea, were first sent to the academy, for a term of nine months, to prepare for their final examination, which practice was continued until 1847. In that year, a board of officers recommended a course of four years at the academy—viz., two years before and two years after a cruise at sea. This plan went into operation, but it was soon abandoned, owing to the constant demand at sea for midshipmen during the Mexican war, and it was not until 1851 that the present uninterrupted course of four years at the academy was inaugurated.

Candidates for the Naval Academy are appointed upon the recommendation of members of Congress, and each state and territory is entitled to a number of appointments corresponding with its congressional representatives. Candidates are admitted between the 20th of September and the 1st of October of each year, and, if successful in the preliminary examination, are permitted to assume the naval uniform, and, in the capacity of acting midshipmen, begin their career on the school-ship "Constitution." This noble old frigate, lately become an adjunct to the Naval Academy, is the home of the fourth class, during the first year of the course.

The entire corps of acting midshipmen now at the Naval Academy is about two hundred strong, and is divided into four classes, three of which occupy the quarters on shore. During the summer vacation, two of the classes are drafted on board the practice-ship to make a cruise in the Atlantic Ocean, and they return well versed in the duties of an officer and a sailor, and in the rigging and evolutions of a ship. During the course of four years they are subjected to eight severe examinations, and, if successful in all, they receive a midshipman's warrant; then they go to sea for two years, and return once more to the academy for their final examination. Thus, the term of a midshipman's apprenticeship is six years, at the expiration of which he receives the warrant of a passed-midshipman, and is then left to carve out his own destiny.

The academy is governed by a captain in the navy, assisted by an executive officer and several lieutenants, who are charged with the discipline of the establishment and the instruction of the midshipmen in strictly professional branches. The other departments of instruction are intrusted to competent professors, and the academy is supplied with a valuable library and scientific apparatus, which aid materially in the education of the "future hope of the navy."

CHAPTER XI.

NORMAL SCHOOLS AND OTHER INSTITUTIONS AND AGENCIES FOR THE PROFESSIONAL TRAINING OF TEACHERS.

TEACHING was not recognized as a science or an art in this country until long after what are termed *par excellence* the learned professions. Indeed, it is not by any means yet admitted to its proper dignity as such; and of special schools of preparation for it, only one can date back more than about forty years, viz., Mr. Hall's, established in 1823.

During the colonial period of the United States, and indeed until within cotemporary memory, teachers were expected to be supplied for many of the more advanced village or district schools, from educational institutions of the higher grades, mainly from the colleges, many of whose students were in the habit of teaching during the winter term. The remaining public schools, in the country at least, were commonly kept by persons who had received no other education than the same class of schools had furnished.

The principal agencies introduced in modern times for the professional training of teachers, setting apart the actual incidental practice already mentioned, by college students and graduates of district schools, and also systematized books on the theory and practice of education,* may be enumerated as 1. Teachers' Associations; 2. Educational Periodicals; 3. Normal Schools; 4. Teachers' Institutes; which agencies respectively first commenced their operations within the United States, in the order named; the two latter, however, in the same year, with an interval of only about four months.

Of Teachers' Associations for professional improvement, the earliest in this country, so far as is known, was the "Middlesex County Association for the Improvement of Common Schools," formed at Middletown, Connecticut, in 1799. The "Incorporated Society of Teachers," in the city of New York, of which Albert Picket was president, and John W. Picket, his brother, corresponding secretary, was incorporated in 1811. The Essex County (Mass.) Teachers' Association was established in August, 1830, by teachers from that county, with a constitution and officers. It is still in existence, and has maintained its series of semi-annual meetings and of lectures unbroken to the present time. The Western College of Teachers, a useful and influential body, was formed in 1831, by the influence of the brothers Picket, Samuel Lewis, and other early friends of education in Ohio and the West.

Far the most prominent and influential, however, of all the existing educational associations in the country, is the American Institute of Instruction. The formation of this body was the ultimate result of a movement which commenced by a meeting of teachers and friends of education at Boston, March 15th to 18th, 1830. This meeting debated and resolved upon a "permanent as-

* The following is a list of some of the earlier American publications on the principles and methods of education:—

ABBOTT, J. *The Teacher.*

ALCOTT, W. A. *History of First District School of Hartford. Word to Primary School Teachers. Confessions of a Schoolmaster. Slate and Blackboard Exercises.*

BEECHER, MISS C. E. *Suggestions on Female Education.*

BURTON, W. *The District School as it Was.*

DAVIS, E. *Manual for Teachers.*

EMERSON, G. B. *The Schoolmaster.*

GRISCOM, J. *Monitorial Instruction.*

HALL, S. *Lectures on School Keeping. Lectures to Female Teachers.*

PAGE, D. P. *Theory and Practice of Teaching.*

PALMER, T. H. *Prize Essay on Teaching.*

POTTER, A. *The School.*

RUSSELL, W. *Suggestions on Education. Manual of Mutual Instruction.*

sociation of persons engaged and interested in the business of instruction;" and, in pursuance of its votes, an adjourned meeting was held at Boston in August following, at which its constitution and name were adopted, and its first course of lectures delivered. It was incorporated in 1831 by the legislature of Massachusetts, and has received an annual grant from that state. Its series of annual meetings is still continued, and its accompanying series of annual volumes of lectures has now reached the 31st, and includes a valuable mass of useful theoretical and practical discussions.

During the period of educational interest which produced the American Institute of Instruction, many conventions and meetings of teachers and friends of education assembled in different parts of the country, to consult and debate upon means of improvement for schools and teachers. Among the more earnest and efficient of these may be named the Windham County (Conn.) Convention, which met in 1826; the Hartford Society for the Improvement of Common Schools, formed in 1827, and among whose members were Messrs. Hooker, Gallaudet, W. C. Woodbridge, and others; the Pennsylvania Society for the Promotion of Public Schools, formed in 1828; and the Convention of the Teachers of New York, which met at Utica in 1832. These bodies frequently possessed scarcely more than an annual existence, meeting from year to year in pursuance of a new call. Their efforts, however, and the evident capacities of such organizations for usefulness, led directly to the subsequent formation of that class of educational societies known as "State Teachers' Associations." Of these, the Massachusetts State Teachers' Association, and the Rhode Island Institute of Instruction, were organized in 1845; the Ohio State Teachers' Association in 1847; and others have followed, until at present there are no less than twenty-seven State Teachers' Associations, some of them acting with remarkable efficiency for the professional improvement of teachers. In connection with these state bodies, county associations exist in several states, some of them enjoying state aid, and many of them useful co-laborers in the educational field with the state associations with which they are affiliated.

The first proposition in this country for a periodical to be devoted to education was made by Rev. Samuel Bacon, a native of Sturbridge, Massachusetts, who, in 1812, issued the prospectus of a periodical, to be known as *The Academical Herald and Journal of Education.* Mr. Bacon subsequently resumed this idea, but gave it up again upon the appearance of the first actual American educational periodical, *The Academician.* This was a large octavo, issued semi-monthly, at New York, during the years 1818–19, and edited by Albert Picket and John W. Picket, afterward the well-known early influential members of the "Western College of Teachers."

This field of labor now remained unoccupied until the appearance of the *American Journal of Education,* commenced January 1st, 1825, at Boston, Mr. T. B. Wait publisher, and edited by Professor William Russell. With its continuation, the *American Annals of Education,* this well-known and valuable journal appeared until the end of 1839, completing an entire series of fourteen octavo volumes.

In January, 1836, appeared the first number of the *Common School Assistant,* a quarto monthly, edited by J. Orville Taylor, and which was published at Albany, and afterward at New York, during four years and four volumes, and part of a fifth, ending in 1840. This periodical was energetically and usefully edited, was taken and read throughout the country, and did a good work in its day and generation for the cause of common schools.

Mr. Taylor also did much for the cause of education by publishing a *Common School Almanac,* and by delivering forcible and apt addresses on educational subjects in many states of the Union.

In August, 1838, appeared at Hartford, Connecticut, the first number of the quarto *Connecticut Common School Journal,* edited by Henry Barnard, Secretary of the Board of Commissioners of Common Schools. This periodical was published during four years, ending in consequence of the strange reactionary rally which abolished the board in 1842. It contained the state public educational documents of its day, beside a great quantity of valuable selections and original articles. A second series in octavo form was commenced by Mr. Barnard in 1850, covering substantially the same ground, and continued by him until January, 1854, when he surrendered its care to the Connecticut State Teachers' Association, which still publishes it. The interval between 1843 and 1850 was covered by the publication of the *Jour-*

nal of the Rhode Island Institute of Instruction, embodying the official documents and action of Mr. Barnard in that state as commissioner of public achools.

In August, 1855, Mr. Barnard issued the first number of his *American Journal of Education*, published at Hartford, quarterly, in octavo. The plan contemplated a series of at least ten volumes, of about 800 pages, to constitute an encyclopædia of educational materials of permanent value, illustrative of the history, biography, theory, and practice of all departments of education, both in this country and in other parts of the world, as well as a record of cotemporary educational facts and progress. In the progress of this plan hitherto, the ten volumes already completed have included over 300 cuts on school architecture, more than forty singularly fine portraits of eminent American teachers and educators, a still larger number of memoirs, and over 1600 pages on the comparatively new and most important department of methodology.

The earliest suggestion of institutional provision for the specific professional training of teachers seems to have been that of Elisha Ticknor, in an article in the *Massachusetts Magazine* for June, 1789, for county schools under able masters, to teach English grammar, Latin, Greek, rhetoric, geography, mathematics, etc., "in order to fit young gentlemen for college and school keeping."

The first proposition for a separate and exclusive teachers' seminary was, however, set forth by the late Professor Denison Olmsted, in an oration at receiving his master's degree, at commencement, 1816, on the "State of Education in Connecticut." This was to be a state institution, to train teachers for the state public schools. Professor Olmsted's prosecution of his plan was prevented by his accepting a professorship in North Carolina.

Seven years afterward, in March, 1823, Rev. Samuel Read Hall opened at Concord, Vermont, the first teachers' seminary in the United States; an unpretending little school, planned in consequence of his own observations upon the wants of teachers, intended for the improvement of teachers in and near his own town, and including a model class of juvenile pupils.

During the years 1824–5, Messrs. Thomas H. Gallaudet of Hartford, Connecticut; James G. Carter of Lancaster, Massachusetts; and Walter R. Johnson of Germantown, Pennsylvania, issued various pamphlets and newspaper articles, ably urging the necessity, practicability, and advantages of institutions for the professional training of teachers.

In February, 1826, a committee was appointed by the legislature of Massachusetts to report a plan for an institution to instruct in practical arts and sciences. This committee included in the plan recommended by them a department for the professional training of teachers. This scheme was not, however, carried into operation.

In the next year, 1827, Governor Clinton recommended to the legislature of the state of New York the establishment of a normal school, and an act was passed for that purpose. It was, however, strongly opposed by Hon. John C. Spencer, who succeeded in preventing it from going into operation, and in causing the adoption instead of the plan of teachers' departments in academies.

The earliest instance of a teachers' institute in this country, though not then so named, was the experimental one gathered at Hartford, Connecticut, in October, 1839, by the means and at the expense of the then superintendent of common schools in Connecticut, in order to prove the practicability and usefulness of the plan. The result was entirely satisfactory. A similar class, or "temporary normal school," was successfully conducted during eight weeks by Mr. Stephen R. Sweet, at Kingsboro, Fulton county, New York, commencing on the 6th of September, 1842. J. S. Denman, Esq., school superintendent of Tompkins county, New York, urged a similar class upon the attention of the Tompkins County Teachers' Association in October, 1842, and a teachers' institute, supposed by him to be the first in the state and in the world—and probably the first expressly so called—was opened under his direction in that county in April, 1843, and profitably conducted during two weeks.

Institutes were held in many places in New York during the following five years, under the auspices of school officers and teachers; and at the end of that time, in November, 1847, an act of the legislature made them part of the legal school system, and provided a trifling annual appropriation to aid in holding them in each county.

Under the influence of earnest efforts by teachers and educators during 1846, the legislature of Connecticut, in May, 1847, made an appropriation which enabled the superintendent, Hon. S. P. Beers, to provide for the holding of institutes in each county of the state in the following autumn; and they have since formed part of the state system for training teachers.

Institutes were introduced into Massachusetts in the autumn of 1846, as part of the comprehensive school reform which spread through that state under Horace Mann's secretaryship of the Board of Education. Those of 1846 were held in consequence of Hon. Edmund Dwight's gift of $1000 for the purpose. In the next year the legislature appropriated a sum to continue the plan, and they were thus incorporated into the public school system of the state of Massachusetts.

The economy and efficiency of this agency in training teachers were so great and manifest, that they quickly spread into the other eastern states, and into many of the middle and western ones; and at present may be considered a fixed feature of the American system of special training for teachers. In 1859, it was estimated that upward of 20,000 teachers were assembled under this plan of organization for instruction in their professional duties.

CHAPTER XII.

SCHOOLS OF SCIENCE FOR ENGINEERS, GEOLOGISTS, ETC.

For many years the government school for training army officers, founded in 1802, and known as the United States Military Academy at West Point, stood alone as a seminary for advanced education, in which classical instruction yielded its pre-eminence to mathematical and scientific culture. In 1824, the Rensselaer Polytechnic Institute was founded at Troy, N. Y., and furnished civilians with the means of education in some measure corresponding to but yet much lower than the military school at West Point. More than twenty years afterward, in 1846, the corporation of Yale College established two professorships, which soon formed the nucleus of the Yale Scientific School; and about the same time a gift of $50,000, subsequently increased to double that amount, by Abbott Lawrence, enabled the corporation of Harvard University to establish in 1847 the Lawrence Scientific School. Within a short time Dartmouth College was enabled to go forward in the same direction, by a bequest of $50,000 received from Abiel Chandler, at his decease in 1851, endowing the Chandler Scientific School. As these three institutions naturally form a group by themselves, providing instruction of an advanced character in several different branches of science, a brief sketch will be given of each one; but there are a variety of less advanced schools, and of schools devoted to a single practical object, like the agricultural schools at Lansing, Mich., and Ovid, N. Y., which will be noticed under their appropriate head.

In August, 1846, the corporation of Yale College established two professorships, one of agricultural chemistry, the other of chemistry applied to the arts; to the first of which was appointed John Pitkin Norton; to the latter Benjamin Silliman, Jr. At the same time a committee was appointed to consider the expediency of forming a "Department of Philosophy and the Arts" in connection with the university. In August, 1847, this committee reported that it was expedient to form such a department, for the instruction of other than undergraduate students. Accordingly, the department was organized for the purpose of providing instruction in philosophy, philology, history and natural science, etc. The branches of chemistry and engineering were embraced in one section, under the title of the Yale Scientific School. The professors, before appointed, entered on their duties in the autumn of 1847. In 1852, the corporation established in this department the degree of Bachelor of Philosophy, to be conferred after a two years' connection with the school, and a satisfactory examination in at least three branches of study. In September, 1852, the school suffered a severe loss in the death of its devoted friend, Professor J. P. Norton, who bequeathed to it his collection of books and apparatus. New professorships have from time to time been established, and additional instructors appointed, but the school has lacked until 1860 sufficient accommodations and the pecuniary means necessary for expansion. By the liberality of Joseph E. Sheffield, Esq., of New Haven, it is now provided with a spacious building, especially adapted to its purposes, and a fund of $100,000 for sustaining its courses of instruction. To the latter fund other gentlemen have contributed. This building (first opened in September, 1860) contains, besides the usual lecture rooms, extensive analytical and metallurgical laboratories, and halls for agricultural and technological museums. Opportunity is afforded in the school for pursuing a general scientific course, extending through three years, or special courses in physics, chemistry, industrial mechanics, and engineering, which occupy two years each.

The degree of Bachelor of Philosophy is now conferred on those who have completed either the general course or one of the special courses in the scientific school, and have passed a satisfactory examination. The degree of Civil Engineer is conferred on those who have completed, besides the special course in engineering, a higher course of one year. It is also proposed to confer a higher degree, that of Doctor of Philosophy, on those who in their residence and their scholarship conform to the requirements of the department. In February, 1860, a course of agricultural lectures was given under the patronage of the school. The faculty of the school now consists of the president of the college, a professor of civil engineering, a professor of natural history, a professor of general and applied chemistry, a professor of industrial mechanics and physics, a professor of organic chemistry, a professor of modern languages, a professor of metallurgy, and a professor of analytical and agricultural chemistry, besides certain assistants.

In 1846, the project of a Scientific School, to be connected with Harvard University, was first publicly announced, and the plans laid before Hon. Abbott Lawrence of Boston, a distinguished merchant of wealth and public spirit. In June, 1847, he offered to the college the munificent sum of $50,000, "for the purpose of teaching the practical sciences." This gift was to be applied for the erection of suitable buildings, and the purchase of apparatus, the residue to form a fund for the support of professors.

On this foundation the school was commenced the same year; Professor Horsford, already connected with the university, filling the chair of chemistry; Professor Agassiz, of Switzerland, being called to that of zoölogy and geology, and Lieut. Eustis, of the army, to that of engineering. In 1849, a laboratory, then unsurpassed even in Europe in its conveniences for practical instruction, was erected and furnished; and in 1850 a building was constructed for the temporary accommodation of the departments of zoölogy, geology, and engineering. Besides the professors already mentioned, instruction is given by the college professors in mathematics, physics, botany, comparative anatomy and physiology, and mineralogy. The school is essentially a combination of independent departments, each having exclusive control of its own internal arrangements, and sustaining a complete course of instruction for itself. At the death of Mr. Lawrence, August 18, 1855, the school received by bequest, as a second gift, the sum of $50,000, to increase its facilities for instruction and research. Connection with the school for at least a single year, in attendance on the prescribed course of studies, in one or more departments, and a satisfactory public examination, are essential to taking the degree of Bachelor of Science.

An estate valued at $350,000 was bequeathed to Harvard College in 1842 by Mr. Benjamin Bussey, of Roxbury, Mass. (to be received after the death of certain relatives), one half of which, including his mansion and farm, was to be appropriated to the establishment of an agricultural school under the direction of the college.

The Chandler Scientific School, connected with Dartmouth College, at Hanover, N. H., was established in 1851, in acceptance of a gift of $50,000, bequeathed to the trustees, for this purpose, by Abiel Chandler. He was a wealthy merchant of Boston, Mass., who was born in 1778 in Concord, N. H., and died in Walpole, N. H., March 22d, 1851. By the will of the founder, instruction is to be given in "mechanics and civil engineering, the invention and manufacture of machinery, carpentry, masonry, architecture, and drawing, the investigation of properties and uses of materials employed in the arts, the modern languages, and English literature, together with bookkeeping." The school was opened in 1852, and the course of study occupies four years; for the general course in the fourth year, may be substituted a civil engineering course or a commercial course.

Those completing the regular course of four years, and passing a satisfactory examination, are entitled to the degree of Bachelor of Science.

Resident graduates will be instructed in the following advanced subjects, through an additional course of one or two years: Analytical chemistry, analytical and celestial mechanics, application of mechanics to carpentry and masonry, mechanical agents, geodesy, practical astronomy, the arts of design with reference to the useful arts.

The demand for instruction in chemistry beyond the requirements of the general college course, has led to a modification of the requirements of many of our colleges and universities. Among the schools included in the University of Virginia, is one of chemistry, in which department a systematic course of practical instruction is given in qualitative and quantitative analysis. The laboratory is open, and an instructor gives his personal attention to the students therein, for eight hours daily, five days in the week.

CHAPTER XIII.

SCHOOLS OF AGRICULTURE.

THE first plan of an agricultural school or college in the English language, which we have met with, was published in 1651 by "Master Samuel Hartlib," to whom Milton addressed his Tractate on Education, and to whom the Parliament of England gave a pension for his disinterested efforts to advance the agricultural and educational interests of the commonwealth. It was nearly two hundred years before an institution of this character was established by individual enterprise, without the aid of any public grant, in the British dominions.

The Agricultural College of the State of Michigan was established in 1855, in accordance with a provision of the revised constitution of the state, adopted in 1850. The legislature in 1855, and again in 1857, provided for the purchase of land and the endowment and management of the institution. A tract of 676 acres, lying three and a half miles east from Lansing, the state capital, was purchased, and a building with accommodations for 80 pupils was erected and dedicated May 13th, 1857. The faculty includes a president, and professors of mathematics, chemistry, physiology and entomology, natural science, English literature, and farm economy and horticulture. The tuition is free (except a matriculation fee of $5), and the students are required to labor three hours a day on the farm, for which they receive a compensation which is allowed in payment of board. The course of professional instruction embraces two years, and includes—I. Theory and Practice of Agriculture—II. Agricultural Chemistry—III. Civil and Rural Engineering—IV. Botany and Vegetable Physiology—V. Zoölogy and Animal Physiology. There is a preparatory course of one year, designed for candidates who have not pursued elsewhere the preliminary studies required in English language, geography and arithmetic, for entrance.

The State University of Michigan at Ann Arbor provides a scientific course, occupying four years, and embracing mathematics, astronomy, geology, zoölogy, botany, chemistry, mineralogy, philosophy, rhetoric, history and modern languages. The School of Engineering, connected with the institution, receives students who have completed the second and third years of the scientific course, and devotes two years to their instruction in engineering. The only charge to the student, from whatever part of the country he may come, is an admission fee of ten dollars.

The Maryland Agricultural College was established and endowed by the state legislature in 1856. The college farm is about two and a half miles north of Bladensburg, in Prince George's county. The faculty includes a president, and five professors, viz.: one of the science of agriculture, including chemistry, geology, etc.; one of the exact sciences, one of languages, one of philosophy, history, etc., and one of natural history, botany, etc. The student, in connection with his course, is obliged to labor on the farm.

The agricultural college now established near Ovid, Seneca Co., N. Y., took its rise from plans started as early as 1837. Nothing definite was accomplished until, in 1844, a charter for an agricultural college was obtained from the legislature; after further delays, in 1856, the sum of $40,000 was appropriated to the college by the legislature, on condition that a like sum be raised by private subscription. This was speedily accomplished, and a tract of some 400 acres purchased. Preparation is making for the accommodation of a large number of pupils.

The Farmers' High School of Pennsylvania was founded by the agricultural society of the state, with a fund of $10,000, accumulated from its annual exhibitions up to the autumn of 1854. The legislature passed an act of incorporation, and a board of trustees was organized; after various private

was the first in the country to admit pupils of both sexes to an entire equality of intellectual training. In any event, both this school and his previous one at Northampton afforded to both boys and girls an education of uncommon value for the period.

When that famous teacher, Caleb Bingham, removed to Boston, in 1784, he did so with the design of opening there a school for girls, who were, singularly enough, at that time excluded from the public schools. Mr. Bingham's enterprise was successful, and was also the means of revolutionizing the unfair school system of the city, and of introducing a plan which, though variously imperfect, at least provided some public instruction for girls.

In 1792, Miss Pierce opened a school for girls at Litchfield, Connecticut, which continued in operation for forty years, and educated large numbers of young ladies from all parts of the country. In the same year, at Philadelphia, was incorporated one of the first, if not the first, female academies in this country.

From about 1797 to 1800, Rev. William Woodbridge, father of the well-known author and educator W. C. Woodbridge, taught a young ladies' school, at first at Norwich, and afterward at Middletown, Conn.

In 1816, Mrs. Emma Willard commenced her endeavors to secure for women the opportunity of acquiring a grade of education corresponding to that which colleges furnish to the other sex. The eminent success and excellence of her celebrated school at Troy are well known; and an important consequence of her labors was, that female seminaries were admitted to receive aid from the literature fund of the state of New York, on the same terms with the academies.

From 1818 to 1830, Rev. Joseph Emerson conducted a young ladies' school of high reputation and efficiency, successively at Byfield and Saugus, Mass., and Wethersfield, Conn. In 1823, George B. Emerson, Esq., opened a young ladies' school at Boston, probably with a more complete and efficient outfit and apparatus than any which had preceded it.

The well-known school of John Kingsbury, Esq., an institution of similar grade and excellence, was opened at Providence, R. I., in 1828.

In 1822, Miss Catherine E. Beecher opened a school for young ladies at Hartford, Conn., which she conducted with eminent success for ten years. She afterward taught for a short period at Cincinnati, but her labors for female education have subsequently consisted in various publications, and in the management of an extended scheme for a system of Christian female education, including a national board, high schools, and normal schools; which has resulted in the establishment of several valuable institutions.

In 1825, at Wilbraham, Mass., was opened the first of the Methodist Conference seminaries; institutions whose plan has substantially followed that of the Wilbraham Seminary, which was drawn up by Rev. Wilbur Fiske, its first principal.

Miss Z. P. Grant and Miss Mary Lyon, both pupils of Rev. Joseph Emerson, were associated in the conduct of an excellent school for young ladies at Ipswich, Mass. The energetic and persevering labors of Miss Lyon, with the purpose of establishing a permanent Protestant school of high grade for young ladies, resulted in the establishment of the celebrated seminary at South Hadley, which was opened in 1837.

The present era in the history of female education in the United States is perhaps most strikingly characterized by the number of large and largely endowed institutions of a high grade, which have been established in various parts of the country. One of them is the Mount Holyoke Female Seminary, at South Hadley, just mentioned. The Packer Collegiate Institute at Brooklyn, N. Y., another of them, had previously existed as the Brooklyn Institute; and received its present name in consequence of the munificent gift of $85,000 by Mrs. Harriet L. Packer of that city. The whole property represents a value of $150,000. A still more magnificent endowment is that of the Vassar Female College at Poughkeepsie, N. Y., for which the vast sum of $408,000 has been given by Matthew Vassar, Esq., of that city.

A characteristic of the female education of the present period is the practice of admitting pupils of both sexes to institutions for secondary and superior education; to the high schools of cities, to academies, to the normal schools, and even in one or two institutions of the collegiate grade. Another one is the increasing regard which is paid to the employment of female teachers, and to their thorough preparatory training for that duty, in institutions partly or wholly for that purpose. On the whole, the department of female education is, at present, attracting as much attention, and improving as rapidly, as any other.

CHAPTER XVIII.

SCHOOL-HOUSES, APPARATUS, AND TEXT-BOOKS.

In no department of instruction has the work of improvement been so general, so rapid, or so thorough as in the material outfit of the school. Within a quarter of a century a revolution has been wrought in public opinion and action in respect to the location, construction, ventilation, warming, furniture, and equipment generally, of school-houses, and more than thirty-five millions of dollars have been expended for these objects within this short period.

SCHOOL-HOUSES AS THEY WERE.

SCHOOL-HOUSES AS THEY ARE.

COUNTRY DISTRICT SCHOOL-HOUSE.

VILLAGE SCHOOL-HOUSE.

VIEW OF GIRARD COLLEGE.

PACKER COLLEGIATE INSTITUTE.

Fig. 2. GARDEN FRONT.

Fig. 3. INTERIOR OF CHAPEL.

NORWICH (CONN) FREE ACADEMY.

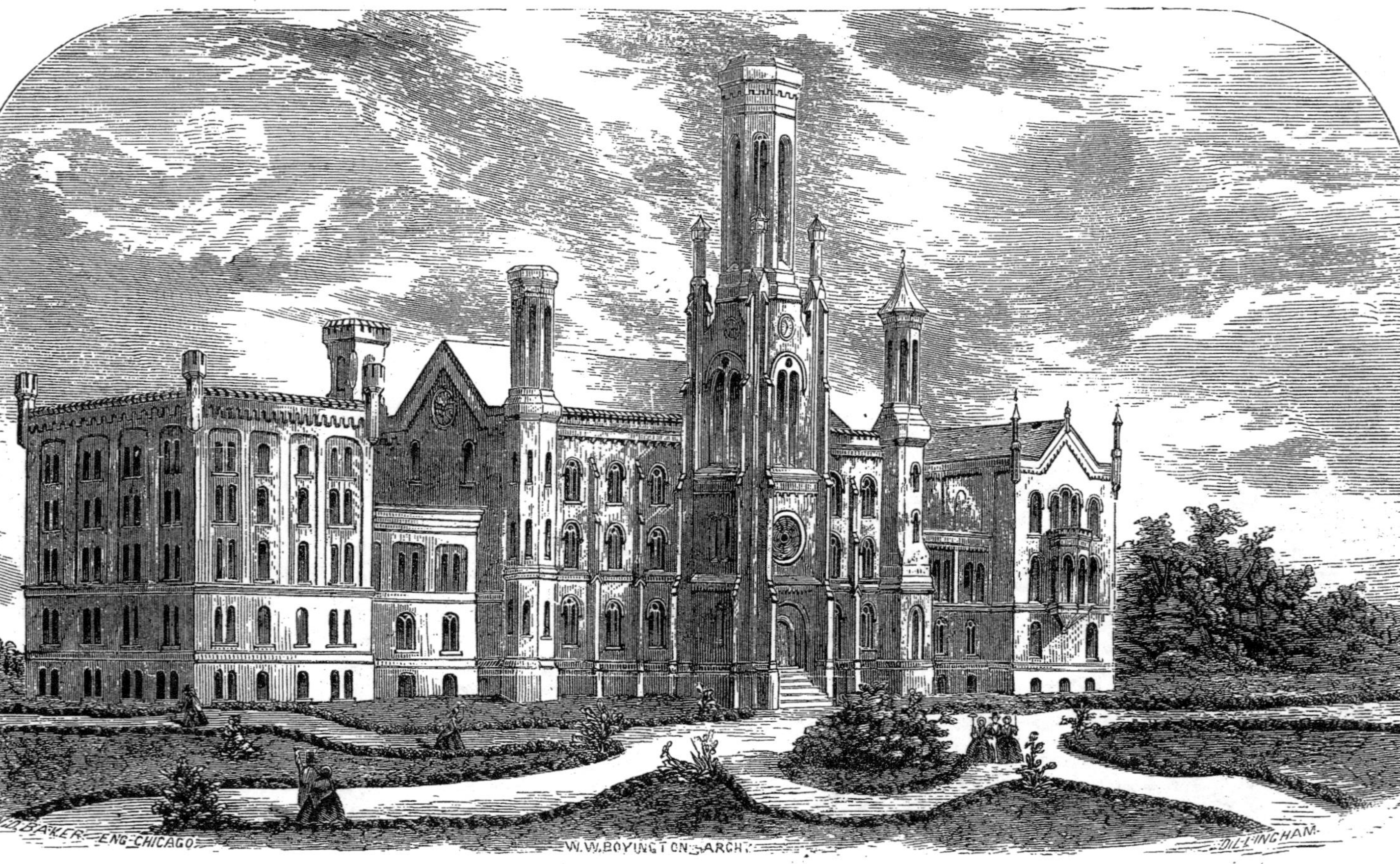

CHICAGO CITY UNIVERSITY.

SCHOOL-BOOKS.

The improvement in the authorship and manufacture of text-books, from the Primer to the Manuals of our colleges and scientific schools, within the last half century is immense. We will refresh the memory of some of our readers by reproducing a few of the tough subjects and illustrations with which they or their fathers were painfully familiar.

The Horn-book.

Few of us have had the satisfaction of learning our letters after the manner described by Prior:—

"To master John the English maid
A Horn-book gives of gingerbread;
And that the child may learn the better,
As he can name, he eats the letter."

To many, even a picture of the old-fashioned Horn-book—the Primer of our ancestors, consisting of a single leaf pasted on a board, and covered in some instances with thin

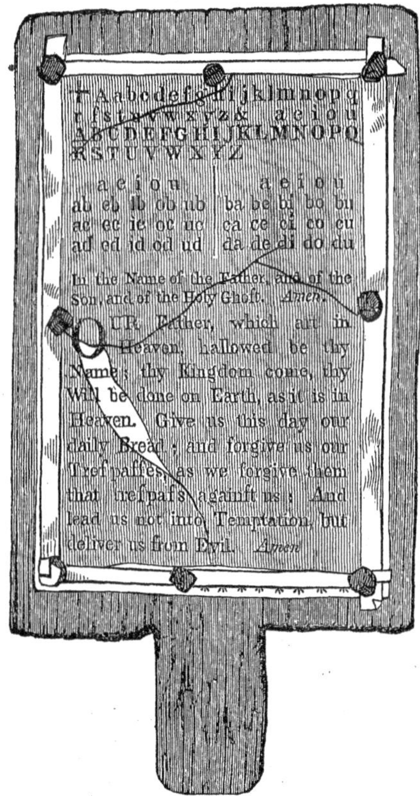

HORN-BOOK OF THE EIGHTEENTH CENTURY.

transparent horn to preserve it from being torn or soiled—will be new. The following description and the accompanying cut we copy from Barnard's *American Journal of Education*, for March, 1860:—

Shenstone, who was taught to read at a dame school near Halesowen, in Shropshire, in his delightfully quaint poem of the *Schoolmistress*, commemorating his venerable preceptress, thus records the use of the Horn-book:—

"Lo! now with state she utters her command;
Eftsoons the urchins to their tasks repair;
Their books of stature small they take in hand,
Which with pellucid horn secured are
To save from finger wet the letters fair."

Cowper thus describes the Horn-book of his time:—

"Neatly secured from being soiled or torn
Beneath a pane of thin translucent horn,
A book (to please us at a tender age
'Tis called a book, though but a single page),
Presents the prayer the Saviour deigned to teach,
Which children use, and parsons—when they preach."
Tirocinium, or a Review of Schools, 1784.

In "*Specimens of West Country Dialect*," the use of the Horn-book is thus shown:—

"Commether *Billy Chubb*, an breng the hornen book. Gee ma the vester in tha windor, yor *Pal came!*—What! be a sleepid—I'll wâke ye. Now, *Billy*, there's a good bway! Ston still there, and mind what I da zâ to ye, an whaur I da point. Now; criss-cross, girt â, little a—b—c—d. That's right, *Billy;* you'll zoon lorn the criss-cross-lain; you'll zoon auvergit Bobby Jiffry—you'll zoon be a *scholard*. A's a pirty chubby bway—Lord lov'n!"

New England Primer.

Of the New England Primer we can give no earlier specimen than the edition of 1777, embellished with a portrait of John Hancock, Esq., who was at that time President of the Continental Congress.

The Honorable JOHN HANCOCK, Efq;
Prefident of the *American* CONGRESS.

We must not omit the painfully interesting group of John Rogers in the burning faggots, with his wife and nine or ten children—including the one at the breast—a problem which has puzzled many a schoolboy's brain:

MR. JOHN ROGERS, minifter of the gofpel in *London*, was the firft martyr in Queen MARY's reign, and was burnt at *Smithfield*, *February* 14, 1554.—His wife with nine small children, and one at her breast following him to the ftake; with which forrowful fight he was not in the leaft daunted, but with wonderful patience died courageoufly for the gofpel of JESUS CHRIST.

We are fortunate in being able to present our readers with an exact transcript of the four pages of the first illustrated alphabet printed in this country. Some of our readers may recognize their old friends of the later editions of the Primer, in which "Young Timothy" and "Zaccheus he" were drawn to nature less severely true. The whole belongs to that department of literature which "he who runs may read, and he who reads will run."

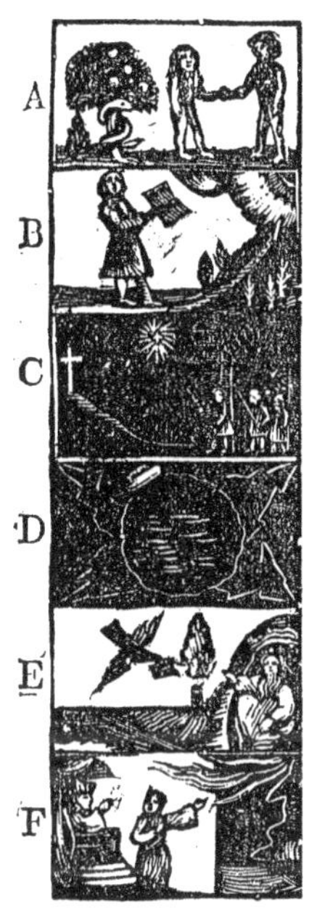

A In ADAM'S Fall
We ſinned all.

B Heaven to find,
The Bible Mind.

C Chriſt crucify'd
For ſinners dy'd.

D The Deluge drown'd
The Earth around.

E ELIJAH hid
By Ravens fed.

F The judgment made
FELIX afraid.

N NOAH did view
The old world & new

O Young OBADIAS,
DAVID, JOSIAS
All were pious.

P PETER deny'd
His Lord and cry'd.

Q Queen ESTHER ſues
And ſaves the *Jews*.

R Young pious RUTH.
Left all for Truth.

S Young SAM'L dear
The Lord did ſear.

G As runs the Glass,
Our Life doth pass.

H My Book and Heart
Must never part.

I JOB feels the Rod,—
Yet bleſſes GOD.

K Proud Korah's troop
Was ſwallowed up

L LOT fled to *Zoar*,
Saw fiery Shower
On *Sodom* pour.

M MOSES was he
Who *Israel's* Hoſt
Led thro' the Sea.

T Young TIMOTHY
Learnt ſin to fly.

U VASTHI for Pride,
Was ſet aſide.

W Whales in the Sea,
GOD's Voice obey.

X XERXES did die,
And ſo muſt I.

Y While youth do chear
Death may be near.

Z ZACCHEUS he
Did climb the Tree
Our Lord to ſee.

WEBSTER'S SPELLING BOOK.

FEW books have done more to give uniformity to the orthography of the language or to fill the memory of successive generations with wholesome truths than Webster's Spelling Book. Who can forget his first introduction to those four-and-twenty characters, standing in stiff upright columns, in their roman and italic dress, beginning with little *a*, and ending with that nondescript "*and per se;*" or his first lesson in combining letters,

ba be bi bo bu by

Or his joy in reaching words of two syllables,

ba ker bri er ci der

Or his exultation in learning to "know his duty" in those "Lessons of Easy Words" beginning,

No man may put off the law of God:

Or the more advanced steps, both in length of words and stubborn morality, in pursuit of

The wick-ed flee

And closing his spelling career with

Om pom pa noo suc
Mich il li mack a nack

And

Ail to be troubled
Ale malt liquor

In this hasty glance at this famous text book, we have designedly passed over the fables commencing with the Rude Boy and ending with Poor Tray, that we might introduce them all unabridged with their unique illustrations.

Of the Boy that ſtole Apples.

AN old man found a rude boy upon one of his trees ſtealing Apples, and deſired him to come down; but the young Sauce-box told him plainly he would not. Won't you? ſaid the old Man, then I will fetch you down; ſo he pulled up ſome tufts of Graſs, and threw at him; but this only made the Youngſter laugh, to think the old Man ſhould pretend to beat him down from the tree with graſs only.

Well, well, ſaid the old Man, if neither words nor graſs will do, I muſt try what virtue there is in Stones; ſo the old Man pelted him heartily with ſtones; which ſoon made the young Chap haſten down from the tree and beg the old Man's pardon.

MORAL.

If good words and gentle means will not reclaim the wicked, they muſt be dealt with in a more ſevere manner.

The Country Maid and her Milk Pail.

WHEN men ſuffer their imagination to amuſe them, with the proſpect of diſtant and uncertain improvements of their condition, they frequently ſuſtain real loſſes, by their inattention to thoſe affairs in which they are immediately concerned.

A country Maid was walking very deliberately with a pail of milk upon her head, when ſhe fell into the following train of reflections: The money for which I ſhall ſell this milk will enable me to increaſe my ſtock of eggs to three hundred. Theſe eggs, allowing for what may prove addle, and what may be deſtroyed by vermin, will produce at leaſt two hundred and fifty chickens. The chickens will be fit to carry to market about Chriſtmas, when poultry always bears a good price; ſo that by May Day I cannot fail of having money enough to purchaſe a new Gown. Green—let me conſider—yes, green becomes my complexion beſt, and green it ſhall be. In this dreſs I will go to the fair, where all the young fellows will ſtrive to have me for a partner; but I ſhall perhaps refuſe every one of them, and with an air of diſdain, toſs from them. Tranſported with this triumphant thought, ſhe could not forbear acting with her head what thus paſſed in her imagination, when down came the pail of milk, and with it all her imaginary happineſs.

The Cat and the Rat.

A CERTAIN Cat had made ſuch unmerciful havoc among the vermin of her neighbourhood, that not a ſingle Rat or Mouſe ventured to appear abroad. Puſs was ſoon convinced, that if affairs remained in their preſent ſituation, ſhe muſt be totally unſupplied with proviſions. After mature deliberation, therefore, ſhe reſolved to have recourſe to ſtratagem. For this purpoſe ſhe ſuſpended herſelf to a hook with her head downwards, pretending to be dead. The Rats and Mice, as they peeped from their holes, obſerving her in this dangling attitude, concluded ſhe was hanging for ſome miſdemeanour; and with great joy immediately ſallied forth in queſt of their prey. Puſs, as ſoon as a ſufficient number were collected together, quitting her hold, dropped into the midſt of them; and very few had the fortune to make good their retreat. This artifice having ſucceeded ſo well, ſhe was encouraged to try the event of a ſecond. Accordingly ſhe whitened her coat all over, by rolling herſelf in a heap of flour, and in this diſguiſe lay concealed in the bottom of a meal tub. This ſtratagem was executed in general with the ſame effect as the former. But an old experienced Rat, altogether as cunning as his adverſary, was not ſo eaſily enſnared. I don't much like, ſaid he, that white heap yonder: Something whiſpers me there is miſchief concealed under it. 'Tis true it may be meal; but it may likewiſe be ſomething that I ſhould not reliſh quite ſo well. There can be no harm at leaſt in keeping at a proper diſtance; for caution, I am ſure, is the parent of ſafety.

The Fox and the Swallow.

ARISTOTLE informs us, that the following Fable was spoken by Eſop to the Samians, on a debate upon changing their miniſters, who were accuſed of plundering the commonwealth.

A Fox ſwimming acroſs a river, happened to be entangled in ſome weeds that grew near the bank, from which he was unable to extricate himſelf. As he lay thus expoſed to whole ſwarms of flies, which were galling him and ſucking his blood, a ſwallow, obſerving his diſtreſs, kindly offered to drive them away. By no means, ſaid the Fox; for if theſe ſhould be chaſed away, which are already ſufficiently gorged, another more hungry ſwarm would ſucceed, and I ſhould be robbed of every remaining drop of blood in my veins.

The Fox and the Bramble.

A FOX, cloſely purſued by a pack of Dogs, took ſhelter under the covert of a Bramble. He rejoiced in this aſylum; and for a while, was very happy; but ſoon found that if he attempted to ſtir, he was wounded by thorns and prickles on every ſide. However, making a virtue of neceſſity, he forbore to complain; and comforted himſelf with reflecting that no bliſs is perfect; that good and evil are mixed, and flow from the ſame fountain. Theſe Briers, indeed, ſaid he, will tear my ſkin a little, yet they keep off the dogs. For the ſake of the good then let me bear the evil with patience; each bitter has its ſweet; and theſe Brambles, though they wound my fleſh, preſerve my life from danger.

The Partial Judge.

A FARMER came to a neighbouring Lawyer, expreſſing great concern for an accident which he ſaid had juſt happened. One of your Oxen, continued he, has been gored by an unlucky Bull of mine, and I ſhould be glad to know how I am to make you reparation. Thou art a very honeſt fellow, replied the lawyer, and wilt not think it unreaſonable that I expect one of thy Oxen in return. It is no more than juſtice, quoth the Farmer, to be ſure; but what did I ſay? —I miſtake—It is *your* Bull that has killed one of *my* Oxen. Indeed! ſays the Lawyer, that alters the caſe; I muſt inquire into the affair; and if—And *if!* ſaid the Farmer—the buſineſs I find would have been concluded without an *if*, had you been as ready to do juſtice to others, as to exact it from them.

The Bear and the two Friends.

TWO Friends, ſetting out together upon a journey, which led through a dangerous foreſt, mutually promiſed to aſſiſt each other if they ſhould happen to be aſſaulted. They had not proceeded far, before they perceived a Bear making towards them with great rage.

There were no hopes in flight; but one of them, being very active, ſprung up into a tree; upon which the other, throwing himſelf flat on the ground, held his breath and pretended to be dead; remembering to have heard it aſſerted, that this creature will not prey upon a dead carcaſs. The bear came up, and after ſmelling to him ſome time, left him and went on. When he was fairly out of ſight and hearing, the hero from the tree called out—Well, my friend, what ſaid the bear? he ſeemed to whiſper you very cloſely. He did ſo, replied the other, and gave me this good piece of advice, never to aſſociate with a wretch, who in the hour of danger, will deſert his friend.

The Two Dogs.

HASTY and inconſiderate connections are generally attended with great diſadvantages; and much of every man's good or ill fortune, depends upon the choice he makes of his friends.

A good-natured Spaniel overtook a ſurly Maſtiff, as he was travelling upon the high road. Tray, although an entire ſtranger to Tiger, very civilly accoſted him; and if it would be no interruption, he ſaid, he ſhould be glad to bear him company on his way. Tiger, who happened not to be altogether in ſo growling a mood as uſual, accepted the propoſal; and they very amicably purſued their journey together. In the midſt of their converſation, they arrived at the next village, where Tiger began to diſplay his malignant diſpoſition, by an unprovoked attack upon every dog he met. The villagers immediately ſallied forth with great indignation, to reſcue their reſpective favourites; and falling upon our two friends, without diſtinction or mercy, poor Tray was moſt cruelly treated, for no other reaſon, but his being found in bad company.

The following cuts, sketched from WILLSON'S Series of "School and Family Readers," with the accompanying explanations, show the great degree of advancement made, not only in the artistic beauty of the Illustrations contained in the latest published of our Reading-Books, but, more especially, in the successful attempt to combine *instruction in reading* with *advancement in useful knowledge.*

From the First Reader.

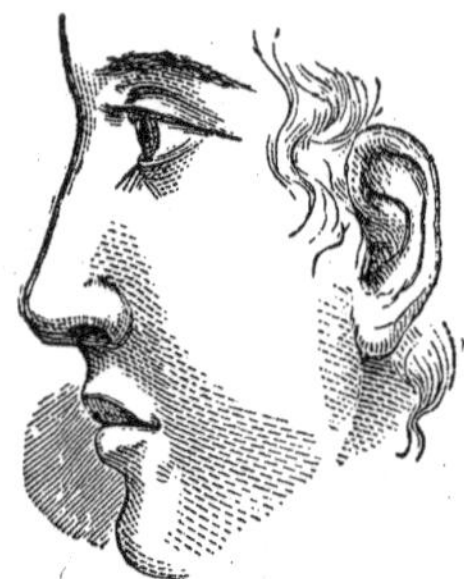

Eye, Nose, Ear, Mouth, Face.

Arm, Hand, Boot, Foot, Shoe.

The Eagle's Nest.

The leading principle developed in the SECOND READER (but which also runs throughout the entire Series) is the early cultivation of the *Perceptive Faculties* by lessons drawn from a great variety of objects and scenes which are represented to the eye of the pupil.

The THIRD READER of the Series, after a brief synopsis of the "Elements of Elocution," is divided into Four Parts:—PART I., "Stories from the Bible," beautifully and bountifully illutsrated.—PART II., "Moral Lessons."—Part III., "First Division of Animal Life," embracing the Mammalia; and PART IV., "Miscellaneous." The following four illustrations give the pupil a general idea of the four great divisions of the Animal Kingdom.

I. Vertebrates.

II. Articulates.

III. Mollusks.

IV. Radiates.

ANIMALS OF THE SEAL KIND.—1. Common Seal, *Phoca vitulina.* 2. Sea-Bear, *Phoca ursina.* 3. Sea-Lion, *Phoca jubata.* 4. Walrus, or Sea-Horse, *Trichechus rosmarus.*

The subject of the *Mammalia,* in the THIRD READER, is illustrated by more than two hundred figures of Animals, many of them in groups, with *Scales of Measurement* showing their comparative sizes, as in the Animals of the Seal kind in the annexed engraving. This we believe to be a new feature, even in zoological works, and it is one that is eminently useful.

An attempt has been made—and, it is believed, successfully—to invest the subject of animal life with a great degree of *interest* for children; to *popularize* it to their capacities; to give all desirable variety to the lessons, as exercises in reading; and to convey as much positive *information* as would be compatible with these requisites for a good Reading-Book. Numerous interesting incidents of animal life, illustrating traits of character, habits, &c., and both poetical and prose selections, effectually relieve the descriptions of that *sameness* of style and matter which is found in most zoological works.

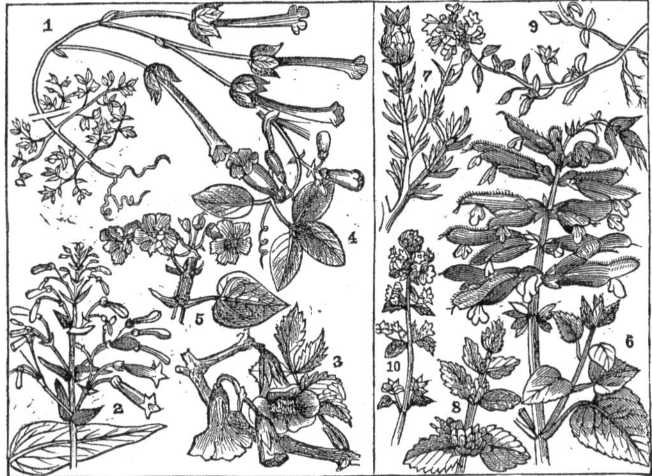

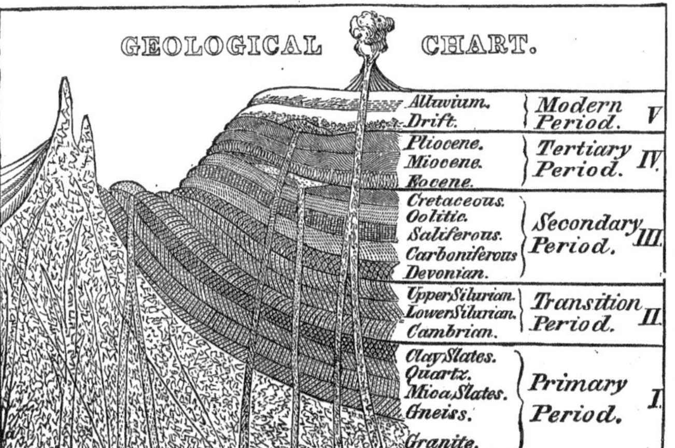

The Fourth Reader, in addition to Miscellaneous Selections, has divisions or "Parts" appropriated to "Human Physiology and Health," "Ornithology, or Birds," "Vegetable Physiology, or Botany," "Natural Philosophy," and "Sacred History," in all which there is great literary variety, well adapted for reading lessons; and, moreover, the beautiful illustrations teach *useful facts*. One of the cuts from "Ornithology," showing the forms, relative sizes, &c., of the "Climbing Birds," is here given.

The Fifth Reader, which is the highest in the Series thus far published, has, in addition to the Miscellaneous Divisions embracing a variety of the best literary selections, the eleven following "Parts."

1. "Elocutionary;" 2. "Herpetology, or Reptiles;" 3. "Second Division of Human Physiology and Health;" 4th, "Second Division of Vegetable Physiology, or Botany; 5. "Ichthyology, or Fishes;" 6. "Civil Architecture;" 7. "Second Division of Natural Philosophy; 8. "Physical Geography;" 9. "Chemistry;" 10. "Geology;" 11. "Ancient History." We have room to introduce only one illustration from each of two of these divisions.

The Botanical Illustration here given represents the Trumpet-Flower and Labiate Families; another cut shows the features which specially characterize these families, but for which we have not room here. The Classification of Plants, in accordance with the *Natural System*, is shown chiefly by such interesting illustrations as these, which certainly accomplish far more than pages of description. Moreover, the economical uses of plants are not overlooked, and the entire treatment of the subject is well calculated to cultivate, in early life, a taste for the successful study of Nature. In the department of Ichthyology, 125 species of fish are figured. Physical Geography, Architecture, Geology, &c., have their appropriate illustrations, all teaching useful facts in science, but without the dryness which usually accompanies scientific detail.

Of the very successful manner in which the above subjects have been made to combine the *literary variety* required in Reading-Books for youth, with *instruction in useful knowledge*, we have not room to speak here; but we commend a critical examination of the books themselves — in their design, plan, and execution—to every one interested in the subject of Educational Progress.

What a contrast between these and our earlier Reading-Books! The simple fact that publishers can now *afford* to illustrate, so elaborately, books designed for use in our *Common Schools*, speaks volumes for the cause of Popular Education.

SCHOOL APPARATUS.

APPARATUS AND EQUIPMENT OF THE DISTRICT SCHOOL AS IT WAS.

SPECIMENS OF APPARATUS OF THE SCHOOL AS IT IS.

CHAPTER XIX.

LIBRARIES.

At the close of the Revolution, there were very few public libraries in the country; hardly any, indeed, away from the colleges and large towns, and even these, few and small as they were, were not generally accessible. The oldest of them all was that of Harvard University, which commenced with the bequest of Harvard's books in 1638, but had been completely destroyed by fire in 1764. Great efforts were made to restore it, and before the commencement of the Revolution about $20,000 and considerable quantities of books had been contributed for that purpose. It could, however, hardly have had more than 10,000 or 12,000 volumes at that period. The only other college libraries then in existence (all of them small, but two or three of them containing many valuable works,) were the library of Yale College, founded in 1700, which had received important additions from Bishop Berkeley and other English gentlemen; the very small library of William and Mary, at Williamsburg, Va., founded, perhaps, two or three years earlier; that of the University of Pennsylvania, founded in 1749, also small, but valuable; that of New Jersey College, at Princeton, founded in 1746; that of King's, now Columbia, College, founded in 1757, and containing at the close of the Revolution not more than 2000 volumes; and the few hundred volumes which had been collected, as nuclei of libraries, in Brown University from and after 1768, Dartmouth College from 1769, and Rutgers College from 1770 to the close of the war. Of proprietary libraries, the oldest and best was the Philadelphia Library Company and Loganian Collection, founded by Benjamin Franklin in 1731, which in 1783 contained about 5000 volumes. The Redwood Library at Newport, R. I., incorporated in 1747, though not a large collection, possessed considerable value to the classical and theological student. The New York Society Library, founded in 1754, had attained to considerable size prior to the war, but suffered much from the vandalism of the British soldiers, its books being carried off by the knapsackful and bartered for grog. In 1795 it had only 5000 volumes. The Charleston Library Society was founded a year or two earlier than the New York Society, and at the commencement of the war had between five and six thousand volumes, aside from the library of Mr. Mackenzie, bequeathed to it about the same time. In 1778, however, this fine collection was almost entirely destroyed by fire, a small portion of the books only being rescued from the flames, and of these many being broken sets. The Providence Athenæum, founded in 1753, the Salem Athenæum in 1760, and the Portland Athenæum in 1765, small collections, but well selected, the special library of the American Philosophical Society at Philadelphia, and a state library of three or four hundred volumes, at Concord, New Hampshire, complete the catalogue of public libraries of any considerable importance at the close of the war of the Revolution.

The period immediately subsequent to the war was not favorable to the multiplication or growth of libraries; for, being among the outgrowths of an opulent and luxurious civilization, we could hardly look for their increase amid the poverty and financial revulsions which continued till nearly the close of the last century. Between 1783 and 1800, ten colleges and one theological seminary were founded, and some of them —as, for instance, Bowdoin, Georgetown, D. C., Williams, Dickinson, Transylvania, and the University of North Carolina—now possess respectable libraries, but they have been mainly accumulated within the last forty years. Of other libraries, we can find no record of even one, of any importance, founded in this period.

In the period between 1800 and the close of the war of 1812, there were five colleges and two theological seminaries organized, all of which now have libraries of considerable importance. To this period also belong the beginnings of the Boston Athenæum, now the fourth library in the country in the number of its volumes, the first library of Congress, which was destroyed by the British in 1814, the noble collection of the New York Historical Society, and the commencement of the special libraries of the American Antiquarian Society at Worcester, and the American Academy of Natural Sciences at Philadelphia.

The war of 1812 was followed by a period of severe financial distress, and it was not till about 1818 that any considerable efforts were made for the establishment of libraries. Between 1818 and the present time, not only have more than one hundred colleges been organized, each of which has a library of some size, and many of them from 10,000 to 25,000 volumes, but there have also been established more than twenty theological seminaries, with considerable collections of books; most of the state libraries, beginning with the valuable State Library at Albany, of over 50,000 volumes, the Congressional, Astor, Smithsonian, Boston Public Library, and other free libraries; most of the libraries of the learned societies, and the extensive collections of the historical societies, three or four proprietary libraries of some note, all of the subscription libraries, known as mercantile, institute, mechanics', or apprentices' libraries, and those connected with young men's Christian associations and with churches. Within the same period also, and mainly within twenty years past, great numbers of special libraries—scientific, commercial, agricultural, mining, humanitarian, or devoted to the promotion of particular departments of art or literature—have been founded, while in all the states Sunday School libraries, and in many of them school-district, town, and academical libraries have been formed. Prior to 1840, there were many instances in which writers who desired to investigate certain periods of history, or certain sciences or arts, were compelled to visit Europe in order to procure from the great libraries of England or the continent the necessary facts. The necessity for this is now nearly obviated. The great libraries of Cambridge, Boston, New York, Philadelphia, and Washington, though neither of them so complete as they should be, yet together furnish material for the preparation of works in most departments of science, literature, or art, and they are every year becoming more and more full in the topics heretofore deficient.

The best free library in this country, and the largest, is the Astor Library of New York. It was founded by the bequest of $400,000 by John Jacob Astor, of which $75,000 was to be appropriated for the building, $120,000 for the first purchase of books, and the remainder invested, and the interest applied to the management and increase of the library. The original building, with its furniture and shelving, opened in 1854, cost about $120,000, the excess over $75,000 being from accrued interest. The $120,000 expended for books purchased about 80,000 volumes. The shelf-room (13,000 feet) being likely to prove insufficient for the wants of the library, William B. Astor, Esq., the son of the founder of the library, purchased a lot adjoining the north side of the library, 80 by 120 feet, and erected an additional building, somewhat larger than the original one, which he presented to the trustees. Mr. Astor has also, at different times, made considerable donations for the purchase of books. The present number of volumes in the library is somewhat more than 120,000, nearly all acquired by purchase. In his long and careful bibliographical preparation for purchasing this library, in his judicious selections, and careful expenditures, Dr. Cogswell, the librarian-in-chief, has established a claim to the gratitude of all scholars.

The library of Harvard University has grown up since 1764, when the original library was destroyed by fire, by numerous donations of books, and, in quite a number of instances, of entire libraries, as well as by donations and bequests of money from friends. These donations and bequests cannot fall much short of $150,000, and it has now a fund of $26,000, the interest of which is applicable to the purchase of books, and the sum of $5000 per year, for five years from 1859, pledged by William Gray, Esq., to be applied to the same purpose. The various collections of books in Gore Hall (the library building) include not only the college library proper, but also the society libraries, and the libraries of the divinity, law, and medical schools. The whole number of volumes is about 125,000, but the library is very miscellaneous in character, and incomplete in certain departments. The considerable sums it now has at command for purchases are applied to make good its deficiencies as far and as fast as possible.

The Boston City Library, a free public library, now ranks third in this country. It was founded in 1848, in accordance with a law of Massachusetts providing for the establishment of town libraries. Hon. Josiah Quincy, jr., then mayor of the city, gave $5000 toward it; Mr. Bigelow gave $1000; Mr. Everett and Mr. Winthrop, large donations of books; Mr. Joshua Bates, of London, $50,000, besides several thousand volumes; Mr. Jonathan Phillips, $10,000; and others, smaller sums. The building, erected at a cost of $363,000 by the city of Boston, is one of the finest library rooms in the world. The present number of volumes is a little more than 100,000, and is increasing at the rate of 8000 volumes per annum. During the present year (1861) also, it will

BOSTON CITY LIBRARY. EXTERIOR.

BOSTON CITY LIBRARY. INTERIOR.

receive the fine library bequeathed to it by the late Theodore Parker, consisting of nearly 18,000 volumes.

The Boston Athenæum ranks fourth in the number of its volumes, is peculiarly rich in the transactions of learned societies, and has a considerable portion of General Washington's library. It has now about 75,000 volumes, and has cost for its building and books full $300,000. Though a proprietary library, it is practically free to the public for consultation. It was founded in 1806, but its principal growth has been within the last twenty-five years.

The library of Congress, which was nearly destroyed by fire in 1851, has since been restored and largely increased. The purchases being made under the direction of a committee of the two Houses, comprising their most eminent scholars, are judicious, and the library, which contains about 65,000 volumes, is one of the best for reference and consultation in the country. The library of the House of Representatives, also in the Capitol, contains about 40,000 volumes.

The Philadelphia Library Company and Loganian Collection is another of the proprietary libraries which are accessible to the public for consulting purposes free of charge. Though founded 130 years ago, its growth has been mainly achieved during the present century. In 1800, it contained only 7000 or 8000 volumes, while its present number is about 70,000.

The New York Mercantile Library is the largest of the subscription and lending libraries which are found in most of the considerable towns of the United States. It possesses a fine edifice in Astor Place, which cost nearly $240,000, and the rent of that portion of the building not occupied for library purposes and reading-rooms, will give it, when its debt is liquidated, a considerable annual fund in addition to its receipts for membership. Its reading-room is the largest in the country, though the free reading-room of the Cooper Institute very nearly approaches it. Its library, though intended mainly for popular readers rather than scholars, contains a very considerable collection of valuable works of reference. Its present number of volumes is about 60,000.

The New York State Library at Albany is by far the largest of all the state libraries, and is especially valuable for its fine collection of works on American history and on the natural sciences. It was founded in 1818, but its principal increase has been since 1845, at which time the Warden collection of works on America was purchased and incorporated in the library. The late Dr. T. Romeyn Beck superintended it for many years, and to his judicious purchases it is indebted for much of its value. Its present number of volumes is not far from 55,000.

The library of the Smithsonian Institution at Washington, though not so large as some others, numbering little more than 35,000 volumes, is a very valuable collection. The aim of Dr. Henry, the secretary of the institution, has been to make it particularly full in those departments in which other libraries are deficient. Its books are loaned to eminent scholars at a distance, when needed for the preparation of works of importance. For some years it received a copy of all copyright books in the country.

The American Antiquarian Society at Worcester has an exceedingly valuable collection on American antiquities. Founded in 1812, by the late Isaiah Thomas, who was for twenty years its president, and who gave it about 9000 volumes, it has now about 26,000 volumes, many of them unique in this country.

The New York Historical Society, founded in 1804, has a very valuable library of about 30,000 volumes, mainly confined to American history and literature; a museum of American relics and antiquities; a large picture gallery; and has recently purchased the fine collection of Egyptian antiquities procured by the late Dr. Abbott.

The American Academy of Natural Sciences at Philadelphia has a museum of natural history of nearly 30,000 specimens, and a library of about 27,000 volumes, more complete in natural history than any other, and also containing a very full collection of the revolutionary literature of France, presented them by Mr. William Maclure.

Two other foundations for libraries are deserving of notice: that of George Peabody, Esq., for the Peabody Institute at Baltimore, which contemplates a library in connection with a gallery of the fine arts, a musical conservatory, etc., the entire endowment amounting to $600,000; and that of the late David Watkinson, of Hartford, Connecticut, who left, in 1857, the sum of $100,000 to found a library of reference in connection with the Connecticut Historical Society, and also made that library his residuary legatee.

These are the most remarkable public libraries of the country. There are, according to the latest returns, 3 libraries containing over 100,000 volumes each; 9 containing over 50,000 volumes each; 19 containing 30,000 volumes or more; 26 containing 25,000 volumes or more; 41 containing over 20,000; and 120 containing 10,000 or more.

The total aggregate of volumes in college, state, national, proprietary, subscription, free, and town libraries, is not far from 3,800,000, and is increasing with great rapidity.

There are, besides these, in many of the states, school-district and academic libraries, containing a very large aggregate amount of books. In the state of New York, the number of volumes in the academic libraries reporting to the Board of Regents exceeds 125,000; and the number of volumes in the common-school libraries exceeds 1,500,000. Massachusetts, New Hampshire, Connecticut, Ohio, Michigan, Indiana, Illinois, Wisconsin, and Iowa, also make provision for such libraries, and have large numbers of them. The latest school returns indicate that the number of volumes in this class of libraries is not far from 4,000,000.

Another class of libraries, containing in the aggregate a vast number of volumes, and in many cases works of considerable size and value, are the Sunday School libraries. Few of these contain less than 200 volumes, and many of them have 1000 or more. More than 4000 different works have been published for these libraries within a few years past by the publishing societies and private publishers, and large drafts are also made by the larger schools on English publications and those intended for adults. Estimating the number of these schools at 35,000, or about two thirds the number of churches (an estimate considerably below the truth), and the volumes in each library at 200, we have an aggregate of 7,000,000 volumes collected in these humble libraries.

As might be expected, the rapid growth of public libraries has stimulated gentlemen of wealth and intellectual tastes to collect private libraries of considerable extent, and in many cases devoted to some specialty. Perhaps the largest of these private collections is that of James Lenox, Esq., of New York, which is especially rich in early works and in Bibles.

One of the most singular is that of John Allan, Esq., of the same city, which contains a very considerable collection of books which have been interleaved and illustrated by the collector, with choice engravings of the persons or events described, often to the number of some hundreds in each volume.

There are in the city of New York alone not less than 25 private libraries containing more than 10,000 volumes each, and in Boston a still larger number. Philadelphia has also many very choice private libraries.

Some of these private collections are very complete on American local history. Noticeable among these are the libraries of Peter Force, Esq., of Washington, D. C.; George Brinley, Esq., of Hartford, Connecticut; George W. Greene, of Providence, R. I.; and Messrs. George Bancroft, J. C. Brevoort, W. J. Davis, H. C. Murphy, William Menzies, and J. R. Brodhead, of New York. The library of Hon. Henry Barnard, at Hartford, Connecticut, is more complete on the subject of education than any other in the country; that of W. Parker Foulke, Esq., of Philadelphia, is very full on prisons and prison discipline, and that of S. Austin Allibone, Esq., of the same city, on English literature and criticism; that of David N. Lord, of New York, on ecclesiastical and polemic literature; that of Professor Charles Anthon, of the same city, contains a fine collection of classics and works on classical literature; that of G. W. Pratt, also of New York, on Oriental languages and literature; that of C. L. Bushnell, on numismatics; that of J. A. Stevens, jr., on the literature of the Middle Ages; those of Messrs. W. P. Chapman and R. G. White, on dramatic and especially Shakspearian literature; that of D. W. Fiske, on Scandinavian literature; that of George Folsom, on history and geography; that of R. M. Hunt, on architecture; and those of Archbishop Hughes, Rev. Dr. Forbes, Rev. Dr. Hatfield, and Rev. Dr. Bethune, on theology, ecclesiastical biography, and patristic literature.

There are in connection with many of our benevolent and humane institutions special libraries containing a few hundred or thousand volumes devoted to the particular work of those institutions. Thus, the American Asylum for the Deaf and Dumb, at Hartford, and the New York Institution for the Deaf and Dumb, have each a very considerable collection of works on deaf mute instruction; the American Bible Society has a fine collection of Bibles in all languages; and the American Bible Union, a valuable collection of works on biblical criticism and exegesis, procured for the use of its translators. The collection of books of reference procured for the use of the editors of the New American Cyclopædia is very extensive and complete, surpassing, in these particulars, any library in the country.

The following table gives the name of every considerable public library in the United States, and its number of volumes, according to the latest reports :—

PRINCIPAL PUBLIC LIBRARIES IN THE UNITED STATES, WITH THE NUMBER OF VOLUMES IN EACH IN 1860, AS NEARLY AS CAN BE ASCERTAINED.

I.—LIBRARIES OF COLLEGES, THEOLOGICAL SEMINARIES, ETC.

*Colleges.**

When founded.	Name.	Location.	No. of volumes.
1638,	Harvard College	Cambridge, Mass	125,000
1692,	William and Mary	Williamsburg, Va	53,000
1700,	Yale College	New Haven, Conn	67,000
1746,	College of New Jersey	Princeton, N. J	24,000
1749,	University of Pennsylvania	Philadelphia, Penn	5,100
1757,	Columbia College	New York City, N. Y	20,000
1768,	Brown University	Providence, R. I	37,000
1769,	Dartmouth College	Hanover, N. H	34,000
1770,	Rutgers College	New Brunswick, N. J	12,000
1781,	Washington College	Lexington, Va	6,500
1783,	Dickinson College	Carlisle, Penn	24,000
1784,	St. John's College	Annapolis, Md	8,000
1785,	Charleston College	Charleston, S. C	5,200
1785,	Franklin College	Athens, Ga	18,500
1789,	Hampden Sidney College	Prince Edward's Co., Va	7,200
1789,	University of North Carolina	Chapel Hill, N. C	21,000
1791,	University of Vermont	Burlington, Vt	13,000
1792,	Georgetown College	Georgetown, D. C	36,000
1793,	Williams College	Williamstown, Mass	20,000
1794,	Bowdoin College	Brunswick, Me	27,500
1795,	Union College	Schenectady, N. Y	16,000
1798,	Transylvania University	Lexington, Ky	14,000
1800,	Middlebury College	Middlebury, Vt	14,000
1801,	University of South Carolina	Columbia, S. C	24,000
1802,	Jefferson College	Cannonsburg, Penn	10,000
1804,	Ohio University	Athens, Ohio	5,300
1806,	University of East Tennessee	Knoxville, Tenn	8,500
1806,	University of Nashville	Nashville, Tenn	10,000
1809,	Miami University	Oxford, Ohio	8,500
1812,	Hamilton College	Clinton, N. Y	13,000
1817,	Alleghany College	Meadville, Penn	10,000
1819,	University of Virginia	Charlottesville, Va	30,000
1819,	St. Joseph's College	Bardstown, Ky	9,000
1820,	Waterville College	Waterville, Me	10,000
1821,	Columbian College	Washington, D. C	8,000
1821,	Amherst College	Amherst, Mass	26,000
1823,	Centre College	Danville, Ky	6,000
1825,	Trinity College	Hartford, Conn	14,000
1825,	Hobart Free College	Geneva, N. Y	14,000
1826,	Kenyon College	Gambier, Ohio	14,000
1826,	Western Reserve College	Hudson, Ohio	9,000
1830,	Spring Hill College	Spring Hill (near Mobile), Ala	7,500
1831,	University of Alabama	Tuscaloosa, Ala	12,000
1831,	University of New York	New York, N. Y	5,000
1831,	Wesleyan University	Middletown, Conn	13,000
1832,	Pennsylvania College	Gettysburg, Penn	11,000
1832,	Denison University	Granville, Ohio	5,200
1832,	Randolph-Macon College	Boydon, Va	8,000
1832,	Hanover College	South Hanover, Ind	5,600
1832,	St. Louis University	St. Louis, Mo	22,000
1833,	Wabash College	Crawfordsville, Ind	10,000
1833,	Delaware College	Newark, Del	10,000
1835,	Marietta College	Marietta, Ohio	16,000
1835,	McKendree College	Lebanon, Ill	5,800
1836,	Franklin and Marshall College	Lancaster, Penn	19,000
1837,	University of Michigan	Ann Arbor, Mich	10,000

* Those containing less than 5000 volumes are not noticed.

When founded.	Name.	Location.	No. of volumes.
1837,	Indiana Asbury University	Greencastle, Ind.	10,000
1838,	Wake Forest College	Forestville, N. C.	5,200
1838,	Emory and Henry College	Washington Co., Va.	9,000
1840,	Davidson College	Mecklenburg Co., N. C.	6,000
1840,	St. John's College	Fordham, N. Y.	16,000
1840,	Mercer University	Penfield, Ga.	9,000
1840,	Georgetown College	Georgetown, Ky.	7,000
1842,	St. James's College	Washington Co., Md.	10,000
1842,	Ohio Wesleyan University	Delaware Co., Ohio	10,500
1843,	Holy Cross	Worcester, Mass.	6,500
1845,	Centenary College	Jackson, La.	6,500
1845,	Wittenberg University	Springfield, Ohio	6,500
1846,	Madison University	Hamilton, N. Y.	8,000
1847,	St. Mary's College	Wilmington, Del.	6,000
1848,	Free Academy	New York	15,000
1848,	State Normal School	Albany, N. Y.	8,000
1848,	University of Mississippi	Oxford, Miss.	5,000
1849,	Lawrence University	Appleton, Wis.	15,000
1850,	Rochester University	Rochester, N. Y.	5,500
1854,	Tufts' College	Mildford, Mass.	8,000
1857,	Loyola College	Baltimore, Md.	20,000
	Santa Clara College	Santa Clara, Cal.	10,000
	Theological Seminaries.		
1784,	Theological Seminary Reformed Dutch Church	New Brunswick, N. J.	7,000
1791,	St. Mary's Theological Seminary	Baltimore, Md.	10,000
1808,	Andover Theological Seminary	Andover, Mass.	21,500
1812,	Princeton Theological Seminary	Princeton, N. J.	11,000
1816,	Divinity School	Cambridge, Mass.	8,700
1816,	Bangor Theological Seminary	Bangor, Me.	10,500
1817,	Episcopal General Theological Seminary	New York	12,000
1820,	Hamilton Theological Seminary	Hamilton, N. Y.	8,000
1821,	Auburn Theological Seminary	Auburn, N. Y.	6,000
1821,	South-Western Theological Seminary	Marysville, Tenn.	6,000
1822,	Episcopal Theological School	Fairfax Co., Va.	7,500
1825,	Newton Theological Institution	Newton, Mass.	5,500
1825,	Wittenberg Theological Seminary	Gettysburg, Penn.	10,000
1825,	German Reformed Theological Seminary	Mercersburg, Penn.	6,000
1827,	Theological Department Kenyon College	Gambier, Ohio	6,500
1828,	Western Theological Seminary	Alleghanytown, Penn.	10,000
1828,	Theological Seminary	Columbia, S. C.	17,500
1829,	Lane Seminary	Cincinnati, Ohio	11,000
1832,	New Albany Theological Seminary	New Albany, Ind.	4,000
1834,	Theological Institute	East Windsor, Conn.	5,000
1836,	Union Theological Seminary	New York	18,000
1844,	Western Theological School	Meadville, Penn.	8,000
1850,	Rochester Theological Seminary	Rochester, N. Y.	6,000
	Medical Schools and Hospitals.		
1755,	Pennsylvania Hospital Library	Philadelphia, Pa.	11,000
1765,	Medical Department Pennsylvania University	" "	5,000
1791,	New York Hospital Library	New York	7,000
1807,	New York College of Physicians and Surgeons	"	1,800
1831,	University Medical School	"	4,500
	Law Schools and Libraries.		
1817,	Dane Law School	Cambridge, Mass.	14,000
1845,	New York State and National Law School	Poughkeepsie, N. Y.	3,000
	New York Law Library	New York	6,500
	Social Law Library	Boston	6,000
1802, 1841,	Law Association	Philadelphia	5,000

II.—STATE LIBRARIES.

When founded.	Name.	Location.	No. of volumes.
1770,	New Hampshire State Library	Concord	6,500
1816,	Pennsylvania " "	Harrisburg	15,500
1817,	Ohio " "	Columbus	18,500
1818,	New York " "	Albany	55,000
1824,	New Jersey " "	Trenton	9,000
1825,	Indiana " "	Indianapolis	20,000

When founded.	Name.	Location.	No. of volumes.
1826,	Maryland State Library	Annapolis	22,000
1826,	Massachusetts " "	Boston	13,000
1828,	Virginia " "	Richmond	18,000
1829,	Missouri " "	Jefferson City	8,000
1834,	Kentucky " "	Frankfort	10,000
1836,	Maine " "	Augusta	17,000
1836,	Wisconsin " "	Madison	7,500
1848,	Connecticut " "	Hartford	7,500
	Tennessee " "	Nashville	9,000
	Mississippi " "	Jackson	8,000
	Louisiana " "	Baton Rouge	10,000
	North Carolina " "	Raleigh	7,000
	California " "	Sacramento	14,000
	III.—PUBLIC OR ENDOWED LIBRARIES.		
1747,	Redwood Library	Newport, R. I.	4,500
1800, 1815, 1851,	Library of Congress	Washington, D. C.	65,000
	Library of House of Representatives	" "	40,000
	Library of State Department	" "	18,000
	Library of War Department	" "	10,000
	Copyright Library	" "	13,500
	Library of Patent Office	" "	10,000
1839,	Astor Library	New York	120,000
1848, 1852,	City Public Library	Boston	100,000
1849,	Smithsonian Institution	Washington, D. C.	35,000
1838,	National Institute	" "	5,000
1852,	Free Library	New Bedford, Mass.	13,000
1857,	City Library	Springfield	7,000
	Bowditch Library	Boston	3,000
	United States Mint	Philadelphia	2,500
	Graham Institute Library	Brooklyn, N. Y.	10,000
	IV.—LIBRARIES OF LEARNED SOCIEITES.		
1742,	American Philosophical Society	Philadelphia, Penn	26,000
1812,	American Antiquarian Society	Worcester, Mass	26,000
1812,	American Academy of Natural Sciences	Philadelphia	27,000
	American Academy of Arts and Sciences	Boston	9,500
	American Oriental Society	New Haven	2,000
	American Geographical and Statistical Society	New York	3,000
	American Natural History Society	Boston	6,500
1824,	Franklin Institute	Philadelphia	6,000
	American Institute	New York	8,000
	New England Genealogical Society	Boston	14,000
	Lyceum of Natural History	New York	3,000
	V.—LIBRARIES OF HISTORICAL SOCIETIES.		
1804,	New York Historical Society	New York	30,000
	Maryland " "	Annapolis	20,000
	Massachusetts " "	Boston	8,000
	Connecticut " "	Hartford	11,000
	Georgia " "	Milledgeville	8,000
	New Jersey " "	Newark	2,500
	Ohio " "	Columbus	2,000
	Wisconsin " "	Madison	4,500
	Chicago " "	Chicago	7,500
	VI.—PROPRIETARY LIBRARIES.		
1731,	Library Company and Loganian Collection	Philadelphia	70,000
1748,	Charleston Library Society	Charleston, S. C.	25,000
1753, 1831, 1836,	Athenæum	Providence, R. I.	23,000
1754,	Society Library	New York	44,000
1760,	Athenæum	Salem, Mass	14,000
1765,	Athenæum	Portland, Me.	10,000
1806,	Athenæum	Boston, Mass.	75,000

When founded.	Name.	Location.	No. of volumes.
1813,	Athenæum	Philadelphia, Penn	15,000
1817,	Athenæum	Portsmouth, N. H.	9,000
	Library Company	Baltimore, Md	17,500
	Library Society	Boston, Mass	16,000
	VII.—MERCANTILE, INSTITUTE, LYCEUM, ETC., LIBRARIES.		
	Membership and library privileges secured by a small annual, semi-annual, or quarterly subscription.		
1820,	Mercantile Library	New York	60,000
1820,	Mercantile Library	Boston, Mass	22,500
	Apprentices' Library	New York	30,000
1819,	Apprentices' Library	Philadelphia, Pa	18,000
1821,	Mercantile Library	" "	16,000
1835,	Mercantile Library	Cincinnati, O	24,000
1838,	Young Men's Institute	Hartford, Ct	15,500
	Young Men's Institute	New Haven	12,000
	Mercantile Library	Baltimore, Md	16,000
1846,	Mercantile Library	St. Louis, Mo	15,000
	Mercantile Library	Portland, Me	2,500
1858,	Mercantile Library	Brooklyn, N. Y.	16,500
	Mercantile Library	San Francisco, Cal	12,000
	Apprentices' Library	Boston, Mass	6,000
	Apprentices' Library	Charleston, S. C	14,000
	Mechanics' Institute	New York	4,000
	Mechanics' Institute	Chicago, Ill	5,000
	Mechanics' Institute	Cincinnati	13,000
1860,	Women's Library	New York	6,000
	VIII.—PUBLIC AND HIGH SCHOOL AND SEMINARY LIBRARIES.		
	High School Library	Providence	21,000
	Public School Library	New Orleans	11,000
1839,	Central High School	Philadelphia	2,000
1853,	Central High School	Cincinnati	14,000
	United States Military Academy	West Point, N. Y.	17,500
	United States Naval Academy	Annapolis, Md	8,000
	Spingler Institute	New York	3,000
	Rutgers Institute	" "	3,500
	IX.—MISCELLANEOUS LIBRARIES.		
1817,	American Asylum for Deaf and Dumb	Hartford, Ct	1,800
1818,	New York Institution for Deaf and Dumb	New York	4,500
1815,	American Bible Society	" "	2,000
1850,	American Bible Union	" "	5,000
1838,	American and Foreign Bible Society	" "	1 600
1822,	American Board C. F. Missions	Boston	6,000
	German Society	Philadelphia	12,000
	Orthodox Friends' Library	"	6,000
	Hicksite Friends' Library	"	5,000
	Boston Library	Boston	16,000
	Washington Library	Washington, D. C.	13,000
	Southwark Library Company	Philadelphia, Penn	10,000
	Wagner Free Institute	" "	8,000
	American Sunday School Union	" "	7,000
	Maryland Institute	Baltimore	12,000
	Congregational Library Association	Boston	4,500

CHAPTER XX.

LYCEUMS, MECHANICS' INSTITUTES, YOUNG MEN'S INSTITUTES, ART UNIONS, ETC.

The name of *Lyceum* is one of ancient origin, having been first bestowed on the place where Aristotle gave his instructions, from its connection with the temple of Apollo Lycius. In more modern times it has been applied to schools where the philosophy of Aristotle was taught, and to institutions in which the instruction was given mainly by lectures. In 1786 it was given, in France, to an institution of the nature of a museum, at which daily lectures were delivered by La Harpe. This was discontinued in 1794, in consequence of the French Revolution. During the present century the name has been applied in France to collegiate schools answering very nearly to our colleges or public high schools.

The Conservatory of Arts and Trades at Paris, organized in 1796, by Vaucanson, is an example of the higher class of lyceum in its more extended sense. It has thirteen galleries of materials and machines, and courses of lectures, scientific and practical, which are largely attended during the winter by the working classes.

The origination of the lyceum as a means of mutual instruction in this country is due, in the first instance, to Benjamin Franklin. His "club for mutual improvement" was founded in Philadelphia in 1727, and after forty years' existence became the basis of the American Philosophical Society, one of the highest scientific societies on this continent. There may have been, and probably were, other societies for mutual improvement organized in different towns and cities of the country, during the hundred years that followed the organization of Franklin's club; but there are no records of any such in the possession of the public, previous to 1824, when Timothy Claxton, an English mechanic, succeeded in founding one, or rather in modifying a reading society, which had been in existence for five years, into what was really a lyceum, in the village of Methuen, Mass. Its exercises were weekly, and in the following order: the first week, reading by all the members; the second week, reading by one member selected for the purpose; the third week, an original lecture; the fourth week, discussion. In 1826, Mr. Josiah Holbrook, then of Derby, Conn., communicated to the *American Journal of Education*, then conducted by Mr. William Russell, his views on the subject of "*Associations of Adults for the Purpose of Mutual Education*," in which were contained the germs of the plan of the *Lyceum*, as subsequently developed by him in his lectures and publications. From the first, his views were of wider scope than the organization of a mere local association; they comprehended the establishment of such associations in every town and village, and their union, by representation, in county, state, and national organizations. They contemplated also, not only mutual instruction in the sciences, but the establishment of institutions for the education of youth in science, art, and morals; the collection of libraries, and of cabinets of minerals and other articles of natural or artificial production, to be increased and enlarged by mutual exchanges, by the different associations. Lectures and practical agricultural occupation, the results of which, it was supposed, would materially diminish the cost of instruction, also formed a part of his programme.

The first association formed in accordance with this plan was organized at Millbury, Mass., by Mr. Holbrook himself, in November of the same year, and was called "Millbury Lyceum, No. 1, Branch of the American Lyceum." Other towns soon after organized lyceums, and these were combined a few months later into the Worcester County Lyceum. Not long after, the Windham County, Conn., Lyceum, with its constituent town lyceums, was established; Rev. Samuel J. May, then of Brooklyn, Conn., rendering valuable assistance in the work.

From this time onward to his death in 1854, Mr. Holbrook devoted his whole energies in one way and another to the promotion of these institutions, and to such measures in connection with the cause of education as should promote mutual instruction in children as well as adults. By scientific tracts, by newspapers and other publications, by the manufacture of school apparatus, and by the collection of small cabinets of minerals, to serve as *nuclei* for larger cabinets, by scholars' fairs, by lectures, and long journeys, and by appeals to the members of Congress and of the state legislatures, he succeeded in rousing a powerful and continued interest in the subject of mutual instruction, which, if it did not accomplish all his own plans, at least gave a wonderful impulse to the general intellectual culture of the nation. The lyceums he founded have passed away, at least in their original form, but in their places, and in a great measure as an indirect result of his labors, we have in every considerable town or village debating societies, young men's institutes, mechanics' institutes, library associations—the three latter often with circulating libraries, courses of lectures, and classes for instruction in science, art, and languages, and often with schools attached for the instruction of the children of the members. We have also lecture foundations, either connected with our colleges or professional schools, or independent, in which courses of instruction in physical science, history, literature, or the laws of language, are communicated to popular audiences.

In rendering the scientific lecture a popular institution, our country is greatly indebted to the late John Griscom, LL.D., Prof. B. Silliman, Sr., and Rev. Henry Wilbur. Dr. Griscom delivered his first course of popular lectures on chemistry in New York city in the winter of 1808; they were largely attended, and were continued for a long series of years. Prof. Silliman commenced popular lecturing on the same subject in New Haven about the same time, in connection with his professional courses. He subsequently delivered popular courses of lectures on chemistry and on geology in most of the large cities of the country. Within the last fifteen or twenty years, Prof. Edward Hitchcock, of Amherst College, and several other eminent geologists, have given courses on geology to popular audiences. Prof. Guyot has lectured on physical geography; Messrs. Mann, Barnard, Page and others, on educational topics; Hon. George P. Marsh on language; Professor Lieber and others on commerce, and other prominent scholars on other subjects. The Lowell Institute at Boston, founded by the munificence of the Hon. J. A. Lowell, gives annually free courses of lectures to large audiences on the most important branches of moral, intellectual, and physical science, and from the liberality of its compensation to the lecturers, induces elaborate and conscientious preparation on their part, and the benefit of this preparation inures also to other audiences, to which these lectures are repeated. It has unfortunately been the custom for a few years past of the young men's institutes, mercantile library associations, and other institutions giving courses of lectures through the winter season, to select lecturers who would amuse rather than instruct their audiences, and hence this mode of public instruction has become gradually less and less efficient, and the chief advantages resulting from these institutions have been the use of their circulating libraries, and their classes of instruction and debate. A revolution, however, is now gradually taking place in this respect; lectures on physical science are more frequently incorporated in the courses, and the highest talent is employed in the illustration of these sciences. The lectures of Professors Doremus, Draper, and Silliman, jr., on chemistry; of Mitchel, Youmans, and Loomis on astronomy, and of Agassiz, Henry, and others on geology, have uniformly attracted large audiences, and have led to the study of these sciences.

The Smithsonian Institution, which combines some of the features of the lyceum, in its public lectures, classes, and museum, with its other objects, will be spoken of at length in another place. Its influence in promoting scientific research has been widely felt.

One of the noblest enterprises connected with this class of institutions is the Cooper Union of New York city. The founder with princely liberality has erected an immense building, occupying an entire block, of the most substantial character. A portion of this building is rented, and the proceeds of the rental go to sustain a free reading-room as extensive as any in the country, a picture gallery, a library, schools of design for male and female pupils, and classes for instruction in sciences, the mechanic arts, and languages, all of which have rooms and instruction free, under the most competent teachers. Courses of lectures on scientific subjects for the working classes also form a part of the plan of Mr. Cooper.

Mr. George Peabody has also made a most liberal endowment, amounting in all to about $600,000, for an institution at Baltimore, to include a public library, courses of lectures on science, art, and literature, prizes for scholarship in the high schools, an academy of music, and a gallery of art.

The number of institutions coming under the general head of lyceums in the United States, is very great; throughout the Northern states every city and every considerable town has some organization of the kind, all of them having their courses of lectures, and most of them debates, essays, readings, or classes of instruction. To them is attributable in no inconsiderable degree the very general prevalence of oratorical talent in our country, and that ability for impromptu argument and discussion, the faculty of "thinking on our legs," as an English writer not inaptly terms it. While much of the instruction communicated by lectures must necessarily be superficial, and is often wanting in accuracy, it cannot be denied that they have contributed much to the diffusion of general information and culture.

CHAPTER XXI.

INSTITUTIONS FOR THE INSTRUCTION OF THE DEAF AND DUMB.

THE capacity of the deaf-mute to receive instruction was not generally acknowledged anywhere till the latter part of the last century. Individual instances of education of those laboring under this infirmity had indeed occurred as early as the middle of the 16th century, and perhaps even at a still earlier date, but no considerable attempts had been made to instruct them previous to the efforts of Pereira, Heinicke, De l'Epée, and Braidwood, all of whom taught deaf and dumb pupils, between 1742 and 1760. Of these, Heinicke and De l'Epée alone are deserving of the honor of being reckoned the founders of a great philanthropic movement. The former attempted the instruction of deaf-mutes by teaching them to articulate; the latter by the manual alphabet, and a development of the natural language of signs. De l'Epée's processes were greatly improved by the Abbé Sicard, and Bebian, a pupil of Sicard.

Deaf-mute instruction was not attempted in this country till about the year 1816. In a few instances children of wealthy parents, suffering under this infirmity, had been sent to England for instruction by the Braidwoods, father and sons, who held in their own family the monopoly of deaf-mute teaching, though adopting substantially the processes of Heinicke, and who charged a very high price for the education of each pupil. The father of one of these American pupils, in a work entitled "*Vox oculis subjecta*," published in 1783, lauded in high terms the instruction of the Messrs. Braidwood.

In 1814, Rev. Thomas H. Gallaudet, a young clergyman of Hartford, Conn., became deeply interested in the case of Alice Cogswell, the little daughter of Dr. M. F. Cogswell, a neighbor of his, who had lost her hearing in infancy, and having devoted much thought and investigation to the subject of the number and condition of the deaf-mutes of that state, was desirous of doing something for their education. Dr. Cogswell and other benevolent gentlemen in Hartford furnished the means of sending him to England, to learn the art of teaching deaf-mutes, and he sailed from New York for Liverpool, May 25, 1815. Arrived in England he found the elder Braidwood dead, and the mother, sons, and other relatives, who had now established three schools, unwilling to enlighten him as to their processes, unless he would pay 1500 dollars, remain a year as an assistant in one of their schools, and take the grandson of the first Braidwood, a drunken vagabond, as a partner in the institution to be established in America. Rejecting these terms, as unworthy of the pioneers in a great benevolent enterprise, Mr. Gallaudet had almost determined to return home, when he met the Abbé Sicard in London, and was most cordially invited by him to come to Paris and acquire his methods of teaching, receiving from him the necessary private instructions to enable him to accomplish this object more rapidly. This generous offer was promptly accepted by Mr. Gallaudet, and after three months of close application he returned to America, bringing with him M. Laurent Clerc, an educated deaf-mute, and one of Sicard's most successful teachers. It was now determined to establish a school for deaf-mute instruction, as soon as the necessary funds could be obtained. For this purpose, Messrs. Gallaudet and Clerc travelled extensively through the Eastern and Middle states, everywhere receiving a warm welcome. In the spring of 1817, about $12,000 had been contributed and pledged, to which the Connecticut legislature subsequently added $5000 more.*

The school was opened in rented buildings, April 15, 1817, having been chartered in May, 1816, by the legislature under the name of "The Connecticut Asylum for the Deaf and Dumb." An application was made to Congress for a grant, as it was supposed, in the general ignorance concerning the number of deaf-mutes, that one asylum would be sufficient for the whole country, and that body donated a township of land in Alabama, which, under wise and careful management, has produced a fund of over $300,000, the interest of which is applied to the reduction of the annual expenses of the institution, and enables the directors to furnish board and tuition to their pupils at the low price of $100 per annum. After the reception of this grant, the name of the institution was changed to "The American Asylum for the Deaf and Dumb."

Thomas Braidwood, the grandson of the founder of the first English school for deaf-mutes, to whom we have already referred, had come to Virginia as early as 1811, and had attempted to establish there a school for the deaf and dumb, but his habits were

* This sum was a few years later expended by the Asylum in the education of indigent deaf-mutes natives of Connecticut.

such that all the assistance offered him was of no avail, and after a time he returned to England; Mr. Gallaudet's efforts incited the family to make another trial, but he was so thoroughly a vagabond, that it again proved unsuccessful. M. Gard, a teacher of deaf-mutes at Bordeaux, and himself a deaf-mute, also offered to come to New York, in 1816, and establish an institution there, on the plan of Sicard, but the project fell through.

Meantime, philanthropic persons in New York city were desirous of establishing an institution for the benefit of the deaf-mutes of the city and state, and an act of incorporation for such an institution was passed on the 15th of April, 1817, the same day that the school at Hartford was opened. Among the most active promoters of this enterprise were Dr. Samuel Akerly, Dr. Samuel L. Mitchill, De Witt Clinton, Silvanus Miller, Peter Sharpe, and Rev. James Milnor, D.D.

The course of the American Asylum at Hartford was prosperous from the first. Mr. Gallaudet was a man of genius, and possessed the ability to originate and carry into effect new methods of instruction, and to modify the processes in use in the French schools. In these measures he was efficiently seconded by M. Clerc, and by a corps of young but able teachers whom he had gathered around him, and imbued with his spirit. Prominent among these teachers were Messrs. William C. Woodbridge, Lewis Weld, Harvey P. Peet, Isaac Orr, and William W. Turner.

The New York Asylum had adverse fortunes to contend with at first. It was opened in May, 1818. Its first principal was Rev. A. O. Stansbury, who had been for a few months previous the steward of the American Asylum, and was but imperfectly qualified for his duties; the greater part of the pupils were day scholars, and attended irregularly; the assistant teachers were half-educated deaf-mutes; an attempt was made to teach articulation, but it proved a failure. Mr. Loofborrow, who succeeded Mr. Stansbury in 1821, possessed intelligence and energy, but he had few competent assistants, and the state legislature which had made appropriations for the support of deaf-mute pupils, was becoming dissatisfied with the condition of the institution, as compared with those at Hartford and Philadelphia. In 1830, an entire change was effected. The asylum was located on Fiftieth street, where buildings were erected for it; day scholars were no longer admitted; the inefficient teachers were dismissed, and Mr. Harvey P. Peet, then one of the ablest of the teachers in the American Asylum, elected principal. Mr. Peet entered upon his duties in February, 1831, and though at first compelled to perform all classes of duties, his genius, tact, and indefatigable labor soon brought order out of chaos, and enabled him to place the institution in the very first rank. In 1853, the property of the institution on Fiftieth street was sold, the buildings being too small for the accommodation of their pupils, and being subject to encroachment from the rapid increase of population in their vicinity. A new location, comprising 37 acres, was purchased on Washington Heights, about nine miles from the City Hall, and overlooking the Hudson river. On this site a magnificent building has been erected, much the finest and most perfect in its arrangements of any asylum for deaf-mutes in the world. It has cost, including the grounds, nearly $600,000, and will accommodate about 500 pupils. Mr. (now Dr.) Peet is still at the head of it, and his eldest son, Mr. Isaac Lewis Peet, is the efficient vice principal.

The Pennsylvania Institution was founded at Philadelphia in 1820, by David Seixas and Mr. Lewis Weld, one of the teachers at the American Asylum, became its principal in 1822. In 1830, Mr. Gallaudet resigned the charge of the American Asylum, and Mr. Weld was elected his successor, and was followed at Philadelphia by Mr. Abraham B. Hutton, who had been one of the teachers of the institution. This school has enjoyed continuous prosperity. The Kentucky School is located at Danville, and was founded in 1823. Mr. J. A. Jacobs, who is still at its head, was its first, and has been its only principal. He, too, had previously been a teacher at the American Asylum. It has a moderate endowment arising from the sale of lands granted to it by Congress. The Ohio Institution was established in 1829, and has had three principals—Messrs. Hubbell, Cary, and Stone. The first and last were from Hartford, the second from the New York Institution. The Virginia Institution, organized at Staunton, was the first in this country which combined the instruction of deaf-mutes and the blind in one institution. Such a combination is not uncommon in Europe, and five other asylums

AMERICAN ASYLUM FOR DEAF AND DUMB, HARTFORD, CONN.

have followed the example in this country. The best authorities, however, regard the plan as objectionable in many respects.

The other institutions for the instruction of deaf-mutes (there are in all twenty-three) have been organized since 1844. Most of them are state institutions, and though generally well managed, partisan politics have, in some instances, materially impaired their efficiency and usefulness.

Provision has been made, in nearly all the states, for the education of the indigent deaf and dumb, so that no person of suitable age, suffering from this infirmity, need go uninstructed, if they, or their friends, will apply to the state authorities; yet of the nearly 3000 deaf-mutes of school age in the United States, but about 2000 are under instruction. The greatest deficiency, however, is in the new states, and will be remedied in the course of a few years.

The term of instruction varies from six to ten years. Seven years is the usual term in most of the states; but in the American Asylum, the New York Institution, and, we believe, the Pennsylvania Institution, a high class has been established, into which those who give evidence of superior abilities, and desire for higher scholarship, are admitted by examination, and pursue an additional course of three years. The course of study, including this period of three years, embraces the topics of a very thorough English and mathematical education. Other languages than English are not usually taught. From these classes most of the deaf-mute teachers are now drawn.

The intellectual and moral condition of uninstructed deaf-mutes is one of extreme, almost rayless ignorance. Careful inquiry in some thousands of cases has demonstrated that, unless communicated by friends versed to some extent in the language of signs, they have no idea of a Supreme Being, of the origin of the objects of nature, of their own possession of a soul, of death, or a future existence. The mind is almost a blank, and the few thoughts they possess are merely such as concern their food, drink, and rest, and the objects with which they are constantly brought in contact. It is obvious, then, that the mental condition of a child of ten or twelve years of age, deaf from birth, and consequently dumb, is below that of a child of three years who can hear and speak. The child who possesses all its faculties has, before entering school, acquired a very considerable fund of ideas, and the words for their intelligent expression; so that the teacher has comparatively little occasion to communicate ideas to him, except on topics connected with his studies, and these he can clothe in words which the child already understands.

In the case of the deaf-mute, on the other hand ideas, even on many common and simple subjects, must be first communicated to him, and that not in words, for as yet these are entirely incomprehensible, but in the language of pantomime and gesture. He is next to be made to comprehend the laws of construction and connect words, either written, or spelled by the manual alphabet, with the ideas already acquired (a long and painful process,) and then, through the two *media* of words and signs, to be taught the elements of science.

The system of Heinicke and the Braidwoods, a system still, with some modifications, taught in Germany and some other European countries, had for its basis the dogma that ideas could only be expressed or communicated by means of words; and hence with great difficulty and pains, even in the flexible German tongue, the deaf-mute was taught to articulate words, whose meanings he did not understand, and then, as step by step he connected ideas with the simplest of them, these were made the means of conveying to him the meaning of those more abstract and difficult. In this way three or four years were consumed before the pupil was prepared to acquire the facts of science, or the knowledge of his moral obligations.

The plan of De l'Epée, modified by Sicard and Bebian, had little in common with that of Heinicke. Their fundamental principle was, that "words have no natural or necessary connection with the ideas of which they are the signs, and that in the natural language of signs or pantomime, improved and enlarged as it can be, there is a complete substitute for them." No attempt was made at teaching articulation, but words were taught by means of signs, and these once acquired, were made the medium of further instruction by ordinary text-books. In order to teach words more readily, M. Sicard introduced what he denominated *methodical signs*, that is, a peculiar gesture for each word, which the pupil was taught. It is obvious that if the vocabulary of the deaf-mute was to be as large as that of ordinary intelligent speaking persons, the number of these arbitrary signs (for it is to be understood that these differed almost as much from the ordinary signs as the latter from words, the natural signs representing ideas, and the methodical signs single words) must be very great, some thousands at least, and to retain them in memory was a very fatiguing task for both pupil and teacher.

The American system of instruction of deaf-mutes differs materially from both the preceding, and this difference originated partly with Mr. Gallaudet and the teachers trained up under him, and is partly the result of the experience and observation of the eminent teachers who have been, and still are, engaged in deaf-mute instruction.

In establishing the American Asylum, Mr. Gallaudet combined the principle of Heinicke, of the connection of ideas with words, with that of De l'Epée, that the natural language of signs must be elevated to as high a degree of excellence as possible in order to serve as the medium for giving the ideas clearly and explaining them accurately; but he added to these another which had never before been applied to deaf-mute instruction, viz., that the process of learning words might be greatly facilitated by leading the pupils to reflect on their own sensations, ideas, and mental processes. With the earliest lessons he imparted in the names of sensible objects, he was accustomed to endeavor to open communication with them, by means of the sign-language, in regard to the feelings and emotions excited by these objects, and, if possible, to connect them with something in the pupil's past experience. From this, the deaf-mute was naturally led on to think of the feelings and emotions of others, thence, by a natural transition, to the idea of God as a Creator and benefactor, and finally to a knowledge of his law, and the final destiny of man. The result of this has been that pupils in this country (for this plan has been generally adopted in our American institutions) are made acquainted with the simple truths of religion and morality in one year, a period in which, in the European institutions, they have scarcely advanced beyond the knowledge of sounds and the names of sensible objects, qualities, and actions, or the most common phrases. Apart from the high religious importance of this process, it brings moral motives to bear earlier, and renders the government of the pupils easier, while it aids them in the formation of correct habits. The conducting of the daily and weekly devotional exercises in the sign-language was another peculiarity introduced by Mr. Gallaudet.

Methodical signs were used to a considerable extent by Mr. Gallaudet and the earlier instructors of American institutions, but were not regarded as so indispensable by them as by the French teachers. Of late years they are less employed than formerly, and are made to indicate phrases rather than words, while the manual alphabet is regarded as of more value in teaching than it was thirty years ago. An advance has also been made, of great importance, by the introduction, by Mr. I. Lewis Peet, of the New York Institution, of manual and written symbols for those ultimate constituents of the sentence which form so considerable a portion of spoken and written language. By this means written language is taught with much greater facility than formerly. The establishment of high classes has also been an important step in the progress of deaf-mute education, furnishing, as it does, the deaf and dumb the opportunity of attaining to as high intellectual culture as those enjoy who are in the possession of all their faculties.

In 1850, the number of deaf-mutes in the United States was 9803, or one in 2345.

Some of the educated deaf and dumb in this country have attained to considerable distinction. Laurent Clerc, the companion of Gallaudet, belongs by his birth and education rather to France than America, yet he has passed more than forty years in this country, and though now retired in a healthful and happy old age, from active duty, is deservedly esteemed and honored. Thomas Brown, the President of the American Association of Deaf-Mutes, is a vigorous and able writer, as are also John T. Burnett and James Nack. The latter has distinguished himself as a poet of no mean ability, and the former has been a frequent and welcome contributor to several of our ablest reviews. Mrs. Mary Toles Peet, the wife of the accomplished vice principal of the New York Institution, though young, is entitled to a very high rank among the most gifted of our female poets. Colonel David M. Phillips, of New Orleans, in spite of his infirmity, was for many years one of the most accomplished military officers of the South. John Carlin, as an artist, and Albert Newsam, as an engraver, have few superiors in their respective professions. The monument to Mr. Gallaudet, designed by the former and engraved by the latter, is one of the most admirable and appropriate monumental structures. Mr. Levi S. Backus was for several years the able and successful manager of a periodical in central New York.

We present a table of the deaf and dumb institutions of the country, with their statistics to the present year (1860). There is also a deaf-mute institution in California, and one erecting at Faribault, Minnesota.

CHAPTER XXII.

INSTITUTIONS FOR THE INSTRUCTION OF THE BLIND.

The instruction of the blind had never been attempted on any considerable scale, in any part of the world, till Valentin Haüy, in 1784, commenced in Paris, France, his school for blind pupils. Individuals who were blind had indeed educated themselves by the assistance of friends; but the great majority of those who suffered from this affliction were left to a life of dependence and depression, and often became beggars. The efforts of Haüy, and his invention of an embossed alphabet, to enable the blind to read, led to the foundation of a school for the blind, supported by the French government, in 1791, and to the organization of similar schools in England, Prussia, Austria, and Russia about the same period. In these schools, reading and music, and some of the simpler mechanic arts, such as knitting, mat-weaving, basket-making, etc., were taught.

The first attempts to establish schools for the blind in this country were made about 1830. Dr. J. D. Fisher, in 1829, obtained an act of incorporation for an institution for the instruction of the blind from the Massachusetts legislature, and in 1831 Dr. Samuel Akerley and Mr. Samuel Wood, a benevolent merchant in New York, in conjunction with some other gentlemen, made an application to the New York legislature for a similar act, which was granted. Soon after this movement was made, Dr. John D. Russ, who had just returned from a mission to Greece, whither he had borne the contributions of American citizens to the suffering Greeks, and who on his way home had visited some of the European blind institutions, identified himself with it, and eventually became the principal of the school for the blind in New York city, which was established in 1832, under the charter already named.

In Boston, Dr. Samuel G. Howe, who had also been actively engaged in the cause of the Greeks, and who, like Dr. Russ, had visited the European institutions for the blind, entered with great zeal upon the work of establishing a school for their instruction,

PENNSYLVANIA ASYLUM FOR THE BLIND.

and made a beginning, we believe, under Dr. Fisher's charter, in 1832. The liberal gift, by Colonel T. H. Perkins, of his valuable mansion house in Pearl street, Boston, to this school, on condition of the raising of $50,000 by the public, soon secured to the institution a liberal endowment.

The year succeeding, an institution for the blind was established in Philadelphia through the efforts of Messrs. Roberts, Vaux, and others, at the head of which was placed an intelligent and philanthropic Prussian, Mr. Julius Friedlander, who had been engaged in teaching the blind at Berlin, under the celebrated Zeunė.

The first efforts of the American instructors of the blind were devoted to the improvement of the alphabet of raised letters, used in printing for the blind, with a view to the preparation of books for them. There were considerable difficulties to be overcome in the accomplishment of this work; the letters must have salient angles; each letter must differ sufficiently from every other to be easily recognized by the touch; yet the size of the letters must be small, or the books printed for the blind would be too cumbrous and expensive. The forms of letters used in Europe did not answer these requirements satisfactorily. Haüy's type, if well embossed, could be read with tolerable facility, but it was much too large, and its size could not be reduced without impairing its legibility; Guillié's was not legible at all; Gall's varied too much from the ordinary form of letter to be desirable, and the other attempts at uniting the requisite qualities failed. Each of the three American superintendents devoted his leisure to the work. Mr. Friedlander devised an alphabet, known in England as the Allston or Sans-serif Alphabet, neat in form and easily read, but somewhat too large. Dr. Russ invented one combining the advantages of Gall's triangular alphabet with the Illyrian letter, and with characters to make it phonetic, but it was somewhat defective in legibility; and Dr. Howe, after repeated trials, constructed what is now known as the Boston letter, which in size, distinctness, and legibility so far surpassed every previous effort, that it has now come into general use in Europe and America. Two other subjects interested these American pioneers in the work of instructing the blind: the recognition by the state legislatures of the right of blind youth to the advantages of an education, and the extension of the course of study so far as to give their pupils a good English education, instructing them, at the same time, in such mechanic arts as might enable them to support themselves after leaving the institution.

At the time of the organization of these

schools, the institutions for the blind in Great Britain, and most of those on the continent of Europe, taught nothing but reading and the mechanic arts, except in the case of those who possessed musical talents, who received such instructions in music as would enable them to play upon the piano or organ, and to sing; but the ordinary branches of elementary education were entirely neglected. The American superintendents determined that their pupils should receive a good common-school education, and if possible something beyond this, and they have succeeded. The period of instruction varies in the institutions for the blind in the United States from five to eight years. In the larger and older institutions it is usually eight years, and includes a course of mathematics and belles-lettres as extensive as that in most of the colleges in the country, and a thorough course of musical training, both vocal and instrumental. The languages are not usually taught. There are now twenty-four of these institutions in the United States. The Ohio Institution at Columbus was founded in 1837, and that of Virginia at Staunton in 1839; the others have all been organized since 1842. To all these establishments there are attached work-rooms, in which the pupils are employed in the manufacture of mattresses, mats, baskets, paper boxes, brooms, brushes, or the simpler articles of cabinet work.

To many of the blind, music furnishes not only a recreation but a means of support. Their ear, long trained to the discrimination of sounds, and their touch, rendered delicate by the acquisition of the art of reading, give them peculiar facilities for the attainment of musical skill; and the concentration of their minds upon it, undisturbed by observation of what is passing around them, adds to their advantages. It is not, therefore, remarkable, that many of them should have attained to great eminence in musical science. The Pennsylvania Institution has been specially remarkable for the musical attainments of its pupils. Its weekly concerts are attended by from 1200 to 1500 of the music-loving inhabitants of that city, and the receipts from these concerts furnish a liberal fund to aid the poorer graduates in commencing an independent life. Many of these pupils find speedy and remunerative employment as organists, choir singers, members of orchestras or bands, or piano-teachers and tuners.

The great cost of printing books for the blind has rendered the supply scanty and the number of books small. The American Bible Society has printed an edition of the Scriptures in the Boston letter, and grants are made from time to time to institutions for the blind. The American Tract Society has also printed a few of its smaller books in the same letter. Aside from these, there are not more than fifty works printed for the blind in England and America, except a few in arbitrary characters, which of course are of no general value. Among these fifty is a cyclopedia to be completed in twenty volumes, but of which only eight or nine have yet been issued. Repeated applications have been made to the general government to make an appropriation either of money or lands, to furnish a fund for the establishment of a press for the blind, but the bills reported have always been defeated. Within the past year a "Printing House for the Blind" has been established at Louisville, Kentucky, endowed in part by private benefactions, and in part by appropriations from the several states. Its managers propose to go on in the manufacture of books for the blind, using the Boston letter, and making grants to the blind of each state in a ratio corresponding to the amount contributed by that state.

Owing in part to this paucity of books the educated blind seldom use the books in the raised letter subsequent to their graduation, except the Scriptures, but depend mostly upon the reading aloud of others for their information and instruction.

Writing has always been a difficult and irksome task to the blind; and various devices have been proposed to facilitate this labor, but hardly any of them have proved satisfactory. The plan adopted by the late William H. Prescott of using a frame of wires over the paper, enabled them to write in straight lines, but no corrections could be made, nor could the scribe read what he had written. The use of inks which would leave an elevated surface has been tried, but without much satisfaction; small printing machines have also been used, but are not convenient.

Within a few years past another process has been introduced, which, despite the apparent objections to it, proves far more serviceable and convenient than any other yet devised. By this invention, known as "Braille's system," from its inventor, M. Louis Braille, a French teacher of the blind, they are soon enabled to read and write with great facility, and by the addition of a single character, music can be printed or copied by the blind far more readily than a seeing person can do it in the ordinary way. The plan is based upon a series of fundamental signs, comprising the first ten letters of the alphabet; none of these consist of less than two nor more than four dots. A second series is formed by placing one dot at the left of each fundamental sign; a third by placing two dots under each sign; a fourth by placing one dot under the right of each. These signs designate, besides the alphabet, the double vowels, peculiar compound sounds like *th*, and the marks of punctuation. By prefixing a sign consisting of three dots, the fundamental signs are used as numerals; by prefixing another the last seven represent musical characters, and by a sign peculiar to each octave the necessity of designating the key to each musical sentence is avoided.

The apparatus consists of a board, in a frame like that of a double slate, the surface of which is grooved horizontally and vertically by lines one eighth of an inch apart; on this the paper is fastened by shutting down the upper half of the frame, and the points are made with an awl or bodkin, through a piece of tin perforated with six holes, an eighth of an inch apart. The perforations are made from right to left, in order that the writing when reversed may read from left to right. Books and music are now printed for the blind on this system. Five or six of our larger institutions have adopted it.

Some of the blind institutions in this country have attached to them workshops for the adult blind, especially those who have graduated at these institutions, where certain advantages of shop-rent, machinery, material at wholesale prices, and in some instances board at a reduced rate, or a moderate pension, are allowed, by way of equalizing the difference between them and the working classes who possess all their faculties. In one instance, in Philadelphia, an asylum has been provided for the aged and infirm blind, where, beguiling the weariness of the passing hours by such light toil as they can readily accomplish, they may pass the evening of life in comfort and happiness.

The ratio of the blind to the entire population was, according to the last census, 1 to 2328, which would give not far from 13,000 as the present number in the country. Estimating one fifth of these as of school age, there should be 2600 in the different institutions. The number actually connected with them does not exceed 1300. As most of the states have made provision for supporting poor blind children at these institutions, a provision available on application to the governor or secretary of state, this number should be largely increased.

We have the testimony of some of the most eminent European teachers of the blind, that our larger institutions are superior to any of those in Europe in the thoroughness and extent of their teaching, and in the spirit of self-dependence with which they inspire their pupils. We insert a table giving a view of the present condition of the blind institutions in this country so far as can be ascertained. There is also an institution for the blind incorporated in California.

CHAPTER XXIII.

INSTITUTIONS FOR THE TRAINING OF IDIOTS.

These belong to the class of humanitarian efforts which have become so numerous during the past hundred years, and which have embraced in their scope the infirm, the orphan, the unfortunate, the vicious, and those who, from deprivation of one or more of their faculties, or feebleness of all of them, have become dependent upon others.

An effort is said to have been made by Vincent de Paul, one of the noblest and purest men in the Roman Catholic Church, more than two hundred years ago, to instruct a few adult imbeciles at the priory of St. Lazarus, in Paris, but with very slight success. The attempt was not repeated till 1818, when an idiot child, dumb from idiocy, was admitted as a pupil at the American Asylum for the Deaf and Dumb at Hartford. He was considerably improved during a residence of a year there; but not being properly a deaf-mute, and not being capable of going on with their classes, he was dismissed. He had, however, learned the sign-language sufficiently to be able to communicate his wants by it. Other imbeciles were subsequently, at various times, admitted to that and some other institutions for the blind and for deaf-mutes in this country prior to 1840. Most of these received some benefit from incidental instruction and intercourse with the pupils of these institutions. In Great Britain, as early as 1819, Dr. Richard Poole, of Edinburgh, published an Essay on Education, in which he urged the importance of attempting to educate and improve idiot children, and called for the organization of an institution for imbeciles. Efforts were made in France, from 1824 to 1838, by several eminent men, to instruct a few of these unfortunates, but with comparatively slight success. They were taught to imitate others in a few motions, and to repeat a few words by rote, but, left to themselves, soon relapsed into their previous hopeless condition. In 1838, Dr. Edward Seguin, a friend and pupil of the celebrated surgeon Itard, who had himself long contemplated the possibility of idiot instruction, commenced teaching a few idiot children in Paris. Unlike those who preceded him in this work, he had studied carefully, in all its bearings and relations, the subject of idiocy; and having become satisfied that it was only a prolonged infancy, in which the infantile grace and intelligence having passed away, there remained only the feeble muscular development and mental weakness of that stage of growth, he sought to follow nature in his processes for the development of the enfeebled body and mind. In these efforts he was far more successful than his predecessors. In 1846, he published his treatise on the Treatment of Idiocy, which is still the text-book of all teachers of imbeciles.

About the same time that Dr. Seguin commenced his school in Paris, a young Swiss physician of Zurich, Dr. Louis Guggenbühl, attempted with success the training of some Cretin* children, on the Abendberg, above Interlachen. The success of these two philanthropists led others in Prussia, Austria, the smaller German states, Sardinia, and England, to establish similar schools for the training of these hitherto neglected children.

The first movements for idiot training in this country were made almost simultaneously in New York and Massachusetts; that in New York having slightly the precedence, though the first schools were organized in Massachusetts. Dr. F. F. Backus of Rochester, elected to the state Senate of New York in the autumn of 1845, had become interested in the accounts of the schools of Seguin and Guggenbühl, and informing himself as fully as possible in regard to them, made a report to the Senate, in the session of 1846, accompanying it with resolutions providing for the establishment of a training school. These passed the two Houses, but were reconsidered and lost in the lower House. During the same winter, on the motion of Judge Byington, in the Massachusetts legislature, a commission was appointed, consisting of the mover, and Dr. S. G. Howe and Gilman Kimball, Esq., to investigate the condition of the idiots and imbeciles of the state. In 1848, as a result of the reports of this commission, the Massachusetts School for Imbecile and Feebleminded Youth was chartered, but was not organized till October of that year. It is under the general superintendence of Dr. S. G. Howe. Meantime, in July, 1848, Dr. H. B. Wilbur, a young physician of Barre, Mass., had opened a private school for imbecile and backward children in that town. In 1851 an experimental Asylum for Idiots was established at Albany, N. Y., and Dr. Wilbur was appointed its superintendent. Three years later, this gave place to the New York State Asylum for Idiots at Syracuse, for which the state erected a noble edifice, and provided for the training of the indigent imbecile children of the state. In 1852, the Pennsylvania Training School for Idiots and Imbeciles was organized at Germantown, Penn.; but in 1859 it was removed to Media, Penn., where a large and well-provided asylum has been erected for it. It is under the care of Dr. Joseph Parish. In 1857, the Ohio State School for Idiots was established at Columbus, and Dr. R. J. Patterson took charge of it. The original school at Barre passed into the hands of Dr. George Brown when Dr. Wilbur removed to Albany, and still maintains its early efficiency. Besides this, there are two other private schools for imbeciles: one in New York, under the charge of Mr. J. B. Richards, who was formerly connected with the Massachusetts and Pennsylvania institutions, and one in Lakeville, Litchfield county, Conn., under the care of Dr. H. M. Knight, established in 1858.

Several of the other state legislatures have agitated the subject, and will, probably, eventually establish schools.

Of those already in existence, the asylum in Syracuse, of the state institutions, and that at Barre, of the private ones, have been the

* The Cretin is an imbecile whose physical degeneration is greater, though his mental condition is more hopeful, than that of the idiot. The disease, Cretinism, is supposed to be caused by the impregnation of the springs with magnesian salts, and is very common in mountainous districts.

ASYLUM FOR IDIOTS, SYRACUSE.

most successful, and, in the opinion of competent and unprejudiced judges, are superior to any of the European institutions. Dr. Seguin, the founder of the Paris school, has been in this country much of the time for twelve years past, and has rendered efficient service in the introduction of the best methods of instruction.

The processes employed in the training of idiots in our American institutions all grew out of Seguin's fundamental theory, "that idiocy is a prolonged infancy;" and the course pursued by nature in developing the infant into the healthy, robust, intelligent child, is closely followed. In many cases, the muscular system is feeble, and unequally and imperfectly developed; this is carefully invigorated by attention to diet, frequent bathing, and such exercise as shall strengthen the muscles, while subordinating them to the control of the will. The attention is fixed, and taught to distinguish form, size, and color by the presentation of objects of bright colors, and of varied form and bulk. The irregular muscular movements, often the result of habit, are controlled by gymnastic exercises with dumb-bells, ladders, etc., and by military exercises, which exact the attention and careful action of the hands, feet, head, and eye. Numbers are taught by the *object* method, and reading by the *word* system and the use of pictures. As in deaf-mute instruction, the effort is made, at the earliest possible moment, to direct the thoughts inward, to lead the child to watch and express his own feelings and emotions, and then to guide him to observe the emotions of others, and soon to learn something of his Creator, and his own moral nature and destiny. It is remarkable with what facility the simple truths of morality and religion are perceived, even by very weak intellects. Their progress in these is much more rapid than in intellectual studies; yet many of the pupils in the best institutions learn to read passably well, to write a good hand, and generally to spell correctly; become familiar with the principal facts of geography, with the elements of grammar, and arithmetic as far, perhaps, as compound numbers. A few make still greater progress, but these are the exceptions, not the rule.

It is, perhaps, too soon to decide very confidently what will be the results of idiot instruction; but this much is tolerably certain, that a proportion not exceeding one fourth, and these often apparently the worst cases when admitted, will become so far improved as to perform the ordinary duties of life and citizenship nearly as well as the masses generally; another fourth will improve so much as to be capable of working intelligently, under the supervision of others, but not of any considerable independent action—these will, under favorable circumstances, nearly or quite support themselves; another fourth will be greatly improved in their habits, and will require but little attention, though unable to do much toward their own support; while the remainder, though often, perhaps, as promising as any at first, will be little, if at all, improved.

The number of idiots and imbeciles in the country has never been satisfactorily ascertained, and in the nature of the case cannot be, from the reluctance of friends, in many cases, to admit their condition. Careful investigations made in some of the states, and in single counties in others, would indicate that here, as in Europe, the number is but little less than that of the insane, or, in round numbers, one in 600.

CHAPTER XXIV.

INSTITUTIONS FOR THE EDUCATION AND TRAINING OF ORPHANS.

Some of the Roman emperors and many of the bishops and pastors of the early Christian Church interested themselves in the care of orphans, but during the dark ages this as well as other charities was neglected and forgotten, and it was not till the sixteenth century that any attempts were made to establish orphan asylums. During the seventeenth century they became quite numerous both among Protestants and Roman Catholics, and few large towns were without one or more orphan houses. The Moravians in particular were specially tender of the fatherless, and in all their settlements of considerable size established houses for them. In the last years of the seventeenth century, August Hermann Franke established his orphan house at Halle, which still exists, and is one of the largest orphan asylums in the world.

In this country orphan houses were established by the Moravians in Pennsylvania and Georgia, early in the eighteenth century. In 1740 the celebrated George Whitefield laid the foundation of his orphan house at Bethesda, about ten miles from Savannah, Georgia. After many pecuniary difficulties it finally attained to a prosperous condition during his life, and he added to it an academy, and purposed, could a charter have been obtained, to establish a college in connection with it.

The number of orphan asylums established previous to the commencement of the present century was, however, very small. There were no very large cities, and it was only in the large cities that orphans unfriended were so numerous as to require considerable buildings for their shelter and domicile. In New York city the first orphan asylum grew out of the "Society for the Relief of Widows with Small Children," and owes its origin to the zeal and energy of the late Mrs. Joanna Bethune. It was founded in 1806, and at first it was attempted to place the children in families, but their number soon rendered this difficult, and after renting premises for a time they erected an asylum in Bank street, and in 1840 removed to their new edifice on the banks of the Hudson, between Seventy-third and Seventy-fourth streets. It is largely endowed.

Subsequently other institutions for orphans have been established in that city, some of them amply endowed either by legacies, or by the increased value of the property on which they were originally erected, while others are dependent, in part, on annual contributions, or on grants from the city treasury or Board of Education. There are now ten of these institutions in New York city and four in the adjacent city of Brooklyn, aside from the Home for the Friendless and other preventive and reformatory institutions, a large part of whose inmates are orphans; and aside, also, from the Randall's Island Nursery, where the last year about 1200 children—orphans, half orphans, or children of intemperate and criminal parents—were cared for. In all these institutions in the city of New York not less than 4000 children are domiciled.

There are now asylums for orphans in nearly every town of 10,000 inhabitants in the country, and in the larger cities there are usually several. Thus there are nine or ten in Philadelphia, three in Baltimore, and five in Boston. One of the most remarkable of these, both on account of the magnificence of its edifice and the largeness of its endowment, is the Girard College for orphans at Philadelphia. It was founded by the bequest of a tract of land and two millions of dollars by Stephen Girard, a wealthy banker of that city. Mr. Girard left minute directions in his will in regard to the building and management of the charity. It is located on a lot comprising forty-one acres of land, surrounded by a wall ten feet in height. The grounds are laid out as play-grounds, gardens, grass-plots, etc. The buildings are all of marble. The principal one is in the form of a Corinthian temple, 169 feet long, 111 wide, and 97 high, and has a portico of thirty-four marble columns each 55 feet high. One of the smaller buildings is used as a laboratory, bakery, etc. The other four are each 125 feet long, 52 feet wide, and two stories in height. The whole cost of the buildings was $1,930,000. The officers are a president, secretary, two professors, five male and twelve female teachers, a physician, matron, assistant matron, and steward. The college was opened in January, 1848. As many poor white male orphans as the endowment can support are admitted, between the ages of six and ten years, fed, clothed, and educated, and between the ages of fourteen and eighteen bound out to mechanical, agricultural, or commercial occupations. No ecclesiastic, missionary, or minister of any sect whatever, is to hold any connection with the college or be admitted to the premises even as a visitor. The number of pupils on the foundation is a little over 350, and the annual expenditure about $60,000.

This is but one of several munificent foundations for orphans in that city. The Burd Orphan Asylum recently founded there for orphans between four and eight years of age, and primarily those of Episcopal parentage, has an endowment of about half a million dollars.

At Zelienople, Butler county, in western Pennsylvania, a farm school for orphans from Lutheran families, was established in 1854, and is under the charge of a superintendent trained to his work in the Institute of Brothers connected with the Rough House, Dr. Wichern's reformatory at Horn, near Hamburg. This is, so far as we are aware, the first distinct effort in this country to train orphan children distinctively to agricultural or horticultural pursuits.

The ordinary course of instruction in most of these institutions embraces the common branches of English education, and in many of them some mechanical pursuit is taught and practised for four or five hours each day. There is reason to believe that, in many cases, the mode of life and the regularity and formality of the course of training, has too much tendency to render the children *automata*, and unfit them to some extent for the hardships, the frequent changes, and the sudden temptations to which they are exposed after leaving the institutions. Where they are placed in private families while yet quite young, this evil is not so likely to follow as where they are retained, as they are in some asylums, to the age of sixteen.

No estimate, either of the amount permanently invested or of the annual current expenses of these institutions in this country can be given, nor even any near approximation to an estimate. The permanent investment is to be reckoned by millions, and possibly by tens of millions; the annual expenditure in New York city alone, reaches nearly or quite half a million of dollars.

CHAPTER XXV.

PREVENTIVE AND REFORMATORY INSTITUTIONS.

Although there are occasional indications that individual philanthropists, like the benevolent Cardinal Odescalchi at Rome, and Sir Matthew Hale in England, had clear perceptions of the evil of leaving vagrant and morally endangered children as well as juvenile delinquents, exposed to the temptations to a vicious life, yet apart from a school established partially for them by the former in 1586, there seems to have been no serious movement in their behalf prior to the establishment of the school and home for vagrant and vicious boys at Rome, by Giovanni Borgi, (better known as Tata Giovanni, or Papa John,) in 1786 or 1787, and the organization of the "Philanthropic Society for the Prevention of Crime" at London in 178[illegible] This last, originally established on the family plan, soon became a large establishment in which a great number of boys were congregated and employed in different branches of manufacture, having also a probationary school of reform for the more vicious and criminal of its inmates. In 1846, the location was changed and the whole system modified. A large farm was purchased at Red Hill, near Reigate, Surrey, agriculture and horticulture substituted for mechanical and manufacturing pursuits, and the family system for the congregated. Since that period the number of family reformatories, as they are called, has greatly increased in Great Britain. On the continent the eminent success of the agricultural and horticultural reformatories of Mettray, Horn, Ruysselede, and many others of more recent origin, has attracted general attention.

In this country the first institution intended for the reformation of vicious and criminal children, was the "New York House of Refuge for Juvenile Delinquents," incorporated in 1824 and opened January 1, 1825. Its founders were John Griscom, Isaac Collins, James W. Gerard, and Hugh Maxwell, all at the time members of a "Society for the Prevention of Pauperism and Crime," which had been formed in 1818. These gentlemen were aided and encouraged by others whose names appear on the list of corporators, and who were through life noteworthy for their hearty participation in works of philanthropy. The institution thus founded has had a steady growth, as the rapid increase of population in the city has been attended by a more than corresponding augmentation of the number of juvenile delinquents. At the end of thirty-six years from its first opening it occupies a tract of between thirty and forty acres on the southern end of Randall's Island, in the East River, and its colossal buildings, erected at an expense of not far from $450,000, furnish ample accommodations for school-rooms, lodging-rooms, dining-rooms, and workshops for 750 children, and actually hold in durance nearly 700.

In 1826 a "House of Reformation," on a similar plan, was established in Boston, and, in 1828, a "House of Refuge" in Philadelphia. Similar institutions have since been organized in New Orleans, Rochester, N. Y., Westboro', Mass., Cincinnati, Providence, Pittsburg, West Meriden, Conn., St. Louis, Baltimore, and perhaps some other cities.

The distinguishing characteristics of these institutions are, that those committed to them have generally been arrested for crime, and have either been sentenced to the House of Refuge, in lieu of a sentence to jail or state prison, or have been sent to these institutions without sentence, in the hope of their reformation. They are supported, directly or indirectly, from the public treasury (the New York house, besides an appropriation of $40 per head from the state comptroller, received last year $8000 from the city treasury, over $5000 from the Board of Education for its schools, and about $7500 from theatre licenses). In most, or all of them, the children are employed in some branch of manufacture, or some mechanic art, for from five to eight hours per day, and receive from three to five hours' instruction in school. In all there is more or less religious and moral instruction imparted, having in view their permanent reformation from evil habits and practices. In all, or nearly all, they are confined at night in cell-like dormitories, into which they are securely locked, and their labor, during the day, is under strict supervision, and is generally farmed out to contractors. High walls and a strict police are mainly relied on to prevent escape, and the attempt to do so, or any act of insubordination, is usually punished with considerable though not perhaps unmerited severity. The managers generally possess and exercise the power of indenturing those children who, after a longer or shorter stay, seem to be reformed, even though the period of their sentence has not been completed. A considerable number who have been sent to the House of Refuge on complaint of their parents are, after a time, delivered to them on application; but a large proportion of these do not do well. Of the others, it is believed that from fifty to seventy-five per cent. reform, at least so far as to become quiet and law-abiding citizens. Of those who do not reform, some, after discharge at the end of their term, are soon recommitted; others are sent to sea, and perhaps amid the hardships of a sailor's life become reformed; others return to the vicious associations from which they were originally taken, and after a few months or years of crime, find their place among the inmates of the county or convict prisons, meet a violent death, or fill a drunkard's grave.

These institutions necessarily combine something of the character of a prison with that of the school, and while their main object is the reformation rather than the punishment of the young offender, they retain so many penal features that they are objects of dread and dislike to many parents and guardians whose children or wards would be materially benefited by their discipline.

This feature of their management has led

to the establishment of another class of reformatories which, though sometimes assuming similar names, are essentially different both in the character of their inmates and in the methods adopted for their reformation. These methods are indeed quite diverse in the institutions coming under this general head, and are to some extent the reflection of the differing views of those who have charge of them.

The subjects taken in charge by these reformatories are somewhat younger on the average than those of the houses of refuge; they are for the most part only guilty of vagrancy and the vicious habits of a street life, or at the worst, of petty pilferings and thefts; they have not been, in most instances, tried for any crime against the laws, or if they have, their tender age has justified the magistrate in withholding a sentence.

When admitted to the reformatory, which is usually done on a magistrate's warrant, they undergo a thorough ablution, and are clothed in plain, neat garments having no distinguishing mark, are well fed, and carefully taught and watched over, and the utmost pains are taken to eradicate their evil habits, and to make them feel that their teachers and those who have them in charge are their best friends and seek their good. Their past history is never alluded to, and is generally known only to the superintendent. In these establishments there are no dormitory cells, and severe punishment is seldom found necessary. The labor of the pupils is seldom regarded as a matter of much importance, though in some instances three, four, or five hours a day are spent in some light employment. From these institutions escapes are unfrequent, and in most cases the children form a strong attachment for their teachers. In some instances they are broken up into groups or families of twenty or thirty persons, each having its "house father" and mother, and its "elder brother," if the pupils are boys, and its matron or "mother," and elder sister or aunt, if they are girls. These officers teach them and perform the duties indicated by their titles in such a way as to supply, as far as possible, the place of those natural relations of whose judicious influence they are deprived. One of these reformatories is a ship, and the pupils are taught all the duties required of an able-bodied seaman, and the order and discipline are similar to those of the naval school ships. They are taught, in addition to ordinary common-school studies, navigation, and after a few months' instruction are in demand for the mercantile marine, where they not unfrequently are rapidly promoted.

In most of these institutions the pupils remain in the reformatory a shorter average period than those who are inmates of the houses of refuge. In the New York Juvenile Asylum, one of the most successful of these reformatories, they are usually indentured or discharged in six or twelve months. In the State Industrial School for Girls at Lancaster, Mass., comparatively few remain over a year. These institutions are usually supported by the large cities, though in a few instances they are state institutions. The labor of the children being of but little account, the expense per head per annum is somewhat greater than in the houses of refuge, but the number of reformations is also greater, and may with considerable certainty be estimated at from seventy-five to eighty-five per cent. Among these institutions we may name the "New York Juvenile Asylum," the "State Industrial School for Girls" at Lancaster, Mass., the "Massachusetts School Ship," the "Asylum and Farm School" at Thompson's Island, Boston, the "State Reform School" at Cape Elizabeth, Maine, the "Reform School" at Chicago, and the "State Reform Farm" at Lancaster, Ohio. In the last, which is the first attempt at the introduction of the family or group system for boys in this country, fruit culture is to be the principal employment of the inmates, and the term of residence will be longer than at most of the others.

In our large cities there is still another class of children for whom a preventive education is necessary; they are not criminal, they have not generally acquired vicious habits, but they are *morally endangered.* They are often orphans or half orphans, and frequently homeless; many of them are children of foreign parents of the lower classes, and have had no opportunities of education; some are the offspring of vicious or intemperate parents. The greater part of them obtain a precarious livelihood by begging, sweeping crossings, boot blacking, selling newspapers, statuettes, fruit, or small wares, or organ-grinding. They are all exposed to strong temptations to evil, and have acquired a kind of defiant independence from being driven so early to take care of themselves.

For these children it has been felt that some provision must be made to prevent them from falling into vicious and criminal courses, and becoming depredators upon society, and to give them the opportunity of becoming good and intelligent citizens. The measures necessary to accomplish these results have been the subject of much discussion; and amid the experimenting which has been the result of this discussion, much good and some evil have been done. Industrial schools have been established, mainly for girls, in which reading and the elements of geography and arithmetic, vocal music, and the use of the needle in plain work, are taught; and the furnishing of one or two meals a day and plain clothing when needed, are made the inducements to attendance. For the newsboys and other young vendors of petty wares, a lodging house has been opened in New York city, and evening instruction given, the boys paying six cents each for their lodging. On the Sabbath a free dinner is provided for those who will attend and receive religious instructions; evening schools are also established, where those who are engaged in their little employments during the day, may receive intellectual and moral training.

In the worst quarters of New York and Philadelphia, missions and houses of industry have been founded, in which schools are kept through the week, much after the plan of the industrial schools already described, and where homeless forsaken children, and those whose parents are vicious and degraded, are clothed, boarded, instructed, and made to know the comforts of a home. It is obvious, however, that the greatest kindness which can be done to these children is to remove them from the influence of the temptations to which they have been exposed, and hence, most of these institutions send their children to homes in the country, after more or less preparatory training, as fast as good places can be found for them. In many cases, they are adopted by those in whose charge they are placed, and find in their foster parents more tender affection and care than they have ever known before. In other cases, they meet with less sympathy and love, and return to the great city and its temptations again.

In 1853, a "Children's Aid Society" was organized in New York city, mainly through the efforts of Mr. Charles L. Brace, one of whose principal objects is the location of this class of children in good homes at the West and elsewhere. Several of these societies have since been formed in other large cities. The original society at New York has the oversight of industrial schools, boys' meetings, the newsboys' lodging house, etc., and gathers from all quarters these morally endangered children, and sends them into the country in companies of forty or fifty; its agents having secured situations for them. About 800 are thus sent out annually.

Still another class of organizations intended for the benefit of these hapless children, though devoting its attention mainly to two classes of them, the very young children, infants and children under ten years, and girls of thirteen years and over, who are homeless and out of employment, are the Homes for the Friendless, of which there are now twelve in the United States. The first of these originated with the American Female Guardian Society, in New York, and was the result of the efforts of the directors of that society to rescue these classes from ruin. It assumed its present form in 1847, and has had nearly 10,000 inmates; 683 were received as members of its schools and workrooms in 1859, and 674 were employed in the home workrooms, and furnished with situations; 640 girls were taught in its industrial schools, and 560 families aided.

These institutions are all of them maintained principally by private contributions, though most of them, in the large cities, receive school moneys, to aid in sustaining their schools, from the city or state, and some of them receive occasional grants from the state or city treasuries.

It is impossible to ascertain, with any considerable certainty, the exact percentage of children from these institutions, who eventually turn out well. In most of them, the failures are the exceptions, and the number of these is not large. The Home for the Friendless in New York city keeps up a correspondence relative to each child sent out, until their majority, unless they die before that time. This correspondence demonstrates that full 90 per cent. grow up virtuous and well behaved. This percentage is larger than can safely be predicated of the other institutions, inasmuch as the children are for the most part received into the home at a very early age, and have not acquired the evil habits of those who are older, before coming under the influence of these charities. In the Children's Aid Societies, Houses of Industry, etc., the percentage reformed is large, but not definitely ascertainable.

There is still another class of reformatory institutions not intended for children, but for that unfortunate class of women who, having led lives of unchastity, have become penitent for their sins and desire to return to the paths of virtue. This department of reform has been less actively promoted here than in Europe, and especially in Great Britain, but there are in most of our large cities Magdalen Asylums, or institutions otherwise designated, but intended for this class. New York has one of these asylums, Boston two, and Philadelphia three, one of which, the Rosine Asylum, founded in 1847, is a very active and useful organization.

The number of Houses of Refuge, or institutions of that class, is fourteen. The cost of their buildings and grounds is about $2,050,000, and the annual cost of their maintenance not far from $340,000.

Of the Juvenile Asylums, &c., there are seven, the cost of buildings and grounds is not far from $450,000, and the annual expenses of maintenance about $130,000.

The number of institutions of the third class cannot be definitely ascertained. Few or none of them are established or entirely maintained by the state or city governments, and some are altogether private enterprises. There are fifteen of them in the city of New York alone, and two or three in Brooklyn, five or six in Philadelphia, and a considerable number in smaller cities and towns. Some of these occupy leased buildings, others own their edifices.

The buildings and grounds of the New York Home for the Friendless cost nearly $60,000, and of the Five Points House of Industry, about $40,000. The annual expenses of seven of the more important of the preventive and reformatory institutions in New York city, were about $114,000. It would probably be safe to estimate the total permanent investment of all these organizations at not less than three millions of dollars, which we are satisfied is below the reality, and the current annual expenditure at not less than $750,000.

That these institutions have not yet attained to their highest degree of efficiency, and that they are not fully adequate to the reformation and preventive education of the vast number of morally endangered, vagrant, and criminal children of the country, is undoubtedly true; but among the evidences of national progress in our country since the commencement of its independent existence, there is none which reflects greater credit upon its philanthropy than the establishment and maintenance of so many institutions of reformation and preventive education.

TABLE OF EDUCATIONAL STATISTICS OF THE UNITED STATES IN 1850.

STATES AND TERRITORIES.	Colleges.					Academies.					Public Schools.					White Persons.		
				Annual Income.					Annual Income.					Annual Income.				
	Number.	Teachers.	Pupils.	Returned.	Estimated.	Number.	Teachers.	Pupils.	Returned.	Estimated.	Number.	Teachers.	Pupils.	Returned.	Estimated.	Returned as in Colleges, Academies, and Public Schools.	Attendi'g School as returned by Families.	Persons over 20 years who cannot read or write.
Alabama	5	55	567	$41,255	$48,530	166	380	8,290	$164,165	$224,279	1,152	1,195	28,380	$315,602	$390,989	37,237	62,778	33,757
Arkansas	3	14	150	3,100	3,100	90	126	2,407	27,937	34,308	353	355	8,493	43,763	68,411	11,050	23,350	16,819
California	....	....	....	....	....	6	5	170	14,270	20,392	2	2	49	3,600	14,700	219	992	5,118
Columbia, Dist. of	2	36	218	24,000	24,000	47	126	2,333	84,040	84,040	22	34	2,169	14,232	14,232	4,720	6,103	1,457
Connecticut	4	56	738	53,639	53,639	202	329	6,996	145,967	152,120	1,656	1,787	71,269	231,220	231,220	79,003	82,433	4,739
Delaware	2	16	144	17,200	17,200	65	94	2,011	47,832	53,498	194	214	8,970	43,861	43,861	11,125	14,216	4,536
Florida	....	....	....	....	....	34	49	1,251	13,089	22,742	69	73	1,878	22,386	31,777	3,129	4,746	3,859
Georgia	13	84	1,535	105,430	105,430	219	318	9,059	108,983	184,849	1,251	1,265	32,705	182,231	190,235	43,299	77,015	41,200
Illinois	6	35	442	13,300	15,389	83	160	4,244	40,488	47,678	4,052	4,248	125,725	349,712	356,416	130,411	181,969	40,054
Indiana	11	61	1,069	43,350	43,350	131	233	6,185	63,520	73,219	4,822	4,860	161,500	316,955	329,095	168,754	220,034	70,540
Iowa	2	4	100	2,000	2,000	33	46	1,111	7,980	11,180	740	828	29,556	51,492	52,620	30,767	35,456	8,120
Kentucky	15	100	1,773	131,461	131,461	330	600	12,712	252,617	306,507	2,234	2,306	71,429	211,852	215,068	85,914	130,917	66,687
Louisiana	6	41	629	85,750	85,750	143	354	5,328	193,077	283,003	664	822	25,046	349,679	362,412	31,003	32,838	21,221
Maine	3	21	282	14,000	17,784	131	232	6,648	51,187	64,966	4,042	5,540	192,815	315,436	318,597	199,745	185,941	6,147
Maryland	13	98	1,127	113,714	122,403	223	503	10,787	232,341	239,083	898	986	33,111	218,836	221,817	45,025	60,447	20,815
Massachusetts	6	85	1,043	107,901	121,929	403	521	13,436	310,177	354,521	3,679	4,443	176,475	1,006,795	1,010,346	190,924	220,781	27,539
Michigan	3	22	308	14,000	14,000	37	71	1,619	24,947	31,953	2,714	3,231	110,455	167,806	168,764	112,382	105,754	7,912
Mississippi	11	45	862	42,400	47,652	171	297	6,628	73,717	144,732	782	826	18,746	254,159	267,821	26,236	48,803	13,405
Missouri	9	65	1,009	79,528	88,277	204	368	8,829	143,171	183,403	1,570	1,620	51,754	160,770	168,961	61,592	95,245	36,281
New Hampshire	1	18	273	11,000	11,000	107	183	5,321	43,202	52,591	2,381	3,013	75,643	166,944	167,938	81,237	88,148	2,957
New Jersey	4	49	470	79,700	79,700	225	453	9,844	227,588	300,242	1,473	1,574	77,930	216,672	220,340	88,244	89,775	14,248
New York	18	174	2,673	148,258	217,267	887	3,136	49,328	810,332	1,015,249	11,580	13,965	675,221	1,472,657	1,486,423	727,222	687,874	91,293
North Carolina	5	29	513	40,700	40,700	272	403	7,822	187,648	222,695	2,657	2,730	104,095	158,564	158,564	112,430	100,591	73,566
Ohio	26	180	3,621	125,792	145,292	206	474	15,052	149,392	201,077	11,661	12,886	484,153	743,074	751,576	502,826	512,278	61,030
Pennsylvania	22	134	3,520	286,805	318,070	524	914	23,751	467,843	570,501	9,061	10,024	413,706	1,348,249	1,362,949	440,977	498,111	66,928
Rhode Island	1	12	283	23,000	23,000	46	75	1,601	32,748	37,423	416	518	23,130	100,481	100,481	25,014	28,359	3,340
South Carolina	8	43	720	104,790	104,790	202	333	7,467	205,489	205,489	724	739	17,838	200,600	200,600	26,025	40,293	15,684
Tennessee	18	83	1,705	65,307	67,689	264	404	9,928	155,902	175,926	2,680	2,819	104,117	198,518	200,253	115,750	146,130	77,522
Texas	2	7	165	1,000	4,125	97	137	3,389	39,384	79,732	349	360	7,946	44,088	94,554	11,500	19,369	10,525
Vermont	5	30	464	21,558	21,558	118	257	6,864	48,935	56,159	2,731	4,173	93,457	176,111	179,181	100,785	92,152	6,189
Virginia	12	73	1,343	159,790	162,574	317	547	9,068	234,372	351,007	2,930	2,997	67,353	314,625	341,279	77,764	109,711	77,005
Wisconsin	2	8	75	4,700	4,700	58	86	2,723	18,796	19,899	1,423	1,529	58,817	113,133	113,874	61,615	56,354	6,361
Territories. Minnesota	....	....	....	....	....	1	1	12	140	....	....	....	....	....	....	12	207	649
Territories. N. Mexico	....	....	....	....	....	1	1	40	....	....	....	....	....	....	....	40	466	25,085
Territories. Oregon	....	....	....	....	....	29	44	842	20,888	24,495	3	4	80	3,927	3,927	922	1,875	157
Territories. Utah	1	....	....	....	....	13	....	....	2,050	2,221	13	....	....	11,512	11,512	....	2,035	153
Total	239	1,678	27,821	1,964,428	2,142,359	6,085	12,260	263,096	4,644,214	5,831,179	80,978	91,966	3,354,011	9,529,542	9,8[illegible]0,793	3,644,928	4,063,046	962,898

CHRONOLOGICAL TABLE OF AMERICAN COLLEGES.

Corporate name.	Location.	Date.	No. of Professors.	No. of Students.	Vols. in Library.
Harvard University	Cambridge, Mass	1636	24	420	125,000
William and Mary	Williamsburg, Va	1693	6	60	53,000
Yale	New Haven, Ct	1700	21	523	67,000
College of New Jersey	Princeton, N. J	1746	19	314	24,000
University of Pennsylvania	Philadelphia, Pa	1749	12	129	5,100
Columbia	New York, N. Y	1754	12	173	14,000
Brown University	Providence, R. I	1764	10	212	35,000
Dartmouth	Hanover, N. H	1769	16	304	33,699
Rutgers	New Brunswick, N. J	1770	6	110	12,000
Washington	Lexington, Va	1781	8	75	6,200
Dickinson	Carlisle, Pa	1783	8	134	23,493
Washington	Chestertown, Md	1783	5	70	1,200
St. John's	Annapolis, Md	1784	6	115	8,000
Franklin	Athens, Ga	1785	10	113	18,250
Charleston	Charleston, S. C	1785	6	37	5,000
University of North Carolina	Chapel Hill, N. C	1789	15	450	21,000
Hampden-Sidney	Prince Edward Co., Va	1789	5	128	7,000
University of Vermont	Burlington, Vt	1791	7	104	13,000
Bowdoin	Brunswick, Me	1792	9	219	27,048
Georgetown	Georgetown, D. C	1792	25	260	36,000
Williams	Williamstown, Mass	1793	11	240	19,700
Washington	Washington Co., La	1795	3	22	1,800
Union	Schenectady, N. Y	1795	15	320	15,500
Greenville	Greenville, Tenn	1796	2	20	3,500
Transylvania	Lexington, Ky	1798	8	..	14,000
Middlebury	Middlebury, Vt	1800	6	103	13,500
South Carolina	Columbia, S. C	1801	8	202	24,000
Jefferson	Canonsburg, Pa	1802	10	215	10,000
Ohio University	Athens, Ohio	1804	6	154	5,000
East Tennessee	Knoxville, Tenn	1806	..	..	8,000
University of Nashville	Nashville, Tenn	1806	8	104	9,666
Washington	Washington, Pa	1806	6	103	3,900
Miami University	Oxford, Ohio	1809	8	121	8,100
Hamilton	Clinton, N. Y	1812	9	131	12,500
Alleghany	Meadville, Pa	1817	6	104	9,600
St. Joseph's	Bardstown, Ky	1819	15	60	8,600
University of Virginia	Charlottesville, Va	1819	14	417	30,000
Waterville	Waterville, Me	1820	6	117	10,000
Amherst	Amherst, Mass	1821	15	242	26,000
Columbian	Washington, D. C	1821	8	66	7,500
Trinity	Hartford, Ct	1823	9	56	13,500
Centre	Danville, Ky	1823	5	180	5,600
Franklin	New Athens, Ohio	1824	4	85	2,000
Hobart Free College	Geneva, N. Y	1825	7	108	13,550
Western Reserve	Hudson, Ohio	1826	7	48	8,451
Kenyon	Gambier, Ohio	1826	10	129	13,384
Georgetown	Georgetown, Ky	1829	8	171	7,000
Indiana State University	Bloomington, Ind	1830	6	115	2,200
Florence Wesleyan	Florence, Ala	1830	5	112	2,000
Mount St. Mary's	Emmetsburg, Md	1830	24	126	4,000
Illinois	Jacksonville, Ill	1830	7	70	3,660
Wesleyan University	Middletown, Ct	1831	7	140	13,000
University of Alabama	Tuscaloosa, Ala	1831	9	120	12,000
University of City of New York	New York, N. Y	1831	16	138	4,300
Lafayette	Easton, Pa	1832	6	100	4,000
Hanover	South Hanover, Ind	1832	5	45	5,400
Dolbear's Commercial	New Orleans, La	1832	10	375	..
Randolph-Macon	Boydon, Va	1832	6	130	8,000
St. Louis University	St. Louis, Mo	1832	18	134	22,000
Denison	Granville, O	1832	7	73	5,000
Delaware	Newark, Del	1833	6	50	10,000
Wabash	Crawfordsville, Ind	1833	7	40	9,600

CHRONOLOGICAL TABLE OF AMERICAN COLLEGES.—*Continued.*

Corporate name.	Location.	Date.	No. of Professors.	No. of Students.	Vols. in Library.
Jackson	Columbia, Tenn.	1833	5	84	4,400
Oberlin	Oberlin, Ohio	1834	8	110	4,000
Norwich University	Norwich, Vt.	1834	4	80	1,650
Pennsylvania	Gettysburg, Pa.	1834	7	154	11,000
Shurtleff	Upper Alton, Ill.	1835	6	40	1,900
McKendree	Lebanon, Ill.	1835	6	99	5,500
Marietta	Marietta, Ohio	1835	6	56	16,000
Franklin and Marshall	Lancaster, Pa.	1836	6	96	19,000
University of Michigan	Ann Arbor, Mich.	1837	17	282	10,000
St. Charles	St. Charles, Mo.	1837	6	50	1,000
Knox	Galesburg, Ill.	1837	7	56	3,300
Emory	Oxford, Ga.	1837	6	126	1,700
Emory and Henry	Washington Co., Va.	1838	5	54	8,470
Oglethorpe	Milledgeville, Ga.	1838	5	100	4,500
Wake Forest	Forestville, N. C.	1838	5	76	5,000
University of State of Missouri	Columbia, Mo.	1839	10	102	3,500
Mercer University	Penfield, Ga.	1839	7	140	8,700
Wesleyan Female	Macon, Ga.	1839	11	188	2,450
Virginia Military Institute	Lexington, Va.	1839	13	150	4,000
Richmond	Richmond, Va.	1840	7	93	1,800
Davidson	Mecklenburg Co., N. C.	1840	7	112	5,600
Bethany	Bethany, Va.	1841	10	124	1,700
St. James's	Washington Co., Md.	1842	14	52	9,500
Holy Cross	Worcester, Mass.	1843	8	75	6,500
Masonic	Lexington, Mo.	1844	3	28	1,200
Franklin	Near Nashville, Tenn.	1844	6	106	3,500
Cumberland University	Lebanon, Tenn.	1844	11	165	4,000
Centenary	Jackson, La.	1845	11	103	5,200
Wittenberg	Springfield, Ohio	1845	5	59	6,200
Madison University	Hamilton, N. Y.	1846	9	145	7,457
St. John's	Fordham, N. Y.	1846	19	43	15,465
Kentucky Military Institute	Franklin Springs, Ky.	1846	9	154	3,000
Beloit	Beloit, Wis.	1847	8	60	3,500
St. Mary's	Wilmington, Del.	1847	7	..	5,500
St. Charles's	Ellicott's Mills, Md.	1848	8	104	450
Union	Murfreesboro', Tenn.	1848	6	150	4,500
University of Mississippi	Oxford, Miss.	1848	9	175	5,000
Howard	Marion, Ala.	1848	6	83	3,000
Lawrence University	Appleton, Wis.	1849	10	100	15,000
University of Louisiana	New Orleans, La.	1849	7	..	..
University, at Lewisburg	Lewisburg, Pa.	1850	6	55	4,000
Urbana University	Urbana, Ohio	1850	8	21	3,500
Carroll	Waukesha, Wis.	1850	5	20	926
University of Rochester	Rochester, N. Y.	1850	8	165	5,200
Madison	Sharon, Miss.	1851	5	102	450
Mississippi College	Clinton, Miss.	1851	7	50	3,750
Wisconsin University	Madison, Wis.	1851	7	30	1,900
Aranama	Goliad, Tex.	1852	3	75	1,800
Racine	Racine, Wis.	1852	6	17	1,700
Milwaukee Female	Milwaukee, Wis.	1852	4	36	729
Polytechnic	Philadelphia, Pa.	1853	8	58	..
Antioch	Yellow Springs, Ohio	1853	12	98	4,200
Tufts	Medford, Mass.	1854	5	54	8,000
Ohio Wesleyan University	Delaware, Ohio	1854	8	147	10,450
Santa Clara	Near San Jose, Cal.	1855	..	..	..
Iowa State University	Iowa City, Iowa	1855	4	..	200
Iowa Wesleyan University	Mount Pleasant, Iowa	1855	9	..	..
Semple Broaddus	Centre Hill, Miss.	1856	4	75	..
Indiana Asbury University	Greencastle, Ind.	1857	8	100	10,000
Kentucky	Harrodsburg, Ky.	1858	8	156	1,600
University of Chicago	Chicago, Ill.	1860	9	20	2,000

THEOLOGICAL SCHOOLS.

Name.	Place.	Denomination.	Commenced operations.	No. Professors.	Students near 1859-1860.	Number educated.	Volumes in Library.
Th. Sem. Dutch Ref. Church....	N. Brunswick, N. J..	Dutch Ref....	1784	3	50	179	7,000
St. Mary's Seminary...........	Baltimore, Md.......	Rom. Catholic.	1791	6	27	..	10,000
Theological School............	Canonsburg, Pa......	Asso. Church.	1792	2	33	147	2,000
Theological Seminary..........	Andover, Mass.......	Congregation..	1807	5	110	1,206	21,259
Theol. Sem. Presbyt. Church....	Princeton, N. J.......	Presbyterian..	1812	5	153	1,626	11,000
Bangor Theological Seminary...	Bangor, Me.........	Congregation..	1816	4	40	330	10,500
Divinity School, Harv. Univ....	Cambridge, Mass....	Cong. Unit....	1816	2	17	295	8,700
Hartwick Seminary............	Hartwick, N. Y.....	Lutheran.....	1816	2	5	52	1,250
Georgetown College...........	Georgetown, D. C...	Rom. Catholic.	1816	3	12	..	2,000
Theol. Inst. Episc. Church......	New York, N. Y.....	Prot. Episcop.	1817	5	58	430	11,963
Hamilton Theol. Seminary......	Hamilton, N. Y.....	Baptist	1820	3	24	262	7,500
Theol. Sem. of Auburn.........	Auburn, N. Y.......	Presbyterian..	1821	4	30	580	6,000
Southwest Theol. Seminary.....	Maryville, Tenn.....	Presbyterian..	1821	2	24	90	6,000
Theol. Dep. Yale College.......	New Haven, Conn...	Congregation..	1822	5	27	680	..
Epis. Theol. School of Virginia..	Fairfax Co., Va.....	Prot. Episcop.	1822	4	47	356	7,500
Union Theological Seminary....	Prince Ed. Co., Va...	Presbyterian..	1824	3	20	175	4,000
N. Hampton Theol. Seminary...	New Hampton, N. H.	Baptist......	1825	2	36	..	2,000
Theological Institution.........	Newton, Mass......	Baptist.......	1825	4	33	201	5,500
Wittenberg Theol. Seminary....	Gettysburg, Pa......	Evang. Luth..	1825	3	25	250	10,000
German Reformed.............	Mercersburg, Pa.....	Germ. Ref. Ch.	1825	2	18	121	6,000
Furman Theol. Seminary.......	Fairfield Dist., S. C..	Baptist.......	1826	2	30	30	1,000
Theol. Dep. Kenyon College....	Gambier, Ohio......	Prot. Episcop.	1827	4	23	91	6,500
Theological Seminary..........	Pittsburg, Pa.......	Asso. Ref.....	1828	3	35	85	1,500
Theological Seminary..........	Columbia, S. C......	Presbyterian..	1828	4	42	249	17,260
Western Theol. Seminary.......	Alleghany, Pa......	Presbyterian..	1828	5	140	537	10,000
Theol. Dep. St. Louis Univ.....	St. Louis, Mo.......	Rom. Catholic.	1829	4	14	86	4,000
Lane Seminary...............	Cincinnati, Ohio.....	Presbyterian..	1829	3	36	257	10,500
Theol. Dep. West. Res. College..	Hudson, Ohio.......	Presbyterian..	1830	3	14	..	79
Virginia Baptist Seminary......	Richmond, Va......	Baptist.......	1832	3	67	..	1,000
Granville Theol. Department....	Granville, Ohio......	Baptist.......	1832	2	8	..	500
New Albany Theol. Seminary...	Hanover, Ind.......	Presbyterian..	1832	3	15	156	4,000
Theol. Inst. of Connecticut......	East Windsor, Conn..	Congregation..	1834	3	17	151	5,000
Gilmanton Theol. Seminary.....	Gilmanton, N. H....	Congregation..	1835	3	23	69	4,300
Theological Seminary..........	Lexington, S. C.....	Lutheran.....	1835	2	10	20	1,800
Oberlin Theol. Department.....	Oberlin, Ohio.......	Congregation .	1835	3	24	157	500
Alton Theol. Seminary.........	Upper Alton, Ill.....	Baptist.......	1835	.	..	..	..
Union Theological Seminary....	New York, N. Y....	Presbyterian..	1836	5	106	211	18,000
Theol. Sem. Ass. Ref. Church...	Newburg, N. Y.....	Ass. Ref. Ch..	1836	1	11	143	3,200
Theol. Sem. Ass. Ref. Church...	Oxford, Ohio	Asso. Ref....	1839	1	12	31	1,500
Nashotah Theol. Seminary......	Nashotah, Wisc.....	Prot. Episcop.	1841	8	49	46	3,000
Western Theol. School.........	Meadville, Pa.......	Cong. Unit...	1844	4	17	60	8,000
Western Bapt. Theol. Institution.	Georgetown, Ky.....	Baptist.......	1845	2	12	180	500
Wittenberg..................	Springfield, Ohio....	W. Lutheran..	1845	1	6	49	..
Theol. Sem. of Mercer Univ.....	Penfield, Ga........	Baptist.......	1846	2	13	..	2,200
Meth. Gen. Bib. Institute.......	Concord, N. H......	Methodist....	1847	3	40	..	2,000
Howard Theol. Institution......	Marion, Ala........	Baptist.......	1848	1	6	..	1,000
Bibl. Dep't Ohio Wesl. Univ....	Delaware, Ohio.....	Methodist....	1849	1	11	..	..
Rochester Theol. Seminary.....	Rochester, N. Y.....	Baptist.......	1850	3	36	50	5,500
Danville Theol. Seminary.......	Danville, Ky........	Presbyterian..	1853	4	52	115	..
Theol. Dep. Lewisburg Univ....	Lewisburg, Pa......	Baptist.......	1855	2	12	20	..
Theol. School, Cumb. Univ......	Lebanon, Tenn......	Cumb. Presby.	1855	2	33	..	..

LAW SCHOOLS.

Name.	Place.	Founded.	Professors.	Students 1859–60.	Graduates.	Vols. in Library.
William and Mary College	Williamsburg, Va.	1730	1	..	..	..
Dane Law School, H. Univ.	Cambridge, Mass.	1817	3	150	1,005	14,500
Law School, Yale College	New Haven, Conn.	1820	2	28	122	2,200
Law School, Univ. of Virginia	Charlottesville, Va.	1825	2	109	247	2,000
Law School, Cincinnati College	Cincinnati, Ohio	1833	3	85	512	3,000
Indiana State University	Bloomington, Ind.	1840	1	18	78	..
North Carolina University	Chapel Hill, N. C.	1845	2	23	..	..
N. Y. State and National L. S.	Poughkeepsie, N. Y.	1845	4	119	..	3,000
Cumberland University	Lebanon, Tenn.	1847	3	188	79	500
University of Pennsylvania	Philadelphia, Pa.	1850	3	60	80	..
University of Albany	Albany, N. Y.	1851	3	129	85	State lib.
Indiana Asbury University	Greencastle, Ind.	1853	1	16	50	..
Maynard L. S. Hamilton College	Clinton, N. Y.	1853	1	9	36	500
University of Mississippi	Oxford, Miss.	1857	1	35	33	1,000
Kentucky Military Inst.	Franklin Springs	1858	1	20	..	.
Law School, Col. College	New York, N. Y.	1859	3	30	..	2,000
University of Michigan	Ann Arbor	1859	3	90	24	1,000
University of Louisiana	New Orleans, La.	..	3	..	..	..
University of Louisville	Louisville, Ky.	..	3	..	..	..

MEDICAL SCHOOLS.

Name.	Place.	Founded.	Prof.	Stud'ts.	Graduates.	Lectures commence.
Med. Dep. Univ. Penn.	Philadelphia, Pa.	1765	9	453	7,100	Early in October.
Medical School, Harv. Univ.	Boston, Mass.	1782	6	104	1,125	1st Wedn. in Nov.
N. H. Medical School	Hanover, N. H.	1797	6	50	928	Thurs. after Com't.
Coll. Phys. & Surg., N. Y.	New York, N. Y.	1807	6	219	852	1st Mon. in Nov.
Med. School, Univ. Md.	Baltimore, Md.	1807	6	100	909	October 31st.
Medical Inst. Yale College	New Haven, Ct.	1813	6	45	709	September.
Castleton Medical College	Castleton, Vt.	1818	7	104	555	4th Thurs. in Aug.
Med. Dep. Transylv. Univ.	Lexington, Ky.	1818	.	..	1,351	..
Medical College of Ohio	Cincinnati, Ohio.	1819	8	130	331	1st Mon. in Nov.
Medical School of Maine	Brunswick, Me.	1820	7	50	880	Early in February.
Med. Dep. Univ. Vt.	Burlington, Vt.	1821	6	49	163	Last of February.
Nat. Med. Col., Columbia Col.	Wash'gton, D. C.	1821	8	17	86	4th Mon. in Oct.
Berkshire Medical School	Pittsfield, Mass.	1823	5	103	473	1st Th. in Sept.
Jefferson Medical College	Philadelphia, Pa.	1824	7	514	2,036	1st Mon. in Nov.
Washington Med. College	Baltimore, Md.	1827	6	25	..	1st Mon. in Nov.
Med. School, Univ. Va.	Charlottesville.	1827	5	99	35	1st October.
Med. College of Georgia	Augusta, Ga.	1830	7	115	124	2d Mon. in Nov.
Med. Faculty, Univ. N. Y.	New York, N. Y.	1831	9	300	1,715	3d Mon. in Oct.
Med. Coll. State of S. C.	Charleston, S. C.	1833	8	158	..	2d Mon. in Nov.
Geneva Medical College	Geneva, N. Y.	1834	9	22	935	1st Wednes. in Oct.
Vermont Medical College	Woodstock, Vt.	1835	8	91	350	1st Th. in March.
Med. Dep. Univ. Louisiana	N. Orleans, La.	1835	9	333	..	3d Mon. in Nov.
St. Louis Medical College	St. Louis, Mo.	1836	10	128	..	1st Thurs. in Nov.
Med. Dep. Univ. Louisville	Louisville, Ky.	1837	.	..	53	..
Med. Dep. Hamp. Sid. Coll.	Richmond, Va.	1838	7	90	40	October 13.
Albany Medical College	Albany, N. Y.	1839	8	114	58	1st Tues. in Oct.
Med. Dep. Penn. College	Philadelphia, Pa.	1839	8	150	35	2d Tues. in Oct.
Rush Medical College	Chicago, Ill.	1842	6	70	16	1st Mon. in Nov.
Med. Dep. West. Reserve Coll.	Cleveland, Ohio.	1844	8	67	640	1st Wed. in Nov.
Med. Dep. of Missouri Univ.	Columbia, Mo.	1846	7	103	13	1st Mon. in Nov.
Starling Medical College	Columbus, Ohio.	1847	8	124	53	1st Mon. in Nov.
Med. Dep. State Univ.	Keokuk, Iowa.	1849	6	80	64	1st Mon. in Nov.
Med. Dep. Univ. Nashville	Nashville, Tenn.	1850	8	436	669	1st Mon. in Oct.
West. Coll. Homœpath. Med.	Cleveland, Ohio.	1850	8	62	17	1st Mon. in Nov.
University of Michigan	Ann Arbor	1850	9	164	305	1st Mon. in Oct.
Med. Dep. Georgetown Coll.	Wash'gton, D. C.	1851	8	36	10	4th Mon. in Oct.
Med. Dep. E. Tenn. Univ.	Knoxville, Tenn.	1856	8	..	..	October.
Med. Dep. State Univ.	Madison, Wisc.	1856	6	..	..	..
Philadelphia Coll. of Med.	Philadelphia, Pa.	..	7	75	250	..
Winchester Med. Coll.	Winchester, Va.	..	5	..	..	1st Mon. in Oct.

STATISTICS OF DEAF AND DUMB INSTITUTIONS IN THE UNITED STATES.—1860.

Name of Institution.	Location.	Date of opening.	Number of deaf-mute pupils.	State beneficiaries.	Cost of building and grounds.	Annual amount received from states.	Amount from paying pupils.	Ordinary current expenses.	Permanent funds.	Annual charge to paying pupils.	No. of instructors, including principal.	No. of D. M. Instructors.	No. of female teachers.	No. educated previous to 1860.	Remarks.
American Asylum for Deaf and Dumb.	Hartford, Ct. .	1817	226	205	$ 75,000	$22,265	$2,100	38,288	$307,000	$100	19	5	6	1,243	
N. York Institution for Deaf and Dumb	N. York city.	1818	303	265	600,000	48,783	4,309	48,659	None.	150	16	7	2	1,153	
Pennsylvania " " " "	Philadelphia. .	1820	218	182	120,000	22,722	2,227	25,000	None.	140	12	3	..	970	
Kentucky " " " "	Danville.	1823	78	70	66,000	15,444	350	14,658	22,000	105	6	2	1	409	
Ohio " " " "	Columbus. . . .	1829	159	156	35,000	20,000	400	20,000	None.	100	9	3	..	606	
Virginia Institution for Deaf, Dumb, and Blind, ...	Staunton.	1839	75	..	75,000	25,000	..	25,000	None.	130	6	3	1	130	
Indiana Institution for Deaf and Dumb	Indianapolis . .	1844	182	182	132,000	28,250	..	30,000	Land.	100	10	5	2	291	
Tennessee " " " "	Knoxville. . . .	1845	61	60	41,780	13,000	130	13,000	None.	130	5	2	1	16	
North Carolina Institution for Deaf, Dumb, and Blind, ...	Raleigh.	1845	68	..	..	8,000	..	..	None.	..	3	2	..	..	
Illinois Institution for Deaf and Dumb	Jacksonville. .	1846	205	205	200,000	27,000	..	27,000	None.	100	10	4	1	100	
Georgia Asylum " " "	Cave Spring Floyd Co.	1846	29	29	18,500	8,000	1,750	8,500	None.	175	4	1	..	83	
South Carolina Asylum for Deaf, Dumb, and Blind, ...	Cedar Spring.	1849	16	16	45,000	7,728	None.	7,728	None.	150	3	1	2	41	
Missouri Institution for Deaf and Dumb.	Fulton.	1851	80	75	55,400	10,800	..	11,750	None.	100	5	4	..	55	
Louisiana Institution for Deaf, Dumb, and Blind.	Baton Rouge.	1852	56	..	200,000	17,600	..	14,590	None.	..	5	..	..	..	
Wisconsin Institution for Deaf and Dumb.	Delavan.	1852	70	68	67,000	11,000	200	11,200	None.	100	6	2	1	..	
Michigan Asylum for Deaf, Dumb, and Blind.	Flint.	1854	70	70	154,000	7,000	..	7,000	None.	100	4	2	..	..	Expenses for both departments.
Iowa Institution for Deaf and Dumb.	Iowa City. . .	1855	50	50	Rent. build.	8,000	..	4,500	None.	140	4	2	..	..	
Mississippi " " " "	Jackson.	1855	49	49	10,500	9,000	..	8,272	..	150	4	3	..	38	
Texas " " " "	Austin.	1857	30	30	9,000	9,000	..	..	100,000 acr. state lands.	..	2	1	1	..	
Columbian Institution for Deaf, Dumb, and Blind.	Washington D. C.	1857	27	24	12,000	7,500	450	6,896	None.	150	5	1	1	..	6 blind pupils.
Alabama Institution for Deaf and Dumb.	Talladega. . . .	1858	24	18	20,000	5,000	840	5,000	None.	140	3	1	1	6	

GENERAL VIEW OF BLIND INSTITUTIONS IN THE UNITED STATES, 1860.

Name of Institution.	Location.	Cost, or estimated value of buildings and grounds.	Date of opening.	Number of pupils.	Annual amount received from states.	Annual current expenses.	Charge to paying pupils.	Number of instructors.	No. of blind instructors.	Number of graduates.	Remarks.
Perkins Institution and N. England Asylum.	Boston, Mass.	$100,000	1832	85	$17,000	$20,000	$200	6	3	405	30 graduates furnished work on premises.
New York Institution for the Blind	New York	300,000	1832	210	22,000	30,000	550	26	18	650	
Pennsylvania " " " "	Philadelphia	175,000	1833	157	26,850	30,000	200	16	8	258	A "Home" for infirm graduates, 16 inmates.
Ohio " " " "	Columbus	50,000	1837	120	16,500	16,500	120	9	2	250	
Virginia Institution for Deaf, Dumb, and Blind	Staunton	75,000	1839	42	25,000	28,000	130	9	..	125	
Kentucky Institution for Blind	Louisville	70,000	1842	50	9,000	9,000	140	4	1	75	
Tennessee Institution for Blind	Nashville	15,000	1844	36	7,620	7,642	200	5	3	..	
Indiana Institution for Blind	Indianapolis	100,000	1847	66	15,000	15,000	100	4	1	..	
Illinois Institution for Blind	Jacksonville	80,000	1849	65	12,000	12,000	100	4	0	67	
Wisconsin Institution for Blind	Janesville	60,000	1850	36	8,000	8,000	..	4	1	15	
Missouri Institution for Blind	St. Louis	45,000	1851	52	10,000	9,000	200	4	1	43	
Mississippi Institution for Blind	Jackson	11,000	1848	20	7,000	7,000	..	..	..	..	
Georgia Academy for Blind	Macon	66,000	1852	26	6,000	6,700	200	3	1	5	
Iowa Institution for Blind	Vinton	19,000	1853	23	5,000	5,000	..	3	..	..	
Louisiana Institution for Deaf, D., and Blind.	Baton Rouge	128,000	1852	14	3,550	3,550	250	..	..	..	
Maryland Institution for Blind	Baltimore	35,000	1854	25	4,800	5,000	100	5	3	3	
Columbian Institution for Deaf, Dumb, and Blind	Washington, D. C.	12,000	1857	..	..	..	..	..	..	..	Only 6 blind pupils.
Michigan Asylum for Deaf, Dumb, and Blind	Flint	154,000	1854	25	7,000	7,000	100	3	..	..	
North Carolina Institution for Deaf, Dumb, and Blind	Raleigh	20,000	1848	18	12,000	12,500	175	3	..	..	
South Carolina Institution for Deaf, Dumb, and Blind	Cedar Spring	45,000	1855	17	7,728	7,728	150	2	1	..	
Arkansas Institute for the Blind	Arkadelphia	..	1859	10	..	..	..	..	..	..	
Texas Institute for Blind	Austin	Rented buildg's.	1856	..	..	..	..	..	..	..	100,000 acres of land granted by the state.
Alabama " " "	Mobile	..	..	..	..	..	..	..	..	..	
Institution for colored Deaf Mutes and Blind	Niagara Falls	..	1860	..	..	..	..	..	..	..	

INDEX TO COMMENDATIONS.

No. 1.

Hon. Josiah Quincy.

No. 2.

President E. Hitchcock, Amherst College.

No. 3.

President J. Cummings, Wesleyan University.

No. 4.

President Girard College.

No. 5.

President Genesee College.

No. 6.

President Cambridge University.

No. 7.

President of Marietta College.

No. 8.

President University of Rochester.

No. 9.

President of Brown University.

No. 10.

President University of Wisconsin.

No. 11.

President Columbia College, New York.

No. 12.

President of Tufts College.

No. 13.

President of Dartmouth College.

No. 14.

Chancellor Tappan, Michigan University.

No. 15.

President Vermont University.

No. 16.

President of Williams' College.

No. 17.

President Trinity College.

No. 18.

President Woolsey, Yale College.

No. 19.

John McLean, Princeton College.

No. 20.

Professor Johnson, Yale College.

No. 21.

Professor H. Smith, Lane Theological Seminary.

No. 22.

Professor W. C. Fowler, Amherst College.

No. 23.

Professor B. Silliman, Yale College.

No. 24.

New York Times.

No. 25.

New York Examiner.

No. 26.

New York Observer.

No. 27.

Hunt's Merchants' Magazine.

No. 28.

Secretary Board of Trade, Philadelphia.

No. 29.

Secretary Board of Trade, Boston.

No. 30.

New Englander.

No. 31.

Philadelphia Inquirer.

No. 32.

Boston Transcript.

No. 33.

New York Herald.

No. 34.

Boston Post.

No. 35.

Principal American Asylum.

No. 36.

John D. Philbrick, Superintendent Massachusetts Schools.

No. 37.

Boston Journal.

No. 38.

Philadelphia Evening Journal.

No. 39.

The Homestead.

No. 40.

Phila. Daily Evening Bulletin.

No. 41.

Secretary Board of Education, Boston, Massachusetts.

No. 42.

S. S. Randall, Superintendent, New York.

No. 43.

New England Farmer.

No. 44.

Frank Leslie.

No. 45.

R. G. Dana, Mercantile Agency, New York.

No. 46.

Evening Post, New York.

No. 47.

Benson J. Lossing.

No. 48.

New York Journal of Commerce.

No. 49.

W. H. Wells, Chicago.

No. 50.

Harvey P. Peet, Superintendent, New York.

No. 51.

Boston Cultivator.

No. 52.

American Journal of Science and Arts.

No. 53.

Springfield Republican.

No. 54.

Isaac Ferris, Chancellor University, New York.

No. 55.

J. M. Mathews, Chancellor University, New York.

No. 56.

Professor E. W. Horsford, Cambridge University.

No. 57.

President Hobart College, Geneva.

No. 58.

President Indiana State University

EXTRACTS FROM COMMENDATIONS.

No. 1.

From Hon. Josiah Quincy, former President of Cambridge University.

L. Stebbins, Esq.: *Sir*,—I have received the "Eighty Years' Progress of the United States," and have examined it, not with that attention which its nature, novelty, curiosity, and general apparent accuracy naturally claim, but with that degree of examination, which at the age of *ninety*, was compatible with an eyesight dimmed by years, and systematically avoiding all labors of supererogation. With this deduction from the value of my judgment, I readily express to you my opinion of the work. It seems to me of extraordinary merit, and considering the number, variety, and importance of the subjects it embraces, of surprising accuracy and reliableness for information. The names of the authors of the respective subjects being given, and their established adequacy and talent being known, gives uncommon accuracy to their statements, and an authenticity to the work seldom attained in publications of such a general character. No expense, apparently, has been spared to render it worthy of public confidence and patronage, which I cordially wish you: both of which I regard it as eminently deserving.

Respectfully, I am yours,

Josiah Quincy.

Boston,

No. 2.

From Pres. Hitchcock, late of Amherst College.

I have examined the work entitled "*Eighty Years' Progress of the United States,*" sufficiently to satisfy myself that it is a work of superior merit. Acquainted as I am with several of the authors, I know that they would never suffer productions of this sort to go forth over their names, unless they possess high merit. The work contains a vast amount of information, which every intelligent man can hardly do without, and which, by the aid of numerous drawings, is here presented in an attractive form. With the aid of this work, any one can well understand the present advanced state of all the great industrial and economical arts in our country, and be able to see how they have grown up from their early and rude beginnings. I know not where else, save by almost infinite labor, this knowledge can be obtained.

Edward Hitchcock.

No. 3.

From the President of the Wesleyan University, Middletown, Conn.

I have examined, with much pleasure and profit, the work entitled "Eighty Years' Progress." It contains a great amount and variety of information, printed in an attractive style, on subjects of the highest importance. It is eminently a practical work, and brings within the reach of all, stores of knowledge heretofore inaccessible to most readers. The novelty of the title, the great truths illustrated and established, give it increased attractiveness and usefulness. The patriot and the philanthropist will be encouraged by its perusal and stimulated to greater exertions to secure further progress in all good things in our country and throughout the world.

The enterprising publisher has not spared expense in the manufacture of the work. The printing and the abundant illustrations are in the highest style of rt. One of the best illustrations of "Eighty Years' Progress," would be found in the comparison of the mechanical execution of this work with that of any work issued eighty years ago.

Joseph Cummings,
President of Wesleyan University.

No. 4.

From President of Girard College, Philadelphia, Pa.

Dear Sir,—I have been interested and instructed by the perusal of your national work, entitled "Eighty Years' Progress" for a copy of which I am indebted to your courtesy.

An illustrated history of the various branches of industry and art in the United States, prepared with the ability and truthfulness which characterizes this work, will be highly acceptable to all classes of readers. In its artistic and mechanical execution, nothing has been left to be desired. I am not acquainted with any work in which so much reliable information on so great variety of subjects may be found in so small a compass. It is emphatically a book for the people.

Yours respectfully,

William H. Allen.

No. 5.

From the President of Genesee College.

Lima, *November* 6,

With as much care as my time would allow, I have examined the work of Mr. Stebbins, entitled "Eighty Years' Progress." It contains a large amount of valuable information, in just the form to be circulated widely among the people. It is in fact a brief and interesting history of our progress as a nation, in both science and the arts. I am willing that my name and influence should aid in its circulation.

J. MORRISON REED.

I fully concur in the above.

JAMES L. ALVISON,
Professor in Genesee College.

No. 6.

From the President of Cambridge University.

CAMBRIDGE, *Oct.* 31,

Dear Sir,—I have examined the work called "*Eighty Years' Progress*," with such attention as I could give it. I am not competent to verify the statements of many parts, but the names of the gentlemen who contributed some of the most important portions seems to be a sufficient guaranty of their accuracy. I have no doubt the volumes contain much valuable information on the practical arts and industrial interests of the country.

C. C. FELTON.

No. 7.

From the President of Marietta College, Ohio.

Dear Sir,—The work on the "*Eighty Years' Progress of the United States*" was received by mail a few days since. I have given what attention I could to it, and write you now, as I am expecting to be absent from home for some days.

The examination of this work has given me much pleasure. The idea of furnishing this most valuable knowledge in a comparatively small compass, was a most happy one. As a people we want information—reliable information. We need to know our own history, in art and science, as well as in government. The people of one section should know how those of others live—the progress of one should be made known to all.

The idea of the work you have undertaken seems to have been well carried out, as well as happily conceived. On a great variety of topics, in which all the people are interested, you have furnished a large amount of valuable information. All, except those of the lowest grade of intelligence, will avail themselves of the opportunity to secure this volume, and, unlike many books, the more it is examined the more valuable will it seem. I anticipate for it a wide circulation.

I feel great interest in the character of the books distributed through the country. We teach our young people, at great cost, to read. Many, having acquired the art, have no disposition to use it; and others read nothing that has any value. Good books, *books*—not newspapers, they will take care of themselves—should be in every house. Hence, I favor school libraries, as an easy and cheap method of putting good books into the hands of the young. For a like reason I rejoice in the purchase, by families, of all good works.

This work on the Progress of the United States, will serve a most excellent purpose in two ways. It may be taken up at any time to employ a few leisure moments, and it serves as an encyclopædia for reference.

Please accept my thanks for the volume, and my best wishes for its wide-spread distribution.

Yours truly, J. W. ANDREWS.

L. STEBBINS, Esq., Worcester, Mass.

No. 8.

From the President of the University of Rochester, N. Y.

I have looked over, somewhat hastily, the work entitled "Eighty Years' Progress." The plan seems to me excellent, the idea of presenting in a short compilation the present state and rate of progress of the various industrial arts is one which can not fail to be thought worthy. In general, the work seems to be successfully and correctly done. In such a work it is impossible to avoid errors, and the prejudices and interests of the different compilers may be occasionally seen. Notwithstanding this, the work seems to me well worthy the patronage of the public.

M. B. ANDERSON,
Pres. University of Rochester.

No. 9.

From the President of Brown University, Providence, R. I.

I have examined those parts of the "Eighty Years' Progress of the United States" on which my studies and observation have enabled me to form an intelligent judgment, and find, compressed within a small compass, a vast amount of valuable information, well selected and well arranged. It furnishes ample means of comparison on the subjects of which it treats, and will, I think, prove to be a valuable book of reference.

Very respectfully, your ob't serv't,
B. SEARS.

No. 10.

From President READ, University of Wisconsin.

I have examined, with a pleasure I can hardly express in too strong terms, your "Eighty Years' Progress of the United States." During the few days the work has been on my table it has saved me, in the examination of facts, labor worth many times the cost of the volume. For the school library the business man, the scholar, or the intelligent family, it will be found a cyclopædia presenting, in a most interesting form, the progress of the various arts of civilized life during the period of our national existence. I most heartily recommend the work.

Very truly yours,
DANIEL READ.

No. 11.

From the President of Columbia College, N. Y.

Sir,—I thank you for the copy of "Eighty Years' Progress of the United States," published by you.

It seems to me of great value as containing information of interest, more or less, to all, and not easily accessible, except to varied labor and research.

The idea, too, of illustrating national progress, not by war, nor annexation, nor diplomatic legerdemain, but by the advance in the institutions of learning, in useful inventions, in the growth of manufactures, agriculture, and commerce, in all the arts of peace, in morals and civilization, in the inner life, so to speak, of the people themselves, seems to me both original and founded in the true notion of progress.

I trust you will derive abundant reward for your praiseworthy adventure.

Your obedient servant,
CH. KING,
Pres. of Columbia College.

MR. STEBBINS.

No. 12.

From the President of Tufts College.

January 27,

MR. STEBBINS: *Dear Sir*,—I was led to expect much from the title of your work, called "Eighty Years' Progress," and resolved to give it a careful examination. I have been richly repaid for the time thus spent, in the great pleasure and profit I have derived from its perusal. Heartily thanking you for this generous contribution to generous knowledge, I trust you may reap a rich reward for your efforts. JOHN P. MARSHALL.

No. 13.

From the President of Dartmouth College.

January 20,

L. STEBBINS, ESQ.: *Dear Sir*,—I received some days ago your very handsome work, "Eighty Years' Progress of the United States," but have found leisure only within a day or two to examine its contents. Those persons who have been longest on the stage can best appreciate the amazing contrasts in the state of the country which you describe, but one who, like myself, can recognize the history of half the period, can testify to the faithfulness and fullness of your exhibition of the growth and power of this great country.

Accept my sincere thanks for the work, and the opinion that on the subjects treated it will be found an invaluable authority by all who study its pages. I trust it may have an extensive distribution. Very respectfully yours,
O. P. HUBBARD.

No. 14.

From Chancellor TAPPAN, State University of Michigan.

January 25,

MR. STEBBINS: *Sir*,—I have the honor to acknowledge the receipt of a copy of the work recently published by you, entitled "Eighty Years' Progress," for which please accept my hearty thanks.

It was not to be expected that this work could be made to contain an adequate view of the progress of our country during eighty years. But you have presented the public with this large work, filled with interesting and valuable matter on this subject, as much, perhaps, as could be compressed into it. I hope this work will find a wide circulation, and thus become a public benefit in a literal sense.

I am very respectfully yours, etc.,
HENRY P. TAPPAN.

No. 15.

From the President of the Vermont University, Burlington.

I have only had time to dip into your "*Eighty Years' Progress*" here and there. But I have been pleased and instructed, and am sure the book must be very valuable. My children are very much interested in it. Yours very truly,
CALVIN PEASE.

No. 16.

From the President of Williams' College.

Dear Sir,—I have no hesitation in saying that the work proposed to be done in the "*Eighty Years' Progress*" has been well done. For those who wish a book of the kind, yours cannot fail to be *the* book. Respectfully yours,
MARK HOPKINS.

MR. L. STEBBINS.

No. 17.

From President of Trinity College, Hartford, Conn.

Dear Sir,—I have to thank you for a copy of your work on the Progress of the United States. It treats of some matters with which I am familiar, and of some with which I am not familiar; but I think I can honestly say, with regard to both, that they are so presented as to be at once interesting and instructive to the general reader.

Your obedient servant,
SAMUEL ELIOT.

HARTFORD, *October* 4,

No. 18.

From Pres. WOOLSEY, Yale College, New Haven, Conn.

YALE COLLEGE, *Nov.* 15,

MR. L. STEBBINS: *Dear Sir*,—Your book is a good and useful one, but it is not my practice to recommend books.

Your obedient servant,
T. D. WOOLSEY.

No. 19.

COLLEGE OF NEW JERSEY, PRINCETON, *Jan.* 28,

Dear Sir,—Your "Eighty Years' Progress of the United States," I regard as a valuable publication, richly meriting the attention of the general reader, as well as the more careful examination of the student interested in observing the advancement of our country in the useful arts and learning.

Very respectfully yours,
JOHN MCLEAN.

L. STEBBINS, Esq.

No. 20.

From Prof. JOHNSON, Yale College, New Haven, Conn.

L. STEBBINS, ESQ.: *Dear Sir*,—I have examined "Eighty Years' Progress," with interest, especially the excellent chapter on agriculture. In my opinion, the work is one of much value, and deserves a wide circulation. Yours, etc.,

S. W. JOHNSON,
Prof. of Analytical and Agricultural Chemistry in the Sheffield Scientific School of Yale College.

No. 21.

From Rev. Dr. SMITH, Lane Theological Seminary, Ohio.

MR. L. STEBBINS: *My Dear Sir*,—I have run my eyes with great interest over your beautiful work, "*Eighty Years' Progress.*" It contains, in a condensed yet attractive form, a mass of information touching the progress and present condition of our country. It is, moreover, information of which every man, at some time, feels the need; and it would be a grand contribution both to the intelligence and patriotism of our whole population, if you could succeed in placing a copy of it in every family of the land. I shall place your book on my table for constant reference.

Wishing you all success in your enterprise,
I am very truly yours,
HENRY SMITH,
Prof. Ch., Hist. and Sac. Rhetoric.

No. 22.

From Professor FOWLER, of Amherst College, Editor of the University Edition of Webster's Dictionary, Series of Classical Books, etc.

The work which you placed in my hands, entitled "Eighty Years' Progress of the United States," I have taken time to examine, in order that I might learn its intrinsic value. I find that the subjects selected are such, and the manner of treatment such, as to supply a felt want in the public mind, which, in its own progress, was demanding higher and better help than it enjoyed before the publication of your work. This might be inferred from the bare mention of the subjects and the authors. These subjects are treated by these writers with that correctness of the statement of the general principles, and with that fullness of detail which make the work just what it ought to be as a guide to the people. Every young man who wishes to elevate his mind by self-culture, ought to read this work carefully.

Yours respectfully,
WILLIAM C. FOWLER.

No. 23.

From Prof. B. SILLIMAN, Yale College, New Haven, Ct.

I have carefully looked through your rich and faithful work, observing the copious tables of contents, glancing at every page of the work, and at all the numerous illustrations, with occasional reading of paragraphs. A more thorough examination it has not been hitherto in my power to make; but even this general survey has left on my mind the decided conviction that you have performed an important service to your country in thus mapping out and condensing and explaining the wonderful progress made in this country, during four-fifths of a century, in all the most important arts of life. My own recollections—my years having been coeval with the entire period covered by your work—sustain your statements regarding the extreme simplicity of our early domestic arts—cheap in mechanical aids but prodigal of time. Now productive industry, aided by successful inventions, fills all our regions where free labor has full scope for action, with innumerable results which are fully equal to our wants, even in the present crisis, leaving also a large redundancy of articles for export, especially in the department of agriculture, and in not a few important mechanical arts.

Your work of closely printed pages of double columns, with a fair paper and a clear and distinct type, with its numerous engravings, defended also by a strong and neat binding, presents a valuable book of reference; a manual to be consulted by the agriculturist and artist, as well as by the man of science and the historian of progress. Wishing to yourself and your worthy coadjutors full success,

I remain, dear sir, yours very respectfully
B. SILLIMAN.

NEW HAVEN, *October* 8,

No. 24.

From the New York Times.

"*Eighty Years' Progress of the United States.*"—If at all inclined to doubt that a great deal of useful information may be bound up in a comparatively small compass by a judicious compiler, in the very handsome work before us, we should find sufficient logic to make us devout believers. The writers have ranged through the wild fields of agriculture, commerce, and trade; very little that develops the material prosperity of a country, and marks its growth, has escaped their industrious research. Undoubtedly, minute criticism might detect slight errors, but in a work of so comprehensive a character, strict accuracy would seem almost unattainable. The statistics given are full and clearly arranged; the grouping of the subjects, and the evident method which the authors have observed in the accomplishment of their not inconsiderable task, are worthy of all praise. The work is one which we particularly need, as it is a lamentable fact that few people are so deficient in general knowledge of facts relative to growth and development of their native country, as ours. The Englishman generally has an arsenal of statistics at his fingers' ends; he can tell you when the first shaft was sunk in the first mine; when the first loom was erected in Manchester. The panoply of facts in which he is arrayed makes him rather a ponderous and far from sprightly companion, at times; but then he always proves formidable as an adversary. Germans, too, have nearly every thing by rote that relates to their own country. Frenchmen are quick to learn, but they have not very retentive memories generally, and are very apt to forget all, and more, than they once knew. It may be urged in extenuation of our national delinquency, as regards a knowledge of our own country, that our country grows too fast for our memories to keep pace with it, and that a Yankee can arrive by guessing at what others, less favored in this respect, can only reach by delving in authorities; but, on the whole, it is better to trust to actual knowledge of facts, and under any circumstances such books as these are good things to have in the library.

No. 25.

From the New York Examiner.

"*Eighty Years' Progress of the United States,*" by eminent literary men, who have made the subjects of which they have written their special study.

The citizen who desires to comprehend fully how the country in which we live has, under the fostering influences of a good government, the enterprise of an energetic people, and above all, the blessing of God, grown from a handful of people to one of the leading powers in the world, should purchase and read carefully this work. It is no catchpenny affair. The men who have prepared the narratives of progress in the various departments of agriculture and horticulture, commerce, manufactures, banking, education, science, art, and the matters which go to make "home" so emphatically an American word, are not novices, penny-a-liners, who write on any or all subjects, with or without an understanding of them, for the sake of their daily bread —but men of high reputation, who have made the subjects they discuss the topics of a life's study. Every subject which will admit of it is finely illustrated, and tables of statistics, carefully prepared from the latest sources, show the present condition of each department, and demonstrate, as only figures can, how great the advance which has been made in each. As a work of reference, not less than as a deeply interesting book for family reading, it will be a treasure to any household that may obtain it.

No. 26.

From the New York Observer.

"*Eighty Years' Progress of the United States.*"—the above rather formidable title-page is quite a full exposition of the contents of this large work, which contain a vast amount of scientific, historical, and statistical matter, and which constitute a valuable encyclopædia, as well as history of the progress of the country, during the last eighty years. Many of the most extended articles are by eminent scientific and practical men, who have devoted themselves largely to the subjects on which they have written.

The subjects are not treated briefly, but in detail, rendering the work valuable as a book of reference as well as for general reading. Such a review as we have in this work may well excite wonder, gratitude, and hope. The history of no other country can furnish a parallel.

No. 27.

From Hunt's Merchants' Magazine, edited by I. Smith Homans, Secretary of the Chamber of Commerce of the State of New York.

"*Eighty Years' Progress of the United States.*"—The first eighty years of the national existence were illustrated by no brilliant military exploits, such as for the most part make up the history of most countries of the Old World, but the American people did not the less on that account assume a marked character, and a first rank among the nations of the earth. Their success in ship-building and commerce at once placed them on a level with the greatest maritime nations. The inventive genius and untiring industry of the people soon revolutionized the manufacturing industry of the world, by the ready application of new mechanical powers to industrial arts; and if the extent and cheapness of land for a time supplied the scarcity of labor in agricultural departments, it did not prevent the multiplication of inventions, which have not only added immensely to home production, but have greatly aided that of European countries. The development of these industries forms the true history of American greatness, and the work of Mr. Stebbins has given a world of information upon each branch of the subject, in a most authentic and attractive form. The chapters on ship-building, commerce, and internal transportation, present to the reader a mass of valuable information as astonishing for the magnitude of the results produced as interesting in the narrative. We know of no other work which, in the compass of two handsome volumes, contains such varied and comprehensive instruction of a perfectly reliable character. They form almost a complete library in themselves.

No. 28.

From the Secretary of Board of Trade, Philadelphia.

L. Stebbins, Esq.: *Dear Sir,*—I examined with interest the volumes published by you, entitled "*Eighty Years' Progress,*" and found them particularly valuable. The design struck me very favorably, and the execution of the several parts could not have been intrusted to more competent hands. The last eighty years of the history of the United States has been one of unexampled progress, and it is now more than ever important to bring in review before the people of every section the leading facts of this marvellous progress.

Very respectfully yours,

Lorin Blodget.

No. 29.

From the Secretary of the Board of Trade, Boston.

My Dear Sir,—My many cares just now have prevented me from a comparison of the statistical matter contained in the "*Eighty Years' Progress*," with official tables in my possession, as well as an examination of some other things, concerning which authorities differ, but I *have* found time to acquaint myself with the general topics and objects of the work, and do not hesitate to declare that I have not read more interesting pages for years. Indeed, the best informed among us, cannot, as it seems to me, fail to find much that is new, while to the young and to those who lack the means of research, so authentic and well-digested account of our country's "Progress," will be of immense service. We all boast of our wonderful march in commerce, in manufactures, in mechanics, and in the arts; and here we have it, step by step, in "facts and figures," and in brief and pithy narrative.

With all my heart, I hope that the sale will be extensive, and that you may be well rewarded for your outlay of time and capital.

Very truly, your friend,

LORENZO SABINE.

L. STEBBINS, Esq., Hartford, Conn.

No. 30.

From the New Englander, New Haven, Conn.

"*Eighty Years' Progress of the United States.*"—In this very large octavo work there is presented in a compact and easily accessible form an amount of valuable information with regard to the progress which the people of the United States have made in all the various channels of industry since the days when they were British colonists, which is not to be found in any other single work with which we are acquainted. Each one of these subjects is amply illustrated with engravings. The different chapters have been prepared by well-known literary men who have each made the subjects about which they have written the study of years. We have examined the work repeatedly and with much care during the past three months, and each time have been impressed anew with its value. There is not an intelligent family in the nation who would not be interested and instructed by it, and find it a most convenient book of reference with regard to every thing pertaining to the industrial interests of the country.

No. 31.

From the Philadelphia Inquirer.

"*Eighty Years' Progress of the United States.*"—To any one desiring at a glance a comprehensive view of the various channels of educational industry in commerce, manufactures, agriculture, statistics, etc., they are invaluable. They are profusely illustrated with elegant engravings in the highest style of artistic merit. The volumes redound with statistical and miscellaneous information of a standard character and permanent value. The expense of publishing a work of this character must have been very large, but we feel confident that a discriminating public have not been overestimated.

There are among the peculiar characteristics of our people, wide-spread opinions prevailing, that books sold by subscription are of a necessity more expensive than when purchased in a general way at the counter of a publishing house. This is evidently an error that could easily be subverted by a little demonstration, and the publishers' remarks in the preface are to the point, and effective. We know of hardly any book or books which are within the reach of every-day life, that we would sooner advise a friend to purchase. Its value will be unimpaired for a lifetime.

No. 32.

From the Boston Transcript.

"*Eighty Years' Progress of the United States.*"—This work is the result of much careful research, exercised by many minds on a variety of important subjects. They show the industrial and educational steps by which the people of the United States have risen from their colonial condition to their present position among the nations of the world. They give, in a historical form, the progress of the country in agriculture, commerce, trade, banking, manufactures, machinery, modes of travel and transportation, and the work is intended to be sold by subscription, and will doubtless have a large circulation. It ought to be in every house in the land. It is more important than ordinary histories of the country, as it exhibits all the triumphs of the practical mind and energy of the nation, in every department of science, art, and benevolence. It is a storehouse of important and stimulating facts, and its interest can hardly be exhausted by the most persistent reader.

No. 33.

From the N. Y. Herald.

"*Eighty Years' Progress of the United States*," by eminent literary men.—The object of this work, as set forth in its preface, is to show the various channels of industry through which the people of the United States have arisen from a British colony to their present national importance. This is done by treating separately the improvements effected in agriculture, commerce, trade, manufactures, machinery, modes of travel, transportation, etc. The preparation of these different articles has been intrusted to writers whose pursuits qualified them to handle them exhaustively, and the result is the assemblage of a vast amount of statistical and other information which is not to be found in the same collective and condensed form in any other work extant.

No. 34.

From the Boston Post.

"*Eighty Years' Progress of the United States*, showing the various channels of industry through which the people of the United States have arisen from a British colony to their present National Importance," is the title of a new and exceedingly valuable work. The work gives in a historical form the vast improvements made in agriculture, commerce, trade, manufacturing, etc., together with a large amount of statistical and other information. It is illustrated with numerous engravings, and altogether forms a most valuable and instructive companion to the writer, the business man, or the student.

No. 35.

From Wm. W. Turner, Principal of the American Asylum for Deaf and Dumb, Hartford, Conn.

I have examined your new national work entitled "Eighty Years' Progress of the United States," and find that the information it contains on the wide range of subjects treated of must make it exceedingly valuable as a standard book of reference. The names of the writers of the different articles afford a sufficient guaranty that the facts and statements may be relied on as correct. I consider the work a very important accession to this department of literature, and have no doubt that it will find its way into the library of every private gentleman and every public institution.

Very truly yours,
Wm. W. Turner.

No. 36.

From John D. Philbrick, Superintendent Common Schools, Massachusetts.

I have examined the "*Eighty Years' Progress*" with great satisfaction. I consider it a work of great value, and it is one which I should be very unwilling to spare from my library. It is not only such a book as the literary or professional man would like to possess, but it is a book for every household, and for every school library.

Very truly yours,
John D. Philbrick.

No. 37.

From the Boston Journal.

"*Eighty Years' Progress of the United States.*"—In this elaborate and valuable work the progress of the United States is illustrated by historical sketches of the rise and development of agriculture, commerce, trade, manufactures, modes of travel and transportation. The authors will be recognized as fully competent to treat upon the above subjects, and their sketches have great interest and value, as well for the facts which they present, as in illustrating the rapid progress of the United States in all that conduces to material wealth and national prosperity. The work abounds in valuable statistical information, and is interesting for perusal, and useful for reference.

No. 38.

From the Philadelphia Evening Journal.

"*Eighty Years' Progress of the United States,*" by eminent literary men.—The work treats of the various channels of industry through which the people of the United States have arisen from a British colony to their present national importance. It treats of the vast improvements made in agriculture, commerce, trade, manufacturing, machinery, modes of travel and transportation, etc., etc.

No. 39.

From the Homestead, Agricultural Journal, Hartford, Ct.

"*Eighty Years' Progress of the United States.*"—The title conveys but a faint idea of the great amount of information contained in these volumes, and no cursory glance can more than convince the reader that they possess great value as an encyclopædia of arts and progress in civilization. The names of the authors of the more important articles, several of whom are known to us personally and highly respected, are a guaranty that their work is well done, and statements reliable. Our limited space forbids an extended notice, but before noticing especially the agricultural departments, we must add, that to every one who takes it up it is one of the most fascinating of books, a most remarkable quality in a book so statistical in its character.

The article of progress in Agriculture is by Chas. L. Flint, Secretary of the Massachusetts Board of Agriculture, and is a most able and interesting collection of facts in regard to the remarkable progress of this country since the Revolution.

No. 40.

From the Philadelphia Daily Evening Bulletin.

Mr. L. Stebbins,—After carefully examining your valuable publication, "Eighty Years' Progress of the United States," and having on various occasions, in our professional business, tested its accuracy as a work of reference, we are able to bear testimony to its character. No work that we have ever seen gives such spirited, comprehensive, and correct views of the progress of our country in political strength, in commerce, agriculture, manufactures, and all branches of industry and art. The work has been prepared with extreme care; the various subjects are treated with intelligence, and the style of composition proves that the writers are men of education, who have thoroughly informed themselves on the subjects they discuss. The illustrations and the typography add much to the attractions of a work that should be in the hands of all who take an interest in the growth of our country, and feel a patriotic pride in its prosperity.

We are very respectfully, your ob't serv'ts,
Peacock, Chambers & Co.

No. 41.

From the Secretary of Board of Education.

Boston, Mass., *Sept.* 6,

Dear Sir,—I beg leave to thank you for your noble work entitled "Eighty Years' Progress."

After such an examination as I have been able to give, I do not hesitate to pronounce it a work of unusual interest and value.

As a depository of facts illustrative of the progress of our country in the departments of industry, it is invaluable.

Its wide circulation, at this eventful period, cannot fail to arouse and deepen that patriotic love of our institutions which is the pressing demand of the hour. Respectfully yours,

J. WHITE.

L. STEBBINS, Esq.

No. 42.

From S. S. RANDALL, City Superintendent Public Schools, New York.

MR. L. STEBBINS: *Dear Sir*,—The great pressure of official engagements has hitherto prevented my acknowledgment of the receipt of the very beautiful and interesting work published by you—"Eighty Years' Progress of the United States." I have not had time to peruse them thoroughly, but take great pleasure in stating that, so far as I have looked into them, the plan and general execution of the work seem to me to be admirable, and well adapted to the wants, as well of the rising generation, as of our fellow-citizens generally. I cheerfully recommend it to the favorable regard of school officers, parents, teachers, and others, as a very valuable compend of scientific and historical knowledge, and as a work well worthy of a place in every school or private library.

No. 43.

From the New England Farmer, Boston.

"*Eighty Years' Progress of the United States.*"—This volume contains an immense amount of valuable and interesting information concerning the rise and development of agriculture, commerce, trade, manufactures, travel and transportation, the arts, and other prominent interests of this country. This information is contained in a series of essays by gentlemen, either and all of whom will be recognized as competent to illustrate the subject upon which he writes.

No. 44.

From Frank Leslie.

After copying the entire title-page, the notice proceeds thus:

Such is the comprehensive title of an elegantly printed work which covers a very wide range of subjects of special American interest. The work is, in fact, an industrial and statistical history of the country since its independence, encyclopædic in character and arrangement, but yet sufficiently complete for every practical purpose. It may be regarded as an epitome of the publication of the Census and the Patent Office, and of the proceedings of our Industrial Societies, compact in form, convenient for reference, and deserving a place in the hands of every reading and reflecting man in the country.

No. 45.

From R. G. DANA, Mercantile Agency, New York.

From a cursory glance at its contents I feel warranted in saying it possesses information of much value and usefulness to all classes.

Very respectfully, R. G. DANA.

No. 46.

From the Evening Post, New York.

"*Eighty Years' Progress of the United States.*"—The range of subjects treated in this work is very full; the writers upon them are well selected with regard to specialties, and their manner of handling is always interesting, frequently thorough. The system pursued is not encyclopædic, but historical, and, so far as possible, exhaustive. The growth of our agricultural prosperity, with particular regard to improvements made in breeds and machinery, and the dissemination of scientific knowledge among farmers, is well recited, and this department forms one of the most attractive features of the book.

No. 47.

From B. J. LOSSING, the Historian.

Sir,—I have examined, with great satisfaction, your work entitled "*Eighty Years' Progress of the United States.*" It is a work of inestimable value to those who desire to know, in minute detail, something more of the history of the country than the events of its political and industrial life as exhibited in the politician's manual, and the bold statements of the census; especially at this time, when the civilized world is eagerly asking what we are and what we have been, that the old governments may attempt to solve the more important question, to them, what we *will* be. Your work, in fact and logical prophecy, furnishes an answer of which any people may be justly proud. Surely, no nation of the earth has ever experienced such bounding progress as this; and in the last eighty years, as exhibited in your work, we see ample prophecies of the future, of strength, influence, leadership among the nations, such as the eye of faith employed by the fathers, dimly saw. No American can peruse your pages without feeling grateful for the privilege of being an American citizen.

I will use a very trite phrase and say, with all sincerity, I wish your work could go "into every family in our land," to increase their knowledge and to strengthen their patriotism.

Yours respectfully,

BENSON J. LOSSING.

No. 48.

From the New York Journal of Commerce.

"*Eighty Years' Progress of the United States.*"—The plan is extensive, and appears to be judiciously carried out. The work is divided into departments, to each of which has been devoted his laborious attention, producing a readable, and at the same time valuable and instructive, summary of the advances made. This plan necessarily comprises a very complete history of the arts and sciences for the past century. In many of them it covers the whole period from the earliest time at which they were known to man, for the century has been productive of new arts, and has furnished mankind with not a few totally new inventions. To digest the contents of the book so as to give a reader even a hint of its comprehensiveness would be impossible.

The book is well fitted for the family reading, and valuable as a source of interest and instruction to the young, while in the business office and counting-room of every merchant, banker, and professional man it would answer a thousand daily questions.

No. 49.

Office of Superintendent of Public Schools, Chicago.

"*Eighty Years' Progress.*"—The work which you have prepared with so much care and labor, presenting the progress of our country during the last eighty years, is peculiarly adapted to gratify and instruct all classes of citizens. No work could be offered to the public at the present time more worthy of a place in family libraries, and school libraries, than the one which you now present.

Yours truly,
W. H. Wells,
Sup. of Public Schools.

No. 50.

From the Superintendent of the Institution of the Deaf and Dumb, New York.

It is only recently that I could find time, from the pressure of official duties, to examine the splendid national work, "*Eighty Years' Progress.*" By the way, I observe that, as you give much information concerning early colonial times, you have in fact given over two and a half centuries of progress. The work strikes me as a production of great value and universal interest. While the statesman will find a mass of statistical information, which, by its arrangement and the able commentary accompanying it, will assist very materially in the correct solution of many politico-economical problems, men actively engaged in almost any pursuit, agricultural, commercial, mining, education, the arts of design, the mechanic arts, etc., will each find much information, both curious and useful.

Hoping for your undertaking all the success it deserves, I remain, very respectfully yours,

Harvey P. Peet.

No. 51.

From the Boston Cultivator.

"*Eighty Years' Progress.*"—There is a work which has been published recently, having the above title, and which, because of these magnificent words, of course, arrests the attention of every wise man. Eighty years' progress? Eighty years of progress in the life of an individual would make a rare record, pregnant with the most practical and important considerations; but the eighty years' progress of which we speak, are the years of a nation, or the progress of many *millions* of individuals, and hence how widely shall we have to open our eyes, if it be faithfully written, and we would take it all in so as to recognize the details of advancement made by a mighty people. The people, whose brilliant destiny is indicated in the above title, are those of the United States, and though we are among and of them, unless by long and constant and vigorous pursuit of the special end, we, ourselves, can have no adequate idea of the real extent of our progress, unless it be summed up from the material, as well as the political history of the period about which we inquire, in some work or works combining the knowledge of many whose observation and reading are large in opportunities and in improvement.

We, as a people, are noted in Christendom as having an undue proportion of self-esteem, and an immodest desire to express it as often as we may find an audience. The Americans, we confess, are, in much, superficial, and their real and unparalleled rapidity of progress is too much and too frequently taken for granted as the basis of adulatory discourse; and because of this, the old European, familiar from his youth with the fixed sources of his power, and with ease and grace weighing or rejecting questions he knows from the outset are or are not determinable, naturally looks with *discredit* upon the live Yankee who "guesses" everything, and when urged to state the real ground of his boasting, only covers his superficial knowledge of his own country and history by his agility in bombast and fleeing the point in new gratulation and a keen thrust which forces an adverse judgment. And the ignorance which leads Americans to a substitution of their wit, also leads those of other nations to suspect the foundation of their boasted power and national resources and importance.

There is but one way to cure this, and that is eminently practical and desirable. It is for the people of our country to study their own history more thoroughly, and not their political history only, but the history of their material progress. There are few good books in which to find this; but there is one which has been put forth by L. Stebbins, which is especially adapted to this object; and a more instructive, interesting, and popular work is rarely found.

No. 52.

From the American Journal of Science and Arts, New Haven, Conn.

"*Eighty Years' Progress of the United States,*" by eminent literary men.—This compendium of national statistics forms a valuable handbook of reference, to which all who possess it will have frequent occasion to turn for information in respect to the progress and condition of the great elements of growth and development in the history of the United States during eighty years past. The value of the book as a work of reference would have been much enhanced by a more frequent reference to authorities and original sources of information. But taken as it is, it supplies a great desideratum, and its pains-taking publisher, Mr. Stebbins, deserves our thanks for so valuable a contribution to our resources in this department of statistics.

No. 53.

From the Springfield Republican.

Our citizens are offered a large and expensive work, giving the industrial progress of the United States during the eighty years of their national existence. It is embellished by numerous engravings, and the letter-press is prepared by writers of eminence in the various departments of which it treats. It is sold to subscribers only.

No. 54.

From ISAAC FERRIS, D. D., Chancellor of the University in New York.

I have looked into the work entitled "Eighty Years' Progress of the United States," and am happy to unite with the worthy men who have examined it, in commending it to my friends.

NEW YORK. ISAAC FERRIS.

No. 55.

From J. M. MATHEWS, D. D., Ex-Chancellor of the University in New York.

The object of the work is highly commendable; and, so far as I have been able to examine it, has been executed with ability and fidelity. I freely commend it to public patronage.

NEW YORK. J. M. MATHEWS.

No. 56.

From Prof. E. W. HOSFORD, of Cambridge University.

It is a work of very great value for popular reference. The articles having been prepared by writers who have made specialties of the subjects upon which they have written, are, as a consequence, eminently attractive. I find them an unfailing source of valuable information and important suggestion.

In the way of illustrations what could be more significant than the group of agricultural implements of 1790, contrasted with the mowing, reaping, raking, and threshing machines of 1860; or than the Franklin printing press as compared with the Hoe printing press?

The author of the article on Steam and Steamboats, renders a most acceptable service, in placing on record the just claims of John Fitch and Oliver Evans.

Let me congratulate you on having found so many able contributors, and in having procured so valuable a work.

No. 57.

From A. JACKSON, D. D., President Hobart College, Geneva.

I have examined, as far as time would allow, your new work, entitled "Eighty Years of Progress." I think it a very convenient book of reference, and a valuable addition to our statistical knowledge. I have already found it a very useful work to consult, and I gladly add it to our College Library, where it well deserves a place.

No. 58.

From C. NUTT, D. D., President of the Indiana State University, Bloomington, Ind.

I have examined your recently published work entitled "Eighty Years' Progress;" and from the examination I have been able to give it, I believe that it merits richly the highest commendation. The great variety and importance of the subjects, the felicitous style in which they are clothed, and their numerous and beautiful illustrations, render this work peculiarly attractive. They embrace subjects of great and universal utility, and deeply interesting to all classes of community. Every profession and calling in life is here exhibited, with the latest improvements in every department of industry and art. The advancement made during eighty years, in the American republic, is unparalleled in the history of the world; and will remain a proof to all coming generations, of the blessings of free institutions, and the capability of man, under a system of self-government, for an almost indefinite progress in civilization. This work should be in every library, public and private, and in the hands of every citizen.

www.ingramcontent.com/pod-product-compliance
Lightning Source LLC
LaVergne TN
LVHW020930110826
845150LV00004B/815

* 9 7 8 1 4 2 5 5 5 3 3 9 5 *